THE POEMS OF
Samuel Johnson

THE POEMS OF

Samuel Johnson

EDITED BY

DAVID NICHOL SMITH

AND

EDWARD L. McADAM

SECOND EDITION

OXFORD
AT THE CLARENDON PRESS
1974

Oxford University Press, Ely House, London W. 1

GLASGOW NEW YORK TORONTO MELBOURNE WELLINGTON
CAPE TOWN IBADAN NAIROBI DAR ES SALAAM LUSAKA ADDIS ABABA
DELHI BOMBAY CALCUTTA MADRAS KARACHI LAHORE DACCA
KUALA LUMPUR SINGAPORE HONG KONG TOKYO

First published 1941
Second Edition 1974

Printed in Great Britain
at the University Press, Oxford
by Vivian Ridler
Printer to the University

PREFACE

As the aims and method of this edition are stated at the conclusion of the Introduction, this Preface deals only with the collaboration of the two editors and the assistance which they have received. They began their work on Johnson's poems independently, one of them many years ago. In 1913 he arranged with the Clarendon Press for an edition, and was able in that year to describe it as being in preparation. When its progress was checked by the events of the next five years, some parts had been completed more or less as they are now printed. But work interrupted is not always easily resumed, and this editor, while continuing to collect material for a volume which he never doubted to see published, found many obstacles to making a good end. Meanwhile the other editor had been at work on Johnson's poems and had prepared an edition which helped to win for him the Doctor's degree of Yale University. The decision was soon taken to bring out a joint edition, and summer vacations were thereafter spent busily in Oxford. In many sections one or other of the two editors has necessarily played the greater part, but they have everywhere consulted each other, and there is no page for which they do not share responsibility. What was checked in its early stages by one European conflagration is thus now completed in the midst of another, when we may remember the lessons of *The Vanity of Human Wishes*.

The delay cannot be regretted, for during these years more additions have been made to our information about Johnson than at any time since the publication of Boswell's *Life*. Manuscripts which were not suspected to exist have become public or accessible by passing to new owners; and in this process much has been learned about the poems, and their number has been increased. The editors are under a great debt to the private collectors or trustees of libraries who have permitted the use of manuscripts in their possession or keeping, and feel that the particular obligations stated in the introductory notes to the poems demand also this general acknowledgement. Their gratitude will be shared by all readers of this volume.

One debt calls for separate mention. In the winter of 1936–7 the senior editor enjoyed the hospitality and privileges extended to

Associate Members of the Huntington Library in Southern California. There he found the value of *Thraliana* as a storehouse of
information about Johnson's minor poems, and as an authority for
their texts. Fortunately this remarkable record of the gay and
the serious in the life of the clever woman who was Johnson's
kindest and most disappointing friend is soon to be published, but
the many quotations here printed had then to be taken from the
manuscript, which was read with the excitement of discovery. At
the same time the Huntington Library provided the true text of
Johnson's 'Short Song of Congratulation', his verses upon Sir John
Lade—a major among the minor poems.

It is a pleasure to the editors to recall the assistance which they
have received from friends who are known by their own work on
Johnson and his circle—R. W. Chapman, J. L. Clifford, A. T.
Hazen, F. A. Pottle, L. F. Powell, and C. B. Tinker; and from other
friends who, if not publicly sealed of the tribe, have shown a liking
for Johnsonian questions—N. Ault, C. H. Collins Baker, H. W.
Garrod, C. T. Onions, H. R. St. J. Sanderson, and P. Simpson.
Special thanks are due to Professor Garrod for the interest which he
has taken in the Latin poems.

December, 1940

ACKNOWLEDGEMENTS

FOR permission to consult and publish manuscript material acknowledgements are due to the Henry W. and Albert A. Berg Collection in the New York Public Library, Astor, Lenox, and Tilden Foundation; the Cornell University Library; the Edward L. Doheny Collection in the Library of St. John's Seminary, Camarillo, California; the Folger Shakespeare Library; the Horace Howard Furness Memorial Library in the University of Pennsylvania; the Harvard College Libraries; to Mr. Arthur A. Houghton, Jr., of New York; to Mrs. Mary C. Hyde of Somerville, New Jersey; to Mr. Herman W. Liebert of New Haven, Connecticut; to the Pierpont Morgan Library, New York; the Yale University Library; the National Library of Australia, Canberra; the Bodleian Library; the British Museum; the Cambridge University Library; to Major C. Congreve; to the Earl of Crawford and Balcarres; the City Council of Lichfield; the Lincolnshire Archives Office at Lincoln; Messrs. William Heinemann, Ltd.; the Hornby Collection in the Liverpool Public Library; the Central Library, Manchester; the John Rylands Library; the National Library of Wales; the Master and Fellows of Pembroke College, Oxford; the William Salt Library, Stafford; the Suffolk Record Office, Bury St. Edmunds; the Victoria and Albert Museum; and to the Hon. Mrs. Helen Mildmay-White.

The reviser is indebted to the staffs of these institutions and to the assistance of many individuals, especially to Mr. Donald D. Eddy, Mr. Richard Hatchwell, Mrs. Mary C. Hyde, Mr. Alan T. McKenzie, Mr. J. C. Maxwell, Mr. E. V. C. Plumptre, Mr. and Mrs. Frederick A. Pottle, Mr. William K. Wimsatt, Miss Marjorie G. Wynne, and Mr. K. K. Yung.

CONTENTS

INTRODUCTION

I

JOHNSON'S first extant poem was written at Lichfield School in 1725; his last was written in the room where he died, almost sixty years later. He never prepared the collection of his writings which he had contemplated when he reserved to himself the right of printing one edition of *The Vanity of Human Wishes*.[1] A few days before his death he told John Nichols, when talking of 'a regular edition of his own works', that 'he had power, from the booksellers, to print such an edition, if his health admitted it, but had no power to assign over any edition, unless he could add notes, and so alter them as to make them new works'.[2] How many of his poems he would have deemed worthy of a place in an authorized collection we can only speculate. When he was consulted about the pieces to be included in a collection of the writings of his friend John Hawkesworth, he replied: 'I am for letting none stand that are only relatively good, as they were written in youth. The buyer has no better bargain when he pays for mean performances by being told that the author wrote them when young.'[3] He would not have been less rigorous in the choice of his own writings. The early verses which he had outgrown, as well as the occasional verses which were preserved by his friends, and the verses which he wrote in his later years to ease the tedium of sleeplessness, would have been left for others to garner. Perhaps in only one respect would he have lightened the task of his editors. He would have removed their doubts of the text to follow for the poems which he had selected.

Boswell intended to bring out a complete edition of the poems, as he stated in a note to the 'Chronological Catalogue of the Prose Works' prefixed to the third edition of the *Life*:

I do not here include his Poetical Works; for, excepting his Latin Translation of Pope's Messiah, his London, and his Vanity of Human Wishes imitated from Juvenal; his Prologue on the opening of Drury-Lane Theatre by Mr. Garrick, and his Irene, a Tragedy, they are very

[1] See p. 110.
[2] *The Gentleman's Magazine*, June 1791, p. 499; Boswell, *Life*, iv. 409.
[3] Letter to John Ryland, 12 April 1777. (*Letters*, ed. Chapman, ii. 168, no. 514.)

numerous, and in general short; and I have promised a complete edition of them, in which I shall with the utmost care ascertain their authenticity, and illustrate them with notes and various readings.[1]

This promise he had made in a note towards the end of the second edition of the *Life*, where he speaks of two English odes, written by Johnson at an early period, 'which will appear in my edition of his Poems'.[2] But the edition remained only a project. His growing ill health, his revision of the *Life*, and his concern with English politics and law precluded serious work on Johnson's poems.

His project shows how well aware he was of the shortcomings of the collected edition which had been published by George Kearsley, the bookseller, within a few weeks of Johnson's death, and the much more important edition included by Sir John Hawkins in 1787 in the eleventh volume of Johnson's *Works*. Most of Johnson's poems printed during his lifetime had appeared anonymously, some without his knowledge; and anonymous poems had been reprinted as his by editors of collections or magazines with whom he had no demonstrable connexion. Kearsley, who kept his eye on the market, had little time to give to textual problems or questions of authorship, and used what he found ready to hand. Hawkins added some new poems from Johnson's papers, but of the forty-five English poems in *Works* 1787 (excluding *Irene*), twenty-one were taken directly from Kearsley; four which were in Kearsley were taken from different sources. Sixteen were taken from Mrs. Piozzi's *Anecdotes*, 1786, and one from Anna Williams's *Miscellanies*, 1766; the remaining three were printed from manuscripts or from a combination of sources. Subsequent editors were to fail to take Boswell's announcement as a warning. They followed Hawkins, and, though they made corrections and additions, were never systematic in revising his texts; and they did not examine if all the poems which they printed were by Johnson. In the present volume the attempt is at last made to provide such an edition as Boswell described, with the advantage of the manuscripts and the information which have become available since his day. He had intended to begin, as far as was possible, from the beginning.

---

[1] *Life*, i. 16 n. 1.
[2] *Life*, ed. 1793, iii. 649; ed. 1934, iv. 375.

II

Five of Johnson's poetical works were published by themselves—*London*, 1738; the Prologue inaugurating Garrick's managership of Drury Lane Theatre in 1747; *The Vanity of Human Wishes*, 1749; *Irene*, 1749; and the Prologue written for a benefit performance of *Comus* in 1750. Other pieces were printed in periodicals, in miscellanies or works of joint authorship, or in his own prose works.

His first poem to be published, his Latin translation of Pope's *Messiah*, appeared in 1731 in an Oxford *Miscellany*, where it is said to be 'by Mr Johnson, a Commoner of Pembroke College'. No English poem of his was printed till 1738, when his *London*, though anonymous, began to make him known. During his active connexion with *The Gentleman's Magazine*, from 1738 to 1743, he contributed to it several short pieces, all likewise anonymous, and in 1747 he supplied a group of six pieces, the authorship of which has long been doubtful.[1] The Drury Lane Prologue of that year added to the reputation which he had gained by *London*, and in 1748 both were included—with new readings in *London*—in Dodsley's *Collection of Poems*. When *The Vanity of Human Wishes* appeared in 1749, with his name for the first time on a title-page, his reputation as a poet was established. Dodsley reprinted it in the fourth volume of his *Collection* in 1755, and again the text contained new readings. The *Collection* was to run to six volumes, but nothing more by Johnson has been identified. Mrs. Thrale recorded that he also wrote 'a Copy of Verses in Dodsley which he never would tell me, though he trusted me with secrets of far greater importance'.[2] But without any additional poem, Dodsley's revised reprints of *London* and *The Vanity of Human Wishes* form with the unrevised Drury Lane Prologue the most important group of Johnson's poems issued during his lifetime. Other corrections that he made in *London* and *The Vanity of Human Wishes* remained in manuscript at his death. In the edition of these two poems published at Oxford in 1759 under the title *Two Satires*, the texts were taken from Dodsley's *Collection*, and there is no evidence that Johnson was in any way concerned in this reprint which may have been promoted by Thomas Warton.

Two short poems[3] were reprinted in 1763 in Fawkes and Woty's

---

[1] See pp. 94–104. [2] *Thraliana*, ii. 81; ed. 1941, p. 205.
[3] 'The Winter's Walk' and the ode beginning 'Stern winter now by spring repress'd': see pp. 100 and 101.

Poetical Calendar, the first 'supplement' to Dodsley's *Collection*.
Johnson showed his interest in this publication by writing for its
last volume his 'Account of William Collins'; but his interest may
not have extended beyond the reprints of Collins's poems.[1] The
editors had searched the magazines for poems descriptive of the
months of the year, and from *The Gentleman's Magazine* for 1747,
it seems, they took two winter pieces which happened to be by
Johnson, though a new reading in one of them may be taken as
evidence that at some stage he was consulted. They did not give the
name of the author of either. They also included a few pieces which
were afterwards wrongly ascribed to Johnson.

In 1766 Johnson helped through the press the *Miscellanies in
Prose and Verse* published for the benefit of his blind friend Anna
Williams. As she had not herself written enough to make up a volume,
he secured contributions from Percy, Mrs. Thrale, and others, and
collected altogether some forty pieces. So as not to diminish her
credit for the volume, he gave no names, though a general statement
of indebtedness is made in the Advertisement, which he wrote
for her. He took first place with his poem *The Ant*, and included
five pieces which he had already printed, not always in the same
form, in periodicals.[2] His editorial control of this volume has set
problems which neither Boswell nor Malone was able to solve with
only the evidence of style to guide them. Passages undoubtedly in
his manner occur in poems which cannot be given to him as a whole.
He admitted that he had revised one of Miss Williams's pieces so
thoroughly that little remained of the original.[3] This volume ranks
second in importance among the publications of his lifetime containing a group of his poems.

[1] These reprints form the fullest collection of Collins's poems that had yet been made.
They are in the last two volumes. It is by no means improbable that Johnson had something to do with the attention paid by the editors to the poems of 'poor dear Collins'.

[2] 'To Miss —— On her giving the Author a Gold and Silk net-work Purse', 'An
Epitaph on Claudy Phillips', 'An Ode on Friendship', 'A translation of the Latin
Epitaph on Sir Thomas Hanmer', and 'To Miss —— On her playing upon the Harpsichord'. See pp. 96, 89, 36, 94, 97. The last of these had been printed in *The Museum*, the
others in *The Gentleman's Magazine*.

[3] 'On the Death of Stephen Grey': see p. 431. For other poems in this volume
ascribed to Johnson in whole or in part see pp. 445–70. Several annotated copies
have not notably improved on the attributions of Boswell and Malone; these are Mrs.
Thrale's (at Lichfield), Malone's (Dyce Collection), two of Thomas Percy's (1. Hyde
Collection, 2. Queen's University, Belfast), and James Boswell the Younger's (Yale); but
see A. T. Hazen, *Johnson's Prefaces and Dedications* (1937), pp. 213–15, and *Life*, ii. 479.

The success of Dodsley's *Collection* continued to lead to imitations and continuations. Another 'Supplement', of unknown editorship, but sometimes wrongly assigned to Moses Mendez because of its misleading title-page, appeared in 1767 and contained two poems[1] correctly said to be by Johnson. The *Collection* published by George Pearch in two volumes in 1768 included only one of Johnson's poems, the Prologue to *Comus*. But the enlarged edition of 1770 in four volumes attributed to him a group of twelve poems,[2] among them three by Hawkesworth, and four of which the author is not known. In the editions of 1775 and 1783, which were edited by Isaac Reed,[3] four of the twelve pieces were omitted for no obvious reason, and three of these were Johnson's. With the edition of 1770 the false attribution of minor pieces became regular. If Johnson knew of it, he was indifferent.

Six poems—*London*, *The Vanity of Human Wishes*, and four Prologues—are given in *Miscellaneous and Fugitive Pieces* issued by Tom Davies in two volumes at the end of 1773, with a third volume a month or two later. Johnson knew nothing of this publication till it appeared, though it consists mainly of his writings, the first volume being composed entirely of them. The six poems, which are in the second volume, form a more substantial collection than any that had yet been made; but they are mere reprints, and have no textual interest.

Other publications before his death with reprints of more than one of his poems are *The Theatrical Bouquet*, 1778, with four Prologues, and *English Prologues and Epilogues*, 1779, with two. In *The New Foundling Hospital for Wit*, 1784, four poems are said to be his, two of them correctly.[4]

III

These were the collections on which Kearsley could draw when Johnson's death, on 13 December 1784, made him decide on publishing an edition of the poems. He had shared in *Johnsoniana, or*

[1] 'The Winter's Walk' and 'Epitaph on Claudius Phillips'. See pp. 100, 89.
[2] See pp. 94–100.
[3] See E. L. McAdam, 'Pearch's *Collection of Poems*', in *The Bodleian Library Record*, April 1940, p. 153.
[4] The early verses 'On a Sprig of Myrtle', and 'On the Death of Dr. Levet': see pp. 49, 232.

a Collection of Bon Mots, &c. by Dr. Johnson, and Others in 1776, and had brought out by himself in 1781, likewise without permission, *The Beauties of Johnson*, a prose selection which kept on selling for several years; and now he lost no time in being ready with a *Life of Johnson* (anonymous, but by William Cooke), the preface to which is dated 28 December. On the last two pages of this book he gave a list of 'Poems of Dr Johnson's now printing in one volume, by G. Kearsley'. It was evidently intended to elicit further titles for the forthcoming collection. Two titles, both copied carelessly from Davies's *Miscellaneous and Fugitive Pieces*, were named in the Errata for deletion. But Kearsley was too easily content with the six new titles which he had secured before *The Poetical Works of Samuel Johnson, now first collected* was published on 15 February 1785. Someone had drawn his attention to three early pieces in *The Gentleman's Magazine* which had not been reprinted—'Stella in Mourning', 'To Lady Firebrace', and 'To Lyce'—and perhaps also to the verses 'On a sprig of Myrtle', and the translation of Pope's 'Messiah'; the late verses 'On the Death of Dr. Levet' he could have known for himself, for they were to be found in several magazines. Someone also had supplied notes for the preface. In all probability this was John Nichols, who had entered on his control of *The Gentleman's Magazine* a few years previously, and whose note on Lady Firebrace was taken over by Kearsley. But Kearsley claimed too much for his volume when he said that it 'not only called out all my industry, but that of my friends'. Except for the above-named poems and *Irene*, he relied in the main on the collections of Dodsley, Pearch, and Davies. He included all the poems given to Johnson, rightly or wrongly, in Pearch's *Collection* of 1770. Of poems assembled in this manner, the texts could not be trustworthy. One point, however, he has to his credit as an editor. He had printed the translation of Pope's *Messiah* from the Oxford *Miscellany* of 1731; but a better text was printed in *The St. James's Chronicle* for 22 January 1785, and he cancelled three leaves in order to substitute it. His attractive little volume provided a useful collection to which others, and he himself, were to add. A pirated reprint, by Osborne and Griffin, was published in the same year.

In this year also new poems by Johnson began to appear. Boswell included in his *Journal of a Tour to the Hebrides* the three Latin poems which Johnson had written or begun, as well as the Latin translation of Dryden's lines on Milton which he had in part recited, while they were on their travels; and he printed them from Johnson's manuscript or dictated copy, or Mrs. Thrale's transcript. By this time Mrs. Thrale, now Mrs. Piozzi, was at work on her *Anecdotes of the late Samuel Johnson, LL.D.*, which appeared in March 1786. She had been careful in preserving the verses which Johnson had dictated or addressed to her, or thrown off on the spur of the moment when in her company; and these she copied into *Thraliana*. Johnson was himself responsible for this heterogeneous collection of anecdote, gossip, and intimate details. 'It is many years', she thus begins, 'since Doctor Samuel Johnson advised me to get a little Book, and write in it all the little Anecdotes which might come to my Knowledge, all the Observations I might make or hear, all the Verses never likely to be published, and in fine ev'ry thing which struck me at the time. Mr Thrale has now treated me with a Repository,— and provided it with the pompous title of Thraliana.' Johnson could not have foreseen much that it was to contain, but he did on one occasion say to her, 'so you have writ out my translation of the Dove in the Thraliana, I warrant'.[1] He was not perturbed that she was keeping verses which he would never publish. On her marriage to Piozzi she took this 'Repository' with her to Italy, and there she extracted from it the material for much of her *Anecdotes*. Except one couplet, omitted inadvertently,[2] she took from it all the verses of which she alone had copies. With the dispersal of her manuscripts in recent years and their acquisition by great libraries—notably the John Rylands Library and the Henry E. Huntington Library— more accurate versions than she printed are now available; but we owe to her the preservation of over twenty pieces. The value of this addition to Johnson's verse may be underestimated because many of the pieces are trivial. They show him in his lighter, happier mood, even in 'a fit of frolicsome gaiety',[3] and nowhere is better illustrated what in the *Anecdotes* she called his 'almost Tuscan power of improvisation'; 'Baretti and I', she says in *Thraliana*, 'were talking one day of the Art of Improvisation; Johnson, says he, can do it as well as any Italian of us all if he pleases.'[4] It was not in her

[1] See p. 213.
[2] See p. 200. The couplet is widely separated in *Thraliana* from the other pieces.
[3] *Thraliana*, iii. 205; ed. 1941, p. 451.
[4] *Anecdotes*, p. 165; *Thraliana*, ii. 89; ed. 1941, p. 209.

nature to be a careful transcriber. The slight verbal differences between the versions in *Thraliana* and the *Anecdotes* are not to be explained by her absence in Italy while the book was going through the press. *Thraliana* often gives a better reading; and it sometimes states the occasion of the verses, and supplies names which had to be omitted in print.

Two of her later works contained further verses by Johnson. At the conclusion of her *Letters to and from the late Samuel Johnson, LL.D.*, 1788, she printed one of his Latin poems[1] and the translation of the 'metres' in *The Consolation of Philosophy* which she had made at his instigation and with his assistance, and carefully distinguished his work from her own. In *British Synonymy*, 1794, she published the full text of the verses on Sir John Lade, following not the original manuscript but the transcript in *Thraliana*. She had given only one stanza in the *Anecdotes*.

Almost all the new poems in the *Tour to the Hebrides* and the *Anecdotes* were included by the next editor, Sir John Hawkins. As an executor he could make use of Johnson's papers, and he therefore determined on a full biography; but he also agreed to superintend for the booksellers the first comprehensive collection of Johnson's various writings. The edition appeared in 1787, the 'Life' forming the first volume, and the poems the second half of the eleventh and last. Hawkins began the division of the poems into two groups, English and Latin or Greek, and seems to have confined his attention to the former. He took over all the poems in Kearsley's edition, added to them from Miss Williams's *Miscellanies* and the *Anecdotes*, and printed three[2] for the first time. The task of collecting the thirty-nine minor poems—some of which are not Johnson's—he cannot have found exacting; and it is much to be regretted that while he had control of Johnson's papers he did not use them in a way to inspire confidence. He spent most care on *London* and *The Vanity of Human Wishes*. In these he introduced several new readings and notes, the sources of which were not stated; but most of them are now thought to have been written by Johnson in the margins of early copies. Once or twice he restored a reading which Johnson had discarded.

---

[1] See p. 190.

[2] 'To Miss Hickman, playing on the Spinet', the translation of Horace, Odes, IV. vii, and the wrongly entitled 'On seeing a Bust of Mrs Montague': see pp. 53, 264, 219. He took the 'Epitaph on Phillips' from the *Miscellanies*, but printed *The Ant* from 'the original in Dr. Johnson's own hand-writing'.

The editor of the Latin poems—certainly of some, and probably of all—was Bennet Langton. 'Of the Latin pieces in the last of these volumes', says Hawkins, 'many were composed in those intervals of ease which during his last illness he at times experienced: others, and those the greater number, were the employment of his thoughts when, being retired to rest, the powers of sleep failed him. . . . The originals, as they were from time to time committed to writing, were by him delivered to Mr Langton, with directions to publish them; and it is to that gentleman that we owe the pleasure of perusing, in this form, these the most recent effusions of his genius, and latest evidences of his piety.'[1] 'During his sleepless nights', says Boswell, 'he amused himself by translating into Latin verse, from the Greek, many of the epigrams in the *Anthologia*. These translations, with some other poems by him in Latin, he gave to his friend Mr. Langton, who, having added a few notes, sold them to the booksellers for a small sum, to be given to some of Johnson's relations, which was accordingly done; and they are printed in the collection of his works.'[2] Johnson had long looked upon Langton as the friend who was most interested in his Latin compositions. In 1774 he had asked Langton to send him a copy of one of his Latin translations, the manuscript of which Mrs. Thrale had been obliged to surrender.[3] Langton was probably entrusted with the choice of the poems most worthy of preservation. But the plan of Hawkins's edition required that all the Latin poems should be collected, whether printed or not, and Langton—who was a better scholar than Hawkins—may have been held responsible for this larger task. It was not performed methodically: dates on the manuscripts seem regularly to have been ignored and omitted. The arrangement of the poems was haphazard, and the proof-reading was careless. Langton's work as an editor may have been finished when he handed his material to Hawkins, or the printer. He had added a few notes; and when a manuscript contained alternative readings, he had decided between them, and in one poem had recorded them.[4] If he ventured occasionally on an emendation, that liberty may have been within the terms of Johnson's directions.

[1] Hawkins, *Life*, 1787, p. ix.   [2] *Life*, ed. 1934, iv. 384.
[3] See p. 197.
[4] As in the 'Verses upon Inchkenneth', p. 195, and the translation of the Collect for Ash Wednesday, p. 229. The alternatives are recorded in the 'Prayer on losing the Power of Speech', p. 237.

When his version differs from an earlier printed version, evidence is lacking that he had manuscript authority.[1] The few extant manuscripts which he used bear signs of having passed through the hands of the printers;[2] and faults in the Latin are sometimes to be explained by the printer's difficulty with Johnson's writing.[3] Langton seems as a rule not to have made transcripts, but his own interpretation of Johnson's hand is written above each word, apparently by some amanuensis, perhaps one of his children.

Despite its many shortcomings, Hawkins's collection holds an outstanding place in the editorial history of Johnson's poems. A few additions were printed in the supplementary volume—'Vol. xiv'—issued in 1788 (and probably edited by Isaac Reed);[4] but Hawkins had provided what his successors, down to the Oxford edition of 1825, were to accept with scant scrutiny; and for many of the poems he, or Langton, remains our sole authority. Kearsley appropriated twenty-two of the English pieces for the 'considerably enlarged' edition of the *Poetical Works* which he published in 1789. When Johnson's poems were added in 1790 to a new edition of *The Works of the English Poets*, the series for which he had written the 'Prefaces Biographical and Critical' afterwards called *The Lives of the Poets*, the printer reproduced the English and Latin texts, and the notes, from the collection of 1787.

The next large contribution was made by Boswell in his *Life* in 1791. He printed from the original manuscripts seven schoolboy poems[5] and the epigram on Colley Cibber as Johnson had dictated it; and he added much information about the poems generally, some of it derived directly from Johnson. He was the first to recognize the problem of doubtful authorship, though he is not always to be trusted when he had to depend on internal evidence; and unfortunately his prejudice against Mrs. Thrale led him to cast too much doubt on what she had said. His texts, like hers, show signs of hasty transcription. His interest in the poems increased as

---

[1] As in the translation of Pope's *Messiah*, p. 43, and the 'Ode upon the Isle of Skye', p. 192.

[2] See p. 241. All used by Langton bear a large '×'.

[3] As in 'Spes', l. 6, p. 236.

[4] The Latin translation of Dryden's Epigram on Milton; the 'Ode on Friendship'; the Epilogue (Latin and English) to the *Carmen Seculare* of Horace; and the Latin translation of the Epitaph on Prince Madoc, of doubtful authorship. See pp. 42, 36, 218, 448.

[5] See pp. 1–2.

new manuscripts were brought to his notice. In 1791 he had been content with a selection of Johnson's early pieces; the seven which he gave are now known to have been selected from a group of thirteen. By 1793 he had come to think of his complete edition. Of the value of the information which it would have contained there can be no question; but there is good reason to think that, unless he had enjoyed the assistance of Malone, it might not have been equally distinguished by the accuracy of its texts.

IV

Hawkins's edition was unfavourably reviewed by Arthur Murphy in four articles in *The Monthly Review*, and when Hawkins was dead the booksellers secured Murphy for their second edition, which was published in 1792 in twelve volumes. Hawkins's *Life* was abandoned, and its place was taken by Murphy's shorter and more readable if not so well-informed *Essay on the Life and Genius of Dr. Johnson*. With it the poems formed the first volume. But if Murphy had any share in the new arrangement of 'Murphy's edition', as it is generally called for convenience, he displayed little interest in the poems beyond what he said of them in his *Essay*. They were reprinted from Hawkins's edition, mostly page for page, with the notes and the mistakes. Three of the shorter English pieces were omitted,[1] and nothing was added. And nothing was added in the editions of 1796 and 1801. The first editor to incorporate poems from Boswell's *Life* was Robert Anderson in *The Poets of Great Britain*, 1795.

On Murphy's death Alexander Chalmers was called in by the booksellers for the edition of 1806, but his first serious work on the poems was done in the edition of 1816. By recording the more striking variants in *London* and *The Vanity of Human Wishes*, and making use of Johnson's corrected copies of these poems, or more probably the transcript of the corrections which was made by James Boswell the younger,[2] he ranks as the first textual critic. Boswell supplied him with notes—some of them textual—on two poems[3]

---

[1] Murphy thought that the lines on Mrs. Montagu were not by Johnson: see p. 219. The other two pieces were evidently omitted as being too trivial—'The tender infant' p. 184, and 'Wear the gown', p. 224.

[2] See pp. 64–5 and 112–13.

[3] The translation from the *Medea* of Euripides, beginning 'The rites deriv'd from ancient days', and 'Friendship': see pp. 220 and 36.

not hitherto included, and it may be that the credit of all the textual work, small in bulk but good so far as it goes, rightly belongs to Malone's collaborator in the great Variorum edition of Shakespeare. In the edition of 1823 a few more poems were added, one of them being the verses on Sir John Lade.[1] None of Chalmers's three editions can have added appreciably to the labours of his busy life; but he was a better editor than Murphy, and better than his immediate successor.

The obvious merits of the edition published at Oxford[2] in 1825 are typographical. The claim made in the prospectus that it would be superior to preceding editions in beauty of execution may have been fulfilled, but not the other claim that it would be superior in correctness of text. It was printed from the 12° edition of 1824. The anonymous editor was Francis Pearson Walesby, who a few years later was appointed Professor of Anglo-Saxon.[3] The bulk of his work on the poems consisted of prefatory observations on the two Satires and *Irene*, but in the few notes which he supplied he included two poems in Boswell's *Life* which Chalmers had missed, and one of these—the Greek epitaph on Goldsmith—had nowhere been reprinted.[4] Other poems were left still ungathered. No editor had yet made so good use of the *Life* as Anderson in 1795, but his collection lay outside the main process of accumulation.

The year 1825 marks the end of the first period of editorial activity.[5] The standard editions had been provided which were to suffice for the nineteenth century. From time to time new verses and new

---

[1] Chalmers had added it to Johnson's poems in *The Works of the English Poets*, 1810, vol. xvi, but not in the edition of 1816.

[2] This edition was the first of the 'Oxford English Classics', a series which was not published by the Clarendon Press but was one of Pickering's ventures. The imprint is usually 'Oxford. Printed for William Pickering, London; and Talboys and Wheeler, Oxford.' To justify the name of the series, the prospectus announced that 'No Author will be published without the assistance of some Graduate Member of the University of Oxford'.

[3] See *The Times*, 7 August 1858, p. 9.

[4] See p. 198. The other is the epigram on Colley Cibber (p. 92). It had been reprinted by Anderson.

[5] During this period the poems were published by themselves in 'Cooke's Edition', 1797; by Thomas Park in 'Sharpe's Edition of the British Poets', 1805, Supplement, 1808 (combined 1811); in the United States 1805, 1810, and 1816; and with a Life by F. W. Blagdon, 1806, 1815, 1820. None of these collections has any importance in the history of the text.

details were to be published, as by Croker in his notes to Boswell's
Life or by correspondents to *Notes and Queries*, but till the end of
the century, and even later, the total contribution to the study of the
poems was small and no new collection showed any advance.
Birkbeck Hill might have edited them, had he been encouraged.
In 1892, when forwarding to a friend a letter which he had received
from America, he wrote: 'I have often thought of an edition of
Johnson's poems which, as the writer suggests, should include all his
minor verse, such as his translations of Latin and Greek verse in
the Rambler etc. I fear however that in this country the sale would
be very slight, whatever might be the case in America.' His notes
on the poems in his edition of Boswell's *Life* are not his best, and
he did better to turn to the *Johnsonian Miscellanies* and *The Lives
of the Poets*. For many years now the most useful work on Johnson's
poems has been done in educational editions of the Satires or in
letters and articles in periodicals.

V

The manuscripts used by Hawkins, Langton, and Boswell
disappeared, and of the majority little seems to be discoverable; but
many have been found and are in libraries and private collections—
mainly in America—where they are no longer hidden; and some
are of poems that are otherwise unknown. Some forty holograph
manuscripts have survived:

Translation of Virgil, *Pastoral* v (p. 5)[1]
Translation of Horace, *Odes* II. xiv (p. 11)
Translation of Horace, *Odes* II. xx (p. 12)
Translation of Horace, *Epode* II (p. 13)
Translation of Addison's 'Battle of the Pygmies and the Cranes'
    (p. 22)[2]
Festina Lentè (p. 28)
Upon the Feast of St Simon & St Jude (p. 29)
Mea nec Falernæ &c. (p. 40)
Adjecere Bonæ &c. (p. 41)
Aurora est Musis Amica (p. 41)
To Miss Hickman playing on the Spinet (p. 53)

[1] Lines 32–52 only.   [2] Lines 97–117 and 140–70 only.

London (p. 60)[1]
The Vanity of Human Wishes (pp. 110, 415)[2]
Epitaph on Hogarth (p. 181)
Psalmus 117 (p. 182)
Γνῶθι σεαυτόν (p. 187)
On Recovering the Use of his Eyes (p. 191)
Ode to Mrs. Thrale 'Permeo terras' (p. 193)
Tetrastick on Goldsmith (p. 198)
Greek Epigram on Sir Thomas More (p. 457)
Charade on Thomas Barnard (p. 205)
Waltoni Piscator Perfectus (p. 208)
Ad T.L. M.D. (p. 215)
Latin translation from Euripides (p. 223)
A Short Song of Congratulation (p. 225)
Ex Anglico: Epitaph on Robin of Doncaster (p. 227)[3]
Ex Anglico: Distich on Lycoris (p. 227)[3]
On Mrs. Thrale (p. 229)
A Summons to Dr. Lawrence (p. 229)
Translation of the Collect for Ash Wednesday (p. 229)
Jejunium et Cibus (p. 230)
Nugæ Anapæsticæ (p. 231)
Prayer for 1 January 1784 (p. 240)
Translation of the *Greek Anthology*, 7. 151 (p. 243)
Translation of the *Greek Anthology*, 7. 553 'Zosima' (p. 245)
Translation of the *Greek Anthology*, 10. 30 (p. 253)
Translation of the *Greek Anthology*, 10. 113 (p. 255)
Septem Ætates (p. 260)
'Luce collustret mihi pectus almâ' (p. 260)
Translation of Horace, *Odes* IV. vii (p. 264)
First draft of 'Irene' (p. 368)
Drafts of part of Act V of 'Irene' (p. 404)

The emergence of several of these manuscripts since 1941 gives reason to hope that others may from time to time be added to the list.[4]

---

[1] Imperfect, comprising lines 99–106, 148–51, and 194–263; p. 412 below.
[2] See the complete transcript appended to this edition, p. 415 below.
[3] Both these items are on the same piece of paper.
[4] See *A Preliminary Handlist of Documents and Manuscripts of Samuel Johnson*, Oxford Bibliographical Society: Occasional Publications No. 2, 1967.

At the same time, and in greater numbers, manuscripts not in Johnson's own hand have become accessible. Mrs. Thrale's transcripts, either in *Thraliana* or by themselves, have almost the value of originals when they are her copies of what Johnson dictated to her. Most are in *Thraliana* but separate copies survive of

Translations from Boethius (p. 169)
In Theatro (p. 179)
Epitaph on Hogarth (p. 181)
Motto for the Collar of Banks's Goat (p. 183)
Verses to Dr Lawrence (p. 190)
Oda, 'Permeo terras' (p. 193)
French Distichs (p. 199)
To Mrs Thrale on her thirty-fifth year (p. 204)
A Short Song of Congratulation (p. 225)

What Boswell took down survives in his journals and the papers associated with his biographies of Johnson, which he carefully preserved and which are now in the Library of Yale University. Among those papers are transcripts of early Johnsonian verses made by Edmund Hector, and others made by James Ross, Boswell's, servant, from originals of schoolboy compositions. Hector supplied Boswell with transcripts of

On a Daffodill (p. 2)
Translation of Horace, *Odes* I. xxii, 'Integer Vitæ' (p. 8)
To a Young Lady on her Birth-Day (p. 31)
The Young Author (p. 32)
An Epilogue to *The Distrest Mother* (p. 34)
On a Lady leaving her Place of Abode (p. 52)

John Wentworth, Johnson's Stourbridge schoolmaster, preserved twelve school exercises by Johnson. William Bowles of Heale arranged with Wentworth's nephew for them to be lent to Boswell, who had copies made by James Ross. In some cases the originals have also survived (asterisked)

Translation from Virgil, *Pastoral* I (p. 4)
Translation of the first Hymn to Daphnis in Virgil, *Pastoral* V
   (p. 5)
*Translation of the second Hymn from Virgil, *Pastoral* V (p. 7)
Translation of Horace, *Odes* II. ix (p. 10)

*Translation of Horace, *Odes* II. xiv (p. 11)
*Translation of Horace, *Odes* II. xx (p. 12)
*Translation of Horace, *Epode* II (p. 13)
Translation of Horace, *Epode* XI (p. 17)
Translation of the Dialogue between Hector and Andromache (p. 18)
Translation of Addison's Battle of the Pygmies and the Cranes (p. 22)[1]
*Festina Lente (p. 28)
*Upon the Feast of St Simon & St Jude (p. 29)

Other transcripts were made by Baretti (pp. 168, 201), Fanny Burney (pp. 216–17), Elizabeth Carter (p. 232), Samuel Lysons (p. 225), Thomas Percy (pp. 92, 134, 183), Frances Reynolds (pp. 232, 443), and Lady Mary Wortley Montagu (p. 36); and some by or for David Garrick (p. 88) and Henry Hervey (pp. 96, 97, and 99). In several cases these copies are the only authorities.

In addition to the five poems published by themselves and the translations of the mottoes in *The Rambler* and *The Adventurer*, about thirty pieces—some of them only couplets—were printed during Johnson's lifetime. Most of them were contributed to *The Gentleman's Magazine* between 1738 and 1747. After 1755, the year in which he revised *The Vanity of Human Wishes* and completed the *Dictionary*, the only new poems that he could have seen in print were—as far as is known—*The Ant*, the Prologues to *The Good Natur'd Man* and *A Word to the Wise*, the Epilogues to the *Carmen Seculare*, the translation of a short passage in the *Medea* of Euripides contributed to Burney's *History of Music*, and 'On the Death of Dr. Robert Levet'. Some of the earlier poems were to reappear with new readings in such collections as Duncombe's *Horace in English Verse*[2] and Anna Williams's *Miscellanies*. The circumstances in which the minor poems were printed did not make for textual accuracy; and in all his poems, as Boswell found,[3] he was prepared to make alterations. The corrections which he left for *London* and *The Vanity of Human Wishes* show that he did not consider either of these poems to have reached its final form.

---

[1] Boswell seems to have failed to return the whole of the original manuscript of this piece, for a leaf from it is preserved in the Boswell papers (p. xxiii n. 2, *ante*).

[2] See p. 8.   [3] See *The Vanity of Human Wishes*, l. 138.

VI

In 1941 the late David Nichol Smith and Edward L. McAdam could fairly consider themselves as pioneers in the editing of Johnson's poems. Since then advances in Johnsonian studies have led to the enlargement of the canon of his works, and at the same time textual criticism has developed new standards of editing. For the *Yale Edition of the Works of Samuel Johnson*, vol. vi (1964), the late E. L. McAdam, aided by Mr. George Milne, prepared a modernized text of the whole body of Johnson's verse as it was then known. Their edition reflected the many discoveries of new pieces made in the intervening twenty-three years. Those discoveries meant that the 1941 Oxford English Text of Johnson's poems had fallen behind the progress of Johnsonian scholarship, so that its recent going out of print has afforded the opportunity for a reconsideration of the canon and the texts.

In preparing the texts for this edition the original documents or photographs of them have been consulted and the readings have been carefully checked. In all instances the reviser has tried to reconstitute the texts without regard to the versions of his predecessors, though it has been gratifying to find how often, despite his wish to avoid their influence, he has come eventually to agree with them.

Each poem is preceded by a list of all the known authorities for its text, whether holographs, transcripts, or publications. The attempt has been made to record every appearance in print of Johnson's poems during his lifetime. Occasionally later publications have been recorded when they have been of some interest or significance. Many reprints were far from authoritative, but the lists sometimes yield unexpected evidence of the extent to which the poems were known.

Johnson's manuscripts have been followed whenever they were available, and likewise all published texts that he is known to have revised. All the variants have been recorded fully with the exception of minor spelling differences and of variants in punctuation. Some readings have no significance beyond showing how errors crept in and became for a while the usual reading.

The introductory notes state what is known about the occasion and composition of the poems, and explain the relation of the different versions. Together they form a collection of the main facts in Johnson's career as a poet. They also deal with the problems of authorship. Eighteen pieces of which the authorship is doubtful, though most of them are probably not by Johnson, are printed together as an appendix; another appendix gives a list of thirty-three pieces which at one time or another have been ascribed to him wrongly or with no good reason.

The former editors printed a transcript of Johnson's drafts of *Irene* believing it to be the only surviving draft of any of his major works. To it can now be added a further portion of the play, part of a draft of *London*, and the whole draft of *The Vanity of Human Wishes*, which are here printed by kind permission of Mrs. Mary Hyde.

The arrangement of 1941 followed the first editor, George Kearsley, in placing the major poems in the first place, but thereafter it printed the poems in chronological order. Such an arrangement has seemed hard to justify and so in this revision all the poems have been placed in chronological order, generally by date of composition, but where that is uncertain then by date of publication. *Irene* has been kept separate from the main series because its composition stretches over at least thirteen years, and because, as a play, it does not so comfortably fit into the sequence of poems. The whole collection is now more readily associated with the author's life and career to form a historical record of the poetic mind of Samuel Johnson.

EARLY POEMS

SEVEN of Johnson's early poems written during his schooldays or shortly afterwards were printed by Boswell (*Life*, 1791, i. 17–23; ed. 1934, i. 5–16). These he selected from the 'considerable collection' which he obtained 'by the favour of Mr. Wentworth, son of one of his masters, and of Mr. Hector, his school-fellow and friend'. Wentworth was the nephew of John Wentworth, the master of the Grammar School at Stourbridge (see A. L. Reade, *Johnsonian Gleanings*, iii. 153, 156); Edmund Hector, familiarly called 'Mund', was Johnson's school-fellow at Lichfield and his chief friend in the days of his early struggles in the Midlands.

From Hector, Boswell received information about seven poems in a letter of 1 February 1785 (*The Correspondence and other Papers of James Boswell relating to the making of the 'Life of Johnson'*, ed. M. Waingrow, 1969, pp. 47–9). Transcripts by Hector of five of them are in the Boswell papers at Yale, but of two ('An Ode on Friendship' and 'To Laura') there are none. Four of the pieces mentioned by Hector were published in *The Gentleman's Magazine*, xiii (July 1743), pp. 376, 378, 380 ('An Ode on Friendship', 'The Young Author', 'To Laura', and the translation of Horace, *Odes* I. xxii, 'Integer Vitæ'). The revision of the texts before publication is evidence for Johnson's responsibility for their appearance in the *Magazine*, and so it is probable that Hector did not have the original manuscripts; that he did not supply Boswell with transcripts of 'An Ode on Friendship' and 'To Laura' may mean that he not only did not have the originals but that he had no copies either.

In 1791 Hector wrote again to Boswell telling him that he had found two more of 'the Dr.'s Odes' which he promised to transcribe and send (Waingrow, *Correspondence*, p. 440), but when he did send them on 31 October 1791 (ibid., p. 449) only one ('An Ode on a Lady leaving her Place of Abode') was new, the other was a second transcription of 'On a Daffodill'. One further version of a poem was sent by Hector to Boswell on 9 January 1794: 'Lately in looking over some papers I meant to burn, I found the original manuscript of the Myrtle, with the date on it, 1731, which I have inclosed' (Waingrow, *Correspondence*, p. 575). This manuscript was released from the Boswell papers at the sale of the books of James Boswell the Younger in 1825 and is recorded again in the Pocock sale in 1875 when it was bought by Thomas Thorpe of none of the pieces mentioned or transcribed by Hector is Johnson's manuscript known to have survived, and it may be presumed that in some cases Johnson had them and in others Hector kept them, but they were eventually lost. Hector's estate devolved to the families of Shipperdson and Meysey-Thompson, but no Johnsonian manuscripts have emerged from those sources.

How long Johnson was at Stourbridge as Wentworth's pupil and assistant is uncertain. Boswell states that 'he remained at Stourbridge for little more than a year', and that he then 'loitered for two years' at Lichfield before he went

to Pembroke College in October 1728. He appears to have gone to Stourbridge
after the Whitsuntide vacation of 1726 (*Johnsonian Gleanings*, iii. 155). If Boswell
is correct in saying that he was there for little more than a year, he did not leave
before Whitsuntide 1727; but in that case Boswell's 'two years' at Lichfield
(Hawkins had said 'about two years') is only a loose description of a period of
seventeen months at most. In any case some if not all of the pieces preserved
by Wentworth may be dated 1726, and none can be shown to be later than 1727.

Boswell gained access to Wentworth's collection by the agency of William
Bowles of Heale, who wrote on 9 November 1787: 'I sent by the coach this evening
12 exercises of Dr Johnson and 2 of a schoolfellow of his: they are numbred,
and Mr Wentworth begs to have the MSS returned to him' (Waingrow, *Correspondence*, p. 244; cf. also pp. 203, 228, and 238). Six numbered originals and an
unnumbered fragment of a seventh of these pieces survive, and it is possible
to reconstruct a list of the twelve pieces: [1] Translation from Virgil, *Pastoral* I;
[2], 3 Translations of the Hymns to Daphnis from Virgil, *Pastoral* V; 4 Translation of Horace, *Epode* II [5] Translation of Horace, *Epode* XI; [6] Translation
of Horace, *Odes* II. ix; 7 Translation of Horace, *Odes* II. xiv; 8 Translation of
Horace, *Odes* II. xx; 9 'Festina Lentè'; 10 'Upon the Feast of St Simon & St
Jude'; [11] Translation of part of the Dialogue between Hector and Andromache; [12] Translation of Addison's 'Battle of the Pygmies and the Cranes'.
(Bracketed numbers are inferred, but the extant numbers are left plain.) From
the number '3' on the original of the second 'Hymn' it is evident that the two
parts from *Pastoral* V were regarded by Wentworth as distinct items. As befits
schoolboy exercises most are translations, and it is fair to suppose that 'Festina
Lentè' and 'Upon the Feast of St Simon & St Jude' were both prescribed
themes.

ON A DAFFODILL, THE FIRST FLOWER
THE AUTHOR HAD SEEN THAT YEAR

Transcript by Edmund Hector, sent to Boswell on 1 February 1785 (Boswell
    MS. C. 1606).
Transcript by Edmund Hector, sent to Boswell on 31 October 1791 (Boswell
    MS. C. 1531).
Works, vi (Yale edn., 1964), 3–4.

Sending the first transcript Hector wrote: 'The Daffodaill was wrote between
his 15th and 16th Year. As it was not characteristick of the Flower He never
much lik'd it.' (Waingrow, *Correspondence*, pp. 47–51). The same letter adds
important information about Johnson's early poems:

'Integer Vitæ was translated at School. The next Year some Young Ladies at Lich.
had a mind to act The Distress'd Mother, for whom he wrote the Epilogue and gave it
me to convey privately to them. The Ode on Friendship was much about the same time.

'To a Lady, on her Birth-day, was made, as I was present, almost impromptu. As
was the Epigram, the first line being propos'd by Dr James, the company call'd upon
him to finish it.

'The Young Authour I shou'd have mentiond before the two last.'

Johnson's fifteenth birthday was 7 September 1724; the verses were perhaps written in the spring of the following year.

The two transcripts differ in minor features. The first was written by Hector when he was just seventy-seven; his hand is firm, consistent, fluent, and clear; any errors are likely to be the result of haste or inattention. The second was written when he was eighty-four; the hand is shaky but clear with each letter formed carefully and separately. Although Hector is a less efficient writer in 1791 with a few errors arising from lack of co-ordination ('srivlings' in l. 23), he was writing more slowly and probably paying more attention to his copy. For these reasons the second transcript is preferred here, with its occasional lapses corrected from 1785.

On a Daffodill, the first Flower the Author had seen that Year

H AIL! lovely Flower, first honour of the Year,
   Hail! beauteous earnest of approaching Spring;
Whose early buds unusual glories wear,
And of a fruitfull year fair omens bring.

Be thou the favourite of the indulgent Sky,   5
Nor feel th' inclemencies of Wintry Air,
May no rude blasts thy sacred bloom destroy;
May Storms howl gently o'er, and learn to spare.

May lambent Zephyrs gently wave thy head,
And balmy Spirits thro' thy foliage play,   10
May the Morns earliest tears on thee be shed
And Thou impearl'd with dew, appear more gay.

May throngs of beauteous Virgins 'round thee crowd,
And view thy charms with no malignant Eyes;
Then scorn those flow'rs, to which the Ægyptians bow'd,   15
Which prostrate Memphis own'd her deities.

Title. *1785*; *not in 1791*.   2 beauteous] beautious *1785*; beauteoust *1791*   3 Buds . . . Glories *1785*   4 fruitfull] *in 1785 Hector first wrote* faithfull   6 the *1785*   8 o're *1791*   10 And] May *1791*   11 earlies *1791*   13 beautious *1791*   15 Flowers *1785*   bowd *1791*   16 Deities *1785*

If mix'd with these, divine Cleora smile,
Cleora's smiles a genial warmth dispence,
New verdure ev'ry fading leaf shall fill,
And Thou shalt flourish by her influence.   20

But while I sing, the nimble moments fly,
See! Sol's bright Chariot seeks the Western Main,
And Ah! behold the shriveling blossoms die,
So late admir'd, and prais'd, alas! in vain.

With grief this emblem of Mankind I see,   25
Like one awakned from a pleasing dream,
Cleora's self fair Flower shall fade like thee;
Alike must fall the Poet and his Theme.

TRANSLATION OF VIRGIL
'PASTORAL' I

Transcript by James Ross in the Boswell Papers, Yale University Library.
Boswell, *Life*, 1791, i. 18 (1934, i. 51).

In *Adventurer* 92 (22 September 1753) Johnson gave a critique of Virgil's
Pastorals in which he wrote:

'The first and the tenth pastorals, whatever be determined of the rest, are sufficient to
place their author above the reach of rivalry. . . . But notwithstanding the excellence of
the tenth pastoral, I cannot forbear to give the preference to the first, which is equally
natural and more diversified.'

Virgil's Pastoral the 1st

MELIBÆUS.

How, Tit'rus, you, supine and careless laid,
    Play on your Pipe beneath this Beechen shade;
While wretched we about the World must roam,
And leave our pleasing fields and native home,

18 dispense *1785*   19 leafe *1791*   22 See Sol's *1791*   23 srivlings *1791*
26 awaken'd *1785*

Title. *Ross*   1 How] Now *Boswell*

17. *Cleora* see p. 52, *post*, and *The Rambler*, No. 15. The name recurs in the lost
Adversaria: 'I near dull —— Cleora, a lady dreaded for her elegance and knowledge,
came by chance; I shone' (Hawkins, *Life of Johnson*, p. 456 n.).

Here at your ease you sing your amorous flame,   5
And the Wood rings with Amarillis' name.

TITYRUS.

Those blessings, friend, a deity bestow'd,
For I shall never think him less than God;
Oft on his Altar shall my firstlings lie,
Their blood the consecrated stones shall dye: 10
He gave my flocks to graze the flowery meads,
And me to tune at ease th' unequall reeds.

MELIBÆUS.

My admiration only I expres'd,
(No spark of envy harbours in my breast)
That when confusion o'er the Country reigns,   15
To you alone this happy state remains.
Here I, though faint myself, must drive my Goats,
Far from their antient fields and humble cots.
This scarce I lead, who left on yonder rock
Two tender kids, the hopes of all the flock.   20
Had we not been perverse and careless grown,
This dire event by omens was foreshown;
Our trees were blasted by the Thunder stroke,   ⎫
And left-hand crows, from an old hollow oak,   ⎬
Foretold the coming evil by their dismal croak.   ⎭   25

TRANSLATION FROM VIRGIL
'PASTORAL' V

Holograph manuscript of ll. 32–48, 53–6 (Second 'Hymn') in the Hornby
 Collection, Liverpool Public Library.
Transcript by James Ross in the Boswell Papers, Yale University Library.
Works, vi (Yale edn., 1964), 6–7.

The holograph translates ll. 56–71 and 76–8 of the fifth Eclogue; the transcript translates ll. 56–75. Since the last four lines are on the verso of the holo-

6 Amerillis *Ross*   9 Alter . . . lye *Ross*   12 the *Ross*   17 tho' *Ross*
21 carless *Ross*

6. The original of this line, 'Formosam resonare doces Amarillida silvas', was praised
by Johnson in 1763, 'All the modern languages (said he) cannot furnish so melodious
a line' (*Life*, i. 460).

graph, it seems that Ross simply failed to turn over. The holograph is severely
trimmed and has probably lost Johnson's ll. 49–53 at the foot of the leaf.

In his criticism of the pastorals in *Adventurer* 92 Johnson wrote of the
original:

'The fifth contains a celebration of Daphnis, which has stood to all succeeding ages as
the model of pastoral elegies. To deny praise to a performance which so many thousands have laboured to imitate, would be to judge with too little deference for the
opinion of mankind: yet whoever shall read it with impartiality, will find that most of
the images are of the mythological kind, and therefore easily invented; and that there
are few sentiments of rational praise, or natural lamentation.'

The Hymns to Daphnis from the fifth Pastoral of Virgil

MOPSUS

THE Nymphs bewail'd poor Daphnis hapless death
    Evn in the bloom of life depriv'd of Breath
The limpid streams with ruefull murmurs flow
And all the withering woods confess their woe
While his sad Mother frantick with despair   5
Accus'd the Gods and curs'd each luckless star
That day that mournfull day, no chearfull song
With pleasing sound allur'd the rural throng
The sympathising Cattle hung their Heads
Nor crop'd the tastfull herb, nor trac'd the verdant meads   10
Touch'd with thy fate Numidias Lyons roar
And spread their echoing Grief from Shore to Shore
By Daphnis skill th' Armenian Tigers broke
Endur'd the stinging lash, and tamely bore the Yoke
Daphnis with Ivy wreath'd the Jav'lins round   15
And trod to Bacchus' praise the Mystick ground
As vines the Elms, as grapes adorn the vine ⎫
As corn the fields, as Bulls the Herds of Kine ⎬
So much our splendour was encreas'd by thine ⎭
Now, at thy fall incens'd the rural Gods   20
Withdraw their Cars and seek the blesst abodes
In vain the lab'ring Hind manures the plain
The banefull weeds spring up, and choak the grain

Title. *Ross*   10 trac'd the] trac'd ye *Ross*   14 stinging] Shuging *Ross*
19 emcreas'd *Ross*   21 blesst] blesstd *Ross*

Now each parterre with thorny Brakes is fill'd
Where late the lilies mix'd with violets smil'd   25
Ye Swains! bestrow the ground with leaves and spread
O'er all the warbling founts a cooling shade
On his dead body let a tomb be plac'd
And be the stone with this inscription grac'd
'Here fairer than his flock the Shepherd lyes   30
'Whose fame from earth resounded to the Skies.'

[MENALCAS]

Now beauteous Daphnis cloath'd with heav'nly light,
Shuns Pluto's Kingdoms and the Realms of Night.
Beneath his feet admires each shining Star,
And sees the Motions of th' Harmonious Sphere.   35
Pleasure in ev'ry Nymph and Shepherd reigns,
And banish'd Sorrow flies the joyous Plains.
The harmless Wolves no more our Cattle fear,
No toils shall intercept the nimble Deer.
Rocks send their acclamations to the Skie,   40
And Woods and Mountains hail the Deity.
Attend my prayers propitious, hear my vow, ⎞
Here have I rais'd four sacred altars, two   ⎬
To great Latona's Son, and two to you.   ⎠
Two Bowls with oyl and Milk I'll yearly crown,   45
And pour them on the consecrated Stone.
Then we with wine will drown our troubles, laid
If winter by the fire; if Summer, in the Shade.
Thyrsis while   sings shall   the Gods
That range lascivious through the lonsome Roads   50
When to the Nymphs the Swain due homage pays
Libations he shall pour to Daphnis praise
While Boars the rocks, while Fish the Rivers love,
While Bees shall feed on Thyme, and Birds shall haunt the grove
Thou shalt with Bacchus equal honours share,   55
The Swains shal pay their vows, and thou shalt hear their prayer.

35 Spher *Ross*   39 entercept *Ross*   40 Skies *Ross*   43 alters *Ross*
48 by the Shade *Ross*   53–6 *omitted by Ross*

49. Cantabunt mihi Damoetas et Lyctius Ægon: | Saltantes Satyros imitabitur
Alphesibœus. Virg. *Ecl.* v. 72–3. Ross left the blanks.

TRANSLATIONS OF HORACE
'ODES', Book I. xxii

Transcript by Edmund Hector in the Boswell Papers, Yale University Library.
The Gentleman's Magazine, July 1743, p. 380.
The Scots Magazine, July 1743, p. 318.
The Works of Horace in English Verse . . . ed. William Duncombe, 1757, i. 82;
2nd. ed. 1767, i. 88-9. Boswell, *Life*, 1791, i. 18 (1934, i. 51).

Boswell printed his version of the translation which Johnson made at school,
from Hector's transcript; but he was unaware of its two later forms. Johnson
revised it on sending it in 1743 to *The Gentleman's Magazine*, and this version
was more seriously revised for inclusion in the translation of Horace edited by
Duncombe in 1757. (Cf. *Life*, iii. 314.) It is there said to be 'By S. J.', and is
wrongly marked as having 'never been printed'; in the second edition Johnson
is named.
The first and last forms are here given in full.

(FIRST VERSION)

Translation of HORACE. *Book* I. *Ode* xxii.

T HE man, my friend, whose conscious heart
    With virtue's sacred ardour glows,
Nor taints with death the envenom'd dart,
    Nor needs the guard of Moorish bows:

Though Scythia's icy cliffs he treads,   5
    Or horrid Africk's faithless sands;
Or where the fam'd Hydaspes spreads
    His liquid wealth o'er barbarous lands.

For while by Chloe's image charm'd,
    Too far in Sabine woods I stray'd;   10
Me singing, careless and unarm'd,
    A grizly wolf surprised, and fled.

No savage more portentous stain'd
    Apulia's spacious wilds with gore;

Title. Integer Vitæ Translated. *Hector*   Variants in *The Gentleman's Magazine*, 1743:
Title. *From* HORACE. *Integer Vitæ*, &c.   2 ardor   3 th' envenom'd   5 cliff
6 torrid   8 barb'rous   12 furious wolf approach'd and   13 No beast
more dreadful ever stain'd

None fiercer Juba's thirsty land,   15
    Dire nurse of raging lions, bore.

Place me where no soft summer gale
    Among the quivering branches sighs;
Where clouds condens'd for ever veil
    With horrid gloom the frowning skies: 20

Place me beneath the burning line,
    A clime deny'd to human race;
I'll sing of Chloe's charms divine,
    Her heav'nly voice, and beauteous face.

(FINAL VERSION)

To ARISTIUS FUSCUS

THE Man, my Friend, whose conscious Heart
    With Virtue's sacred Ardour glows,
Nor taints with Death th' envenom'd Dart,
    Nor needs the Guard of *Moorish* Bows.

O'er icy *Caucusus* he treads,   5
    Or torrid *Afric*'s faithless Sands,
Or where the fam'd *Hydaspes* spreads
    His liquid Wealth thro' barbarous Lands.

For while in *Sabine* Forests, charm'd
    By *Lalagé*, too far I stray'd,   10
Me singing, careless and unarm'd,
    A furious Wolf approach'd, and fled.

No Beast more dreadful ever stain'd
    Apulia's spacious Wilds with Gore;
No Beast more fierce *Numidia*'s Land,   15
    The Lion's thirsty Parent, bore.

15 (First Version)   None e'er more fierce *Numidia*'s land,
                The lyon's thirsty parent, bore.

17 summer's   18 quiv'ring

Place me where no soft Summer Gale
　　Among the quivering Branches sighs,
Where Clouds, condens'd, for ever veil
　　With horrid Gloom the frowning Skies:　　　20

Place me beneath the burning Zone,
　　A Clime deny'd to human Race;
My Flame for *Lalagé* I'll own;
　　Her voice and Smiles my Song shall grace.

24 Voice, her Smiles, *Duncombe*²

TRANSLATION OF HORACE
'ODES'. Book II. ix

Transcript by James Ross in the Boswell Papers, Yale University Library.
Boswell, *Life*, 1791, i. 18 (1934, i. 52).

CLOUDS do not always veil the skies,
　　Nor showrs immerse the verdant plain;
Nor do the Billows always rise,
　　Or storms afflict the ruffled Main.

Nor, Valgius, on th' Armenian Shores　　　5
　　Do the chain'd waters always freeze;
Not always furious Boreas roars,
　　Or bends with violent force the Trees.

But you are ever drown'd in tears,
　　For Mystes dead you ever mourn;　　　10
No setting Sol can ease your cares,
　　But finds you sad at his return.

The wise experienc'd Grecian Sage
　　Mourn'd not Antilochus so long;
Nor did King Priam's hoary age　　　15
　　So much lament his Slaughter'd Son.

Leave off, at length, these woman's sighs,
　　Augustus' num'rous trophies sing;
Repeat that Princes victories,
　　To whom all Nations tribute bring.　　　20

1 viel *Ross*　　　2 imerse *Ross*　　　11 care *Ross, Boswell*　　　13 sage *Boswell, 1791*
15 Priams *Ross*　　　17 of *Ross*

Niphates rolls an humbler wave,
  At length th' undaunted Scythian yields,
Content to live the Roman's Slave,
  And scarce forsakes his native fields.

TRANSLATION OF HORACE
'ODES', Book II. xiv

Manuscript in the Johnson Museum, Lichfield.
Transcript by James Ross in the Boswell Papers, Yale University Library.

The manuscript is in the collection of autograph letters (p. 66) formed by Thomas George Lomax of Lichfield, and presented by his son, Alderman Alfred Charles Lomax, to the Johnson Museum, Lichfield, on the occasion of the bicentenary celebration in 1909.

The last four lines and the signature were reproduced in facsimile by Boswell as a specimen of Johnson's handwriting 'when at School, in his 16th year' (*Life*, 1791, ii. conclusion). They were printed in a letter to *Notes and Queries* of 24 July 1858 (II. vi. 67; cf. 99) by T. G. Lomax, who there stated that the manuscript had been sent to him by a lady in Scotland, and that it had been found 'on looking over the papers of a lately deceased nobleman'.

The poem is written on both sides of a small sheet of paper (ll. 21-8 verso), and is signed.

Horace. Book 2ᵈ. Ode 14

ALASS, dear Friend, the fleeting years
    In everlasting Circles run,
In vain you spend your vows and prayers,
They roll, and ever will roll on.

Should Hecatombs each rising Morn   5
On cruel Pluto's Altar dye,
Should costly Loads of incense burn,
Their fumes ascending to the Skie;

You could not gain a Moments breath,
Or move the haughty King below,   10
Nor would inexorable Death
Defer an hour the fatal blow.

21 roll's *Ross*   23 Romans' *Boswell, 1791*; Romans *Ross*

6 Alter *Ross*

2. Cf. Watts's hymn 'Awake our Souls, away our Fears' (1707), ll. 11–12.

In vain we shun the Din of war,
And terrours of the Stormy Main,
In vain with anxious breasts we fear   15
Unwholesome Sirius' sultry reign;

We all must view the Stygian flood
That silent cuts the dreary plains,
And cruel Danaus' bloody Brood
Condemn'd to everduring pains.   20

Your shady Groves, your pleasing wife,
And fruitfull fields, my dearest Friend,
You'll leave together with your life,
Alone the Cypress shall attend.

After your death, the lavish heir   25
Will quickly drive away his woe,
The wine you kept with so much care
Along the marble floor shall flow.

TRANSLATION OF HORACE
'ODES', Book II. xx

Manuscript in the Hyde Collection.
Transcript by James Ross in the Boswell Papers, Yale University Library.

   The manuscript is reproduced in the *R. B. Adam Library*, 1929, i, after p. 189.
The poem is written on two sides of a small sheet of paper (ll. 16–24 verso) in
Johnson's youthful handwriting, and is signed.

Horace Book 2ᵈ Ode 20ᵗʰ

Now with no weak unballast wing
   A Poet double-form'd I rise,
From th' envious world with scorn I spring,
And cut with joy the wond'ring Skies.

19 Danæus *Ross*

   16. Cf. Pope's Homer, *Iliad*, xiii. 424: 'In Sirius' sultry reign'.

   1. 'Unballast', a late instance of this form of the participle which was passing out of
use in the seventeenth century and is not recognized by Johnson in his *Dictionary*.
Addison has 'th'unballass'd vessel' in his early translation of the story of Phæton from
Ovid's *Metamorphoses*, l. 187 (*Works*, 1721, i. 157).

Though from no Princes I descend, 5
Yet shall I see the blest abodes,
Yet, great Mæcenas, shall your friend
Quaff Nectar with th' immortal Gods.

See! how the mighty Change is wrought!
See! how whate'er remain'd of Man 10
By plumes is viel'd; see! quick as thought
I pierce the Clouds a tunefull Swan.

Swifter than Icarus Ill flie
Where Lybia's swarthy offspring burns,
And where beneath th' inclement Skie 15
The hardy Scythian ever mourns.

My Works shall propagate my fame,
To distant realms and climes unknown,
Nations shall celebrate my Name
That drink the Phasis or the Rhône. 20

Restrain your tears and cease your cries,
Nor grace with fading flours my Herse,
I without fun'ral elegies
Shall live for ever in my verse.

TRANSLATION OF HORACE
'EPODE' II

Manuscript in the Hyde Collection.
Transcript by James Ross in the Boswell Papers, Yale University Library.

The manuscript is reproduced in facsimile in the *R. B. Adam Library*, 1929, i, after p. 189. The paper has been folded down the middle, and the translation is written on the left-hand side of two pages, the right-hand side being used for corrections. The writing is very small, and sometimes difficult to read. The

20 Pha   *Ross*   22 flowrs . . . Hearse *Ross*

corrections are unusually numerous. The manuscript has the appearance of a
first draft, but is signed.

Horace. Epode the 2*ᵈ*.

B LEST as th' immortal Gods is he
  Who lives from toilsome bus'ness free,
Like the first race in Saturns reign
When floods of Nectar stain'd the main,
Manuring with laborious hand   5
His own hereditary Land,
Whome no contracted debts molest
No griping Creditors infesst.
No trumpets sound, no Soldiers cries,
Drive the soft Slumbers from his eyes,   10
He sees no boist'rous Tempests sweep
The Surface of the boiling Deep,
Him no contentious suits in law
From his belov'd retirement draw,
He ne'er with forc'd Submission waits   15
Obsequious, at his Patrons gates;
But round the lofty Poplar twines
With artfull hand the teeming vines,
Or prunes the barren boughs away;
[Or] sees from far his Bullocks play   20
Or drains the Labour of the Bees,
Or sheers the Lambkins snowy fleece.
Or when with golden Apples crown'd
Autumn o'erlooks the smiling Ground
When rip'ning fruits perfume the year,   25
Plucking the blushing Grape and Pear,
Gratefull, rewards the Deities,
That, fav'ring, listen to his cries.

1 Blesst *Ross*   7–8 Whome . . . infesst. *in margin*   8 infest *Ross*   10 Drivs
Ross; from *above* for *struck out*   11 boist'rous *above* Northern *struck out*   17 twins
Ross   20 far *inserted above line*
27–8 Gratefull . . . cries. *in margin, instead of*
        Rewards the fav'ring Deities,
        That grant his Prayers, and hear his cries. *struck out*

Beneath some spreading Ilex Shade
On some green bank supinely Laid,   30
Where Riv'lets gently purl along
And, murm'ring, balmy Sleep prolong,
Whilst each Musician of the Grove
Lamenting warbles out his love,
In pleasing Dreams he cheats the Day   35
Unhurt by Phœbus fi'ry ray.
But when increas'd by Winter shours
Down cliffs the roaring Torrent pours
The grizly foaming Boar surrounds
With twisted toils, and op'ning hounds;   40
[So]metimes the greedy Thrush to kill
[He] sets his nets, employs his skill.
With secret springes oft ensnares
The screaming Cranes and fearfull Hares.
Would not these pleasures soon remove   45
The bitter pangs of slighted love?
If to compleat this heav'nly Life
A frugal, chast, industrious, Wife,
Such as the Sun-burnt Sabines were,
Divide the burden of his care,   50
And heap the fire, and milk the Kine
And crown the bowl with new-prest wine
And waiting for her weary lord
With unbought dainties load the board;
I should behold with scornfull eye   55
The studied arts of Luxury:

29 spreading Ilex *above* venerable *struck out*   Ilex] Trees *Ross*   36 fi'ry] sultry
Ross
39–40 The grizly ... hounds *lightly struck out*;

      The foaming Boar he then with op'ning hounds
      And twisted *in margin more heavily struck out*

41 Sometimes *Ross*   45 Would ... soon *below* Such Pleasures quickly would *struck
out*   52 heap] sweap *Ross*   56 Studied *above* various *struck out*; studied *om.
in Ross*

40. *op'ning*, i.e. giving voice.
49. 'Such the Sabine *Matrons* were' (Dryden, *Ep.* 2).

No fish from the Carpathian coast
By Eastern Tempests hither tost,
Nor Lybian fowls, nor Snipes of Greece,
So much my Appetite would please   60
As herbs of which the forrests nigh
Wholsome variety supply.
Then to the Gods, on solemn days,
The farmer annuall honours pays
Or feasts on Kids the Wolves had kill'd   65
And frighted, left upon the field.
How pleas'd he sees his Cattle come,
Their dugs with milk distended, home!
How pleas'd beholds his Oxen bow
And faintly draw th' inverted Plow.   70
His chearfull Slaves, a num'rous band,
Around in beauteous order stand.

Thus did the Us'rer Alphius praise,
With transports kindled, rural ease,
His money he collected strait,   75
Resolv'd to purchase a retreat.
But still desires of sordid gain   ⎫
Fix'd in his canker'd breast remain: ⎬
Next Month he sets it out again.   ⎭

57–62 No fish . . . supply. *in margin, instead of*

        Whate'er the swarthy Lybian boasts,
        Whate'er from India spicy coasts
        Driv'n hither by inclement skies
        I once admir'd, I'd then despise:
        The painted meads and Forrests nigh
        Can more delicious food supply. *struck out*

57 fish from the *instead of* fishes from ('es' *struck out*: the *above the line*)   59 Snipes]
Ships *Ross*   61 forrests *after* fields *struck out*   63 Then] When *Ross*   on solemn
days *om. in Ross*   67 How pleas'd *above* Joyfull *struck out*   69 How pleas'd
beholds his *above* He sees the wearied *struck out*   72 beautous *Ross*   77 still
inserted above the line

TRANSLATION OF HORACE
'EPODE' XI

Transcript by James Ross in the Boswell Papers, Yale University Library.
Works, vi (Yale edn., 1964), 10–12.

The Yale editors, recognizing a six-line stanzaic form, departed from the transcript and printed the text in stanzas. That Ross's transcript of 'Upon the Feast of St Simon & St Jude' ignored Johnson's stanzas and indentations is warrant for supposing them necessary. In the absence of punctuation in the transcript, stops have been introduced sparingly.

Horace Epode

PETTIUS, no more I verses write
  My Bosom glows with fiercer fire
No more I sing, no more delight
  To handle the melodious Lyre
Venus, the sacred Sisters dispossest   5
Invades my soul, and rages in my breast.

Thrice has December strip'd the tree
  And thrice deform'd the verdant year
Since from Inachia's charms set free
  I first foresook the scornfull fair   10
I then (my cheeks still glow with shame) was grown
The sport of Boys, and scandall of the town.

No feasts could e'er my cares dispell
  Sighs issued from my heaving breast
The pains I labour'd to conceal   15
  My silence and my groans confess'd.
Then when repeated bowls unlock'd the Heart
To thee I told the causes of my smart

To thee I then with tears complain'd
  That all the fair their favours sold   20
No wit nor honesty could stand
  Against th' omnipotence of Gold
And wish'd my rising anger could remove
Those anxious fears that fan'd the flame of Love.

1 Pethus . . . veres *Ross*   5 dispossesst *Ross*   7 strip'd] chip'd *Ross*

Then would I free from torments live   25
   And quit Inachia's venal charms
Nor with too powerfull Rivals strive
   But take another to my arms.
Thus I t' effect this mighty change design'd
And 'gainst the pow'r of Venus steeld my mind   30

But being counsell'd to go home
   And see my Mistress face no more
Confus'd about the streets I roam
   And stop'd unwilling at her door
Then to the inclement skies expos'd I sat   35
And sigh'd and wept at her relentless gate.

Lyciscus whose soft arms excell
   A Girls, inflames me with desire
Nor counsells nor reproach expell
   The raging of the kindled fire   40
But the next blooming virgins beauteous face
Or Boy, whose snowy neck the flowing ringlets grace.

TRANSLATION FROM 'THE ILIAD'

Transcript by James Ross in the Boswell Papers, Yale University Library.
Boswell, *Life*, 1791, i. 19 (1934, i. 53), ll. 60–89.

  This schoolboy translation from Homer appears to be wholly independent
of Pope's translation; it owes more to Dryden's version of the same passage
(1693). The original is *Iliad*, vi, ll. 440–65.

  Boswell imposed his own punctuation on the passage he printed.

Translation of part of the Dialogue between HECTOR *and* ANDROMACHE; *from the Sixth Book of* HOMER'S ILIAD

H ECTOR, this heard without a Moments stay
   Back through the City trod his former way
Soon as the chief approach'd the Scæan Gate
About to rush into the field of fate

26 quit] quite *Ross*

Title. The Dialogue between Hector and Andromache from the Sixth Book of the
Iliad, *altered by Boswell*   3 scæn *Ross*

He met Andromache his beauteous Wife   5
Far dearer than his own or Fathers Life
Whose Sire Eëtion in Cilicia reign'd
Where Hypoplacus' lofty shades extend
The Nurse attending bore a lovely Boy
Pledge of their love and source of all their Joy   10
By Hector call'd Scamandrius from the God
That laves proud Ilion with his rapid flood
But call'd Astyanax because his Sire
Alone preserv'd the town from Grecian fire
From Hector's breast each gloomy trouble flies   15
And secret pleasures sparkled in his eyes
Mournfull Andromache the silence broke
Her tears in shou'rs descending as she spoke
  Why gen'rous warriour will you rashly run
On dangers which your safety bids you shun   20
Forgetfull of your Wife forgetfull of your Son
Soon shall you fall by num'rous Hosts opprest
And Grecian spears shall quiver in your Breast
But, Ah! before arise that hapless day
May I lye cold beneath a Load of Clay   25
While Hector lives I tast of ev'ry Joy
With Hectors life away my pleasures fly
My Father fell by fierce Achilles hand
Whose direfull rage destroy'd my native land
Pleas'd with the conquest, he forbore the spoil   30
And Burnt him decent on a funerall pile
The Nymphs bewail'd his fall with loud Lament
And planted Elms around his Monument
By that dire sword my sev'n brave Brothers dy'd
All stemm'd in one sad day the Stygian Tyde   35
Among their flocks the blooming Heroes fell
And stain'd with blood Pelides vengefull steel
My Mother who alone escap'd the grave
The victor hither brought, A royall Slave
Soon as with Gold appeas'd, He set her free   40
To tast again the sweets of Liberty

Provok'd Diana with a vengefull Dart
Ended her wretched life and pierc'd her heart
But dearest Hector while thou liv'st I see
A Father, Brother, Husband all in thee   45
Rush not impetuous to the bloody fray
Nor tempt the dangers of this deathfull day
Think shouldst thou fall how wretched shall we be
A Widow I, an helpless Orphan he
Within the town assemble all thy powers   50
And man the walls and fortifie the tow'rs
Where the wild fig trees join their darksom shade
The Bravest of the Greeks the wall invade
Th' Atridae there and Tydeus mighty Son
Idomeneus and Godlike Telamon   55
Thrice to the wall their dreadfull Hosts have led
And thrice to mount the Battlements assay'd
Whether urg'd on by Seers from Heav'n inspir'd
Or their own Souls with hopes of Vict'ry fir'd.
She ceas'd, then Godlike Hector answer'd kind   60
His various plumage sporting in the wind
    That post, and all the rest shall be my care
But shall I then forsake th' unfinish'd war?
How would the Trojans brand great Hectors name!
And one base action sully all my fame   65
Acquir'd by wounds, and Battles bravely fought!
Oh! how my soul abhors so mean a thought.
Long since I learn'd to slight this fleeting breath,
And view with chearfull eyes approaching death.
The inexorable Sisters have decreed   70
That Priam's house, and Priam's self shall bleed:
The day will come, in which proud Troy shall yield,
And spread its smoaking ruins o'er the field.
Yet Hecuba's, nor Priam's hoary age,
Whose blood shall quench some Grecian's thirsty rage,   75
Nor my brave Brothers, that have bit the Ground,
Their souls dismiss'd through many a ghastly Wound
Can in my bosom half that grief create,
As the sad thought of your impending fate:

42 Provock'd *Ross*

When some proud Grecian Dame shall tasks impose,   80
Mimick your tears, and ridicule your woes;
Beneath Hyperia's waters shall you sweat,
And, fainting, scarce support the liquid weight:
Then shall some Argive loud insulting cry,
Behold the wife of Hector, guard of Troy!   85
Tears, at my name, shall drown those beauteous eyes,
And that fair Bosom heave with rising sighs!
Before that day, by some brave Hero's hand,
May I lye slain and spurn the Bloody sand.
    Hector, this speaking with extended hand   90
From the fair Nurse Astyanax demands
The child starts back affrighted at the Blaze
Of light reflected from the polish'd brass
And in his Nurses bosom hides his face
The Parents smil'd the Chief his helm unbound   95
And plac'd the beamy terror on the ground
Then kist his Son and raising to the Skies
In fervent prayer addrest the Deities
    Immortal Gods! and thou allmighty Jove
That reign'st supreme among the Pow'rs above   100
Propitious hear my prayers, protect the Boy
Grant him like me to guard the walls of Troy
Let distant regions echo with his name
And his more glorious acts eclipse his Fathers fame
May then his Mothers heart with joys oerflow   105
And may she ne'er returning sorrows know
    The Chief this spoke into the Mothers arms
Returns his child, she views his infant charms
Tumultuous passions strugle in her breast
And joy and sorrow stand by turns confest   110
This Hector saw, his soul was touch'd with grief
He grasp'd her hand endeav'ring kind relief,
    Ah! let not tears down that fair count'nance rowl
Restrain your sorrows, calm your troubled soul
Your sighs are spent in vain, if fates withstand   115
Hector shall perish by no warriours hand
But if by their irrevocable doom

88 Heroes *Ross*   92 affrighed *Ross*
8127022   D

My death is now decreed my death will come
The Bravest Hero, and the fearfull'st Slave
Shall sink alike into the gloomy grave   120
Hence to the Palace and your Maids repair ⎫
There let the web and distaff be your care ⎬
To Men belongs the dreadfull work of war.   ⎭
   Then on his brow the mighty Soldier plac'd
His shining helm with nodding horse hair grac'd   125
Swifter than Lightning to the fight he flies
Andromache looks back with weeping eyes
Then sought the Palace where the menial train
Shed floods of tears, and sympathiz'd in pain
With dolefull cries their living lord they mourn   130
Nor from the Battle look for his return.

TRANSLATION OF ADDISON'S 'BATTLE OF THE PYGMIES AND THE CRANES'

Manuscript of ll. 97–117 and 140–70, in Yale University Library.
Transcript by James Ross in the Boswell Papers, Yale University Library.
Modern Language Review, xxxi, January 1936, p. 60 (contributed by Dorothy Moody).

The two holograph fragments of Johnson's translation of Addison's *ΠΥΓΜΑΙ-ΟΓΕΡΑΝΟΜΑΧΙΑ, sive Prælium inter Pygmæos et Grues commissum,* are written on both sides of part of a folio leaf which was discovered among the Boswell papers at Malahide Castle and passed into the Isham Collection (Pottle, *Catalogue,* No. 468). Each fragment represents about one-eighth of Addison's poem (ll. 97–113, 134–59). The last seven lines, with Johnson's signature, are written along the right-hand margin. What has been preserved is the lower half of the second leaf. Boswell says nothing about this translation although he had a complete transcription.

Lines 48–9 contain the couplet referred to by Johnson in the anecdote told by Steevens in *The St. James's Chronicle,* 13 January 1785, and *The European Magazine,* January 1785, p. 51 (*Miscellanies,* ed. Hill, ii. 314):

'To a gentleman who expressed himself in disrespectful terms of Blackmore, one of whose poetick bulls he happened just then to recollect, Dr. Johnson answered,—I hope, Sir, a blunder, after you have heard what I shall relate, will not be reckoned decisive against a poet's reputation: When I was a young man, I translated Addison's Latin

---

125. Cf. Pope's Homer, *Iliad,* xv. 567: 'with nodding horse-hair formidably grac'd'.

poem on the Battle of the Pigmies and the Cranes, and must plead guilty to the following couplet:

> Down from the guardian boughs the nests they flung,
> And kill'd the yet unanimated young.

And yet I trust I am no blockhead. I afterwards changed the word *kill'd* into *crush'd*.'

In his *Life of Addison*, para. 11, Johnson characterized the original:

'Three of his Latin poems are upon subjects on which, perhaps, he would not have ventured to have written in his own language. *The Battle of the Pigmies and Cranes*; *The Barometer*; and *a Bowling-green*. When the matter is low or scanty, a dead language, in which nothing is mean because nothing is familiar, affords great conveniences; and by the sonorous magnificence of Roman syllables, the writer conceals penury of thought and want of novelty, often from the reader, and often from himself.'

The Battle of the Pygmies and Cranes

FEATHER'D Battalions, Squadrons on the wing
And the sad fate of Pygmie Realms I sing
Direct O Goddess, my advent'rous song
In warring Colours shew the warring throng
Teach me to range my troopes in just array   ⎱   5
Whilst beaks and swords engage in bloody fray   ⎬
And paint the horrors of the dreadfull day   ⎰
In pompous Numbers ancient Heroes rise
Their growing fame re'echoes to the skies
Who hath not heard of Argo's valiant crew?   10
How great Achilles godlike Hector slew?
How Turnus by Æneas sword expir'd?
Or how before Nassau the Gallick troops retir'd?
Who has not read the Theban Brothers Hate?
And wept unhappy Pompeys hapless fate?   15
I first attempt in never-dying lays
To propagate the Pygmie Heroes praise
While in my verse the shrilling trumpets sound
I'll sing the Chiefs dispensing fate around
In vain from heavens black Concave, like a Cloud   20
Fresh foes descending glut their swords with blood
Where radiant Phoebus rising from the Sea
Dispells the darkness with his golden ray
In a low vale by rocks that pierce the skies
Guarded from all but winged enemies   25

Title. *Ross*   11 Achillis *Ross*

In former ages while upheld by fate
Securely flourish'd the Pygmiean state
The fruitfull fields th' industrious People till'd
And with laborious crouds the Plains were fill'd
Now, wand'ring o'er the Cliffs the Traveller　　　　30
Small bones and mangled bodies scatter'd there
Affrighted views; and looking o'er the plain
With horrour counts the number of the Slain
The victor Cranes the conquer'd realms possess
Scream in the nests and brood their young in peace　　35
Not so, while long th' undaunted race maintain'd
Against th' invading Birds their native land
Whatever Crane confiding in his might
Dar'd have provok'd a foe to single fight
Soon forth in arms had some bold soldier stood　　　40
Soon had the wrathfull faulchion drank his blood
Oft from behind they wounded them with darts
Or fix'd the pointed Arrows in their hearts
When e'er the lab'ring Bird with anxious care
Had form'd her nest and plac'd her burthen there　　45
Some furious soldier would approach that bore
Death in his look, and hands imbru'd in gore
Who to the ground the shatter'd Building flung
And crush'd the yet unanimated young
From hence the seeds of Discord first arose　　　　50
The Pygmies thus exasperate their foes
Hence Men and Birds promiscuous press'd the sand
And Death exulting stalk'd along the land
Not the Mæonian Bard in lofty strain
Sung such a war when in a miry fen　　　　　　55
Fiercely contending two vast armies stood
And dy'd their Bulrush-spears in mutual blood

---

51 exasp'rated *Ross*

---

47. *imbru'd.* Under 'Imbue' in the *Dictionary* Johnson wrote, 'This word which seems wanted in our language, has been proposed by several writers, but not yet adopted by the rest.' Cf. p. 141, *post.*
53. Cf. Dryden: 'Pass'd all their precious Hours in Plays and Sports,
　　　　　Till Death behind came stalking on, unseen.'
　　(*The Flower and the Leaf*, 566–7; quoted in *Dictionary*, s.v. 'stalk'.)

Here with dead Mice the marsh was strow'd around
There frogs crept croaking o'er the swampy ground
Wounded and spent, in vain they strive to rise   60
Or lift themselves into the wonted skies
But now alass! the fatall hour drew nigh
In which the Pygmie wept his cruelty
The injur'd Cranes their Murther'd offspring mourn
And with fell rage and secret anguish burn   65
When all conspiring leave Mæons lake
And warm Cäyster's flowing banks forsake
To Mareotis fen the rumour flies
From Isther's flood unnumberd flocks arise
Which whet their beaks, for flight their wings prepare   70
Sharpen their claws, and meditate the war
These when o'er Winters sway, prevail'd the spring
Together rise and shoot upon the wing
Astonish'd Nations view with wild affright
The dark Horizon ravish'd from their sight   75
Meantime the Pygmies with undaunted hearts
Temper their swords and point their missive darts
The steely troops embodied closely stand
Their wings extend themselves across the Land
Then rises the brave Leader of their hosts   80
Who matchless Strength and Bulk Gygantick boasts
Of aspect stern for in his face he wears
The prints of claws and honourable scars
With rage implacable he still persue'd
The feather'd race and thirsted for their blood   85
Soon as their young began to draw their breath
He tore them down and trampled them to death
This forc'd the Cranes to utter dolefull moans
And Strymons hollow banks resounded with their groans
But now their cruel enemies draw near   90
And first a sound invades th' astonish'd ear

64 ofspring *Ross*   78 clossly *Ross*   89 St ymons *Ross*

77. Cf. Dryden: 'In vain with Darts a distant War they try,
            Short, and more short the missive Weapons fly.'
(*Cymon and Iphigenia*, 623-4; quoted in *Dictionary*, s.v. 'missive'.)

Quickly the Cranes appear before their eyes
Thick clouds of hostile Birds obscure the skies
Above their heads th' embattled Squadrons hung
And scarce the lab'ring air sustain the throng   95
The fearless Pygmies view them from afar
Rage with disdain, and hope th' approaching war
Not long they stood, when stooping from their height
The Cranes with beaks and claws provoke the fight.
Thick from their wounded wings the feathers fly,   100
Beneath Pygmæan steel what numbers dye!
Breathless at length they leave th' unfinish'd war
And hang aloft suspended in the air.
But their lost strength and vigour soon return
They clap their wings, and with new fury burn;   105
Then, swift as thought, by headlong anger driv'n
Descend, impetuous, from the vault of Heav'n.
Their foes the shock sustain in Battle skill'd,
And victory hangs doubtfull o'er the field.
Here lies a fowl transfix'd with many a wound   110
That strugling pants, and rowls her eye-balls round.
There a stout warriour fainting gasps for breath
And grasps the bloody sand involv'd in death.
Swords, arms and wings are scatter'd o'er the plain
On ev'ry side rise mountains of the slain,   115
Whose mortal wounds pour forth a purple flood,
The plain contested flows with mingled blood.
The valiant Prince with unresisted force
Where'er the Battle rages bends his course
That day what legions by his faulchion bled!   120
His arm alone rais'd Bulwarks of the dead
Before his face the frighted Cranes gave way
He turn'd awhile the fortune of the day
Till thither an huge Bird the tumult drew
Who caught the Chief, ev'n in his soldiers view   125

106 anger] fury *Ross*   111 round] sound *Ross*   112 gasps] graspt *Ross*
116 mortall *Ross*   117 with mingled blood *om. in Ross*

97. Cf. Dryden: 'Raging with high Disdain, repeats his Blows . . .' (Trans. of Ovid, *Met.* xii. 178).
113. Cf. Pope's Homer, *Iliad*, xiii. 645, 'furious grasps the bloody dust in death'.

In his fell claws, then into th' air he springs
The joyfull Cranes triumphant clap their wings;
While the sad Pygmies mourn with weeping eyes
Their Godlike Hero strugling in the skies.
   Now bleeds the war afresh, the Crane from high   130
Forcefull descending, strikes his enemy
Then flies aloft, th' astonish'd warriours feel
The wound, and, furious wave the shining steel
The Birds elude the stroke with cautious care
Its useless force the weapon spends in air   135
Such was the horrour of the dreadfull fight
As when great Briareus with matchless might
Hurling vast Mounts against the Realms above
Shook headlong from his throne imperial Jove
In rat'ling storms huge Promontories flie   140
And Bolts and rocks encounter in the Skie,
At length deform'd with many a grizly wound
Th' enormous Gyants smoke upon the Ground.
O'erpowr'd and faint the Pygmies scarce sustain
Their foes attacks, and wield their arms with pain.   145
Part turn their Backs, part seiz'd with wild surprise
Utter sad groans and lamentable cries.
Impending death they strive to 'scape in vain
For fear retards their flight, the cruell Crane
Scatters their breathless bodies o'er the plain.   150
Thus fell the Pygmie state, which long had stood
Secure, and triumph'd oft' in hostile blood.
To ev'ry empire bounds the Gods ordain
The limits fix'd they strive to pass in vain;
So by their great decree Assyria fell   155
And Persia felt the force of Grecian steel;
Not Rome itself that held the world in awe
Could cancell their irrevocable Law.

---

135 It's *Ross*   140 *om. in Ross*   142 grizly wound *om. in Ross*   148 Em-
pending *Ross*   149 cruel *Ross*   150 Plain *Ross*

142. Cf. Dryden: 'Close by each other laid they press'd the Ground,
        Their manly Bosoms pierc'd with many a griesly Wound.'
    (*Palamon and Arcite*, i. 149–50; quoted in *Dictionary*, s.v. 'grisly'.)
143. Cf. Pope, *Odyssey*, xi. 738 (quoted *post*, p. 230).

Now in the Realms below the Pygmie shades
Mix'd with old Heroes trace the flow'ry meads,   160
And wander sportive o'er th' Elysian plain:
Or if old womens tales may credit gain,
When pale-fac'd Cynthia sheds her silver light
Dispelling the black horrors of the Night,
The Shepherds oft' see little ghosts glide by   165
And shades of Pygmies swim before their eye.
They call them Fairies; these now free from care
And giv'n to mirth, the Cranes no longer fear,
But move their numrous arms to Musicks sound,
And tread in mystick rings the mossie ground.   170

FESTINA LENTE

Manuscript in the Hyde Collection.
Transcript by James Ross in the Boswell Papers, Yale University Library.

The manuscript is written on one side of a quarto sheet, and signed.
The title suggests that the poem was an original composition on a theme that
was perhaps prescribed by Wentworth.

Festina Lentè

WHATEVER course of Life great Jove allots,
    Whether you sit on thrones, or dwell in cots,
Observe your steps; be carefull to command
Your passions; guide the reins with steady hand,
Nor down steep cliffs precipitately move   5
Urg'd headlong on by hatred or by love:
Let Reason with superiour force controul
The floods of rage, and calm thy rufled soul.
Rashness! thou spring from whence misfortunes flow!
Parent of ills! and source of all our woe!   10
Thou to a scene of bloodshed turn'st the Ball,
By thee wholl citys burn, wholl nations fall!
By thee Orestes plung'd his vengefull dart
Into his supplicating mothers heart.

170 mossie *Ross*

Hurry'd to death by thee, Flaminius fell, 15
And crowds of godlike Romans sunk to hell.
But cautious Fabius from impending fate
Preserv'd the reliques of the Latian state
From bold invaders clear'd th' Italian lands
And drove the swarthy troops to their own barren sands. 20

UPON THE FEAST OF ST. SIMON
AND ST. JUDE

Manuscript in the Hyde Collection.
Transcript by James Ross in the Boswell Papers, Yale University Library.

This poem is written on the left-hand half of both sides of a folio sheet, the right-hand half being left for corrections, but none were made. It was printed for the first time by the courtesy of Mr. Howard Eric, of Stamford, Connecticut. Like the other early poems that have survived in manuscript, it is signed.

As the poem belongs to the group preserved by Wentworth, we may assume that it was written at his suggestion, or at least with his knowledge; and the guess may be hazarded that it was written for 28 October 1726.

It stands by itself not merely among Johnson's early poems but among all his poems, both in its metrical form and in the scope allowed to 'extatick fury'. Its stanza is that of the *Song to David*, which was not written till more than thirty years later, but the stanza was not uncommon among minor Augustan poets, e.g. Denham, Stepney, Parnell, Fenton, and Walsh (whose Imitation of Horace, *Odes*, III. iii (1705), is not dissimilar in tone to Johnson's verses), and it will also be found in Akenside's *Odes* and Elizabeth Carter's 'Ode to Wisdom' (1746) which Richardson printed in *Clarissa*.

Upon the feast of St Simon & St Jude

O F Fields with dead bestrew'd around,
  And Cities smoaking on the ground
    Let vulgar Poets sing,
Let them prolong their turgid lays
With some victorious Heroe's praise 5
    Or weep some falling King.

While I to nobler themes aspire,
To nobler subjects tune my lyre;
    Those Saints my numbers grace

Who to their Lord were ever dear,   10
To whom the church each rolling year
   Her solemn honours pays.

In vain proud tyrants strove to shake
Their faith, or force them to forsake
   The Steps their Saviour trod;   15
With breasts resolv'd, they follow'd still
Obsequious to his heav'nly will
   Their master and their God.

When Christ had conquer'd Hell and fate
And rais'd us from our wreched state,   20
   O prodigy of Love!
Ascending to the skies he shone
Refulgent on his starry throne
   Among the Saints above.

Th' Apostles round the world were sent,   25
Dispensing blessings as they went,
   Thro' all the spacious ball;
Far from their happy native home
They, pleas'd, thro' barb'rous nations roam
   To raise them from their fall.   30

Where Atlas was believ'd to bear
The weight of ev'ry rolling sphere,
   Where sev'nmouth'd Nilus roars,
Where the darkvisag'd Natives fry,
And scarce can breath th' infected sky,   35
   But bless the Northern shoars,

Simon by gen'rous Zeal inspir'd,
With ardent love of virtue fir'd,
   There trod the Lybian sands,
Though fierce Barbarians threatend death   40
And Serpents with their poys'nous breath
   Infest the barren Lands.

25 was sent *Ross*   27 Thr' *Ross*   28 frome *Ross*   34 Native *Ross*
40 threatned *Ross*   41 Serpants *Ross*

Nor there confin'd his active Soul;
But where the Realms beneath the Pole
    In clouds of Ign'rance mourn,   45
Thither with eager hast he runs
And visits Britain's hardy Sons
    Ah! never to return!

Nor whilst she Simons acts persues
Art thou forgotten by the Muse,   50
    Most venerable Jude!
Where Tigris beats his sounding shore
The haughty Persian in thy gore
    His wrathfull sword imbru'd.

Thrice happy Saints—where do I rove?   55
Where doth extatick fury move
    My rude unpolish'd song;
Mine unharmonious verse profanes
Those names which in immortal strains
    Angelick choirs have sung.   60

TO A YOUNG LADY ON HER BIRTHDAY

Transcript by Edmund Hector in the Boswell Papers, Yale University Library.
Boswell, *Life*, 1791, i. 20 (1934, i. 53).

Boswell gives this note: 'Mr. Hector informs me, that this was made almost
impromptu, in his presence.' We are not told who the young lady was. Text from
Hector's transcript.

To a Young Lady on her Birth-Day

THIS Tributary Verse receive my fair,
    Warm with an Ardent Lover's fondest Pray'r
May this returning Day for ever find
Thy form more Lovely, more Adorn'd thy Mind,

45 Ign'rance *omitted by Ross*

48. 'SIMONEM ZELOTEM Evangelii doctrinam *ad Occidentalem Oceanum,
Britannicasque insulas* pertulisse, author est Nicephorus Callisti. Eundem *in Britannica
crucifixum, occisum et sepultum esse,* tradit in Synopsi Dorotheus.' Usher, *Britannicarum
Ecclesiarum Antiquitates,* 1687, p. 4.

All Pains, all cares may fav'ring Heav'n remove,   5
All, but the Sweet Solicitudes of Love.
May Powerful Nature join with graceful Art,
To point each Glance, and force it to the Heart.
O then, when conquer'd Crowds confess thy Sway,
When even Proud Wealth and Prouder Wit obey,   10
My Fair be mindful of the Mighty Trust,
Alas! 'tis hard for Beauty to be just.
Those Sovereign Charms with Strictest care employ,
Nor give the generous Pain, the Worthless joy,
With his own Form acquaint the forward Fool,   15
Shewn in the faithful Glass of Ridicule,
Teach mimick Censure her own faults to find, ⎫
No more let Coquets to themselves be blind,   ⎬
So shall Belinda's Charms improve Mankind. ⎭

THE YOUNG AUTHOR

Transcript by Edmund Hector in the Boswell Papers, Yale University Library.
The Gentleman's Magazine, July 1743, p. 378.
The Scots Magazine, July 1743, p. 319.
Boswell, *Life*, 1791, i. 21 (1934, i. 54).

The earliest form of this piece is printed by Boswell from Hector's transcript,
with a note of the variant readings. It was a revised version which Johnson
sent to *The Gentleman's Magazine* in 1743. Boswell pointed out that it was there
printed 'with many alterations'. Hector's transcript bears the footnote, 'This he
inserted in the Gentleman's Magazine, 17   '.

The piece may be regarded as an early study for the passage on the scholar's
life in *The Vanity of Human Wishes*, but was perhaps written under the influence
of his prematurely leaving Oxford in December 1729. Hector noted that it
'was wrote in his 20th year' (Waingrow, *Correspondence*, p. 49 n.). If any significance can be attached to the reference to over-hasty publication (l. 20) it can
perhaps be read as an allusion to the supposed early edition of his translation of
Pope's *Messiah* (*post*, p. 43), though that was against his will.

Text from *The Gentleman's Magazine*.

7 grateful *Boswell*

---

18. 'coquet' becomes 'coquette' in Boswell's second edition. Johnson gives 'coquette'
in the *Dictionary*, but places the accent on the first syllable.

The Young Author

WHEN first the peasant, long inclin'd to roam,
Forsakes his rural seats and peaceful home,
Charm'd with the scene the smiling ocean yields,
He scorns the flow'ry vales and verdant fields;
Jocund he dances o'er the wat'ry way,   5
While the breeze whispers and the streamers play.
Joys insincere! thick clouds invade the skies,
Loud roars the tempest, high the billows rise,
Sick'ning with fear he longs to view the shore,
And vows to trust the faithless deep no more.   10
   So the young author panting for a name,
And fir'd with pleasing hope of endless fame,
Intrusts his happiness to human kind,
More false, more cruel than the seas and wind.
'Toil on, dull croud, in extacy, he cries,   15
'For wealth or title, perishable prize;
'While I these transitory blessings scorn,
'Secure of praise from nations yet unborn.'
This thought once form'd, all counsel comes too late,
He plies the press, and hurries on his fate;   20
   Swiftly he sees the imagin'd laurels spread,
He feels th' unfading wreath surround his head;
Warn'd by another's fate, vain youth, be wise,
These dreams were *Settle*'s once and *Ogilby*'s.
   The pamphlet spreads, incessant hisses rise,   25
To some retreat the baffled writer flies,

Variants in the transcript which were followed by Boswell without division into paragraphs.
Title. Author *Hector*] Authour *Boswell* (*also* 11)   2 seats] Sports   3 Charm'd]
Pleas'd   4 flow'ry vales and verdant] verdant Meads and flow'ry   5 Jocund
he dances] Then dances jocund   wat'ry] watery   6 *After this line Hector gave
two omitted couplets:*

> Unbounded Prospects in his Bosom roll,
> And future Millions lift his rising Soul,
> In blissfull dreams he Digs the Golden Mine,
> And raptured sees the Newfound Ruby shine.

8 roars the tempest . . . billows rise] roar the Billows . . . Waves arise   11 for a
name] after Fame   12 And the long honours of a lasting Name   14 and] or
15 extacy] Extacies   16 Title's perishable   17 these] those   18 nations] Ages
20 plies the] flies to   22 He feels th'] And feels the   24 These] Those

Where no sour criticks damn, nor sneers molest,
Safe from the keen lampoon and stinging jest;
There begs of heav'n a less distinguish'd lot;
Glad to be hid, and proud to be forgot.   30

EPILOGUE TO 'THE DISTREST
MOTHER'

Transcript by Edmund Hector in the Boswell Papers, Yale University Library.
Boswell, *Life*, 1791, i. 22 (1934, i. 55).

Boswell gives this note: 'Some young ladies at Lichfield having proposed to
act "The Distressed Mother", Johnson wrote this, and gave it to Mr. Hector
to convey it privately to them.' Hector gave the information to Boswell in his
letter of 1 February 1785 (see p. 1, *ante*) and prefaced his account with the
phrase 'The next Year', that is, after the translation of 'Integer Vitæ' at School.
The implication is not clear, but must predate Johnson's going up to Oxford,
and may connect the poem with the period between his leaving Lichfield School
in the latter part of 1725 and his going to Stourbridge in early summer 1726.

The Distrest Mother, an imitation of Racine's *Andromaque* by Ambrose Philips,
was produced in March 1712. That Johnson should have written an Epilogue
for it is the more interesting in the light of what he was to say about the original
Epilogue in his *Life of Philips*: 'It was concluded with the most successful
Epilogue that was ever yet spoken on the English theatre. The three first nights
it was recited twice; and not only continued to be demanded through the run,
as it is termed, of the play, but whenever it is recalled to the stage, where by
peculiar fortune, though a copy from the French, it yet keeps its place, the
Epilogue is still expected, and is still spoken.' It was nominally by Budgell, but
Addison's revision is said to have made 'quite another thing' of it. Mrs. Oldfield
spoke it in the character of Andromache. See *The Spectator*, No. 341.

Text from Hector's transcript of 1785.

AN EPILOGUE
intended to have been spoken by a LADY
who was to personate the GHOST of
HERMIONE

Yᴇ Blooming Train who give despair or Joy,
Bless with a Smile or with a Frown destroy,
In whose fair Cheeks destructive Cupids wait,
And with unerring Shafts distribute Fate,

27 damn, nor] snarl, no   28 keen] tart

Whose Snowy Breasts, whose animated Eyes,   5
Each Youth admires tho' each admirer dies;
Whilst you deride their Pangs in barb'rous play, ⎫
Unpitying see them weep, and hear them Pray, ⎬
And unrelenting Sport Ten Thousand lives away. ⎭
For you ye fair I quit the gloomy Plains,   10
Where Sable Night in all her Horror reigns,
No fragrant Bow'rs, no delightful Glades,
Receive th' unhappy Ghosts of Scornful Maids.
For kind, for tender Nymphs the Myrtle blooms,
And weaves her bending boughs in pleasing Glooms,   15
Perennial Roses deck each Purple Vale,
And Scents ambrosial breath in every Gale;
Far hence are banish'd Vapours, Spleen and Tears,
Tea, Scandal, Ivory Teeth and Languid Airs,
No Pug nor favourite Cupid there enjoys   20
The balmy Kiss for which poor Thyrsis dies:
Form'd to delight they use no foreign Arms,
Nor Tort'ring Whalebones pinch them into Charms,
No Conscious Blushes there their Cheeks inflame,
For those who feel no Guilt can know no Shame,   25
Unfaded Still their former Charms they Shew,
Around them pleasures wait, and Joys for ever New.
But cruel Virgins meet Severer Fates,
Expell'd and exil'd from the blissful Seats,
To dismal Realms, and Regions void of Peace,   30
Where furies ever howl and Serpents hiss.
O'er the sad Plains Perpetual Tempests Sigh,
And Pois'nous Vapours, blackning all the Sky,
With livid hue the Fairest Face o'ercast,
And every Beauty Withers at the blast,   35
Where e'er they fly their Lovers Ghosts persue,
Inflicting all those Ills which once they knew,
Vexation, Fury, Jealousy, Despair,
Vex ev'ry Eye and every Bosom tear,
Their foul deformities by all descry'd   40
No Maid to flatter and No Paint to hide;

36. Hector has 'Lover's'. Johnson must have written 'lovers'. The apostrophe in the plural (s') did not become regular till about the end of the century.

Then Melt ye Fair, while Crouds around you sigh,
Nor let Disdain sit low'ring in your Eye,
With Pity soften every awful Grace,
And Beauty Smile Auspicious in each Face,   45
To ease their pains exert your Milder Power,
So shall you Guiltless reign and all Mankind adore.

FRIENDSHIP; AN ODE

Transcript, ? 1740, in the handwriting of Lady Mary Wortley Montagu in an
album belonging to her (ff. 50ᵛ, 51), and now in the possession of the Earl of
Harrowby (MS. 255).
The Gentleman's Magazine, July 1743, p. 376.
The Scots Magazine, July 1743, p. 319.
Anna Williams, *Miscellanies in Prose and Verse*, 1766, p. 90.
The London Magazine, June 1766, p. 321.
The Gentleman's Magazine, June 1785, p. 477.
Works, 1788, xiv. 547.
Boswell, *Life*, 1791, i. 84 (1934, i. 158).
Works, 1816, i. 409.

This poem was first printed in *The Gentleman's Magazine* along with Johnson's 'Young Author' and his translation of Horace's 'Integer Vitæ'. Boswell
was the first to reprint it as it had then appeared, and introduced it thus:

I should think myself much wanting, both to my illustrious friend and my readers,
did I not introduce here, with more than ordinary respect, an exquisitely beautiful Ode,
which has not been inserted in any of the collections of Johnson's poetry, written by
him at a very early period, as Mr. Hector informs me, and inserted in the Gentleman's
Magazine of this year (1743; *Life*, i. 158).

Another version, which Boswell overlooked, had been included in Anna
Williams's *Miscellanies*; and yet another version had been contributed to *The
Gentleman's Magazine* in 1785 by 'B. W.', who says:

I do not believe the following Verses have ever appeared in print; but I am not certain
of it. They were written by the worthy Dr. Johnson, in his younger days, at the request
of Mrs. Porter, his future wife.

Johnson's authorship of the poem 'at a very early period' and 'in his younger
days' before his marriage (i.e. before July 1735) is thus attested by Hector and
'B. W.' independently but it probably reflects Johnson's feelings as he was about
to leave home for Oxford, and as he was leaving his friend Hector behind.

The poem was copied by Lady Mary Wortley Montagu into an album containing current verse. The contents and the evolving handwriting indicate that she
filled this album between the years 1712 and 1762. She afterwards inserted
a few dates and names of authors, and to one poem towards the conclusion she
added the date 1743; but there is no reason for placing her transcription of John-

son's poem later than 1740. Her version was not derived from the printed version of 1743, and must have been taken from a manuscript now lost.

Lady Louisa Stuart was the first to draw attention to the presence of this poem in her grandmother's album. Writing in 1837, at the age of eighty, she quoted the whole poem, not quite accurately, in her 'introductory anecdotes' in Lord Wharncliffe's edition of Lady Mary's Works (i. 53–4), and attributed it to Mary Astell, who died in 1731. But there is no mention of Mary Astell in the album, and the ascription of this poem to her must be put down to a lapse of memory. Of the author or date of the poem Lady Mary says nothing. (In Harrowby MS. 81, ff. 139–40, is an answer 'To Clio, Occasion'd by Her Verses upon Friendship', but so commonplace a topic makes it impossible to associate the piece with Johnson's verses.)

The poem as she transcribed it has the heading 'Ode on Friendship address'd to the Lady —'; and in the third line Friendship is said to be 'To W—— and to Angels given,'—a reading which does not agree well with the argument of the poem, and has the appearance of being substituted by an admirer intent on paying her a compliment. The fifth stanza differs wholly from the fifth stanza in the printed version of 1743, but is devoid of the obvious purpose to be expected in a substitution.

The explanation of the difference is supplied by the version published by 'B. W.' in 1785. He was wrong in thinking that he was printing the poem for the first time, but the terms of his letter leave no doubt that he was following an early manuscript. His version contains the two stanzas which might have been taken for alternatives but are now seen to belong equally to the poem as it was originally written, containing seven stanzas in all. Lady Mary's version has stanzas 1, 2, 3, 5, 6, 7; *The Gentleman's Magazine* of 1743 has stanzas 1, 2, 3, 5, 4, 7.

The stanza omitted in *The Gentleman's Magazine* may have been cut out by the editor or printer, so that the poem could be fitted in at the bottom of the second column of the closely packed page. The fifth stanza is there made to conclude with a long dash. The obvious if not the only meaning to be attached to this dash is that something has been omitted.

The resemblance of the version in Lady Mary's album (the third line excepted) to the version printed in 1766 in Anna Williams's *Miscellanies* cannot so easily be explained. Johnson must then have made use of a manuscript, and in all probability one that he had not seen for many years. There is no means of knowing whether it contained six or seven stanzas, but the poem as he printed it in 1766 omits the stanza which is omitted in the album.

Of no other poem by Johnson can we deduce the existence of so many written copies. Two were used by him for the printed texts of 1743 and 1766, and a third was used by B. W. in 1785. Lady Mary's copy alone survives, and it must have been taken from yet another copy. We can only guess how it came to her hands. She is not known ever to have seen Johnson, and the social circles in which they moved were far apart. Her only known reference to him concerns *The Rambler* and is not complimentary. She cannot have suspected that the essayist whom she described as a packhorse following in the beaten road of his predecessors was the author of a poem which she had thought worth transcribing

into her private album. It was not wholly as he had written it, and she may have
been attracted by the inserted flattery. But who of Johnson's friends was at once
on such terms with him as to know his unpublished poem and on such terms with
her? Savage had dedicated his *Miscellaneous Poems* to her in 1726, and in 1729
in *The Wanderer* (Book V. 72) he had praised

Fair Wortley's angel-Accent, Eyes, and Mind.

Till we learn more about Savage's later life his use of Johnson's poem must
remain only a surmise; but could it be established, we should know that Lady
Mary transcribed the poem after Easter 1738, for Johnson did not become the
friend of Savage till after he had written *London*. Perhaps she saw it through the
agency of Lord Hervey's younger brother, Johnson's friend, Henry Hervey Aston.

The text is here given in its full form of seven stanzas, as printed in *The
Gentleman's Magazine* in 1785.

AN

ODE on FRIENDSHIP

F RIENDSHIP! peculiar boon of heav'n,
   The noble mind's delight and pride,
To Men and Angels only giv'n,
   To all the lower world deny'd;

While Love, a stranger to the blest,   5
   Parent of thousand wild desires,
The human and the savage breast
   Inflames alike with raging fires.

With bright, but oft destructive gleam,
   Alike o'er all his lightnings fly;   10
Thy lambent glories only beam
   Around the fav'rites of the sky.

Directress of the brave and just,
   O guide me through life's darksome way,
And let the tortures of mistrust   15
   On selfish bosoms only prey.

Title, *1766*. Ode on Friendship address'd To the Lady—*1740*: Friendship; an Ode
1743: Dr. Johnson upon Friendship *1785*   1 boon] Gift *1740*, *1766*   3 To W——
and to Angels given *1740*   5 a stranger to] unknown amongst *1740*: unknown among
1743, *1766*   6 thousand wild] Rage and hot *1740*, *1766*   desire *1740*   7 savage
. . . human *1743*   8 Inflames] Torments *1743*   raging] equal *1740*, *1766*   Fire *1740*
9 gleam] gloom *1743*   13–16 *Om. 1740, 1766*: after ll. 17–20 *1743*   14 me] us
1743   16 prey.—— *1743*

Thy gentle flows of guiltless joys
  On fools and villains ne'er descend;
In vain for thee the monarch sighs,
  And hugs a flatterer for a friend.   20

When Virtues kindred Virtues meet,
  And sister souls together join,
Thy pleasures, permanent as great,
  Are all transporting, all divine.

Oh, must their ardours cease to glow   25
  When souls to blissful climes remove?
What rais'd our Virtues here below,
  Shall aid our Happiness above.

TO LAURA

The Gentleman's Magazine, July 1743, p. 378.
Boswell, *Life*, 1791, i. 84 (1934, i. 157).

    This quatrain was ascribed to Johnson by Boswell with this note: 'Mr. Hector was present when this Epigram was made impromptu. The first line was proposed by Dr. James, and Johnson was called upon by the company to finish it, which he instantly did.' James perhaps proposed not only the first line, but the first couplet. It was probably composed in the later 1720s or early 1730s when Johnson was much in Hector's company and when the other verses published in the *Magazine* for July 1743 were also composed. See p. 36 *ante*, and Hector's letter to Boswell, 1 February, 1785, p. 1 *ante*.

    James and Hector were both Johnson's school-fellows. In the same year as this epigram appeared Johnson wrote the Dedication for James's *Medicinal Dictionary*, and they remained close friends till James's death in 1776. Cf. Allen T. Hazen, 'Samuel Johnson and Dr. Robert James', *Bulletin of the Institute of the History of Medicine*, vol. iv, No. 6, June 1936, pp. 455–65; and his *Samuel Johnson: Prefaces and Dedications* (New Haven, 1937), pp. 68–73.

19 monarch] tyrant *1743*   20 And] Who *1740*   21–4 *Om. 1743*   22 sister-souls *1740, 1766*   23 permanent as great] lasting, as they're great *1740*   25 Oh, must their ardours] Oh may this Flame neer *1740*: Nor shall thine ardours *1743*: O! Shall thy flames then *1766*   26 When souls] till you *1740*   blissful] happier *1740, 1766*   27 our] your *1740*   Virtue *1740, 1743, 1766*   28 our] yr *1740*

23 Johnson accepted this pronunciation of 'great' in his *Plan of a Dictionary*, 1747, p. 13.

Ad Lauram parituram Epigramma

ANGLIACAS inter pulcherima *Laura* puellas,
   Mox uteri pondus deposita grave,
Adsit, *Laura*, tibi facilis *Lucina* dolenti;
   Neve tibi noceat prænituisse Deæ.

COLLEGE VERSES

Manuscript in the Library of Pembroke College, Oxford. (Facsimile in Boswell, *Life*, ed. Hill, 1887, i, after p. 60.)
Boswell, *Life*, ed. Croker, 1831, i. 44; (1934, i. 271 n.)

These verses were part of an undergraduate exercise. They are written on a folded sheet: a Latin prose composition—under the title

'— Mea nec Falernæ
Temperant Vites, neque Formiani
Pocula Colles.' (Horace, *Od.* I. xx)

—occupies the first of the four small quarto pages, and the verses, with a shortened title, follow on the third page, and are signed 'Johnson'. They are here printed from the manuscript. Croker, who was the first to print them (with translations), remarks that 'it may be surmised that the college beer was at this time indifferent'.

Mea nec Falernæ &c.

QUID mirum Maro quod dignè canit arma Virumque,
   Quid quod putidulùm nostra Camœna sonat?
Limosum nobis Promus dat callidus haustum,
   Virgilio vires Uva Falerna dedit.
Carmina vis nostri scribant meliora Poetæ?   5
   Ingenium jubeas purior haustus alat.

Manuscript in the Library of Pembroke College, Oxford.
Boswell, *Life*, ed. Croker, 1831, i. 44.

This second undergraduate manuscript is similar to the first: the verses are written on the third of four pages, and follow a Latin prose composition on the

---

3. *Promus.* Presumably John Hopkins (*Johnsonian Gleanings*, v. 42–3) whose artfulness is corroborated by his career and a note in the college buttery books: 'Est Croeso diti Solers vel ditior Hopkins.'

first page with the title 'Adjecere bonæ paulo plus artis Athenæ' (Horace, *Ep.* II. ii. 43). The verses have a shortened title, but are not signed. Croker remarks that 'Johnson repeated this idea in *ΓΝΩΘΙ ΣΕΑΥΤΟΝ*, but not, as the editor thinks, so elegantly as in the epigram'.

Adjecere bonæ &c.

QUAS Natura dedit dotes, Academia promit,
   Dat Menti propriis Musa nitere bonis.
Materiam Statuæ sic præbet Marmora Tellus,
   Saxea Phidiacâ spirat imago manu.

AURORA EST MUSIS AMICA

Manuscript owned by Major C. Congreve, deposited in the Bodleian Library. *Works*, vi (Yale ed. 1964), 28.

The manuscript is signed and bears a number of alterations in Johnson's hand. It is a small piece of paper, roughly torn (3×4 in.), and the handwriting is cramped making decipherment difficult. It derives from Charles Congreve, one of Johnson's Lichfield schoolfellows and later a contemporary at Oxford. It might have been written either as a school or a college exercise, but the latter seems the more likely for the title recurs frequently in surviving undergraduate 'themes' preserved in Pembroke College library.

Aurora est Musis Amica

CUM caput Hesperiis attollit Phœbus ab undis,
   Atque Æthra ambiguâ pallida luce rubet;
Harmoniâ tellus completur lata, per agros
   Curas mulcentes dulcè queruntur aves.
Rorem, qui segetes, geniali et gramina succo   5
   Nutrit mane, putes esse Heliconis aqua,
Tunc vati facilem se præbet Apollo, Sybillae
   Vix majore Deus corda furore quatit.

---

4 queruntur] 'qu' *missing*

Title. Compare the close of Milton's first *Prolusion* 'Utrum Dies an Nox praestantior sit'. The idea was perhaps commonplace, cf. *Janua Linguarum* (London, 1615), pp. 16–17, No. 256, 'Aurora musis apta: the morning is fit for studie'.

4 *dulce queruntur aves*: cf. Ovid, *Amores*, III. i. 4. See also Horace, *Epode*, ii. 26 'queruntur in silvis aves', which is translated by Johnson, p. 15 *ante*.

Carmine præbentur bellantia Numina digne
  Assurgitque epicis Pagina docta modis.   10
Hinc annis panguntur Delenda Poemata nullis
  Queis majus pretium sæcula lapsa dabunt.
Quid mirum? cum saxa movet statuasque tacentes
  Ignis quem Phœbi naribus efflat equus,
Quos pulsata sonos edit lyra pollice, primis   15
  Percussa a radiis Memnonis ora dabant.

TRANSLATION OF DRYDEN'S EPIGRAM
ON MILTON

Transcript by Boswell in his Manuscript Journal (Yale).
Thraliana, ii (1777–8), p. 94; ed. K. Balderston, 1941, p. 213.
Boswell, *Journal of a Tour to the Hebrides*, 1785, p. 87. (*Life*, v (1964), 86.)
Piozzi, *Anecdotes*, 1786, p. 72.
Works, 1788, xiv. 545.
Works, 1823, i. 414.

Boswell thus alludes to this translation in his original *Journal* under the date
22 August 1773 (ed. Pottle and Bennett, p. 60):

'I observed a family could not expect a poet but in a hundred generations. "Nay,"
said Mr. Johnson, "not one family in a hundred can expect a poet in a hundred generations." Then repeated "Three poets," etc., and part of a Latin translation of it done at
Oxford—perhaps his own. I must ask.'

In a footnote to the published *Tour*, dated 2 May 1778, Boswell says that
Johnson acknowledged the translation and dictated it to him. Boswell made slight
modifications in his proofs to the capitals and punctuation of the manuscript
version.

Text as given by Boswell in 1785.

9 praebentur] describit *crossed out*   11 panguntur *uncertain reading* palpantur
Works pateuntur *is improbable*   nullis *crossed out*; nullis] scribit *and* pangit *crossed*
out   14 Quem Efflant quem rem Phœbi naribus ignis equi *crossed out*

---

11. *panguntur*. The line is unmetrical, but there is no doubt of the last two syllables.
Mr. E. V. C. Plumptre writes: 'Johnson wrote at first "hinc annis nullis delenda poemata
scribit" having in mind the *vates* of line 7 as subject. Then realising that the laws of
prosody do not allow *-ata scr-*, he altered to *poemata pangit*: a good if hackneyed
verb which I think is more likely than *palpare*. But recognizing that a passive verb would
be more in place than an active one whose subject was scarcely obvious, and since
panguntur clearly won't do at the end, he seized a suitable spondaic word *nullis* and made
the exchange. The MS. evidence is clear that *panguntur* was left unscannable in the
middle.'

16 *Percussa*. Professor W. K. Wimsatt happily proposed this reading which satisfies
the sense and almost all the graphical difficulties of the word.

Quos laudet vates Graius Romanus et Anglus
Tres tria temporibus secla dedere suis.
Sublime ingenium Graius; Romanus habebat
Carmen grande sonans; Anglus utrumque tulit.
Nil majus Natura capit: clarare priores 5
Quæ potuere duos tertius unus habet.

TRANSLATION OF POPE'S MESSIAH

John Husbands, *A Miscellany of Poems*, Oxford, [October] 1731, p. 111.
The Gentleman's Magazine, April 1752, p. 184.
The Grand Magazine of Magazines, xxii (April 1752), 184–5.
The Scots Magazine, August 1752, p. 405.
De Hollandsche Wysgeer . . . Te Amsterdam. 1759, I. i. 'Tweede Deel', pp. 230–3.
Edward Popham, *Selecta Poemata Anglorum Latina*, 1776, iii. 16, and 1779,
p. 304.
Thraliana, iv (1781–6), p. 155; ed. 1941, p. 576.
The St. James's Chronicle, 22 January 1785.
Poetical Works, 1785 (two issues), p. 180.
Works, 1787, xi. 398.

This translation was made as a Christmas exercise on the suggestion of William
Jorden, Johnson's tutor at Pembroke College, As Johnson is shown by the buttery
books of the college to have been in residence at Christmas 1728 but to have
left by 12 December 1729, by which time Jorden had also left to be inducted
into the rectory of Standon, Staffordshire, there can be no doubt that Christmas
1728 is the date of the poem. John Husbands, who included the poem in his
Miscellany in 1731, was a fellow of Pembroke from June 1728 till his death in
November 1732. (See A. L. Reade, *Johnsonian Gleanings*, v, 123–9, 158–9, 194.
See also R. S. Crane, 'An Early 18th Century Enthusiast for Primitive Poetry—
John Husbands', *Modern Language Notes*, xxxvii (1922), 27–36.)

According to Boswell, who got his information from Johnson's friend and
contemporary John Taylor, the translation was 'first printed for old Mr. Johnson, without the knowledge of his son, who was very angry when he heard of it'.
Nothing more is known of this printing, and our earliest text is in Husbands's
Miscellany. A revised version was published in *The Gentleman's Magazine* for
April 1752, in parallel columns with Pope's poem. Johnson usually revised his
early pieces before allowing them to be included in the *Magazine*, and the new
readings in this version must be held to have had his authority. The version in
The Scots Magazine is identical. As printed by Edward Popham in his Latin
collection in 1776 the poem contains several variants, and is dated 1750—

1, 3 Graius] Græcus *1788, 1823*

which may at first appear to be an error for 1752; but some of the variants
cannot be explained as the emendations of an editor, and point to the use of an
earlier text than that of *The Gentleman's Magazine* and even of the *Miscellany*.
In *The St. James's Chronicle* for 22 January 1785 the poem was printed with this
introduction:

> 'Several inaccurate Copies of the Latin Version of Pope's *Messiah*, by the late
> Dr. Samuel Johnson, having been handed about, I enclose you one corrected by his
> own Hand.'

This version is not free from misprints but contains four good new readings.
That they were made by Johnson need not be doubted, but when they were
made is not known. All that can be said is that they are corrections of the text in
The Gentleman's Magazine.

Although Kearsley's edition of the *Poetical Works* is not known to have been
published before 15 February 1785, the writer of the note in *The St. James's
Chronicle* may have seen some early copies. Kearsley had used Husbands's text,
corrected by his errata. He published a second issue of this edition almost
immediately, as is shown by the comparative rarity of the first, and the offending
pages (179–84) were cancelled. The version of the poem which he substituted
follows that in *The St. James's Chronicle*. In his second edition (1789) the poem
is reprinted from the second issue of the first edition, and a new note says that
'for a correct copy of this Translation, the Editor is indebted to Mr. Steevens'.
It would thus appear that George Steevens was the writer of the note in *The
St. James's Chronicle* and the sender of the copy corrected by Johnson's own
hand. Earlier in the same month he had contributed to that periodical the
anecdotes of Johnson which were at once republished in *The European Magazine*.

The text printed in the *Works* in 1787 by Langton, who provided most of the
Latin poems in that edition and is understood to have been the editor of them
all, contains three readings in Husbands's *Miscellany* rejected in *The Gentleman's
Magazine*, three first found in *The St. James's Chronicle*, and—apart from misprints—one reading that is new. Perhaps he made use of a discarded manuscript.

Mrs. Thrale obtained a copy from Richard Graves in October 1783, and
transcribed it carelessly into *Thraliana* (p. 576). It was taken from Husbands's
Miscellany.

Pope is said to have remarked that 'The writer of this poem will leave it
a question for posterity, whether his or mine be the original' (Hawkins, *Life*,
p. 13). Joseph Warton, however, asserts in his edition of Pope (1797, 1. 105 n.)
that the translation 'has been praised and magnified beyond its merits', and points
out expressions which he thought 'reprehensible'.

The text here printed follows that in *The St. James's Chronicle* and the *Poetical
Works* of 1785 (second issue), with slight corrections.

Four other Latin translations of Pope's *Messiah* were published during
Johnson's lifetime: by Usher Gahagan, 1748; by Richard Onely, 1749; by
Thomas Tyrwhitt, 1753; and by William Bermingham, Naples, 1760.

Johnson's Latin was rendered into English (apparently in ignorance of Pope's
original) by W. Meickle, *The Messiah, a Poem translated from the Latin of
Dr. Johnson, by W. Meickle*, 1834.

MESSIA

TOLLITE concentum, *Solymææ* tollite nymphæ!
Nil mortale loquor, cœlum mihi carminis alta
Materies; poscunt gravius cœlestia plectrum.
Muscosi fontes, silvestria tecta, valete,
Aonidesque Deæ, et mendacis somnia *Pindi.*   5
Tu mihi, qui flammâ movisti pectora sancti
Stidereâ *Isaiæ*, dignos accende furores!
   Immatura calens rapitur per sæcula vates,
Sic orsus—Qualis rerum mihi nascitur ordo!
Virgo! virgo parit! felix radicibus arbor   10
Jessæis surgit, mulcentesque æthera flores
Cœlestes lambunt animæ; ramisque columba,
Nuncia sacra Dei, plaudentibus insidet alis.
Nectareos rores, alimentaque mitia cœlum
Præbeat, et tacitè fœcundos irriget imbres!   15
Huc fœdat quos lepra, urit quos febris, adeste!
Dia salutares spirant medicamina rami.
Hic requies fessis; non sacrâ sævit in umbrâ
Vis boreæ gelida, aut rapidi violentia solis.
'Irrita vanescent priscæ vestigia fraudis,'   20
Justitiæque manus pretio intemerata bilancem
Attollet reducis; bellis prætendet olivas
Compositis Pax alma suas, terrasque revisens
Sedatas niveo Virtus lucebit amictu.
Volvantur celeres anni! Lux purpuret ortum   25
Expectata diu! Naturæ claustra refringens
Nascere, magne puer! Tibi primas, ecce! corollas

(The two issues of *Poetical Works*, 1785, are designated *1785*¹ and *1785*²)

Title: Messia. Ex alieno ingenio Poeta, ex suo tantum Versificator. Scalig. Poet. *Husbands*
3 graves *1785*¹   8 Immatura] Ille futura *Popham*   18 sacrâ] sacra hac *Popham*
19 rapidi] nimii *Popham*   24 Sedatas] Pacatas *Husbands, Gent. Mag., Popham*

Title (variants). J. C. Scaliger, *Poetics*, VI. iv., ed. 1561, p. 308.

2–3. *cœlum . . . materies*: 'reprehensible', Joseph Warton.

7. *dignos accende furores*: 'reprehensible', id.

11–12. 'Badly translated', id. (i. 96 n.). The original reads 'Whose sacred flow'r with fragrance fills the skies'.

20. This line is within inverted commas in all prints before 1787. 'Irrita' and 'priscæ Vestigia fraudis' are from Virgil's fourth eclogue, ll. 14 and 31.

Deproperat tellus, fundit tibi munera, quicquid
Carpit *Arabs*, hortis quicquid frondescit eois.
Altius, en! *Lebanon* gaudentia culmina tollit,   30
En! summo exultant nutantes vertice silvæ.
Mittit aromaticas vallis *Saronica* nubes,
Et juga *Carmeli* recreant fragrantia cœlum.
Deserti lætâ mollescunt aspera voce,
Auditur Deus! ecce Deus! reboantia circum   35
Saxa sonant Deus; ecce Deus! deflectitur æther
Demissumque Deum tellus capit; ardua cedrus,
Gloria silvarum, dominum inclinata salutet!
Surgite convalles, tumidi subsidite montes!
Sternite saxa viam, rapidi discedite fluctus!   40
En! quem turba diu cecinerunt enthea, vates,
En! SALVATOR adest; vultus agnoscite cæci
Divinos, surdas sacra vox permulceat aures!
Ille cutim spissam visus hebetare vetabit,
Reclusisque oculis infundet amabile lumen,   45
Obstrictasque diu linguas in carmina solvet.
Ille vias vocis pandet, flexusque liquentis
Harmoniæ purgata novos mirabitur auris.
Accrescunt tremulis tactu nova robora nervis:
Consuetus fulcro innixus reptare bacilli   50
Jam saltu capreas, jam cursu provocat euros.
Non planctus, non mœsta sonant suspiria, pectus
Singultans mulcet, lachrymantes terget ocellos.
Vincla coercebunt luctantem adamantina mortem,
Æternoque orci dominator vulnere languens   55
Invalidi raptos sceptri plorabit honores.
Ut quà dulce strepunt scatebræ, quà læta virescunt

33 Et juga] Culmina *Popham*   34 Deserti lætâ *Husbands, 1785¹, 1787*] Deserti
latâ *Gent. Mag., St. Jas., 1785²*: Deserta et læta *Popham*   43 surdos *1787 in error*
49 tremulis] teneris *1787*   51 Jam . . . jam] Nunc . . . nunc *Husbands, 1785¹, 1787*
53 tergit *Husbands, 1785¹, 1787*   57 strepent *St. Jas. 1785², 1787*

32. Tom Warton records that Johnson quoted this line on his visit to Oxford in 1754:
'As we were leaving the College, he said, "Here I translated Pope's Messiah. Which do
you think is the best line in it?—My own favourite is, 'Vallis aromaticas fundit Saronica
nubes'." I told him I thought it a very sonorous hexameter. I did not tell him it was
not in the Virgilian style.' (Boswell, *Life*, i. 272.) 'Reprehensible', Joseph Warton.
   44. *Ille cutim . . . vetabit:* 'reprehensible', id.

Pascua, quà blandum spirat purissimus aer
Pastor agit pecudes, teneros modo suscipit agnos,
Et gremio fotis selectas porrigit herbas,   60
Amissas modo quærit oves, revocatque vagantes;
Fidus adest custos, seu nox furat horrida nimbis,
Sive dies medius morientia torreat arva:
Postera sic pastor divinus sêcla beabit,
Et curas felix patrias testabitur orbis.   65
Non ultra infestis concurrent agmina signis,
Hostiles oculis flammas jaculantia torvis;
Non litui accendent bellum, non campus ahenis
Triste coruscabit radiis; dabit hasta recusa
Vomerem, et in falcem rigidus curvabitur ensis.   70
Atria, pacis opus, surgent, finemque caduci
Natus ad optatum perducet cœpta parentis.
Qui duxit sulcos, illi teret area messem,
Et seræ texent vites umbracula proli.
Attoniti dumeta vident inculta coloni   75
Suave rubere rosis, sitientesque inter arenas
Garrula mirantur salientis murmura rivi.
Per saxa, ignivomi nuper spelæa draconis,
Canna viret, juncique tremit mutabilis umbra.
Horruit implexo quà vallis sente, figuræ   80

62 horrida] humida *Husbands, Gent. Mag., Popham*   63 morientia] languentia
Popham   77 Garrula . . . murmura] Murmura . . . garrula *Husbands, 1785*[1]
79 mutabilis] variabilis *Husbands, Gent. Mag., Popham, 1787*

62. Warton cites 'furat horrida membris' as 'reprehensible', but 'membris' is not
found in any known text.

79. Warton says that he was once present at a dispute on the merits of Johnson's Latin
verse 'betwixt a person of great political talents and a scholar who had spent his life
among the Greek and Roman classics. Both were intimate friends of Johnson. The
former, after many objections had been made to this translation by the latter, quoted
a line which he thought equal to any he ever had read.

—juncique tremit variabilis umbra.
The green reed trembles—

The Scholar (Pedant if you will) said, there is no such word as variabilis in any classical
writer. Surely, said the other, in Virgil; variabile semper fœmina.—You forget, said the
opponent, it is varium et mutabile.' (Pope, 1797, i. 105.) The politician was probably
Burke, and the scholar may have been Joseph Warton himself. Warton had not used
Johnson's corrected text when he marked the expression as 'reprehensible', for 'variabilis' had been replaced by 'mutabilis'.

Surgit amans abies teretis, buxique sequaces
Artificis frondent dextræ; palmisque rubeta
Aspera, odoratæ cedunt mala gramina myrto.
Per valles sociata lupo lasciviet agna,
Cumque leone petet tutus præsepe juvencus.   85
Florea mansuetæ petulantes vincula tigri
Per ludum pueri injicient, et fessa colubri
Membra viatoris recreabunt frigore linguæ.
Serpentes teneris nil jam lethale minantes
Tractabit palmis infans, motusque trisulcæ   90
Ridebit linguæ innocuos, squamasque virentes
Aureaque admirans rutilantis fulgura cristæ.
Indue reginam, turritæ frontis honores
Tolle, *Salema*, sacros, quam circum gloria pennas
Explicat, incinctam radiatæ luce tiaræ!   95
En! formosa tibi porrecta per atria proles
Ordinibus surgit densis, vitamque requirit
Impatiens, lentéque fluentes increpat annos.
Ecce! peregrinis fervent tua limina turbis;
Barbarus, en! clarum divino lumine templum   100
Ingreditur, cultuque tuo mansuescere gaudet.
Cinnameos cumulos, *Nabathæi* munera veris,
Ecce! cremant genibus tritæ regalibus aræ.
Solis *Ophyræis* crudum tibi montibus aurum
Maturant radii, tibi balsama sudat *Idume*.   105

82 palmisque rubeta] Spinetaque Palmis *Husbands, 1785*[1]   86 mannetæ *Husbands*
89 minantes] micantes *Husbands, Gent. Mag., 1787*   91 squamasque virentes]
squamas viridantes *Popham*: equamasque *Husbands*   96 porrecta] spatiosa *Husbands*,
Gent. Mag., Popham, 1787   102 Cinnameos cumulos . . . munera] Cinnameis
cumulis . . . munere *Popham*

81-2. *buxique . . . dextræ:* 'reprehensible', Warton.

86. The errors *mannetæ*, for *mansuetæ*, and *equamasque* for *squamasque* (l. 91) in
Husbands are evidence of its proximity to Johnson's manuscript, in which, at this period,
he uses the short *s* initially and medially; but cf. the erroneous *deferet* (114).

87-8, *fessa . . . linguæ:* 'reprehensible', id.

89. 'nil jam lethale minantes' represents Pope's 'harmless'. Of all Popham's variants
'minantes' alone reappears in the corrected text; but 'micantes' ('darting', 'flashing
forth') is so bold a usage as to look like a misprint—though it is found in the two earliest
texts, and in Langton's.

102. This is one of the lines in which Popham's reading points to the use of an
inferior text.

Ætheris, en! portas sacro fulgore micantes
Cœlicolæ pandunt, torrentisque aurea lucis
Flumina prorumpunt; non posthac sole rubescet
India nascenti, placidæve argentea noctis
Luna vices revehet; radios pater ipse diei   110
Proferet archetypos; cœlestis gaudia lucis
Ipso fonte bibes, quæ circumfusa beatam
Regiam inundabit, nullis cessura tenebris.
Littora deficiens arentia deseret æquor,
Sidera fumabunt, diro labefacta tremore   115
Saxa cadent, solidique liquescent robora montis:
Tu secura tamen confusa elementa videbis,
Lætaque *Messià* semper dominabere rege,
Pollicitis firmata Dei, stabilita ruinis.

ON A SPRIG OF MYRTLE

The Museum, 1747, ii. 429 (Numb. xxvi, 14 March 1747).
The Union: or Select Scots and English Poems, 'Edinburgh', 1753, p. 117; also
   London, 1759, 1766, and Dublin, 1761.
Samuel Derrick, *A Collection of Original Poems*, 1755, p. 183.
The London Chronicle, 1 October 1768.
The Gentleman's Magazine, September 1768, p. 439.
The Scots Magazine, September 1768, p. 487.
The London Magazine, October 1768, p. 549.
The Annual Register, 1768, p. 248.
A Companion for a Leisure Hour . . . By Several Gentlemen. 1769, p. 151.
The Gentleman's Magazine, April 1779, p. 205.
The Weekly Magazine, 12 May 1779.
The Westminster Magazine, May 1779, p. 273.
The Scots Magazine, May 1779, p. 268.
The Poetical Works of Hammond (British Poets), Edinburgh, 1781, p. x.
The Festival of Wit, 1783, p. 161.
The Universal Magazine, March 1784, p. 156.
The New Foundling Hospital for Wit, 1784, 1786, vi. 59.
Poetical Works, 1785, p. 170.
Piozzi, *Anecdotes*, 1786, p. 33. (4 edns.)
A Dictionary of the English Language, By Samuel Johnson, L.L.D., London,
   Jarvis, 1786, i. a3ʳ.
Works, 1787, xi. 363.

107 torrentisque] crescentis et *Popham*: torrentis *1787*   114 deferet *Husbands*
119 Pollicitis firmata Dei,] Firmiùs ac ipsis Mundi *Popham*

Joshua Edkins, *A Collection of Poems . . . mostly Original*, Dublin, 1789, p. 16. Boswell, *Life*, 1791, i. 42 (1934, i. 92).

These verses appeared in *The Museum* anonymously. In *The Union*, a collection formed by Thomas Warton at Oxford and published with an Edinburgh imprint in 1753, they were said to be 'By Mr. Hammond'. When Derrick printed them in his *Collection* two years later, he placed them among the poems which he had received from 'a man of fashion' whom he was not permitted to name. They were first tentatively attributed to Johnson in *The London Chronicle* for 1 October 1768, where they are called 'Verses, said to have been written by Samuel Johnson, L. L. D. at the request of a Gentleman, to whom a Lady had given a Sprig of Myrtle'; and they were given with the same title in *The Gentleman's Magazine* for September. But by an editorial oversight they were reproduced from *The Union* and attributed to Hammond in *The Gentleman's Magazine* for April 1779. In the next number a correspondent who signed himself '*Eugenio*' (John Nichols) stated emphatically that they were '*not* written by Mr. Hammond, but by Dr. Johnson'. They were included in the *Poetical Works* in 1785, and in 1794 Boswell, who had followed a printed text in 1791 and 1793, received from Edmund Hector 'the original manuscript', of which, however, he made no use.

When Johnson's authorship of the verses was no longer doubtful, a controversy arose about their origin. In the *Poetical Works* they were said to have been 'written at Birmingham soon after he left the college, at the request of a friend who aspired to the character of a poet with his mistress' (Advertisement, p. iii). Then Mrs. Piozzi in her *Anecdotes* gave her account of what Johnson had told her, basing it on what she had written in *Thraliana* (ii. 9; ed. 1941, p. 163) in 1777:

'one Day in the Year 1768 I saw some Verses with his Name in a Magazine, these are they—I thought they were not his [here is pasted a cutting from *The Gentleman's Magazine* for September] so I asked him;—A young fellow replied he about forty Years ago had a Sprig of Myrtle given him by a Girl he courted, and asked me to write him some Verses upon it. I promised he but forgot; and when the Lad came a Week after for them, I said I'll go fetch them so ran away for five Minutes, and wrote the nonsense you are so troubled about; and which these Blockheads are printing now so pompously with their L: L: D.'

Against this in the margin she wrote 'Edmund Hector of Birmingham'. But Boswell preferred to accept the story which he received from Miss Anna Seward of Lichfield, and quoted from a letter which she had sent to him asserting that the verses were composed at her grandfather's house and addressed by Johnson to Lucy Porter. In the first number of *The Gentleman's Magazine* to be published after the appearance of the *Life*, Boswell's selection of Miss Seward as his guide met with the authoritative comment of John Nichols. Since 1778 Nichols had been a proprietor of the *Magazine*, and the attribution of the verses to Hammond in 1779 had led to a talk about them with Johnson, which he now reported in a letter (May 1791, p. 396):

'It happened that the verses in question were communicated to the Magazine for 1779, p. 205, as the production of Mr. Hammond; and, on my shewing them to Dr. Johnson

May 6, 1779, he told me they were neither Mr. Hammond's, nor Mr. Derrick's, to whom they had also been ascribed. "I wrote them, Sir, added the Doctor, more than 40 years ago, when I was at Birmingham, at the request of a friend; who, having frequently teazed me for the verses, I went one day up stairs as if to fetch them, and wrote them in the short space of time it required to have actually done so."'

No less authoritative was a private letter from the 'friend' himself, Edmund Hector. Boswell gave the true story of the verses in the second edition of the *Life*, and acknowledged that Mrs. Piozzi 'is not always inaccurate'. But he had now to deal with Miss Seward. She was not prepared to doubt what she had believed all her life, and she stated her case in *The Gentleman's Magazine* for October 1793 (p. 875). Boswell replied (p. 1009); and what he called their 'awkward and unpleasant squabling' continued till he received another letter from Hector, and printed it in the *Magazine* for January 1794 (p. 34):

'The true history (which I could swear to) is as follows. Mr. Morgan Graves, the elder brother of a [worthy] clergyman near Bath [Richard Graves, author of *The Spiritual Quixote*], with whom I was acquainted, waited upon a lady in this neighbourhood, who, at parting, presented him the branch. He shewed it me, and wished much to return the compliment in verse. I applied to Johnson, who was with me, and in about half an hour dictated the verses which I sent to my friend.' (9 January 1794; Waingrow, *Correspondence*, p. 575.)

With this letter, which is reprinted in full in the third edition of the *Life*, Hector enclosed 'the original manuscript', written by himself at Johnson's dictation. He says that it bore the date 1731. As he retained it till 1794, what Morgan Graves received was, as might be expected, a copy. The 'original manuscript', together with Hector's letter to Boswell, was recorded as lot 76 in Sotheby's sale of the library of Lewis Pocock on 10 May 1875, and was bought by Thomas Thorpe for 16 shillings.

The later texts derive from that in *The London Chronicle*, but the inferior reading in l. 7 does not give it authority over *The Museum* with which Johnson was certainly concerned. The new readings in 1785 are apparently editorial, and were reproduced by Hawkins. Mrs. Piozzi, never a scrupulous transcriber, introduced a new reading, and Boswell copied her.

On a LADY'S *presenting a Sprig of* MYRTLE *to a* GENTLEMAN

WHAT Fears, what Terrors does thy Gift create!
Ambiguous Emblem of uncertain Fate!
The Myrtle, Ensign of supreme Command,
(Consign'd by *Venus* to *Melissa*'s Hand)

Title. *Museum*: On a Lady's . . . Gentleman *Union*: On the Authors receiving a Sprig of Myrtle from a young Lady. By Mr. Hammond *Derrick*: Verses, written at the request of a Gentleman to whom a Lady had given a Sprig of Myrtle. *1785. See also introductory note.* 1 Fears] hopes *Lond. Chron. &c.* thy] this *1785* 2 uncertain] my future *Derrick* 4 to Venus by *1785*

Not less capricious than a reigning Fair,   5
Oft favors, oft rejects the Lover's Care.
In Myrtle Groves oft sings the happy Swain,
In Myrtle Shades despairing Ghosts complain;
The Myrtle crowns the happy Lovers Heads,
Th' unhappy Lovers Graves the Myrtle spreads;   10
Oh! then the Meaning of thy Gift impart,
And cure the Throbbings of an anxious Heart;
Soon must this Bough, as you shall fix his Doom,
Adorn *Philander*'s Head, or grace his Tomb.

ON A LADY LEAVING HER PLACE OF ABODE

Transcript by Edmund Hector in the Boswell Papers, Yale University Library. *Works*, vi (Yale ed. 1964), 38–9.

Hector sent his transcript to Boswell on 31 October 1791, with his second copy of the *Daffodill* (p. 2, *ante*). He added 'mark'd 1731'. In his letter to Boswell of 9 August 1791 (Waingrow, *Correspondence*, p. 440) he intimated his intention of sending the two pieces:

'I will transcribe for you if you think proper Two of the Dr.s Odes, which I have found, one very early wrote of seven Stanza's [i.e. *Daffodill*] the other of four to a Young Lady— Sister to the Gentleman the Myrtle was wrote for.'

Although this poem contains only three stanzas, it can hardly be doubted that it is the ode meant. The young lady, 'Cleora', was therefore a sister of Morgan Graves. Graves had four brothers among whom was Richard, author of *The Spiritual Quixote*, 1773, and two sisters: Elizabeth who died at the age of nine, and Mary, born in 1714. She married in 1748 the Revd. John Tayler (1700–74), Rector of Weston Turville with Bedgrove, Bucks., and died there in 1779. She was a beautiful and gracious young lady, the ornament of a small literary coterie at her family home at Mickleton, Glos., where for a time Shenstone was in love with her. (His verses to 'Selinda' are addressed to her, and his own copy of his *Poems upon Various Occasions*, Oxford 1737, now at Yale, shows that the book was dedicated to her.) In 1731 she was seventeen, and if Hector knew Morgan Graves well enough to call him 'my friend' (p. 51, *ante*) then Johnson could well have been known to them both. Another probable common acquaintance was Henry Hervey. The occasion of this poem remains undiscovered.

5 a] the *Derrick*   6 Now grants, and now rejects *Piozzi, Boswell*: the poet's pray'r *Derrick*: a lover's pray'r *Lond. Chron. &c.*: prayer *Piozzi*   7 Groves] shades *Lond. Chron. &c.*   9–10 *om. Derrick* 10 lover's grave *Piozzi*[1]: lovers' grave *Piozzi*[2–4], *Boswell*   12 cure] ease *Lond. Chron. &c.*   throbbing *Derrick*   13 must] shall *Derrick*   bough] sprig *1785*   his] its *1785*

An Ode on a Lady leaving her place of abode.
almost impromptu

W̲HEN the departing Sun resigns,
  The Northern Shores to Clouds and frost
The chill Inhabitant repines,
In half a Year of darkness lost.

Cleora thus regretted flies,   5
Fair source of wit, and love, and mirth
Withdraws the influence of those Eyes,
Which gave a thousand pleasures birth.

Not long the happy Russians mourn,
Revolving Springs their frost repay   10
O would Cleora thus return,
And bless me with continu'd day.

TO MISS HICKMAN PLAYING ON
THE SPINET

Manuscript in the Hyde Collection.
Transcript by Malone in his copy of Boswell's *Life*, 1807 (British Museum
  10854. d. 3).
Works, 1787, xi. 371.
  The manuscript, which is reproduced in facsimile in *The R. B. Adam Library*
(vol. i, after p. 189), bears the following note on the back:

> Written by the late Dʳ. Samuel Johnson
> on my Mother, when Miss Hickman, playing
> on the Spinet
>
>   J Turton

The poem was first printed by Hawkins, who states that it was communicated
to him by Dr. Turton.
  Dorothy Hickman (born 13 February 1714) was the daughter of Gregory
Hickman (1688–1748) of Stourbridge, to whom Johnson sent his first known
letter on 30 October 1731. Johnson had been befriended by Hickman in an
unsuccessful application for the post of usher in the Grammar School of Stourbridge, and the letter shows that Hickman had been struck with his facility in

9 the happy the *Hector*

making verses, and had suggested that a new theme might be found in the recent failure. To this Johnson replied 'that versifying against one's inclination is the most disagreeable thing in the world, and that one's own disappointment is no inviting subject' (*Letters*, i. 1). The verses to Dorothy Hickman may have been written during the visit to Stourbridge in 1731, when she was aged seventeen.

Johnson was connected with the Hickmans by marriage. His uncle Dr. Joseph Ford married the widow of Dorothy's grandfather, and his uncle Nathaniel Ford married one of Dorothy's aunts (see Aleyn Lyell Reade, *The Reades of Blackwood Hill*, 1906, pp. 149, 150, and pedigrees XXVII and XXIX).

Dorothy Hickman married Dr. John Turton, of Wolverhampton, in 1734, and was the mother of Dr. John Turton, the fashionable London physician who attended Goldsmith in his last illness.

The text here given follows the manuscript.

To Miss Hickman playing on the Spinet

B RIGHT Stella, form'd for universal Reign,
  Too well You know to keep the Slaves You gain.
When in Your Eyes resistless Lightnings play,
Aw'd into Love, our conquer'd hearts obey,
And yield, reluctant, to despotick Sway.   5
But when your Musick sooths the raging pain,
We bid propitious Heav'n prolong your reign,
We bless the Tyrant, and we hug the Chain.
     When old Timotheus struck the vocal String,
Ambitious Fury fir'd the Grecian King: 10
Unbounded Projects lab'ring in his Mind,
He pants for room, in one poor World confin'd.
Thus wak'd to rage by Musick's dreadfull Pow'r,
He bids the Sword destroy, the Flame devour.
Had Stella's gentle touches mov'd the Lyre,   15
Soon had the Monarch felt a nobler fire,
No more delighted with destructive War,
Ambitious only now to please the Fair,
Resign'd his Thirst of Empire to her Charms,
And found a Thousand Worlds in Stella's Arms.   20

10 Ambitious Fury] Ambition's fury *Works, misreading the manuscript*

9–20. Suggested by Dryden's *Alexander's Feast*.

TO SYLVANUS URBAN

Editor of *The Gentleman's Magazine*

The Gentleman's Magazine, March 1738, p. 156, and 1784, verso of title-leaf of Part I.
Shaw, *Memoirs of Johnson*, 1785, p. 34.
A Dictionary of the English Language. By Samuel Johnson, L.L.D., London, Jarvis, 1786, i. a4^r.
Hawkins, *Life of Johnson*, 1787, p. 90.
Works, 1787, xi. 388.
Boswell, *Life*, 1791, i. 56 (1934, i. 113).

The poem is understood to have been Johnson's first contribution to *The Gentleman's Magazine*, where it appeared unsigned [In some reprints it is signed 'S.J.'], with an introductory note about the attacks on Cave by rival booksellers:

'All Men of Sense, as far as we can find, having condemn'd the rude Treatment given Mr Urban by certain Booksellers, whose Names are not worth the mention already made of them; we hope it will not be thought any Ostentation, to let the Reader see a few of the Pieces sent in his favour by Correspondents of all Degrees ...'

A translation signed 'Briton' followed in May (p. 268), and another, according to Nichols by William Jackson of Canterbury, was printed on the verso of the title-page of Part II, 1784. Shaw prints another translation (pp. 36–7), provided 'by a friend'. Hawkins and Boswell reprinted the first translation. In a note to the proof reader Boswell wrote: 'Be sure to compare Urbane etc both latin and english with the original' (see R. W. Chapman in *Johnson and Boswell Revised*, 1928, p. 24).

Ad URBANUM

U RBANE, nullis fesse laboribus,
   URBANE, nullis victe calumniis,
    Cui Fronte Sertum in Erudita
      Perpetuo viret et virebit;

Quid moliatur Gens Imitantium,   5
   Quid et minetur, sollicitus parum,
    Vacare solis perge Musis,
      Juxta Animo Studiisque felix.

1. Murphy cites the beginning of Casimir's Ode to Pope Urban:
        Urbane, regum maxime, maxime
        Urbane vatum.

'The Polish poet was, probably, at that time in the hands of a man who had meditated the history of the Latin poets' (*Essay*, 1792, p. 42). The resemblance is confined to the first word, and the metre; though Johnson knew Casimir, cf. *Life of Cowley*, para. 137.

Linguæ procacis plumbea Spicula,
Fidens, Superbo frange Silentio;   10
Victrix per obstantes catervas
Sedulitas animosa tendet.

Intende nervos fortis, inanibus
Risurus olim nisibus Æmuli;
Intende jam nervos, habebis   15
Participes operæ Camœnas.

Non ulla Musis Pagina gratior,
Quam quæ severis ludicra jungere
Novit, fatigatamque nugis
Utilibus recreare Mentem.   20

Texente Nymphis serta Lycoride,
Rosæ ruborem sic Viola adjuvat
Immista, sic Iris refulget
Æthereis variata fucis.

TO RICHARD SAVAGE

The Gentleman's Magazine, April 1738, p. 210.
The London Magazine, November 1741, p. 565.
Boswell, *Life*, 1791, i. 88 n. (1934, i. 162 n.).

This epigram immediately precedes Johnson's Greek epigram to Eliza in *The Gentleman's Magazine*. It was attributed to Johnson in *The London Magazine*, to which it was probably sent by Savage; it follows two longer poems which are there said to be inserted at Savage's desire. Boswell was assured that Johnson wrote it, and Nichols agreed in the Preface to the General Index to *The Gentleman's Magazine*, 1821, p. xxi. Croker attacked the attribution (*Life*, 1831, i. 138 n. 2).

This epigram may cast doubt on Johnson's reported statement that he did not know Savage when he wrote *London*. On the other hand, the epigram cannot be taken to show more than slight and recent acquaintance; and *London* had been offered to the publisher a few weeks before the epigram was printed. It may be that Johnson met Savage in April 1738. See note on *London*, l. 2 *post*.

16 opera *Works*

Ad RICARDUM SAVAGE, *Arm.*
Humani Generis Amatorem.

H UMANI studium generis cui pectore fervet,
O! colat humanum Te foveatque genus!

ON A RIDDLE BY ELIZA

The Gentleman's Magazine, April 1738, p. 210.
Works, 1787, xi. 397.

In an undated letter which Johnson sent to Cave before 6 April 1738, he says, 'I have composed a Greek Epigram to Eliza, and think she ought to be celebrated in as many different languages as Lewis le Grand' (*Life*, 1934, i. 122). The epigram is an answer to a long English riddle by Elizabeth Carter in the February issue of *The Gentleman's Magazine*, 1738, p. 99.

Boswell marked both the Greek epigram and the Latin translation as acknowledged by Johnson, but erroneously attributed them to the following year (*Life*, i. 140).

Εἰς τὸ τῆς ᾿ΕΛΙΣΣΗΣ περὶ τῶν ᾿Ονείρων Αἴνιγμα

Τ Ἡι Κάλλους δυνάμει τί τέλος; Ζεὺς πάντα δέδωκεν
Κύπριδι, μήδ᾿ αὐτοῦ Σκῆπτρα μέμηλε Θεῷ.
᾿Εκ Διός ἐστιν ὄναρ, θεῖός ποτ᾿ ἔγραψεν ῞Ομηρος,
᾿Αλλὰ τόδ᾿ εἰς θνητοὺς Κύπρις ἔπεμψεν ῞Οναρ·
Ζεὺς μοῦνος φλογόεντι πόλεις ἔκπερσε κεραυνῷ,   5
῞Ομμασι λαμπρὰ Διὸς Κύπρις ὄϊστὰ φέρει.

In ELIZÆ ÆNIGMA

Q UIS formæ modus imperio? *Venus* arrogat audax
Omnia, nec curæ sunt sua sceptra *Jovi.*
Ab *Jove Mæonides* descendere Somnia narrat:
Hæc veniunt *Cypriæ* Somnia missa *Deæ.*
Jupiter unus erat, qui stravit fulmine gentes;   5
Nunc armant *Veneris* lumina tela *Jovis.*

---

1 generis studium *London Mag.*

---

2 μὴδ᾿ *GM*   5 Ζεὺς *GM*

TO ELIZABETH CARTER

Montagu Pennington, *Memoirs of Elizabeth Carter*, 1807, i. 271 n.

This quatrain was printed by Pennington with this introduction: 'The following Epigram by Dr. Johnson, found among Mrs. Carter's papers, in his own hand-writing, and evidently addressed to her, has never, I believe, been published before.' Without more information it is impossible to date these verses, which may have been written almost any time after 1738.

QUID mihi cum cultu? Probitas inculta nitescit,
  Et juvat ingenii vita sine arte rudis.
Ingenium et mores si pulchra probavit Elisa,
  Quid majus mihi spes ambitiosa dabit?

TO A LADY WHO SPOKE IN DEFENCE OF LIBERTY

The Gentleman's Magazine, April 1738, p. 211; May 1787, p. 441.
The London Magazine, September 1739, p. 462.
Thraliana, iv (1781–6), pp. 95, 267; ed. 1941, pp. 538, 671.
Piozzi, *Anecdotes*, 1786, p. 157.
Hawkins, *Life of Johnson*, 1787, p. 316.
Works, 1787, xi. 396.
Boswell, *Life*, 1791, ii. 258 n. (1934, iii. 341 n.).

The manuscript of '*Johnson's lines to Miss Aston*' was lot 179 in the Johnston sale at Messrs. Puttick and Simpson's, 12 August 1863.

This epigram was addressed to Molly Aston. Boswell calls her 'a violent Whig', and adds that it was written 'in answer to her high-flown speeches for *Liberty*'. Johnson dictated it to Mrs. Thrale in July 1782 when talking about happiness, and what she then wrote in *Thraliana* she expanded into a characteristic account in the *Anecdotes*:

'When Mr Thrale once asked him which had been the happiest period of his past life? he replied, "it was that year in which he spent one whole evening with M—y As—n. That indeed (said he) was not happiness, it was rapture; but the thoughts of it sweetened the whole year." I must add, that the evening alluded to was not passed *tête-a-tête* [as she had said in *Thraliana*], but in a select company, of which the present Lord Kill-morey was one. "Molly (says Dr Johnson) was a beauty and a scholar, and a wit and a whig; and she talked all in praise of liberty: and so I made this epigram upon her—She was the loveliest creature I ever saw!!!"'

Mary Aston, familiarly known as 'Molly', was the second daughter of Sir Thomas Aston, of Aston, Cheshire, third baronet. Her elder sister Catherine married the Hon. Henry Hervey, Johnson's friend, and her younger sister Magdalen married Gilbert Walmesley. Born 25 December 1706, she married David Brodie, captain in the Royal Navy, in 1753, and died about 1765. (See

A. L. Reade, *Johnsonian Gleanings*, v. 249 and vi. 186; her portrait is reproduced as the frontispiece to vi.) She is mentioned several times by Boswell, once as having explained a question in economics which had puzzled Johnson and Lord Kames (*Life*, iii. 340).

Verses by her are preserved in Johnson's handwriting. She had refused to give a copy to a cousin when Johnson, having only once heard them, twelve lines in all, asked for a bit of paper and wrote them down. The manuscript is now in the Bodleian Library (MS. Don. c. 56, f. 73).

In the second edition of the *Life*, 1793 (iii. 131), Boswell quotes from a correspondent [Revd. John Brickdale Blakeway] of *The Gentleman's Magazine* who thought that Johnson was indebted to an epigram in *Menagiana*, ed. 1716, iii. 377:

> On s'étonne ici que Caliste
> Ait pris l'habit de Moliniste.
> Puisque cette jeune beauté
> Ote à chacun sa liberté,
> N'est-ce pas une Janseniste?

Abraham Hayward (*Autobiography . . . of Mrs. Piozzi*, 2nd ed., 1861, i. 51 n.) suggested that Johnson may have had Propertius in mind: 'Nullus liber erit si quis amare volet.' (*Elegies*, II. xxiii. 24, 'De Amoris Servitute'.) In Johnson's copy of Camden's *Remaines*, 1636 (in the Folger Shakespeare Library), he has adjusted the punctuation of an epitaph on p. 416:

'A Gentleman who dwelt at Bermington in Holland, wrote this Distich in Latin upon his wife buried at Westerkeale in Lincolnshire

> Quæ pia, quæ prudens, quæ provida, pulchra suasisti,
> Vxor in æternium, chara MARIA vale.'

The similarities may be more readily granted than the debt, though it is certain that Johnson had read Camden at Oxford (*Life*, iii. 304).

A translation by T. Knight was published in *The London Magazine* for September 1739. Mrs. Thrale made an impromptu translation when the distich was dictated to her (*Thraliana*, p. 539, *Anecdotes*, p. 157, MS. Rylands Eng. 647/119). Others are given by Hawkins, by Boswell, and by Murphy, *Monthly Review*, May 1787, p. 369. For two Italian translations see *Thraliana*, p. 671.

Text and title from *The Gentleman's Magazine*, 1738.

To a Lady *who spoke in Defence of* LIBERTY

LIBER ut esse velim, suasisti, pulchra *Maria*:
Ut maneam liber, pulchra *Maria*, vale.

Title. Ad foeminam quandam generosam quæ libertatis causæ in sermone patrocinata fuerat. *1787*   2 liber maneam, *London Mag.*

LONDON

London was published on 13 May 1738. (The draft manuscript bears the note '12 May'.) All that is known of the poem before this date is to be learned from four letters sent by Johnson to Cave, the proprietor and printer of *The Gentleman's Magazine*, and included by Boswell in the *Life* (i. 120–3). About the end of March it was submitted to Cave for publication. Cave thought well of it, and was willing to print it, but suggested that Dodsley might publish it. 'I was to day', writes Johnson, 'with Mr. Dodsley, who declares very warmly in favour of the paper you sent him, which he desires to have a share in, it being, as he says, *a creditable thing to be concerned in*. I knew not what answer to make till I had consulted you, nor what to demand on the Author's part, but am very willing that, if you please, he should have a part in it, as he will undoubtedly be more diligent to disperse and promote it.' This, from the last of the four letters, was written on or before 6 April, as is shown by a note in another hand on the back. The poem was printed by Cave and published by Dodsley. The first edition was probably of 500 copies (see Johnson's undated letter to Cave, *Letters*, ed. Chapman, i. 10, no. 6). Of the four authorized folio editions of 1738–9 only the second was slightly revised (p. 64 *post*). In all four the same type was reused and reimpressed, but on each occasion the compositors deliberately respaced the setting, a procedure which ensured that they could claim full payment for each printing.

In another of the letters Johnson had offered to Cave to defray the expenses of printing on condition of receiving the profits, should there be any. But Dodsley proposed to buy the whole copyright, and bought it for ten guineas. 'I might perhaps have accepted of less', Johnson said long afterwards to Boswell, 'but that Paul Whitehead had a little before got ten guineas for a poem, and I would not take less than Paul Whitehead.'

It was commonly believed during Johnson's lifetime that he had found difficulties in getting *London* published. Samuel Derrick spoke of them in his 'Fortune. A Rhapsody' (*A Collection of Original Poems*, 1755, p. 218):

> Will no kind patron Johnson own?
> Shall Johnson, friendless, range the town?
> And ev'ry publisher refuse
> The offspring of his happy Muse.

He added this footnote: 'Sam. Johnson, one of the most elegant writers of the age, Author of the New English Dictionary, at first could scarcely find a Bookseller, who would publish his fine imitation of Juvenal's third satire.' A similar statement was made in Cooke's *Life of Johnson* (1785, p. 10) and in Shaw's *Memoirs of the Life and Writings of the late Dr. Samuel Johnson* (1785, pp. 31, 46); but the four letters printed by Boswell give it no support.

Johnson insisted that the passages in Juvenal's satire[1] which he had followed

---

[1] See E. A. and L. D. Bloom in *Huntington Library Quarterly*, xxiv (1970–1), 1–23, 115–39.

most directly 'must be subjoined at the bottom of the Page, part of the beauty of the performance (if any beauty be allow'd it) consisting in adapting Juvenal's Sentiments to modern facts and Persons'. Herein he was following a common habit and in particular the example of Pope, who in the original editions of some of his Imitations of Horace had the corresponding passages in the original printed on the left-hand page. It was during the decade in which *London* appeared that the art of poetic imitation reached its highest excellence. Reviewing its history, long after its greatest vogue had passed, Johnson wrote thus in his *Life of Pope*:

'This mode of imitation, in which the ancients are familiarised by adapting their sentiments to modern topicks, by making Horace say of Shakespeare what he originally said of Ennius, and accommodating his satires on Pantolabus and Nomentanus to the flatterers and prodigals of our own time, was first practised in the reign of Charles the Second by Oldham and Rochester, at least I remember no instances more ancient. It is a kind of middle composition between translation and original design, which pleases when the thoughts are unexpectedly applicable and the parallels lucky. It seems to have been Pope's favourite amusement, for he has carried it further than any former poet.'

In writing *London*, Johnson was aware of entering into competition with Pope; and comparison was invited by the fact that Pope's *One Thousand Seven Hundred and Thirty Eight, a Dialogue something like Horace*, appeared on the same day. Since both were published by Dodsley the coincidence may have been more than accidental. With Pope's example before him, he was able to excel the imitation of the Third Satire of Juvenal which Oldham had written in 1682.

There is little in common between Oldham's and Johnson's poems, beyond the similarity unavoidable in imitations of the same original. The harsh cadence of a rugged line, which Oldham still believed proper to effective satire, had passed out of favour by Johnson's day. Oldham lacerates; Johnson's purpose is rather to affront. Again, what was pre-eminently a social satire expressing disgust with the inequalities, the follies, and the rottenness of city life, and exalting by contrast the conditions which are surmised to prevail in the country, becomes in Johnson's hands largely a political satire. His antipathy to Walpole's administration is given free scope in the allusions to excise, the abuse of pensions, the tyranny of the licensing laws, and the servitude of a thoughtless age—allusions which anticipate not only some of the definitions in the *Dictionary*, but also the theme of two ironical pamphlets which he published in the following year, *Marmor Norfolciense* and *A Compleat Vindication of the Licensers of the Stage*. A good commentary on this political element is supplied by an article in *The Craftsman* published on the same day as *London*, and reprinted in *The Gentleman's Magazine*. It begins with a reference to Juvenal, and deals with some of the same topics as the poem. *London* could be regarded by the 'patriots' as a political manifesto. The rapid and steady sale, which called for the second edition in a week and the third in two months, is not to be attributed solely to poetic merit.

None the less it is clear that Johnson had read Oldham's satire, and that phrases had dwelt in his memory.[1] Boswell pointed out two coincidences

---

[1] An edition of 'Oldham's Poems, with notes, historical and critical' appears in Johnson's list of projected works, 'Designs' (*Life*, iv. 381 n.).

> . . . the Common-shore,
> Where *France* does all her Filth and Ordure pour (*Oldham*),
> The common shore of Paris and of Rome (l. 94);

and,

> No Calling or Profession comes amiss,
> A needy *Monsieur* can be what he please (*Oldham*),
> All sciences a fasting Monsieur knows (l. 115).

These are not 'the only instances', as Boswell said, but they are the most striking. Oldham's English parallels to the Latin facts and persons are occasionally echoed by Johnson, and notably in this passage:

> Happy the times of the old *Heptarchy*,
> Ere *London* knew so much of Villany:
> Then fatal Carts thro *Holborn* seldom went,
> And *Tyburn* with few Pilgrims was content:
> A less, and single Prison then would do,
> And serv'd the City, and the Country too.

So Oldham; and thus Johnson:

> Scarce can our Fields, such Crowds at *Tyburn* die,
> With Hemp the Gallows and the Fleet supply . . . .
> A single Jail, in *Alfred*'s golden Reign,
> Could half the Nation's Criminals contain (l. 242).

Such similarities suggest unconscious recollection. The closest likeness happens to be to Dryden's translation. There we find—

> All things the hungry *Greek* exactly knows:
> And bid him go to Heav'n, to Heav'n he goes.

Johnson, making freer play with Juvenal's 'in caelum jusseris', says—

> All Sciences a fasting Monsieur knows,
> And bid him go to Hell, to Hell he goes (l. 116).

When Goldsmith included *London* in *The Beauties of English Poesy* (1767), he prefixed to it the following note:

'This poem of Mr. Johnson's is the best imitation of the original that has appeared in our language, being possessed of all the force and satyrical resentment of Juvenal. Imitation gives us a much truer idea of the ancients than even translation could do.'

These words suggest that Goldsmith was thinking of more poems than Oldham's, and he may have had in mind two ventures to which the excellence of *London* should have been a deterrent—Samuel Derrick's *The Third Satire of Juvenal, translated into English Verse* (1755), and Edward Burnaby Greene's *The Satires of Juvenal Paraphrastically Imitated, and adapted to the Times* (1763). His verdict still holds true. Johnson himself, however, came to think that his adaptations had not always been adequate. The passage on Orgilio's flaming palace, he admitted, was 'no picture of modern manners, though it might be true at Rome'. He too, like Pope, had no choice but to make the Frenchman represent the Greek of the classical satires. 'We conquered France, but felt our captive's charms', says Pope, imitating Horace; and Johnson writes 'I cannot bear a French metropolis'. There were traces of French influence in the London of

George II, as there may be now, but Voltaire did not mistake it for 'a French metropolis', nor did Johnson himself.

He had his own experience in mind when he said in his *Life of Pope* that 'between Roman images and English manners there will be an irreconcileable dissimilitude, and the work will be generally uncouth and party-coloured; neither original nor translated, neither ancient nor modern'. This is truer of *London* than of Pope's Imitations of Horace, or of his own mature *Vanity of Human Wishes*. But the dissimilitude did not trouble his contemporaries, who were attracted by the force and point of the modern allusions. What struck Pope most in the poem was its promise. The unknown author, he said, 'will soon be déterré'.

EDITIONS AND TEXT

Holograph manuscript of lines 99–106, 147–50, 198–263 in the Hyde Collection.

London: A Poem, In Imitation of the Third Satire of Juvenal. . . . London: Printed for R. Doddesley . . . MDCCXXXVIII. Folio. Published 13 May 1738.[1] (Facsimile, Scolar Press 1970.)

London: A Poem, . . . The Second Edition . . . Printed for R. Dodsley . . . MDCCXXXVIII. Folio. Published about 20 May 1738.

London: A Poem, . . . The Second Edition . . . Printed for R. Dodsley . . . MDCCXXXVIII. Octavo. [Despite the imprint, actually printed and published in Edinburgh by Ruddiman; *teste* D. F. Foxon.]

London: A Poem, . . . Dublin: Reprinted by and for George Faulkner. MDCCXXXVIII. Octavo.

London: A Poem, . . . The Third Edition . . . Printed for R. Dodsley . . . MDCCXXXVIII. Folio. Published 15 July 1738.

London: A Poem, . . . The Fourth Edition . . . Printed for R. Dodsley . . . MDCCXXXIX. Folio.

Dodsley, *Collection of Poems*, 1748, i. 101; second ed., 1748, i. 192; also 1751, '55, '58, '63, '65, '66, '70, '75, '82. (The basis of all texts to 1785, except 1750.)

London: A Poem, . . . The Fifth Edition. London: Printed by E. Cave at St. John's Gate, and sold by R. Dodsley in Pallmall, 1750. Price 1s. Where may be had, Price 1s The Vanity of Human Wishes, being the 10th Satire of Juvenal, imitated by the same Author. Quarto.

Two Satires. By Samuel Johnson, A.M. Oxford, 1759. [Two states, with variant titles and minor differences in the text.]

The Art of Poetry on a New Plan, 1761, ii. 116.

The Beauties of English Poesy, Selected by Oliver Goldsmith, 1767, i. 59.

A Select Collection of Poems, Edinburgh, 1768, 1772, i. 50.

Davies, *Miscellaneous and Fugitive Pieces*, 1773, 1774, ii. 300.

D. Junii Juvenalis et A. Persii Flacci Satiræ, ed. Knox, 1784, p. 373.

Poetical Works, 1785, p. 1.

Works, 1787, xi. 319.

---

[1] Minor features in an early state of the first edition are detailed by Mr. R. R. Allen in *Papers of the Bibliographical Society of America*, lx (1966), 214–15.

Poetical Works, 1789, p. 1.

(Sixty-six lines, selected from different parts of the poem, were printed in *The Gentleman's Magazine* for May 1738, p. 269.)

Three editions published during Johnson's lifetime have independent value,—the first; the second folio, which has two new readings (ll. 65, 198); and Dodsley's edition of 1748, which has three more (ll. 59, 122, 251). Emendations which Johnson left in manuscript, as well as others for which the authority is not known, were incorporated by Hawkins in 1787.

The 'fifth' edition issued in quarto in 1750 as a companion to *The Vanity of Human Wishes* is a reprint of the first edition and ignores Johnson's corrections. But on a copy of this inferior edition Johnson wrote notes and variants, forgetful of the changes that he had already made. This copy came to the hands of Hawkins, and was used by him for his text of 1787. In his *Life of Johnson* (p. 57) he says that 'the poem was finished, as appears by a manuscript note of the author in his own corrected copy, in 1738'. Boswell, apparently following him carelessly, says that Johnson 'has marked upon his corrected copy of the first edition of it, "Written in 1738"' (*Life*, i. 120). There would be little point in such an inscription on a copy dated 1738 on the title-page. Whether or not an annotated copy of any edition was ever seen by Boswell, the annotated copy of the fifth edition was certainly seen by James Boswell the younger, who transcribed the annotations into his copy of the 1789 edition of Johnson's poems, not earlier, as an inscription shows, than 1793. 'These notes and various readings', he says, 'I have transcribed from Johnson's own handwriting on a copy of the 5th edition.' We can thus account for four of the new readings in Hawkins's text (ll. 5, 131, 218, 241), and five of its explanatory notes.[1] But Johnson had written six. They are here set out consecutively; their matter and tone suggest that they were written many years after 1750:

(54) The invasions of the Spaniards were defended in the houses of Parliament.

(59) The licensing act was then lately made.

(72) The paper which at that time contained apologies for the Court.

(173) The Spaniards at this time were said to make claim to some of our American provinces.

(194) This was by Hitch a Bookseller justly remarked to be no picture of modern manners, though it might be true at Rome.

(245) A cant term in the House of Commons for methods of raising money.

The fifth of these notes was first printed, from a 'MS note in Dr. Johnson's hand-writing', in the collected edition of 1816 by Alexander Chalmers, but it must surely have been supplied, as other notes then were, by the younger Boswell. On the sale of Boswell's books in 1825 his annotated volume passed to J. W. Croker, and is now in the Nichol Smith Collection of the National Library of Australia, Canberra. The copy of the fifth edition with Johnson's notes has disappeared. A reconsideration of the significance of Boswell's notes

[1] A copy of the first edition, 1738, in the Berg Collection of the New York Public Library has all the readings adopted by Hawkins written in an early hand. The handwriting is neither Johnson's nor Hawkins's, nor apparently that of James Boswell jun., but it is certainly of the eighteenth century.

by A. D. Moody (*The Library*, xxvi (1971), 22–38) suggests that they may have been over-valued.

The text of 1748 is here followed because it embodies changes made on two revisions, but the new readings which Johnson subsequently left in manuscript are inserted, and his notes are added under the lines to which they refer. Typographical errors are corrected.

L O N D O N:

A

P O E M,

In IMITATION of the

THIRD **SATIRE** of *JUVENAL.*

✿✢✿✢✿✢✿✢✿✢✿✢✿✢✿✢✿✢✿✢✿✢✿✢✿✢✿✢✿✢✿✢✿✢✿✢

- - - - - - - - - *Quis ineptæ*
Tam patiens Urbis, tam ferreus ut teneat se ?
JUV.

✿✢✿✢✿✢✿✢✿✢✿✢✿✢✿✢✿✢✿✢✿✢✿✢✿✢✿✢✿✢✿✢✿✢✿✢

L O N D O N:

Printed for *R. Doddesley,* at *Tully*'s Head in *Pall-Mall.*
MDCCXXXVIII.

LONDON:

A POEM

In IMITATION of the

THIRD SATIRE of *JUVENAL*

Quis ineptæ
Tam patiens urbis, tam ferreus ut teneat se?

JUV. [Sat. I. 30–1.]

[a]THO' Grief and Fondness in my Breast rebel,
    When injur'd THALES bids the Town farewell,
Yet still my calmer Thoughts his Choice commend,

JUV. SAT. III.

[a]*Quamvis Digressu veteris confusus Amici;*
Laudo, tamen, vacuis quod Sedem figere Cumis
Destinet, atque unum Civem donare Sibyllæ. (Ver. 1–3.)

Epigraph: E. L. and L. D. Bloom, 'Johnson's *London* and Its Juvenalian Texts',
and 'Johnson's *London* and the Tools of Scholarship', *Huntington Library Quarterly*,
xxiv (1970–1), 1–23, 115–39.

2. Hawkins identified Thales with Richard Savage, who left London for Swansea
in July 1739. 'The event is antedated in the poem of "London"; but in every particular,
except the difference of a year, what is there said of the departure of Thales must be
understood of Savage, and looked upon as true history' (*Life*, 1787, p. 86; cf. p. 56),
Boswell declared this conjecture to be groundless: 'I have been assured, that Johnson
said he was not so much as acquainted with Savage when he wrote his *London*' (*Life*, i.
125 n.). Then Chalmers pointed out that Boswell had stated Johnson to be the author
of the complimentary lines 'Ad Ricardum Savage' printed in *The Gentleman's Magazine*
for April 1738 (see p. 56). 'This surely implies previous acquaintance with Savage, for
Dr. Johnson would not have praised a stranger in such terms; and gives a very strong
probability to Sir John Hawkins's conjecture. That Savage did not set out for Wales
until the following year, is a matter of little consequence, as the intention of such a
journey would justify the lines alluding to it' (*Works*, 1806, i. 145). These three state-
ments cover all the ground of a long controversy: see *The Gentleman's Magazine*,
December 1840, p. 612, and *Life*, i. 125. For a complete account of Savage see C. R.
Tracy, *The Artificial Bastard* (Toronto, 1953). Thales' function in the poem is
more important than his identity, but the controversy continues, see F. V. Bernard,
Notes and Queries, September 1958, 398–9, and August 1964, 293–6. Savage did not
set out for Wales till July 1739. There seems to be no evidence that he thought of going
there till many months after the publication of *London*. The Rev. John Hussey wrote
the following note in his copy of Boswell's *Life*: 'Johnson told me that London was
written *many years* before he was acquainted with Savage and that it was even *published*
before he knew him—of which I informed Mr. Boswell—who did not think proper to
believe me—Johnson also said that by Thales he did not mean any particular person.'
Thales corresponds to Juvenal's Umbricius, who leaves for the country in disgust
at the life in Rome.

I praise the Hermit, but regret the Friend,
Resolved at length, from Vice and LONDON far,   5
To breathe in distant Fields a purer Air,
And, fix'd on CAMBRIA's solitary shore,
Give to St. DAVID one *true Briton* more.

  bFor who would leave, unbrib'd, *Hibernia*'s Land,
Or change the Rocks of *Scotland* for the *Strand?*   10
There none are swept by sudden Fate away,
But all whom Hunger spares, with Age decay:
Here Malice, Rapine, Accident, conspire,
And now a Rabble Rages, now a Fire;
Their Ambush here relentless Ruffians lay,   15
And here the fell Attorney prowls for Prey;
Here falling Houses thunder on your Head,
And here a female Atheist talks you dead.

  cWhile THALES waits the Wherry that contains
Of dissipated Wealth the small Remains,   20
On *Thames*'s Banks, in silent Thought we stood,
Where GREENWICH smiles upon the silver Flood:
Struck with the Seat that gave *ELIZA Birth,
We kneel, and kiss the consecrated Earth;
In pleasing Dreams the blissful Age renew,   25
And call BRITANNIA's Glories back to view;

b—— *Ego vel* Prochytam *præpono* Suburræ.
Nam quid tam miserum, tam solum vidimus, ut non
Deterius credas horrere Incendia, Lapsus
Tectorum assiduos, et mille Pericula sævæ
Urbis, & Augusto recitantes Mense Poetas? (5–9.)
c*Sed, dum tota Domus Rhedâ componitur unâ,*
Substitit ad veteres Arcus.—(10, 11.)
  * Queen Elizabeth born at Greenwich.

---

5 Resolved at length *Johnson MS. correction, 1787* (Resolv'd)] Who now resolves
1738–85   18 there *GM*   21 Banks] bank *1763–82*

  9–14. These lines were taken by Boswell to show the prejudice of a 'true-born English-man' against Ireland and Scotland. But Johnson is contrasting the simplicity of rural life in a poor country with the dangers and vices of the town.

  16. Quoted in the first edition of the *Dictionary*, s.v. 'prowl', and modestly said to be 'Anon.'; omitted in the edition of 1773.

  20. Quoted in the *Dictionary*, with 'poor' for 'small', s.v. 'dissipate'.

  21–4. Johnson was lodging at Greenwich when he wrote the poem. He visited it with Boswell on 30 July 1763, when Boswell read aloud these lines 'with enthusiasm'; no comment of Johnson's is recorded.

Behold her Cross triumphant on the Main,
The Guard of Commerce, and the Dread of *Spain*,
Ere Masquerades debauch'd, Excise oppress'd,
Or *English* Honour grew a standing Jest.   30
    A transient Calm the happy Scenes bestow,
And for a Moment lull the Sense of Woe.
At length awaking, with contemptuous Frown,
Indignant THALES eyes the neighb'ring Town.
    ᵈSince Worth, he cries, in these degen'rate Days,   35
Wants ev'n the cheap Reward of empty Praise;
In those curst Walls, devote to Vice and Gain,
Since unrewarded Science toils in vain;
Since Hope but sooths to double my Distress,
And ev'ry Moment leaves my Little less;   40
While yet my steady Steps no ᵉStaff sustains,
And Life still vig'rous revels in my Veins;
Grant me, kind Heaven, to find some happier Place,
Where Honesty and Sense are no Disgrace;
Some pleasing Bank where verdant Osiers play,   45
Some peaceful Vale with Nature's Paintings gay;
Where once the harass'd BRITON found Repose,
And safe in Poverty defy'd his Foes;

> ᵈ*Hic tunc* Umbricius: *Quando Artibus, inquit, honestis*
>   *Nullus in Urbe Locus, nulla Emolumenta Laborum,*
>   *Res hodie minor est, here quam fuit, atque eadem Cras*
>   *Deteret exiguis aliquid, proponimus illuc*
>   *Ire fatigatas ubi* Dædalus *exuit Alas;*
>   *Dum nova Canities* ———— (21–6.)
> ᵉ   ———— *et Pedibus me*
>   *Porto meis, nullo Dextram subeunte Bacillo.* (27–8.)

---

35 he cries] my friend *GM*   37 these *GM*; Vice and Cain *Nickell copy* (*cf. p.* 63
n. 1 *ante*)   41 steady *edd. 1–5*: steddy *1748, 51, 55*   46 paintings] painting
GM 1755–8

---

29. *excise*. Thus defined in the *Dictionary*: 'A hateful tax levied upon commodities, and adjudged not by the common judges of property, but wretches hired by those to whom excise is paid.' Cf. *The Idler* 65, and *Life*, i. 295 n.

35. The rest of the poem is a speech by Thales.

41. 'Steady' is the spelling in the *Dictionary*.

47. *Briton*. A reference to the Anglo-Saxon and Danish invasions: contrast 'Briton' in l. 119.

Some secret Cell, ye Pow'rs, indulgent give.
^fLet —— live here, for —— has learn'd to live.   50
Here let those reign, whom Pensions can incite
To vote a Patriot black, a Courtier white;
Explain their Country's dear-bought Rights away,
And plead for Pirates* in the Face of Day;

> ^f *Cedamus Patriâ: vivant* Arturius *istic*
> *Et* Catulus: *maneant qui Nigrum in Candida vertunt.* (29–30.)
> * The invasions of the Spaniards were defended in the houses of Parliament.

49. This line need not imply religious retirement. Johnson later told Boswell, 'I have thought of retiring, and have talked of it to a friend; but I find my vocation is rather to active life' (*Life*, v. 63).

50. The blanks cannot be filled satisfactorily. The line requires a monosyllable, but that is the only clue. Johnson may not have had any one person in mind.

51. *pensions.* 'An allowance made to any one without an equivalent. In England it is generally understood to mean pay given to a state hireling, for treason to his country' (*Dictionary*). When Johnson received his own pension, these definitions, and the 'distant hints and dark allusions' in this poem were turned to account by Wilkes in *The North Briton* (No. 12, 21 August 1762): 'It is a matter of astonishment that *no notice* has till now been taken of him by government for some of the most *extraordinary* productions, which appeared with the name of *Samuel Johnson*; a name sacred to *George and Liberty*. No man, who has read only one poem of his, *London*, but must congratulate the good sense and discerning spirit of the minister [Bute], who bestows such a part of the public treasure on this distinguished friend of the public, of his master's family, and of the constitution of this country. The rewards are *now* most judiciously given to those who have supported, not to those who have all their lives written with bitterness, and harangued with virulence, against the government. With all due deference to the first minister's discernment, I rather think that Mr. *Johnson* (as merit *of this kind* must now be rewarded) might have been better provided for in another way: I mean at the board of *Excise*.'

54. *pirates.* Spain had at this time the legal right to regulate the traffic with her American possessions, and the activity with which she enforced the search of English merchant vessels created a popular indignation which was steadily augmented after the affair of 'Jenkins's ear' in 1731 till in 1739 Walpole was forced against his will into a naval war with Spain. Cf. *The Craftsman* of 13 May 1738: 'I would only possess my Countrymen with Strength of Mind, not to be diverted from the Maintenance of the old Laws and Interests of *their Country*, by any arguments. For if we have received much Damage, and suffer'd more Disgrace, from the *Spaniards*; if many of our *poor Countrymen* are now living in a State of *Slavery* amongst them, more like *Beasts of Burthen* than *Christians*, or *human Creatures*; if We have been abused, insulted, and tortured by Them; if when a *Remedy* is humbly begg'd, which should be offer'd, it is still deny'd; to what Purpose shall a *distress'd Englishman* go and hear a *fine set Speech*? ... If I should happen to be wrong in my Judgment, upon this Occasion, I have at least a Multitude of *wise* and *honest Men* on my side; which I deem more honourable than to receive 500 *l.* per *Ann.* to force and torture Rhetorick, in order to prove a longer Forbearance in the *Spanish Affair* beneficial to this Nation.' Cf. also Pope's *Epistle to Augustus*, l. 2, and *One Thousand Seven Hundred and Thirty-Eight*, ll. 17, 18.

With slavish Tenets taint our poison'd Youth, 55
And lend a Lye the confidence of Truth.
    ᵍLet such raise Palaces, and Manors buy,
Collect a Tax, or farm a Lottery,
With warbling Eunuchs fill a licens'd* Stage,
And lull to Servitude a thoughtless Age. 60
    Heroes, proceed! What Bounds your Pride shall hold?
What Check restrain your Thirst of Pow'r and Gold?
Behold rebellious Virtue quite o'erthrown,
Behold our Fame, our Wealth, our Lives your own.
    To such, a groaning Nation's Spoils are giv'n, 65
When publick Crimes inflame the Wrath of Heav'n:
    ʰBut what, my Friend, what Hope remains for me,
Who start at Theft, and blush at Perjury?
Who scarce forbear, tho' BRITAIN's Court he sing,
To pluck a titled Poet's borrow'd Wing; 70
A Statesman's Logic, unconvinc'd can hear,

   ᵍ *Queis facile est Ædem conducere, Flumina, Portus,*
     Siccandam Eluviem, portandum ad Busta Cadaver. ——
     Munera nunc edunt. —— (31–6.)
   ʰ *Quid* Romæ *faciam? mentiri nescio: Librum,*
     Si malus est, nequeo laudare & poscere. —— (41–2.)
     * The licensing act was then lately made.

---

58 farm] form *1748²*   59 a licens'd] our silenc'd *edd. 1–5, 1787*   ᵍ Quod facile
Nickell copy of *1 (cf. p.* 63 *n.* 1 *ante).*   65 a groaning nation's spoils are giv'n] the
Plunder of a Land is giv'n *edd. 1, 5, 1787*

56. Quoted in the *Dictionary*, s.v. 'truth' as '*Anonymous*'; removed from ed. 4.

59. *warbling eunuchs.* A reference to the Italian opera, then at the height of its popularity.

a licens'd stage. The Act requiring all plays to be licensed before performance (10 George II, c. 28) had come into force on 24 June 1737. It ordered that 'no Person shall, for Hire, Gain, or Reward, act, perform, represent, or cause to be acted, performed, or represented any new Interlude, Tragedy, Comedy, Opera, Play, Farce, or other Entertainment of the Stage, or any Part or Parts therein; or any new Act, Scene, or other Part added to any old Interlude, Tragedy, Comedy, Opera, Play, Farce, or other Entertainment of the Stage, or any new Prologue or Epilogue, unless a true Copy thereof be sent to the Lord Chamberlain of the King's Household for the time being fourteen Days at least before the acting, representing, or performing thereof.' The Act was introduced to suppress satire on Walpole's government. The original editions of *London* read 'our silenc'd stage'; but in 1748 Walpole was out of power, Garrick was joint patentee and manager of Drury Lane, and Johnson could no longer properly refer to the theatre as 'silenc'd'.

And dare to slumber o'er the *Gazetteer*;*
Despise a Fool in half his Pension drest,
And strive in vain to laugh at *H——y*'s jest.

ⁱOthers with softer Smiles, and subtler Art,   75
Can sap the Principles, or taint the Heart;
With more Address a Lover's Note convey,
Or bribe a Virgin's Innocence away.

Well may they rise, while I, whose Rustic Tongue
Ne'er knew to puzzle Right, or varnish Wrong,   80
Spurn'd as a Beggar, dreaded as a Spy,
Live unregarded, unlamented die.

ᵏFor what but social Guilt the Friend endears?
Who shares *Orgilio*'s Crimes, his Fortune shares.

ˡBut thou, should tempting Villainy present   85

> ⁱ —— *Ferre ad Nuptas, quæ mittit Adulter,*
> *Quæ mandat norint alii: Me Nemo Ministro*
> *Fur erit, atque ideo nulli Comes exeo.* —— (45–7.)
> ᵏ *Quis nunc diligitur nisi conscius?* ——
> *Charus erit* Verri, *qui* Verrem *tempore, quo vult,*
> *Accusare potest.* —— (49–54.)
> ˡ   —— *Tanti tibi non sit opaci*
> *Omnis Arena* Tagi, *quodque in Mare volvitur Aurum,*
> *Ut Somno careas.* —— (54–6.)
> * The paper which at that time contained apologies for the Court.

---

74 H——y's] Clodio's *1787*   81 Begger *edd. 2–4, 1748*¹

---

72. *the Gazetteer*, i.e. *The Daily Gazetteer*, the official newspaper of Walpole's ministry, founded in 1735. Cf. Johnson's *Compleat Vindication of the Licensers of the Stage*, 1739, p. 28: 'I cannot but indulge myself a little by dwelling on this pleasing Scene, and imagining those *Halcyon-days* in which no Politicks shall be read but those of the *Gazetteer*, nor any Poetry but that of the Laureat.'

74. H——y's, perhaps Hervey's—John Lord Hervey (1696–1743), supporter of Walpole and confidant of the Queen, the 'Sporus' of Pope's *Epistle to Arbuthnot*. His brother 'Harry Hervey' was one of Johnson's early friends (*Life*, i. 106); see pp. 84, 96 ff. Professor Donald J. Greene (*The Politics of Samuel Johnson*, 1960, pp. 307–8) doubts the identification with Hervey, and suggests the Rev. John ('Orator') Henley (1692–1756). He adduces Mrs. Thrale's doubt (*Johnsonian Miscellanies*, i. p. 254), and Pope's characterization of Henley as 'Zany of thy Age' (*The Dunciad*, iii. 206). The authority for Hawkins's reading 'Clodio's jest' is not known. Possibly the change was made by Johnson late in life, when the particular allusion had lost its point. For 'Clodio' cf. Pope's *Epistle to Cobham*, 179 ff.

81. *beggar*. The *Dictionary* gives 'beggar', but says 'it is more properly written *begger*'. Cf. l. 201.

All *Marlb'rough* hoarded, or all *Villiers* spent;
Turn from the glitt'ring Bribe thy scornful Eye,
Nor sell for Gold, what Gold could never buy,
The peaceful Slumber, self-approving Day,
Unsullied Fame, and Conscience ever gay.   90
ᵐThe cheated Nation's happy Fav'rites, see!
Mark whom the Great caress, who frown on me!
LONDON! the needy Villain's gen'ral Home,
The Common Shore of *Paris* and of *Rome*;
With eager Thirst, by Folly or by Fate,   95
Sucks in the Dregs of each corrupted State.
Forgive my Transports on a Theme like this,
ⁿI cannot bear a *French* metropolis.
ᵒIllustrious EDWARD! from the Realms of Day,
The Land of Heroes and of Saints survey;   100
Nor hope the *British* Lineaments to trace,
The rustic Grandeur, or the surly Grace;
But lost in thoughtless Ease, and empty Show,
Behold the Warriour dwindled to a Beau;
Sense, Freedom, Piety, refin'd away,   105
Of FRANCE the Mimic, and of SPAIN the Prey.
   All that at home no more can beg or steal,
Or like a Gibbet better than a Wheel;

ᵐ *Quæ nunc Divitibus Gens acceptissima nostris,*
   Et quos præcipue fugiam, properabo fateri. (58–9.)
ⁿ ——— *Non possum ferre*, Quirites,
   Græcam *Urbem.* ——————— (60–1.)
ᵒ Rusticus *ille tuus sumit Trechedipna*, Quirine,
   Et ceromatico fert Niceteria Collo. (67–8.)

94 shore] sewer *1758, 1763–82, 1787*   103 But] Now *GM*

86. *Marlborough.* 'That is no longer doubted, of which the nation was then first informed, that the war was unnecessarily protracted to fill the pockets of Marlborough,
and that it would have been continued without end if he could have continued his annual
plunder' (*Life of Swift*, § 46, ed. Hill, iii. 18).
   Villiers,—George Villiers (1628–87), second Duke of Buckingham, the 'Zimri' of
Dryden's *Absalom and Achitophel.* Cf. Pope's *Of the Use of Riches*, 1732, ll. 299–314.
   94. See introductory account for the corresponding passage in Oldham's satire.
Shore is changed in Dodsley's *Collection*, 1758, to 'sewer'. In the *Dictionary* Johnson
says that 'shore' is 'properly *sewer*', and 'sewer' is 'now corrupted to *shore*'.
   99. *Edward.* Edward III, victor at Crécy; Henry V, at Agincourt (l. 120).
   106. Quoted in the *Dictionary*, s.v. 'mimick', as by '*Anon.*'.
   108. *gibbet . . . wheel*, the English and French methods of execution. The guillotine
replaced the wheel at the Revolution.

Hiss'd from the Stage, or hooted from the Court,
Their Air, their Dress, their Politicks import;   110
PObsequious, artful, voluble and gay,
On *Britain*'s fond Credulity they prey.
No gainful Trade their Industry can 'scape,
qThey sing, they dance, clean Shoes, or cure a Clap;
All Sciences a fasting Monsieur knows,   115
And bid him go to Hell, to Hell he goes.

rAh! what avails it, that, from Slav'ry far,
I drew the Breath of Life in *English* Air;
Was early taught a *Briton*'s Right to prize,
And lisp the Tale of HENRY's Victories;   120
If the gull'd Conqueror receives the Chain,
And Flattery subdues when Arms are vain?

sStudious to please, and ready to submit,
The supple *Gaul* was born a Parasite:
Still to his Int'rest true, where'er he goes,   125
Wit, Brav'ry, Worth, his lavish Tongue bestows;
In ev'ry Face a Thousand Graces shine,
From ev'ry Tongue flows Harmony divine.

tThese Arts in vain our rugged Natives try, ⎫
Strain out with fault'ring Diffidence a Lye, ⎬   130
And get a Kick for awkward Flattery. ⎭

p *Ingenium velox, Audacia perdita, Sermo*
   Promptus, —— (73–4.)
q *Augur, Schænobates, Medicus, Magus: omnia novit*
   Græculus esuriens, in Cælum, jusseris, ibit. (77–8.)
r *Usque adeo nihil est, quod nostra Infantia Cælum*
   Hausit Aventini? (84–5.)
s *Quid? quod Adulandi Gens prudentissima, laudat*
   Sermonem indocti, Faciem deformis Amici? (86–7.)
t *Hæc eadem licet & nobis laudare: sed illis*
   Creditur. (92–3.)

120 tale] tales *1755–82*   122 flattery subdues . . . vain?] what their Armies lost,
their Cringes gain? *edd. 1–5:* flattery prevails *1787*   vain. *1748*   125 goes,] goes.
edd. 3, 4, 1748   131 get *Johnson MS. correction, 1787*] gain *1738–85*   aukward
edd. 3, 4, 1748, 1751–85

116. Cf. Dryden's translation, 'And bid him go to Heav'n, to Heav'n he goes'; see
introductory account, and Boswell, *Life*, iii. 357.
122. *subdues.* The authority for Hawkins's variant 'prevails' is not known.
129–31. The only instance of a triplet in Johnson's mature verse.

Besides, with Justice, this discerning Age
Admires their wond'rous Talents for the Stage:
[u]Well may they venture on the Mimic's art,
Who play from Morn to Night a borrow'd Part;   135
Practis'd their Master's Notions to embrace,
Repeat his Maxims, and reflect his Face;
With ev'ry wild Absurdity comply,
And view each Object with another's Eye;
To shake with Laughter ere the Jest they hear,   140
To pour at Will the counterfeited Tear;
And as their Patron hints the Cold or Heat,
To shake in Dog-days, in *December* sweat.
   [x]How, when Competitors like these contend,
Can surly Virtue hope to fix a Friend?   145
Slaves that with serious Impudence beguile,
And lye without a Blush, without a Smile;
Exalt each Trifle, ev'ry Vice adore,
Your Taste in Snuff, your Judgment in a Whore;
Can *Balbo*'s Eloquence applaud, and swear   150
He gropes his Breeches with a Monarch's Air.
   For Arts like these preferr'd, admir'd, carest,
They first invade your Table, then your Breast;
[y]Explore your Secrets with insidious Art,
Watch the weak Hour, and ransack all the Heart;   155
Then soon your ill-plac'd Confidence repay,
Commence your Lords, and govern or betray.

> [u] *Natio Comœda est. Rides? majore cachinno*
>   *Concutitur, &c.* (100–1.)
> [x] *Non sumus ergo pares: melior, qui semper & omni*
>   *Nocte dieque potest alienum sumere vultum,*
>   *A facie jactare manus: laudare paratus,*
>   *Si bene ructavit, si rectum minxit Amicus.* (104–7.)
> [y] *Scire volunt Secreta Domûs, atque inde timere.* (113.)

144 *No paragraph division 1748, 1751–85*

150. *Balbo.* There are no grounds for identifying this 'stammerer' with any one speaker.

151. *gropes*, used in the obsolete sense 'to touch with the hand, take hold of, grasp'. This line is quoted in the *Oxford English Dictionary* as the latest example of this use.

      ᶻBy Numbers here from Shame or Censure free,
All Crimes are safe, but hated Poverty.
This, only this, the rigid Law persues,   160
This, only this, provokes the snarling Muse.
The sober Trader at a tatter'd Cloak,
Wakes from his Dream, and labours for a Joke;
With brisker Air the silken Courtiers gaze,
And turn the varied Taunt a thousand Ways.   165
ᵃOf all the Griefs that harrass the Distrest,
Sure the most bitter is a scornful Jest;
Fate never wounds more deep the gen'rous Heart,
Than when a Blockhead's Insult points the Dart.
      ᵇHas Heaven reserv'd, in Pity to the Poor,   170
No pathless Waste, or undiscover'd Shore?
No secret Island in the boundless Main?
No peaceful Desart yet unclaim'd by SPAIN?*
Quick let us rise, the happy Seats explore,
And bear Oppression's Insolence no more.   175
This mournful Truth is ev'ry where confest,
ᶜSLOW RISES WORTH, BY POVERTY DEPREST:

> ᶻ —— *Materiem præbet causasque Jocorum*
> *Omnibus hic Idem? si fœda et scissa lacerna, &c.* (147-8.)
> ᵃ Nil habet *infelix Paupertas durius in se,*
> *Quam quod ridiculos Homines facit.* (152-3.)
> ᵇ   —— *Agmine facto*
> *Debuerant olim tenues migrasse* Quirites. (162-3.)
> ᶜ Haud *facile emergunt, quorum Virtutibus obstat*
> *Res angusta Domi, sed* Romæ *durior illis*
> *Conatus* ——
>   —— *Omnia* Romæ
> *Cum pretio* ——
> *Cogimur, & cultis augere peculia servis.* (164-89.)

   * The Spaniards at this time were said to make claim to some of our American
provinces.

---

158 *No paragraph division edd. 1, 5*   160 persues *edd. 1, 2, 5*   161 snarling]
darling *edd. 3, 4*   Muse.] Muse; *ed. 1*   166 grief *1751-63*

158-77. In this section of *London* Johnson most clearly voices his own feelings. He
follows Juvenal's 'res angusta domi', but he speaks from experience.

160. 'Persues', the spelling of the first, second, and fifth editions, is not sanctioned in
the *Dictionary*, which gives 'pursue', though 'persue' is the spelling of Johnson's letters.
Similarly 'harrass' (ll. 47, 166) and 'desart' (l. 173), though found in all the early
editions, appear in the *Dictionary* in the modern spelling, like 'aukward'.

But here more slow, where all are Slaves to Gold,
Where Looks are Merchandise, and Smiles are sold,
Where won by Bribes, by Flatteries implor'd, 180
The Groom retails the Favours of his Lord.
But hark! th' affrighted Crowd's tumultuous Cries
Roll thro' the Streets, and thunder to the Skies;
Rais'd from some pleasing Dream of Wealth and Pow'r,
Some pompous Palace, or some blissful Bow'r, 185
Aghast you start, and scarce with aking Sight
Sustain th' approaching Fire's tremendous Light;
Swift from pursuing Horrors take your Way,
And Leave your little ALL to Flames a Prey;
dThen thro' the World a wretched Vagrant roam, 190
For where can starving Merit find a Home?
In vain your mournful Narrative disclose,
While all neglect, and most insult your Woes.
eShould Heaven's just Bolts *Orgilio*'s Wealth confound,*
And spread his flaming Palace on the Ground, 195
Swift o'er the Land the dismal Rumour flies,
And publick Mournings pacify the Skies;
The Laureat Tribe in servile Verse relate,
How Virtue wars with persecuting Fate;
fWith well-feign'd Gratitude the pension'd Band 200

d ———— *Ultimus autem,*
Ærumnæ cumulus, quod nudum, & frusta rogantem
Nemo cibo, nemo hospitio, tectoque juvabit. (209–11.)
e *Si magna* Asturici *cecidit Domus, horrida Mater,*
Pullati Proceres. ——— (212–13.)
f —— *Jam accurrit, qui Marmora donet,*
Conferat Impensas: hic, &c.
Hic Modium Argenti. ——— (215–20.)
* This was by Hitch a Bookseller justly remarked to be no picture of modern manners,
though it might be true at Rome. [*Works*, 1816, ed. A. Chalmers, i. 204.]

198 servile] venal *edd. 1, 5, 1787* 200 pennon'd *Nickell copy of 1* (*cf. p.* 63 *n.* 1 *ante*)

186. *aking*—changed in 1765 to 'aching'. The verb is historically 'ake', and the substantive 'ache', and for the assimilation of the two forms Johnson's *Dictionary* appears
to be largely responsible: see the *O.E.D.* But Johnson enters both spellings of the verb
and gives the greater prominence to 'ake', though he says it is 'more grammatically
written *ache*'.
194 note. Charles Hitch, bookseller in Paternoster-row, was one of the publishers of
the *Dictionary*. He was Master of the Stationers' Company in 1758, and died in 1764.
See Nichols, *Literary Anecdotes*, iii. 390.

Refund the Plunder of the beggar'd Land.
See! while he builds, the gaudy Vassals come,
And crowd with sudden Wealth the rising Dome;
The Price of Boroughs and of Souls restore,
And raise his Treasures higher than before.   205
Now bless'd with all the Baubles of the Great,
The polish'd Marble, and the shining Plate,
g*Orgilio* sees the golden Pile aspire,
And hopes from angry Heav'n another Fire.

 h*Could'st* thou resign the Park and Play content,   210
For the fair Banks of *Severn* or of *Trent*;
There might'st thou find some elegant Retreat,
Some hireling Senator's deserted Seat;
And stretch thy Prospects o'er the smiling Land,
For less than rent the Dungeons of the *Strand*;   215
There prune thy Walks, support thy drooping Flow'rs,

---

 g —— *Meliora ac plura reponit*
  Persicus *Orborum lautissimus*. —— (220–1.)
 h *Si potes avelli* Circensibus, *optima* Soræ,
  Aut Fabreteriæ *Domus, aut* Frusinone *paratur*,
  Quanti nunc Tenebras unum conducis in Annum.
  Hortulus hic ————
  Vive Bidentis amans, & culti Villicus Horti,
  Unde Epulum possis centum dare Pythagoræis. (223–9.)

---

201 begger'd edd. *1–5*, *1748¹* (*cf. l.* 81) h *Unde Epitum Nickell copy of 1* (*cf. p.* 63
n. 1 *ante*)

---

 203. *dome*, simply 'building'; cf. *The Vanity of Human Wishes*, l. 139.
 212. *elegant*. Johnson defines 'elegant' in the *Dictionary* as 'pleasing with minuter beauties', and in illustration gives this line—from memory: 'There may'st thou', &c.
 215. *the dungeons of the Strand*. Hawkins thought that this reference was the result of Johnson's having lived in Exeter Street in March 1737 (*Life*, 1787, p. 57). But Johnson's 'seeming abhorrence' does not need this explanation.
 216–23. Johnson's praise of the blessings of a country life should be read in connexion with a passage in his *Life of Savage* (1744, p. 145): 'As he was ready to entertain himself with future Pleasures, he had planned out a Scheme of Life for the Country, of which he had no Knowledge but from Pastorals and Songs. He imagined that he should be transported to Scenes of flow'ry Felicity, like those which one Poet has reflected to another, and had projected a perpetual Round of innocent Pleasures, of which he suspected no Interruption from Pride, or Ignorance, or Brutality. With these Expectations he was so enchanted, that when he was once gently reproach'd by a Friend for submitting to live upon a Subscription, and advised rather by a resolute Exertion of his Abilities to support himself, he could not bear to debar himself from the Happiness which was to be found in the Calm of a Cottage, or lose the Opportunity of listening, without Intermission, to the Melody of the Nightingale, which he believ'd was to be

Direct thy Rivulets, and twine thy Bow'rs;
And, while thy Grounds a cheap Repast afford,
Despise the Dainties of a venal Lord:
There ev'ry Bush with Nature's Music rings,   220
There ev'ry Breeze bears Health upon its Wings;
On all thy Hours Security shall smile,
And bless thine Evening Walk and Morning Toil.
    [i]Prepare for Death, if here at Night you roam,
And sign your Will before you sup from Home.   225
    [k]Some fiery Fop, with new Commission vain,
Who sleeps on Brambles till he kills his Man;
Some frolick Drunkard, reeling from a Feast,
Provokes a Broil, and stabs you for a Jest.
    [l]Yet ev'n these Heroes, mischievously gay,   230
Lords of the Street, and Terrors of the Way;

[i] —— *Possis ignavus haberi,*
   Et subiti Casus improvidus, ad Cœnam si
   Intestatus eas. —— (272-4.)
[k] *Ebrius et petulans, qui nullum forte cecidit,*
   Dat Pœnas, Noctem patitur lugentis Amicum
   Peleidæ. —— (278-80.)
[l] —— *Sed, quamvis improbus Annis,*
   Atque Mero fervens, cavet hunc, quem coccina Læna
   Vitari jubet, et Comitum longissimus Ordo,
   Multum præterea Flammarum, atque ænea Lampas. (282-5.)

218 grounds *Johnson MS. correction, 1787*] Beds *1738-85*   223 thine] the *Dublin
1738*: thy *1755-82*   226, 230 *New paragraphs 1748[2], 1751-85*

heard from every Bramble, and which he did not fail to mention as a very important
Part of the Happiness of a Country Life.' But this passage need not be taken as evidence
for the identification of Thales with Savage. It is a satirical companion piece to the
praises of the country in the poem, and at the end of the second act of *Irene*; and in
neither the play nor the poem was he expressing his own feelings. With the country
he associated disappointment and failure. See also *The Rambler*, No. 135, *The Adventurer*, No. 126, and *The Idler*, Nos. 16 and 71, and R. W. Ketton-Cremer, 'Johnson
and the Countryside' in *Johnson, Boswell, and their Circle: Essays Presented to L. F.
Powell* (Oxford, 1965), pp. 65-75.

    223. *thine evening*: altered in 1755 to 'thy evening'. But in the same year Johnson said
in his *Dictionary* (A Grammar of the English Tongue—Of Pronouns), '*mine* and
thine were formerly used before a vowel, as *mine amiable lady*; which though now dis-
used in prose, might be still properly continued in poetry'.
    227. *brambles*: 'Taken, in popular language, for any rough prickly plant' (*Dictionary*);
in modern usage, 'thorns'.
    231. Quoted in the *Dictionary*, s.v. 'terror', as by '*Anonym.*' and removed from ed. 4.

Flush'd as they are with Folly, Youth and Wine,
Their prudent Insults to the Poor confine;
Afar they mark the Flambeau's bright Approach,
And shun the shining Train, and golden Coach.   235
     [m]In vain, these Dangers past, your Doors you close,
And hope the balmy Blessings of Repose:
Cruel with Guilt, and daring with Despair,
The midnight Murd'rer bursts the faithless Bar;
Invades the sacred Hour of silent Rest,   240
And leaves, unseen, a Dagger in your Breast.
     [n]Scarce can our Fields, such Crowds at *Tyburn* die,
With Hemp the Gallows and the Fleet supply.
Propose your Schemes, ye Senatorian Band,
Whose *Ways and Means** support the sinking Land;   245
Lest Ropes be wanting in the tempting Spring,
To rig another Convoy for the K——g.
     [o]A single Jail, in ALFRED's golden Reign,
Could half the Nation's Criminals contain;
Fair Justice then, without Constraint ador'd,   250

> [m] *Nec tamen hoc tantum metuas: nam qui spoliet te*
>   *Non deerit: clausis Domibus, &c.* (302-3.)
> [n] *Maximus in Vinclis Ferri modus: ut timeas, ne*
>   *Vomer deficiat, ne Marræ et Sarcula desint.* (310-11.)
> [o] *Felices Proavorum Atavos, felicia dicas*
>   *Secula, quæ quondam sub Regibus atque Tribunis*
>   *Viderunt uno contentam Carcere* Romam. (312-14.)
> * A cant term in the House of Commons for methods of raising money.

---

241 leaves *Johnson MS. correction, 1787* plants *1738-85*   247 k—g] king *1782,*
1787

---

240. Quoted in the *Dictionary*, s.v. 'rest', as by '*Anonym.*' and removed from ed. 4.
242. *Tyburn*: the place of execution till 1783, near which now stands the Marble Arch.
247. 'The nation was discontented at the visits made by the king to Hanover' (Hawkins).
248. The legend of Alfred's 'golden reign' derives from William of Malmesbury's *Gesta Regum Anglorum*, ii. 122 (ed. Stubbs, 1887, i. 130): 'Si quis autem reus . . . transfugeret, omnes ex centuria et decima regis multam incurrerent. Hoc commento pacem infudit provinciæ; ut etiam per publicos aggeres, ubi semitæ in quadrivium finduntur, armillas aureas juberet suspendi, quae viantium aviditatem riderent, dum non essent qui eas abriperent.' It was given currency by Spelman's *Life of Alfred*, ed. Hearne, 1709, p. 114.

Held high the steady Scale, but deep'd the Sword;
No Spies were paid, no *Special Juries* known,
Blest Age! But ah! how diff'rent from our own!
    PMuch could I add,—but see the Boat at hand,
The Tide retiring, calls me from the Land: 255
qFarewel!—When Youth, and Health, and Fortune spent,
Thou fly'st for Refuge to the Wilds of *Kent*;
And tir'd like me with Follies and with Crimes,
In angry Numbers warn'st succeeding Times;
Then shall thy Friend, nor thou refuse his Aid,   260
Still Foe to Vice, forsake his *Cambrian* Shade;
In Virtue's Cause once more exert his Rage,
Thy Satire point, and animate thy Page.

p *His alias poteram, & plures subnectere Causas:*
    Sed Jumenta vocant. ——— (315–16.)
q —— *Ergo vale Nostri memor, & quoties te*
    Roma *tuo refici properantem reddet* Aquino,
    Me quoque ad Eleusinam Cererem, *vestramque* Dianam
    Convelle a Cumis: *Satirarum Ego, ni pudet illas,*
    Adjutor gelidos veniam caligatus in Agros. (318–22.)

251 Held ... sword] Sustain'd the Ballance, but resign'd the Sword *edd. 1–5*: Held ...
but sheath'd the sword *1787*: Held ... but dropp'd the sword *MS. note in Yale copy
of 1763, A Classical Arrangement of Fugitive Pieces, v. 1796*   253 ah] ha *Dublin
1738*   262 exert] forsake *1759*

251. *deep'd the sword.* Johnson's intention was to show Justice in her traditional
posture, holding the sword with the point resting on the ground or pointing downwards;
she suspended punishment, for which there was no occasion in a golden age, but she did
not give up her power to punish. The reading of the early editions—'resign'd the sword'
—did not express this meaning. The reading printed by Hawkins is a clarification.
Dodsley's 'deep'd' may be a misreading of 'drop'd', for Johnson's 'ro' and 'ee' are easily
confused. 'Drop' in the sense of 'lower', as 'to drop the voice, the eyes', is familiar; it
is also properly used in fencing. 'Deep' as a transitive verb is not recorded in the *O.E.D.*
after the early sixteenth century, but the reading 'deep'd the sword' is found in no fewer
than twenty issues of the poem between 1748 and 1789. If Johnson wrote 'dipp'd', the
printer was not likely to mistake it for 'deep'd'. The objection to 'drop'd the sword' is
that it would normally be taken to mean 'let fall the sword'. Cf. *Taxation no Tyranny*,
§ 10, 'dropping both the sword and balance from our hands'.

POEMS, 1738–1749

TO ELIZA PLUCKING LAUREL

The Gentleman's Magazine, August 1738, p. 429.

These verses are ascribed to Johnson on the authority of Boswell's statement that he contributed to *The Gentleman's Magazine* in 1739 (a mistake for 1738) 'an Epigram both in Greek and Latin to Eliza, and also English verses to her' (*Life*, i. 140). The Greek and Latin epigrams were printed in the number for April 1738 (see above, p. 57). The English verses of August are a translation of yet another epigram published in July, which Croker attributed to Johnson on stylistic grounds. Mrs. G. Hampshire in *Notes and Queries*, June 1972, pp. 221–2, cites a letter from the Revd. Nicholas Carter to his daughter Elizabeth on 13 August 1738, which must refer to the Latin epigram, not only from the sense of his remarks, but because the August number of the Magazine was not published until the end of that month: 'Peggy sent me Johnson's Epigram which is very pretty: & is esteemed so here. Peggy saies she can construe it.'

The translation bears the signature 'Urbanus' and is preceded by two other translations, the first signed 'Alexis' and the second said to be by 'Mr S——n D——k', i.e. Stephen Duck. If 'Urbanus' stood for anyone in particular he was Edward Cave. The explanation may be that Johnson thought little of the two other translations and proceeded—as on other occasions—to extemporize something better, and then used 'Urbanus' in the sense of 'the office of Sylvanus Urban', or 'Editor'.

Eliza is Elizabeth Carter. Her answers in Latin and English are printed immediately below the verses of Urbanus. (Cf. M. Pennington, *Memoirs of . . . Mrs. Elizabeth Carter*, 2nd ed. 1808, i. 38, 73.) In a letter of July 1738 to Mrs. Underdown, Elizabeth Carter reports a visit to Twickenham and a walk round Pope's garden, 'The Lawrels are intespers'd about with the most agreeable wildness, & the Trees grow with as much freedom as in a forest . . .' Johnson was not one of the party. See *Notes and Queries*, June 1972, loc. cit.

Ad ELISAM *POPI* Horto Lauros carpentem.

ELYSIOS *Popi* dum ludit læta per hortos,
    En avida lauros carpit *Elisa* manu.
Nil opus est furto. Lauros tibi, dulcis *Elisa*,
    Si neget optatas *Popus*, *Apollo* dabit.

To ELIZA *plucking Laurel in Mr* POPE'S *Gardens*

As learn'd *Eliza*, sister of the Muse,
  Surveys with new contemplative delight
Pope's hallow'd glades, and never tiring views,
  Her conscious hand his laurel leaves invite.

Cease, lovely thief! my tender limbs to wound,   5
  (Cry'd *Daphne* whisp'ring from the yielding tree;)
Were *Pope* once void of wonted candour found,
  Just *Phœbus* would devote his plant to thee.

TO LADY FIREBRACE

The Gentleman's Magazine, September 1738, p. 486.
The Gentleman's Magazine, January 1785, pp. 5–6.
Poetical Works, 1785, p. 171.
Works, 1787, xi. 364.
Works, 1788, xiv. 498–500.

A reference to these trifling verses while they were still unwritten occurs in one of Johnson's letters to Cave: 'The verses to Lady Firebrace may be had when you please, for you know that such a subject neither deserves much thought, nor requires it' (*Life*, i. 136). Evidently they were written at the desire of Cave, and perhaps with the jocular purpose of encouraging a correspondent who had on several occasions celebrated the beauties of Bury St. Edmunds but had been silent for some months. His last contributions were in February 1738 (pp. 98, 99), one of them signed 'W. B.' and the other 'W. B——n'. His name had been given in full as 'W. Bryan' in December 1735 (p. 733). Nothing appears to be known of him beyond what is stated in 'The Autobiography of Sylvanus Urban' (*The Gentleman's Magazine*, September 1856, p. 273):

'He was a well-known character in Bury St. Edmund's, who went by the name of Count Bryan; and who had written several poetical pieces which were inserted in the Magazine, some of which are now curious for the allusions they make to the principal families then resident in his neighbourhood.' See vol. i, p. 445; iii. 657; v. 323, 325, 733; viii. 98, 99.

The following note is given in the 1785 edition of Johnson's poems:

This lady was Bridget, third daughter of Philip Bacon, Esq. of Ipswich, and relict of Philip Evers, Esq. of that town; she became the second wife of Sir Cordell Firebrace, the last Baronet of that name, (to whom she brought a fortune of 25,000 £) July [October] 26, 1737. Being again a widow in 1759, she was a third time married, April 7, 1762, to William Campbell, Esq. uncle to the present Duke of Argyle, and died July 3, 1782.

This note was first published in *The Gentleman's Magazine*, 1785, pp. 5–6, and repeated, with the signature 'N[ichols]', in *Works*, 1788, xiv. 498. See also *The Gentleman's Magazine*, 1737, p. 637, 1759, p. 146, and 1782, p. 359; G. E. C., *Complete Baronetage*, iv. 175; and A. L. Reade, *Johnsonian Gleanings*, vi. 154–6. Sir Cordell Firebrace (1712–59) was M.P. for Suffolk from 1735 till his death.

Johnson had no associations with Suffolk that have been recorded, and for all that the verses tell us he may never have seen Lady Firebrace, but his friend Henry Hervey, later Aston, was a younger son of the Earl of Bristol whose seat was at Ickworth near Bury St. Edmunds.

Text from *The Gentleman's Magazine*, 1738.

To Lady F——ce *at* Bury *Assizes*

AT length must *Suffolk*'s beauties shine in vain,
So long renown'd in *B——n*'s deathless strain?
Thy charms at least, fair *F——e*, might inspire
Some zealous bard to wake the sleeping lyre.
For such thy beauteous mind, and lovely face, 5
Thou seem'st at once, bright nymph, a Muse and Grace.

ON THOMAS BIRCH

The Gentleman's Magazine, December 1738, p. 654.
Works, 1787, xi. 397.

This epigram was written when the Rev. Thomas Birch was editing *The General Dictionary, Historical and Critical* (1734–41), and contributing to it several hundred biographies. See J. M. Osborn, 'Thomas Birch and the General Dictionary', *Modern Philology*, August 1938, p. 25. Boswell marks the epigram as having been acknowledged by Johnson, but erroneously places it in 1739 (*Life*, i. 140).

Εἰς ΒΙΡΧΙΟΝ

ΕΙΔΕΝ Ἀληθείη πρώην χαίρουσα γράφοντα
Ἡρώων τε βίους Βίρχιον, ἠδὲ Σοφῶν,
Καὶ βίον, εἶπεν, ὅταν ῥίψῃς θανάτοιο βέλεσσι,
Σοῦ ποτε γραψόμενον Βίρχιον ἄλλον ἔχοις.

¹ *Suffolk*'s] Suffolk *1785, 1787*

TO POSTERITY

AN ANCIENT PROPHETICAL INSCRIPTION

Marmor Norfolciense: or an Essay on an Ancient Prophetical Inscription, In Monkish Rhyme, Lately Discover'd near Lynn in Norfolk, 1739, p. 8.
The Gentleman's Magazine, May 1739, p. 269; June, p. 324.
The London Magazine, May 1739, p. 244.

These political verses are the nucleus of Johnson's *Marmor Norfolciense,* published in April 1739.

'In this performance', says Boswell, 'he, in a feigned inscription, supposed to have been found in Norfolk, the county of Sir Robert Walpole, then the obnoxious prime minister of this country, inveighs against the Brunswick succession, and the measures of government consequent upon it. To this supposed prophecy he added a Commentary, making each expression apply to the times, with warm Anti-Hanoverian zeal.' (*Life,* i. 141.)

Johnson's method corresponds to Swift's in *The Windsor Prophecy,* but his *Marmor Norfolciense* is a more elaborate performance. Whereas Swift feigns to have come upon a prophecy 'written in a black Old English Letter . . . about two hundred years ago', and printed it as a broadside, Johnson discovers an older prophecy of uncertain date, inscribed on stone in rhyming Latin verse, and this he edits with a translation and an ironically serious commentary in a pamphlet of some fifty pages. *Marmor Norfolciense* is Johnson's most bitter and sustained attack on the government of Sir Robert Walpole. The verses may be read as a companion piece to the loftier political passages in *London.*

The whole pamphlet was reprinted in 1775, with notes by 'Tribunus' (Francis Webb, 1735-1815), without Johnson's knowledge, when he was enjoying his pension and supporting the government of George III, and again reprinted in 1820. But an adaptation of the English verses, in which the satire is directed against George III's minister, the Earl of Bute, had been printed before that in *The New Foundling Hospital for Wit,* 1769, iii. 29.

The original edition remains the sole authority for the text, modified by a few marginal corrections in Johnson's own copy in Manchester Central Library.

POST-GENITIS

CUM Lapidem hunc, magni
Qui nunc jacet Incola stagni,

Vel Pede Equus tanget,
Vel Arator vomere franget,

Sentiet ægra Metus,   5
Effundet Patria Fletus,

Littoraque ut Fluctu,
Resonabunt Oppida Luctu:

Nam fœcunda rubri
Serpent per Prata Colubri,   10

Gramina vastantes,
Flores Fructusque vorantes,

Omnia fœdantes,
Vitiantes, et spoliantes;

Quanquam haud pugnaces,   15
Ibunt per cuncta minaces,

Fures absque Timore,
Et pingues absque Labore.

Horrida dementes
Rapiet Discordia Gentes,   20

Plurima tunc Leges
Mutabit, plurima Reges

Natio, conversâ
In Rabiem tunc contremet Ursâ

Cynthia, tunc latis   25
Florebunt Lilia Pratis,

Nec fremere audebit
Leo, sed violare timebit,

Omnia consuetus
Populari Pascua lætus.   30

Ante Oculos Natos
Calcatos et Cruciatos

Jam feret ignavus,
Vetitâque Libidine pravus.

32 Calcatos *corrected in Johnson's hand in his own copy*: Calceatos *1739*

En quoque quod Mirum,   35
Quod dicas denique dirum,

Sanguinem Equus sugit,
Neque Bellua victa remugit.

To POSTERITY

WHENE'ER this Stone, now hid beneath the Lake,
  The Horse shall trample, or the Plough shall break,
Then, O my Country! shalt thou groan distrest,
Grief swell thine Eyes, and Terror chill thy Breast.
Thy Streets with Violence of Woe shall sound,   5
Loud as the Billows bursting on the Ground.
Then thro' thy Fields shall scarlet Reptiles stray,
And Rapine and Pollution mark their Way.
Their hungry Swarms the peaceful Vale shall fright
Still fierce to threaten, still afraid to fight;   10
The teeming Year's whole Product shall devour,
Insatiate pluck the Fruit, and crop the Flow'r:
Shall glutton on the industrious Peasants Spoil,
Rob without Fear, and fatten without Toil.
Then o'er the World shall Discord stretch her Wings,   15
Kings change their Laws, and Kingdoms change their Kings.
The Bear enrag'd th' affrighted Moon shall dread;
The Lilies o'er the Vales triumphant spread;

---

10 fierce] *misprinted* fieree   13 peasant's *Gent. Mag., London Mag.*
18 triumphant] *misprinted* triumphan   25 vein *G.M.*

7–14. The familiar attack on the standing army.

17. 'The Terror created to the Moon by the Anger of the Bear, is a strange Expression, but may perhaps relate to the Apprehensions raised in the *Turkish* Empire, of which a Crescent or new Moon is the imperial Standard, by the increasing Power of the Empress of *Russia*, whose Dominions lie under the Northern Constellation called the *Bear*' (*Marmor Norfolciense*, 1739, pp. 36, 37).

18. 'The Lillies borne by the Kings of *France* are an apt Representation of that Country; and their flourishing over wide extended Valleys, seems to regard the new Increase of the *French* Power, Wealth and Dominions, by the Advancement of their Trade, and the Accession of *Lorain*' (*M.N.*, p. 37). By the treaty of Vienna, November 1738, the duchy of Lorrain was to pass to France on the death of Stanislaus, the father-in-law of Louis XV.

Nor shall the Lyon, wont of old to reign
Despotic o'er the desolated Plain,   20
Henceforth th' inviolable Bloom invade,
Or dare to murmur in the flow'ry Glade;
His tortur'd Sons shall die before his Face,
While he lies melting in a lewd Embrace;
And, yet more strange! his Veins a Horse shall drain,   25
Nor shall the passive Coward once complain.

PROLOGUE TO GARRICK'S 'LETHE'

Transcript in the Folger Shakespeare Library.
The Times Literary Supplement, 4 January 1947, p. 9.
Works, vi (Yale ed. 1964), 67.

The transcript, in an unidentified hand, was discovered by Miss Mary E.
Knapp and first published in *The Times Literary Supplement*. It bears a docket
by Garrick: 'Prologue by Mr. Sam: Johnson for Lethe when first it was wrote
for Drury Lane at Giffard's Benefit.' Giffard's benefit was 15 April 1740. *Lethe*
was Garrick's first venture as a playwright (the drafts and early printings are in
the Huntington Library and the British Museum), but in 1740 he was still in
partnership with his brother Peter in the wine trade. Henry Giffard (1699–1772),
actor and manager of the theatre in Goodman's Fields until its closure by the
Licensing Act of 1737, was at this time making efforts to reopen. It was in his
touring company at Ipswich in July 1741 that Garrick made his stage début.

Text from the manuscript with the expansion of contracted forms.

PRODIGIOUS Madness of the writing Race!
Ardent of Fame, yet fearless of Disgrace.
Without a boding Tear, or anxious Sigh,
The Bard obdurate sees his Brother die.
Deaf to the Critick, Sullen to the Friend,   5
Not One takes Warning, by another's End.

3 Tear] fear *TLS, Works*

19–26. Commonplaces of the opposition to Walpole and the Court. England is
'represented as not daring to touch the Lillies, or murmur at their Growth' (*M.N.*, p. 38);
'tortur'd Sons' refers to the war with Spain. Cf. *London*, l. 54, n.
25. 'I might observe that a Horse is borne in the Arms of H——. But how then does
the Horse suck the Lyon's Blood? Money is the Blood of the Body politic.—But my
Zeal for the present happy Establishment will not suffer me to pursue a Train of Thought
that leads to such shocking Conclusions. The Idea is detestable, and such as, it ought
to be hoped, can enter into the Mind of none but a virulent Republican, or bloody
Jacobite' (*M.N.*, p. 41). The horse courant of Saxony was on the royal arms of England
from the death of Anne to the accession of Victoria.

Oft has our Bard in this disastrous Year,
Beheld the Tragic Heroes taught to fear.
Oft has he seen the indignant Orange fly,
And heard th' ill Omen'd Catcall's direful Cry.   10
Yet dares to venture on the dangerous Stage,
And weakly hoped to 'scape the Critick's Rage.
  This Night he hopes to shew that Farce may charm,
Tho' no lewd Hint the mantling Virgin warm,
That useful Truth with Humour may unite,   15
That Mirth may mend, and Innocence delight.

EPITAPH ON CLAUDY PHILLIPS

The Gentleman's Magazine, September 1740, p. 464.
The Norfolk Poetical Miscellany, 1744, i. 363.
Carteret's *Miscellany*, 1752, i. 363 (a reissue of prec.).
The Poetical Miscellany, 1754, i. 363 (another issue of prec.).
W. Toldervy, *Select Epitaphs*, 1755, ii. 222.
John Hackett, *Select and Remarkable Epitaphs*, 1757, i. 125.
The Festoon [ed. Richard Graves], 1766, p. 152.
Anna Williams, *Miscellanies in Prose and Verse*, 1766, p. 23.
Collection of the most Esteemed Pieces of Poetry (Mendez), 1767, p. 209, and 1770, p. 165.
The Court Miscellany, November 1767, p. 610.
The Annual Register, 1767, p. 252.
The Weekly Magazine, Edinburgh, 15 June 1769.
T. Webb, *A new select Collection of Epitaphs*, 1775, i. 79.
The Gentleman's Magazine, December 1779, p. 608.
The Scots Magazine, January 1780, p. 42.
Garrick, *Poetical Works*, 1785, ii. 480.
Works, 1787, xi. 367.
Poetical Works, 1789, p. 205.
Boswell, *Life*, 1791, i. 78 (1934, i. 149).

  This epitaph is signed 'G.' in *The Gentleman's Magazine*, like the piece immediately preceding it, and was therefore sometimes supposed to be by Garrick. It was first said to be by 'S. Johnson' in Hackett's *Epitaphs* in 1757. See also *The Letters of David Garrick*, ed. D. M. Little and G. M. Kahrl, 1963,

---

9 idignant *Transcript*: poignant *TLS, Works*

---

  10. *Catcall*: 'A squeaking instrument, used in the playhouse to condemn plays', *Dictionary*.

ii. 897–9, no. 799: Garrick to Boswell, 14 September 1773. All doubt was set at rest by Boswell:

'It has been ascribed to Mr. Garrick, from its appearing at first with the signature G; but I have heard Mr. Garrick declare, that it was written by Dr. Johnson, and give the following account of the manner in which it was composed. Johnson and he were sitting together; when, amongst other things, Garrick repeated an Epitaph upon this Philips by a Dr. Wilkes, in these words:

> Exalted soul! whose harmony could please
> The love-sick virgin, and the gouty ease;
> Could jarring discord, like Amphion, move
> To beauteous order and harmonious love;
> Rest here in peace, till angels bid thee rise,
> And meet thy blessed Saviour in the skies.

Johnson shook his head at these common-place funeral lines, and said to Garrick, "I think, Davy, I can make a better". Then, stirring about his tea for a little while, in a state of meditation, he almost extempore produced the following verses: "Phillips, whose touch" etc.' (*Life*, i. 148.)

Wilkes's epitaph is inscribed on the memorial tablet which was placed by public subscription in the porch of St. Peter's Church, Wolverhampton, shortly after Philips's death, and it follows these words:

> Near this Place lies
> Charles Claudius Phillips
> Whose absolute Contempt of Riches
> and inimitable Performance upon the Violin
> made him the Admiration of all that knew him
> He was born in Wales
> made the tour of Europe
> and after the Experience of both Kinds of Fortune
> Died in 1732

The inscribed version differs in several places from the version given by Boswell; for example, the last line reads 'And join thy Saviour's Consort (i.e. concert) in the Skies'. Johnson's epitaph is inscribed on another stone which was placed underneath sometime after 1800.

Dr. Richard Wilkes (1691–1760) began practice as a physician at Wolverhampton in 1720 and attained to eminence in his profession. His epitaph on himself, his portrait, and his account of Phillips are in Salt's *History of Staffordshire*, 1801, ii. 147–8, Appendix, p. 18.

Johnson's epitaph may have been sent to *The Gentleman's Magazine* by Garrick; but as Johnson was then actively engaged on the *Magazine* the 'G' is more probably a careless repetition from the previous piece. Hawkins says that the lines are recognized as Johnson's 'in a memorandum of his handwriting'. The memorandum has disappeared.

An adaptation of the epitaph as a glee for three voices ('O thou whose notes cou'd oft remove the pangs of woe or hapless Love', etc.) was set to music by Henry Harington: see *A Collection of Catches*, Edinburgh [1780], vol. iii, p. 92, and *A Favourite Collection of Songs* [1780?].

It is here printed as contributed to Miss Williams's *Miscellanies*.

An Epitaph on Claudy Phillips, a Musician

PHILLIPS! whose touch harmonious could remove
 The pangs of guilty pow'r, and hapless love,
Rest here distrest by poverty no more,
Find here that calm thou gav'st so oft before;
Sleep undisturb'd within this peaceful shrine,   5
Till angels wake thee with a note like thine.

TRANSLATION OF GREEK EPIGRAMS

Gentleman's Magazine, December 1740, p. 595.
The Idler, 1767, ii. 299, 300.
Works, 1787, xi. 419, 420.

In his *Essay on Epitaphs* Johnson included two inscriptions found in the *Greek Anthology* (vii. 553 and 676), 'one upon a Man whose Writings are well known, the other upon a Person whose Memory is preserved only in her EPITAPH, who both lived in Slavery, the most calamitous Estate in human Life'. To each he added a Latin translation in verse and an English translation in prose. The verses are included among the translations from the *Anthology* which he made late in life: see pp. 245–6.

> ZOSIMA, quæ solo fuit olim corpore Serva,
> Corpore nunc etiam libera facta fuit.

> 'Zosima, who in her Life could only
> 'have her Body enslaved, now finds her
> 'Body likewise set at Liberty.'

> SERVUS *Epictetus*, mutilatus corpore vixi
> Pauperieque Irus, curaque prima Deum.

> 'Epictetus, who lies here, was a Slave
> 'and a Cripple, poor as the Begger in the
> 'Proverb, and the Favourite of Heaven.'

Title. An Epitaph upon the celebrated Claudy Philips, Musician, who died very poor *G.M. 1740*: On Claudius Phillips, an excellent Musician at Bridgnorth, Salop; who died very poor *Toldervy*: Epitaph on Claude Phillips, an Itinerant Musician *1787, 1789* &c. 1 Philips *G.M., Festoon, Webb, Boswell 1793* 2 and] or *Hackett, Mendez, Webb, Boswell* 3 oppress'd *Mendez* 4 Here find *G.M., Toldervy, Hackett, Festoon, Mendez, Webb, Boswell* 5 Rest undisturb'd within this humble *Mendez*

Zosima. Johnson also used the name in *The Rambler*, No. 12.

ON COLLEY CIBBER

Boswell, *Life*, 1791, i. 78 (1934, i. 149).
Works, 1825, i. 132 n.

Boswell tells us that Johnson dictated this epigram to him at the inn at Blackshiels on 21 November 1773 when they were concluding their tour in Scotland. He had heard it repeated by Garrick. He says in his *Journal* (v. 350) that 'imperfect copies are gone about', and in the *Life* (i. 149) that the epigram 'has never yet appeared'; but he did not know its exact date. Hill assigned it to 1741, believing it to have been suggested by that year's Birthday Ode, which ends with this chorus:

> While thus our Master of the Main
> Revives Eliza's glorious Reign,
> The great Plantagenets look down,
> And see your Race adorn your Crown.

(See *The Gentleman's Magazine* for October 1741, p. 549.) But the satire applies to all the Odes of Cibber, who was Laureate from 1730 to 1757. In October 1734 he was ridiculed for a Birthday Ode which was almost exactly the same as his composition of the previous year.

The Rev. John Hussey wrote the following note in his interleaved copy of Boswell's *Life*: 'I have heard Johnson speak respectfully and with kindness of Colley Cibber.'

AUGUSTUS still survives in Maro's strain,
    And Spenser's verse prolongs Eliza's reign;
Great George's acts let tuneful Cibber sing;
For Nature form'd the Poet for the King.

TRANSLATION OF POPE'S VERSES ON HIS GROTTO[1]

The Gentleman's Magazine, October 1743, p. 550.
Transcript, *c.* 1775, by or for Thomas Percy (Bodleian Library, MS. Percy 87).
Works, 1787, xi. 406.

Boswell marked this translation as acknowledged by Johnson (*Life*, 1934, i. 157), and Langton included it among Johnson's Latin poems. A prefatory note in *The Gentleman's Magazine* states that it was hastily written:

'Tho' several translations of Mr. *Pope*'s Verses on his grotto have already appear'd, we hope that the following attempt, which, we are assured, was the casual amusement of half an hour, during several solicitations to procede, will neither be unacceptable to our readers, nor (these circumstances consider'd) dishonour the persons concerned by a hasty publication.'

---

[1] Cf. *Life of Pope*, para. 119.

Hill argued that this translation could not be Johnson's, as he 'was not the man to allow that haste of performance was any plea for indulgence' (*Life*, i. 157 n.); but Johnson did not ask for indulgence, and the joint witness of Boswell and Langton remains unshaken.

Pope's verses were first published in *The Gentleman's Magazine* for January 1741. Dodsley published in October 1743 a sixteen-page pamphlet containing the verses and two anonymous Latin translations with one in Greek by Walter Harte. Neither Latin version resembles Johnson's.

The text is taken from *The Gentleman's Magazine*. The authority for Langton's variants is not known, but they are found in Percy's transcript.

Verses on a Grotto by the River Thames at Twickenham, composed of Marbles, Spars, and Minerals. By Mr POPE. Latine Redditum.

QUISQUIS iter tendis, vitreas qua lucidus undas
  Speluncæ late *Thamesis* prætendit opacæ,
Marmoreo trepidant qua lentæ in fornice guttæ,
Crystallisque latex fractus scintillat acutis,
Gemmaque luxuriæ nondum famulata nitenti   5
Pendet, et incoquitur tectum sine fraude metallum:
Ingredere O!—Magnam pura cole mente parentem,
Auriferasque, auri metuens, scrutare cavernas.
Ingredere! *Egeriæ* sacrum en tibi panditur antrum!
Hic, in se totum longe per opaca futuri   10
Temporis *Henricum* rapuit vis vivida mentis;
Hic pia *Vindamius* traxit suspiria, in ipsa
Morte memor patriæ; hic *Marcmonti* pectore prima
Cœlestis fido caluerunt semina flammæ.
Temnere opes pretium sceleris, patriamque tueri   15
Fortis, ades, solus tangas venerabile limen.

3 Marmoreâ *Some edd. of GM, 1787*   6 Pendet] Splendet *1787*   7 Magnam]
rerum *1787*   13 Marmonti *1787*   16 solus tangas] tibi sponte patet *1787*

11. *Henricum*—Henry St. John, Viscount Bolingbroke.
12. *Vindamius*—Sir William Wyndham.
13. *Marcmonti*—the Earl of Marchmont.

EPITAPH ON SIR THOMAS HANMER

The Gentleman's Magazine, May 1747, p. 239.
W. Toldervy, *Select Epitaphs*, 1755, ii. 192.
John Hackett, *Select and Remarkable Epitaphs*, 1757, ii. 148.
Anna Williams, *Miscellanies in Prose and Verse*, 1766, p. 94.
Pearch, *Collection of Poems*, 1770, iii. 251.
T. Webb, *A new select Collection of Epitaphs*, 1775, i. 52, ii. 209.
Poetical Works, 1785, p. 188.
Works, 1787, xi. 369.

This is the first of a group of six poems which are printed in *The Gentleman's Magazine* for May 1747, each over the signature '***'. The authorship of some of them has been questioned (see *Life*, i. 177), but in a manuscript note signed 'J. R.' and dated March 1788 they are said to have been 'given to me by Johnson ... in Mr. Hawkesworth's absence, who then generally compiled Cave's poetical Miscellany'. 'J. R.' is John Ryland, Hawkesworth's brother-in-law, and his testimony may be accepted as final (*Life*, i. 242, iv. 1934, 435; Nichols, *Literary Anecdotes*, ix. 500. A more recent challenge, on stylistic grounds, was made by Professor Arthur Sherbo in *Review of English Studies*, xvii (1966), 382–90). The attribution of some to Johnson is corroborated by his occasional citation from them in the *Dictionary*, where he commonly designates his own work as anonymous. The note is written on a stray leaf from *The Cabinet of Genius*, 1788, containing 'The Winter's Walk'. Its discovery was announced by J. Reading in a letter to *The Times Literary Supplement* of 11 September 1937.

The poem was first assigned to Johnson in Pearch's *Collection*, but was omitted in the edition of 1775.

Hanmer died in May 1746 and was buried in the church of Hanmer in Flintshire, where he is commemorated in the Latin epitaph on which the poem is based. It is printed in *The Gentleman's Magazine* before the poem. It was written by Robert Freind, who had been Hanmer's tutor at Christ Church, Oxford, and was appointed Headmaster of Westminster School a year or two before his pupil was elected Speaker of the House of Commons.

The poem is not a 'translation', and hardly even a 'paraphrase'. Though the words 'Or rather a Paraphrase' are part of the title in *The Gentleman's Magazine*, the poem is an original composition on the lines suggested by the lapidary prose of the epitaph.

The text is taken from Miss Williams's *Miscellanies*.

A TRANSLATION
OF THE LATIN EPITAPH
On Sir THOMAS HANMER
WRITTEN BY DOCTOR FREIND

THOU, who survey'st these walls with curious eye,
Pause at this tomb where HANMER's ashes lie;
His various worth, through varied life attend,
And learn his virtues, while thou mourn'st his end.
His force of genius burn'd in early youth, 5
With thirst of knowledge, and with love of truth;
His learning, join'd with each endearing art,
Charm'd ev'ry ear, and gain'd on ev'ry heart.
Thus early wise, th' endanger'd realm to aid,
His country call'd him from the studious shade; 10
In life's first bloom his publick toils began,
At once commenc'd the Senator and Man.
In bus'ness dext'rous, weighty in debate,
Thrice ten long years he labour'd for the State;
In ev'ry speech persuasive wisdom flow'd, 15
In ev'ry act refulgent virtue glow'd.
Suspended faction ceas'd from rage and strife,
To hear his eloquence, and praise his life.
Resistless merit fix'd the Senate's choice,
Who hail'd him Speaker, with united voice. 20
Illustrious age! how bright thy glories shone,
When HANMER fill'd the chair, and ANN the throne.
Then, when dark arts obscur'd each fierce debate,
When mutual frauds perplex'd the maze of State,
The moderator firmly mild appear'd, 25
Beheld with love, with veneration heard.
This task perform'd, he sought no gainful post,
Nor wish'd to glitter at his country's cost;

Title. Written by Doctor Freind.] Or rather a Paraphrase. *G.M.*; Friend *Miscellanies.*
2 at] on *G.M.*

20. Speaker of the House of Commons 1714–15.

Strict, on the right he fix'd his steadfast eye,
With temp'rate zeal, and wise anxiety;   30
Nor e'er from virtue's path was lur'd aside,
To pluck the flow'rs of pleasure or of pride.
   Her gifts despis'd, corruption blush'd and fled,
And fame pursu'd him, where conviction led.
Age call'd at length his active mind to rest,   35
With honour sated, and with cares opprest;
To letter'd ease retir'd, and honest mirth,
To rural grandeur, and domestick worth;
Delighted still to please mankind, or mend,
The Patriot's fire yet sparkled in the friend.   40
   Calm conscience then his former life survey'd,
And recollected toils endear'd the shade;
Till nature call'd him to the gen'ral doom,
And virtue's sorrow dignify'd his tomb.

TO MISS —— ON HER GIFT OF
A NET-WORK PURSE

Transcript made by or for Henry Hervey, or Aston, in the possession of the
   Marquis of Bristol (deposited in the Suffolk Record Office, Bury St. Edmunds).
The Gentleman's Magazine, May 1747, p. 239.
Anna Williams, *Miscellanies*, 1766, p. 10.
Pearch, *Collection of Poems*, 1770, iii. 250.
St. James's Chronicle, 25 January 1785.
The London Magazine, May 1785, p. 353.
Poetical Works, 1785, p. 167.
Works, 1787, xi. 356.

   This poem is signed '***' in *The Gentleman's Magazine*. It was first attributed
to Johnson in Pearch's *Collection*, but was omitted in the edition of 1775.
Malone ascribed it to Johnson in his annotated copy of Miss Williams's *Miscellanies* (now in the Dyce Collection, Victoria and Albert Museum), from which
the text is here taken.
   It is one of four poems by Johnson which are found in a collection of transcripts made by or for his friend Henry Hervey (who changed his name to
Aston in 1744 when his wife, the sister of Molly Aston, succeeded to the family
estates). In this transcript it is addressed 'To Miss Carpenter'. Similarly, the

31 paths *1785, Works*   lur'd] turn'd *G.M.*

37. His edition of Shakespeare occupied him for several years and appeared in 1743–4.

poem 'To Miss —— On her playing upon the Harpsicord' is addressed 'To
the Honble Miss Carpenter'. Hervey's own verses, 'The Female Drum' (Dodsley's *Collection*, 1758, iii. 183–8), are also 'Address'd to the Honourable Miss
Carpenter'.

Alicia Maria Carpenter (1729–94) was the only daughter of the second Lord
Carpenter, and was married on 12 March 1751 to the Earl of Egremont. Hervey,
who had taken orders in 1743 after an undistinguished and spendthrift career in
the army, induced Johnson to write for him the sermon which he delivered at
St. Paul's before the Sons of the Clergy on 2 May 1745 (see L. F. Powell in
The Times of 25 November 1938); and it may be that Johnson again helped him
by writing two poems which he could send to an accomplished and attractive
girl in her teens.

To Miss ——
On her giving the Author a Gold and Silk
net-work Purse of her own weaving

THOUGH gold and silk their charms unite,
   To make thy curious web delight,
In vain the vary'd work would shine,
If wrought by any hand but thine,
Thy hand that knows the subtler art,   5
To weave those nets that catch the heart.
   Spread out by me, the roving coin,
Thy nets may catch, but not confine,
Nor can I hope thy silken chain
The glitt'ring vagrants shall restrain;   10
Why, SYLVIA, was it then decreed,
The heart, once caught, should ne'er be freed?

TO MISS —— ON HER PLAYING UPON
THE HARPSICHORD

Transcript made by or for Henry Hervey, or Aston, in the possession of the
   Marquis of Bristol (deposited in the Suffolk Record Office, Bury St. Edmunds).
The Museum, 1746, ii. 178 (Numb. xviii, 22 November 1746).
Anna Williams, *Miscellanies*, 1766, p. 104.

Title. To Miss ——] To Stella *St. James's Chron., Lond. Mag.*   2 thy] the *G.M.*
7 out by me] for their prey *G.M., Hervey transcript*   coin *G.M.*: coin, *Hervey, Miscel-*
lanies.   8 catch] snare *G.M., Hervey*   11 SYLVIA] Stella *St. James's Chron.,*
Lond. Mag., Poems, Works.

Pearch, *Collection of Poems,* 1770, iii. 253; 1775, iii. 247; 1783, iii. 249.
Poetical Works, 1785, p. 168.
Works, 1787, xi. 357.

In *The Museum* and in Hervey's transcript this poem is addressed to Miss Carpenter. It may be read as a companion piece to the poem on the network purse. Both are included in Miss Williams's *Miscellanies.* Malone thought that it was 'perhaps' by Johnson. It was first said to be by Johnson in Pearch's *Collection,* 1770.

Text from the *Miscellanies.*

To MISS ——
On her playing upon the Harpsicord in a Room hung with some Flower-Pieces of her own Painting

WHEN STELLA strikes the tuneful string
   In scenes of imitated Spring,
Where Beauty lavishes her pow'rs
On beds of never-fading flow'rs,
And pleasure propagates around   5
Each charm of modulated sound,
Ah! think not, in the dang'rous hour,
The nymph fictitious, as the flow'r;
But shun, rash youth, the gay alcove,
Nor tempt the snares of wily love.   10
    When charms thus press on ev'ry sense,
What thought of flight, or of defence?
Deceitful Hope, and vain Desire,
For ever flutter o'er her lyre,
Delighting, as the youth draws nigh,   15
To point the glances of her eye,
And forming, with unerring art,
New chains to hold the captive heart.
    But on these regions of delight,
Might Truth intrude with daring flight,   20

Title To Miss *** *Miscellanies*: To the Hon. Miss Carpenter *Museum, Hervey transcript* (Honble)   Harpsichord *Museum, 1785, 1787* ('Harpsicord' in the *Dictionary*)
7 hour] Bower *Museum, Hervey*   18 chains to hold] Tortures for *Museum, Hervey*
19 those *1785, 1787*

5-6. Quoted, as '*Anon.*', in the *Dictionary*, s.v. 'modulate'.

Could STELLA, sprightly, fair and young,
One moment hear the moral song,
Instruction with her flow'rs might spring,
And Wisdom warble from her string.
   Mark, when from thousand mingled dyes   25
Thou see'st one pleasing form arise,
How active light, and thoughtful shade,
In greater scenes each other aid;
Mark, when the diff'rent notes agree
In friendly contrariety,   30
How passion's well-accorded strife
Gives all the harmony of life;
Thy pictures shall thy conduct frame,
Consistent still, though not the same,
Thy musick teach the nobler art   35
To tune the regulated heart.

STELLA IN MOURNING

Transcript made by or for Henry Hervey, or Aston, in the possession of the
  Marquis of Bristol (deposited in the Suffolk Record Office, Bury St. Edmunds).
The Gentleman's Magazine, May 1747, p. 239.
Poetical Works, 1785, p. 170.
Works, 1787, xi. 361.

   The evidence for Johnson's authorship is the signature '***' in *The Gentleman's Magazine*, from which the text is here taken. See p. 94.

STELLA *in* MOURNING

WHEN, lately, *Stella*'s form display'd
   The beauties of the gay brocade,
The nymphs, who found their pow'r decline,
Proclaim'd her, not so fair as fine.
'Fate! snatch away the bright disguise,   5
'And let the goddess trust her eyes.'

---

21 Could] Wou'd *Museum*.

     5 Fate Snatch'd *Hervey transcript*

   31–2. Quoted, as by '*Johnson*', in the *Dictionary*, s.v. 'strife'; removed from ed. 4.

Thus blindly pray'd the fretful fair,
And fate malicious heard the pray'r.
But brighten'd by the sable dress,
As virtue rises in distress,   10
Since *Stella* still extends her reign,
Ah! how shall envy sooth her pain?
  Th' adoring youth, and envious fair,
Henceforth shall form one common pray'r,
And Love and Hate alike implore   15
The skies, that *Stella* mourn no more.

THE WINTER'S WALK

Transcript made by or for Henry Hervey, or Aston, in the possession of the
  Marquis of Bristol (deposited in the Suffolk Record Office, Bury St. Edmunds).
The Gentleman's Magazine, May 1747, p. 240 (two editions).
Fawkes and Woty, *The Poetical Calendar*, 1763, i. 17.
Collection of the most Esteemed Pieces of Poetry (Mendez), 1767, p. 208, and 1770,
  p. 164.
The Court Miscellany, November 1767, p. 607.
The London Magazine, December 1767, p. 643.
The Universal Magazine, December 1767, p. 329, and November 1779, p. 263.
The Scots Magazine, December 1767, p. 643.
The Annual Register, 1767, p. 265, and 1779, p. 175.
The Weekly Magazine, Edinburgh, 22 June 1769.
Pearch, *Collection of Poems*, 1770, iii. 244; 1775, iii. 242; 1783, iii. 244.
The Oxford Magazine, January 1773, p. 26.
The Lady's Poetical Magazine, 1781, i. 176.
Poetical Works, 1785, p. 162.
Works, 1787, xi. 355.
The Cabinet of Genius, 1788 (with 'Stella' as frontispiece to poem).

  This poem is signed '***' in *The Gentleman's Magazine*. It was first said to be
by Johnson in the *Collection* of 1767. Boswell remarks that 'it has never been
controverted to be his'.
  The reprint in *The Poetical Calendar* contains a new reading in the last
line, and there is no reason for holding that it was not introduced by Johnson.
Boswell thought that the original form was 'more Johnsonian. . . . A horrour
at life in general is more consonant with Johnson's habitual gloomy cast of
thought' (*Life*, i. 179). To this Croker replied that 'Johnson's habitual horror
was not of life, but of death' (*Life*, 1831, i. 154 n.).
  Text from *The Gentleman's Magazine*, except last line.

The WINTER'S WALK

BEHOLD my fair, where-e'er we rove,
   What dreary prospects round us rise,
The naked hills, the leafless grove,
   The hoary ground, the frowning skies.

Nor only through the wasted plain,   5
   Stern winter, is thy force confest,
Still wider spreads thy horrid reign,
   I feel thy pow'r usurp my breast.

Enliv'ning hope, and fond desire,
   Resign the heart to spleen and care,   10
Scarce frighted love maintains his fire,
   And rapture saddens to despair.

In groundless hope, and causeless fear,
   Unhappy man! behold thy doom,
Still changing with the changeful year,   15
   The slave of sunshine and of gloom.

Tir'd with vain joys, and false alarms,
   With mental and corporeal strife,
Snatch me, my *Stella*, to thy arms,
   And screen me from the ills of life.   20

AN ODE

The Gentleman's Magazine, May 1747, p. 240.
Fawkes and Woty, *The Poetical Calendar*, 1763, iv. 3.
Pearch, *Collection of Poems*, 1770, iii. 236.
Poetical Works, 1785, p. 155.
Works, 1787, xi. 350.

   This poem is signed '***' in *The Gentleman's Magazine*. It was first attributed
to Johnson in Pearch's *Collection*, from which it was omitted in the edition of
1775. Boswell thought that the 'learned description of the gout' was 'very

3 hills] hill *Mendez, Pearch, 1785, Works*   5 through . . . , is] thought . . . in *Pearch,
1785, Works 1787–1801*   11 his] her *G.M.* (some edd.), *Fawkes and all later
texts*   20 And screen . . . ills] And hide . . . sight *G.M., Hervey transcript, as an
alternative to* For there are all the Joys of Life.

characteristic'; but he found a difficulty in the footnote, 'The Author being ill of the Gout', for 'Johnson was not attacked with that distemper till at a very late period of his life'. He suspected a poetical fiction. 'Why may not a poet suppose himself to have the gout', he asks, 'as well as suppose himself to be in love?' (*Life*, i. 179).

The footnote may have been supplied by 'J. R.', who sent the poem to the press (see p. 94), in the belief that readers of the *Magazine* would welcome some explanation of 'arthritic tyranny'.

Text from *The Gentleman's Magazine*.

An ODE

STERN winter now, by spring repress'd,
Forbears the long-continu'd strife,
And nature, on her naked breast,
    Delights to catch the gales of life.

Now, o'er the rural kingdom roves   5
    Soft Pleasure with her laughing train,
Love warbles in the vocal groves,
    And vegetation paints the plain.

Unhappy! whom to beds of pain
    Arthritic tyranny consigns,   10
Whom smiling nature courts in vain,
    Tho' rapture sings, and beauty shines.

Yet, tho' my limbs disease invades,
    Her wings Imagination tries,
And bears me to the peaceful shades,   15
    Where ——'s humble turrets rise.

Here stop, my soul, thy rapid flight,
    Nor from the pleasing groves depart,
Where first great nature charm'd my sight,
    Where wisdom first inform'd my heart.   20

Title] Spring. An Ode. *1785, Works*   8 paints] plants *Pearch, 1785, Works*

7–8. Quoted in the *Dictionary*, s.v. 'vegetation', as '*Anonymous*'.
10. '*The Author being ill of the Gout*' added as a footnote in *The Gentleman's Magazine*; omitted in *The Poetical Calendar*.

Here let me thro' the vales pursue
　　A guide, a father, and a friend;
Once more great nature's work review,
　　Once more on wisdom's voice attend.

From false caresses, causeless strife,   25
　　Wild hope, vain fear, alike remov'd,
Here let me learn the use of life,
　　Then best enjoy'd, when most improv'd.

Teach me, thou venerable bow'r,
　　Cool meditation's quiet seat,   30
The gen'rous scorn of venal pow'r,
　　The silent grandeur of retreat.

When Pride, by guilt, to greatness climbs,
　　Or raging factions rush to war,
Here let me learn to shun the crimes   35
　　I can't prevent, and will not share.

But, lest I fall by subtler foes,
　　Bright wisdom teach me *Curio*'s art,
The swelling passions to compose,
　　And quell the rebels of the heart.   40

TO LYCE

The Gentleman's Magazine, May 1747, p. 240.
Poetical Works, 1785, p. 172.
Works, 1787, xi. 364.

　　This is the last of the six pieces signed '***', in *The Gentleman's Magazine*; see p. 94. Boswell had doubts if it was by Johnson:

'I have also some difficulty to believe that he could produce such a group of *conceits* as appear in the verses to Lyce, in which he claims for this ancient personage as good a right to be assimilated to *heaven*, as nymphs whom other poets have flattered; he therefore ironically ascribes to her the attributes of the *sky*, in such stanzas as this: "Her teeth the *night* with *darkness* dies" etc.' (*Life*, i. 179.)

23 work review] works review *Fawkes*: work renew *Pearch*: works renew *1785*, *Works*
28 Then] When *Pearch*, *1785*, *Works*

Boswell's hesitation has been shared by others. The piece is unlike Johnson in spirit. But it is a free imitation of Horace's Ode iv. 13, and it may be early work. The note by 'J. R.' suggests that the group of six poems was given to help him over an editorial difficulty, and Johnson may well have collected stray pieces that he had by him.

Text from *The Gentleman's Magazine*; in line 12 some editions have 'rain' in error for 'show'rs'.

To LYCE, *an elderly Lady*

YE nymphs whom starry rays invest,
   By flatt'ring poets giv'n;
Who shine, by lavish lovers drest,
   In all the pomp of heav'n;

Engross not all the beams on high,   5
   Which gild a lover's lays,
But as your sister of the sky,
   Let *Lyce* share the praise.

Her silver locks display the moon,
   Her brows a cloudy show,   10
Strip'd rainbows round her eyes are seen,
   And show'rs from either flow.

Her teeth the night with darkness dyes,
   She's starr'd with pimples o'er,
Her tongue like nimble lightning plies,   15
   And can with thunder roar.

But some *Zelinda* while I sing
   Denies my *Lyce* shines,
And all the pens of *Cupid*'s wing
   Attack my gentle lines.   20

Yet spite of fair *Zelinda*'s eye,
   And all her bards express,
My *Lyce* makes as good a sky,
   And I but flatter less.

THE DRURY-LANE PROLOGUE

Prologue and Epilogue, spoken at the opening of the Theatre in Drury-Lane 1747. London: Printed by E. Cave at St. John's Gate; sold by M. Cooper in Pater-Noster-Row, and R. Dodsley Pall-mall. M,DCC,XLVII. (Price 6d.) 4°. (Facsimile, New York, 1902). [Two states of title: with and without '(*Price 6d.*).']
Prologue . . . Drury-Lane 1747. London: Printed by W. Webb, near St. Paul's. 4°. (Pirated edition; type-facsimile, Oxford, 1924.)
The Gentleman's Magazine, October 1747, p. 490.
Dodsley, *Collection of Poems*, 1748, iii. 150; ed. 2, 1748, i. 206; also 1751, '55, '58, '63, '65, '66, '70, '75, '82.
Elphinston, *A Collection of Poems*, 1764, p. 114.
A Select Collection of Poems, Edinburgh, 1768, 1770, i. 62.
Davies, *Miscellaneous and Fugitive Pieces*, 1773, 1774, ii. 291.
The Gentleman and Lady's Weekly Magazine, Edinburgh, 1774, p. 2.
The Theatrical Bouquet, 1778, 1780, p. 300.
A Collection and Selection of English Prologues and Epilogues, 1779, iii. 120.
Davies, *Life of Garrick*, 1780, i. 108.
Poetical Works, 1785, p. 173.
Hawkins, *Life of Johnson*, 1787, p. 196.
Works, 1787, xi. 344.

The Prologue was written to inaugurate Garrick's managership of Drury-Lane on Tuesday 15 September 1747. Johnson is reported by George Steevens to have said of it:

'The whole number [of lines] was composed before I threw a single couplet on paper. . . . I did not afterwards change more than a word in it, and that was done at the remonstrance of Garrick. I did not think his criticism just, but it was necessary he should be satisfied with what he was to utter.' (*Johnsonian Miscellanies*, ii. 313.)

According to an advertisement in *The General Advertiser* for 8 October 1747, Garrick hoped that the publication of the Prologue would be 'considered as a proof of his desire to compensate the disappointment' of the audience at his having been disabled by illness from speaking it 'when it was demanded'. Advertisements in the same paper show that he spoke it only during the first week of his management, on 15, 16, 17, and 19 September.

The Prologue was first printed with Johnson's name in Dodsley's *Collection*. The Epilogue was written by Garrick.

Text from the first edition.

PROLOGUE

AND

EPILOGUE,

SPOKEN AT THE OPENING OF THE

THEATRE

IN

DRURY-LANE 1747.

LONDON:

Printed by E. CAVE at St *John's Gate*; sold by M.
COOPER in *Pater-Noster-Row*, and R. DODSLEY
Pall-mall.   M,DCC,XLVII.   (*Price 6d.*)

PROLOGUE

Spoken by Mr. GARRICK,

At the Opening of the Theatre in *Drury-Lane* 1747.

WHEN Learning's Triumph o'er her barb'rous Foes
First rear'd the Stage, immortal SHAKESPEAR rose;
Each Change of many-colour'd Life he drew,
Exhausted Worlds, and then imagin'd new:
Existence saw him spurn her bounded Reign,   5
And panting Time toil'd after him in vain:
His pow'rful Strokes presiding Truth impress'd,
And unresisted Passion storm'd the Breast.

Then JOHNSON came, instructed from the School,
To please in Method, and invent by Rule;   10
His studious Patience, and laborious Art,
By regular Approach essay'd the Heart;
Cold Approbation gave the ling'ring Bays,
For those who durst not censure, scarce cou'd praise.
A Mortal born he met the general Doom,   15
But left, like *Egypt*'s Kings, a lasting Tomb.

8 unresisted] unresisting *Davies 1773–4, 1780*   12 essay'd] assail'd *Dodsley 1758–82,
Davies 1773–4, 1780*

3–6. Cf. Edward Young, *Epistle to Lord Lansdowne*, 1713, p. 20:

> He made One Nature and Another found,
> Both in his Page with Master-strokes abound:
> His Witches, Fairies, and Enchanted Isle,
> Bid us no longer at our Nurses smile.

6. 'Drinking tea one day at Garrick's with Mr. Langton, he was questioned if he was not somewhat of a heretick as to Shakespeare; said Garrick, "I doubt he is a little of an infidel."—"Sir, (said Johnson) I will stand by the lines I have written on Shakespeare in my Prologue at the opening of your Theatre." Mr. Langton suggested, that in the line

> And panting Time toil'd after him in vain,

Johnson might have had in his eye the passage in the "Tempest", where Prospero says of Miranda,

> She will outstrip all praise,
> And make it halt behind her.

Johnson said nothing. Garrick then ventured to observe, "I do not think that the happiest line in the praise of Shakespeare". Johnson exclaimed (smiling) "Prosaical rogues! next time I write, I'll make both time and space pant".' (*Life*, iv. 25, and p. 378 n., *post.*)

The Wits of *Charles* found easier Ways to Fame,
Nor wish'd for JOHNSON's Art, or SHAKESPEAR's Flame;
Themselves they studied, as they felt they writ,
Intrigue was Plot, Obscenity was Wit.   20
Vice always found a sympathetick Friend;
They pleas'd their Age, and did not aim to mend.
Yet Bards like these aspir'd to lasting Praise,
And proudly hop'd to pimp in future Days.
Their Cause was gen'ral, their Supports were strong,   25
Their Slaves were willing, and their Reign was long;
Till Shame regain'd the Post that Sense betray'd,
And Virtue call'd Oblivion to her Aid.

Then crush'd by Rules, and weaken'd as refin'd,
For Years the Pow'r of Tragedy declin'd;   30
From Bard, to Bard, the frigid Caution crept,
Till Declamation roar'd, while Passion slept.
Yet still did Virtue deign the Stage to tread,
Philosophy remain'd, though Nature fled.
But forc'd at length her antient Reign to quit,   35
She saw great *Faustus* lay the Ghost of Wit:
Exulting Folly hail'd the joyful Day,
And Pantomime, and Song, confirm'd her Sway.

18 Flame;] Flame, *1747*   32 while] whilst *1785, 1787*   roar'd] soar'd *Davies*
1773–4   37 joyful] joyous *1785, 1787*

17. Cf. Pope, *Epistle to Augustus*, l. 107, 'the Wits of either Charles's days'; and *The Idler*, No. 69, 'The Wits of Charles's time had seldom more than slight and superficial views'.

23–4. Quoted in the *Dictionary*, s.v. 'pimp'; removed from ed. 4.

35–8. Similarly Pope in *The Dunciad*, iii. 301–8, had spoken of pantomime and song as the destroyers of the legitimate drama:

> Already Opera prepares the way,
> The sure fore-runner of her [i.e. Dulness's] gentle sway. . . .
> To aid our cause, if Heav'n thou can'st not bend,
> Hell thou shalt move; for Faustus is our friend.

The Life and Death of Doctor Faustus, made into a Farce, by William Mountfort, was reprinted in 1720. *Harlequin Doctor Faustus* was one of the commonest of the farces which, in Pope's words, 'it was the custom to act at the end of the best Tragedies, to spoil the digestion of the audience'. Dick Minim echoes the Prologue; he 'wondered what was become of the comick genius which supplied our ancestors with wit and pleasantry, and why no writer could be found that durst now venture beyond a Farce' (*The Idler*, No. 60).

But who the coming Changes can presage,
And mark the future Periods of the Stage?—   40
Perhaps if Skill could distant Times explore,
New *Behns*, new *Durfeys*, yet remain in Store.
Perhaps, where *Lear* has rav'd, and *Hamlet* dy'd,
On flying Cars new Sorcerers may ride.
Perhaps, for who can guess th' Effects of Chance?   45
Here *Hunt* may box, or *Mahomet* may dance.
    Hard is his lot, that here by Fortune plac'd,
Must watch the wild Vicissitudes of Taste;
With ev'ry Meteor of Caprice must play,
And chase the new-blown Bubbles of the Day.   50
Ah! let not Censure term our Fate our Choice,
The Stage but echoes back the publick Voice.
The Drama's Laws the Drama's Patrons give,
For we that live to please, must please to live.
    Then prompt no more the Follies you decry,   55
As Tyrants doom their Tools of Guilt to die;
'Tis yours this Night to bid the Reign commence
Of rescu'd Nature, and reviving Sense;
To chase the Charms of Sound, the Pomp of Show,
For useful Mirth, and salutary Woe;   60
Bid scenic Virtue form the rising Age,
And Truth diffuse her Radiance from the Stage.

45 for . . . Chance? *within brackets 1748–1787*   the effects *Davies 1773–4, 1780*

46. Edward Hunt, a light-weight pugilist, who defeated the Life-guardsman Hawksley, at Broughton's Amphitheatre, on 11 June 1746. See Pierce Egan's *Boxiana* (1812), i. 67–9. Johnson approved of boxing (*Johnsonian Miscellanies*, i. 149; *Life*, v. 229).

Mahomet, 'a rope-dancer, who had exhibited at Covent-Garden theatre the winter before, said to be a Turk' (Hawkins).

59. All editions agree in reading 'chase' but it is possible that Johnson actually wrote 'change'.

61. Quoted in the *Dictionary*, s.v. 'scenick', as by '*Anonym.*'.

THE VANITY OF HUMAN WISHES

The Vanity of Human Wishes, the first work to bear Johnson's name on the title-page, was published in quarto on 9 January 1749. 'I wrote', said Johnson, 'the first seventy lines . . . in the course of one morning, in that small house beyond the church at Hampstead. The whole number was composed before I committed a single couplet to writing' (*Works*, 1787, xi. 212). The poem was in the hands of Dodsley by November 1748. The receipt for fifteen guineas was printed by Boswell from a copy given to him by James Dodsley in 1786, and is here printed from the original, now in the Hyde Collection:

Novr. 25th 1748

I received of Mr Dodsley fifteen Guineas for which I assign to him the right of copy of an imitation of the tenth Satire of Juvenal written by me; reserving to myself the right of printing one Edition.

Sam: Johnson.

The poem was printed by Cave, who in the following year printed the quarto edition of *London*. In his supplement to *The Gentleman's Magazine* for 1748, published in January 1749, Cave quoted 110 lines of the poem, with the following note:

'On *Jan.* 9, was published, long wish'd, another *satire* from *Juvenal*, by the author of *London*; tho' it belongs not properly to this year, we cannot resist the pleasure of entertaining our readers with some passages from it on this *first* opportunity.'

Boswell corroborates Hawkins's statement that seventy lines of the poem were composed in one day; he says that he heard the statement from Johnson's own lips (*Life*, i. 192). In another passage he reports that Johnson said, when talking of the difficulty of making verses,

'I have generally had them in my mind, perhaps fifty at a time, walking up and down in my room; and then I have written them down, and often, from laziness, have written only half lines. I remember I wrote a hundred lines of *The Vanity of Human Wishes* in a day' (ii. 15).

He also told Boswell that he had the satires of Juvenal 'all in his head' (i. 193). This habit of composition warns us of the danger of assigning *The Vanity of Human Wishes* to a definite date, and there are indications in the poem itself that it may not all have been written at the same time. The great passages are complete in themselves and lose nothing by being taken out of their setting. The thought of the vanities of life was never long absent from Johnson's mind. His schoolboy verses on 'The Young Author', which he revised for publication in *The Gentleman's Magazine* of July 1743, are a first sketch for the finished picture of the ills that assail the life of the scholar. His Wolsey and Charles XII of

Sweden, though suggested by Juvenal's Sejanus and Hannibal, are independent studies of the vanity of political ambition and military prowess. From a letter written in June 1742 we learn that he was then engaged on a drama on 'Charles of Sweden'. But we must assign to the year 1748 the casting of the poem in its final form. The religious exhortation of the conclusion enforces the lesson of his prose tale *The Vision of Theodore, the Hermit of Teneriffe*, published in Dodsley's *Preceptor* in April 1748.

In *London* he had the corresponding passages in Juvenal printed at the foot of the page; here he was content to cite only the numbers of the verses. The difference indicates the greater maturity of *The Vanity of Human Wishes*. Imitation though it is, the freedom and the sincerity of the treatment make it an original poem. The difficulty of what he called, in his *Life of Pope*, the irreconcilable dissimilitude between Roman and English manners is overcome so successfully that the poems of Juvenal and Johnson have to be regarded, not as model and copy, but as companion studies of the same subject.

Only one separate edition of *The Vanity of Human Wishes* was published in Johnson's lifetime. After 1755 the poem was available in Dodsley's *Collection*, but the absence of any reprint during these six years is remarkable. There are no grounds for holding that the size of the edition was unusually large. *London* had gone into three editions in two months.

Garrick's comment on the poem may have expressed the view of many of his contemporaries when the poem appeared:

'When Johnson lived much with the Herveys, and saw a good deal of what was passing in life, he wrote his *London*, which is lively and easy. When he became more retired, he gave us his *Vanity of Human Wishes*, which is as hard as Greek. Had he gone on to imitate another satire, it would have been as hard as Hebrew' (Boswell, *Life*, i. 194).

The contemporary allusions in *London*, and the direct bearing of the poem as a whole on the political and social conditions of the day, had contributed to its immediate success. *The Vanity of Human Wishes* appealed rather to the more deliberate public that could appreciate its stateliness in general description and the wisdom of its calmer mood. It did not serve any passing purpose, and today it has lost no part of its meaning. Now that time has blunted here and there the edge of the earlier satire, the superiority of *The Vanity of Human Wishes* is no longer in doubt.

There had been many verse renderings of Juvenal's tenth satire before Johnson's poem, but of Johnson's debt to any of these there can be no question. The only renderings of Juvenal to which he anywhere refers are Stapylton's, Holyday's, and Dryden's, and the imitation of the third satire by Oldham. Dryden's translation he knew well, but his knowledge of it is even less evident in *The Vanity of Human Wishes* than in *London*. 'The peculiarity of Juvenal', he said in his *Life of Dryden*, 'is a mixture of gaiety and stateliness, of pointed sentences, and declamatory grandeur'; and he pointed out where the translation by Dryden and his associates was deficient. He was fully aware of the special quality of his own work when he proceeded to say, 'it is therefore perhaps possible to give a better representation of that great satirist, even in those parts which Dryden himself has translated'. But he added,—'some passages excepted,

which will never be excelled'. He must have had in mind Dryden's rendering
of the opening lines of this satire, where he himself was not at his best:

> Look round the Habitable World, how few
> Know their own Good; or knowing it, pursue.
> How void of Reason are our Hopes and Fears!
> What in the Conduct of our Life appears
> So well design'd, so luckily begun,
> But, when we have our wish, we wish undone?

EDITIONS AND TEXT

Holograph manuscript in the Hyde Collection. (See p. 415, *post.*)

The Vanity of Human Wishes. The Tenth Satire of Juvenal, Imitated By
Samuel Johnson. London: Printed for R. Dodsley at Tully's Head in Pall-
Mall, and Sold by M. Cooper in Pater-noster Row. M.DCC.XLIX. Quarto.
Published 9 January 1749. (Type facsimile, Oxford, 1927. Facsimile
Augustan Reprint Soc. No. 22, 1950; Scolar Press, 1970)

[*The Gentleman's Magazine*, xviii. 1748, Supplement, 598–9 quotes largely.]

Dodsley, *Collection of Poems*, 1755, iv. 156. Also 1758, '63, '65, '66, '70, '75, '82.

Two Satires. By Samuel Johnson, A.M. Oxford, 1759. [Two states with variant
titles.]

A Select Collection of Poems, Edinburgh, 1768, i. 248; 1772, i. 246.

Davies, *Miscellaneous and Fugitive Pieces*, 1773, 1774, ii. 312.

The Lady's Poetical Magazine, 1781, ii. 266.

D. Junii Juvenalis et A. Persii Flacci Satiræ, ed. Knox, 1784, p. 380.

Poetical Works, 1785, p. 22.

Poetical Works, Osborne and Griffin, 1785, p. 20.

Works, 1787, xi. 331.

Poetical Works, 1789, p. 22.

The text of the original edition of 1749 and the revised text in Dodsley's
Collection of 1755 are alone authoritative. All the others published during Johnson's lifetime derive from the latter, and are mere reprints in which he had
no part.

Annotations in the younger James Boswell's copy of the edition of 1789 show
that Johnson left a revised copy of the first edition of the poem—as of the fifth
edition of *London*—with marginal corrections not incorporated in Dodsley's
text. Boswell simply states that the text of 1789 is 'Compared with the 1st
Edition'; but besides noting the original readings he records five manuscript
corrections which Johnson never printed:

> (41. New) Corrected to n*o*w
> (167. 'scape) scaped alterd to scapes
> (268. And yield) Diffuse cor MSS.
> (293. in) with cor MSS.
> (298. could) shall cor M.

These corrections were probably made shortly after 1749 in preparation for
a second edition which was not required. That they antedate the revision in 1755

is indicated by line 167, where *'scaped* is altered to *'scapes* because the rest of the passage is in the present tense; but as *vulgar* is generally plural, the edition of 1755 reads *'scape*. It seems unlikely that these corrections should have been made in reverse order, i.e. that Johnson having once improved the reading *'scaped* to *'scape*, should at some time after 1755 have made an inferior correction. The other four manuscript corrections he appears to have forgotten; but it is not impossible that all the five were made about the time when he revised the fifth edition of *London*. But for a reconsideration of the significance of Boswell's notes, see A. D. Moody in *The Library*, xxvi (1971), 22–38.

Johnson revised the poem carefully for its inclusion in Dodsley's *Collection*, and made changes in over twenty lines. One of them is the substitution of *patron* for *garret* (l. 160), occasioned by Lord Chesterfield's treatment of him while compiling his *Dictionary* and made about the same time as he wrote his famous letter to Chesterfield. He will not readily be credited with having sanctioned the omission of this couplet in the account of Wolsey (ll. 103, 4):

> Turn'd by his Nod the Stream of Honour flows,
> His Smile alone Security bestows.

It comes at the bottom of a page in the original edition (p. 10, B1ᵛ), and must have been omitted by mistake.[1] On the other hand, we may attribute to him the deletion of this couplet in the account of the dangers that wait on Beauty (after l. 330):

> An envious Breast with certain Mischief glows,
> And Slaves, the Maxim tells, are always Foes.

Not a good couplet in itself, it adds nothing to the force of the passage, and even checks the run of the sense.

Hawkins, who worked on Dodsley's text, restored the first of the two omitted couplets, and, whimsically, six of the readings of the first edition. He used the copy with Johnson's manuscript corrections, and introduced all the five of which we have record. But he also included three readings for which his authority is not known.

An unknown revision is implied by the record of lot 302 in the Dillon sale at Sotheby's, 7 June 1869, which included a copy of the 1749 edition 'with an additional couplet at page 18 in the autograph of Johnson'. Page 18 includes lines 209–24.

The version of 1755 is the basis of the present text. The first of the omitted couplets is restored, and the second is consigned to the footnotes. Johnson's corrections known to have been left in manuscript are incorporated. Typographical errors are corrected.

---

[1] For arguments against the retention of this couplet, see A. Sherbo, *Notes and Queries*, 10 May 1952, 205–6, and A. D. Moody, loc. cit.

THE
VANITY
OF
HUMAN WISHES.

THE

Tenth Satire of *Juvenal*,

IMITATED

By *SAMUEL JOHNSON.*

LONDON:

Printed for R. Dodsley at Tully's Head in Pall-Mall, and Sold by M. Cooper in Pater-noster Row.

M.DCC.XLIX.

THE

VANITY

OF

HUMAN WISHES.

The TENTH SATIRE *of JUVENAL* Imitated.

[a]LET Observation with extensive View,
    Survey Mankind, from *China* to *Peru*;
Remark each anxious Toil, each eager Strife,
And watch the busy Scenes of crouded Life;
Then say how Hope and Fear, Desire and Hate,   5
O'erspread with Snares the clouded Maze of Fate,
Where wav'ring Man, betray'd by vent'rous Pride,
To tread the dreary Paths without a guide,

[a] *Ver.* 1–11.

---

8 Guide; *1749, 1755*

1, 2. In *Memoirs of the Life and Writings of the late Dr. Samuel Johnson*, 1785, by the Rev. William Shaw, a short series of 'brief strictures' begins thus (p. 51): 'Let observation survey the world, from China to Peru, and we must allow its *view to be extensive*, whether the poet tells us so or not.' Coleridge is reported to have said in the sixth of his *Lectures on Shakespeare and Milton*, 5 December 1811, 'as much as to say "Let observation with extensive observation observe mankind extensively"' (ed. J. Payne Collier, 1856, p. 42; cf. *Table Talk*, 21 April 1811, ed. 1835, ii. 354). Wordsworth made the same criticism in conversation, as Hazlitt tells us in *The Spirit of the Age*, 1825; and so did De Quincey in his essay on *Rhetoric*, 1828. Byron wrote in his *Diary* on 9 January 1821: 'I remember an observation of Sharpe's, (the *Conversationist*, as he was called in London, and a very clever man,) that the first line of this poem was superfluous, and that Pope . . . would have begun at once, only changing the punctuation—"Survey mankind from China to Peru"' (ed. R. E. Prothero, 1904, v. 161). Byron may have heard this criticism in conversation, but Richard Sharp had made it in a letter of 4 February 1808 (*Letters and Essays*, 1834, p. 36). Even Tennyson, who admired Johnson's grave earnestness, asked why he did not say 'Let observation, with extended observation, observe extensively' (*Tennyson, a Memoir, by his son*, 1897, ii. 73). For a spirited defence of this couplet, see Saintsbury, *History of Criticism*, 1904, iii. 223.

China to Peru. Cf. Boileau, *Sat.* viii. 3, 'De Paris au Pérou, du Japon jusqu'à Rome,' thus rendered by Oldham, 1682, 'Throughout the Globe from *London* to *Japan*'; Sir William Temple, *Of Poetry*, 1690, *ad fin.*, 'in all Nations from *China* to *Peru*'; Soame Jenyns, *Epistle to Lord Lovelace*, 1735, 'From frozen Lapland to Peru' (Dodsley, 1748, iii. 157, or 129); Thomas Warton, the elder, *Of the Universal Love of Pleasure*, 'All human Race, from China to Peru' (*Poems*, 1748, p. 16). Cf. *Notes and Queries*, 21 October 1944, 188–9, and 27 October 1951, 479.

As treach'rous Phantoms in the Mist delude,
Shuns fancied Ills, or chases airy Good.   10
How rarely Reason guides the stubborn Choice,
Rules the bold Hand, or prompts the suppliant Voice,
How Nations sink, by darling Schemes oppres'd,
When Vengeance listens to the Fool's Request.
Fate wings with ev'ry Wish th' afflictive Dart,   15
Each Gift of Nature, and each Grace of Art,
With fatal Heat impetuous Courage glows,
With fatal Sweetness Elocution flows,
Impeachment stops the Speaker's pow'rful Breath,
And restless Fire precipitates on Death.   20
    ^bBut scarce observ'd the Knowing and the Bold
Fall in the gen'ral Massacre of Gold;
Wide-wasting Pest! that rages unconfin'd,
And crouds with Crimes the Records of Mankind,
For Gold his Sword the hireling Ruffian draws,   25
For Gold the hireling Judge distorts the Laws;
Wealth heap'd on Wealth, nor Truth nor Safety buys,
The Dangers gather as the Treasures rise.
    Let Hist'ry tell where rival Kings command,
And dubious Title shakes the madded Land,   30
When Statutes glean the Refuse of the Sword,
How much more safe the Vassal than the Lord,
Low sculks the Hind beneath the Rage of Pow'r,
And leaves the wealthy Traytor in the *Tow'r*,

^b *Ver.* 12–22.

---

10 Good. *1749, 1755*   12 Voice, *1749, 1755*   21 observ'd the . . . Bold,
1749, 1755   25 Hireling, *1749*   32 Lord, *1749, 1755*   34 wealthy
traytor] bonny Traytor *1749*

15. *Fate wings*, &c., i.e. the afflictive dart is feathered with every wish, with each gift
of nature, and with each grace of art.

22. *massacre of gold*, the destruction caused by wealth: 'sed plures nimia congesta
pecunia cura strangulat' (Juvenal).

31. Cf. Addison, *The Campaign*, l. 192:

          Refuse of swords, and gleanings of a fight.

34. *the wealthy traytor.* The change from 'the *bonny Traytor*' of the first edition
removed the definitely Scottish allusion at a time when the Jacobite rising of 1745 was
no longer fresh in memory. The Earl of Cromartie, the Earl of Kilmarnock, Lord
Balmerino, and Simon Fraser Lord Lovat were brought to the Tower of London for

Untouch'd his Cottage, and his Slumbers sound,   35
Tho' Confiscation's Vulturs hover round.
    The needy Traveller, serene and gay,
Walks the wild Heath, and sings his Toil away.
Does Envy seize thee? crush th' upbraiding Joy,
Encrease his Riches and his Peace destroy,   40
Now Fears in dire Vicissitude invade,
The rustling Brake alarms, and quiv'ring Shade,
Nor Light nor Darkness bring his Pain Relief,
One shews the Plunder, and one hides the Thief.
    cYet still one gen'ral Cry the Skies assails,   45
And Gain and Grandeur load the tainted Gales;
Few know the toiling Statesman's Fear or Care,
Th' insidious Rival and the gaping Heir.
    dOnce more, *Democritus*, arise on Earth,
With chearful Wisdom and instructive Mirth,   50
See motley Life in modern Trappings dress'd,
And feed with varied Fools th' eternal Jest:
Thou who couldst laugh where Want enchain'd Caprice,
Toil crush'd Conceit, and Man was of a Piece;
Where Wealth unlov'd without a Mourner dy'd,   55
And scarce a Sycophant was fed by Pride;
Where ne'er was known the Form of mock Debate,
Or seen a new-made Mayor's unwieldy State;

c *Ver.* 23–7.   d *Ver.* 28–55.

36 hover round] clang around *1749*   40 destroy, *1749, 1755*   41 Now
Johnson MS. correction, 1787] New *1749, 1755*   45 one] the *1749*   47 or] and
GM   51 motly *1755*   55 dy'd; *1749, 1755*

their part in the rising, and the first three were beheaded on Tower Hill on 18 August
1746, the last on 9 April 1747. 'Bonny' is said in the *Dictionary* to be 'a word now almost
confined to the Scottish dialect'. Cf. *Life*, i. 180.
    36. *hover round*, substituted for 'clang around' because the vultures of the law need not
be noisy. For 'clang' as applied to the shrill cries of birds, cf. *Paradise Lost*, xi. 831, 'The
haunt of Seales and Orcs, and Sea-mews clang' (quoted in the *Dictionary*), and vii. 422.
    40. Cf. Johnson's *Annals* (*Works*, Yale ed., i (1958), 14).
    46. *load the tainted gales*. In the *Dictionary* Johnson cites Thomson's *Autumn*,
l. 364, 'the Spaniel struck Stiff by the tainted Gale'.
    48. Cf. Dryden, 'I neither will, nor can Prognosticate / To the young, gaping Heir,
his Father's Fate' (trans. Juvenal, *Sat.* iii. 81–2).
    51. *motley*, so in the *Dictionary*.

8127022   K

Where change of Fav'rites made no Change of Laws,
And Senates heard before they judg'd a Cause;   60
How wouldst thou shake at *Britain*'s modish Tribe,
Dart the quick Taunt, and edge the piercing Gibe?
Attentive Truth and Nature to descry,
And pierce each Scene with Philosophic Eye.
To thee were solemn Toys or empty Shew,   65
The Robes of Pleasure and the Veils of Woe:
All aid the Farce, and all thy Mirth maintain,
Whose Joys are causeless, or whose Griefs are vain.
    Such was the Scorn that fill'd the Sage's Mind,
Renew'd at ev'ry Glance on Humankind;   70
How just that Scorn ere yet thy Voice declare,
Search every State, and canvass ev'ry Pray'r.
    ᵉUnnumber'd Suppliants croud Preferment's Gate,
Athirst for Wealth, and burning to be great;
Delusive Fortune hears th' incessant Call,   75
They mount, they shine, evaporate, and fall.
On ev'ry Stage the Foes of Peace attend,
Hate dogs their Flight, and Insult mocks their End.
Love ends with Hope, the sinking Statesman's Door
Pours in the Morning Worshiper no more;   80
For growing Names the weekly Scribbler lies,
To growing Wealth the Dedicator flies,
From every Room descends the painted Face,
That hung the bright *Palladium* of the Place,
And smoak'd in Kitchens, or in Auctions sold,   85
To better Features yields the Frame of Gold;

ᵉ *Ver.* 56–107.

---

63 decry *1755* (*corrected 1787*)

---

73. Parallel with Swift's *To Doctor D-l-y, on the Libels Writ against him*, 1730,
93 'croud about Preferment's Gate.' Cf. C. B. Ricks in *Review of English Studies* xi
(1960), 413.
    78. *dogs.* This line is quoted from memory in the *Dictionary*,—'Hate dogs their rise,
and insult mocks their fall'.
    81. *the weekly scribbler*, in the political journals, which were generally published once
a week and were taking the place of the pamphlet as the normal organ of political propa-
ganda. See *Johnson's England*, 1933, ii. 335–40.

For now no more we trace in ev'ry Line
Heroic Worth, Benevolence Divine:
The Form distorted justifies the Fall,
And Detestation rids th' indignant Wall.   90
    But will not *Britain* hear the last Appeal,
Sign her Foes Doom, or guard her Fav'rites Zeal?
Through Freedom's Sons no more Remonstrance rings,
Degrading Nobles and controuling Kings;
Our supple Tribes repress their Patriot Throats,   95
And ask no Questions but the Price of Votes;
With Weekly Libels and Septennial Ale,
Their Wish is full to riot and to rail.
    In full-blown Dignity, see *Wolsey* stand,
Law in his Voice, and Fortune in his Hand: 100
To him the Church, the Realm, their Pow'rs consign,
Thro' him the Rays of regal Bounty shine,
Turn'd by his Nod the Stream of Honour flows,
His Smile alone Security bestows:
Still to new Heights his restless Wishes tow'r,   105
Claim leads to Claim, and Pow'r advances Pow'r;
Till Conquest unresisted ceas'd to please,
And Rights submitted, left him none to seize.
At length his Sov'reign frowns—the Train of State
Mark the keen Glance, and watch the Sign to hate.   110

92 Zeal; *1749, 1755*   103–4 *not in 1755, restored 1787*

---

93. *remonstrance*, alluding to the Grand Remonstrance presented to Charles I, 1 December 1641.

97. *septennial ale*. This couplet is cited in the *Dictionary* as '*Anonym.*' Johnson cancelled it in the fourth edition (1773) of the *Dictionary*. Parliaments were septennial from 1716 (1 Geo. 1, Stat. 2, Cap. 38) to the Parliament Act of 1910. 'At the end of every seven years comes the Saturnalian season, when the freemen of Great Britain may please themselves with the choice of their representatives' (*The Patriot* (1774), para. 2). Cf. also *Life*, ii. 73.

99–120. If Johnson's Wolsey is indebted to any one work more than another, it is *Henry VIII*. A description so condensed and generalized of a theme so well known cannot have a 'source', but some of the details suggest recollection of the Shakespearian play. Shakespeare's Fall of Wolsey is quoted at length in Dodsley's *Preceptor* (published 7 April 1748), i. 70–3; a work with which Johnson was connected. But he was, at this time, reading extensively for the *Dictionary*. See C. B. Ricks, 'Wolsey in *The Vanity of Human Wishes*', *Modern Language Notes*, lxxiii (1958), 563–8.

103–4. There is no obvious reason why Johnson should have condemned this couplet. Its omission in 1755 may be ascribed to Dodsley's printer. See the introductory account.

Where-e'er he turns he meets a Stranger's Eye,
His Suppliants scorn him, and his Followers fly;
At once is lost the Pride of aweful State,
The golden Canopy, the glitt'ring Plate,
The regal Palace, the luxurious Board,   115
The liv'ried Army, and the menial Lord.
With Age, with Cares, with Maladies oppress'd,
He seeks the Refuge of Monastic Rest.
Grief aids Disease, remember'd Folly stings,
And his last Sighs reproach the Faith of Kings.   120
   Speak thou, whose Thoughts at humble Peace repine,
Shall *Wolsey*'s Wealth, with *Wolsey*'s End be thine?
Or liv'st thou now, with safer Pride content,
The wisest Justice on the Banks of *Trent?*
For why did *Wolsey* near the Steeps of Fate,   125
On weak Foundations raise th' enormous Weight?
Why but to sink beneath Misfortune's Blow,
With louder Ruin to the Gulphs below?
   ^fWhat gave great *Villiers* to th' Assassin's Knife,
And fixed Disease on *Harley*'s closing life?   130

^f *Ver.* 108–13.

---

113 At once is lost] Now drops at once *1749, 1787*   124 The wisest justice] The
richest Landlord *1749*   125 near the steeps] by the Steps *1749*

---

113. *At once is lost*, substituted to avoid the domestic image of 'Now drops . . . the
plate', though Johnson meant vessels of silver, and because of other nouns in this
sentence. Hawkins missed the purpose of the alteration.
   115. Quoted in the *Dictionary*, s.v. 'luxurious', as by '*Anon.*'.
   124. *the wisest justice*. The MS. first read 'wisest Justice', which was then changed to
'wealthiest Landlord', but printed as 'richest Landlord.' This drew the contrast between
wealth accompanied with thirst for power and wealth enjoyed with safer pride on one's
own estates in the country. The reversion to the original reading contrasts the thirst for
power and the unselfish exercise of power for the benefit of one's fellow men. In mentioning the Trent Johnson was thinking of Lichfield.
   125. *near the steeps of fate*. This replaces 'by the Steps of Fate', a difficult phrase which
must be taken to mean 'by fated degrees'. Cf. l. 312 *post* and *The Rambler*, No. 14,
para. 2 'steeps of virtue'. S. I. Tucker in *Notes and Queries*, August 1957, 354.
   129. *Villiers*—George Villiers, first Duke of Buckingham, father of the 'Villiers' in
London, l. 86. On the word 'knife', cf. *The Rambler*, No. 168.
   130. *Harley*—Robert Harley, Earl of Oxford, leader of the Tory party under Queen
Anne; but his bad health for some years before his death in 1724 was not the immediate
result of his exercise of power nor of his fall in 1714 and the unsuccessful attempt at his
impeachment. In his retirement he continued to collect his great library.

What murder'd *Wentworth*, and what exil'd *Hyde*,
By Kings protected, and to Kings ally'd?
What but their Wish indulg'd in Courts to shine,
And Pow'r too great to keep or to resign?
ᵍWhen first the College Rolls receive his Name,   135
The young Enthusiast quits his Ease for Fame;
Through all his Veins the fever of Renown
Burns from the strong Contagion of the Gown;
O'er *Bodley*'s Dome his future Labours spread,
And* *Bacon*'s Mansion trembles o'er his Head;   140

ᵍ *Ver.* 114–32.
* *There is a tradition, that the study of friar Bacon, built on an arch over the bridge, will fall, when a man greater than Bacon shall pass under it.*

137 Through all his Veins] Resistless burns *1749, 1787*   138 Burns *Johnson MS. correction given to Boswell*] Caught *1749, 1787*: Spreads *1755*   140 *Note added 1755*

131. *Wentworth*—Thomas Wentworth, Earl of Strafford, impeached and executed 1641.

Hyde—Edward Hyde, Earl of Clarendon, banished 1667. He spent the last seven years of his life in France. His daughter Anne married the Duke of York, afterwards James II, in 1660, and was mother of Queen Mary and Queen Anne; hence 'to kings ally'd'. 'By kings protected' refers to Wentworth.

135–64. In the description of the lot of the scholar Johnson draws upon his own experience. Mrs. Piozzi describes how he was affected by it when reading the poem to the domestic circle at Streatham: 'When Dr. Johnson read his own satire, in which the life of a scholar is painted, with the various obstructions thrown in his way to fortune and to fame, he burst into a passion of tears one day: the family and Mr. Scott only were present, who, in a jocose way, clapped him on the back, and said, What's all this, my dear Sir? Why you, and I, and *Hercules*, you know, were all troubled with *melancholy*. . . . The Doctor was so delighted at his odd sally, that he suddenly embraced him, and the subject was immediately changed' (*Anecdotes*, 1786, p. 50). Cf. Burton, *Anatomy of Melancholy*, I. II. 3. xv.

138. *Burns from the strong contagion.* Boswell pointed out to Johnson that 'spread' in the next line recurs too soon after 'Spreads from the strong contagion', the reading in the revised text of 1755, and was told to change 'Spreads' to 'Burns'. 'For perfect authenticity', he says, 'I now had it done with his own hand. I thought this alteration not only cured the fault, but was more poetical, as it might carry an allusion to the shirt by which Hercules was inflamed' (*Life*, iii. 357). He adds in a footnote that he deposited the slip of paper in the Bodleian library, but it remained among his papers until 1947 when Lt.-Col. R. H. Isham presented it to the library. 'Burns' is a reversion to the reading of the first edition. Cf. Boswell's Journal, 1779, *Private Papers*, xiii. 213.

139. *Bodley's dome.* In the *Dictionary* the first definition of 'dome' is 'a building, a house, a fabrick'; cf. *London*, l. 203. The line means 'his future writings spread throughout the Bodleian Library', and does not allude to the dome of the Radcliffe Library, now called the Radcliffe Camera, which was not opened till 13 April 1749, and did not become a part of the Bodleian Library till 1860.

140. *Bacon's mansion.* The reputed 'mansion' of Roger Bacon was the gatehouse at the northern end of Grandpont, or Folly Bridge, the bridge over the Thames to the south

Are these thy Views? proceed, illustrious Youth,
And Virtue guard thee to the Throne of Truth,
Yet should thy Soul indulge the gen'rous Heat,
Till captive Science yields her last Retreat;
Should Reason guide thee with her brightest Ray,   145
And pour on misty Doubt resistless Day;
Should no false Kindness lure to loose Delight,
Nor Praise relax, nor Difficulty fright;
Should tempting Novelty thy Cell refrain,
And Sloth effuse her opiate Fumes in vain;   150
Should Beauty blunt on Fops her fatal Dart,
Nor claim the triumph of a letter'd Heart;
Should no Disease thy torpid Veins invade,
Nor Melancholy's Phantoms haunt thy Shade;
Yet hope not Life from Grief or Danger free,   155
Nor think the Doom of Man revers'd for thee:
Deign on the passing World to turn thine Eyes,
And pause awhile from Letters to be wise;
There mark what Ills the Scholar's Life assail,
Toil, Envy, Want, the Patron, and the Jail.   160

150 Sloth effuse her opiate] Sloth's bland Opiates shed their *1749*   158 letters,]
Learning *1749*: learning, *1787*   159 There] Yet *GM*   160 patron] Garret *1749*

of Oxford and near Pembroke College. It was taken down in 1779. See *Notes and Queries*, 20 August 1910 (XI. ii. 158). A view of Bacon's study by M. A. Rooker is the illustration in the Oxford Almanack for 1780; it is reproduced in *The Oxford Historical Pageant*, 1907, along with another from a drawing in the Bodleian Library. The footnote in Dodsley's *Collection* may not have been supplied by Johnson.

145–6. Cf. Pope, *Essay on Criticism*, ll. 211–12:

> If once right reason drives that cloud away,
> Truth breaks upon us with resistless day.

148. This line is quoted in the *Dictionary* under 'relax'.

149. *refrain*, a rare sense not given in the *Dictionary*.

155–6. Quoted in Boswell's *Hebrides*, 11 September 1773. Boswell records his talk with Johnson on 23 September 1777 about 'misery being "the doom of man" in this life', *Life*, iii. 198, *Note-Book*, p. 22.

158. 'Learning' may have been replaced by 'letters' in order to avoid the possible misreading 'learning to be wise'.

160. *the patron*, replacing 'the Garret'. 'After experiencing', says Boswell, 'the uneasiness which Lord Chesterfield's fallacious patronage made him feel, he dismissed the word *garret* from the sad group' (*Life*, i. 264). The letter to Chesterfield was written on 7 February 1755, and the revised version of the poem appeared about the middle of March. In the *Dictionary*, published 15 April, 'Patron' is said to be 'commonly a wretch who supports with insolence, and is paid with flattery'.

See Nations slowly wise, and meanly just,
To buried Merit raise the tardy Bust.
If dreams yet flatter, once again attend,
Hear *Lydiat*'s Life, and *Galileo*'s End.
    Nor deem, when Learning her last Prize bestows   165
The glitt'ring Eminence exempt from Foes;
See when the Vulgar 'scape, despis'd or aw'd,
Rebellion's vengeful Talons seize on *Laud*.
From meaner Minds, tho' smaller Fines content
The plunder'd Palace or sequester'd Rent;   170

---

165 last] lost *1749*   166 foes] woes *1758–85, 1789, 1825*   167 'scape] 'scap'd
1749: 'scapes *Johnson MS. correction, 1787*

161, 2. This couplet is quoted in the *Dictionary* under 'just', removed from ed. 4.

162. *the tardy bust.* Johnson had in mind the bust of Milton which was placed in Westminster Abbey in 1737 by William Benson; see the Prologue to *Comus*, ll. 21–4, and introductory note (p. 137), and cf. *The Dunciad*, iii. 325. But his words have a wider application. The monument to Butler erected in the Abbey in 1721 had induced Samuel Wesley's epigram:

> While Butler, needy Wretch! was yet alive,
> No gen'rous Patron would a Dinner give:
> See him, when starv'd to Death and turn'd to Dust,
> Presented with a Monument Bust!
> The Poet's Fate is here in Emblem shown.
> He ask'd for Bread, and he receiv'd a Stone.
> (*Poems*, 1736, p. 62.)

The monument to Dryden in the Abbey was erected in 1720, and the monument to Shakespeare in 1741.

164. *Lydiat*—Thomas Lydiat (1572–1646), mathematician and Biblical scholar; fellow of New College, Oxford, and rector of Alkerton, Oxfordshire. His works on chronology gave him a European reputation. He was ranked by his contemporaries with Bacon, but he lived and died in poverty. He was not well known when Johnson chose him as the representative of impecunious learning; a short account of him, in illustration of Johnson's allusion, was inserted from the 'General Dictionary' in *The Gentleman's Magazine*, 1748, Supplement, p. 598. Cf. *Life*, i. 194 n.

167. *'scape.* Chalmers has this note: 'This was first written "See, where the vulgar 'scape*d*"; but, as the rest of the paragraph was in the present tense, he altered it to 'scape*s*; but again recollecting that the word *vulgar* is never used as a singular substantive, he adopted the reading of the text [i.e. 'scape]'. See the introductory account.

169. *content*, i.e. content the persecutor, who exacts smaller penalties from meaner minds.

In this passage, and in it alone, Johnson shows his political opinions. It was not 'fatal learning' which led Archbishop Laud to the block in 1645. The passage was attacked with Whig prejudice by Macaulay in his article on Johnson in the *Encyclopædia Britannica*, 1856. Johnson characterized Laud in his Life of Cheynel (1751), para. 12.

Mark'd out by dangerous Parts he meets the Shock,
And fatal Learning leads him to the Block:
Around his Tomb let Art and Genius weep,
But hear his Death, ye Blockheads, hear and sleep.
ʰThe festal Blazes, the triumphal Show,   175
The ravish'd Standard, and the captive Foe,
The Senate's Thanks, the Gazette's pompous Tale,
With Force resistless o'er the Brave prevail.
Such Bribes the rapid *Greek* o'er *Asia* whirl'd,
For such the steady *Romans* shook the World;   180
For such in distant Lands the *Britons* shine,
And stain with Blood the *Danube* or the *Rhine*;
This Pow'r has Praise, that Virtue scarce can warm,
Till Fame supplies the universal Charm.
Yet Reason frowns on War's unequal Game,   185
Where wasted Nations raise a single Name,
And mortgag'd States their Grandsires Wreaths regret
From Age to Age in everlasting Debt;
Wreaths which at last the dear-bought Right convey
To rust on Medals, or on Stones decay.   190
ⁱOn what Foundation stands the Warrior's Pride?
How just his Hopes let *Swedish Charles* decide;
A Frame of Adamant, a Soul of Fire,
No Dangers fright him, and no Labours tire;

ʰ *Ver.* 133–46.   ⁱ *Ver.* 147–67.

174 sleep] weep *Osborne 1785*   191 pride *1755*

173. *Art and Genius.* Oxford University, of which Laud was a benefactor.

175. *festal.* Johnson forgot to include this word in the *Dictionary*.

177. *Gazette's*, commonly accented on the first syllable in the eighteenth century, and so marked in the *Dictionary*.

183. *This pow'r has praise*, i.e. praise has this power, and virtue of itself can hardly arouse this power, without the allurements of fame.

191–222. The account of Charles XII of Sweden is commonly considered the greatest passage of the poem. Johnson had long been interested in Charles and had thought of writing a play about him; in a letter of 10 June 1742 he says, 'I propose to get Charles of Sweden ready for this winter'. Cf. *The Adventurer*, No. 99, para. 10. Charles, who was an ally of the Old Pretender, was a favourite of the Tories; his death in 1718 was a severe blow to Jacobitism.

Voltaire's *Histoire de Charles XII* had been published in 1732 and was well known in England; a translation appeared at once, and was published as a serial in *Read's Weekly Journal* from 29 April 1732.

O'er Love, o'er Fear, extends his wide Domain,   195
Unconquer'd Lord of Pleasure and of Pain;
No Joys to him pacific Scepters yield,
War sounds the Trump, he rushes to the Field;
Behold surrounding Kings their Pow'r combine,
And One capitulate, and One resign;   200
Peace courts his Hand, but spreads her Charms in vain;
'Think Nothing gain'd, he cries, till nought remain,
'On *Moscow*'s Walls till *Gothic* Standards fly,
'And all be Mine beneath the Polar Sky.'
The March begins in Military State,   205
And Nations on his Eye suspended wait;
Stern Famine guards the solitary Coast,
And Winter barricades the Realms of Frost;
He comes, not Want and Cold his Course delay;—
Hide, blushing Glory, hide *Pultowa*'s Day: 210
The vanquish'd Hero leaves his broken Bands,
And shews his Miseries in distant Lands;

---

195 fear,] Force, *1749* fear *1755*   199 pow'rs *1785, 1787*   201 spreads]
spread *1749*   204 be] is *1749*   208 realm *1758–82, 1825*   209 not . . .
and] nor . . . nor *1749, 1787*

---

195. *Fear*. 'Force' in the first edition was a misreading of Johnson's handwriting; his *e* and *o* are often indistinguishable, and his *a* is commonly left open. The couplet (with 'fear') is given in the *Dictionary* under 'lord'.

196. Quoted in the *Dictionary*, s.v. 'unconquered', but removed from ed. 4.

200. *One capitulate*—Frederick IV of Denmark, defeated in the campaign ended by the peace of Traventhal, 1700.

One resign—Augustus II of Poland, deposed 1704, and succeeded by Stanislas I, who was chosen by Charles.

201. Quoted in the *Dictionary*, s.v. 'peace', but removed from ed. 4.

202. Cf. Lucan, *Phars*. ii. 657: 'Nil actum credens, dum quid superesset agendum',—said of Cæsar. Translated by Rowe: 'He reckons not the past, while aught remain'd / Great to be done, or mighty to be gain'd.'

203. *Gothic*, i.e. Swedish, though commonly used in Johnson's time in the sense of Teutonic.

204. *be*, substituted for 'is' because of 'remain' in l. 202. Syntax again is the reason for the inferior 'not . . . and' instead of 'nor . . . nor' in l. 209, where the rhyme could not allow 'delays'.

205. Quoted in the *Dictionary* under 'march', but omitted in ed. 4.

210 ff. After his crushing defeat by Peter the Great at Pultowa, or Poltava, in 1709, Charles fled to Bender in Turkish territory, and remained there till 1714. He fell at the attack on Frederikshald in Norway in 1718.

Condemn'd a needy Supplicant to wait,
While Ladies interpose, and Slaves debate.
But did not Chance at length her Error mend?   215
Did no subverted Empire mark his End?
Did rival Monarchs give the fatal Wound?
Or hostile Millions press him to the Ground?
His Fall was destin'd to a barren Strand,
A petty Fortress, and a dubious Hand;   220
He left the Name, at which the World grew pale,
To point a Moral, or adorn a Tale.
   ^kAll Times their Scenes of pompous Woes afford,
From *Persia*'s Tyrant to *Bavaria*'s Lord.
In gay Hostility, and barb'rous Pride,   225
With half Mankind embattled at his Side,
Great *Xerxes* comes to seize the certain Prey,
And starves exhausted Regions in his Way;
Attendant Flatt'ry counts his Myriads o'er,
Till counted Myriads sooth his Pride no more;   230
Fresh Praise is try'd till Madness fires his Mind,
The Waves he lashes, and enchains the Wind;
New Pow'rs are claim'd, new Pow'rs are still bestow'd,
Till rude Resistance lops the spreading God;

^k *Ver*. 168-87.

214. *While ladies interpose*. Johnson was probably thinking of the part played by
Catherine, the empress of Peter the Great, in July 1711, when, to Charles's indignation,
the Russian army was enabled to escape from certain defeat at the Pruth. One of the
conditions of the treaty was that Peter should not oppose Charles's return to Sweden.

220. *a dubious hand*. Voltaire states that Charles was killed by a cannon-ball and denies
that he was shot by his aide-de-camp, Siker. On Voltaire's statement that 'ce brave
officier fut longtems désespéré de cette calomnie', Nordberg, the Swedish biographer of
Charles, has this note: 'Siker y donna lieu lui-même; car étant tombé à Stockholm en
1722 dans une violente Maladie, qui lui avoit troublé la tête, il disoit aux Médecins, aux
Chirurgiens, et à ceux qui le gardoient, que c'étoit lui qui avoit fait ce fatal coup. Il
ouvroit même ses fenêtres et le crioit au peuple qui passoit dans les rues' (*Histoire de
Charles XII* . . . traduite du Suédois de Monsieur J. A. Nordberg, 1749, iii. 359).

223-54. Johnson has depicted Wolsey in place of Juvenal's Sejanus and Charles XII
in place of Hannibal. He now retains Juvenal's Xerxes, but reinforces the lesson by
adding the contemporary example of 'the bold Bavarian'.

232. *The waves he lashes*, &c., a variation of what Juvenal had said, thus rendered by
Dryden:

     Who whipt the Winds, and made the Sea his Slave.

Boswell preferred Johnson's alteration; see *Life*, ii. 227. Cf. *The Adventurer*, No. 137,
para. 6, and Preface to the *Dictionary*, para. 85.

The daring *Greeks* deride the Martial Shew,   235
And heap their Vallies with the gaudy Foe;
Th' insulted Sea with humbler Thoughts he gains,
A single Skiff to speed his Flight remains;
Th' incumber'd Oar scarce leaves the dreaded Coast
Through purple Billows and a floating Host.   240
   The bold *Bavarian,* in a luckless Hour,
Tries the dread Summits of *Cesarean* Pow'r,
With unexpected Legions bursts away,
And sees defenceless Realms receive his Sway;
Short Sway! fair *Austria* spreads her mournful Charms,
The Queen, the Beauty, sets the World in Arms;   246
From Hill to Hill the Beacons rousing Blaze
Spreads wide the Hope of Plunder and of Praise;
The fierce *Croatian,* and the wild *Hussar,*
And all the Sons of Ravage croud the War;   250
The baffled Prince in Honour's flatt'ring Bloom
Of hasty Greatness finds the fatal Doom,
His foes Derision, and his Subjects Blame,
And steals to Death from Anguish and from Shame.
  [1]Enlarge my Life with Multitude of Days,   255
In Health, in Sickness, thus the Suppliant prays;

[1] *Ver.* 188–288.

235–6 Greek derides . . . heaps *1759*   242 Cæsarean *1785*   250 And] With *1787*

239–40. *Th' incumber'd oar,* &c. Mrs. Rose—the daughter-in-law of Johnson's friend Dr. Rose of Chiswick—told Croker that this was Johnson's favourite couplet: 'Mrs. Piozzi related to me that when Dr. Johnson one day observed that poets in general preferred some one couplet they had written to any other, she replied, that she did not suppose he had a favourite; he told her she was mistaken—he thought his best lines were "The encumber'd oar", &c. (*Life,* ed. Croker, 1831, v. 414).

241–54. Charles Albert, Elector of Bavaria, asserted his claim to the imperial crown on the death of Charles VI in 1740, and after overrunning the 'defenceless realms' of Upper Austria and Bohemia, was crowned as Charles VII in 1742; but he became a puppet in the hands of his allies and died discredited in 1745. Johnson's prose account of the war of the Austrian succession and of the part played in it by Maria Theresa, 'fair Austria', will be found in his 'Memoirs of Frederick III, King of Prussia' published in *The Literary Magazine,* 1756.

249. *Hussar,* used in Johnson's time only in the strict sense of a 'Hungarian light-horseman'. Cf. G. Rothenburg, *Notes and Queries,* ccix (August 1964), 296–8.

250. Hawkins's authority for *with* is not known.

255 ff. These lines on old age may be compared with what Johnson said about the same time in *The Rambler,* Nos. 41, 50, and 69.

Hides from himself his State, and shuns to know,
That Life protracted is protracted Woe.
Time hovers o'er, impatient to destroy,
And shuts up all the Passages of Joy: 260
In vain their Gifts the bounteous Seasons pour,
The Fruit autumnal, and the vernal Flow'r,
With listless Eyes the Dotard views the Store,
He views, and wonders that they please no more;
Now pall the tastless Meats, and joyless Wines,   265
And Luxury with Sighs her Slave resigns.
Approach, ye Minstrels, try the soothing Strain,
Diffuse the tuneful Lenitives of Pain:
No Sounds alas would touch th' impervious Ear,
Though dancing Mountains witness'd *Orpheus* near;   270
Nor Lute nor Lyre his feeble Pow'rs attend,
Nor sweeter Musick of a virtuous Friend,
But everlasting Dictates croud his Tongue,
Perversely grave, or positively wrong.
The still returning Tale, and ling'ring Jest,   275
Perplex the fawning Niece and pamper'd Guest,
While growing Hopes scarce awe the gath'ring Sneer,
And scarce a Legacy can bribe to hear;
The watchful Guests still hint the last Offence,
The Daughter's Petulance, the Son's Expence,   280
Improve his heady Rage with treach'rous Skill,
And mould his Passions till they make his Will.
    Unnumber'd Maladies his Joints invade,
Lay Siege to Life and press the dire Blockade;
But unextinguish'd Av'rice still remains,   285
And dreaded Losses aggravate his Pains;
He turns, with anxious Heart and cripled Hands,
His Bonds of Debt, and Mortgages of Lands;

---

262 Vernal *1749*   268 Diffuse *Johnson MS. correction, 1787*] And yield *1749, 1755*
270 witness'd] witness *1758–82*   271 pow'rs] pow'r *1759, 1785*   283 his joints]
each Joint *1749*

---

271. *attend*, attend to, regard. This older use is illustrated in the *Dictionary* by *The Merchant of Venice*, v. i. 103: 'The crow doth sing as sweetly as the lark When neither is attended.' This passage echoes lines from the same scene in Shakespeare.
281. *improve*, increase, augment, a use not recorded in the *Dictionary*.

Or views his Coffers with suspicious Eyes,
Unlocks his Gold, and counts it till he dies.   290
But grant, the Virtues of a temp'rate Prime
Bless with an Age exempt from Scorn or Crime;
An Age that melts with unperceiv'd Decay,
And glides in modest Innocence away;
Whose peaceful Day Benevolence endears,   295
Whose Night congratulating Conscience cheers;
The gen'ral Fav'rite as the gen'ral Friend:
Such Age there is, and who shall wish its end?
Yet ev'n on this her Load Misfortune flings,
To press the weary Minutes flagging Wings: 300
New Sorrow rises as the Day returns,
A Sister sickens, or a Daughter mourns.
Now kindred Merit fills the sable Bier,
Now lacerated Friendship claims a Tear.
Year chases Year, Decay pursues Decay,   305
Still drops some Joy from with'ring Life away;
New Forms arise, and diff'rent Views engage,
Superfluous lags the Vet'ran on the Stage,

293 with *Johnson MS. correction*, 1787] in *1749, 1755*   298 shall *Johnson MS. correction*, 1787] could *1749, 1755*

291–8. Johnson is said by Mrs. Piozzi to have had his mother in mind when writing this passage: 'So excellent was her character, and so blameless her life, that when an oppressive neighbour once endeavoured to take from her a little field she possessed, he could persuade no attorney to undertake the cause against a woman so beloved in her narrow circle: and it is this incident he alludes to in the line of his Vanity of Human Wishes, calling her

The general favourite as the general friend.

Nor could any one pay more willing homage to such a character, though she had not been related to him, than did Dr. Johnson on every occasion that offered: his disquisition on Pope's epitaph placed over Mrs. Corbet is a proof of that preference always given by him to a noiseless life over a bustling one.' (*Anecdotes*, 1786, p. 8.)

293–4. Cf. Dryden, *The State of Innocence* (1677), v. i. 349–50, 'Still quitting ground, by unperceived decay / And steal from life, and melt away.' (G. J. Kolb, *Modern Language Notes*, lxxiv (1959), 212–13.)

304. This line is quoted in the *Dictionary* under 'lacerate', with 'Here' for 'Now'.

308. *Superfluous . . . stage.* Cf. *The Rambler*, No. 207, 'The Folly of continuing too long upon the Stage'. With these words Scott concludes the farewell note at the end of *Castle Dangerous*, and they were the last that he wrote for the press: see Lockhart, *Life of Scott*, end of chap. xx. Scott declared that 'he had more pleasure in reading *London* and *The Vanity of Human Wishes* than any other poetical composition he could mention' (ibid.).

Till pitying Nature signs the last Release,
And bids afflicted Worth retire to Peace.   310
  But few there are whom Hours like these await,
Who set unclouded in the Gulphs of fate.
From *Lydia*'s monarch should the Search descend,
By *Solon* caution'd to regard his End,
In Life's last Scene what Prodigies surprise,   315
Fears of the Brave, and Follies of the Wise?
From *Marlb'rough*'s Eyes the Streams of Dotage flow,
And *Swift* expires a Driv'ler and a Show.
  ᵐThe teeming Mother, anxious for her Race,
Begs for each Birth the Fortune of a Face: 320
Yet *Vane* could tell what Ills from Beauty spring;
And *Sedley* curs'd the Form that pleas'd a King.

  ᵐ *Ver.* 289–345.

---

316 wise! *1792*

---

  313. *Lydia's monarch*, Croesus. See Herodotus, i. 30–3.
  317. Marlborough suffered two paralytic strokes in 1716 and died in 1722. Swift's closing years are described with some minuteness in the *Life of Swift*.
  321. *Vane*. In a note in the fifth edition of Boswell's *Life*, 1807, i. 172, Malone says that this line has been generally misunderstood: 'The lady mentioned . . . was not the celebrated Lady Vane, whose memoirs were given to the publick by Dr. Smollett [*Peregrine Pickle*, ch. lxxxi], but Anne Vane, who was mistress to Frederick Prince of Wales, and died in 1736, not long before Johnson settled in London. Some account of this lady was published, under the title of *The Secret History of Vanella*, 8vo. 1732. See also *Vanella in the Straw*, 4to. 1732.' For evidence of the misunderstanding see *The Gentleman's Magazine*, 1788, pp. 368, 461, and 1789, p. 403.
  Anne Vane (1705–36) was the daughter of Gilbert Vane, second Lord Barnard. After her death her notoriety was challenged by her distant connexion Frances Anne, Lady Vane (1713–88), wife of the second Viscount Vane. Though the latter was better known in 1749, it is as certain that Johnson would not thus have referred to one who was still living as it is improbable that at that time she was disposed to moralize on the ills that spring from beauty.
  322. *Sedley*. Catherine Sedley (1657–1717), only child of Sir Charles Sedley, was mistress of the Duke of York, afterwards James II, and was created by him Countess of Dorchester in 1686. (See Dorset's verses on her: 'Tell me, Dorinda, why so gay,' and: 'Proud with the spoils of royal cully . . .'.) Her father's resentment made him a supporter of the Revolution. 'I am even with King James in point of civility', he is reported to have said, 'for as he made my daughter a countess, so I have helped to make his daughter a queen', referring to Mary, the wife of William III.
  Lord Hailes told Johnson that 'he was mistaken in the instances he had given of unfortunate fair ones', and for 'Vane' proposed 'Shore' (i.e. Jane Shore) and for 'Sedley' proposed 'Valière' (i.e. Mlle de la Vallière, mistress of Louis XIV). See Boswell's *Hebrides*, 17 August 1773. Anna Seward said that 'not even Dr. Johnson himself' could tell her who was meant by Sedley. 'I knew at the time I wrote the poem', she reports

Ye Nymphs of rosy Lips and radiant Eyes,
Whom Pleasure keeps too busy to be wise,
Whom Joys with soft Varieties invite,   325
By Day the Frolick, and the Dance by Night,
Who frown with Vanity, who smile with Art,
And ask the latest Fashion of the Heart,
What Care, what Rules your heedless Charms shall save,
Each Nymph your Rival, and each Youth your Slave? 330
Against your Fame with Fondness Hate combines,
The Rival batters, and the Lover mines.
With distant Voice neglected Virtue calls,
Less heard, and less the faint Remonstrance falls;
Tir'd with Contempt, she quits the slipp'ry Reign,   335
And Pride and Prudence take her Seat in vain.
In croud at once, where none the Pass defend,
The harmless Freedom, and the private Friend.
The Guardians yield, by Force superior ply'd;
By Int'rest, Prudence; and by Flatt'ry, Pride.   340
Now Beauty falls betray'd, despis'd, distress'd,
And hissing Infamy proclaims the rest.
      [n]Where then shall Hope and Fear their Objects find?

[n] *Ver.* 346–66.

---

330 *After this line 1749 has:*

          An envious Breast with certain Mischief glows,
          And Slaves, the Maxim tells, are always Foes.

340 By . . . by] To . . . to *1787*   341 Now] Here *1749, 1787*

---

him to have said shortly before his death, 'but the history has now escaped my recollection'. This was only a weary reply to a tiresome questioner. See *The Gentleman's Magazine*, 1800, pp. 5, 131.

330. On the omission of the couplet which came after this line in the first edition, see the introductory account.

338. Quoted as '*Anon.*', in the *Dictionary*, s.v. 'private', but removed from ed. 4.

340. *By . . . by.* The authority for the change to 'To . . . to' in Hawkins's edition is not known.

343–68. Johnson's earnest religion transforms the Stoic conclusion of Juvenal's satire. In *The Idler*, No. 41, which was written at the time of his mother's death, he speaks of the insufficiency of Stoic virtue: 'The Precepts of *Epicurus*, who teaches us to endure what the Laws of the Universe make necessary, may silence but not content us. The dictates of *Zeno*, who commands us to look with indifference on external things, may dispose us to conceal our sorrow, but cannot assuage it. Real alleviation of the loss of friends, and rational tranquillity in the prospect of our own dissolution, can be received

Must dull Suspence corrupt the stagnant Mind?
Must helpless Man, in Ignorance sedate,   345
Roll darkling down the Torrent of his fate?
Must no Dislike alarm, no Wishes rise,
No Cries attempt the Mercies of the Skies?
Enquirer, cease, Petitions yet remain,
Which Heav'n may hear, nor deem Religion vain.   350
Still raise for Good the supplicating Voice,
But leave to Heav'n the Measure and the Choice,
Safe in his Pow'r, whose Eyes discern afar
The secret Ambush of a specious Pray'r.
Implore his Aid, in his Decisions rest,   355
Secure whate'er he gives, he gives the best.
Yet when the Sense of sacred Presence fires,
And strong Devotion to the Skies aspires,
Pour forth thy Fervours for a healthful Mind,
Obedient Passions, and a Will resign'd;   360
For Love, which scarce collective Man can fill;
For Patience sov'reign o'er transmuted Ill;
For Faith, that panting for a happier Seat,
Counts Death kind Nature's Signal of Retreat:

346 Roll . . . torrent] Swim . . . Current *1749*   348 attempt] invoke *1787*
352–4 choice, . . . pray'r.] Choice. . . . Pray'r. *1749*, *1755*: choice. . . . pray'r, *1782*.
357 when . . . fires] with . . . prest *1749*   358 And . . . to the skies aspires] When
. . . fills thy glowing Breast *1749*   364 Counts] Thinks *1749*

only from the promises of him in whose hands are life and death, and from the assurance of another and better state, in which all tears will be wiped from the eyes, and the whole soul shall be filled with joy. Philosophy may infuse stubbornness, but Religion only can give Patience.' Cf. *The Vision of Theodore, the Hermit of Teneriffe*, published in Dodsley's *Preceptor* in April 1748, and *The Rambler*, No. 32 (7 July 1750). Boswell says that 'were all the other excellencies of this poem annihilated, it must ever have our grateful reverence from its noble conclusion'. Macaulay, on the other hand, thought that Johnson here 'has fallen decidedly short of the sublimity of his Pagan model'.

345. See Motto to *The Rambler*, No. 105, p. 146, *post*.

346. *darkling*, said in the *Dictionary* erroneously to be 'a participle, as it seems, from *darkle*, which yet I have never found'. Strictly an adverb meaning 'in the dark', as in Shakespeare and Milton, it came to be used as an adjective in eighteenth-century poetry.

348. *attempt*. Hawkins's authority for 'invoke' is not known.

362. This line is quoted in the first three editions of the *Dictionary* under 'transmute', but not in the fourth.

364. *kind Nature's signal of retreat*. It was not always thus that Johnson looked on death: see in particular Boswell's *Life*, ii. 106.

These Goods for Man the Laws of Heav'n ordain,   365
These Goods he grants, who grants the Pow'r to gain;
With these celestial Wisdom calms the Mind,
And makes the Happiness she does not find.

368. Cf. the lines contributed by Johnson to the conclusion of Goldsmith's *Traveller* (p. 438), and *The Life of Savage*, 1744, § 167: 'It were doubtless to be wished . . . that men would secure themselves from being disappointed in their endeavours after happiness by placing it only in virtue, which is always to be obtained.'

The characteristic ending of Johnson's poem is far removed from Juvenal's closing lines:

> Nullum numen habes si sit prudentia, nos te,
> nos facimus, Fortuna, deam caeloque locamus.

They are thus rendered by Dryden:

> Fortune was never worshipp'd by the Wise;
> But, set aloft by Fools, usurps the Skies.

Johnson appears to have been more familiar with the other reading 'Nullum numen abest, si sit prudentia': see Piozzi, *Anecdotes*, p. 218, and Boswell, *Life*, iv. 180.

POEMS, 1750–1784

NEW PROLOGUE TO 'COMUS'

A New Prologue spoken by Mr Garrick, Thursday, April 5, 1750. At the Representation of Comus, for the benefit of Mrs Elizabeth Foster, Milton's Grand-Daughter, and only surviving Descendant. London: Printed for J. Payne and J. Bouquet in Pater-noster-Row. M,DCC,L. For Mrs Elizabeth Foster. Folio

Reprinted, Edinburgh, 1750. 8°.

The Gentleman's Magazine, April 1750, p. 183.

The Scots Magazine, April 1750, p. 179.

The London Magazine, May 1750, p. 231.

Elphinston, *A Collection of Poems*, 1764, p. 113.

Transcript, *c.* 1765, by Thomas Percy (Bodleian Library: Percy 87).

Pearch, *Collection of Poems*, 1768, i. 306; 1770, i. 313; 1775, iii. 234; 1783, iii. 236.

Davies, *Miscellaneous and Fugitive Pieces*, 1773, 1774, ii. 296.

A Collection and Selection of English Prologues and Epilogues, 1779, iii. 226 (wrongly ascribed to Garrick).

Poetical Works, 1785, p. 175.

Works, 1787, xi. 346.

In the Postscript which Johnson contributed to Lauder's *Essay on Milton* (1750) he tells how, in reading Newton's edition of *Paradise Lost*, then recently published, he first heard of Mrs. Foster:

'. . . one passage, at the conclusion of the life of MILTON, excited in me too much pity and indignation to be suppressed in silence.

"*Deborah*, MILTON's youngest daughter," says the editor, "was married to Mr. *Abraham Clarke*, a weaver in *Spittle-fields*, and died in *August* 1727, in the 76th year of her age. She had ten children. *Elizabeth*, the youngest, was married to Mr. *Thomas Foster*, a weaver in *Spittle-fields*, and had seven children, who are all dead; and she herself is aged about *sixty*, and *weak* and *infirm*. She seemeth to be a *good plain sensible woman*...; in all probability MILTON's whole family will be *extinct* with her, and he can *live* only in his writings. And *such is the caprice of fortune*, this *grand-daughter* of a MAN, who will be an everlasting glory to the nation, has now for *some years*, with her husband, kept a *little chandler's or grocer's shop, for their subsistence*, lately at the lower *Holloway*, in the road between *Highgate* and *London*, and at present in *Cock Lane*, not far from *Shoreditch Church*."

That this relation is true, cannot be questioned:—but, surely, the honour of letters, the dignity of sacred poetry, the spirit of the *English* nation, and the glory of human nature, require—that it should be true no longer. In an age, in which statues are erected to the honour of this great writer, in which his effigy has been diffused on medals, and his work propagated by translations, and illustrated by commentaries; in an age, which, amidst all its vices, and all its follies, has not become infamous for want of charity: it may be, surely, allowed to hope, that the living remains of MILTON will be no longer suffered to languish in distress. It is yet in the power of a great people, to reward the poet whose name they boast, and from their alliance to whose genius, they claim some kind of superiority to every other nation of the earth; that poet, whose works may possibly be read when every other monument of *British* greatness shall be obliterated; to reward him—not with pictures, or with medals, which, if he sees, he sees with contempt, but—with tokens of gratitude, which he, perhaps, may even now consider as not unworthy the regard of an immortal spirit. And, surely, to those, who refuse their names to no other scheme of expence, it will not be unwelcome, that a SUBSCRIPTION is proposed, for relieving, in the languor of age, the pains of disease, and the contempt of poverty, the grand-daughter of the author of PARADISE LOST.'

The Postscript was followed by a list of the booksellers to whom subscriptions might be paid. All this was reprinted in *The Gentleman's Magazine* for December 1749, p. 563.

Johnson then persuaded Garrick to give a performance of *Comus* for the benefit of Mrs. Foster (*Gentleman's Magazine*, 1750, p. 152), and wrote the Prologue for the occasion. He also drew attention to the performance in a letter to *The General Advertiser* of 4 April 1750 (Boswell, *Life*, i. 227):

'Sir,

That a certain Degree of Reputation is acquired merely by approving the Works of Genius, and testifying a Regard to the Memory of the Authours, is a Truth too evident to be denied; and therefore to ensure a Participation of Fame with a celebrated Poet, many who would perhaps have contributed to starve him when alive, have heaped expensive Pageants upon his Grave.

It must indeed be confess'd, that this Method of becoming known to Posterity, with Honour, is peculiar to the Great, or at least to the Wealthy; but an Opportunity now offers for almost every Individual to secure the Praise of paying a just Regard to the illustrious Dead, united with the Pleasure of doing good to the Living. To assist industrious Indigence struggling with Distress, and debilitated by Age, is a Display of Virtue, and an Acquisition of Happiness and Honour.

Whosoever then would be thought capable of Pleasure in reading the Works of our incomparable MILTON, and not so destitute of Gratitude as to refuse to lay out a Trifle in a rational and elegant Entertainment for the Benefit of his living Remains, for the Exercise of their own Virtue, the Increase of their Reputation, and the pleasing Consciousness of doing good, should appear at Drury-Lane Theatre To-morrow, April 5, when Comus will be perform'd for the Benefit of Mrs. Elizabeth Foster, Grand-daughter to the Author, and the only surviving Branch of his Family.

N.B. There will be a new Prologue on the Occasion written by the Author of Irene, and spoken by Mr. Garrick . . .'

The performance was originally arranged for Wednesday, 4 April, but was postponed to the following night, when the theatre was expected to be fuller. Johnson wrote thus of it in his *Life of Milton*:

'She had so little acquaintance with diversion or gaiety, that she did not know what was intended when a benefit was offered her. The profits of the night were only one hundred and thirty pounds, though Dr. Newton brought a large contribution; and twenty pounds were given by Tonson, a man who is to be praised as often as he is named. . . . This was the greatest benefaction that *Paradise Lost* ever procured the author's descendents; and to this he who has now attempted to relate his Life, had the honour of contributing a Prologue.'

Mrs. Foster died 9 May 1754, at Islington, in her sixty-sixth year (*The Public Advertiser*, 15 May 1754; *Gentleman's Magazine*, 1754, p. 243).

Text from the first edition.

A NEW
PROLOGUE

SPOKEN BY

Mr GARRICK,

Thursday, *April* 5, 1750.

AT THE

REPRESENTATION of COMUS,

FOR THE BENEFIT OF

Mrs ELIZABETH FOSTER,

MILTON's

Grand-Daughter, and only surviving Descendant.

LONDON:

Printed for J. PAYNE and J. BOUQUET in Pater-noster-Row.
M,DCC,L.

For Mrs ELIZABETH FOSTER.

A NEW

PROLOGUE

SPOKEN AT THE

Representation of COMUS.

YE patriot Crouds, who burn for *England*'s Fame,
　　Ye Nymphs, whose Bosoms beat at MILTON's Name,
Whose gen'rous Zeal, unbought by flatt'ring Rhimes,
Shames the mean Pensions of *Augustan* Times;
Immortal Patrons of succeeding Days,　　　　　　　　5
Attend this Prelude of perpetual Praise!
Let Wit, condemn'd the feeble War to wage
With close Malevolence, or public Rage;
Let Study, worn with Virtue's fruitless Lore,
Behold this Theatre, and grieve no more.　　　　　　10
This Night, distinguish'd by your Smile, shall tell,
That never BRITON can in vain excel;
The slighted Arts Futurity shall trust,
And rising Ages hasten to be just.

　At length our mighty Bard's victorious Lays　　　15
Fill the loud Voice of universal Praise,
And baffled Spite, with hopeless Anguish dumb,
Yields to Renown the Centuries to come.
With ardent Haste, each Candidate of Fame
Ambitious catches at his tow'ring Name:　　　　　　20
He sees, and pitying sees, vain Wealth bestow
Those pageant Honours which he scorn'd below:
While Crowds aloft the laureat Bust behold,
Or trace his Form on circulating Gold,

11 Smile] smiles *1785, 1787*　　　12 Briton] Britain *1785, 1787*　　　23 Bust] Dust
first edition, corrected in MS. in most copies　　　24 on] in *Percy*

21–4. Compare the passage on 'pictures' and 'medals' in the Postscript quoted
on p. 134.
Bust. See *The Vanity of Human Wishes*, l. 162, and note.
circulating gold. In addition to employing Rysbrack to erect the monument in
Westminster Abbey, Benson engaged John Sigismund Tanner to engrave a medal
commemorating the erection of the monument. See *Medallic Illustrations of the
History of Great Britain*, 1911, Plate CLIV.

Unknown, unheeded, long his Offspring lay,   25
And Want hung threat'ning o'er her slow Decay.
What tho' she shine with no MILTONIAN Fire,
No fav'ring Muse her morning Dreams inspire;
Yet softer Claims the melting Heart engage,
Her Youth laborious, and her blameless Age: 30
Hers the mild Merits of domestic Life,
The patient Suff'rer, and the faithful Wife.
Thus grac'd with humble Virtue's native Charms
Her Grandsire leaves her in *Britannia*'s Arms,
Secure with Peace, with Competence, to dwell,   35
While tutelary Nations guard her Cell.
Yours is the Charge, ye Fair, ye Wise, ye Brave!
'Tis yours to crown Desert—beyond the Grave!

TRANSLATIONS OF MOTTOES AND QUOTATIONS IN 'THE RAMBLER'

The mottoes in *The Rambler*, as in *The Tatler* and *The Spectator*, were given without translation in the original issues. Steele had begun No. 370 of *The Spectator* (5 May 1712) by remarking that:

'Many of my fair Readers, as well as very gay and well-received Persons of the other Sex, are extremely perplexed at the *Latin* Sentences at the Head of my Speculations; I do not know whether I ought not to indulge them with Translations of each of them.'

But he and Addison continued to provide no assistance in the sheets that were served up at tea-tables and in coffee-houses. Assistance had to be sought elsewhere. A little book had just appeared called *The Motto's of the Five Volumes of Tatlers, and the Two Volumes of the Spectator, Translated into English* (April 1712); and it was to be supplemented as new volumes of the collected numbers of *The Spectator* were published. It was reissued in 1735 as *The Mottoes of the Spectators, Tatlers and Guardians*, and in 1737 with the mottoes of *The Freeholder* added.

Johnson thus conformed to the established custom in leaving his mottoes untranslated in the original folio issues; but when *The Rambler* was reprinted in duodecimo (vols. i–iv, January 1752; vols. v and vi, July 1752) each volume was furnished with translations of its mottoes in six additional pages; and similarly six pages of translations were prefixed to each of the two volumes of the 1753 collection of the folio numbers. The translations were first printed immediately below the mottoes and quotations in the Dublin reprint of 1752; of the editions with which Johnson was directly concerned, the first to include them in this manner was the edition of 1756.[1]

It is questionable whether Johnson would not have been content to leave the mottoes untranslated had not James Elphinston translated them in the edition which he brought out at Edinburgh. 'With a laudable zeal', says Boswell, 'at once for the improvement of his countrymen, and the reputation of his friend, he suggested and took charge of an edition of these essays at Edinburgh, which followed progressively the London publication.' Elphinston's rare edition has many points of interest. It is the only edition which reproduces the text of *The Rambler* as it first appeared in the folio numbers, and though its occasional variants were once thought to imply revision by Johnson those have since been shown to derive from variant states of the folios;[2] and it was the first edition to be published in volumes: Nos. 1–158 being collected in six very small octavos by November 1751 while they were still uncollected by the London publishers. But the chief interest attaches to the 'Version of the Mottoes' which is appended to each of the six volumes, and of which Elphinston was the sole author. Johnson read these versions and saw where they could be bettered; and before Elphinston brought out the last two of his eight volumes (July 1752) the last volumes of Johnson's own revised edition had appeared with Johnson's authorized translations of all the mottoes and quotations in the 208 numbers. In his last two volumes Elphinston adopted the translations in the London edition.

Johnson's list, unlike Elphinston's, is composite. He selects renderings from well-known authors, relies on some of his acquaintances for others, and himself provides the remainder. The evidence for his authorship, apart from style, is the absence of attribution to any other writer. Johnson was always punctilious in acknowledging assistance, and what he leaves unassigned is to be accepted as his own. He adopted thirty-six of Elphinston's translations, introducing new readings in some of them.[3] The Rev. Francis Lewis, of Chiswick—of whom all that Boswell could learn was that 'he lived in London and hung loose upon society'—supplied thirty-four. Two were by Anna Williams (Nos. 75 and 172). Two others (Nos. 150 and 166) were by 'E. C.'—initials which are expanded in the edition of 1756, not into Elizabeth Carter but, unexpectedly, into 'Edw. Cave'. A large number are from Francis's *Horace* and from Dryden's *Virgil* or *Juvenal*. Of about two hundred and sixty verse renderings Johnson himself supplied over sixty.

The translations for Nos. 31–57 are reprinted in *The Gentleman's Magazine* for October 1752, pp. 468–70 (in continuation of Nos. 1–30 by Elphinston, September 1750, pp. 406–9), and begin with the following note:

---

[1] The habit of inserting the translation immediately under the Latin or Greek in reprints of the periodical essays had begun in the forties, e.g. *The Freeholder*, 1744. But in original issues the Greek or Latin continued to be given without translation, e.g. *The Adventurer*, 1752–4, and *The Connoisseur*, 1754–6. The quotations in *The Idler* have remained untranslated.

[2] C. B. Bradford, 'The Edinburgh Ramblers', *Modern Language Review*, xxiv (1939), 241–4, rebutted by Professor A. Strauss, *The Rambler* (*Works*, Yale ed., iii (1969), p. xxxiv).   [3] The most serious changes are in the motto of No. 130. See p. 442.

'The translations signed *J.E.* were previously published in the *Edinburgh* edition; those signed *J.* are by the author, and those *F. Lewis*, by the Rev. *Francis Lewis* of *Chiswick*, and the others are from the books cited.'

The translations 'signed J.' correspond to those which are unsigned in the duodecimo and folio editions of 1752 and 1753. Further confirmation that the unsigned translations in these editions are by Johnson is provided by a note written by Thomas Percy about 1764 in his copy of the 1756 edition: 'Those without any annexed name by the Author himself' (Bodleian: Percy, 77–80).

The reprint in *The Gentleman's Magazine* for October 1752 concludes with Johnson's new translation of the mottoes to Nos. 7 and 12, and with the wish that 'he would oblige the world with more of his poetical compositions'. The former, from Boethius, was singled out for quotation by Boswell, as showing how well Johnson would have executed a translation of this philosophical poet (*Life*, i. 139).

Johnson told Boswell that he intended to add to his two imitations of Juvenal's satires, 'for he had them all in his head' (*Life*, i. 193). His translations of the mottoes preserve a few fragments, and fewer than might have been expected. He gives Dryden's rendering oftener than his own.

Many of the translations are only single lines, and some might lose their point if printed without the original Latin or Greek, but all have a right to be brought together and included, among his poetical works.

NUMB. 6. SATURDAY, APRIL 7, 1750

Ni vitiis pejora fovens
  Proprium deserat ortum.   [BOETHIUS, III. vi.]

  UNLESS the soul, to vice a thrall,
  Desert her own original.[1]

NUMB. 7. TUESDAY, APRIL 10, 1750

O qui perpetuâ mundum ratione gubernas,
Terrarum cœlique sator!——
Disjice terrenæ nebulas & pondera molis,
Atque tuo splendore mica! Tu namque serenum,
Tu requies tranquilla piis. Te cernere, finis,
Principium, vector, dux, semita, terminus, idem.   BOETHIUS [III. ix].

  O THOU whose pow'r o'er moving worlds presides,
  Whose voice created, and whose wisdom guides,
  On darkling man in pure effulgence shine,
  And chear the clouded mind with light divine.

  [1] Cf. Johnson's translation from Boethius, *post*, p. 173.

'Tis thine alone to calm the pious breast   5
With silent confidence and holy rest:
From thee, great God, we spring, to thee we tend,
Path, motive, guide, original, and end.

Numb. 8. Saturday, April 14, 1750

——*Media inter prælia semper*
Sideribus, cœlique plagis, superisque vacavi.   [LUCAN, x. 185–6.]

AMID the storms of war, with curious eyes
I trace the planets and survey the skies.

Numb. 10. Saturday, April 21, 1750

Posthabui tamen illorum mea seria ludo.   VIRG. [*Ecl.* vii. 17].

FOR trifling sports I quitted grave affairs.

Numb. 12. Saturday, April 28, 1750

——*Miserum parvâ stipe focilat, ut pudibundos*
Exercere sales inter convivia possit.——
————*Tu mitis, & acri*
Asperitate carens, positoque per omnia fastu,
Inter ut æquales unus numeraris amicos,
Obsequiumque doces, & amorem quæris amando.
                                    LUCANUS, *ad* Pisonem [126–132].[1]

UNLIKE the ribald, whose licentious jest
Pollutes his banquet and insults his guest;
From wealth and grandeur easy to descend,
Thou joy'st to lose the master in the friend:
We round thy board the cheerful menials see,   5
Gay with the smile of bland equality;
No social care the gracious lord disdains;
Love prompts to love, and rev'rence rev'rence gains.

---

[1] See Baehrens, *Poetae Latini Minores*, 1879, i. 230.

NUMB. 17. TUESDAY, MAY 15, 1750

——*Ridetque sui ludibria trunci.* [LUCAN, ix. 14.]

AND soaring mocks the broken frame below.

NUMB. 21. TUESDAY, MAY 29, 1750

Terra salutiferas herbas, eademque nocentes,
Nutrit; & urticæ proxima sæpe rosa est.
OVID [*Rem. Amor.* 45].

OUR bane and physic the same earth bestows,
And near the noisome nettle blooms the rose.

NUMB. 32. SATURDAY, JULY 7, 1750

Leniter ex merito quicquid patiare ferendum est. [OVID, *Her.* v. 7.]

LET pain deserv'd without complaint be borne.

NUMB. 33. TUESDAY, JULY 10, 1750

Quod caret alternâ Requie durabile non est. OVID [*Her.* iv. 89].

ALTERNATE rest and labour long endure.

NUMB. 39. TUESDAY, JULY 31, 1750

Infelix—nulli bene nupta marito. AUSONIUS [*Epit. Heroum* xxx].

UNBLEST, still doom'd to wed with misery.

NUMB. 45. TUESDAY, AUGUST 21, 1750

Ἥπερ μεγίστη γίγνεται σωτηρία,
Ὅταν γυνὴ πρὸς ἄνδρα μὴ διχοστατῇ,
Νῦν δ' ἐχθρὰ πάντα. EURIPIDES [*Medea* 14].

THIS is the chief felicity of life,
That concord smile on the connubial bed;
But now 'tis hatred all.——

Numb. 46. Saturday, August 25, 1750

——*Genus, et proavos, et quæ non fecimus ipsi,*
Vix ea nostra voco.   Ovid [*Met.* xiii. 140–1].

Nought from my birth or ancestors I claim;
All is my own, my honour and my shame.

Numb. 48. Saturday, September 1, 1750

——*Projecere animam! quam vellent æthere in alto*
Nunc & pauperiem, & duros tolerare labores!
[Virg. *Aen.* vi. 436–7.]

For healthful indigence in vain they pray,
In quest of wealth who throw their lives away.

Numb. 54. Saturday, September 22, 1750

Tu-ne etiam moreris? Ah! quid me linquis, Erasme,
Ante meus quam sit conciliatus amor?
J. C. Scaliger [*Epit. in Laud. Erasmi*].

Art thou too fall'n? ere anger could subside
And love return, has great *Erasmus* died?

Numb. 65. Tuesday, October 30, 1750

————*Garrit anilis*
Ex re fabellas.———— Hor. [*Sat.* ii. vi. 77].

The chearful sage, when solemn dictates fail,
Conceals the moral council[1] in a tale.

—χείμαρροι ποταμοὶ κατ᾽ ὄρεσφι ῥέοντες
Ἐς μισγάγκειαν συμβάλλετον ὄβριμον ὕδωρ,
Τῶνδε τέ τηλόσε δοῦπον ἐν οὔρεσιν ἔκλυε ποιμήν.
[Hom. *Il.* iv. 452–5.]

Work'd into sudden rage by wintry show'rs,
Down the steep hill the roaring torrent pours;
The mountain shepherd hears the distant noise.

---

[1] counsel 1756.

NUMB. 67. TUESDAY, NOVEMBER 6, 1750

Αἱ δ' ἐλπίδες βόσκουσι φυγάδας, ὡς λόγος
Καλῶς βλέπουσιν ὄμμασι, μέλλουσι δέ.
EURIP. [*Phoen.* 396–7].[1]

EXILES, the proverb says, subsist on hope.
Delusive hope[2] still points to distant good,
To good that mocks approach.

NUMB. 71. TUESDAY, NOVEMBER 20, 1750

Τὸ ῥόδον ἀκμάζει βαιὸν χρόνον. ἢν δὲ παρέλθῃ,
Ζητῶν εὑρήσεις οὐ ῥόδον, ἀλλὰ βάτον.   [*Anthol.* xi. 53.][3]

SOON fades the rose; once past the fragrant hour,
The loiterer finds a bramble for a flow'r.

NUMB. 81. TUESDAY, DECEMBER 25, 1750

Discite Justitiam moniti—— VIRG. [*Aen.* vi. 620].

HEAR, and be just.[4]

NUMB. 82. SATURDAY, DECEMBER 29, 1750

Omnia Castor *emit, sic fiet ut omnia vendat.* MART. [VII. xcvii].

WHO buys without discretion, buys to sell.

NUMB. 83. TUESDAY, JANUARY 1, 1751

Nisi utile est quod facias stulta est gloria. PHAEDRUS [III. xvii. 12].

ALL useless science is an empty boast.

---

[1] Substituted in the duodecimo edition, 1752, for: Ἔλπις καὶ σὺ τύχη μέγα χαίρετε. *Epigr. vetus* [*Greek Anthol.* ix. 49].

[2] Cf. *The Rambler*, No. 2, para. 8: 'The Understanding of a Man, naturally sanguine, may, indeed, be easily vitiated by too luxurious an Indulgence of the Pleasures of Hope ...' (folio ed.), 'On the Death of Levet', l. 1, *post*, p. 233, and *Vanity of Human Wishes*, 9–10, *ante*, p. 116.

[3] Translated by Johnson into Latin also: see his 'Translations from the Greek Anthology', *post*, p. 256.   [4] Cf. *Adventurer* 14, *post*, p. 156.

NUMB. 85. TUESDAY, JANUARY 8, 1751

Otia si tollas periere Cupidinis *arcus*
Contemptæque jacent, et sine luce faces.
OVID [*Rem. Amor.* 139–40].

AT busy hearts in vain love's arrows fly;
Dim, scorn'd, and impotent, his torches lie.

NUMB. 89. TUESDAY, JANUARY 22, 1751

Dulce est disipere in Loco. HOR. [*Od.* IV. xii. 28].

WISDOM at proper times is well forgot.

NUMB. 90. SATURDAY, JANUARY 26, 1751

In tenui labor. VIRG. [*Georg.* iv. 6].

WHAT toil in slender things!

NUMB. 93. TUESDAY, FEBRUARY 5, 1751

—— *Experiar quid concedatur in illos*
Quorum Flaminiâ tegitur cinis atque Latinâ. JUV. [i. 170–1].

MORE safely truth to urge her claim presumes,
On names now found alone on books and tombs.

NUMB. 96. SATURDAY, FEBRUARY 16, 1751

Quod si Platonis *musa personat verum,*
Quod quisque discit, immemor recordatur. BOETHIUS [III. xi. 15].

TRUTH in platonic ornaments bedeck'd,
Inforc'd we love, unheeding recollect.

NUMB. 104. SATURDAY, MARCH 16, 1751

——*Nihil est quod credere de se*
Non possit—— JUV. [iv. 70–1].

NONE e'er rejects hyperbolies of praise.

NUMB. 105. TUESDAY, MARCH 19, 1751

——*Animorum*
Impulsu, et cæcâ magnâque cupidine ducti. Juv. [x. 350–1].

VAIN man runs headlong, to caprice resign'd;
Impelled by passion, and with folly blind.[1]

NUMB. 106. SATURDAY, MARCH 23, 1751

——*Non unquam dedit*
Documenta fors majora, quam fragili loco
Starent superbi.—— [SENECA, *Troad.* 4–6.]

INSULTING chance ne'er call'd with louder voice,
On swelling mortals to be proud no more.

NUMB. 111. TUESDAY, APRIL 9, 1751

Φρονεῖν γὰρ οἱ ταχεῖς, οὐκ ἀσφαλεῖς.
SOPHOC. [*O. T.* 617].

DISASTER always waits an[2] early wit.

NUMB. 117. TUESDAY, APRIL 30, 1751

Quàm juvat immites ventos audire cubantem—
Aut, gelidas hybernus aquas cùm fuderit auster,
Securum somnos, imbre juvante, sequi! [TIBUL. I. i. 45–8.]

HOW sweet in sleep to pass the careless hours,
Lull'd by the beating winds and dashing show'rs!

NUMB. 122. SATURDAY, MAY 18, 1751

Nescio qua natale solum dulcedine cunctos
Ducit. OVID [*Pont.* I. iii. 35].

BY secret charms our native land attracts.

---

[1] Not from *The Vanity of Human Wishes*; see ll. 345–6.
[2] Misprinted 'on' by Hawkins, &c.

NUMB. 127. TUESDAY, JUNE 4, 1751

Cœpisti melius quàm desinis: ultima primis
    Cedunt: dissimiles hic vir, et ille puer.   OVID [*Her.* ix. 23–4].

SUCCEEDING years thy early fame destroy;
Thou, who began'st a man, wilt end a boy.

NUMB. 128. SATURDAY, JUNE 8, 1751

Αἰὼν δ' ἀσφαλὴς
Οὐκ ἐγένετ', οὔτ' Αἰακίδᾳ παρὰ Πηλεῖ,
Οὔτε πὰρ' ἀντιθέῳ
Κάδμῳ. λέγονταί γε μὰν βροτῶν
"Ολβον ὑπέρτατον οἳ
Σχεῖν.   PIND. [*Pyth.* iii. 153–8].

FOR not the brave, or wise, or great,
E'er yet had happiness compleat;
Nor *Peleus*, grandson of the sky,
    Nor *Cadmus*, scap'd the shafts of pain,
Though favour'd by the pow'rs on high,
    With ev'ry bliss that man can gain.

NUMB. 129. TUESDAY, JUNE 11, 1751

——*Nunc, o nunc, Dædale, dixit,*
    Materiam, qua sis ingeniosus, habes.
Possidet en terras, et possidet æquora Minos:
    Nec tellus nostræ, nec patet unda fugæ.
Restat iter cœlo: cœlo tentabimus ire.
    Da veniam cœpto, Jupiter alte, meo.
            OVID [*Ars Am.* ii. 33–8].

NOW *Dædalus*, behold, by fate assign'd,
A task proportion'd to thy mighty mind!
Unconquer'd bars on earth and sea withstand;
Thine, *Minos*, is the main, and thine the land.
The skies are open—let us try the skies:
Forgive, great *Jove*, the daring enterprize.

NUMB. 132. SATURDAY, JUNE 22, 1751

—— *Dociles imitandis*
Turpibus ac pravis omnes sumus.—— JUV. [xiv. 40–1].

THE minds of mortals, in perverseness strong,
Imbibes with dire docility the wrong.

NUMB. 135. TUESDAY, JULY 2, 1751

Cælum non animum mutant. HOR. [*Ep.* I. xi. 27].

PLACE may be chang'd; but who can change his mind?

NUMB. 138. SATURDAY, JULY 13, 1751

——*tecum libeat Mihi sordida rura*
Atque humiles habitare casas, et figere cervos.
VIRG. [*Ecl.* ii. 28–9].

WITH me retire and leave the pomp of courts
For humble cottages and rural sports.

NUMB. 139. TUESDAY, JULY 16, 1751

—— *Sit quod vis simplex duntaxat et unum.* HOR. [*Ars Poet.* 23].

LET ev'ry piece be simple and be one.

NUMB. 140. SATURDAY, JULY 20, 1751

——*Quis tam* Lucili *fautor inepte est*
Ut non hoc fateatur? HOR. [*Sat.* I. x. 2–3].

WHAT doating bigot to his faults so blind,
As not to grant me this, can *Milton* find?

NUMB. 141. TUESDAY, JULY 23, 1751

Hilarisque, tamen cum pondere, virtus. STAT. [*Silv.* II. iii. 65].

GREATNESS with ease, and gay severity.

NUMB. 143. TUESDAY, JULY 30, 1751

Imperet bellante prior, jacentem
  Lenis in hostem. HOR. [*Car. Sec.* 51].

LET *Cæsar* spread his conquests far,
Less pleas'd to triumph than to spare.

NUMB. 153. TUESDAY, SEPTEMBER 3, 1751

Turba Remi sequitur fortunam, ut semper, et odit
Damnatos.   JUV. [x. 73].

THE fickle crowd with fortune comes and goes;
Wealth still finds followers, and misfortune foes.[1]

NUMB. 156. SATURDAY, SEPTEMBER 14, 1751

Nunquam aliud natura, aliud sapientia dicit. JUV. [xiv. 321].

FOR wisdom ever echoes nature's voice.

NUMB. 160. SATURDAY, SEPTEMBER 28, 1751

——*Inter se convenit ursis.* JUV. [xv. 164].

BEASTS of each kind their fellows spare;
Bear lives in amity with bear.

NUMB. 161. TUESDAY, OCTOBER 1, 1751

Οἴη γὰρ φύλλων γενεή, τοίηδε καὶ Ἀνδρῶν.
                              HOM. [*Il.* vi. 146].

FRAIL as the leaves that quiver on the sprays,
Like them man flourishes, like them decays.

Quantulacunque estis, vos ego magna voco.
                [OVID, *Amor.* III. xv. 14.]

HOW small to others, but how great to me.

——Ὃς ὑπέρτατα δώματα ναίει. [HESIOD, *Op.* 8.]

THIS habitant th' aerial regions boast.

---

[1] Not from *The Vanity of Human Wishes*; see l. 79.

Numb. 164. Saturday, October 12, 1751

———*Vitium, Gaure, Catonis habes.*   Mart. [ii. lxxxix. 2].

Gaurus, pretends to *Cato*'s fame;
And proves, by *Cato*'s vice, his claim.

Numb. 168. Saturday, October 26, 1751

———*Decipit*
Frons prima multos, rara mens intelligit
Quod interiore condidit cura angulo.
                         Phaedrus [iv. ii. 5–7].

The tinsel glitter, and the specious mein,
Delude the most; few pry behind the scene.

———*Si robora sacra ferirent,*
In sua credebant redituras membra secures.   [Lucan, iii. 430–1.]

None dares with impious steel the grove to rend,
Lest on himself the destin'd stroke descend.

Numb. 169. Tuesday, October 29, 1751

Thebais, multa cruciata lima,
Tentat, audaci fide, Mantuanæ
          Gaudia famæ.   [Statius, *Silv.* iv. vii. 26–8.]

Polish'd with endless toil, my lays
At length aspire to *Mantuan* praise.

Numb. 170. Saturday, November 2, 1751

Confiteor; si quid prodest delicta fateri.   Ovid [*Amor.* ii. iv. 3].

I grant the charge; forgive the fault confess'd.

Numb. 171. Tuesday, November 5, 1751

Tædet cœli convexa tueri.   Virg. [*Aen.* iv. 451].

Dark is the sun, and loathsome is the day.

NUMB. 173. TUESDAY, NOVEMBER 12, 1751

Quo Virtus, quo ferat Error. HOR. [*Ars. Poet.* 308].

NOW say, where virtue stops and vice begins?

NUMB. 176. SATURDAY, NOVEMBER 23, 1751

—— *Naso suspendere adunco.* HOR. [*Sat.* I. vi. 5].

ON me you turn the nose.——

NUMB. 178. SATURDAY, NOVEMBER 30, 1751

Pars Sanitatis velle sanari fuit. SENECA [*Hippolytus*, 248].

TO yield to remedies is half the cure.

NUMB. 180. SATURDAY, DECEMBER 7, 1751

Ταῦτ' εἰδὼς σοφὸς ἴσθι, μάτην δ' Ἐπίκουρον ἔασον
Ποῦ τὸ κενὸν ζητεῖν, καὶ τίνες αἱ μονάδες.
AUTOMEDON [*Anthol.* xi. 50].[1]

ON life, on morals, be thy thoughts employ'd;
Leave to the schools their atoms and their void.

NUMB. 182. SATURDAY, DECEMBER 14, 1751

——*Dives qui fieri vult,*
Et cito vult fieri. JUV. [xiv. 176–7].

THE lust of wealth can never bear delay.

NUMB. 183. TUESDAY, DECEMBER 17, 1751

Nulla fides regni sociis, omnisque Potestas
Impatiens consortis erat. LUCAN [i. 92–3].

No faith of partnership dominion owns;
Still discord hovers o'er divided thrones.[2]

---

[1] For Johnson's Latin translation of the whole epigram, see 'Translations from the Greek Anthology', *post*, p. 255.
[2] Cf. *Adventurer* 45, *post*, p. 159.

Numb. 188. Saturday, January 4, 1752

——*Si te colo*, Sexte, *non amabo*.   Mart. [II. lv. 3].

The more I honour thee, the less I love.

Numb. 199. Tuesday, February 11, 1752

> *Decolor, obscurus, vilis, non ille repexam*
> *Cesariem Regum, nec candida virginis ornat*
> *Colla, nec insigni splendet per cingula morsu;*
> *Sed nova si nigri videas miracula Saxi,*
> *Tunc superat pulchros cultus, & quicquid Eois*
> *Indus Littoribus rubra scrutatur in alga.*
> > Claudianus [xlviii. 10–15].

Obscure, unpriz'd, and dark, the magnet lies,
Nor lures the search of avaricious eyes,
Nor binds the neck, nor sparkles in the hair,
Nor dignifies the great, nor decks the fair.
But search the wonders of the dusky stone,
And own all glories of the mine outdone,
Each grace of form, each ornament of state,
That decks the fair, or dignifies the great.[1]

Numb. 208. Saturday, March 14, 1752

> ‘Ηράκλειτος ἐγώ· τί με ὦ κάτω ἕλκετ' ἄμουσοι;
> Οὐχ ὑμῖν ἐπόνουν, τοῖς δέ μ' ἐπισταμένοις.
> Εἷς ἐμοὶ ἄνθρωπος τρισμύριοι· οἱ δ' ἀνάριθμοι
> Οὐδείς· ταῦτ' αὐδῶ καὶ παρὰ Περσεφόνῃ.
> > Diog. Laert. [IX. i. 16].

Be gone ye blockheads, *Heraclitus* cries,
And leave my labours to the learn'd and wise,
By wit, by knowledge, studious to be read,
I scorn the multitude, alive and dead.[2]

> Αὐτῶν ἐκ μακάρων ἀντάξιος εἴη ἀμοιβή.
> > [Dionysius, *Periegesis*, 1186.]

Celestial pow'rs! that piety regard,
From you my labours wait their last reward.

---

[1] Added in the fourth edition, 1756.
[2] Added in the fourth edition, 1756. Translated into Latin, *post*, p. 242.

THE ANT

Anna Williams, *Miscellanies in Prose and Verse*, 1766, p. 1.
The Monthly Review, June 1766, p. 265.
Works, 1787, xi. 372.
Works, ed. Murphy, 1792, i. 157.

'The Ant' is the first piece in Miss Williams's *Miscellanies*, which Johnson helped to collect and see through the press. Hawkins printed a slightly different version 'from the original in Dr. Johnson's own handwriting'. Boswell says 'I have a copy in his own handwriting' (*Life*, ii. 25), but does not quote it, and we do not know whether it was the copy which Hawkins used or that which had been used for the *Miscellanies*, or neither. Lot 3162 in the Boswell sale at Messrs. Sotheby's, 24 March 1825, was described as 'A Pocket Book, *date in the first leaf*, *April* 14, 1752; containing an Index apparently to a Common Place Book. In the first leaf are the verses paraphrased from Proverbs, entitled "The Ant" *printed in Mrs Williams' Miscellanies*, and which have been said not to be Johnson's; the corrections in this first Sketch prove the fact that they were his. There are other Memoranda and Resolves in the Book.' It was bought by Thorpe for £1. 3s. but has not been traced.

The version in the *Miscellanies* must be taken to have been authorized by Johnson, and was the only one printed during his lifetime. It is here adopted. Hawkins's version has hitherto been followed in collected editions.

Proposals for the *Miscellanies* had been issued as early as September 1750 (see *The Gentleman's Magazine*, 1750, p. 432), and had been written or revised by Johnson; according to William Strahan's printing ledgers the proposals were issued 'at different times'. If the description of the lost Pocket Book is correct. 'The Ant' was written soon after the completion of *The Rambler*.

In the Appendix on Poetic Diction to his Preface to *Lyrical Ballads* (1802), Wordsworth cited this slight production to illustrate the 'extravagant and absurd' features of *poetic diction*.

THE ANT

From PROVERBS, *chap*. vi. *ver.* 6

TURN on the prudent Ant, thy heedful eyes,
  Observe her labours, Sluggard, and be wise.
No stern command, no monitory voice
Prescribes her duties, or directs her choice,
Yet timely provident, she hastes away   5
To snatch the blessings of the plenteous day;

Title. vii. *1766 (misprint)*; paraphrase of Proverbs, Chap. VI. Verses 6, 7, 8, 9, 10, 11.
'Go to the Ant thou Sluggard'. *1787* &c.

When fruitful summer loads the teeming plain,
She gleans the harvest, and she stores the grain.
  How long shall sloth usurp thy useless hours,
Dissolve thy vigour, and enchain thy powers?   10
While artful shades thy downy couch enclose,
And soft solicitation courts repose,
Amidst the drousy charms of dull delight,
Year chases year, with unremitted flight,
Till want, now following fraudulent and slow,   15
Shall spring to seize thee like an ambush'd foe.

TRANSLATIONS OF MOTTOES AND QUOTATIONS IN 'THE ADVENTURER'

Published with the Tables of Contents and Title leaves for the bound volumes of the collected numbers of *The Adventurer* which ran, twice weekly like *The Rambler*, through 140 numbers from Tuesday, 7 November 1752, until Saturday, 9 March 1754. The undertaking was edited by John Hawkesworth, and Johnson contributed only twenty-nine essays.

The controversy over the exact number of essays by Johnson, who commonly is designated by the signature 'T', has been discussed by Dr. L. F. Powell in his Introduction to *Works*, ii (Yale ed. 1963), 323–36. Johnson's responsibility for translations of mottoes and quotations, and for their selection, is advanced by Professor A. Sherbo in his *Samuel Johnson, Editor of Shakespeare, with an Essay on 'The Adventurer'* (Illinois Studies in Language and Literature, No. 42, Urbana, 1956), pp. 145–74. Professor Sherbo argues for Johnson's responsibility for the unsigned translations on the analogy of the argument in favour of his similar responsibility in *The Rambler*.

According to Thomas Percy (in his marked copy of *The Idler*, 1761), Johnson was largely responsible for the selection of the mottoes, and Johnson himself admits some of this responsibility in his letter to Warton of 8 March 1753: 'I speak as one of the fraternity though I have no part in the paper beyond now and then a Motto' (*Letters*, ed. Chapman, i. 48, No. 46).

A certain difficulty arises because, as Professor Sherbo shows, not all of the unsigned Mottoes are by Johnson: No. 81 is by Francis, and No. 126 is from Rowe, but Professor Sherbo's study of the possible sources of the English versions found no certain originals for the others. Though Hawkesworth was no Latinist, Joseph Warton certainly was, and as a contributor ('Z') to the venture, he was certainly capable of translating the mottoes and quotations. He, however, went to the trouble in his edition of Pope, to dissociate himself from them: 'The

8 gleans] crops *1787*   10 Dissolve] Unnerve *1787*   pow'rs? *1787*: pow'rs; *1792*
12 repose. *1787*: repose? *1792*

mottoes prefixed to the papers in the Rambler and Adventurer, were not so happy. The attempt to translate them was absurd' (Pope's *Works*, ed. J. Warton, 1797, i. 282).

Motto for Title-page[1]

——*Tentanda via est; quâ me quoque possim*
Tollere humo, victorque virum volitare per ora.

VIRG. [Georg. iii. 9–10].

ON vent'rous wing in quest of praise I go,
And leave the gazing multitude below.

NUMB. 3. TUESDAY, NOVEMBER 14, 1752

——*Scenis decora alta futuris.*   VIRG. [*Aen.* i. 429].

THE splendid ornament of future scenes.

NUMB. 7. TUESDAY, NOVEMBER 28, 1752

Sit mihi fas audita loqui——   VIRG. [*Aen.* vi. 266].

WHAT I have heard, permit me to relate.

NUMB. 8. SATURDAY, DECEMBER 2, 1752

Durate et vosmet rebus servate secundis.   VIRG. [*Aen.* i. 207].

ENDURE and conquer; live for better fate.

NUMB. 9. TUESDAY, DECEMBER 5, 1752

——'Ἐν προθύροις θῆκε διδασκαλίην.[2]

VET. EPIGR. [Gk. Anthol., Posidippus, 16. 275].

HE hung th' instructive symbol o'er his door.

---

[1] *Motto for title-page.* Also cited, with Dryden's translation in *The Rambler*, No. 87. (See also *Life*, ii. 329.) The same motto recurs on the title of Henry Lucas's 'The Earl of Somerset', 1779, revised by Johnson.

[2] In 1754, the revised second edition, the reading is πρότεροις θῆκη.

Numb. 10. Saturday, December 9, 1752

Da, Pater, augustam menti conscendere sedem;
Da fontem lustrare boni; da, luce repertâ,
In Te conspicuos animi defigere visus!　　　Boet. [iii. 9].

Give me, O Father! to thy throne access,
Unshaken seat of endless happiness!
Give me, unveil'd, the source of good to see!
Give me thy light, and fix mine eyes on thee!

Numb. 12. Saturday, December 16, 1752

Magnum pauperies opprobrium jubet
Quidvis aut facere aut pati.　　　Hor. [*Od.* iii. xxiv. 42–3].

He whom the dread of want ensnares,
With baseness acts, with meanness bears

Numb. 14. Saturday, December 23, 1752

Admonet, et magnâ testatur voce per umbras:
Discite justitiam moniti, et non temnere Divos.
　　　　　　　　Virg. [*Aen.* vi. 619].

Ev'n yet his voice from hell's dread shades we hear—
'Beware, learn justice, and the Gods revere.'[1]

Numb. 16. Saturday, December 30, 1752

Gratior & pulchro veniens in corpore virtus.　　　Virg. [*Aen.* v. 344].

More lovely virtue, in lovely form.

Numb. 18. Saturday, January 6, 1753

Duplex libelli dos est; quod risum movet,
Et quod prudenti vitam consilio monet. Phaedrus [i, Prol. 3].[2]

A two-fold gift in this my volume lies;
It makes you merry, and it makes you wise.

---

[1] Translated in *The Rambler*, No. 81, as 'Hear, and be just' (p. 144 *ante*).
[2] Used as the motto for the collected edition of *The Idler*, 1761.

NUMB. 19. TUESDAY, JANUARY 9, 1753

Quodcunque ostendis mihi sic, incredulus odi. HOR. [*Ars Poet.* 188].
THE monstrous tale, incredulous I hate.

NUMB. 20. SATURDAY, JANUARY 13, 1753

——*Quid violentius aure tyranni.* JUV. [iv. 86].
ROUGH truth soon irritates a tyrant's ear.

NUMB. 21. TUESDAY, JANUARY 16, 1753

Si genus humanum et mortalia temnitis arma;
At sperate Deos memores fandi atque nefandi.
VIRG. [*Aen.* i. 542–3].
OF mortal Justice if thou scorn the rod—
Believe and tremble, thou art judg'd of GOD.

NUMB. 22. SATURDAY, JANUARY 20, 1753

Rursus et in veterem fato revoluta figuram. VIRG. [*Aen.* vi. 449].
HIS native form at length by fate restor'd.

NUMB. 23. TUESDAY, JANUARY 23, 1753

——*Quo fit, ut omnis*
Votivâ pateat veluti descripta tabellâ
Vita—— HOR. [*Sat.* II. i. 32–4].[1]
IN books the various scenes of life he drew,
As votive tablets give the wreck to view.

NUMB. 24. SATURDAY, JANUARY 27, 1753

Longa mora est, quantum noxæ sit ubique repertum,
Enumerare. OVID [*Met.* i. 214–15].
THE various ills ordain'd to man by fate
Where'er he turns, 'tis tedious to relate.

[1] This motto was also used by Boswell on the title of his *Life of Johnson*.

Numb. 26. Saturday, February 3, 1753

Est ardelionum quædam Romæ natio
Gratis anhelans——   Phaedrus [ii. v. 1-2].

Through all the town the busy triflers swarm,
Fix'd without proof, and without int'rest warm.

Numb. 27. Tuesday, February 6, 1753

Νυκτὸς——Αἰθήρτε καὶ 'Ημέρα ἐξεγένοντο.
          Hesiod [*Theog.* 124].

From night arose the sun-shine and the day.

Numb. 28. Saturday, February 10, 1753

Cœlo supinas si tuleris manus
Nascente Lunâ, rustica Phidyle;
Nec pestilentem sentiet Africum
Fœcunda vitis——   Hor. [*Od.* iii. xxiii. 1-2, 5-6].

If rustic Phidyle her prayer renews,
    Her artless prayer, when sacred hours return,
Her vines shall droop beneath no blighting dews,
    Nor southern storms her yellow harvests burn.

Numb. 33. Tuesday, February 27, 1753

——Latet anguis in herba.   Virg. [*Ecl.* iii. 9].[1]

Within the grass conceal'd a serpent lies.

Numb. 34. Saturday, March 3, 1753

Has toties optata exegit gloria pœnas.   Juv. [x. 187].[2]

Such fate persues the votaries of praise.

——Sed quæ præclara et prospera tanti,
Ut rebus lætis par sit mensura malorum! Juv. [x. 97].[3]

See the wild purchase of the bold and vain,
Where ev'ry bliss is bought with equal pain!

---

[1] Also the motto of No. 135 (p. 167 *post*).
[2] Rendered by lines 251-4 of *The Vanity of Human Wishes*.
[3] Cf. lines 111-20 of *The Vanity of Human Wishes*.

NUMB. 37. TUESDAY, MARCH 13, 1753

Calumniari si quis autem voluerit,
Quod arbores loquantur, non tantum feræ;
Fictis jocari nos meminerit fabulis. PHAED. [I, Prol. 5].

LET those whom folly prompts to sneer,
Be told we sport with fable here;
Be told, that brutes can morals teach,
And trees like soundest casuists preach.

NUMB. 40. SATURDAY, MARCH 24, 1753

Solvite tantis animum monstris,
Solvite, Superi; rectam in melius
Vertite mentem. SEN. [*Herc. Fur.* 1063].

O! SAVE ye Gods, omnipotent and kind,
From such abhor'd chimeras save the mind!
In truth's strait path no hideous monsters roar;
To truth's strait path the wand'ring mind restore.

NUMB. 42. SATURDAY, MARCH 31, 1753

——*Sua suique* DEUS *fit dira Cupido.* VIRG. [*Aen.* ix. 185].

OUR lusts are Gods, and what they will is fate.

NUMB. 43. TUESDAY, APRIL 3, 1753

Mobilitate viget—— VIRG. [*Aen.* iv. 175].

ITS life is motion.

NUMB. 45. TUESDAY, APRIL 10, 1753

Nulla fides regni sociis, omnisque potestas
Impatiens consortis erit. LUCAN [i. 92–3].[1]

No faith of partnership dominion owns;
Still discord hovers o'er divided thrones.

---

[1] Also used as the motto for *The Rambler*, No. 183 (p. 151 *ante*).

Numb. 46. Saturday, April 14, 1753

Μισῶ μνήμονα Συμπότην.   Prov. Gr.[1]

FAR from my table be the tell-tale guest.

Numb. 48. Saturday, April 21, 1753

Ibat triumphans Virgo——
Sunt qui rogatam rettulerint preces
Tulisse CHRISTO, *redderet ut reo*
Lumen jacenti, tum invenit halitum
Vitæ innovatum, visibus integris.
                                    PRUDENT. [*Peristeph.* xiv. 52–6].

AS rescu'd from intended wrong,
The modest virgin pac'd along,
By blasting heav'n depriv'd of day
Beneath her feet th' accuser lay:
She mark'd, and soon the pray'r arose
To HIM who bade us love our foes;
By faith inforc'd the pious call
Again relum'd the sightless ball.[2]

Numb. 49. Tuesday, April 24, 1753

                                ——*Flumina libant*
Summa leves——   VIRG. [*Georg.* iv. 54–5].

—— THEY lightly skim,
And gently sip the dimply river's brim.

Juvet integros accedere fontes   [LUCRETIUS, i. 927.]

HIS be the joy t' approach th' untasted springs.

Numb. 50. Saturday, April 28, 1753

Quicunque turpi fraude semel innotuit,
Etiamsi vera dicit, amittit fidem.   PHAED. [I. x. 1–2].

THE wretch that often has deceiv'd,
Though truth he speaks, is ne'er believ'd.

---

[1] The source of the quotation remains unknown.
[2] It may be doubted whether Johnson was the author of these awkward verses.

NUMB. 53. TUESDAY, MAY 8, 1753

Quisque suos patimur Manes. VIRG. [*Aen.* vi. 743].

EACH has his lot, and bears the fate he drew.

NUMB. 54. SATURDAY, MAY 12, 1753

——*Sensim labefacta cadebat*
Relligio—— CLAUDIANUS [*In Ruf.* i. 14].

—— HIS confidence in heav'n
Sunk by degrees——

NUMB. 56. SATURDAY, MAY 19, 1753

——*Multos in summa pericula misit*
Venturi timor ipse mali. LUCANUS [*Phars.* vii. 105–6].

HOW oft the fear of ill to ill betrays!

NUMB. 57. TUESDAY, MAY 22, 1753

——*Nec vox hominem sonat*—— VIRG. [*Aen.* i. 328].

—— O MORE than human voice!

NUMB. 58. SATURDAY, MAY 26, 1753

Te spectem, suprema mihi cùm venerit hora,
Te teneam moriens deficiente manu. TIBULLUS [I. i. 60–1].

BEFORE my closing eyes, dear Cynthia, stand,
Held weakly by my fainting trembling hand.[1]

Cynthia decedens, felicius, inquit, amata
  Sum tibi; vixisti dum tuus ignis eram.
Cui Nemesis, quid, ait, tibi sunt mea damna dolori?
  Me tenuit moriens deficiente manu.
                                    OVID [*Am.* III. ix. 55–8].

BLEST was my reign, retiring Cynthia cry'd:
Not till he left my breast, Tibullus dy'd.
Forbear, said Nemesis, my loss to moan,
The fainting trembling hand was mine alone.

---

[1] Tibullus' beloved was Delia, not Cynthia. The change may have been made under the influence of the quotation from Ovid. Johnson quoted the lines as he lay dying (*Life*, iv. 406–7).

NUMB. 59. TUESDAY, MAY 29, 1753

——Si Pieriâ Quadrans tibi nullus in Arcâ
Ostendatur, ames nomen victumque Machæræ;
Et vendas potius, commissa quod Auctio vendit
Stantibus, Oenophorum, Tripodes, Armaria, Cistas,
Halcyonem Bacchi, Thebas, & Terea Fausti. JUV. [vii. 8–12].

IF not a souse in thy lank purse appear,
Go mount the rostrum and turn auctioneer;
With china crack'd the greedy crowd trepan,
With spurious pictures and with false japan;
Sell the collected stores of misers dead,
Or English peers for debts to Gallia fled.

——Molles ubi reddunt ova columbæ.   [JUV. iii. 202.][1]
WHERE pigeons lay their eggs.

——ou la vertu n'a plus ni Feu ni Lieu;   BOILEAU [*Sat.* i. 24].
WHERE shiv'ring worth no longer finds a home.

NUMB. 60. SATURDAY, JUNE 2, 1753

Jus est et ab hoste doceri.   OVID [*Met.* iv. 428].
OUR foes may teach, the wise by foes are taught.

NUMB. 61. TUESDAY, JUNE 5, 1753

Ploravere suis non respondere favorem
Quæsitum meritis——   HOR. [*Epist.* II. i. 9–10].[2]

EACH inly murm'ring at th' unequal meed,
Repines that merit should reward exceed.

NUMB. 62. SATURDAY, JUNE 9, 1753

O fortuna viris invida fortibus
Quam non æqua bonis præmia dividis.   SENECA [*Herc. Fur.* 524–5].

CAPRICIOUS fortune ever joys,
With partial hand to deal the prize,
To crush the brave and cheat the wise.

---

[1] Not translated in *London.*
[2] Also the motto of *The Rambler,* No. 190, with a translation by Pope.

rari quippe boni; [Juv. xiii. 26.][1]
THE good are few.

NUMB. 65. TUESDAY, JUNE 19, 1753

Et furiis agitatus amor.—— VIRG. [*Aen.* x. 872].
LOVE, which the furies irritate to rage.

NUMB. 66. SATURDAY, JUNE 23, 1753

> *Nolo virum, facili redimit qui sanguine famam:*
> *Hunc volo, laudari qui sine morte potest.*
> MART. [I. viii. 5–6].

NOT him I prize who poorly gains
From death the palm which blood disdains;
But him who wins with nobler strife
An unpolluted wreath from life.

NUMB. 67. TUESDAY, JUNE 26, 1753

Inventas——vitam excoluere per artes. VIRG. [*Aen.* vi. 663].
THEY polish life by useful arts.

NUMB. 68. SATURDAY, JUNE 30, 1753

Nocet empta dolore voluptas. OVID [HORACE, *Epist.* I. ii. 55].
HOW vain the joy for which our pain must pay.

NUMB. 70. SATURDAY, JULY 7, 1753

> *Virtus, repulsæ nescia sordidæ,*
> *Intaminatis fulget honoribus;*
> *Nec sumit aut ponit secures,*
> *Arbitrio popularis auræ.* HOR. [*Od.* III. ii. 17–20].[2]

STRANGER to folly and to fear,
  With pure untainted honour bright,
Virtue disdains to lend an ear
  To the mad people's sense of right.

---

[1] Included in the motto of *The Rambler*, No. 175, with a translation by Creech.
[2] Also used as the motto for *The Rambler*, No. 3, with a translation by Elphinston.

NUMB. 71. TUESDAY, JULY 10, 1753

——*Hominem pagina nostra sapit.*   MART. [x. iv. 10].
WE strive to paint the manners and the mind.

NUMB. 74. SATURDAY, JULY 21, 1753

Insanientis dum sapientiæ
Consultus, erro.   HOR. [*Od.* I. xxxiv. 2–3].[1]
I MIST my end, and lost my way,
By crack-brain'd wisdom led astray.

NUMB. 77. TUESDAY, JULY 31, 1753

Peccare docentes
Fallax historias monet.   HOR. [*Od.* III. vii. 19–20].[2]
To taint th'attentive mind she tries
With tales of exemplary vice.

NUMB. 78. SATURDAY, AUGUST 4, 1753

——*Propter vitam vivendi perdere causas.*   JUV. [viii. 84].[3]
NOR quit for life, what gives to life its worth.

NUMB. 80. SATURDAY, AUGUST 11, 1753

'Ρεῖα δ' ἀριγνωτη πέλεται, καλαὶ δὲ τέ πᾶσαι.
[HOM. *Od.* vi. 108.]
THO' all are fair, she shines above the rest.

NUMB. 82. SATURDAY, AUGUST 18, 1753

Nunc scio quid sit Amor.   VIRG. [*Ecl.* viii. 43].[4]
NOW know I what is love.

---

[1] Included in the motto for *The Rambler*, No. 95, with a translation by Francis. Johnson comments on this Ode in *Life*, iii. 279; iv. 215.

[2] The folio *Adventurer* reads 'movet', which is corrected in the second edition of 1754.

[3] Quoted in *The Rambler*, No. 79, as 'in the language of the *Roman* satirist, to save life by losing all for which a wise man would live'.

[4] Quoted in *The Rambler*, No. 37, with a translation by Dryden and an imitation by Pope.

NUMB. 92. SATURDAY, SEPTEMBER 22, 1753

Cum tabulis animum censoris sumet honesti. HOR. [*Epist.* II. ii. 10].[1]

BOLD be the critic, zealous to his trust,
Like the firm judge inexorably just.

NUMB. 95. TUESDAY, OCTOBER 2, 1753

——*Dulcique animos novitate tenebo.* OVID [*Met.* iv. 284].

AND with sweet novelty your soul detain.

NUMB. 101. TUESDAY, OCTOBER 23, 1753

——*Est ubi peccat.* HOR. [*Epist.* II. i. 63].

—— YET sometimes he mistakes.

NUMB. 104. SATURDAY, NOVEMBER 3, 1753

——*Semita certe*
Tranquillæ per virtutem patet unica vitæ. JUV. [x. 363–4].[2]

BUT only virtue shews the paths of peace.

NUMB. 109. TUESDAY, NOVEMBER 20, 1753

Insanire putas solennia me, neque rides. HOR. [*Epist.* I. i. 101].

YOU think me but as mad as all mankind.

NUMB. 112. SATURDAY, DECEMBER 1, 1753

——*Has pœnas garrula lingua dedit.* OVID [*Am.* II. ii. 44].

SUCH was the fate of vain loquacity.

NUMB. 113. TUESDAY, DECEMBER 4, 1753

——*de l'amour la sensible peinture,*
Est pour aller au cœur la route la plus sure.
BOILEAU [*L'Art poét.* iii. 95–6].

THOSE tender scenes that pictur'd love impart,
Insure success and best engage the heart.

---

[1] The motto of *The Rambler*, No. 88, with a translation by Creech, and included in the motto on the title-page of Johnson's folio *Dictionary*, 1755.
[2] Not translated in *The Vanity of Human Wishes*, but rendered in the closing couplet.

NUMB. 115. TUESDAY, DECEMBER 11, 1753

Scribimus indocti doctique. HOR. [*Epist.* II. i. 117].

ALL dare to write, who can or cannot read.[1]

NUMB. 118. SATURDAY, DECEMBER 22, 1753

——*Animorum*
Impulsu, et cæcâ magnaque cupidine ducti. JUV. [x. 350–1].[2]

BY blind impulse of eager passion driv'n.

NUMB. 123. TUESDAY, JANUARY 8, 1754

—— *Jam protervâ*
Fronte petet Lalage maritum. HOR. [*Od.* II. v. 15–16].

THE maid whom now you court in vain,
Will quickly run in quest of man.

NUMB. 124. SATURDAY, JANUARY 12, 1754

——*Incedis per ignes*
Suppositos cineri doloso. HOR. [*Od.* II. i. 7–8].[3]

WITH heedless feet on fires you go,
That hid in treacherous ashes glow.

NUMB. 127. TUESDAY, JANUARY 22, 1754

——*Veteres ita miratur, laudatque!* —— HOR. [*Epist.* II. i. 64].

THE wits of old he praises and admires.

[1] Translated by Francis in the folio, but replaced by Johnson in the second edition, 1754.
[2] Also the motto of *The Rambler*, No. 105 (p. 146 *ante*), and translated as lines 345–6 in *The Vanity of Human Wishes* (p. 132 *ante*).
[3] Quoted in the *Life of Addison* (para. 98) as 'As the process of these narratives is now bringing me among my contemporaries, I begin to feel myself "walking upon ashes under which the fire is not extinguished" . . .'.

NUMB. 129. TUESDAY, JANUARY 29, 1754

Quicquid agunt homines, votum, timor, ira, voluptas,
Gaudia——   JUV. [i. 85–6].

WHATE'ER excites our hatred, love or joy,
Or hope, or fear, these themes my muse employ.

Invalidique patrum referant jejunia nati.   VIRG. [*Georg.* iii. 128–9].

—— FROM the faint embrace
Unmanly sons arise, a puny race!

NUMB. 130. SATURDAY, FEBRUARY 2, 1754

Qui non est hodie, cras minus aptus erit.   MART. [OVID, *Rem. Amor.* 94].

THE man will surely fail who dares delay,
And lose to-morrow that has lost to-day.

NUMB. 132. SATURDAY, FEBRUARY 9, 1754

——*Ferimur per opaca locorum.*   VIRG. [*Aen.* ii. 725].

—— DRIV'N thro' the palpable obscure.[1]

NUMB. 135. TUESDAY, FEBRUARY 19, 1754

——*Latet anguis in herba.*   VIRG. [*Ecl.* iii. 93].[2]

BENEATH the grass conceal'd a serpent lies.

NUMB. 136. SATURDAY, FEBRUARY 23, 1754

——*Quis talia fando*
Temperet a lacrimis.   VIRG. [*Aen.* ii. 6–7].

AND who can hear this tale without a tear?

---

[1] Cf. *Paradise Lost*, ii. 406.
[2] Also the motto of No. 33 (p. 158 *ante*). The folio *Adventurer* here reads 'Within but 'Beneath' is substituted in the second edition, 1754.

VERSES IN BARETTI'S COMMONPLACE BOOK

Transcript by Giuseppe Baretti in his commonplace book in the library of the University of Pennsylvania (Furness Collection).
Notes and Queries, 4 September 1858, II. vi. 187.

These lines were published in *Notes and Queries* by Cl. Hopper, who writes that 'there was in existence a MS. common-place-book made by Giuseppe Baretti, in which were copies of several letters of Dr. Johnson to him, and the following original verses written by Johnson, and said not to be printed'. They were the 'Rispossa del Johnson' to impromptu verses by Baretti entitled 'Versi improvisati con la penna da Giuseppe Baretti'. The commonplace book was identified by Professor Alan T. McKenzie and described in *Johnsonian News-Letter*, xxviii (September 1968), 7–8, and *Notes and Queries* (September 1971), 336–7.

Baretti came to England in 1751, and in 1755 Johnson wrote for him the preface to his *Introduction to the Italian Language*. This exchange of verses may have taken place at any time thereafter.

Rispossa del Johnson

A T sight of sparkling Bowls or beauteous Dames
    When fondness melts me, or when wine inflames,
I too can feel the rapture fierce and strong
I too can pour the extemporary song;
But though the number for a moment please,   5
Though musick thrills, or sudden sallies seize,
Yet lay the Sonnet for an hour aside,
Its charms are fled and all its power destroy'd;
What soon is perfect, soon alike is past:
That slowly grows which must for ever last.   10

ON LORD ANSON

Thraliana, ii (1777–8), p. 94; ed. 1941, p. 213.
The St. James's Chronicle, 1 January 1785.
The European Magazine, January 1785, p. 58.
Piozzi, *Anecdotes*, 1786, p. 71.

The epigram is introduced in *Thraliana* thus:

'The Verses too which—with the true Gratitude of a Wit—Johnson made at my Lord Anson's, when the Owner with great Politeness walked over the Grounds with him, and shewed him among other Things—a Temple to the Winds, were done Improviso and are pretty enough.'

In the *Anecdotes* Mrs. Piozzi adds that she 'wrote it down from his own lips one evening in August 1772', and that it 'has been falsely printed in many papers since his death'. Croker pointed out that Johnson 'disliked Lord Anson, first as a whig, and also perhaps from local politics, as the Ansons have had a strong party interest in Lichfield' (*Life*, 1848, p. 624 n., and *Johnsonian Gleanings*, viii. 5). Johnson had reviewed his *Voyages* in *The Gentleman's Magazine*, xix (September, October, December 1749) and xx (February, March 1750).

Anson purchased Moor Park in Hertfordshire in 1754 with the wealth which had come to him as prize-money, and erected in the grounds his Temple to the Winds. A photograph of it is given in Robert Bayne's *Moor Park*, 1871, p. 99. The occasion of Johnson's visit is not known, but as Anson died 6 June 1762 the epigram may be dated *c*. 1760.

The only reference to Anson recorded by Boswell was made on 16 March 1779, when Johnson asked the writer of an *Ode to the Warlike Genius of Britain*, 'Why do you praise Anson?'

An unsigned translation followed the couplet in *The St. James's Chronicle*, and no fewer than eight translations in *The European Magazine*.

> GRATUM animum laudo; Qui debuit omnia ventis,
> Quam bene ventorum surgere templa jubet!

TRANSLATIONS FROM BOETHIUS
'DE CONSOLATIONE PHILOSOPHIÆ'

Manuscripts in the John Rylands Library (Ry. Eng. MS. 538), (Bk. II, Metre 2) in the Hyde Collection, and (Bk. III Metre 3) in the Johnson House, London.
Piozzi, *Letters to and from Samuel Johnson*, 1788, ii. 418–24.
The Edinburgh Magazine, April 1788, p. 310. Bk. II, Metre 2, and Bk. III, Metre 6, only.

These translations were added by Mrs. Piozzi to her edition of Johnson's letters, in the preface to which she says:

> 'The verses from Boethius will be accepted as a literary rarity; it was about the year 1765 when our Doctor told me that he would translate the Consolations of Philosophy, but said, I must do the Odes for him, and produce one every Thursday: he was obeyed; and in commending some, and correcting others, about a dozen Thursdays passed away. —Of those which are given here however, he did many entirely himself; and of the others—I suffered my own lines to be printed, that his might not be lost. The work was broken off without completion, because some gentleman, whose name I have forgotten, took it in hand; and against him, for reasons of delicacy—Johnson did not chuse to contend.'

In the unpublished memoirs which she began to write in 1810 under the name *Piozziana*, conveniently called the Mainwaring *Piozziana*, she says (i. 68–70) that they 'went however but a little Way in the Business, because some poor

1 Gratum . . . Qui] Qui nil Virtuti, sed *St. James's Chron., Eur. Mag.*

Author had engaged in the Work—and he fear'd our Publication would be his Hindrance'. (J. L. Clifford, *Hester Lynch Piozzi* (*Mrs. Thrale*), 2nd ed., Oxford, 1968, pp. 57–8.)

The poor author may be identified as Daniel Bellamy, who for over fifty years had picked up a precarious livelihood by his pen. In 1768, to help him in the straitened circumstances of his old age, his son brought out a collection of some of his writings under the title *Ethic Amusements*, and was allowed to dedicate it to the King. 'This sabbath of his days', says his son's preface, 'it is his utmost ambition to maintain with some degree, or, at least, some appearance of decent Independency.' The first place in the volume is given to 'The Comforts of Philosophy' translated by 'William Causton, Esq; and Mr. Bellamy'. It is only a reprint of the translation published by Causton in 1730, with slight editorial additions and a quotation from *The Idler* in its title. Possibly Bellamy found himself unequal to the task of giving a new translation, for he was then eighty years old, but the knowledge that he was busied somehow with a translation was sufficient to make Johnson abandon his project. (Philip Ridpath began his translation of Boethius as early as 1761 and eventually published it in 1785, but he was a Scottish minister, not a 'poor author': see the *Diary of George Ridpath*, ed. Paul, Edinburgh, 1922, p. 367.)

In 1738 Johnson had advised Miss Carter to translate Boethius (*Life*, i. 139), and in 1752 had himself translated three quotations from Boethius in *The Rambler*.

The lines printed in italics, here as in the *Letters*, were composed by Mrs. Thrale, whose translations of I. i, I. iii, I. iv, II. i, II. iii, II. vii, and III. vii are in the Rylands papers.

Texts from the manuscripts, but the punctuation of the printed copy has occasionally been adopted.

BOOK II. METRE 2

THOUGH countless as the Grains of Sand
    That roll at Eurus' loud command;
Though countless as the lamps of night
That glad us with vicarious light;
Fair plenty, gracious Queen, shou'd pour   5
The blessings of a golden Show'r,
Not all the gifts of Fate combin'd
Would ease the hunger of the mind,
But swallowing all the mighty store,
Rapacity would call for more;   10
For still where wishes most abound
Unquench'd the thirst of gain is found;
In vain the shining gifts are sent,
For none are rich without content.

5 Plenty's gracious draft

Book II. Metre 4

Wouldst thou to some stedfast Seat,
Out of Fortune's Pow'r retreat?
Wouldst thou when fierce Eurus blows
Calmly rest in safe Repose?
Wouldst thou see the foaming Main,   5
Tossing rave but rave in vain?
Shun the Mountain's airy Brow,
Shun the Sea-sapp'd Sand below;
Soon th' aspiring Fabric falls,
When loud Auster shakes her Walls,   10
Soon the treachrous Sands retreat,
From beneath the cumbrous Weight;
Fix not where the tempting Height
Mingles Danger with Delight;
Safe upon the rocky Ground,   15
Firm and low thy Mansion found;
There, mid Tempests loudest Roars,
Dashing Waves and shatter'd Shoars,
Thou shalt sit and smile to see
All the World afraid but thee,   20
Lead a long and peaceful Age,
And deride their utmost Rage.

Book III. Metre 1

The prudent Hind intent on Gain
Must clear the Ground to sow the Grain,
And Ceres richest gifts abound
Where late the rankest Weeds were found;
To him whom painful Tastes annoy,   5
Sweet honey yields a double Joy;
The Tempest gives the Calm delight,
The Morning owes her Charms to night;
And thus the Mind tormented long
With wild Vicissitudes of Wrong,   10
Contemns at length the treachrous toys,
And real Happiness enjoys.

BOOK III. METRE 3

Through Gripus Grounds let rich Pactolus roll,
No golden Sands can satisfy his Soul;
Though Chains of Pearl bow down his pensive Head
Though a whole Hecatomb his Acres tread,
No wealth his life from weary care can save,   5
No care his wealth can carry to the grave.

BOOK III. METRE 4

Vainly the Tyrian Purple bright,
Vainly the Pearl's pellucid white,
The Tyrant Nero strove t' adorn,
Who liv'd our hatred and our Scorn;
His Choice our sacred Seats disgracd,   5
His Conduct Human Kind debased:
If such on Earth can Bliss bestow,
Say what is happiness below?

BOOK III. METRE 5

The Man who pants for ample Sway
Must bid his Passions all obey;
Must bid each wild Desire be still,
Nor yoke his Reason with his Will:
For tho' beneath thy haughty Brow   5
Warm India's supple Sons should bow,
Tho' Northern Climes confess thy Sway,
Which erst in Frost and Freedom lay,
If Sorrow pine or Av'rice crave,
Bow down and own thyself a Slave.   10

Book III. Metre 3. The manuscript of this, with lines 5 and 6 as Mrs. Thrale wrote them deleted and with Johnson's couplet added in his own hand, is preserved in the copy of the *Letters* which formerly belonged to Samuel Lysons and is now in the Johnson House, London. A facsimile faces p. 114 of A. M. Broadley's *Dr. Johnson and Mrs. Thrale*, 1910. Johnson's lines replace Mrs. Thrale's:

> Two certain Ills his parting Hours offend
> His Wealth forsakes him, & his Cares attend.

Metre 5. The first four lines of the original were quoted as the motto to *Idler*, 96.

BOOK III. METRE 6

I

All Men throughout the peopled Earth
   From one sublime Beginning spring;
All from one Source derive their Birth
   The same their Parent and their King.

2

At his Command proud Titan glows,   5
   And Luna lifts her Horn on high;
His hand this Earth on Man bestows
   And strews with Stars the spangled Sky.

3

From her high Seats he drew the Soul,
   And in this earthly Case confin'd;   10
To wondring Worlds produc'd the whole,
   Essence Divine with Matter join'd.

4

Since then alike All Men derive
   From God himself their noble Race,
Why should the witless Mortals strive   15
   For vulgar Ancestry and Place?

5

Why boast their Birth before his Eyes,
   Who holds no human Creature mean;
Save him whose Soul enslav'd to Vice
   Deserts her nobler Origin.   20

10 Case] cage *Letters*   19-20. Cf. Johnson's translation of the quotation in *The Rambler*, No. 6 (p. 140).

Book III. Metre 6. 'The next we did together—for a Joke—Stanza by Stanza. I made him take the first of course.' *Piozziana*, loc. cit.

Book III. Metre 12

Happy he whose Eyes have view'd
The transparent Fount of Good;
Happy whose unfetterd Mind
Leaves the Load of Earth behind.
Tho' when Orpheus made his Moan   5
For his lovely Consort gone,

Book III. Metre 12. Johnson used lines 1–2 of the original as the epigraph to his fairy-tale 'The Fountains' (1766). Mrs. Thrale made a complete translation. Johnson dictated his revisions, and she wrote them in the margin, appending his initials to each except lines 37–8 and 53–8. They are all condensations and, with the exception of the last, are introduced in this manner:—'These 8 should be 4 as', 'these 14 should be 8 or 10 at most as', 'These should be 2 only as'. Thereafter she wrote a fair copy, incorporating his revisions. Her discarded passages are printed in italics.

1–4
Happy He of human Race
Who in Truth's pellucid Glass
Virtue's Fountain clear and true
His reflected Face can view.
'Mong all Mortals happy He
Who from worldly Fetters free
Can behold with Brow serene
Fickle Fortune's changing Scene.

5–12
No such Sage poor Orpheus prov'd
When he lost the fair he lov'd,
When he groan'd and when he sigh'd
Till the pitying Woods reply'd,
When his Griefs harmonious Sound
Drew the listning Forests round,
When his sweet lamenting Strain
Stopt the Rivers as they ran,
Made the Hind approach to hear
Tho' the Lyon's self were near,
And attentive to his Woe
Heedless of her former Foe
Made the tim'rous Hare be seen
With the Hound upon the Green.

Johnson's first revision, cancelled:

Tho' when Orpheus sweetly sighing
Woods to evry Sigh replying,
Hebrus heard her Poet groan,
For his lovely Consort gone,
Listning forests learnt the Strain,
Rivers rested as they ran,
Tho' the

6. Six cancelled lines follow:

Listning Forests learnt the Strain
Rivers rested as they ran.

Tho' the Hind approach'd to hear
Where the Lyoness stood near,
And attentive to the Sound
Hares forgot the following hound,   10
Round him danc'd the listning Woods,
Silent Wonder stopt the Floods;
Grief and Madness unrepress'd
Rag'd within the Master's Breast
While t' asswage the Pangs of Love   15
Verse and Music vainly strove;
Now he sighs to heav'n, and now
Rushes on the Realms below.
There he breath'd his am'rous Fire,
There he touch'd his trembling Lyre,   20
Warbling there his softer Sorrows
From his Parent Muse he borrows
Notes to touch each tender Feeling,
Numbers to each Bosom stealing,
Sighs that silent Measure keep,   25
Groans that grieve and Words that weep.
These the hapless Poet tries
To regain his beauteous Prize;
Nor in vain—the Strings obey,
Love and Music bear the sway,   30
Cerberus Rage their Powers disarm,
Stern Alecto feels the Charm,
Tears from fierce Megæra flow;

Tho' the Lyoness and Hind
Were on this occasion join'd
While attracted by the Sound
Hares forgot the foaming Hound.   (MS. 538/44-2.)

11 danc'd] *above* crowd *cancelled*
13-18

Nature thus thro' every Part
Yielded to the Poets Art,
While his Passions kept their Course
Still encreasing in their Force:
Mad with Anger mad with Love
Since no Tears the Gods can move,
Rashly now he speeds his Flight
To the Realms of endless Night
To the murky Shades of Hell
Where eternal Horrors dwell:

While attentive to his Woe
Sudden stops Ixion's Wheel,   35
Hell's fierce Hawk forgets his Meal.
Tantalus astonish'd stood
Scorning now th' o'erflowing Flood,
Till at length stern Pluto cried,
Conquring Poet take thy Bride!   40
Purchased by thy powerful Song,
All her Charms to thee belong;
Only this Command obey,
Look not on her by the way;
Tho' reluctant still refrain,   45
Till the Realms of Light you gain.
But what Laws can Lovers awe?
Love alone to Love is Law:
Just emerging into Light,
Orpheus turn'd his eager Sight,   50

34 *And all Attention reigns below.*—cancelled
36 *his*—Letters, *and Ry. MS. 538–3*] *her MS. HLT*

37–8   *Openmouth'd as when he stood*
                        Near the now-neglected Flood,
                        Fix'd in Wonder at the Sound
                        Thirsty Tantalus is found;

39–46   *And the King at length confest*
                        Soft Emotions in his Breast.
                        Quickly take thy beauteous Bride,
                        Take her hence stern Pluto cried;
                        Vanquish'd by thy Music's Pow'r,
                        Death and Hell their Prey restore:
                        Only this Command obey
                        Look not on her by the Way,
                        Tho' reluctant still refrain
                        Till the Realms of Light you gain.

41 thy] the *Letters*

47–52   *But for Lovers who shall find*
                        Links to last, or Laws to bind?
                        That which feeds their present Flame
                        Love alone is Law to them,
                        Thus, the distant Daylight rising,
                        Orpheus all Behests despising
                        On those fatal Charms to look
                        For which fair Daylight he forsook
                        Turning tow'rd th' Infernal Coast,
                        Look'd Alas! but look'd and lost.

Fondly view'd his following Bride,
Viewing lost and losing died.

To You whose gen'rous Wishes rise
To court Communion with the Skies,
   To you the Tale is told;   55
When grasping Bliss th' unsteady mind
Looks back on what She left behind,
   She faints and quits her hold.

PROLOGUE TO
'THE GOOD NATUR'D MAN'

The Public Advertiser, 3 February 1768.
Lloyd's Evening Post, 3 February 1768.
Goldsmith, *The Good Natur'd Man*, 5 February 1768.
The London Magazine, February 1768, pp. 61, 98.
The Gentleman's Magazine, February 1768, p. 86.
The Annual Register, 1768, p. 223 (2nd series).
The Spouter's Companion; or, Theatrical Remembrancer [*c.* 1770], pp. 46–7.
Davies, *Miscellaneous and Fugitive Pieces*, 1773, 1774, ii. 298.
The Theatrical Bouquet, 1778, 1780, p. 170.
Poetical Works, 1785, p. 177.
Works, 1787, xi. 347.

   The Good Natur'd Man was produced at Covent Garden on 29 January 1768, when the Prologue was spoken by Bensley. The version printed in the newspapers, on 3 February, was no doubt supplied by the playhouse. It appears to be a playhouse revision, made without the knowledge of either Johnson or Goldsmith who would certainly have objected to the reading 'our little Bard'. The version published with the play on 5 February must be taken to be what Johnson wrote, and is here followed with slight corrections.[1] Both versions are given in *The London Magazine* for February.

51–2. Mrs. Thrale laid claim to these lines in *Thraliana*, i. 24, but did not mark them in her transcripts or in *Letters*, 1788. Cf. A. Hayward, *Autobiography of Mrs. Piozzi*, 2nd ed., 1861, ii. 87.
52 losing] loving *in fair copy, and Letters.*
53–8   *To You then whose Sublime Desire*
               Would fain to heav'nly Heights aspire
                  This Fable we address;
               For he whose Eyes once backward cast
               Regrets the Regions that He past
                 Shall ne'er that Heav'n possess.

[1] The bibliography of the early editions is elucidated by W. B. Todd in *Studies in Bibliography*, xi (1958), 133–42.

The Prologue had been a long-standing promise, but according to Boswell Johnson was in no mood when he wrote it to introduce a comedy (*Life*, ii. 42, 45). The gloom of the opening lines is said to have been deepened by the heavy delivery of Bensley. The Prologue was expected to aid Goldsmith in his contest with Kelly, whose *False Delicacy* had just been produced by Garrick at Drury Lane, but it found little favour.

An elaborately unfriendly criticism appeared in *The London Magazine*, of which the chief point was that Johnson borrowed the idea from the Prologue to Kenrick's comedy, *The Widow'd Wife*. The review may have been written by Kenrick, whose play was acted At Drury Lane on 5 December 1767, and was printed the same month. His Prologue is in *The Gentleman's Magazine* for December 1767, p. 604. The similarity of the two Prologues lies in the ideas suggested by the approaching General Election of 1768 in which Johnson was active on behalf of Henry Thrale the M.P. for Southwark. Parliament was dissolved on 11 March.

Prologue to '*The Good Natur'd Man*'

PREST by the load of life, the weary mind
   Surveys the general toil of human kind;
With cool submission joins the labouring train,
And social sorrow loses half its pain:
Our anxious Bard, without complaint, may share   5
This bustling season's epidemic care;
Like Cæsar's pilot, dignified by fate,
Tost in one common storm with all the great;
Distrest alike, the statesman and the wit,
When one a borough courts, and one the pit.   10
The busy candidates for power and fame,
Have hopes, and fears, and wishes, just the same;
Disabled both to combat, or to fly,
Must hear all taunts, and hear without reply.

4 sorrow] sorrow, *Play*   its] it's *Play.*   *After this line, Newspapers have:*
                      Amidst the toils of this returning year,
                      When senators and nobles learn to fear;
5 anxious] little *Newspapers*   6 This] The *Newspapers*   care;] care. *Play*

7 See Lucan, *Phars.* v. 539, and Plutarch, 'Cæsar', ch. 38.

Uncheck'd on both, loud rabbles vent their rage,   15
As mongrels bay the lion in a cage.
Th' offended burgess hoards his angry tale,
For that blest year when all that vote may rail;
Their schemes of spite the poet's foes dismiss,
Till that glad night when all that hate may hiss.   20
This day the powder'd curls and golden coat,
Says swelling Crispin, begg'd a cobbler's vote.
This night our wit, the pert apprentice cries,
Lies at my feet, I hiss him, and he dies.
The great, 'tis true, can charm th' electing tribe;   25
The bard may supplicate, but cannot bribe.
Yet judg'd by those, whose voices ne'er were sold,
He feels no want of ill-persuading gold;
But confident of praise, if praise be due,
Trusts without fear, to merit, and to you.   30

IN THEATRO

Transcript by Mrs. Thrale presented to Boswell, and now in the Harvard
    University Library. (MS. Eng. 1158.)
Transcript by Mrs. Thrale in the Hyde Collection.
Transcript made for Mrs. Thrale now in the John Rylands Library. (MS. Eng.
    543/27.)
Transcript in unidentified hand in the William Salt Library, Stafford.
Thraliana, ii (1777-8), p. 95; ed. 1941, p. 214.
M. Maty, *A New Review*, January 1785, pp. 27-8.
Piozzi, *Anecdotes*, 1786, p. 73.
Works, 1787, xi. 392.

    These verses are introduced thus in Mrs. Piozzi's *Anecdotes*:

'One evening in the oratorio season of the year 1771, Mr. Johnson went with me to
Covent-Garden theatre; and though he was for the most part an exceedingly bad playhouse companion, as his person drew people's eyes upon the box, and the loudness of
his voice made it difficult for me to hear any body but himself; he sat surprisingly quiet,
and I flattered myself that he was listening to the music. When we were got home however he repeated these verses, which he said he had made at the oratorio, and he bid me
translate them.'

---

15 loud rabbles vent their] caprice may vent its *Newspapers*   16 mongrels bay]
children fret *Newspapers*   17 The *Newspapers*   19 The poet's foes their schemes
of spite dismiss *Newspapers*   21-4 *Newspapers omit*   28 ill persuading *Play*
30 merit] candour *Newspapers*

A similar but briefer account introduces the verses in *Thraliana*. The account in the unpublished *Piozziana* (i, 78–9), written about 1810, differs in details:

'His verses composed one Night at the Opera whither he *would absolutely* accompany me, made some Amends for the contemptuous Clatter he made while the Music was going on. . . . It was an English Opera of Doctor Arne and perform'd at Covent Garden Theatre—but such was his Behaviour I little dreamed he was making these Sapphics the while, but the Instant we got home he repeated, and bad me translate them by Breakfast Time next Day.'

Maty had also described the verses as 'written extempore at the Opera in 1771'.

The transcript which she gave to Boswell contains her translation on the reverse, and underneath it is written 'Mrs Thrale gave me this, 1775. James Boswell'. This version of her translation was first printed in *Notes and Queries*, 4 March 1905; the version in her *Anecdotes* was slightly revised.

The oratorio performed at Covent Garden on 8 March 1771 was Handel's *Messiah*; Johnson has been identified among the subscribers to the first edition.

Text from the transcript given to Boswell.

In Theatro

March 8, 1771

TERTII verso quater orbe lustri,
   Quid theatrales tibi, Crispe, pompæ?
Quam decet canos male literatos
          Sera voluptas.

Tene mulceri fidibus canoris?   5
Tene cantorum modulis stupere?
Tene per pictas oculo elegante
          Currere formas?

Inter equales, sine felle liber,
Codices, veri studiosus, inter   10
Rectius vives, sua quisque carpat
          Gaudia gratus.

Lusibus gaudet puer otiosis,
Luxus oblectat Juvenem theatri,
At Seni fluxo sapienter uti   15
          Tempore restat.

2 pompei! *Thraliana*   5 canori? *Thraliana*   9 æquales *Maty, Works*   14 Juvenam
Thraliana   16 Tempora *Anecdotes 2–4 edd.*

EPITAPH ON HOGARTH

Manuscript in the Berg Collection of the New York Public Library.
Garrick Correspondence, 1831, i. 446.
Letters, ed. Hill, i. 186; (ed. Chapman, i. 273, No. 269).
    First stanza only:
Transcript by Mrs. Thrale in the John Rylands Library.
Thraliana MS. i (1776–7), p. 67; ed. 1941, p. 41.
Piozzi, *Anecdotes*, 1786, p. 136.
The Gentleman's Magazine, March 1786, p. 249; February 1789, p. 112.
Works, 1787, xi. 379.

This epitaph was sent in a letter of 12 December 1771 to Garrick, who had
been asked by Mrs. Hogarth to write an epitaph on her husband and had sent
a draft of three stanzas to Johnson for his opinion and help. 'An epitaph is
no easy thing', Johnson replied, and criticized Garrick's verses severely. 'Suppose
you worked upon something like this', he said, introducing his own two stanzas,
which are here printed from the original letter.

Garrick submitted a new draft on 22 December (MS. Hyde; *The Letters of
David Garrick*, ed. D. M. Little and G. M. Kahrl (Cambridge, Mass., 1963),
ii. 778, No. 666). His final version, as inscribed on the monument in Chiswick
Churchyard, runs thus:

> Farewel, great Painter of Mankind!
>   Who reach'd the noblest point of Art,
> Whose *pictur'd Morals* charm the Mind,
>   And through the Eye correct the Heart.
>
> If *Genius* fire thee, Reader, stay:
>   If *Nature* touch thee, drop a Tear;
> If neither move thee, turn away,
>   For HOGARTH's honour'd dust lies here.

'How much prettier', says Mrs. Thrale in *Thraliana*, 'is Johnson's little
Epitaph which he intended for Hogarth than that which Garrick wrote and put
upon his Tombstone.' She must have got her single stanza from Johnson, and
as the variants are too serious to be explained by her inaccuracy, what she
preserved was probably dictated by Johnson on the spur of the moment. She
reproduced it in the *Anecdotes*, and from there it passed into all editions of
Johnson's works.

The first stanza alone did not fulfil Johnson's requirements for a good epitaph.
In his *Dissertation on the Epitaphs of Pope* he said that the omission of the name
of the person commemorated is a fault which 'scarcely any beauty can compensate'. He had brought in Hogarth's name in the second stanza.

THE Hand of Art here torpid lies
        wav'd
That traced th' essential form of Grace,
Here death has clos'd the curious eyes
    That saw the manners in the face.

If Genius warm thee, Reader, stay,   5
    If Merit touch thee, shed a tear,
Be Vice and Dulness far away
    Great Hogarth's honour'd Dust is here.

[Version in *Thraliana* and *Anecdotes*]
THE hand of him here torpid lies
    That drew th' essential Form of Grace;
Here clos'd in Death th' attentive Eyes
    That saw the Manners in the Face.

TRANSLATION OF PSALM 117

Manuscript in the Hyde Collection.
Works, 1787, xi. 403.

    This translation was written in the Johnson diary in the Hyde Collection on
a blank page between the entries for 22 December 1771 and 11 August 1777.

Psalmus 117

ANNI quà volucris ducitur orbita,
  Patrem cœlicolûm perpetuo colunt
Quovis sanguine cretæ
    Gentes undique carmine.

2 That] Who *Rylands transcript*   6 Merit *written above an obliterated word*

2, 5 Patrem] *Regem, with *utrobique Patrem at foot, in line with and after In lecto.
MS.   2 pepetuo MS.

    2. The 'essential form of Grace' is Hogarth's 'one precise line, properly to be called
the line of *Beauty*'; see his *Analysis of Beauty*, 1753, p. 49. It was a 'waving line'; hence
the suggested variant 'wav'd' instead of 'traced', which was too near 'Grace'.

Patrem cujus amor blandior in dies   5
Mortales miseros servat, alit, fovet,
Omnes undique Gentes
Sancto dicite carmine.

In lecto.

MOTTO FOR A GOAT

Thraliana ii (1777-8), p. 95; ed. 1941, p. 213.
Transcript by Mrs. Thrale in the Hyde Collection.
Transcript made for Mrs. Thrale in the John Rylands Library (MS. Eng. 543/ 27).
Transcript by Thomas Percy in the Hyde Collection (dated 'March 1772').
Transcript by Sir Joshua Reynolds in the Hyde Collection.
Piozzi, *Anecdotes*, 1786, p. 70.
Works, 1787, xi. 396.
The European Magazine, July 1789, p. 5.
Boswell, *Life*, 1791, i. 351 (1934, ii. 144).
Letters, ed. Chapman, 1952, i. 275, No. 272.

Boswell printed the distich and a translation 'by a friend' along with this letter from Johnson to Sir Joseph Banks:

'Sir,
I return thanks to you and to Dr. Solander for the pleasure which I received in yesterday's conversation. I could not recollect a motto for your Goat, but have given her one. You, Sir, may perhaps have an epick poem from some happier pen than, Sir,
                                          Your most humble servant,
Johnson's-court, Fleet-street,   Sam. Johnson.'
Feb. 27, 1772.

Dr. L. F. Powell points out that the letter as printed in *The European Magazine*, July 1789, p. 5, is dated 'March 26, 1772' and contains two better readings: 'given her a distich' and 'may some time have an epic poem from some happier hand than that of' (*Life*, 1934, ii. 492). A facsimile of the complete letter including the distich was published at Norwich, by J. M. Johnson, early in the nineteenth century (copy in the Wellcome Historical Medical Library). Its text agrees with Boswell, rather than *The European Magazine*, but reads 'a distich' for 'one'. It is possible there were two copies of the letter (*Letters*, loc. cit.).

The *Anecdotes* gives this account, based on the account in *Thraliana*:

'The inscription on the collar of Sir Joseph Banks's goat which had been on two of his adventurous expeditions with him, and was then, by the humanity of her amiable master, turned out to graze in Kent, as a recompence for her utility and faithful service, was given me by Johnson in the year 1777 I think, and I have never yet seen it printed.'

(The fourth edition of *Anecdotes* differs in very minor details of spelling and accentuation.)

5 blandior *above* lætior *uncancelled MS.*

But, to quote Dr. Powell, 'Banks went round the world once only, with Capt. Cook in the Endeavour. In the so-called "Specimens of a Diary" published by Thomas Byerley ("Stephen Collet") in *Relics of Literature*, 1823, p. 310, it is stated that the goat accompanied Capt. Wallis in the Dolphin (1766–8), and Capt. Cook in the Endeavour (1768–71), and died, at Mile End, 28 April 1772'.

Versus Collari Capræ Domini Banks inscribendi

PERPETUI, ambita bis terra, præmia lactis
Hæc habet altrici Capra secunda Jovis.

PARODIES OF 'THE HERMIT OF WARKWORTH'

The Hermit of Warkworth. A Northumberland Ballad. In three fits or cantos, 1771, was an original poem by Thomas Percy composed in the traditional measure of the old ballads which he had edited in his *Reliques*.

On 20 March 1771 Johnson wrote to Langton: 'Dr. Percy has written a long ballad in many *fits*; it is pretty enough. He has printed, and will soon publish it.' Under the date 3 April 1773 Boswell records that 'the conversation having turned on modern imitations of ancient ballads, and some one having praised their simplicity, he treated them with that ridicule which he always displayed when that subject was mentioned' (*Life*, ii. 212). Three parodies by him have been preserved.

I

Thraliana MS. iii (1778–81), p. 127; ed. 1941, p. 398.
Piozzi, *Anecdotes*, 1786, p. 66.
Works, 1787, xi. 377.

This parody was written in *Thraliana* on 1 August 1779, with this comment: 'These Verses which were meant to make Fun of Dr. Percy's Poem called The Hermit of Warkworth got about, and made Percy angry—but he soon came to himself.' Percy could not be named in the *Anecdotes*: 'Some of the old legendary

Title *Works*; Inscription on the collar of Mr. Banks's Goat; March 27: 1772 *Rylands transcript*   1 Perpetua *Boswell*

---

1. 'Perpetui'—because the goat never failed to give milk. The point is lost in 'perpetua præmia'. See *Notes and Queries*, clxxxiii (1942), 314; cf. also Crinagoras, *Gk. Anthol.* ix, 224.

stories put in verse by modern writers provoked him to caricature them thus one day at Streatham; but they are already well known, I am sure.'

T HE tender infant, meek and mild,
   Fell down upon the stone;
The nurse took up the squealing child,
   But still the child squeal'd on.

II

Boswell's manuscript in the Yale University Library.
The St. James's Chronicle, 13 January 1785.
The European Magazine, January 1785, p. 51.
Cooke, *Life of Johnson*, 1785 (second edition), p. 150.
The London Magazine, April 1785, p. 254.
Hawkins, *Life of Johnson*, 1787, p. 389.
Wordsworth, *Lyrical Ballads*, 1800, Preface.
Cradock, *Literary Memoirs*, 1826, p. 207.
Boswell Papers, vi. 97; ix. 265.
Boswell for the Defence, ed. Wimsatt and Pottle, 1960, pp. 177–8.

Boswell first heard this parody from Garrick on 9 May 1772. Garrick's version was

> With my hat upon my head
> I walked into the Strand;
> And there I met another man
> With his hat in his hand.

On 7 April 1773 Boswell repeated these lines to Johnson, telling him that he had them from Garrick. 'Then he has no ear', said Johnson, and gave Boswell the version here printed. Boswell never published the parody because of Percy's sensitiveness to ridicule. Cradock says:

'I think Dr. Percy had received very great cause to take real offence at Dr. Johnson, who, by a ludicrous parody on a stanza in the *Hermit of Warkworth*, had rendered him contemptible. It was urged, that Johnson only meant to attack the metre; but he certainly turned the whole Poem into ridicule. . . . Mr. Garrick, in the Postscript of a letter to me, soon afterwards asked me, "Whether I had seen Johnson's criticism on the *Hermit*? it is already", said he, "over half the town."' (*The Letters of David Garrick*, ed. Little and Kahrl, 1963, ii. 759, no. 651.)

Steevens (in *The St. James's Chronicle* and *European Magazine*), Hawkins, and Wordsworth mistakenly assumed that the parody was aimed at Percy's *Reliques*. Steevens gives the place of composition as Miss Reynolds's tea table, with Percy present. Wordsworth quoted the parody as Boswell received it from Johnson; where he found it is not known.

2 the] a *Thraliana*   4 still] yet *Thraliana*

I PUT my hat upon my head
  And walk'd into the Strand,
And there I met another man
  Who's hat was in his hand.

III

The St. James's Chronicle, 13 January 1785.
The European Magazine, January 1785, p. 51.
Cooke, *Life of Johnson*, 1785 (second edition), p. 150.
The London Magazine, April 1785, p. 254.
Hawkins, *Life of Johnson*, 1787, p. 389.

According to Steevens this parody was improvised immediately after the
preceding and in Percy's presence: 'And thus he proceeded through several
more stanzas till the Reverend Critic cried out for quarter.'

I THEREFORE pray thee, Renny dear,
  That thou wilt give to me,
With cream and sugar soften'd well,
  Another dish of tea.

Nor fear that I, my gentle maid,   5
  Shall long detain the cup,
When once unto the bottom I
  Have drank the liquor up.

Yet hear, alas! this mournful truth,
  Nor hear it with a frown;—   10
Thou canst not make the tea so fast
  As I can gulp it down.

1 As with my *Steevens, Cooke, Hawkins*   2 I walk'd along the *Steevens, Cooke,
Hawkins*   3 I there did meet *Steevens, Cooke, Hawkins*   4 With his hat in
Steevens, Cooke, Hawkins, Cradock

1 I pray thee, gentle Renny *Hawkins*   3 soften'd] temper'd *Hawkins*   9 alas!]
at last, *Hawkins*

TRANSLATION OF THE BEGINNING OF 'RIO VERDE'

Thraliana MS. ii (1777–8), p. 92; ed. 1941, p. 211.
Piozzi, *Anecdotes*, 1786, p. 66.
Works, 1787, xi. 377.

The brief account of this translation in *Thraliana*—'likewise the famous *Rio Verde* of the Spanish Poet which he render'd Impromptu thus'—is thus expanded in the *Anecdotes*:

'A famous ballad also, beginning *Rio verde, Rio verde*, when I commended the translation of it, he said he could do it better himself—as thus. . . . But Sir, said I, this is not ridiculous at all. "Why no (replied he), why should I always write ridiculously?"'

The Spanish poem (Pérez de Hita, *Guerras civiles de Granada*, xvii) and Percy's translation had been printed in Percy's *Reliques of Ancient English Poetry*, 1765, i. 318–23.

GLASSY water, glassy water,
Down whose current clear and strong,
Chiefs confus'd in mutual slaughter,
Moor and Christian, roll along.

ΓΝΩΘΙ ΣΕΑΥΤΟΝ

Manuscript, in the Yale University Library.
Works, 1787, xi. 389.

The text is taken from the manuscript, which is dated 12 December 1772. The poem was written after Johnson's careful revision of the *Dictionary* for the fourth edition. Beattie alludes to it in his Diary, 24 May 1773: 'I sat two hours with Dr. Samuel Johnson, who was in exceedingly good humour and spirit; showed me some Latin verses he had lately composed, on finishing the last edition of his Dictionary, and allowed me to take a copy' (Margaret Forbes, *Beattie and his Friends*, 1904, p. 78). To judge from its provenance the manuscript was eventually given to Mrs. Thrale.

The allusion to Scaliger is explained by the epigram on dictionary-makers which the younger Scaliger wrote in his Arabic lexicon:

> Si quem dura manet sententia iudicis olim,
>   Damnatum ærumnis suppliciisque caput:
> Hunc neque fabrili lassent ergastula massa,
>   Nec rigidas vexent fossa metalla manus.
> Lexica contexat, nam cætera quid moror? omnes
>   Pœnarum facies hic labor unus habet.

(*Josephi Scaligeri Poemata Omnia*, 1615, Poemata Propria, p. 35.) This epigram is printed in *The Gentleman's Magazine*, 1748, p. 8, and is said by Murphy to have been 'communicated without doubt by Dr. Johnson'; but it was given as a note to an article which was not written by Johnson.

A paraphrastic translation is printed in Murphy's *Essay*, 1792, p. 82.

Γνῶθι σεαυτόν[1]

(*Post Lexicon Anglicanum auctum et emendatum.*)

LEXICON ad finem longo luctamine tandem
   Scaliger ut duxit, tenuis pertæsus opellæ,
Vile indignatus Studium, nugasque molestas,
Ingemit exosus, scribendaque lexica mandat
Damnatis, pœnam pro pœnis omnibus unam.   5
   Ille quidem recte, sublimis, doctus, et acer,
Quem decuit majora sequi, majoribus aptum,
Qui veterum modo facta ducum, modo carmina vatum,
Gesserat et quicquid Virtus, Sapientia quicquid
Dixerat, imperiique vices, cœlique meatus,   10
Ingentemque animo seclorum volverat orbem.
   Fallimur exemplis; temere sibi turba scholarum
Ima tuas credit permitti, Scaliger, iras.
Quisque suum nôrit modulum; tibi, prime virorum,
Ut studiis sperem, aut ausim par esse querelis,   15
Non mihi sorte datum, lenti seu sanguinis obsint
Frigora, seu nimium longo jacuisse veterno,
Sive mihi mentem dederit Natura minorem.
   Te sterili functum cura, vocumque salebris
Tuto eluctatum spatiis Sapientia dia   20
Excipit æthereis, Ars omnis plaudit amica,
Linguarumque omni terra discordia concors
Multiplici reducem circumsonat ore magistrum.
   Me, pensi immunis cum jam mihi reddor, inertis
Desidiæ sors dura manet, graviorque labore   25

11 volverat] volveret *Works*   21 amica] amico *Works*   22 ex *struck out after* omni *MS.*

2 ff. Cf. Preface to *A Dictionary* &c., 1755, penult. para.
22. Cf. *Life of Cowley*, para. 56 and *The Rambler*, No. 167, para. 9; Horace, *Epist.* I. xii. 19.

[1] Cf. *The Rambler*, No. 24.

Tristis et atra quies, et tardæ tædia vitæ.
Nascuntur curis curæ, vexatque dolorum
Importuna cohors, vacuæ mala somnia mentis.
Nunc clamosa juvant nocturnæ gaudia mensæ,
Nunc loca sola placent, frustra te, Somne, recumbens   30
Alme voco, impatiens noctis metuensque diei.
Omnia percurro trepidus, circum omnia lustro,
Si qua usquam pateat melioris semita vitæ,
Nec quid agam invenio; meditatus grandia, cogor
Notior ipse mihi fieri, incultumque fateri   35
Pectus, et ingenium vano se robore jactans.
Ingenium, nisi materiem Doctrina ministret,
Cessat inops rerum, ut torpet, si marmoris absit
Copia, Phidiaci fœcunda potentia cœli.
Quicquid agam, quocunque ferar, conatibus obstat   40
Res angusta domi, et macræ penuria mentis.
   Non Rationis opes Animus, nunc parta recensens,
Conspicit aggestas, et se miratur in illis,
Nec sibi de gaza præsens quód postulet usus
Summus adesse jubet celsa dominator ab arce;   45
Non operum serie, seriem dum computat ævi,
Præteritis fruitur, lætos aut sumit honores
Ipse sui judex, actæ bene munera vitæ;
Sed sua regna videns, loca nocte silentia late
Horret, ubi vanæ species, umbræque fugaces,   50
Et rerum volitant raræ per inane figuræ.

35–41 *These lines were written below the date at the end, and replace the following cancelled lines:*

> Notior ipse mihi fieri, pectusque fateri
> Incultum studiis, et paucis dotibus auctum
> Materies arti, sua desunt arma labori
> Ingeniumque sui cohibet penùria census.
> Nec miratur opes, celsa speculator ab arce
> Congestas animus, lætos aut sumit honores

> (aut *above* neque *struck out*)

37 ministret] ministrat *Works*   42 Rationis . . . recensens *above* Animus sero nimium
dum parta recenset *MS.*   43 Conspicit aggestas *above* Versat opum cumulos *MS.*
44 Nec *above* Non *MS.*   postulet] postulat *Works*   46 Non operum . . . ævi *above*
Non numerat palmas, aut *unfinished.*

38. Cf. Johnson's treatment of this idea when he was an undergraduate, p. 41 *ante.*
41. Cf. Juvenal, *Sat.* iii. 164–5; *London*, 177 (p. 76 *ante*).

Quid faciam? tenebrisne pigram damnare senectam
Restat? an accingar studiis gravioribus audax?
Aut, hoc si nimium est, tandem nova lexica poscam?

12. Dec. 1772

VERSES ADDRESSED TO
DR. LAWRENCE

Transcript by Mrs. Thrale in the John Rylands Library.
Piozzi, *Letters*, 1788, ii. 415.
Mainwaring *Piozziana*, i. 81.

Johnson had serious eye trouble in May and June 1773: see his letter to Mrs. Thrale of 24 May, *Prayers and Meditations* 22 July (*Works*, i (Yale ed. 1958), 157–8), *Life*, ii. 264, and the quotation from Baretti's letter to Mrs. Thrale of 5 June, given in *The R. B. Adam Library*, iii. 15. The verses may be dated about 24 May 1773. 'The copy of verses in Latin hexameters, as well as I remember, which he wrote to Dr. Lawrence, I forgot to keep a copy of', says Mrs. Piozzi in her *Anecdotes*, p. 74; but she included them in her edition of the *Letters*, along with her own translation. In *Piozziana* she says that she 'wrote them down as *he repeated* them . . . so perhaps there may be Mistakes'.

The poem was set up from the transcript now in the John Rylands Library. The title was added by Mrs. Piozzi on sending it to the press.

VERSES *addressed to Dr.* LAWRENCE, *composed*
by Dr. JOHNSON, *as he lay confined with*
an inflamed Eye.

SANGUINE dum tumido suffusus flagrat ocellus,
  Deliciasque fugit solitas solitosque labores;
Damnatus tenebris, lectoque affixus inerti,
Quid mecum peragam, quod tu doctissime posses
Laurenti saltem facili dignarier aure?   5
Humanæ mentis, rerum se pascere formis,
Est proprium, et quavis captare indagine verum
Omnibus unus amor, non est modus unus amoris.
Sunt qui curriculo timidi versantur in arcto,
Quos soli ducunt sensus, solus docet usus;   10

54 tandem *above* etiam *MS*

Qui sibi sat sapiunt, contenti noscere quantum
Vel digiti tractant, oculus vel sentit et auris:
Tantundem est illis, repleat spatia ardua cœli
Materies, vastum an late pandatur inane.
Scire vices ponti facile est, nihil amplius optant   15
Nec quærunt quid, luna, tuo cum fluctibus orbi.
Sic sibi diffisi, lenta experientia cursum
Qua sulcat, reptant tuti per lubrica vitæ.
Altera pars hominum, sanctæ rationis alumni,
Permissum credit nudas sibi sistere causas,   20
Materiemque rudem, magnæque parentis adesse
Conciliis, verique sacros recludere fontes.
Gens illa, impatiens per singula quæque vagandi
Tentat iter brevius, magno conamine summam
Naturæ invadens, mundique elementa refingens   25
Lævia serratis miscens, quadrata rotundis,
Corpora cuncta suis gestit variare figuris,
Particulasque locans, certas certo ordine, pulchram
Compagem edificat, cœlorum atque ætheris ignes
Accendit, rerumque modos ac fœdera ponit.   30
Hi sunt quos animi generosa insania magni
In sublime rapit, queis terra et pontus et aer
Sub pedibus subjecta jacent; queis ultima primis
Nexa patent; hi sunt quos nil mirabile turbat,
Nil movet insolitum, sub legibus omnia fictis   35
Dum statuunt, causisque audent prefigere metam.

ON RECOVERING THE USE OF
HIS EYES

Manuscript in the Hyde Collection.
Works, 1787, xi. 383.

The text is taken from the manuscript which shows that 'Jan.' in the edition
of 1787 is a misprint for 'Jun.'

11 sapient *Rylands*   14 Materies *emend.*: Materia *Rylands, Piozziana, 1788*
19 *New paragraph at head of new page, 1788*   24 ita *Rylands, with* iter *above in another hand*

VITÆ qui varias vices
Rerum perpetuus temperat arbiter,
Læto cedere lumini
Noctis tristitiam qui gelidæ jubet,
Acri sanguine turgidos   5
Obductosque oculos nubibus humidis
Sanari voluit meos,
Et me, cuncta beans cui nocuit dies
Luci reddidit et mihi.
Qua te Laude, Deus, qua prece prosequar?   10
Sacri discipulus Libri
Te semper studiis utilibus colam.
Grates, summe Pater, tuis
Recte qui fruitur muneribus, dedit.

Jun. 20–21. –73

ODE UPON THE ISLE OF SKYE

Transcript by Boswell in his MS. Journal (Yale).
Boswell, *Journal of a Tour to the Hebrides*, 1785, p. 173. (*Life*, v (1964), 155.)
The Gentleman's Magazine, February 1786, p. 156.
Works, 1787, xi. 394.

The text is taken from Boswell's *Journal*. 'I am inclined to think', he says, 'that it was on this day [Sunday, 5 Sept. 1773] he composed the following Ode upon the *Isle of Sky*, which a few days afterwards [9 Sept.] he shewed me at Rasay'. Boswell was allowed on 20 September to take the copy that he printed (*Journal*, ed. Pottle and Bennett, p. 193). In Boswell's transcript the punctuation is slight, most of the pointing appearing in the proofs. The authority of these accidentals may be doubted, as may also be the stanzaic form of which the Ross transcripts (p. 17 *ante*), made under his supervision, take no cognizance. Boswell also frequently supplied or altered titles.

The manuscript has disappeared, but Boswell records the alterations which Johnson had made in l. 2 and in ll. 15, 16. In the version given by Langton in the *Works* the rejected couplet is restored, and other changes are made. It would appear that Langton used the original manuscript but edited it to his own liking.

An unsigned translation was printed in *The Gentleman's Magazine*, February 1786, p. 156; another, by 'B', in April 1792, p. 365; and yet another in *The Scots Magazine*, April 1799, p. 261.

SKIA

PONTI profundis clausa recessibus,
  Strepens procellis, rupibus obsita,
    Quam grata defesso virentem
      Skia sinum nebulosa pandis.

His cura credo sedibus exulat;   5
His blanda certe pax habitat locis:
    Non ira, non mœror quietis
      Insidias meditatur horis.

At non cavata rupe latescere,
Menti nec ægræ montibus aviis   10
    Prodest vagari, nec frementes
      E scopulo numerare fluctus.

Humana virtus non sibi sufficit,
Datur nec æquum cuique animum sibi
    Parare posse, ut Stoicorum   15
      Secta crepet nimis alta fallax.

Exæstuantis pectoris impetum,
Rex summe, solus tu regis arbiter,
    Mentisque, te tollente, surgunt,
      Te recidunt moderante fluctus.   20

ODE ADDRESSED TO MRS. THRALE

Manuscript in the Hyde Collection.
Transcript by Mrs. Thrale in the Hyde Collection (15 August 1777).
Transcript made for Mrs. Thrale in the Rylands Library (MS. Eng. 543/27).
Transcript by Boswell in his manuscript Journal (Yale).

Boswell's MS. includes virtually no punctuation; that was inserted in the proofs of his
Journal of a Tour   Title] ODA *Boswell*   2 'In the manuscript, Dr. Johnson,
instead of *rupibus obsita*, had written *imbribus uvida*, and *uvida nubibus*, but struck them
both out.' *Boswell*   12 E scopulo] In specula *1787*   15, 16 *'Instead of these two
lines, he had written, but afterwards struck out, the following:*

          Parare posse, utcunque jactet
            Grandiloquus nimis alta Zeno.' *Boswell*.

This reading was adopted in 1787   19 surgunt] fluctus *1787* (*printer's error*)
20 recidunt *Malone's Errata*] recedunt *Boswell*: resident *1787*

Transcript in unidentified hand in the Huntington Library.
Thraliana MS. ii (1777-8), p. 97; ed. 1941, p. 215.
Boswell, *Journal of a Tour to the Hebrides*, 1785, p. 177. (*Life*, v (1964), 158.)
Piozzi, *Anecdotes*, 1786, p. 163.
Works, 1787, xi. 394.
Piozzi, *Letters*, 1788, i. 178.

   The original manuscript—which is reproduced in *The R. B. Adam Library*, i, after p. 115—closes with 'Scriptum in Skiâ. Sept. 6' [1773]. Under that date Boswell wrote in the *Journal*: 'Dr. Johnson being fatigued with his journey, retired early to his chamber, where he composed the following Ode, addressed to Mrs. Thrale.' In his letter to Mr. Thrale from Inveraray, 23 October 1773, Johnson says that he has 'inclosed an ode which I wrote in the isle of Sky'. Boswell received his copy from Mrs. Thrale; Johnson had refused to give him one, but added that he 'might get it from her if she pleased' (*Journal*, ed. Pottle and Bennett, p. 136, and M. Hyde, *The Impossible Friendship*, Harvard, 1972, pp. 44-5). The authority for Langton's reading in the last stanza as printed in the *Works* is not known.
   A translation signed 'B' and dated 1786 appeared in *The Gentleman's Magazine*, March 1792, p. 260. Miss Cornelia Knight's translation was printed in Piozzi, *Letters*, 1788, i. 179-80, and by Robert Carruthers in his edition of Boswell's *Journal*, 1851, p. 120. Yet another translation was supplied by Lord Houghton to Hayward's *Autobiography of Mrs. Piozzi*, 1861, i, p. 29, and was reprinted by Hill, *Life*, v. 424.

ODA

Pᴇʀᴍᴇᴏ terras, ubi nuda rupes
  Saxeas miscet nebulis ruinas,
Torva ubi rident steriles coloni
    Rura labores.

Pervagor gentes, hominum ferorum   5
Vita ubi nullo decorata cultu
Squallet informis, tugurîque fumis
    Fœda latescit.

Inter erroris salebrosa longi,
Inter ignotæ strepitus loquelæ,   10
Quot modis mecum, quid agat, requiro,
    Thralia dulcis.

Title] *None, MS., Thraliana, Anecdotes*: Oda *Tour*: Ode, De Skia Insula *1787*: Skia
Huntington transcript   1 rupe *Hyde, Thraliana*   5 gentes *above* terras *erased in*
MS.   7 tigurîque *MS., Hyde, Rylands, Thraliana, Anecdotes* (*corrected in Errata
and ed. 4*), *1787*   9 Errores *Thraliana*   12 Thralia] Thralea *Errata Anec.*
(*also* 19)   dulcis.] dulcis? *Tour*: dulcis! *Hyde*

Seu viri curas, pia nupta, mulcet,
Seu fovet mater sobolem benigna,
Sive cum libris novitate pascit   15
            Sedula mentem;

Sit memor nostri, fideique merces
Stet fides constans, meritoque blandum
Thraliæ discant resonare nomen
            Littora Sciæ.   20
Scriptum in Skiâ. Sept. 6.

VERSES UPON INCHKENNETH

Transcript by Boswell in his MS. Journal (Yale).
Boswell, *Journal of a Tour to the Hebrides*, 1785, p. 407. (*Life*, v (1964), 325–6.)
Works, 1787, xi. 393.

Boswell printed the poem under the date Sunday 17 October 1773: 'Dr. Johnson said, that it was the most agreeable Sunday he had ever passed; and it made such an impression on his mind, that he afterwards wrote the following Latin verses upon Inchkenneth.' Johnson sent them to Boswell in a letter dated 21 January 1775: '. . . as you love verses, I will send you a few which I made upon Inchkenneth; but remember the condition, that you shall not show them, except to Lord Hailes, whom I love better than any man whom I know so little. If he asks you to transcribe them for him, you may do it, but I think he must promise not to let them be copied again, nor to show them as mine.' (*Life*, ii. 293.)

The version printed by Langton in the *Works* is based on an earlier manuscript, was shown to Croker by Langton's grandson in 1831 but has since disappeared. (It was included in lot 242 in a sale at Messrs. Sotheby's, 1 December 1896, and was bought by John Pearson for £12.) Croker says that it bore the date '2d Dec. 1773'. His description of it shows that it was not a fair copy; if the date is correct, Johnson was engaged on the poem after his return to London. What Johnson sent to Boswell in 1775 was evidently a revised version from which two couplets were omitted.

13 cures *Hyde, Thraliana*   15 pascet *Hyde, Tour*   17, 18 merces . . . constans]
solvat Fida mercedem *1787*   21 . . . 1773 *Hyde*

20. 'The classical reader will not have failed to observe how much his [Johnson's] taste, and even his Latinity, have improved since the days of the ode *Ad Urbanum*, and the epigrams to *Savage* and *Eliza*. His verses *In Theatro*, and those in Sky and in Inchkenneth, and this ode to Mrs. Thrale are, if the Editor may venture to give his opinion, much more natural in their thoughts, and more elegant in their expressions, than his earlier attempts in this line.' (Croker, *Life*, 1831, ii. 388 n.)

According to Croker the manuscript proved that one of the lines as printed in 1787 'was manufactured by Mr. Langton from two variations which Dr. Johnson had, it seems, successively rejected'; but Langton gives other readings for which Croker's description of the manuscript does not account.

Boswell's version is here followed. His transcript is barely punctuated, most of the pointing being introduced in the proofs. Johnson generally punctuated only lightly and so the authority of the Boswellian accidentals may be doubted. The indentation of alternate lines was also introduced in the proofs, but Boswell was not usually attentive to such details in his transcripts. The variants in the manuscript are given on Croker's authority (*Life*, 1831, iii. 528).

A translation by Sir Daniel Sandford, written 1833, was printed in Lachlan Maclean's *Account of Iona*, ed. 1841, p. 134, and reprinted in *The Book of Highland Verse*, ed. Dugald Mitchell, 1912, p. 204.

Insula Sancti Kennethi

PARVA quidem regio, sed relligione priorum
   Nota, Caledonias panditur inter aquas;
Voce ubi Cennethus populos domuisse feroces
   Dicitur, et vanos dedocuisse deos.
Huc ego delatus placido per cœrula cursu   5
   Scire locum volui quid daret ille novi.
Illic Leniades humili regnabat in aula,
   Leniades magnis nobilitatus avis:
Una duas habuit casa cum genitore puellas,
   Quas Amor undarum fingeret esse deas: 10
Non tamen inculti gelidis latuere sub antris,
   Accola Danubii qualia sævus habet;
Mollia non deerant vacuæ solatia vitæ,
   Sive libros poscant otia, sive lyram.
Luxerat illa dies, legis gens docta supernæ   15
   Spes hominum ac curas cum procul esse jubet.

Title] Insula Kennethi, Inter Hebridas *1787*   2 Nota] Clara *1787*   inter] intra *Journal* edd. i. ii (misprint)   3 Kennethus *Boswell's transcript; changed in proof*
6 locum . . . ille] locus . . . iste *1787*   9 habuit] tenuit *MS.*: cepit *1787*
10 fingeret] crederet *1787*   11 Non] Nec *1787*   13 deerant] desunt *1787*
15 Luxerat] Fulserat *1787*   15, 16 gens . . . ac . . . cum] qua . . . et . . . gens *1787*
16 jubet] velit *MS. After this line 1787 reads:*

        Ut precibus justas avertat numinis iras
        Et summi accendat pectus amore boni.

8. *Leniades*, i.e. McLean—Sir Allan McLean, the chief of his clan.

Ponti inter strepitus sacri non munera cultus
  Cessarunt; pietas hic quoque cura fuit:
Quid quod sacrifici versavit femina libros,
  Legitimas faciunt pectora pura preces.   20
Quo vagor ulterius? quod ubique requiritur hic est;
  Hic secura quies, hic et honestus amor.

TRANSLATION OF 'BUSY, CURIOUS, THIRSTY FLY'

Works, 1787, xi. 404.

This translation was made before 5 July 1774, when Johnson wrote to Langton: 'If you have the Latin version of *Busy, curious, thirsty fly*, be so kind as to transcribe and send it' (Boswell, *Life*, ii. 281). Mrs. Thrale had been asked to give up her copy: 'he obliged me to resign his translation of the song beginning *Busy, curious, thirsty fly*, for him to give Mr. Langton, with a promise *not* to retain a copy. I concluded he knew why, so never enquired the reason' (*Anecdotes*, p. 75). The manuscript is lost, and the translation survives as Langton printed it.

The English verses were first published in *The Scarborough Miscellany*, 1732, with the title 'The Fly, An Anacreontick'. They were by William Oldys, Johnson's associate on *The Harleian Catalogue*.

S EU te sæva sitis, levitas sive improba fecit,
  Musca, meæ comitem, participemque dapis,
Pone metum, rostrum fidens immitte culullo,
  Nam licet, et toto prolue læta mero.

---

17 sacri non] non sacri *1787*   18 *After this line 1787 reads:*
      Nil opus est æris sacra de turre sonantis
      Admonitu, ipsa suas nunciat hora vices.

19 libros? *1787*   20 Sint pro legitimis pectora pura sacris *cancelled MS.*: Legitimas faciunt pura labella preces *cancelled MS.*: Sint pro legitimis pura labella sacris *1787*.

1 sitis *om. Works 1792–1816*: fames *1823, 1825*.

---

19. 'Miss McLean read the evening service, in which we all joined.' Boswell. Sir Allan's eldest daughter, Maria, is probably meant. She and her younger sister Sibella were at home at the time; Ann, the youngest, was away (*Boswell's Journal of a Tour to the Hebrides*, ed. Pottle and Bennett, 1964, p. 434).

20. Boswell wrote to Johnson on 2 February 1775 that Lord Hailes 'is charmed with your verses on Inchkenneth, says they are very elegant, but bids me tell you he doubts whether 'Legitimas faciunt pectora pura preces' be according to the rubrick: but that is your concern; for, you know, he is a Presbyterian'.

Tu, quamcunque tibi velox indulserit annus,   5
    Carpe diem, fugit, heu, non revocanda dies!
Quæ nos blanda comes, quæ nos perducat eodem,
    Volvitur hora mihi, volvitur hora tibi!
Una quidem, sic fata volunt, tibi vivitur æstas,
    Eheu, quid decies plus mihi sexta dedit!   10
Olim, præteritæ numeranti tempora vitæ,
    Sexaginta annis non minor unus erit.

'TETRASTICK' ON GOLDSMITH

Manuscript of Johnson's letter to Langton, 5 July 1774, in the Hyde Collection.
Boswell, *Life*, 1791, ii. 93 (1934, ii. 282).
R. Bland and J. H. Merivale, *Translations chiefly from the Greek Anthology, with
Tales and Miscellaneous Poems*, 1806, p. 99.
Works, 1825, i. 153 n.
Letters, ed. Chapman, 1952, i. 410–11, No. 358.

Johnson included these verses in his letter to Langton of 5 July 1774, written
on the morning of the day on which he set out on his Welsh tour. Goldsmith
had died on 4 April. They precede by two years the Latin epitaph in Westminster Abbey. Percy sent a copy to Boswell on 6 March 1787 (C. C. Abbott,
Catalogue of Papers at Fettercairn, 1936, p. 110), having 'procured' it from 'Mr.
Archdall' [Richard Archdall]. (See Waingrow, *Correspondence*, pp. 204–5.)
    Boswell printed the lines without accents: see R. W. Chapman, *Johnson and
Boswell Revised*, p. 28. Accents were added in the third edition of the *Life*, 1799,
by Malone. Text from the manuscript, though the accentuation of the last line
is faulty and should read: ποιητήν, ἱστορικόν, φυσικόν.
    A translation is given in William Seward's *Anecdotes*, 1798, ii. 466, and in
Bland and Merivale, *l.c.s.*

> *Τ*ΟΝ τάφον εἰσοράας τὸν Ὀλιβαρίοιο, κονίην
>   Ἄφροσι μὴ σεμνὴν, Ξεῖνε, πόδεσσι πάτει·
> Οἷσι μέμηλε φύσις, μέτρων χάρις, ἔργα παλαιῶν,
>   Κλαίετε ποιήτην, ἱστόρικον, φύσικον.

1 Ωλειβερίοιο *Life 1*: τόν Ο'λιβαρίοιο *Life 2–5*: τὸν Ο'λιβαροιο *Life 6, 1811*   2 παλει.
1806   4 *recte* ποιητήν, ἱστορικόν, φυσικόν

---

6. Cf. the motto of *The Idler*, No. 101: 'Carpe hilaris: fugit heu! non revocanda dies.'

ON THE DUKE OF MARLBOROUGH

Works, 1787, xi. 427.

This cannot be dated; most of the pieces that are known only in Langton's text were written late in Johnson's life.

Langton says that it is a version of a Latin epigram on the great Duke of Marlborough by the Abbé Salvini:

> Haud alio vultu fremuit Mars acer in armis:
> Haud alio Cypriam perculit ore Deam.

> *T*ΟΙΟΣ Ἄρης βροτολοιγὸς ἐνὶ πτολέμοισι μέμηνε,
> Καὶ τοῖος Παφίην πλῆξεν ἔρωτι Θεάν.

FRENCH DISTICHS

Manuscript of Mrs. Thrale's French Journal, 1775, in the John Rylands Library.
Bulletin of the John Rylands Library, July 1931, xv. 486.
The French Journals of Mrs. Thrale and Doctor Johnson, ed. Tyson and Guppy, 1932, p. 79.

On 15 September 1775 Mrs. Thrale set out with her husband and Johnson on their French tour, and on 22 September, when they were at Rouen, she made the following entry in her *Journal*: 'Mr. Johnson has made a little Distich at every Place we have slept at, for example . . .'

> A CALAIS
> Trop de frais.

> S^t. Omer
> Tout est cher.

> Arras
> Helas!

> A Amiens
> On n'a rien.

> Au Mouton[1]
> Rien de Bon.

---

[1] Explained in the Diary as 'The Sign of the Mouton D'Or a(t) Neuf Chatel'.

TRANSLATION OF VERSES FROM
A FRENCH PANTOMIME

Thraliana MS. ii (1777–8), p. 90; ed. 1941, p. 209.
Piozzi, *Anecdotes*, 1786, p. 68.

The original of this impromptu translation is given thus in *Thraliana*:
'These foolish French Verses too—in a Pantomime:
> Je suis Cassandre descendu des Cieux
> Pour vous faire entendre, Mesdames et Messieurs,
> Que Je suis Cassandre deçendu des Cieux—

which he translated thus—Improviso.'

In the *Anecdotes* the first and third lines have 'descendüe', and 'Cassander' in Johnson's translation becomes 'Cassandra'; but 'Bystander' shows that Johnson said 'Cassander'.

The French verses appear to be derived from the seventh Entrée of Benserade's *Balet de Cassandre* (*Œuvres*, 1698, ii. 8):

> Je suis Cassandre
> Descendüe des Cieux,
> Je suis Cassandre,
> Non pas pour vos beaux yeux, &c.

The impromptu may have been made during Johnson's visit to Paris with the Thrales in October 1775. According to the *Anecdotes* the French verses were 'quoted' to him. His own diary records only one visit to a theatre: 'At night we went to a comedy. I neither saw nor heard . . .' (19 October 1775; *Works*, i (Yale ed. 1958), 239–40), but Mrs. Thrale went to the theatre and opera, and she gives her impressions of an allegorical farce (*The French Journals of Mrs. Thrale and Doctor Johnson*, ed. Tyson and Guppy, 1932, p. 140).

I AM Cassander, come down from the Sky,
   To tell each Bystander, what none can deny,
That I am Cassander come down from the Sky.

TRANSLATION OF AN EPIGRAM ON
A DOG

Thraliana, MS. i. 17; ed. 1941, p. 10.

The Latin epigram of which this is a translation is printed in *Menagiana*, ed. 1713, ii. 162:

'Du Belley a fait cette belle Epigramme sur un Chien qui étoit de bonne garde contre les voleurs, mais qui laissoit entrer les Amans sans abboyer:

> *Latratu fures excepi; mutus amantes:*
> *Sic placui Domino; sic placui Dominæ.*'

Menagiana adds an Italian translation, and *Thraliana* gives it also as well as one in French. As the passage occurs near the beginning of *Thraliana*, Johnson's translation—which is introduced with the words 'Johnson translates it thus'—cannot be later than 1776 and may belong to that year. It is not included in the *Anecdotes* or *British Synonymy*. (See Du Bellay, *Poésies françaises et latines*, ed. E. Courbet, 1918, i. 511.) In *Epigrams Ancient and Modern*, ed. J. Booth (1865), p. 306, the Latin is thus translated:

> 'At thieves I bark; at lovers wag my tail!
> And thus I please both Lord and Lady Thrale.'

To Robbers furious, and to Lovers tame,
     I pleas'd my Master, and I pleas'd my Dame.

TRANSLATION OF LINES IN BARETTI'S 'EASY PHRASEOLOGY'

Transcript by Baretti in the collection of the Marquis of Lansdowne.
Thraliana MS. ii (1777–8), p. 91; ed. 1941, p. 210.
Piozzi, *Anecdotes*, 1786, p. 69.
Works, 1787, xi. 378.
Lansdowne, *Johnson and Queeney*, 1932, p. xv, and *The Queeney Letters*, 1934, p. xiii.

'He likewise translated those Pretty Italian Lines of Mr. Baretti at the End of the small Talk very elegantly and all in a Minute' (*Thraliana*, ii. 91). Baretti's lines are:

> Viva! viva la padrona!
> Tutta bella, e tutta buona,
> La padrona è un angiolella
> Tutta buona e tutta bella;
> Tutta bella e tutta buona;
> Viva! viva la padrona!

Baretti's *Small Talk for the use of Young Ladies that wish to learn the colloquial part of the Italian Language* (published as *Easy Phraseology*, &c. with a preface by Johnson) was printed in 1775, and the translation was written in *Thraliana* before the end of 1777. The 'padrona' was Queeney Thrale, whose name, like her mother's, was Hester.

In April 1794 Mrs. Piozzi noted in *Thraliana* (vi. 49; ed. 1941, p. 877) that the verses were 'coming out now set to musick'. In a marginal note in the copy of *Anecdotes* presented to Sir James Fellowes in 1816 she says: 'I heard these verses sung at Mr. Thomas's by three voices, not three weeks ago' (A. Hayward, *Autobiography of Mrs. Piozzi*, 1861, i. 29).

The text is from the *Anecdotes*. Baretti's transcript of the lines, printed in
Lord Lansdowne's *Johnson and Queeney*, reads as follows:

> Long may live our charming Hetty
>   Always young and always pretty:
> Live our charming Hetty long
>   Always pretty always young;
> Always young and always pretty
>   Long may live our charming Hetty!
> Huzza! Huzza! Huzza!

LONG may live my lovely Hetty!
  Always young and always pretty,
Always pretty, always young,
Live my lovely Hetty long!
Always young and always pretty;   5
Long may live my lovely Hetty!

TRANSLATIONS FROM METASTASIO

Thraliana MS. ii (1777–8), pp. 92–4; iv. 100; ed. 1941, pp. 211, 212, 542.
Piozzi, *Anecdotes*, 1786, pp. 166–7.
Works, 1787, xi. 381–2.

These two impromptu translations were written in *Thraliana* towards the end
of 1777 and introduced thus:

'This Italian Song too of Metastasio as Baretti and I were commending it, he turned into
English instantly

> Deh! se piacermi vuoi
> Lascia i Sospetti tuoi,
> Non mi turbar con questo
> Molesto dubitar:
>
> Chi ciecamente crede
> Impegna a serbar Fede;
> Chi sempre Inganno aspetta,
> Alletta ad Ingannar.

. . . Another favourite Passage too in the same Author, which Baretti made his Pupil,
my eldest Daughter, get by heart, Johnson translated into Blank Verse *sur le Champ*:
Baretti wrote it down from his Lips, and I write it now from Baretti's Copy, which is
almost worne out with lying by in the folds.

> Parlata D'Emirena al falso Cortigiano Aquilio—
>   Ah, tu in Corte invecchiasti, . . .'

The first passage is from *La Clemenza di Tito*, I. ii, the second from *Adriano
in Syria*, II. i. Both translations must be earlier than June 1776, when Baretti
left the Thrale household.

The second translation was again inserted in *Thraliana* on 28 August 1782. In her *Anecdotes* Mrs. Piozzi says 'it is probably printed before now, as I think two or three people took copies'. But all the known printed texts derive from the *Anecdotes*, which is here followed.

I

WOULD you hope to gain my heart,
   Bid your teizing doubts depart;
He who blindly trusts, will find
Faith from every generous mind:
He who still expects deceit,   5
Only teaches how to cheat.

II

Grown old in courts, thou art not surely one
Who keeps the rigid rules of ancient honour;
Well skill'd to sooth a foe with looks of kindness,
To sink the fatal precipice before him,
And then lament his fall with seeming friendship: 5
Open to all, true only to thyself,
Thou know'st those arts which blast with envious praise,
Which aggravate a fault with feign'd excuses,
And drive discountenanc'd virtue from the throne:
That leave the blame of rigour to the prince,   10
And of his every gift usurp the merit;
That hide in seeming zeal a wicked purpose,
And only build upon another's ruin.

TRANSLATION OF A DISTICH ON THE DUKE OF MODENA

Thraliana MS. ii (1777-8), p. 89; ed. 1941, p. 209.
Piozzi, *Anecdotes*, 1786, p. 69.
Works, 1787, xi. 379.

Mrs. Thrale included this distich in *Thraliana* towards the end of 1777 and introduced it thus:

'Baretti and I were talking one Day of the Art of Improvisation: Johnson, says he, can

II 2 Who] That *Thraliana* i, ii   4-5 him . . . his] them . . . their *Thraliana* i
8 Excuse *Thraliana* i   9 drive] chase *Thraliana* ii   11 And yet of every *Thraliana* i, ii

do it as well as any Italian of us all if he pleases; I once repeated him these Lines of an Improvisatore spoken when the Duke of Modena ran away for Fear of the Comet

> Se al venir vostro i Principi sen' vanno,
> Deh venga ogni Di,—durate un Anno.—

which he instantly rendered thus. . . .'

A comet was seen in February and March 1742, and in May the Duke of Modena withdrew from his dominions before the attack of the Sardinians (*Gentleman's Magazine*, 1742, pp. 106, 210, 334).

Johnson reminded Mrs. Thrale of the Italian distich in his letter to her of 6 October 1783.

> IF at your coming princes disappear,
> Comets! come every day—and stay a year.

TO MRS. THRALE, ON HER COMPLETING HER THIRTY-FIFTH YEAR

Mrs. Thrale's manuscript in the John Rylands Library (MS. Eng. 543/26).
Thraliana MS. ii (1777–8), p. 91; ed. 1941, p. 211.
Piozzi, *Anecdotes*, 1786, p. 164.
Works, 1787, xi. 380.

Mrs. Thrale was born on 27 January 1740/1. According to *Thraliana* this poem was written for her birthday in 1777:

'And this Year 1777 when I told him it was my Birthday and that I was then thirty five Years old, He repeated me these Verses which I wrote down from his Mouth as he made them.'

A fuller account, less trustworthy in detail, is given in her *Anecdotes*:

'As I went into his room the morning of my birth-day once, and said to him, Nobody sends me any verses now, because I am five-and-thirty years old; and Stella was fed with them till forty-six, I remember. My being just recovered from illness and confinement will account for the manner in which he burst out suddenly, for so he did without the least previous hesitation whatsoever, and without having entertained the smallest intention towards it half a minute before. . . . "And now (said he, as I was writing them down), you may see what it is to come for poetry to a Dictionary-maker; you may observe that the rhymes run in alphabetical order exactly".'

The poem probably belongs to 1776. When copying it into *Thraliana* at the very end of 1777, Mrs. Thrale might easily have underestimated the time that had elapsed since she received it.

Text from Mrs. Thrale's manuscript.

O FT in Danger yet alive
     We are come to Thirtyfive;
Long may better Years arrive,
Better Years than Thirty five;
Could Philosophers contrive   5
Life to stop at Thirtyfive,
Time his Hours should never drive
O'er the Bounds of Thirtyfive:
High to soar and deep to dive
Nature gives at Thirtyfive;   10
Ladies—stock and tend your Hive,
Trifle not at Thirty five:
For howe'er we boast and strive,
Life declines from Thirtyfive;
He that ever hopes to thrive   15
Must begin by Thirty five:
And those who wisely wish to wive,
Must look on Thrale at Thirtyfive.

CHARADE ON THOMAS BARNARD

Manuscript in the library of the Earl of Crawford.
Transcript by Mrs. Thrale in 'Minced Meat for Pyes' (MS. Harvard).
Boswell, *Life*, 1793, i. *xviii (1934, iv. 195).
Letters, ed. Chapman, 1952, ii. 160, No. 506.1.

This charade was written on a card now in the possession of Lord Crawford, and is here printed from a transcript made by Dr. L. F. Powell. The date is Friday, 17 January 1777. Johnson was prevented from dining with the Club on that day for the reason given in his letter to Mrs. Thrale of 15 January, and left the card on Dean Barnard, who was about to go to Ireland. Barnard had been appointed Dean of Derry in 1769 and in 1780 became Bishop of Killaloe.

The charade was printed by Boswell in 1793, among the additions 'recollected and received after the second edition was printed'; and in the third edition it was inserted under the year 1783.

At the top of the card Johnson wrote: 'Mr. Johnson, not being to dine at the Club this day, as he intended, waits on the Dean of Derry to take leave, and wish him a prosperous voyage. Friday Jan: 17th.'

3 Long] Oft *Thraliana*   17 those] all *Anecdotes*

14. Cf. Johnson's letter to Mrs. Thrale, 14 August 1780: 'If you try to plague me, I shall tell you that, according to Galen, life begins to decline from *Thirty-five*.'

Charade!

M Y first, shuts out Thieves from your house or your Room,
My second, expresses a Syrian perfume;
My whole, is a Man in whose converse is shar'd,
The strength of a Bar, and sweetness of Nard.

LINES WRITTEN IN RIDICULE OF
THOMAS WARTON'S POEMS

Thraliana, ii (1777–8), p. 89; ed. 1941, p. 209.
Piozzi, *Anecdotes*, 1786, p. 64.
Works, 1787, xi. 375.

Thraliana gives the name which was suppressed in the *Anecdotes*:

'When Tom Warton published his Poems in Jan: 1777.—nobody read 'em. Warton's Poems are *come out* says Mr. Johnson; yes replied I, and this cold Weather has *struck them in* again: I have written Verses to abuse them says he, but I can repeat but two or three of them, and those you must say nothing of, for I love Thomas look you—tho' I laugh at him.'

Thraliana also contains this marginal note opposite the verses:

'These Verses have of late run about the Town. I gave them Pepys and he has shew'd off with them for a whole Winter.'

W HERESOE'ER I turn my View,
All is strange, yet nothing new;
Endless Labour all along,
Endless Labour to be wrong;
Phrase that Time has flung away,   5
Uncouth Words in Disarray:
Trickt in Antique Ruff and Bonnet,
Ode and Elegy and Sonnet.

PARODY OF THOMAS WARTON

Thraliana ii (1777–8), p. 89; iii (1778–81), p. 126; ed. 1941, pp. 209, 398.
Piozzi, *Anecdotes*, 1786, p. 66.
Works, 1787, xi. 377.
Boswell, *Life*, 1791, ii. 147 (1934, iii. 159).

The full story of the composition of this parody is given by Boswell under the date 18 September 1777 (*Life*, iii. 158–9):

'He observed, that a gentleman of eminence in literature had got into a bad style of poetry of late. "He puts (said he) a very common thing in a strange dress till he does not know it himself, and thinks other people do not know it."
BOSWELL. "That is owing to his being so much versant in old English poetry."
JOHNSON. "What is that to the purpose, Sir? If I say a man is drunk, and you tell me it is owing to his taking much drink, the matter is not mended. No, Sir, ——— has taken to an odd mode. For example; he'd write thus:

> Hermit hoar, in solemn cell,
> Wearing out life's evening gray.

Gray evening is common enough; but *evening gray* he'd think fine.—Stay;—we'll make out the stanza. . . ." '

Boswell added a note on the second stanza:

'When Dr. Johnson and I were sitting *tête-à-tête* at the Mitre tavern, May 9, 1778, he said, "*Where* is bliss", would be better. He then added a ludicrous stanza, but would not repeat it, lest I should take it down. It was somewhat as follows; the last line I am sure I remember:

> While I thus   cried,
>   seer;
> The hoary   reply'd,
> Come, my lad, and drink some beer.

In spring, 1779, when in better humour, he made the second stanza, as in the text. There was only one variation afterwards made on my suggestion, which was changing *hoary* in the third line to *smiling*, both to avoid a sameness with the epithet in the first line, and to describe the hermit in his pleasantry. He was then very well pleased that I should preserve it.'

The two stanzas were inserted in *Thraliana* in the margin opposite the verses beginning 'Wheresoe'er I turn my view', and with this introduction: 'Long after this, he in scorn of the same Author Tom Warton, composed extempore the following comical Lines.' They were inserted a second time on 1 August 1779, when this remark was added:

'They are meant to ridicule Tom Warton; Mr Boswell has 'em however, I remember seeing him write them down one day in our Library at Stretham.'

Warton's name was suppressed in the *Anecdotes* as well as in Boswell's *Life*, from which this text is taken.

H ERMIT hoar, in solemn cell,
        Wearing out life's evening gray;
Smite thy bosom, sage, and tell,
    Where is bliss? and which the way?

3 Smite] Strike *Thraliana* i, ii, *Anecdotes*   4 Where *Thraliana* i, *Boswell*: What *Thraliana* ii, *Anecdotes*.

1, 2. Cf. Warton, Ode on 'The First of April' (*Poems*, 1777, p. 36): The morning hoar, and evening chill.

Thus I spoke; and speaking sigh'd;   5
—Scarce repress'd the starting tear;—
When the smiling sage reply'd—
—Come, my lad, and drink some beer.

TRANSLATION OF A SONG IN
WALTON'S 'COMPLEAT ANGLER'

Manuscript in the Hyde Collection.
Works, 1787, xi. 405.

The manuscript, dated 'Febr. 1777', is reproduced in facsimile in *The R. B.
Adam Library*, i, after p. 189. The lines are a translation of a part of John
Chalkhill's song in *The Compleat Angler* (I. xvi):

> Or we sometimes pass an hour
>   Under a green willow,
> That defends us from a shower,
>   Making earth our pillow;
>   Where we may
>   Think and pray,
>   Before death
>   Stops our breath:
>   Other joys
>   Are but toys,
>   And to be lamented.

Of *The Compleat Angler* Johnson observed 'It is a mighty pretty book!' (*The
Athenæum*, 25 August 1894, p. 257.) Text and title from the manuscript, with
additions to the punctuation.

Waltoni Piscator perfectus

Nunc, per gramina fusi,
    Densâ fronde Salicti
Dum defenditur imber,
Molles ducimus horas.
Hic, dum debita morti   5
Paulum vita moratur,
Nunc rescire priora,
Nunc instare futuris,

7 smiling] hoary *Thraliana* i, ii, *Anecdotes*

Title] E Waltoni Piscatore Perfecto excerptum. *Works*

Nunc summi prece sancta
Patris Numen adire est.   10
Quicquid quæritur ultra,
Cæco ducit amore,
Vel spe ludit inani,
Luctus mox pariturum.[1]
Febr. 1777

PROLOGUE TO
'A WORD TO THE WISE'

The Public Advertiser, 31 May 1777.
The London Chronicle, 31 May 1777.
The St. James's Chronicle, 31 May 1777.
The Westminster Magazine, May 1777, p. 273.
The Gentleman's Magazine, June 1777, p. 286.
The Scots Magazine, June 1777, p. 325.
The London Magazine, July 1777, p. 375.
The Annual Register, 1777, p. 198.
Hugh Kelly, *Works*, 1778, p. x.
The Theatrical Bouquet, 1778, 1780, p. 211.
Poetical Works, 1785, p. 178.
Hawkins, *Life of Johnson*, 1787, p. 518.
Works, 1787, xi. 349.
Boswell, *Life*, 1791, ii. 115 (1934, iii. 114).

A note by the Rev. John Hussey in his copy of Boswell's *Life* (now in the National Library of Australia), states:

'On reading over this Prologue to Dr. Johnson, the morning after it was spoken, the Doctor told me instead of *renew'd hostilities* he wrote *revengeful petulance*, and did not seem pleased with the alteration.'

Hussey had earlier supplied Boswell with 'Memorandums' on Hawkins's *Life of Johnson*. His notes included: 'Prologue for Mrs. Kelly. line 9th for renew'd hostilities, read, resentful petulance.' (Waingrow, *Correspondence*, p. 235). This note made in August 1787 is more probably correct than his later version in which 'revengeful' may be a slip for 'resentful'.

15 *date omitted in Works*

---

[1] 'The metre . . . is a curious choice, as such lines are usually employed in combination with others and not by themselves throughout the whole of a piece. But George Buchanan, whom Johnson called 'a great poetical genius', puts in his tragedy of 'Jephthes' twenty-five consecutive lines of this measure in the mouth of the Chorus.' (Edward Bensly, *Notes and Queries*, 5 September 1925, p. 170.)

As the version in *The Public Advertiser* alone gives *petulance*, that version is here adopted.

Hugh Kelly had died in February 1777 at the age of thirty-eight, and on 29 May the management of Covent Garden gave a performance of his *Word to the Wise* for the benefit of his widow and children. To add importance to the occasion Johnson was asked to write a Prologue. He complied out of kindness, for his opinion of Kelly was not high, and they were not well acquainted. On one occasion Johnson said of him, 'I never desire to converse with a man who has written more than he has read' (*Johnsonian Miscellanies*, ii. 6).

When *A Word to the Wise* was produced at Drury Lane in the first week of March 1770, it met with the organized interruption of Kelly's political opponents, because of his support of the government in his management of *The Public Ledger*. According to Johnson's letter of 2 June 1777 to Mrs. Thrale, 'poor Mrs Kelly had a miserable night. Only fifty pounds' (MS. Hyde). There was nothing political in the play; it was just another sentimental comedy. When published by subscription a few weeks later, it was introduced by an address in which the author replied to his assailants.

The play was revived at Covent Garden on 13 May 1777, without any demonstration of ill will. Johnson's Prologue must have been written in the intervening fortnight before the benefit performance. It was spoken by Thomas Hull, and was 'heard with the most respectful attention, and dismissed with the loudest applause' (*Biographia Dramatica*, 1782, i. 269). See also Hawkins's *Life of Johnson*, p. 518; *Letters*, ed. Chapman, ii. 190, no. 535; *Johnsonian Miscellanies*, i. 432.

Prologue to *'A Word to the Wise'*

THIS night presents a play, which publick rage,
    Or right, or wrong, once hooted from the stage;
From zeal or malice now no more we dread,
For English vengeance *wars not with the dead*.
A generous foe regards, with pitying eye,   5
The man whom fate has laid, where all must lye.
To wit, reviving from its author's dust,
Be kind, ye judges, or at least be just:
Let no resentful petulance invade
Th' oblivious grave's inviolable shade.   10

9 Let] For *Lond. Chron.*, *St. James's Chron.*, *Gent. Mag.*, *Scots Mag.*, *Lond. Mag.*, *West. Mag.*, *Ann. Reg.*, *1785*, *Works*   resentful petulance *Hussey 1787* renew'd hostilities *all except Public Advertiser*; revengeful petulance *Hussey 1791*

4. 'I war not with the dead', Pope's Homer, *Iliad*, vii. 485.

Let one great payment every claim appease,
And him who cannot hurt, allow to please;
To please by scenes unconscious of offence,
By harmless merriment, or useful sense.
Where aught of bright, or fair, the piece displays,   15
Approve it only—'tis too late to praise.
If want of skill, or want of care appear,
Forbear to hiss—the Poet cannot hear.
By all, like him, must praise and blame be found;
At best, a fleeting gleam, or empty sound.   20
Yet then shall calm reflection bless the night,
When liberal pity dignify'd delight;
When pleasure fired her torch at Virtue's flame,
And mirth was bounty with a humbler name.

BURLESQUE OF LINES BY LOPE DE VEGA

Thraliana MS. ii (1777–8), p. 90; ed. 1941, p. 210.
Piozzi, *Anecdotes*, 1786, p. 67.
Works, 1787, xi. 378.

The occasion of this impromptu burlesque is thus described in *Thraliana*:

'Another more humorous Instance of his Powers of Improvisation. I was praising these Verses of Lope de Vega,

> Si a quien los Leones vence,
> Vence una Muger hermosa;
> El de mas flaco s'averguence
> O ella de ser mas furiosa.

They are well enough, replied Johnson, but the Conceit is not clear: the Lady as we all know does not conquer as the Lyon does—'tis merely a Play of Words as if I should say
If the Man etc.'

This passage was written by Mrs. Thrale towards the end of 1777, but how much earlier the verses were made is not known. In his letter to Mrs. Thrale of 2 April 1773 Johnson says, 'To-day I have been learning Spanish of Baretti'; on the other hand, when he was on his visit to Percy at Easton Maudit, North-amptonshire, in the summer of 1764, his regular reading was 'the old Spanish romance of *Felixmarte of Hircania*'. The Spanish quatrain is from Lope's *Arcadia*, iv (*Biblioteca de Autores Españoles*, vol. 38, *Colección . . . de Obras No Dramáticas de Lope . . .* , Madrid, 1926, p. 115).

20 best] last *Kelly's Works, Hawkins's Life, Boswell*   24 a] an *all exc. Pub. Adv.*
Gent. Mag., Scots Mag., West. Mag., Ann. Reg.

The substance of the passage in *Thraliana* is reproduced in the *Anecdotes*, as is also the substance of this continuation:

'This is of the same Species of Humour as his reply to Sheridan who was commending with ridiculous Vehemence the following Line

> Who rules o'er Freemen should himself be free:

to be sure, Sir, replied Johnson hastily, and

> Who drives fat Oxen should himself be fat.'

The line which is parodied concludes Act I of Henry Brooke's *The Earl of Essex*, produced in 1761; the parody appears to have been first printed in the account of Johnson in *The Westminster Magazine* for September 1774, p. 445. (*Life*, iv. 312–13.)

Text from *Thraliana*.

I F the Man who Turneps cries
Cry not when his Father dies;
'Tis a Sign that he had rather
Have a Turnep than a Father.

TRANSLATION OF LINES BY BENSERADE

Thraliana MS. ii (1777–8), p. 94; ed. 1941, p. 213.
Piozzi, *Anecdotes*, 1786, p. 70.
Works, 1787, xi. 379.

This translation was given impromptu, according to *Thraliana*, 'when somebody was praising Benserade's Verses à son lit.

> Theatre des Ris et des Pleurs,
> Lit ou je nais et ou je meurs;
> Tu nous fais voir comment Voisins
> Sont nos Plaisirs et nos Chagrins.'

Mrs. Thrale had already given her own translation in *Thraliana*, i. 206 (ed. 1941, p. 121):

> Bed where first I drew my Breath,
> Bed of Love, and Bed of Death;
> Thine's the Theatre to show
> How near allied are Bliss and Woe.

The first volume of *Thraliana* (September 1776–September 1777) contains no allusion to Johnson's translation, which was apparently made after hers, sometime late in 1777.

3 Sign] proof *Anecdotes*   4 a Father] his father *Anecdotes*

I N bed we laugh, in bed we cry,
And born in bed, in bed we die;
The near approach a bed may shew
Of human bliss to human woe.

TRANSLATION OF ANACREON'S 'DOVE'

Thraliana MS. iii (1777–8), p. 123; ed. 1941, p. 233.
Piozzi, *Anecdotes*, 1786, p. 46.
A Dictionary of the English Language, by Samuel Johnson, *L.L.D.*, London,
Jarvis, 1786, i. a3ʳ.
Works, 1787, xi. 374.

This poem was written in *Thraliana* on 15 January 1778, and is thus
introduced:

'Mr. Johnson told me today that he had translated Anacreon's Dove, and as they were
the first Greek Verses that had struck him when a Boy; so says he they continue to
please me as well as any Greek Verses now I am Three score: I hope added he, I have
done them as well as Frank Fawkes;—seeing me laugh at that—nay nay says he, Frank
Fawkes has done them very finely. here however are Johnson's.'

This was supplemented two months later by the following marginal note:

'25: March. Johnson said to me—so you have writ out my translation of the Dove
in the *Thraliana* I warrant; I have so, said I; but have you mention'd says he that I
intended doing it at sixteen, and never did till I was 68, for that's most remarkable.'

These two passages are the basis of the account in the *Anecdotes*, where it is
added that the poem was taken down to Johnson's dictation: 'if you will get
the pen and ink, I will repeat to you Anacreon's Dove directly.'

There were two copies of Anacreon in the catalogue of Johnson's books:
lot 171, published by the Foulis Press in Glasgow in 1777, and lot 617 from the
same press in 1761. The latter was probably the copy procured for Johnson by
Boswell in 1772 (*Life*, ii. 202). It is now in the Hyde Collection. A copy of the
edition by Joshua Barnes, 1721, inscribed 'Sam: Johnson 1726', is in the library
of the University of Chicago, and 'Anacreon per Baxter' appears in the list of
the books Johnson left behind on going down from Oxford (*Johnsonian Gleanings*, v. 229).

In his *Life of Waller* (1779), Johnson said: 'Genius now and then produces
a lucky trifle. We still read the *Dove* of Anacreon, and *Sparrow* of Catullus . . .'
(ed. Hill, para. 109).

The translation by Francis Fawkes (1720–77) was published in 1760. Johnson
was a subscriber to his *Original Poems and Translations*, 1761. He was the joint
editor of *The Poetical Calendar*, 1763, which contains two of Johnson's poems
and his account of Collins.

The text here printed is from the *Anecdotes*, but the variants in *Thraliana*
have been restored, and occasionally the punctuation.

Anacreon, Ode IX

L OVELY courier of the sky,
   Whence or whither dost thou fly?
Scatt'ring, as thy pinions play,
Liquid fragrance all the way:
Is it business? is it love?   5
Tell me, tell me, gentle Dove.
"Soft Anacreon's vows I bear,
"Vows to Myrtale the fair;
"Grac'd with all that charms the heart,
"Blushing nature, smiling art.   10
"Venus, courted with an ode,
"On the bard her Dove bestow'd.
"Vested with a master's right
"Now Anacreon rules my flight:
"His the letters which you see,   15
"Weighty charge consign'd to me:
"Think not yet my service hard,
"Joyless task without reward:
"Smiling at my master's gates,
"Freedom my return awaits,   20
"But the liberal grant in vain
"Tempts me to be wild again:
"Can a prudent Dove decline
"Blissful bondage such as mine?
"Over hills and fields to roam,   25
"Fortune's guest, without a home,
"Under leaves to hide one's head,
"Slightly shelter'd, coarsely fed?
"Now my better lot bestows
"Sweet repast, and soft repose;   30
"Now the generous bowl I sip
"As it leaves Anacreon's lip,
"Void of care, and free from dread
"From his fingers snatch his bread,

Title. *None Thraliana, Anecdotes*   2 or] and *Anecdotes*   11 with] by *Anecdotes*
15 which] that *Anecdotes*

"Then with luscious plenty gay   35
"Round his chamber dance and play,
"Or from wine as courage springs,
"O'er his face extend my wings;
"And when feast and frolic tire,
"Drop asleep upon his lyre.   40
"This is all;—be quick and go,
"More than all thou canst not know;
"Let me now my pinions ply,
"I have chatter'd like a pye."

TO DR. LAWRENCE

Manuscript in the Huntington Library (HM. 675).
Works, 1787, xi. 391.

Thomas Lawrence, for many years Johnson's physician and friend, was President of the Royal College of Physicians from 1767 to 1774. He retired to Canterbury after a paralytic stroke in 1782, and died there 6 June 1783. 'He was a man of strict piety and profound learning, but little skilled in the knowledge of life or manners, and died without having ever enjoyed the reputation he so justly deserved' (Piozzi, *Anecdotes*, p. 76; cf. Hawkins, *Life*, p. 401).

A translation of the Ode while it was still unpublished was printed in *The Gentleman's Magazine* for December 1784, p. 934, signed 'J. D.'—perhaps John Desmoulins, a witness to Johnson's will and a legatee.

The present text is taken from the manuscript which Lawrence received. Langton apparently used another manuscript, and may have added the explanatory title.

Ad T. L. M.D.

FATERIS ergo quod populus solet
    Crepare væcors, nil sapientiam
  Prodesse vitæ, literasque
    In trepidis dare terga rebus.

Tu, queîs laborat sors hominum, mala   5
Nec vincis acer, nec pateris pius;
  Te mille succorum potentem
    Destituit medicina mentis.

Title] Ad Thomam Laurence, Medicum Doctissimum, Cum filium peregre agentem desiderio nimis tristi prosequeretur. *Works*   4 trepidis] dubiis *Works*

---

44 Cf. the last line of Fawkes's translation, 'I have chatter'd like a Jay'.

Per cæca noctis tædia turbidæ,
Pigræ per horas lucis inutiles, 10
   Torpesque languescisque curis
   Sollicitus nimis, heu! paternis.

Tandem dolori plus satis est datum,
Exsurge fortis, nunc animis opus,
   Te docta, Laurenti, vetustas 15
   Te medici revocant labores.

Permitte summo res hominum Patri,
Permitte fidens, ac muliebribus,
   Amice, majorem querelis,
   Redde tuis, tibi redde, mentem. 20
         Cal. Jun. 1778

A SONG COMPOSED FOR FANNY BURNEY

Fanny Burney's transcript in the Berg Collection, New York Public Library.
Joyce Hemlow, *The History of Fanny Burney*, 1958, p. 114.

According to Fanny Burney's *Diary*, Johnson, whilst at Streatham in November 1778, had a slight fall which led him to joke that he would be nursed by Fanny who should sing to him to soothe his cares. He then recited impromptu, the following verses (*Diary of Fanny Burney*, ed. Austin Dobson, 1904, i. 145). Fanny Burney's transcript was first discovered and published by Professor Joyce Hemlow.

SHE shall sing me a song,
  Of two Day's long
The Woodcock and the sparrow;
Our little Dog has bit his tail
And he'll be Hang'd to-morrow. 5

AN EXTEMPORE ELEGY

Fanny Burney's transcript in the Berg Collection, New York Public Library.
Joyce Hemlow, *The History of Fanny Burney*, 1958, pp. 114-15.

According to Fanny Burney's account this elegy was made extempore, 'Dr. Johnson, Mrs Thrale and myself spouting it out alternately'. The lines are

17 res hominum] quicquid habes *Works*   18 ac] et *Works*   21 *date omitted in Works*

undated, and the extent of the alternate contributions is unknown. They may
have been single lines, couplets, or whole stanzas, though Johnson's responsibility
for the clumsy sixteenth line may be doubted.

i

Here's a Woman of the Town,
   Lies as Dead as any Nail!
She was once of high renown,—
   And so here begins my Tale.

ii

She was once as cherry plump   5
   Red her cheek as Cath'rine Pear,
Toss'd her nose, and shook her Rump,
   Till she made the Neighbours stare.

iii

There she soon became a Jilt,
   Rambling often to and fro'   10
All her life was naught but guilt,
   Till Purse and Carcase both were low.

iv

But there came a country 'Squire
   He was a seducing Pug!
Took her from her friends and sire,   15
   To his own House her did lug.

v

Black her eye with many a Blow,
   Hot her breath with many a Dram,
Now she lies exceeding low,
   And as quiet as a Lamb.   20

EPILOGUE TO HORACE'S 'CARMEN SECULARE'

Baretti, *The Carmen Seculare of Horace* [1779], pp. 9,9.
A Collection and Selection of English Prologues and Epilogues, 1779, iv. 254.
   Translation only.
The European Magazine, June 1787, p. 451.
The Carmen Seculare of Horace. Set to Music by Mr. Philidor. [1788], pp. 18,
   19. (Performed at the installation of the Knights of the Bath; cf. *The Gentle-
   man's Magazine*, lviii (April 1788), p. 459, *s.d.* '19 May'.)
Works, 1788, xiv. 546.
Works, 1823, i. 415.

Towards the end of 1778 Baretti ventured on the experiment of setting
Horace's *Carmen Seculare* to music, and secured the collaboration of Philidor,
who happened then to be in London. On 21 November Johnson said in a letter
to Mrs. Thrale: 'Baretti has told his musical scheme to Burney, and Burney will
neither grant the question nor deny. He is of opinion, that, if it does not fail, it will
succeed, but, if it does not succeed he conceives it must fail.' Three performances
were given at the Free-Masons Hall, in Great Queen Street, near Lincoln's Inn
Fields, on 26 February and 5 and 12 March. 'The Learned and the Elegant',
said the announcement in *The Public Advertiser*, 'are invited to this Exhibition
as to a new Mode of Pleasure, arising from the Union of ancient Poetry with
modern Music.' Financially the exhibition was successful: see Baretti's note,
quoted by Hill, *Life*, iii. 373. See also *The Times Literary Supplement*, 16 August
1941, p. 400.

Baretti was responsible for the choice and arrangement of the words and for
the English translation; and he obtained an Epilogue for the occasion, in both
Latin and English. This Epilogue was first attributed to Johnson in print by
George Colman, in a review of the Rev. William Tasker's translation of the
Carmen Seculare, in *The Monthly Review* for April 1779, p. 315:

'Though the learned have, in general, found Sanadon's arrangement of the odes of
Horace, in order to construct the *Carmen Seculare*, to be more ingenious than solid, yet
it is not wonderful that Sig. Baretti and Mons. Philidor, whose chief object was to
present the Public with a new musical entertainment, should have adopted the idea of
Sanadon, which, by comprehending additional matter, gave more scope to the com-
poser, and afforded at least a longer, if not more rational, amusement to the auditor:
nor is it wonderful, considered in that light, that the Rev. Mr. Tasker should inform us
that "it is Mr. Baretti's edition, without any variation, that is here *attempted* to be
translated." He has, accordingly, followed that edition down to the *Epilogue Baretti*,
as Mr. Tasker calls it, but rather (as we are told it should be styled) the *Epilogus*
Johnsonianus.'

The translation was erroneously attributed to Garrick, who died on 20 January,
in *Prologues and Epilogues*. Both Latin and English were included in the four-
teenth volume of the *Works*.

The Latin and English texts are here printed from the libretto or programme
of the performance. The copy in the Bodleian Library has corrections in the

English Epilogue, which are in a hand that has not been identified, and were adopted in *Prologues and Epilogues*.

Epilogus

QUÆ fausta Romæ dixit Horatius,
Hæc fausta vobis dicimus, Angliæ
Opes, triumphos, et subacti
Imperium pelagi precantes.

Epilogue

SUCH strains as, mingled with the lyre,
Could Rome with future greatness fire,
Ye Sons of England, deign to hear,
Nor think our wishes less sincere.

May ye the varied blessings share   5
Of plenteous peace, and prosp'rous war;
And o'er the globe extend your reign,
Unbounded Masters of the main.

ON SEEING A PORTRAIT OF
MRS. MONTAGU

Works, 1787, xi. 373.

Hawkins's edition is the sole authority for this poem, which was probably printed, like the two which there precede it ('The Ant' and the translation of Horace, *Od*. iv. 7), from Johnson's manuscript. Hawkins entitles it 'On seeing a Bust of Mrs. Montague'. But the first line shows that it was written as an inscription for a framed portrait. The last lot in Johnson's sale catalogue contained a portrait of Mrs. Montagu 'framed and glazed'.

Mrs. Montagu began an annual allowance to Johnson's indigent and blind friend Anna Williams in 1775. Sometime in that year she sat for a cameo by James Tassie, and in 1776 a medallion portrait, probably from the cameo, was published by T. Wright. (The medallion was engraved by Thomas Holloway

2 future greatness] generous ardour *MS. correction, Prol. and Epil.*   3 England]
Britain *MS. corr., Prol. and Epil.*   5 the varied] th' alternate *Prol. and Epil.*
8 Masters] Rulers *MS. corr., Prol. and Epil.*

in 1785; see *The European Magazine*, 1800, ii. 243.) On 15 October 1778 Johnson
wrote to Mrs. Thrale: 'There is a print of Mrs. Montagu, and I shall think
myself very ill rewarded for my love and admiration if she does not give me one;
she will give it nobody in whom it will excite more respectful sentiments.' Writing
again on 18 March 1779, he says 'I called for the print, and got good words'.
The date of the poem is probably 1779. Johnson must have received the portrait
before their temporary estrangement over the *Life of Lyttelton*.

In *The Monthly Review* for July 1787, p. 69, in the course of a review of
Hawkins's edition of the *Works*, Murphy said that 'the verses to Mrs. Montague
are well known to be the production of Mr. Jerningham'. He may have confounded them with the lines on Mrs. Montagu ('Minerva') included in Jerningham's *Poems*, 1796, i. 199. The verses were omitted in Murphy's edition of the
Works, 1792, and were restored by Chalmers in the edition of 1816.

H AD this fair figure which this frame displays,
  Adorn'd in Roman time the brightest days,
In every dome, in every sacred place,
Her statue would have breath'd an added grace,
And on its basis would have been enroll'd,   5
"This is Minerva, cast in Virtue's mould."

TRANSLATIONS FROM THE 'MEDEA'
OF EURIPIDES

Johnson made three translations of a favourite passage in one of his favourite
authors—lines 193–203 of the *Medea* of Euripides: the first seriously for publication, the second in ridicule of the style of another translator, and the third
into Latin.

I

Charles Burney, *General History of Music*, 1782, ii. 340.
A New Review, ed. Maty, August 1782, p. 111.
The Town and Country Magazine, September 1794, p. 386.
The Carlton House Magazine, October 1794, p. 386.
R. Bland and J. H. Merivale, *Translations chiefly from the Greek Anthology, with
Tales and Miscellaneous Poems*, 1806, p. 100.[1]
James Savage, *The Librarian*, December 1808, facsimile of a transcript by
Porson, p. 274.
Works, 1816, i. 411.

This translation appears to have been written specially for Burney's *History of
Music*, where the author is not named. 'I am obliged', says Burney, 'to a learned

---

[1] See H. D. Weinbrot, *Notes and Queries* (November 1967), 410–11.

friend for this elegant translation'. It was first ascribed to Johnson in *The Town and Country Magazine*; and it was first included in Johnson's *Works* in 1816, with this note by James Boswell the Younger: 'It has always been ascribed to Johnson; but to put the matter beyond a doubt, Mr. Malone ascertained the fact by applying to Dr. Burney himself.'

The translation was made before the end of July 1779. On 1 August Mrs. Thrale entered in *Thraliana* that Johnson had translated some verses of Euripides 'seriously' and had 'given them Burney for his History of Musick'. She says that she does not have a copy of the translation, but that it is to be printed in Burney's second volume,—'so no matter for writing it out if one had it,—'tis very elegant I remember'.

T HE rites deriv'd from ancient days
　　With thoughtless reverence we praise,
The rites that taught us to combine
The joys of music and of wine,
And bad the feast, and song, and bowl,　　　　　5
O'erfill the saturated soul;
But n'er the Flute or Lyre apply'd
To cheer despair, or soften pride,
Nor call'd them to the gloomy cells
Where Want repines, and Vengeance swells,　　10
Where Hate sits musing to betray,
And Murder meditates his prey.
To dens of guilt and shades of care
Ye sons of Melody repair,
Nor deign the festive dome to cloy　　　　　　15
With superfluities of joy.
Ah, little needs the Minstrel's pow'r
To speed the light convivial hour;
The board with varied plenty crown'd
May spare the luxuries of sound.　　　　　　　20

II

Thraliana MS. iii (1778–81), pp. 125–6; ed. 1941, p. 397.
Piozzi, *Anecdotes*, 1786, p. 65.
Works, 1787, xi. 376.

This burlesque of the style of Robert Potter, translator of Aeschylus, had been recently composed when it was transcribed into *Thraliana* on 1 August 1779:

'Johnson has been diverting himself with imitating Potter's Æschylus in a translation of some Verses of Euripides—he has translated them seriously besides, and given them

Burney for his History of Musick. Here are the Burlesque ones—but they are a *Caricatura* of Potter whose Verses are obscure enough too. . . . Poor Potter! he does write strange unintelligible Verses to be sure, but I think none as bad as these neither. . . . Johnson has an agreeable Talent of imitating people's Verses, but he will always render them *too* ridiculous.'

For the full story we are indebted to a letter written by Susan Burney to her sister Fanny, also on 1 August 1779, and after a visit to Streatham with her father:

'I followed my father into the library, which was much such a room as I expected;— a most charming one. There sat Mrs. Thrale and Dr. Johnson, the latter finishing his breakfast upon peaches. . . . Dr. Johnson interrupted Mrs. Thrale by telling my father Mrs. Thrale had desired *Mr. Potter* to translate some verses for him, which he (Dr. J.) had before undertaken to do. "How so?" said my father. "*Why Mr. Potter?*" "Nay, Sir, I don't know. It was Mrs. Thrale's fancy." Mrs. Thrale said she would go and fetch them. . . . Then came back Mrs. Thrale, with the *verses*, which she had been copying out. . . . The verses were then given to my father. After he had read the first stanza, "Why, these are none of Potter's!" said he, "these are *worse* than Potter. They beat him at his own weapons." Dr. Johnson and Mrs. Thrale laugh'd very much, and the verses proved to be the *former's*, and were composed, in a comical humour, the evening before, in derision of Potter. They are admirable, you will see them at Streatham, and perhaps procure a copy, which my father could not do. Dr. Johnson is afraid of having them spread about as some other verses were he wrote in the same way to redicule poor Dr. Percy' (*The Early Diary of Frances Burney*, 1889, ii. 256-8).

Potter's translation of Aeschylus was published in 1777 and republished in 1779. Under the date 9 April 1778 Boswell recorded a conversation in which Johnson said, 'I thought what I read of it *verbiage*: but upon Mr. Harris's recommendation, I will read a play. (To Mr. Harris.) Don't prescribe two' (*Life*, iii. 256). It was the first complete translation of Aeschylus into English, and it held its place unchallenged till well into the nineteenth century.

When Johnson wrote this burlesque, Potter was engaged on his complete translation of Euripides, which appeared in 1781-3. There is no reason to think that Potter knew of the parody during Johnson's lifetime, or before its publication in 1786. A story of Johnson's rudeness to Potter when they were introduced by Mrs. Montagu is told, evidently on the authority of Dr. Parr, in E. H. Barker's *Literary Anecdotes*, 1852, i. 1. Potter was the author of *An Inquiry into some Passages in Dr. Johnson's Lives of the Poets, particularly his Observations on Lyric Poetry and the Odes of Gray*, 1783, and *The Art of Criticism, as exemplified in Dr. Johnson's Lives*, 1789. Horace Walpole, writing to Mason on 9 June 1783, pointed out that the true object of the former book was 'to revenge the attack on Lord Lyttelton at the instigation of Mrs. Montagu'.

Text from the *Anecdotes*, corrected by *Thraliana*.

ERR shall they not, who resolute explore
　　Times gloomy backward with judicious eyes;
And scanning right the practices of yore,
　　Shall deem our hoar progenitors unwise.

They to the dome where smoke with curling play   5
   Announc'd the dinner to the regions round,
Summon'd the singer blythe, and harper gay,
   And aided wine with dulcet-streaming sound.

The better use of notes, or sweet or shrill,
   By quiv'ring string, or modulated wind;   10
Trumpet or lyre—to their harsh bosoms chill,
   Admission ne'er had sought, or could not find.

Oh! send them to the sullen mansions dun,
   Her baleful eyes where Sorrow rolls around;
Where gloom-enamour'd Mischief dread the Sun,   15
   And Murder, all blood-bolter'd, schemes the wound.

When cates luxuriant pile the spacious dish,
   And purple nectar glads the festive hour,
The guest, without a want, without a wish,
   Can yield no room to Music's soothing pow'r.   20

III

Works, 1787, xi. 426.

The manuscript is dated, but otherwise differs very little from Langton's
printed text.

Eur. Med. 190–203

Non immerito culpanda venit
   Proavûm væcors insipientia,
Qui convivia lautasque dapes
Hilarare suis jussere modis
Cantum, vitæ dulce levamen.   5
At nemo feras iras hominum,
Domibus claris exitiales,
Voce aut fidibus pellere docuit,

15 dreads the Sun] loves to dwell *Anecdotes, Works*

Queis tamen aptam ferre medelam
Utile cunctis hoc opus esset,   10
Namque ubi mensas onerant epulæ
Quorsum dulcis luxuria soni?
Sat lætitia, sine subsidiis,
Pectora molli mulcet dubiæ
Copia Cœnæ.   15

June 28. –1780

PRAYER ON CHRISTMAS DAY, 1779

Works, 1787, xi. 383.

The manuscript which Langton followed is lost.

Dec. 25, 1779.

NUNC dies Christo memoranda nato
Fulsit, in pectus mihi fonte purum
Gaudium sacro fluat, et benigni
            Gratia Cœli!

Christe, da tutam trepido quietem,   5
Christe, spem præsta stabilem timenti;
Da fidem certam, precibusque fidis
            Annue, Christe.

ON HEARING MISS THRALE
DELIBERATE ABOUT HER HAT

Thraliana MS. iii (1778–81), p. 153; ed. 1941, p. 416.
Piozzi, *Anecdotes*, 1786, p. 165.
Works, 1787, xi. 381.

These lines were written in *Thraliana* on Wednesday 5 January 1780, and are thus introduced:

'Hester was deliberating whether she should put on her fine new dressed hat to dine at Mrs. Montagus next Fryday—*do* my darling says Johnson
            Wear the Gown, etc.'

The lines are cited in the *Anecdotes* as an instance of Johnson's 'almost Tuscan power of improvisation'. Hester, or Queeney, then aged seventeen, is there said to have been 'consulting with a friend about a new gown and dressed hat she thought of wearing to an assembly'.

They were omitted in Murphy's edition of the *Works*, 1792, and were not restored by Chalmers, nor are they in the edition of 1825.

Text from the *Anecdotes*.

W EAR the gown, and wear the hat,
  Snatch thy pleasures while they last;
Hadst thou nine lives like a cat,
  Soon those nine lives would be past.

A SHORT SONG OF CONGRATULATION

Manuscript in the Huntington Library (HM. 2583).
Thraliana MS. iii (1778–81), p. 205; ed. 1941, p. 451.
Piozzi, *Anecdotes*, 1786, p. 196 (4th stanza only).
Transcript by Samuel Lysons (in Johnson House, London).
Piozzi, manuscript of *British Synonymy* in the John Rylands Library.
Piozzi, *British Synonymy*, 1794, i. 359.
The Town and Country Magazine, October 1794, p. 427.
The British Critic, November 1794, p. 511.
The Annual Register, 1794, p. 419.
The Scottish Register, 1795, iii. 301.
The Kentish Register, February 1795, p. 71.
Boswell, *Life*, 1799, iv. 441 (1934, iv. 413).
Chalmers, *English Poets*, 1810, xvi. 611.
Works, 1823, i. 363.

Johnson sent the poem to Mrs. Thrale on 8 August 1780, along with a covering letter in which he says:

'You have heard in the papers how Sir John Lade is come to age. I have enclosed a short song of congratulation, which You must not shew to any body. It is odd that it should come into any bodies head. I hope you will read it with candour, it is, I believe, one of the authours first essays in that way of writing, and a beginner is always to be treated with tenderness.'

The present text is taken from the manuscript, now in the Huntington Library.[1] Previously printed texts all derive from that in *British Synonymy*, which differs in several places both from the original and the transcript in *Thraliana*. A transcript by Lysons inserted in a copy of Mrs. Piozzi's *Letters*, ii. 174, contains additional variants, and may have followed yet another transcript by Mrs. Piozzi.

2 thy] your *Thraliana*

[1] See H. D. Weinbrot in *Huntington Library Quarterly*, xxxiv (1970), 79-80.

John Hoole stated in *The European Magazine* for September 1799 that Johnson repeated the poem to a few friends 'with great spirit' on 30 November 1784, a fortnight before his death, and told them that 'he never gave but one copy'. Boswell quoted this in the first two editions of the *Life*, adding in the second that he had read the poem, presumably in the days when he was on good terms with Mrs. Thrale, and 'found it to be a piece of exquisite satire, conveyed in a strain of pointed vivacity and humour, and in a manner of which no other instance is to be found in Johnson's writings'. But he was unable to quote the poem till it was published in *British Synonymy*, and from this book it was copied into the posthumous third edition of the *Life*.

Sir John Lade was the son of Thrale's sister, and was born after his father's death in the hunting-field. The birth is thus announced in *The Gentleman's Magazine* for August 1759: 'Aug. 1. Relict of Sir John Lade, Bt.—of a son and heir, who is immediately entitled to a very large estate.' He was the young gentleman of Mrs. Piozzi's *Anecdotes* who called out suddenly in the Streatham drawing-room, 'Mr. Johnson, would you advise me to marry?' and received the reply, 'I would advise no man to marry, Sir, who is not likely to propagate understanding.' Thrale and Johnson had some notion of marrying him to Fanny Burney, but in 1787 he married a notorious woman named Laetitia Darby. He followed Johnson's predictions, squandered a great fortune, and died without issue in 1838. Cf. D'Arblay, *Diary*, i. 79; *Johnsonian Miscellanies*, i. 213; *Life*, iv. 412, 552; and W. P. Courtney, *Temple Bar*, February 1902, pp. 199–215.

The resemblance of A. E. Housman's *A Shropshire Lad* to these verses has been often remarked: e.g. George Rylands in *Words and Poetry* (1926), p. 44; W. L. Phelps in *Spectator*, clxi (1938), 21; Charles Norman in *Poetry*, lx (1942), 264–9; and M. Jones in *Transactions of the Johnson Society*, *Lichfield*, December 1959, pp. 12–36.

A Short Song of Congratulation

L ONG-EXPECTED one and twenty
   Ling'ring year, at last is flown,
Pomp and Pleasure, Pride and Plenty
   Great Sir John, are all your own.

Loosen'd from the Minor's tether,   5
   Free to mortgage or to sell,
Wild as wind, and light as feather
   Bid the slaves of thrift farewel.

Title. *From Johnson's letter to Mrs. Thrale*: None, MS., *Thraliana, Synonymy, Boswell*: One and Twenty *1810*: Improviso on a young heir's coming of age. *1823*   2 Years at length are *Lysons*   last] length *Synonymy*   3 Pride and Pleasure, Pomp and Plenty *Thraliana, Synonymy*   4 Sir John] —— —— *Synonymy* all] now *Thraliana, Synonymy* your (thine *erased*)   8 Slaves] Sons *Synonymy, Lysons*

Call the Bettys, Kates, and Jennys
Ev'ry name that laughs at Care,   10
Lavish of your Grandsire's guineas,
Show the Spirit of an heir.

All that prey on vice and folly
Joy to see their quarry fly,
Here the Gamester light and jolly,   15
There the Lender grave and sly.

Wealth, Sir John, was made to wander,
Let it wander as it will;
See the Jocky, see the Pander,
Bid them come, and take their fill.   20

When the bonny Blade carouses,
Pockets full, and Spirits high,
What are acres? What are houses?
Only dirt, or wet or dry.

If the Guardian or the Mother   25
Tell the woes of wilful waste,
Scorn their counsel and their pother,
You can hang or drown at last.

TRANSLATION OF ROBIN OF
DONCASTER'S EPITAPH

Manuscript in the Pierpont Morgan Library, New York.
Works, 1787, xi. 404.

Langton printed this note on the verses: 'These lines are a version of three

9 Bettys] Betsys *Thraliana*: Betseys *Synonymy*: Betsies *Lysons*   10 All the Names
that laugh at *Thraliana*: All the names that banish *Synonymy*, *Lysons*   11 your]
they *Lysons* (the *erased in MS.*)   13-20 *Lysons reverses the order of these stanzas*
13 An all . . . in vice or *Anecdotes*: On Vice or *Thraliana*, *Synonymy*: in vice and
Lysons   15 Here] There *Synonymy* (*printed copy*)   17 Sir John] my lad
Synonymy   18 as] if *Lysons*   19 See . . . see] Call . . . call *Synonymy*, *Lysons*
20 Come my lads and take your fill *Lysons*   21 When] Whilst *Lysons*   25 Should
the guardian friend or mother *Synonymy*: Should the guardian or the Mother *Lysons*
26 woes] spoils *Lysons*   27 counsel and] Counsel scorn *Thraliana*, *Synonymy*:
Nonsense scorn *Lysons*

sentences that are said in the manuscript to be "On the monument of John of Doncaster"; and which are as follows:

> What I gave that I have;
> What I spent that I had;
> What I left that I lost.'

But 'John of Doncaster' is an error for 'Robin of Doncaster'. The lines were carved on the border of an altar-shaped tomb in St. George's Church, Doncaster:

> Howe nowe who is heare
> I Robyn of Doncaster and Margaret my feare
> That I spent that I had
> That I gave that I have That I left that I loste.

In the centre, beneath the date 'A.D. 1579', were the words: 'Quod Robertus Byrkes who in this worlde dyd reyne thre skore yeares and seaven and yet lyved not one.' The monument was raised by Robin himself during the lifetime of his first wife; he lived to marry three other wives, and died in 1590. He was an alderman of Doncaster, and three times mayor.

The monument perished when the church was destroyed by fire in February 1853; but it is fully described in John Edward Jackson's *History of St. George's Church at Doncaster*, 1855, pp. 99–101, and illustrated, Plate viii. The inscription is in T. Webb's *New Select Collection of Epitaphs*, 1775, ii. 1.

Johnson visited the church on his way to Scotland. He quotes the epitaph on 'the monument of Robert of Doncaster' in his letter to Mrs. Thrale of 12 August 1773. The translation may have been made then, and the manuscript may represent a later rewriting.

Several other instances of the same or similar lines are on record, as in Camden's *Remaines*, ed. 1605, p. 53, and Weever, *Ancient Funerall Monuments*, 1631, pp. 423, 581. See Jackson, op. cit., and Joseph Hunter, *South Yorkshire*, 1828, i. 43; and cf. Southey, *The Doctor*, ch. xlii, 1834, ii. 91. The text is taken from the manuscript.

Ex Anglico

HABEO dedi quod alteri
Habuique quod dedi mihi
Sed quod reliqui perdidi.
> Aug 27. –80 DD.

In the manuscript there is also the following distich, in Johnson's handwriting, similarly headed: 'Ex Anglico'. The English version is supplied, perhaps by Langton, on the verso:

> Chloe new marry'd looks on Men no more!
> Why then, 'tis plain for what She looked before!

These lines are from William Walsh's 'Chloe', an epigram, printed in his *Letters and Poems, Amorous and Gallant*, 1692, p. 103. (See *Notes and Queries*, December 1969, 464; and May 1970, 186.)

N UM nova nupta viros cessat spectare Lycoris;
Nonne ita spectârit cur prius illa docet?

Aug −80

ON MRS. THRALE

Manuscript in the John Rylands Library (Eng. MS. 543/23).
The John Rylands Library Bulletin, 1932, p. 60.

This couplet was written by Johnson on an odd scrap of paper, and cannot
be dated. It was too personal to print; but Mrs. Thrale kept it to herself.

H OSTEM odit tacitè, sed amicum ridet apertè
Thralia. Quid mavis? tutius hostis eris.

A SUMMONS TO DR. LAWRENCE

Manuscript in the Huntington Library (HM. 20846).

These lines are the sole contents of a note which Johnson addressed 'To
Dr. Lawrence'. Thus Johnson summoned his doctor to attend one of his
friends—certainly a woman, probably a member of his household, and perhaps
Miss Williams.

They were presumably written before Lawrence's paralytic stroke in March
1782.

P HŒBE fave, ægrotat quæ te colit, ulla nec usquam est
Quam magis exoptes arte valere tua.

TRANSLATION OF THE COLLECT FOR
ASH WEDNESDAY

Manuscript in the Hyde Collection.
Transcript by Boswell in Yale University Library.
Works, 1787, xi. 384.

Johnson wrote alternative readings at the foot of the translation with the note
'Sic corrige'. These were adopted by Langton and are adopted here.

In lecto, die Passionis. Apr. 13. 1781.

Summe Deus, qui semper amas quodcunque creasti,
Judice quo, scelerum est pœnituisse, salus,
Da veteres noxas animo sic flere novato,
Per Christum ut veniam sit reperire mihi.

JEJUNIUM ET CIBUS

Manuscript in the Hyde Collection.
Works, 1787, xi. 388.

Langton omitted the date of this piece and supplied the title. Text from the manuscript.

Serviat ut Menti corpus Jejunia serva,
Ut Mens utatur corpore, sume cibos.

Sept. 16. –81

AN IMITATION OF POPE

Prefaces, Biographical and Critical, to the Works of the English Poets, vii (1781), 'Pope', 289–91.
The Lives of the English Poets, Dublin, 1781, ii. 416–17 [various edns. and issues].
The Lives of the Most Eminent English Poets, 1781, iv. 184–5.
The Lives of the Most Eminent English Poets, 1783, iv. 182–3.
Works, vi (Yale ed. 1964), 309–10.

These lines are cited in the *Life of Pope* to illustrate Johnson's contention that the sound of verse has no necessary connexion with the sense. He wrote:

'Motion, however, may be in some sort exemplified; and yet it may be suspected that even in such resemblances the mind often governs the ear, and the sounds are estimated by their meaning. One of the most successful attempts has been to describe the labour of Sisyphus:

> With many a weary step, and many a groan,
> Up a high hill he heaves a huge round stone;
> The huge round stone, resulting with a bound,
> Thunders impetuous down, and smoaks along the ground.[1]

Who does not perceive the stone to move slowly upward, and roll violently back? But set the numbers to another sense . . . We have surely lost much of the delay, and much of the rapidity.'

The imitation was first attributed to Johnson by the Yale editors in 1964.

2 Cuique loco recti pænituisse mali est *MS*.   3 noxas] culpas *MS*.   4 Christum] Chrisum *MS*.

---

[1] Pope's *Odyssey*, xi. 735–8.

W HILE many a merry tale, and many a song,
　　Chear'd the rough road, we wish'd the rough road long,
The rough road then, returning in a round,
Mock'd our impatient steps, for all was fairy ground.

ANAPÆSTICS ADDRESSED TO
DR. LAWRENCE

Manuscript in the Huntington Library (HM. 20847).
A Voyage to Abyssinia . . . to which are added other tracts, ed. George Gleig,
　(*Works*, xv), 1789, p. 499.

This text is taken from the undated manuscript in the Huntington Library.
The poem is the main part of a letter to Dr. Lawrence (*Letters*, ed. Chapman,
ii. 471–2, no. 770. 1).

Gleig appends the date 'March 21, 1782', but his authority for it is not known.
In the short prose sequel to the poem Johnson says, 'I go to Streatham to-
morrow' (cf. ll. 20–22). His *Prayers and Meditations* show that he was at Streatham
from 21 to 23 March 1782. Gleig's '21' may be a mistake for '20'. In a letter to
Miss Lawrence of 22 May 1782 Johnson asks for a copy of 'those short lines
which I sent to the Doctor'.

Nugæ anapæsticæ in lecto lusæ.
Medico Æger S.

N UNC mihi facilis
　　Liberiori
Cursu Spiritus
Itque reditque;
Nunc minus acris　　　　　　　　　5
Seu thoracem
Sive abdomen
Laniat tussis;
Tantum prodest
Tempore justo　　　　　　　　　10
Secare venam;
Tantum prodest
Potente succo

---

1 song. *1783*　　　2 along. *1783*

Title. cusæ Medico Ægro. S. *Gleig*

Dulce papaver.
Quid nunc superest?   15
Ut modo tentem
Quantum strictam
Mollia laxent
Balnea pellem,
Cras abiturus   20
Quo revocârit
Thralia suavis.
Hoc quoque superest
Ut tibi, gentis
Medicæ Princeps   25
Habeam grates;
Votaque fundam
Ne, quæ prosunt
Omnibus, artes
Domino desint.   30
Vive valeque.

ON THE DEATH OF DR. ROBERT LEVET

Thraliana, iv (1781–6), pp. 86–8; ed. 1941, p. 532.
Transcript by Elizabeth Carter in the Hyde Collection.
Transcript by Frances Reynolds in her manuscript *Recollections* in the Hyde Collection.
Transcript by one of the Burney family in Harvard University library (MS. Eng. 926).
The Gentleman's Magazine, August 1783, p. 695.
The British Magazine and Review, August 1783, p. 136.
The Universal Magazine, August 1783, p. 104.
The London Magazine, September 1783, p. 232.
The Weekly Magazine, 18 September 1783.
The Annual Register, 1783, p. 189.
The Scots Magazine, January 1784, p. 44.
The New Foundling Hospital for Wit, 1784, 1786, vi. 62.
The European Magazine, January 1785, p. 56.
Poetical Works, 1785, p. 184.
Piozzi, *Anecdotes*, 1786, p. 118 (5th stanza only).
Hawkins, *Life*, 1787, p. 554.

14 papaper *MS.*

Works, 1787, xi. 365.

Boswell, *Life*, 1791, ii. 414 (iv. 137).

Levet died on 17 January 1782, in his seventy-seventh year, and the poem was written before 18 April, when it was entered in *Thraliana*:

'Doctor Johnson has been writing Verses on his old Inmate Mr. Levett he tells me: that poor Creature was 84 or 85 years old this Winter, when after an uninterrupted Series of Health he died suddenly by a Spasm or Rupture of some of the Vessells of the Heart. He lived with Johnson as a sort of *necessary Man*, or Surgeon to the wretched Household he held in Bolt Court; where Blind Mrs. Williams, Dropsical Mrs. Desmoulines, Black Francis and his White Wife's Bastard, with a wretched Mrs. White, and a thing that he called Poll, shared his Bounty, and increased his Dirt. Levett used to bleed one, and blister another, and be very useful, tho' I believe disagreable to all: he died while his Patron was with me in Harly Street—and very sorry he was—in his way of being sorry— and he wrote these Verses.'

Other accounts of Levet may be found in *The London Magazine*, September 1783 (signed 'S. Y.'); *The St. James's Chronicle*, 18–20 Jan. 1785; *The Gentleman's Magazine*, Feb. 1785, p. 101 (said to be by George Steevens); and Boswell's *Life*, i. 243 n. 3; iv. 137 n. The memoir signed 'S. Y.' is not by Boswell; see Pottle, *The Literary Career of James Boswell*, p. 299.

Boswell says that on 21 March 1783 Johnson 'repeated to me his verses on Mr. Levett with an emotion which gave them full effect'; but the version which he prints is not said to have been given him by Johnson, or to have been dictated. He adds in a note that Johnson repeated l. 20 to him thus,

And Labour steals an hour to die,

and 'afterwards altered it to the present reading'.

Johnson gave a copy to Miss Reynolds 'with his own hand', but it has disappeared; the transcript which she made for her *Recollections* contains a variant recorded by Hill (*Johnsonian Miscellanies*, ii. 250) but omits stanza 3. A copy given to Hannah More (Roberts, *Memoirs*, i. 278) is also untraced. Another transcript, by Miss Carter, bound in a copy of Johnson's *Journey* is in the Hyde Collection. An undated transcript by John Phillips of the Middle Temple (Bodl. MS. Eng. misc. e. 241 f. 95) is a corrupt descendant from Boswell's text. The 'Burney' transcript at Harvard is equally corrupt. The texts are discussed by S. C. Roberts in *The Review of English Studies*, October 1927, p. 442; that given here is from *The Gentleman's Magazine*.

On the Death of Dr. ROBERT LEVET

CONDEMN'D to hope's delusive mine,
  As on we toil from day to day,
By sudden blasts, or slow decline,
  Our social comforts drop away.

Title. *Dr.*] Mr. *Works*   3 blasts] blast *Thraliana, Carter, Reynolds, Hawkins, Boswell*

1. Cf. motto to *The Rambler*, No. 67, *ante*, p. 144.

Well tried through many a varying year,   5
  See LEVET to the grave descend;
Officious, innocent, sincere,
  Of ev'ry friendless name the friend.

Yet still he fills affection's eye,
  Obscurely wise, and coarsely kind;   10
Nor, letter'd arrogance, deny
  Thy praise to merit unrefin'd.

When fainting nature call'd for aid,
  And hov'ring death prepar'd the blow,
His vig'rous remedy display'd   15
  The power of art without the show.

In misery's darkest caverns known,
  His useful care was ever nigh,
Where hopeless anguish pour'd his groan,
  And lonely want retir'd to die.   20

No summons mock'd by chill delay,
  No petty gain disdain'd by pride,
The modest wants of ev'ry day
  The toil of ev'ry day supplied.

His virtues walk'd their narrow round,   25
  Nor made a pause, nor left a void;
And sure th' Eternal Master found
  The single talent well employ'd.

The busy day, the peaceful night,
  Unfelt, uncounted, glided by;   30
His frame was firm, his powers were bright,
  Tho' now his eightieth year was nigh.

9 fills] fill'd *Osborne and Griffin 1785*   11 arrogance] ignorance *Hawkins's Life*
17 caverns] cavern's *Gent. Mag.*: cavern *Poems, Works*   18 useful care] useful aid
Lond. Mag.: ready help *Boswell*   19 Where] When *Lond. Mag.*   pour'd his]
pours her *Anec.*: pour'd the *Lond. Mag.*   20 retir'd] retires *Anec.*   21 mock'd]
shock'd *Reynolds*   22 gain] gains *Boswell*   25 walk'd] trod *Reynolds*   26 made
. . . left] felt . . . made *Reynolds*   left] felt *Carter*   27 th'] the *Carter, Hawkins's
Life*   28 The] His *New Found. Hosp., Boswell*   29 peaceful] cheerful *Carter*

7. *officious.* Mrs. Piozzi (*British Synonymy*, ii. 79) understood this word in the
modern sense. It here means 'full of good offices'.

Then with no throbbing fiery pain,
No cold gradations of decay,
Death broke at once the vital chain,   35
And free'd his soul the nearest way.

TRANSLATIONS OF FRENCH VERSES ON SKATING

Thraliana, iv (1781–6), p. 108; ed. 1941, p. 548.
Piozzi, *Anecdotes*, 1786, pp. 143–4.
The Gentleman's Magazine, March 1786, p. 249.
Works, 1787, xi. 380.

Mrs. Piozzi told the story of these verses in her *Anecdotes*:

'We had got a little French print among us at Brighthelmstone, in November 1782 of some people skaiting, with these lines written under:

> Sur un mince chrystal l'hyver conduit leurs [vos] pas,
> Le précipice est sous la glace;
> Telle est de nos [vos] plaisirs la légère surface;
> Glissez, mortels, n'appuyez pas.

And I begged translations from every body: Dr. Johnson gave me this [*the first*]; . . .

'He was however most exceedingly enraged when he knew that in the course of the season I had asked half a dozen acquaintance to do the same thing, and said, it was a piece of treachery, and done to make every body else look little when compared to my favourite friends the *Pepyses* . . .'

Johnson made the second translation impromptu after seeing this translation by William Pepys:

> Swift o'er the level how the skaiters slide,
> And skim the glitt'ring surface as they go:
> Thus o'er life's specious pleasures lightly glide,
> But pause not, press not on the gulph below.

The two translations by Johnson were preserved in *Thraliana*, under the date 4 November 1782, along with others. One of these is 'by H. L. T.', and is printed in her *British Synonymy*, 1794, ii. 259. Johnson's own diary records on Monday, 11 November 1782, 'did the French Skating' (*Works*, i (Yale ed. 1958), 349).

The 'little French print' is an engraving by Larmessin of a painting by Lancret. A copy is in the Cannan collection of skating prints in the British Museum. It is reproduced, without the verses, in *The Poetry of Skating*, by Edgar Wood Syers, 1905, p. 42. The verses were by Pierre Roy.

Text from the *Anecdotes*.

---

33 throbbing fiery] throbs of fiery *Thraliana, Carter, Lond. Mag., Boswell*: fiery throbs of *Reynolds*: fiery, throbbing: *Poems, Works*: throb of fiery *Hawkins's Life*   36 free'd] forc'd *Gent. Mag., Ann. Reg., New Found. Hosp., Poems*

I

O'ER ice the rapid skaiter flies,
   With sport above and death below;
Where mischief lurks in gay disguise,
   Thus lightly touch and quickly go.

II

O'er crackling ice, o'er gulphs profound,
   With nimble glide the skaiters play;
O'er treacherous pleasure's flow'ry ground
   Thus lightly skim, and haste away.

CHRIST TO THE SINNER

Works, 1787, xi. 384.

These verses, and almost all the Latin poems which follow, are known only in Langton's text.

In Lecto. Dec. 25, 1782.

SPE non inani confugis,
   Peccator, ad latus meum;
Quod poscis, haud unquam tibi
Negabitur solatium.

ON HOPE

Works, 1787, xi. 395.

The day was Wednesday of Holy Week. The error in the last line indicates that Langton sent the original manuscript to the printer. Johnson's 'ca' could easily be confused with 'lu'.

Spes

Apr. 16, 1783.

HORA sic peragit citata cursum;
   Sic diem sequitur dies fugacem!
Spes novas nova lux parit, secunda

II. 1 On crackling *Thraliana*

Spondens omnia credulis homullis;
Spes ludit stolidas, metuque cæco   5
Lux angit miseros cadens homullos.

PRAYER ON LOSING THE POWER OF SPEECH

Works, 1787, xi. 384.

This prayer was written during the night when Johnson was deprived of speech by a paralytic stroke, and is thus referred to in his letter to Mrs. Thrale of 19 June 1783:

'On Monday the 16th I sat for my picture, and walked a considerable way with little inconvenience. In the afternoon and evening I felt myself light and easy, and began to plan schemes of life. Thus I went to bed, and in a short time waked and sat up, as has been long my custom, when I felt a confusion and indistinctness in my head, which lasted I suppose about half a minute. I was alarmed, and prayed God, that however he might afflict my body, he would spare my understanding. This prayer, that I might try the integrity of my faculties, I made in Latin verse. The lines were not very good, but I knew them not to be very good: I made them easily, and concluded myself to be unimpaired in my faculties.'

Johnson's own diary simply notes: 'I went to bed, and as I conceive, about 3 in the morning, I had a stroke of the palsy.'

Langton notes the different readings in the manuscript, now lost, but does not make clear which Johnson wrote first.

A translation is given in *Notes and Queries*, 14 November 1903, p. 389.

Nocte, inter 16 et 17 Junii, 1783.

S UMME Pater, quodcunque tuum de corpore Numen
  Hoc statuat, precibus Christus adesse velit:
Ingenio parcas, nec sit mihi culpa rogâsse,
  Qua solum potero parte, placere tibi.

CHRISTIANUS PERFECTUS

Works, 1787, xi. 386.
Undated, and known only in Langton's text.

Q UI cupit in sanctos Christo cogente referri,
  Abstergat mundi labem, nec gaudia carnis
Captans, nec fastu tumidus, semperque futuro

6 angit miseros cadens *emend.*: angit, miseros ludens *Works*

Variants in Johnson's MS.   1 tuum ... Numen ... statuat] tuæ ... leges ... statuant]   2 precibus] votis   3 rogâsse] precari   4 placere] litare

Instet, et evellens terroris spicula corde,
Suspiciat tandem clementem in numine patrem.   5
   Huic quoque, nec genti nec sectæ noxius ulli,
Sit sacer orbis amor, miseris qui semper adesse
Gestiat, et, nullo pietatis limite clausus,
Cunctorum ignoscat vitiis, pietate fruatur.
Ardeat huic toto sacer ignis pectore, possit   10
Ut vitam, poscat si res, impendere vero.
   Cura placere Deo sit prima, sit ultima, sanctæ
Irruptum vitæ cupiat servare tenorem;
Et sibi, delirans quanquam et peccator in horas
Displiceat, servet tutum sub pectore rectum: 15
Nec natet, et nunc has partes, nunc eligat illas,
Nec dubitet quem dicat herum, sed, totus in uno,
Se fidum addicat Christo, mortalia temnens.
   Sed timeat semper, caveatque ante omnia, turbæ
Ne stolidæ similis leges sibi segreget audax   20
Quas servare velit, leges quas lentus omittat,
Plenum opus effugiens, aptans juga mollia collo
Sponte sua demens; nihilum decedere summæ
Vult Deus, at, qui cuncta dedit tibi, cuncta reposcit.
   Denique perpetuo contendit in ardua nisu,   25
Auxilioque Dei fretus, jam mente serena
Pergit, et imperiis sentit se dulcibus actum.
Paulatim mores, animum, vitamque refingit,
Effigiemque Dei, quantum servare licebit,
Induit, et, terris major, cœlestia spirat.   30

PRAYERS

Works, 1787, xi. 385, 387, 402.

   Only two of these seven Prayers are dated in Langton's text. Four are based, in whole or in part, on Collects in *The Book of Common Prayer*.

I

PATER benigne, summa semper lenitas,
   Crimine gravatam plurimo mentem leva:
Concede veram pœnitentiam, precor,
Concede agendam legibus vitam tuis.

Sacri vagantes luminis gressus face   5
Rege, et tuere, quæ nocent pellens procul;
Veniam petenti, summe da veniam, pater;
Veniæque sancta pacis adde gaudia:
Sceleris ut expers omnis, et vacuus metu,
Te, mente purâ, mente tranquillâ colam: 10
Mihi dona morte hæc impetret Christus suâ.

II

Æterne rerum conditor,
Salutis æternæ dator;
Felicitatis sedibus
Qui nec scelestos exigis,
Quoscumque scelerum pœnitet;   5
Da, Christe, pœnitentiam,
Veniamque, Christe, da mihi;
Ægrum trahenti spiritum
Succurre præsens corpori,
Multo gravatam crimine   10
Mentem benignus alleva.

III

O Qui benignus crimina ignoscis, pater
Facilisque semper confitenti ades reo,
Aurem faventem precibus O præbe meis;
Scelerum catenâ me laborantem gravi
Æterna tandem liberet clementia,   5
Ut summa laus sit, summa Christo gloria.

IV

Per vitæ tenebras rerumque incerta vagantem
Numine præsenti me tueare pater!
Me ducat lux sancta, Deus, lux sancta sequatur;
Usque regat gressus gratia fida meos.

I. 9 omnis *emend.*: omni *1787–1825*   III. 4 grav[ ] *1787*: gravè *Works 1792–*
1825

III. Cf. the last of the Prayers upon Several Occasions, beginning, 'O God, whose
nature and property is ever to have mercy'.
IV. Cf. the Collect for the seventeenth Sunday after Trinity.

Sic peragam tua jussa libens, accinctus ad omne   5
  Mandatum, vivam sic moriarque tibi.

V

Me, pater omnipotens, de puro respice cœlo,
  Quem mœstum et timidum crimina dira gravant;
Da veniam pacemque mihi, da, mente serena,
  Ut tibi quæ placeant, omnia promptus agam.
Solvi, quo Christus cunctis delicta redemit,   5
  Et pro me pretium, tu patiare, pater.

VI

Manuscript in the Langton Papers, Lincolnshire Archives Office.

Cal. Jan. in lecto, ante lucem. 1784.

Summe Dator vitæ, naturæ æterne Magister,
  Causarum series quo moderante fluit,
Respice quem subigit senium morbique seniles,
  Quem terret vitæ meta propinqua suæ,
Respice inutiliter lapsi quem pœnitet ævi,   5
  Recte ut pœniteat respice, magne Parens.

VII

Jan. 18, 1784.

Summe Pater, puro collustra lumine pectus,
  Anxietas noceat ne tenebrosa mihi.
In me sparsa manu virtutum semina larga
  Sic ale, proveniat messis ut ampla boni.
Noctes atque dies animo spes læta recurset,   5
  Certa mihi sancto flagret amore fides.
Certa vetet dubitare fides, spes læta timere,
  Velle vetet cuiquam non bene sanctus amor.
Da, ne sint permissa, pater, mihi præmia frustra,
  Et colere et leges semper amare tuas.   10
Hæc mihi, quo gentes, quo secula, Christe, piâsti,
  Sanguine, peccanti promereare tuo!

v. 2 dira *Works 1801: om. 1787*   VI. 3 subiget *Works 1792–1825*   VII. 9 promissa
conj.   12 peccanti *emend.*: precanti *1787, &c.*

  v. Cf. the Collect for the twenty-first Sunday after Trinity.
  VI. Cf. the Collect for the second Sunday after Epiphany.

A MEDITATION

Works, 1787, xi. 386.

Feb. 27, 1784.

M ENS mea quid quereris? veniet tibi mollior hora,
In summo ut videas numine læta patrem;
Divinam in sontes iram placavit Jesus;
Nunc est pro pœna pœnituisse reis.

TRANSLATIONS FROM THE GREEK
ANTHOLOGY

Works, 1787, xi. 407.

These translations belong to the winter of 1783–4. Only four are known to survive in manuscript, and three bear dates in Johnson's hand: '84. Jan. 15. op.' (7. 151), '84. Jan. 21. op.' (10. 113), and '84—Jan. 31.' (10. 30); 7. 553 is not dated. In J. W. Croker's sale, Sotheby's 6 May 1858, lot 106 was Johnson's 'Eight copies of small Latin verses; several bearing dates . . .' which were probably some of these translations. Johnson mentioned them in his letter to Mrs. Thrale of 19 April 1784: 'When I lay sleepless, I used to drive the night along by turning Greek epigrams into Latin'; but as he also proposes to borrow her copy of the *Anthology* some of the translations that have been preserved may have been made subsequently. Boswell gives this account:

'During his sleepless nights he amused himself by translating into Latin verse, from the Greek, many of the epigrams in the *Anthologia*. These translations, with some other poems by him in Latin, he gave to his friend Mr. Langton, who, having added a few notes, sold them to the booksellers for a small sum, to be given to some of Johnson's relations, which was accordingly done; and they are printed in the collection of his works' (*Life*, iv. 384).

Malone refers to them thus in his letter to Percy of 2 March 1785: 'Being of late very sleepless, used to amuse himself with turning some Greek Epigrams into Latin, in bed, but I doubt whether productions composed in such a state of mind, are correct enough for publication.'

For most of the epigrams Langton's text gives page references to the edition by Brodæus published at Basle in 1549. Johnson supplied page references on the surviving pieces as 'Br. 326' (7. 151), 'Br. 55' (10. 30), and 'Br. 24' (10. 113). Langton, or an amanuensis, has usually supplied an interlinear transcription perhaps as an aid to the printer, and each piece is marked with a cross, probably as part of some checking system.

Langton arranged the translations for which he knew the references in the order adopted by Brodæus; and that might have been the order in which Johnson wrote them. But they are here arranged under the numbers in modern editions of the *Anthology* since the publication of the edition by Friedrich Jacobs, Leipzig, 1813–17. Langton may not have seen proofs. Typographical errors are corrected, and names of authors are supplied.

Johnson had long been familiar with the *Anthology*. He included Latin translations of two of the epigrams in his *Essay on Epitaphs*, 1740 (see p. 91); he introduced a quotation in the *Dictionary* under 'Grubstreet' (9. 458); and two of the epigrams here translated into Latin (ll. 50 and ll. 53) he quoted in the original Greek in *The Rambler*, Nos. 71 and 180, and afterwards turned into English (see pp. 144 and 151).

5. 67 CAPITO

FORMA animos hominum capit, at, si gratia desit,
  Non tenet; esca natat pulchra, sed hamus abest.

5. 74 (or 73) RUFINUS

FLORIBUS in pratis legi quos ipse, coronam
  Contextam variis, do, Rhodoclea, tibi:
Hic anemone humet, confert narcissus odores
  Cum violis; spirant lilia mista rosis.
His redimita comas, mores depone superbos: 5
  Hæc peritura nitent; tu peritura nites!

6. 1 PLATO

ILLA triumphatrix Graiûm consueta procorum
  Ante suas agmen Lais habere fores,
Hoc Veneri speculum; nolo me cernere qualis
  Sum nunc, nec possum cernere qualis eram.

7. 128 ANONYMOUS

Br[odæus, 1549, p.] 398.

HERACLITUS ego; indoctæ ne lædite linguæ,
  Subtile ingenium quæro, capaxque mei,
Unus homo mihi pro sexcentis, turba popelli
  Pro nullo, clamo nunc tumulatus idem.

6.1. Cited in *The Rambler*, No. 143.
7.128. Translated into English as the motto to *The Rambler*, No. 208, *ante*, p. 152.

7. 136 ANTIPATER

Br. 326.

EXIGUUM en! Priami monumentum; haud ille meretur
Quale, sed hostiles quale dedere manus.

7. 151 ANONYMOUS

84. Jan. 15, op.   Br. 326.

HECTOR dat gladium Ajaci, dat Balteum et Ajax
Hectori, at exitio munus utrique fuit.

7. 239 PARMENIO

Br. 227.

FUNUS Alexandri mentitur fama; fidesque
Si Phœbo, victor nescit obire diem.

7. 265 PLATO

Br. 285.

NAUFRAGUS hic jaceo; contra jacet ecce colonus!
Idem Orcus terræ, sic, pelagoque subest.

7. 282 THEODORIDAS

Br. 344.

NAUFRAGUS hic jaceo; fidens tamen utere velis,
Tutum aliis æquor, me pereunte, fuit.

7. 284 ASCLEPIADES

Br. 344.

UT vis, ponte minax, modo tres discesseris ulnas,
Ingemina fluctus, ingeminaque sonum.
Si forsan tumulum quo conditur Eumarus aufers,
Nil lucri facies; ossa habet et cinerem.

7.151. 2 et *1787*.

7.151. The dated manuscript is in the Edward L. Doheny Collection in the Library
of St. John's Seminary, Camarillo, California.

7.265. The first line is identical with that in the metrical version by Hugo Grotius,
which was not printed till 1795.

7.284. The second couplet is separated from the first by several pages in Langton's
text. Johnson probably wrote them on different scraps of paper.

7. 318 CALLIMACHUS

Br. 301.

QUID salvere jubes me, pessime? Corripe gressus;
Est mihi quod non te rideo, plena salus.

7. 319 ANONYMOUS

ET ferus est Timon sub terris; janitor Orci,
Cerbere, te morsu ne petat ille, cave.

7. 350 ANONYMOUS

Br. 241.

NAUTA, quis hoc jaceat ne percontere sepulchro;
Eveniat tantum mitior unda tibi!

7. 459 CALLIMACHUS

CRETHIDA fabellas dulces garrire peritam
Prosequitur lacrymis filia mœsta Sami,
Blandam lanifici sociam, sine fine loquacem,
Quam tenet hic, cunctas quæ manet, alta quies.

7. 461 MELEAGER

Br. 267.

CUNCTIPARENS tellus, salve, levis esto pusillo
Lysigeni, fuerat non gravis ille tibi.

7. 471 CALLIMACHUS

Br. 399.

AMBRACIOTA, vale lux alma, Cleombrotus infit,
Et saltu e muro Ditis opaca petit:
Triste nihil passus, animi at de sorte Platonis
Scripta legens, solâ vivere mente cupit.

7.461. Brodæus has Ἀυσιγένην, which Johnson must have misread Ἀυσιγένην. The
accepted reading is Αἰσιγένην.
7.471. See also pp. 458–9 post.

7. 538 ANYTE

Br. 223.

QUI jacet hic, servus vixit, nunc, lumine cassus,
  Dario magno non minus ille potest.

7. 553 DAMASCIUS

Br. 322.

ZOSIMA, quæ solo fuit olim corpore serva,
  Corpore nunc etiam libera facta fuit.

7. 560 PAULUS SILENTIARIUS

SÆPE tuum in tumulum lacrymarum decidit imber
  Quem fundit blando junctus amore dolor;
Charus enim cunctis, tanquam, dum vita manebat,
  Cuique esses natus, cuique sodalis, eras.
Heu quam dura preces sprevit, quam surda querelas   5
  Parca, juventutem non miserata tuam!

7. 590 JULIANUS ÆGYPTIUS

Br. 266.

CLARUS Joannes, reginæ affinis, ab alto
  Sanguine Anastasii; cuncta sepulta jacent:
Et pius, et recti cultor: non illa jacere
  Dicam; stat virtus non subigenda neci.

7. 669 PLATO

STELLA mea, observans stellas, Dii me æthera faxint,
  Multis ut te oculis sim potis aspicere.

7.533. 1 qua *1787*; quondam *deleted in MS.*

7.553. Cf. p. 91. The manuscript of this piece, used by Langton, is owned by
Mr. Herman W. Liebert of New Haven, Connecticut.
7.560. Johnson has not translated the first couplet of the original.

7. 676 ANONYMOUS

Br. 399.

SERVUS, Epictetus, mutilato corpore, vixi,
  Pauperieque Irus, curaque summa Deûm.

8. 137 ANONYMOUS

DICITE, Causidici, gelido nunc marmore magni
  Mugitum tumulus comprimit Amphilochi.

9. 13 PLATO JUNIOR

Br. 8.

FERT humeris claudum validis per compita cæcus,
  Hic oculos socio commodat, ille pedes.

9. 18 GERMANICUS CÆSAR

Br. 60.

ME, cane vitato, canis excipit alter; eodem
  In me animo tellus gignit et unda feras,
Nec mirum; restat lepori conscendere cœlum,
  Sidereus tamen hic territat, ecce, canis!

9. 29 ANTIPHILUS

Br. 103.

PUPPE gubernatrix sedisti, Audacia, prima,
  Divitiis acuens aspera corda virum;
Sola rates struis infidas, et dulcis amorem
  Lucri ulciscendum mox nece sola doces.
Aurea secla hominum, quorum spectandus ocellis   5
  E longinquo itidem pontus et orcus erat.

9. 39 MUSICIUS

Br. 18.

AD Musas Venus hæc: Veneri parete, puellæ,
  In vos ne missus spicula tendat amor.
Hæc Musæ ad Venerem: Sic Marti, diva, mineris;
  Huc nunquam volitat debilis iste puer.

7.676. Cf. p. 91 (two variants).

9. 44 PLATO

Br. 162.

HIC, aurum ut reperit, laqueum abjicit, alter ut aurum
Non reperit, nectit quem reperit laqueum.

9. 48 ANONYMOUS

Br. 75.

ANTIOPE satyrum, Danaë aurum, Europa juvencum,
Et cycnum fecit Leda petita Jovem.

9. 50 MIMNERMUS

Br. 167.

VIVE tuo ex animo, vario rumore loquetur
De te plebs audax, hic bene et ille male.

9. 54 MENECRATES

Br. 31.

CUM procul est, optat, cum venit, quisque senectam
Incusat, semper spe meliora videt.

9. 55 LUCILLIUS, or MENECRATES

Br. 31.

OPTARIT quicunque senex sibi longius ævum,
Dignus qui multa in lustra senescat, erit.

9. 65 ANONYMOUS

Br. 70.

TELLURI arboribus ver frondens, sidera cœlo,
Græciæ et urbs, urbi est ista propago, decus.

9. 66 ANTIPATER SIDONIUS

Br. 127.

MNEMOSYNE, ut Sappho mellita voce canentem
Audiit, irata est ne nova Musa foret.

9.54, 55. Langton prints the two translations together, but in reverse order, as if
they formed one epigram. Johnson may have written them on the same paper without
clearly distinguishing them. The epigrams are not combined in the text of Brodæus.
9.55. Cf. *The Rambler*, No. 69, para. 1.

9. 74 ANONYMOUS

Br. 155.

NUNC huic, nunc aliis cedens, cui farra Menippus
    Credit, Achæmenidæ nuper agellus eram.
Quod nulli proprium versat Fortuna, putabat
    Ille suum stolidus, nunc putat ille suum.

9. 110 ALPHEUS

Br. 24.

NUNQUAM jugera messibus onusta, aut
    Quos Gyges cumulos habebat auri;
Quod vitæ satis est, peto, Macrine:
    Mi, nequid nimis, est nimis probatum.

9. 112 ANTIPATER THESSALONICENSIS

Br. 307.

VITAM a terdecimo sextus mihi finiet annus,
    Astra mathematicos si modo vera docent.
Sufficit hoc votis; flos hic pulcherrimus ævi est,
    Et senium triplex Nestoris urna capit.

9. 133 ANONYMOUS

Br. 29.

QUISQUIS adit lectos elatâ uxore secundos,
    Naufragus iratas ille retentat aquas.

9. 138 ANONYMOUS

Br. 126.

ME miserum sors omnis habet; florentibus annis
    Pauper eram, nummis diffluit arca senis;
Queis uti poteram quondam Fortuna negavit,
    Queis uti nequeo, nunc mihi præbet opes.

9.74. Cf. Horace, *Sat.* II. ii. 129-34.
9.138. Cf. *The Rambler*, No. 165, motto.

9. 148 ANONYMOUS

Br. 26.

DEMOCRITE, invisas homines majore cachinno,
  Plus tibi ridendum secula nostra dabunt.
Heraclite, fluat lacrymarum crebrior imber;
  Vita hominum nunc plus quod misereris habet.
Interea dubito; tecum me causa nec ulla   5
  Ridere, aut tecum me lacrimare jubet.

9. 160 ANONYMOUS

EXCEPTÆ hospitio Musæ tribuere libellos
  Herodoto hospitii præmia, quæque suum.

9. 163 ANONYMOUS

FERT humeris, venerabile onus, Cythereius heros
  Per Trojæ flammas, densaque tela, patrem.
Clamat et Argivis: Vetuli, ne tangite, vita
  Exiguum est Marti, sed mihi grande lucrum.

9. 250 ONESTES

BUCCINA disjecit Thebarum mœnia, struxit
  Quæ lyra. Quam sibi non concinit harmonia!

9. 288 GEMINUS

CECROPIDIS gravis hic ponor, Martique dicatus,
  Quo tua signantur gesta, Philippe, lapis.
Spreta jacet Marathon, jacet et Salaminia laurus,
  Omnia, dum Macedûm gloria et arma premunt.
Sint Demosthenicâ ut jurata cadavera voce,   5
  Stabo illis qui sunt, quique fuere, gravis.

9.288. 5. Johnson may have meant 'ut' to be cancelled.

9. 304 Parmenio

Br. 10.

Qui, mutare vias ausus terræque marisque,
  Trajecit montes nauta, fretumque pedes,
Xerxi, tercentum Spartæ Mars obstitit acris
  Militibus; terris sit pelagoque pudor!

9. 359 Posidippus, or Plato Comicus

Br. 26.

Elige iter vitæ, ut possis; rixisque dolisque
  Perstrepit omne forum; cura molesta domi est.
Rura labor lassat; mare mille pericula terrent;
  Verte solum, fient causa timoris opes;
Paupertas misera est; multæ cum conjuge lites   5
  Tecta ineunt; cælebs omnia solus ages;
Proles aucta gravat, rapta orbat, cæca juventæ est
  Virtus, canities cauta vigore caret.
Ergo optent homines, aut nunquam in luminis oras
  Venisse, aut visâ luce repente mori.   10

9. 360 Metrodorus

Elige iter vitæ, ut mavis; prudentia lausque
  Permeat omne forum; vita quieta domi est.
Rus ornat natura; levat maris aspera lucrum;
  Verte solum, donat plena crumena decus;
Pauperies latitat, cum conjuge gaudia multa   5
  Tecta ineunt, cælebs impediere minus;
Mulcet amor prolis, sopor est sine prole profundus;
  Præcellit juvenis vi, pietate senex.
Nemo optet nunquam venisse in luminis oras,
  Aut periisse; scatet vita benigna bonis.   10

9.360. 4 donat *1825*: donet *1787–1823*

9.359. Translated into English in Johnson's *Adventurer*, No. 107, para. 9.
9.360. Translated into English in Johnson's *Adventurer*, No. 107, para. 11.

9. 375 ANONYMOUS

Br. 5.

PECTORE qui duro, crudos de vite racemos
  Venturi exsecuit, vascula prima meri,
Labraque constrictus semesos, jamque terendos
  Sub pedibus, populo prætereunte, jacit,
Supplicium huic, quoniam crescentia gaudia læsit,   5
  Det Bacchus, dederat quale, Lycurge, tibi.
Hæ poterant uvæ læto convivia cantu
  Mulcere, aut pectus triste levare malis.

9. 394 PALLADAS

Br. 126.

MATER adulantum prolesque, Pecunia, curæ,
  Teque frui timor est, teque carere dolor.

9. 444 ERATOSTHENES SCHOLASTICUS

PULCHRA est virginitas intacta, at vita periret,
  Omnes si vellent virginitate frui;
Nequitiam fugiens, servatâ contrahe lege
  Conjugium, ut pro te des hominem patriæ.

9. 523 ANONYMOUS

Br. 11.

SIT tibi, Calliope, Parnassum, cura, tenenti,
Alter ut adsit Homerus, adest etenim alter Achilles.

9. 530 ANONYMOUS

Br. 156.

NON Fortuna sibi te gratum tollit in altum;
  At docet, exemplo, vis sibi quanta, tuo.

9.394. Cf. *The Rambler*, No. 131, para. 9, 'to have it [Gold] is to be in Fear, and to
want it is to be in Sorrow'.

9. 573 AMMIANUS

Br. 24.

TU neque dulce putes alienæ accumbere mensæ,
    Nec probrosa avidæ grata sit offa gulæ;
Nec ficto fletu, fictis solvare cachinnis,
    Arridens domino collacrymansque tuo,
Lætior haud tecum, tecum neque tristior unquam,   5
    Sed Miliæ ridens, atque dolens Miliæ.

9. 577 PTOLEMÆUS

Br. 92.

ÆVI sat novi quam sim brevis; astra tuenti,
    Per certas stabili lege voluta vices,
Tangitur haud pedibus tellus; conviva Deorum
    Expleor ambrosiis exhilarorque cibis.

9. 647 POMPEIUS

Br. 487.

CUM fugere haud possit fractis Victoria pennis,
    Te manet imperii, Roma, perenne decus.

9. 648 MACEDONIUS

Br. 487.

CIVIS et externus grati; domus hospita nescit
    Quærere, quis, cujas, quis pater, unde venis.

9. 654 JULIANUS ÆGYPTIUS

Br. 488.

LATRONES, alibi locupletum quærite tecta,
    Assidet huic custos strenua pauperies.

9. 702 ANONYMOUS

Br. 486.

JUPITER hoc templum, ut, siquando relinquit Olympum,
    Atthide non alius desit Olympus, habet.

9.648. 2 cujas *emend.*: cujus *1787–1825*

10. 26 LUCIANUS

Br. 24.

HORA bonis quasi nunc instet suprema fruaris,
  Plura ut victurus secula, parce bonis:
Divitiis, utrinque cavens, qui tempore parcit,
  Tempore divitiis utitur, ille sapit.

10. 27 LUCIANUS

Br. 75.

IMPIA facta patrans, homines fortasse latebis,
  Non poteris, meditans prava, latere Deos.

10. 28 LUCIANUS

Br. 46.

OMNIS vita nimis brevis est felicibus, una
  Nox miseris longi temporis instar habet.

10. 30 ANONYMOUS

84–Jan 31   Br. 55.

GRATIA ter grata est velox, sin forte moretur
  Gratia vix restat nomine digna suò.

10. 31 LUCIANUS

Br. 26.

NIL non mortale est mortalibus; omne quod est hi
  Prætereunt, aut hos præterit omne bonum.

10. 58 PALLADAS

Br. 27.

TERRAM adii nudus, de terra nudus abibo.
  Quid labor efficiet? non nisi nudus ero.

10.31. 1 hic *1825*

10.26. Cf. *The Rambler*, No. 53, motto.
  10.30. The manuscript of this translation is now in the collection of Mr. Arthur A. Houghton, of New York. The second line is written under 'Ut florem amittat gratia tota perit', which is struck out. To help the compositor, five difficult words in the first line are rewritten above, and all the words in the last line are rewritten below, in a clear and bold hand. (Reproduced in Tregaskis's catalogue, March 1928, p. 15.) Cf. Johnson's letter (no. 929. 1, ed. Chapman) to 'Queeney' Thrale of this date.

10. 60 Palladas

Br. 126.

DITESCIS, credo, quid restat? quicquid habebis
In tumulum tecum, morte jubente, trahes?
Divitias cumulas, pereuntes negligis horas,
Incrementa ævi non cumulare potes.

10. 72 Palladas

Br. 27.

VITA omnis scena est ludusque; aut ludere disce
Seria seponens, aut mala dura pati.

10. 74 Paulus Silentiarius

Br. 19.

PROSPERA sors nec te strepitoso turbine tollat,
Nec menti injiciat sordida cura jugum;
Nam vita incertis incerta impellitur auris,
Omnesque in partes tracta retracta fluit;
Firma manet virtus; virtuti innitere, tutus   5
Per fluctus vitæ sic tibi cursus erit.

10. 84 Palladas

Br. 27.

NATUS eram lacrymans, lacrymans e luce recedo;
Sunt quibus a lacrymis vix vacat ulla dies.
Tale hominum genus est, infirmum, triste, misellum,
Quod mors in cineres solvit, et abdit humo.

10. 93 Palladas

FORTUNÆ malim adversæ tolerare procellas,
Quam domini ingentis ferre supercilium.

10. 98 Palladas

Br. 152.

CUM tacet indoctus, sapientior esse videtur,
Et morbus tegitur, dum premit ora pudor.

10. 108 ANONYMOUS

Br. 56.

SEU prece poscatur, seu non, da Jupiter omne
Magne bonum, omne malum et poscentibus abnue nobis.

10. 113 ANONYMOUS

Br. 24.

NON opto, aut precibus posco ditescere, paucis
Sit contenta mihi vita, dolore carens.

84. Jan 21. op.

10. 119 ANONYMOUS

Br. 24.

RECTA ad pauperiem tendit, cui corpora cordi est
Multa alere, et multas ædificare domos.

10. 123 ÆSOPUS

Br. 27.

QUÆ sine morte fuga est vitæ, quam turba malorum
   Non vitanda gravem, non toleranda facit?
Dulcia dat natura quidem, mare, sidera, terras,
   Lunaque quas et sol itque reditque vias.
Terror inest aliis, mœrorque, et siquid habebis   5
   Forte boni, ultrices experiere vices.

10. 124 GLYCO

Br. 2.

QUANDOQUIDEM passim nulla ratione feruntur
Cuncta, cinis cuncta et ludicra, cuncta nihil.

11. 50 AUTOMEDON

Br. 30.

FÆLIX ante alios nullius debitor æris;
   Hunc sequitur cælebs; tertius, orbe, venis.

10.113. The dated manuscript is in the Cambridge University Library. Cf. Johnson's
letter (no. 926, ed. Chapman) to Mrs. Thrale of this date.
11. 50. Cf. 'The Mottoes and Quotations in *The Rambler*', No. 180, *ante*, p. 151.

Nec male res cessit, subito si funere sponsam,
Ditatus magna dote, recondis humo.
His sapiens lectis, Epicurum quærere frustra   5
Quales sint monades, quà fit inane, sinas.

II. 53 ANONYMOUS

Br. 168.

VITA rosæ brevis est; properans si carpere nolis,
Quærenti obveniet mox sine flore rubus.

II. 118 CALLICTER

Br. 205.

HAUD lavit Phido, haud tetigit; mihi febre calenti
In mentem ut venit nominis, interii.

II. 145 ANONYMOUS

EN Sexto, Sexti meditatur imago, silente;
Orator statua est, statuæque orator imago.

II. 167 POLLIANUS

Br. 256.

CUR opulentus eges? tua cuncta in fœnore ponis.
Sic aliis dives, tu tibi pauper agis.

II. 176 LUCILLIUS

Br. 212.

HERMEM Deorum nuncium, pennis levem,
Quo rege gaudent Arcades, furem boum,
Hujus palestræ qui vigil custos stetit,
Clam nocte tollit Aulus, et ridens ait;
Præstat magistro sæpe discipulus suo.   5

11.53. 1 Vita rosæ *1816*: Vitæ rosa *1787*, &c.

11.53. Cf. 'The Mottoes and Quotations in *The Rambler*', No. 71, *ante*, p. 144.

11. 186 NICARCHUS

Br. 210.

NYCTICORAX cantat lethale, sed ipsa canenti
Demophilo auscultans nycticorax moritur.

11. 213 LEONIDAS

Br. 202.

MENODOTUM pinxit Diodorus, et exit imago,
Præter Menodotum, nullius absimilis.

11. 391 LUCILLIUS

MUREM Asclepiades sub tecto ut vidit avarus,
Quid tibi, mus, mecum, dixit, amice, tibi?
Mus blandum ridens, respondit, pelle timorem;
Hic, bone vir, sedem, non alimenta, peto.

11. 430 LUCIANUS

Br. 262.

QUI pascit barbam si crescit mente, Platoni,
Hirce, parem nitido te tua barba facit.

11. 432 LUCIANUS

Br. 170.

PULICIBUS morsus, restinctâ lampade, stultus
Exclamat: Nunc me cernere desinitis.

13. 3 THEOCRITUS

POETA, lector, hic quiescit Hipponax,
Si sis scelestus, præteri procul marmor:
At te bonum si nôris, et bonis natum,
Tutum hic sedile, et si placet, sopor tutus.

11.186. Cf. the account of 'Suspirius the screech-owl' in *The Rambler*, No. 59.

16 (Appendix Planudea). 1 Damacetus

Br. 2.

Non Argos pugilem, non me Messana creavit;
  Patria Sparta mihi est, patria clara virûm.
Arte valent isti, mihi robore vivere solo est,
  Convenit ut natis, inclyta Sparta, tuis.

16. 16 Anonymous

Br. 96.

Quod nimium est fit ineptum; hinc, ut dixere priores,
  Et melli nimio fellis amaror inest.

16. 87 Julianus Ægyptius

Arti ignis lucem tribui, tamen artis et ignis
  Nunc ope supplicii vivit imago mei.
Gratia nulla hominum mentes tenet, ista Promethei
  Munera muneribus si retulere fabri.

16. 168 Anonymous

Br. 445.

Unde hic Praxiteles? nudam vidistis, Adoni,
  Et Pari, et Anchisa, non alius, Venerem.

16. 209 Anonymous

Br. 451.

Sufflato accendis quisquis carbone lucernam,
  Corde meo accendas; ardeo totus ego.

16. 326 Anonymous

Dat tibi Pythagoram pictor; quod ni ipse tacere
  Pythagoras mallet, vocem habuisset opus.

16. 331 Agathias

Clara Cheroneæ soboles, Plutarche, dicavit
  Hanc statuam ingenio Roma benigna tuo.

Das bene collatos, quos Roma et Græcia jactat,
    Ad Divos paribus passibus ire duces;
Sed similem, Plutarche, tuæ describere vitam   5
    Non poteras, regio non tulit ulla parem.

16. 364 LEONTIUS

MENTE senes olim juvenis, Faustine, premebas,
    Nunc juvenum terres robore corda senex.
Lævum at utrumque decus, juveni quod præbuit olim
    Turba senum, juvenes nunc tribuere seni.

SIMONIDES

Thucydides, vi. 59

PROLEM Hippi, et sua quâ meliorem secula nullum
    Videre, Archidicen hæc tumulavit humus;
Quam, regum sobolem, nuptam, matrem, atque sororem
    Fecerunt nulli sors titulique gravem.

CLEANTHES

Epictetus, *Enchiridion*, ad fin.

ME, rex deorum, tuque, duc, necessitas,
    Quo, lege vestrâ, vita me feret mea.
Sequar libenter; sin reluctari velim,
    Fiam scelestus, nec tamen minus sequar.

UNIDENTIFIED

COGITAT aut loquitur nil vir, nil cogitat uxor,
    Felici thalamo non, puto, rixa strepit.

Simonides. This epigram is in neither the Palatine nor Planudean manuscript of the *Greek Anthology*.

Cleanthes. This epigram likewise is not in the *Anthology*. For Seneca's translation see *Epist. ad Lucilium*, xviii. 107.

THE SEVEN AGES OF THE WORLD

Manuscript in the Hyde Collection.
Works, 1787, xi. 427; (Yale ed. i (1958), 376).

These verses were written in Johnson's Latin diary for 1784, between the entries for 28 and 29 July, and have no connexion with the context.

Septem Ætates

PRIMA parit terras ætas; siccatque secunda;
 Evocat Abramum dein tertia; quarta relinquit
Ægyptum; templo Solomonis quinta superbit;
Cyrum sexta timet; lætatur septima Christo.

A MEDITATION

Manuscript in the collection of Mr. Arthur A. Houghton, of New York.
Works, 1787, xi. 388.

This poem is here printed from a photograph of the manuscript.

Noctu. Aug 8– 84

LUCE collustret mihi pectus almâ,
 Pellat et tristes animi tenebras,
Nec sinat semper tremere ac dolere
   Gratia Christi;

Me Pater tandem reducem benigno   5
Summus amplexu foveat, beato
Me gregi Sanctus socium beatum
   Spiritus addat.

---

3 superbit] supersit *Works 1787–1825* 4 Sexta dolet Babylona, et gaudet *cancelled: above* Cyrum sexta vocat, lætatur *first three words cancelled: below*, Cyrum sexta timet; lætatur septima Christo. *MS.*

---

3 dolore *Works 1787–1810*

---

1. *siccatque*: see Genesis viii. 13, 14.

ON THE STREAM AT STOWE MILL LICHFIELD

Works, 1787, xi. 389.

Stowe Mill was at the east end of Stowe Pool, near St. Chad's Church, and was worked by water from the stream, called Curborough Brook, which flows from the pool to the west of the churchyard. A branch flowing to the east and north of the churchyard is shown in John Snape's map of Lichfield, 1781. This branch no longer exists, but it explains 'diffluentem' in the title of the poem. The mill was demolished in 1856, when the South Staffordshire Waterworks Company converted the pool into a reservoir, and the present St. Chad's Road runs over its site. It is represented in a sketch of 'Stow 1720' inserted in the extra-illustrated copy of Thomas Harwood's *History of Lichfield* in the Gough Collection in the Bodleian Library. The place where Johnson was taught to swim by his father must have been some little distance below the mill, at or near the junction of the branch with the main stream.

The poem, which survives only in Langton's text, cannot be dated accurately, for Johnson paid several visits to Lichfield in later life. The destruction of trees which he laments is not on record, and, to judge from the poem, was more than a periodical lopping of willows; but the available evidence suggests that the bathing-place assumed larger dimensions and greater beauty in his mind's eye as he viewed it through the mist of memory.

In manhood Johnson was a strong swimmer: see Boswell, *Life*, ii. 299, and Piozzi, *Anecdotes*, 1786, p. 113.

In Rivum a Mola Stoana Lichfeldiæ diffluentem

ERRAT adhuc vitreus per prata virentia rivus,
  Quo toties lavi membra tenella puer;
Hic delusa rudi frustrabar brachia motu,
  Dum docuit blanda voce natare pater.
Fecerunt rami latebras, tenebrisque diurnis   5
  Pendula secretas abdidit arbor aquas.
Nunc veteres duris periêre securibus umbræ,
  Longinquisque oculis nuda lavacra patent.
Lympha tamen cursus agit indefessa perennis,
  Tectaque qua fluxit, nunc et aperta fluit.   10
Quid ferat externi velox, quid deterat ætas,
  Tu quoque securus res age, Nise, tuas.

12. The friend whom he addresses as Nisus was in all probability Edmund Hector, the friend alike of his youth and his old age. They met at Birmingham on Johnson's

EPIGRAMS

Works, 1787, xi. 396.

None of these three epigrams is dated. The title given to the first one may have been supplied by Langton (cf. *ante*, p. 230).

Jactura Temporis

I

Hora perit furtim lætis, mens temporis ægra
Pigritiam incusat, nec minus hora perit.

II

Quas navis recipit, quantum sit pondus aquarum,
Dimidium tanti ponderis intret onus.

III

Quot vox missa pedes abit horæ parte secunda?
Undecies centum denos quater adde duosque.

GEOGRAPHIA METRICA

Works, 1787, xi. 428.

Langton gives this footnote: 'To the above Lines (which are unfinished, and can therefore be only offered as a fragment), in the Doctor's manuscript, are prefixed the words, "Geographia Metrica". As we are referred, in the first of the verses, to Templeman, for having furnished the numerical computations that are the subject of them, his work has been accordingly consulted, the title of which is, "A new Survey of the Globe", and which professes to give an accurate mensuration of all the empires, kingdoms, and other divisions thereof,

visits to Lichfield in 1781 and 1784. Hector told Boswell that at their last meeting 'he was very solicitous with me to recollect some of our most early transactions, and transmit them to him, for I perceive nothing gave him greater pleasure than calling to mind those days of our innocence' (*Life*, iv. 375). The poem is an expression of these feelings. Nisus and Euryalus were proverbial for their friendship. (*Aeneid*, v and ix.)

I. Cf. *Rambler*, 108.

II. The load of a ship should be half of the weight of the water which it can hold.

III. Sound travels at the rate of 1,142 feet a second. This figure was arrived at by William Derham in 1708 (*Philosophical Transactions*, 1708, Numb. 313, p. 32), and was accepted throughout the eighteenth century.

in the square miles that they respectively contain. On comparison of the several numbers in these verses with those set down by Templeman, it appears that nearly half of them are precisely the same; the rest are not quite so exactly done.' The notes here given are condensed from Langton's.

Thomas Templeman was a writing-master at Bury St. Edmunds, and his *Survey* was published posthumously in 1729. Johnson's lines might have been written at almost any time thereafter, but Langton's possession of the manuscript is strong evidence that they are late. They are probably contemporary with the last of the preceding epigrams. It would seem that at one time towards the end of his life Johnson found amusement in translating numbers into Latin hexameters.

Geographia Metrica

HIS Tempelmanni numeris descripseris orbem.
Cum sex centuriis Judæo millia septem.
Myrias Ægypto cessit bis septima pingui.
Myrias adsciscit sibi nonagesima septem
Imperium qua Turca ferox exercet iniquum.   5
Undecies binas decadas et millia septem
Sortitur Pelopis tellus quæ nomine gaudet.
Myriadas decies septem numerare jubebit
Pastor Arabs: decies octo sibi Persa requirit.
Myriades sibi pulcra duas, duo millia poscit   10
Parthenope. Novies vult tellus mille Sicana.
Papa suo regit imperio ter millia quinque.
Cum sex centuriis numerat sex millia Tuscus.
Centuriâ Ligures augent duo millia quartâ.
Centuriæ octavam decadem addit Lucca secundæ.   15
Ut dicas, spatiis quam latis imperet orbi
Russia, myriadas ter denas adde trecentis:
Sardiniam cum sexcentis sex millia complent.

6 decadas *1787: Johnson may have written* decades.

2. Templeman sets down the square miles of Palestine at 7,600.
3. The square miles of Egypt are, in Templeman, 140,700.
5. The whole Turkish empire, in Templeman, is computed at 960,057 square miles.
6–11. The Morea, in Templeman, is set down at 7,220 square miles.—Arabia, at 700,000.—Persia, at 800,000.—Naples, at 22,000.
11. Sicily, at 9,400.   12. The Pope's dominions at 14,868.
13. Tuscany, at 6,640.   14. Genoa, at 2,400.   15. Lucca, at 286.
17. The Russian empire, in the 29th plate of Templeman, is set down at 3,303,485 square miles.
18. Sardinia, at 6,600.

Cum sexagenis, dum plura recluserit ætas,
Myriadas ter mille homini dat terra colendas.   20
Vult sibi vicenas millesima myrias addi,
Vicenis quinas, Asiam metata celebrem.
Se quinquagenis octingentesima jungit
Myrias, ut menti pateat tota Africa doctæ.
Myriadas septem decies Europa ducentis   25
Et quadragenis quoque ter tria millia jungit.
Myriadas denas dat, quinque et millia, sexque
Centurias, et tres decadas Europa Britannis.
Ter tria myriadi conjungit millia quartæ,
Centuriæ quartæ decades quinque Anglia nectit.   30
Millia myriadi septem fœcunda secundæ
Et quadragenis decades quinque addit Ierne,
Quingentis quadragenis socialis adauget
Millia Belga novem.
Ter sex centurias Hollandia jactat opima   35
Undecimum Camber vult septem millibus addi.

TRANSLATION OF HORACE
'ODES', Book IV. vii

Manuscript in the Hyde Collection.
Hawkins, *Life*, 1787, 1st ed., p. 574, 2nd ed., p. 575.
Works, 1787, xi. 372.
The European Magazine, March 1787, p. 202.
The County Magazine, Salisbury, March 1787, p. 228.

The manuscript has been reproduced in facsimile in Tregaskis's *Caxton Head Catalogue*, May 1916, and in *The R. B. Adam Library*, i, following p. 189. The poem is written on two sides of a quarto leaf. It is dated 'Nov. 1784'. Hawkins must therefore be wrong in saying that it was written at Ashbourne (*Life*, 1787, p. 574). If Boswell is right in saying 'in the country' (*Life*, iv. 370), it must have been written at Lichfield, or on the return journey to London,

---

28 decadas *1787: Johnson may have written* decades.

---

20. The habitable world, at 30,666,806.
22. Asia, at 10,257,487.
24. Africa, at 8,506,208.
25. Europe, at 2,749,349.
28. The British dominions, at 105,634.
30. England, at 49,450.
32. Ireland, at 27,457.
34. The United Provinces, at 9,540.
35. Holland, at 1,800.
36. Wales, at 7,011.

which Johnson reached on 16 November, within a month of his death. It was
his last English poem.

Text from the manuscript; a comma or full stop has been occasionally inserted at the end of a line (3, 4, 9, 10, 11, 12, 13, 15, and 23).

<blockquote>

THE snow dissolv'd no more is seen,
 The fields, and woods, behold, are green,
The changing year renews the plain,
The rivers know their banks again,
The spritely Nymph and naked Grace   5
The mazy dance together trace.
The changing year's successive plan
Proclaims mortality to Man.
Rough Winter's blasts to Spring give way,
Spring yield[s] to Summer['s] sovereign ray, 10
Then Summer sinks in Autumn's reign,
And Winter chils the World again.
Her losses soon the Moon supplies,
But wretched Man, when once he lies
Where Priam and his sons are laid,   15
Is nought but Ashes and a Shade.
Who knows if Jove who counts our Score
Will toss us in a morning more?
What with your friend you nobly share
At least you rescue from your heir.   20
Not you, Torquatus, boast of Rome,
When Minos once has fix'd your doom,
Or Eloquence, or splendid birth,
Or Virtue shall replace on earth.
Hippolytus unjustly slain   25
Diana calls to life in vain,
Nor can the might of Theseus rend
The chains of hell that hold his friend.

</blockquote>

Nov. 1784

2 behold, *written above* again *struck out* 6 mazy *written above* mazy d *struck out*
10 yield to Summer *MS.* 18 toss] rouse *Hawkins. The misreading is credible from
the MS. and is evidence that Hawkins saw it.* 24 replace on] restore to *Works*

PRAYER

Works, 1787, xi. 403.

The date given by Langton, who presumably found it in the manuscript, was that on which Johnson received the sacrament for the last time, eight days before his death. In all probability this was his last poem. It is a free paraphrase of the collect of the Communion Service. Latin versions of other collects are on pp. 229, 238–40.

Dec. 5, 1784.

S UMME Deus, cui cæca patent penetralia cordis;
  Quem nulla anxietas, nulla cupido fugit;
Quem nil vafrities peccantum subdola celat;
  Omnia qui spectans, omnia ubique regis;
Mentibus afflatu terrenas ejice sordes   5
  Divino, sanctus regnet ut intus amor:
Eloquiumque potens linguis torpentibus affer,
  Ut tibi laus omni semper ab ore sonet:
Sanguine quo gentes, quo secula cuncta piavit,
  Hæc nobis Christus promeruisse velit!   10

IRENE[1]

[1] Reprinted, with omissions and alterations, from *Essays and Studies by Members of the English Association*, xiv, 1929. A further discussion of *Irene* by B. H. Bronson is included in his *Johnson Agonistes and Other Essays*, 1946.

THE STORY

Irene is based on a story in *The Generall Historie of the Turkes*, by Richard Knolles, a book which Johnson always held in the highest regard, and praised in *The Rambler* as displaying 'all the excellencies that narration can admit'. But nowhere was he content to versify Knolles's prose, and from first to last his play is singularly deficient in allusions to be illustrated, or difficulties to be explained, by consulting the material on which he worked. It is the divergencies, not the similarities, that are of interest, and they are characteristic. In general we may say that Johnson was indebted to Knolles for little more than the suggestion of his *Irene*. He did not write with a book lying open before him, but once having found his subject let it take shape in his own mind.

The story which is told by Knolles in over three closely packed folio pages may thus be given here in brief; but there is one paragraph which must be quoted in full, not so much because it wins the attention of every reader and explains Johnson's praise of the narrative style, as because it shows why Johnson could not follow the story as he found it. He gave it a less violent climax, more in harmony with his idea of the moral purpose of the drama.

According to the story, Irene, a Greek of incomparable beauty and rare perfection, was made captive at the sack of Constantinople in 1453, and handed over to the Sultan Mahomet II, who took such delight in her that in a short time she became the mistress and commander of the great conqueror. 'Mars slept in Venus' lap, and now the soldiers might go play.' He neglected the government of his empire till the discontent of his subjects threatened the security of his throne. Mustapha Bassa, his companion from childhood and now his favoured counsellor, thereupon undertook to warn him of his danger, and performed the difficult duty without incurring the effects of his anger. Torn awhile by contrary passions, the Sultan came to a sudden decision, and summoned a meeting of all the Bassas for the next day.

'So the Bassa being departed, he after his wonted manner went in vnto the Greeke, and solacing himselfe all that day and the night following with her, made more of her than euer before: and the more to please her, dined with her; commanding, that after dinner she should be attired with more sumptuous apparell than euer she had before worne: and for the further gracing of her, to be deckt with many most precious jewels of inestimable valour. Whereunto the poore soule gladly obeyed, little thinking that it was her funerall apparell. Now in the meane while, *Mustapha* (altogither ignorant of the Sultans mind) had as he was commanded, caused all the nobilitie, and commanders of the men of warre, to be assembled into the great hall: euerie man much marueiling, what should be the emperors meaning therein, who had not of long so publikely shewed himselfe. But being thus togither assembled, and euerie man according as their minds gaue them, talking diuersly of the matter: behold, the Sultan entred into the pallace leading the faire Greeke by the hand; who beside her incomparable beautie and other the greatest graces of nature, adorned also with all that curiositie could deuise, seemed not now to the beholders a mortal wight, but some of the stately goddesses, whom the Poets in their extacies describe. Thus comming togither into the midst of the hall, and due reuerence vnto them done by al them there present; he stood still with the faire lady in his left hand, and so furiously looking round about him, said vnto them: *I vnderstand of your great discontentment, and that you all murmur and grudge, for that I, ouercome with mine affection towards this so faire a paragon, cannot withdraw my selfe from her presence: But I would faine know which of you there is so temperat, that if he had in his possession a thing so rare and precious, so louely and so faire, would not be thrice aduised before he would forgo the same? Say what you thinke: in the word of a Prince I giue you free libertie so to doe.* But they all rapt with an incredible admiration to see so faire a thing, the like whereof they had neuer before beheld, said all with one consent, That he had with greater reason so passed the time with her, than any man had to find fault therewith. Whereunto the barbarous prince answered: *Well, but now I will make you to vnderstand how far you haue been deceiued in me, and that there is no earthly thing that can so much blind my sences, or bereaue me of reason as not to see and vnderstand what beseemeth my high place and calling: yea I would you should all know, that the honor and conquests of the* Othoman *kings my noble progenitors, is so fixed in my brest, with such a desire in my selfe to exceed the same, as that nothing but death is able to put it out of my remembrance.* And hauing so said, presently with one of his hands catching the faire Greeke by the haire of the head, and drawing his falchion with the other, at one blow strucke off her head, to the great terror of them all. And hauing so done, said vnto them: *Now by this iudge whether your emperour is able to bridle his affections or not.* And within a while after, meaning to discharge the rest of his choller, caused great preparation to be made for the conquest of PELOPONESVS, and the besieging of BELGRADE.'[1]

Such is the story which Johnson transformed in his *Irene*. This simple tale of lust and cruelty became in his hands a drama of the struggle between virtue and weakness. Irene is represented not as a helpless victim of the Sultan's passion, but as the mistress of her fate. Will she sacrifice her creed to attain security and power? She has freedom to decide.

> Wilt thou descend, fair Daughter of Perfection,
> To hear my Vows, and give Mankind a Queen?
>
> .   .   .   .
>
> To State and Pow'r I court thee, not to Ruin:
> Smile on my Wishes, and command the Globe,

—so the Sultan woos her. In order that this freedom may be emphasized, she is placed in contrast to Aspasia, a new character for whom there is no warrant in the original story. Aspasia is the voice of clear and unflinching virtue; and she is rewarded with her escape from slavery in company with the lover of her choice. But Irene yields, and pays the penalty. She hesitates, complies, and half repents, then is betrayed and ordered to die. Her death is exhibited by Johnson as the punishment of her weakness, whereas in Knolles's story it is but the fortuitous conclusion of helpless misfortune. Even in his first serious work the great

[1] *Historie of the Turkes*, 1603, p. 353.

moralist, as he came to be called, converted a record of senseless cruelty into a study of temptation.

When Johnson edited *Twelfth Night* he criticized the marriage of Olivia and the succeeding perplexity as wanting credibility and as failing 'to produce the proper instruction required in the drama, as it exhibits no just picture of life'. It was a juster picture of life that Irene should be strangled at the Sultan's orders for her supposed treachery than decapitated by him without warning and without reason in the presence of his admiring court; and he drew it so that there should be no mistake about 'the proper instruction required in the drama'. In his criticism of *As You Like It* he said that 'by hastening to the end of his work Shakespeare suppressed the dialogue between the usurper and the hermit, and lost an opportunity of exhibiting a moral lesson in which he might have found matter worthy of his highest powers'. Johnson never hastened in his *Irene*, and he never refused the chance of a moral lesson. Much of the interest of this early drama lies in the examples which it provides of his later precepts or observations as a critic, for he held much the same opinions throughout his fifty years as an author; they show change mainly in the confidence with which they are expressed. 'I do not see that *The Bard* promotes any truth, moral or political'— so he said in his Life of Gray; and if we want to know what he meant we may turn to his *Irene*.

Of the political truths it cannot be said—again to quote the Life of Gray— that we have never seen them in any other place; some of them were expressed elsewhere by Johnson himself, and better. The downfall of a nation is due not so much to the strength of the conqueror as to weakness and vice at home,

> A feeble Government, eluded Laws,
> A factious Populace, luxurious Nobles,
> And all the Maladies of sinking States.

Empires are weakened by the lust of conquest and possession:

> Extended Empire, like expanded Gold,
> Exchanges solid Strength for feeble Splendor.

In the perfect state all classes work together for the good of the whole:

> If there be any Land, as Fame reports,
> Where common Laws restrain the Prince and Subject,
> A happy Land, where circulating Pow'r
> Flows through each Member of th' embodied State,
> Sure, not unconscious of the mighty Blessing,
> Her grateful Sons shine bright with ev'ry Virtue;
> Untainted with the Lust of Innovation,
> Sure all unite to hold her League of Rule
> Unbroken as the sacred Chain of Nature,
> That links the jarring Elements in Peace.

This is a good statement of Johnson's Tory creed, and none the worse for the implied satire on the Whigs. It is the only passage in *Irene* in which the political allusion is specific; and it is introduced cautiously, with the responsibility for the anachronism thrown on the broad shoulders of Fame, for it was not the English constitution in the days of the Wars of the Roses that Johnson had in his mind to praise.

The characters are said to be Turks and Greeks, but if they were called by other names the play would lose nothing. They are members, or attendants, of the great family of tragic heroes of Drury Lane, and what they say has no local or racial limits in its application. But the play was suggested by a story that belongs to the year 1456,[1] and there is therefore one allusion to the Renaissance:

> The mighty *Tuscan* courts the banish'd Arts
> To kind *Italia*'s hospitable Shades;
> There shall soft Leisure wing th' excursive Soul,
> And Peace propitious smile on fond Desire;
> There shall despotick Eloquence resume
> Her ancient Empire o'er the yielding Heart;
> There Poetry shall tune her sacred Voice,
> And wake from Ignorance the Western World.

This is the clearest indication of the time of the play, and it may easily be missed. It was sufficient that *Irene* should conform to these great postulates of the regular drama—that human nature is everywhere much the same, and that what may happen at one time may well happen at another. A story laid in Constantinople in the middle of the fifteenth century could be made rich in moral lessons for a London audience of the eighteenth.

Johnson was not the first to make a drama out of Knolles's story. His is the fourth extant play on *Irene* in English. The other three have long been forgotten, and at least one of them is now not easily found:

I. The Tragedy of The unhappy Fair Irene. By Gilbert Swinhoe, Esq; London: Printed by J. Streater, for J. Place, at Furnifals Inn Gate, in Holborn, M.DC.LVIII.

II. Irena, A Tragedy. | Licensed, October 13. 1664. Roger L'Estrange. | London, Printed by Robert White for Octavian Pulleyn Junior, at the sign of the Bible in St Pauls Church-yard near the little North-door. 1664.

III. Irene; Or, The Fair Greek, A Tragedy: As it is Acted at the Theatre Royal in Drury-Lane, By Her Majesty's Sworn Servants. London: Printed for John Bayley at the Judge's Head in Chancery-Lane, near Fleetstreet. 1708. [By Charles Goring].

The interest of these plays lies mainly, and to the reader of Johnson perhaps wholly, in the treatment of the central figure. There is no question of borrowing. None of them owes anything to another, nor did they provide anything to their greater successor. The two earlier plays Johnson may be assumed not to have known; if he happened to know the third, he certainly took nothing from it. Here are four independent renderings of Knolles's story, and four distinct presentations of the character of Irene.

But the story was well known before Knolles wrote his history. There was a fifth play, the lost Elizabethan play by George Peele, described in the *Merrie conceited Jests* as 'the famous play of the Turkish Mahamet and Hyrin the fair

---

[1] According to Knolles's narrative, Irene was captured at the siege of Constantinople in 1453 and murdered just before the siege of Belgrade in 1456. 'This amorous passion indured the space of three continuall yeres' (Painter, *Palace of Pleasure*).

Greek'. Hyrin, or Hiren—a familiar term to the Elizabethans, and long a puzzle to the annotators of Shakespeare—is none other than Irene.

It was Bandello who first told the story in print. He says he heard it from Francesco Appiano, a doctor and learned philosopher, the great-grandson of Francesco Appiano who was doctor to Francesco Sforza II, Duke of Milan, and a contemporary of Mahomet II. It may have little or no foundation in fact; it may well be only a revival of the old story of Alexander, adapted to a century that was much occupied with the amorousness and the cruelty of the Turk. What alone concerns us here is that Bandello made it the subject of his tenth novella, entitled 'Maometto imperador de' turchi crudelmente ammazza una sua donna', and first published in 1554. The story soon spread throughout Europe. A French version was given in 1559 in *Histoires Tragiques Extraictes des Œuvres Italiennes de Bandel, & mises en nostre langue Françoise, par Pierre Boaistuau surnommé Launay, natif de Bretaigne*, and was reprinted in 1564 in Belleforest's continuation and enlargement of Boaistuau's collection. It appeared in English in 1566 as the fortieth novel in Painter's *Palace of Pleasure*. Then it was swept up in the widespread net of the Latin historians of Turkey. Martinus Crusius gave it in his *Turcogræciæ Libri Octo* (Basle, 1584, pp. 101–2), translating it from the French.[1] Joachimus Camerarius, in his *De Rebus Turcicis* (Frankfurt, 1598, p. 60), took it directly from the Italian.[2] In the Latin writers Knolles had authority to include it in his majestic history. But he was not content to work on the somewhat condensed versions which they provided. He had recourse to Painter's *Palace of Pleasure*, and produced a skilful and even masterly rehandling of what he read in that collection of stories.[3]

That the lost Elizabethan play was founded on the novel in *The Palace of Pleasure* is not a rash assumption. Bandello's 'Irenea' had become 'Hyrenée' in the French of Boaistuau, and 'Hyrenee' or 'Hirenee' in the English of Painter; and when Peele brought her on the English stage she was 'Hyrin' or 'Hiren'. From the reference to the play in the *Merrie Jests*, and from the vogue which the word suddenly acquired, we can deduce something of the character of her part.

Johnson missed an opportunity when he edited Shakespeare. He did not suspect the relationship of Pistol's Hiren to the heroine of his own tragedy.[4]

COMPOSITION AND PERFORMANCE

Irene was produced under the name *Mahomet and Irene* at Drury Lane Theatre on Monday, 6 February 1749, and had a run of nine nights, the last performance taking place on Monday, 20 February. It was acted on the intervening Tuesdays (7, 14), Thursdays (9, 16), Saturdays (11, 18), and Monday (13), the theatre

---

[1] 'Excerpsi ex Gallica conuersione partis operum Italicorum Bandeli' (Crusius, 1584, p. 101).

[2] 'Non potui facere quin adiicerem id quod in Italicis narrationibus & de hoc Mahometha traditum reperissem' (Camerarius, 1958, p. 60).

[3] The story as told by Painter is reprinted as the seventeenth and last story in *The Queene of Navarres Tales. Containing Verie pleasant Discourses of fortunate Lovers*, 1597.

[4] See also J. C. Maxwell, '*Othello* and *Irene*', *Notes and Queries* (April 1957), 148.

being closed on the Wednesdays and Fridays. Johnson's three benefit nights were the 9th, 14th, and 20th. None of the theatre bills is known to have been preserved, but in their place we have full announcements in *The General Advertiser*. From it we also learn that *Irene* was published on Thursday, 16 February.[1]

When Arthur Murphy wrote his four articles on Hawkins's edition of Johnson's Works in *The Monthly Review* in 1787, he stated in one of them that *Irene* was acted 'in all thirteen nights', as its run was uninterrupted from Monday the 6th to Monday the 20th. This statement—and much more in these articles— he repeated in his *Essay on the Life and Genius of Johnson* in 1792.[2] He forgot about Lent. In the eighteenth century the London theatres were closed in Lent on Wednesdays and Fridays, and in 1749 Ash Wednesday fell on 8 February.

Though not given to the public till 1749, *Irene* was the earliest of Johnson's more important works. He was engaged on it while running his school at Edial, near Lichfield, and had written 'a great part' before he set out in March 1737 to seek his fortune in London. According to Boswell he had written only three acts before his short stay at Greenwich, and while there 'used to compose, walking in the Park', but did not finish it till his return to Lichfield in the course of the summer to settle his affairs. There is proof, however, that the conclusion had been planned and partly written while he was still at Edial. The manuscript of his first draft—now in the British Museum—contains in haphazard order matter that was ultimately worked up into each of the five acts, or incorporated in them without change. All that can be assigned to the spring and summer of 1737 is the completion and revision of the play.

This manuscript is of particular interest as a draft of one of Johnson's major works; and it shows the effort that *Irene* had cost him. As far as we know he never took such pains again. The subject-matter of each scene is written out in detail; the characters are described—some are named who were afterwards omitted; there are drafts of speeches and page references to authorities. Johnson had read widely in Knolles's *Historie*, and had at least consulted George Sandys's *Relation of a Journey . . . Containing a description of the Turkish Empire*, 1615, Herbelot's *Bibliothèque Orientale*, 1697, and the *Life of Mahomet*, 1697, by Humphrey Prideaux.

Then came the trouble of getting the play brought upon the stage. Peter Garrick, the actor's elder brother, told Boswell what he recollected in 1776, and Boswell jotted down this in his Note Book:

'Peter Garrick told me, that Mr Johnson went first to London to see what could be made of his Tragedy of Irene that he remembers his borrowing the Turkish history (I think Peter said of *him*) in order to take the story of his Play out of it. That he & Mr Johnson went to the Fountain tavern by themselves, & Mr Johnson read it to him—

---

[1] The same paper on 8 and 9 February advertised *Mahomet and Palmira* as 'just published'. It had been published as *Mahomet the Impostor* in 1744, shortly after the death of the author—James Miller.

[2] It is only fair to Murphy to add that if he says 'thirteen nights' in *The Monthly Review* for August 1787, p. 135, he had said 'nine nights' in the April number, p. 290, and reverted to 'nine nights' in his *Life of Garrick*, 1801, i, p. 163.

This Mr Peter Garrick told me at Lichfield Sunday 24 March 1776. . . . He said he spoke to Fleetwood the Manager at Goodman's Fields to receive Irene. But Fleetwood would not read it; probably as it was not recommended by some great Patron.'[1]

Both the Garricks used what influence they had with Charles Fleetwood, the manager of Drury Lane Theatre, and for some time they seemed likely to be successful. In a letter to his wife on 31 January 1740, Johnson reported that

'David wrote to me this day on the affair of Irene, who is at last become a kind of Favourite among the Players. Mr. Fletewood promises to give a promise in writing that it shall be the first next season, if it cannot be introduced now, and Chetwood the Prompter is desirous of bargaining for the copy, and offers fifty Guineas for the right of printing after it shall be played. I hope it will at length reward me for my perplexities.'

It was only the promise of a promise, and Fleetwood was an adept in the art of evasion. Next year we find Johnson so far discouraged by the actors as to turn to the booksellers. Edward Cave, always ready to assist the mainstay of his *Magazine*, wrote thus to Thomas Birch on 9 September 1741:

'I have put Mr Johnson's Play into Mr Gray's Hands, in order to sell it to him, if he is inclined to buy it, but I doubt whether he will or not. He would dispose of Copy and whatever Advantage may be made by acting it. Would your Society, or any Gentleman or Body of men, that you know, take such a Bargain? Both he and I are very unfit to deal with the Theatrical Persons. Fletewood was to have acted it last Season, but Johnson's diffidence or   prevented it.'[2]

Johnson was evidently abandoning hope of ever seeing the play on the stage, and was resigned to get what money he could for it by publication. But John Gray, the bookseller who brought out Lillo's pieces, would not buy it. A further stage in despondency was reached when Johnson was content to lend the manuscript to his friends. 'Keep Irene close, you may send it back at your leisure' is what he wrote to John Taylor, rector of Market Bosworth, on 10 June 1742.

The turn in the fortunes of the play came when David Garrick, his old pupil and friend, assumed the managership of Drury Lane. Garrick had always been anxious to see *Irene* given a chance, and now that he was under a special debt for the great Prologue with which his managership had been inaugurated (as well as for a Prologue for his first play, *Lethe*; cf. p. 88 *ante*), he decided to make it one of the features of the next season. He chose a very strong cast, including Barry, Mrs. Pritchard, Mrs. Cibber, as well as himself; and he provided the further attraction of new dresses and stage-decorations. 'Never', says Hawkins, 'was there such a display of eastern magnificence as this spectacle exhibited.'[3] 'The dresses', says Davies, 'were rich and magnificent, and the scenes splendid and gay, such as were well adapted to the inside of a Turkish seraglio; the view of the gardens belonging to it was in the taste of eastern elegance.'[4] The main difficulty was to induce Johnson to consent to alterations which Garrick knew by

---

[1] *Boswell's Note Book* 1776–1777 (ed. R. W. Chapman), 1925, p. 11.
[2] British Museum, Birch MSS. 4302, f. 109; quoted, with slight inaccuracies, by Boswell, *Life*, i. 153. There is a purposed blank in the manuscript after 'diffidence or'. The 'Society' is the Society for the Encouragement of Learning: see Nichols, *Literary Anecdotes*, ii. 90–7, and *The Library*, December 1938, pp. 263–88.
[3] *Life*, 1787, p. 199.   [4] *Memoirs of Garrick*, 1780, i. 120.

experience to be necessary. He told Boswell long afterwards that Johnson 'not only had not the faculty of producing the impressions of tragedy, but that he had not the sensibility to perceive them'.[1] 'When Johnson writes tragedy', he said to Murphy, '*declamation roars, and passion sleeps*; when Shakespeare wrote, he dipped his pen in his own heart.'[2] Garrick knew that *Irene* would succeed only by the efforts of the players; and Johnson on his part feared that their methods of enlivening the action would detract from the seriousness of his purpose, and obscure the worth of his studied lines. 'Sir,' he said indignantly, 'the fellow wants me to make Mahomet run mad, that he may have an opportunity of tossing his hands and kicking his heels'.[3] We may believe that he was strengthened in his indignation by the recollection of what he had recently written about Savage's experience with Colley Cibber—'having little interest or reputation, he was obliged to submit himself wholly to the players, and admit, with whatever reluctance, the emendations of Mr. Cibber, which he always considered as the disgrace of his performance'.[4] But Garrick insisted, and Johnson had to yield. What these alterations were, there is nothing now to show. The manuscript affords no clue, as it is only a first draft; nor does the book. Most probably the play was printed exactly as it had been written. The claim of George Cawthorne's *British Theatre*, 1796, that the text was 'Regulated from the Prompt Book' is not true of his edition of *Irene*, nor of subsequent reprints of that edition. The one alteration by Garrick of which there is record affects only the action, and it had to be abandoned. This was the strangling of Irene by a bow-string on the stage. The author of a tragedy in which the scene does not change and all is supposed to happen within one day[5] could be trusted not to kill his heroine before the eyes of the audience, and must have consented with no goodwill to so gross a violation of the methods of the regular drama. As events proved, Garrick had gone too far in his desire for stirring action. The strangling of Irene was at once greeted with cries of 'Murder, Murder', though John Bull, as Charles Burney put it,[6] will allow a dramatic poet to stab or slay by hundreds, and her death had to take place as Johnson had designed. From the evidence of a Diary once in the possession of Mrs. Garrick, the change was made after the second night:

Feb. 6, 1749. Irene. Written by Mr. Johnson—went off very well for 4 Acts, the 5th Hiss'd generally.

Feb. 7. Ditto. 5th Act hiss'd again.[7]

Burney and Davies, however, both say that the offence was removed after the first night. Garrick must have been responsible also for the stage-name *Mahomet and Irene*.

The play was received without enthusiasm. The most adverse account is given by Hawkins who, always lukewarm, says that it met with cold applause. Burney,

---

[1] *Life*, i. 198.   [2] *Essay*, 1792, p. 53.   [3] *Life*, i. 196.

[4] *Life of Savage*, 1744, p. 23; *Lives of the Poets*, ed. G. B. Hill, ii. 339.

[5] According to the manuscript the Scene is 'a Garden near the Walls of Constantinople', and the Time is 'Ten days after the taking of it'.

[6] In a note printed in the third edition of Boswell's *Life*.

[7] Sold at Puttick and Simpson's on 11 July 1900, 'Catalogue of Autograph Letters and Documents', p. 16, lot 135.

a man of warmer temperament, who was present at the first performance and several of the others, remembered that it was much applauded the first night and that there was not the least opposition after the death-scene had been removed. But a letter from Aaron Hill to Mallet, written while the play was in the middle of its run, shows that the chief attraction to him—and we may presume to many others—lay in the dresses and the acting:

'I was in town', he wrote on 15 February, 'at the *Anamolous* [sic] Mr. *Johnson's* benefit, and found the Play his proper representative, strong sense, ungrac'd by sweetness, or decorum: Mr. *Garrick* made the *most* of a detach'd, and almost independent character. He was elegantly dress'd, and charm'd me infinitely, by an unexampled silent force of painted action; and by a peculiar *touchingness*, in cadency of voice, from exclamation, sinking into pensive lownesses, that both surpriz'd, and interested! Mrs. *Cibber*, too, was beautifully dressed, and did the utmost justice to her part. But I was sorry to see *Mahomet* (in Mr. B—Y) lose the influence of an attractive *figure* and degrade the awfulness of an imperious *Sultan*, the impressive menace of a martial *conqueror*, and the beseeching *tendernesses* of an amorous *sollicitor*, by an unpointed *restlessness* of leaping *levity*, that neither carried *weight* to suit his *dignity*, nor struck out *purpose*, to express his *passions*.'[1]

Garrick had evidently no difficulty in carrying the performance to the sixth night. In order to carry it to the ninth, so that Johnson might have three third-night benefits, he had recourse to expedients which Johnson cannot have liked. On the seventh night this grave tragedy was supplemented with lighter entertainment. It was not uncommon at this time to add a farce to a serious play, and it is to the credit of *Irene* to have survived to the sixth night without such aid; it was not uncommon also to add dancing; but on the seventh night Garrick added both a farce and dancing—and Scotch dancing. According to the announcement in *The General Advertiser* the play was presented—

With Entertainments of Dancing, particularly
The Scotch Dance by Mr. COOKE, Mad. ANNE AURETTI, &c.
To which (by Desire) will be added a Farce, call'd
The ANATOMIST;
Or, The Sham-Doctor.

On the eighth night the Scotch Dance was repeated, with Garrick's farce *The Lying Valet*; on the ninth there were 'the Savoyard Dance by Mr. Matthews, Mr. Addison, &c.', and Fielding's farce *The Virgin Unmasked*. Short as this run of nine nights may now appear, it compares not unfavourably with other runs about the same time. The twenty nights of *Cato* in April and May 1713 still remained the record for a tragedy. Thomson's *Tancred and Sigismunda* (1745) had nine nights, and his *Coriolanus*, produced immediately before *Irene*, had ten, and Aaron Hill's *Merope*, produced immediately after it, had nine with two additional performances (one 'by particular desire', the other by royal command) at intervals of a week; Moore's *Gamester* (1753) had ten with an eleventh a week later, Young's *Brothers* (1753) had eight, and Glover's *Boadicea* (1753) had ten. The mere number of performances is thus in itself no proof that *Irene* had not succeeded on the stage. A more important indication is that neither Garrick nor any other actor thought of reviving it during Johnson's lifetime. Nor, it

[1] *Works of Aaron Hill*, 1753, ii, pp. 355–6.

would appear, has it ever been acted since, though when it was included in Bell's *British Theatre* it was adorned with a frontispiece representing Miss Wallis as Aspasia—a part which she is not known to have played.

Financially, Johnson had no reason to consider *Irene* a failure. The author of an original play produced at Drury Lane during Garrick's management was given the receipts of a benefit night with a deduction of sixty guineas for the expenses of the house, though the expenses usually came to about ninety.[1] From a manuscript note by Isaac Reed[2] printed by Malone[3] we learn that after the theatre had reserved its hundred and eighty guineas there remained for Johnson as his profit on the three nights £195. 17s. In addition he received from Dodsley £100 for the copyright. (Manuscript dated 8 September 1749, in Pierpont Morgan Library, New York.) After twelve years of disappointment *Irene* thus at last brought Johnson altogether about £300.

Criticisms of *Irene* immediately appeared in periodicals and pamphlets. A long and laudatory letter, which occupies more than a column of *The General Advertiser* of 18 February 1749, speaks of it as 'the best Tragedy, which this Age has produced, for Sublimity of Thought, Harmony of Numbers, Strength of Expression, a scrupulous Observation of Dramatic Rules, the sudden Turn of Events, the tender and generous Distress, the unexpected Catastrophe, and the extensive and important Moral'. The tone of the whole letter and such a statement as 'all who admire *Irene* pay a Compliment to their own Judgment' suggest that it was written with more than a critical purpose. Garrick probably knew something about what was in effect a skilful advertisement, issued at a time when he was taking other means to ensure a third benefit night. A more impartial but equally friendly account is the 'Plan and Specimens of *Irene*' which was published in *The Gentleman's Magazine* for February when the play had been withdrawn. It gives an elaborate analysis of the plot, and after saying that 'to instance every moral which is inculcated in this performance would be to transcribe the whole', cites about a hundred and fifty lines with high praise. The play is censured in respect of the design and the characters, but commended for the justice of the observations and the propriety of the sentiments, in *An Essay on Tragedy, with a Critical Examen of Mahomet and Irene*, an ineffective and now very rare pamphlet published without the author's name by Ralph Griffiths on 8 March. Equally rare is *A Criticism on Mahomet and Irene, In a Letter to the Author*, which was 'printed and sold by W. Reeve, in Fleet-Street; and A. Dodd, opposite St. Clement's Church, in the Strand', and, according to announcements in *The General Advertiser*, was published as early as 21 February.[4]

---

[1] See Garrick's letter to Smollett of 26 November 1757, *Letters*, ed. Little and Kahrl, i. 271, no. 197.

[2] In his copy of Murphy's *Essay on . . . Johnson*, 1792, p. 52 (Brit. Mus. T.1563). See J. F. Woodruff in *Notes and Queries* (February 1971), 61–2.

[3] Boswell's *Life of Johnson*, 6th edition, 1811, i. p. 176. The note was supplied to Malone, the editor of this edition, by Alexander Chalmers. The receipts for the three benefit nights were £177. 1s. 6d., £106. 4s. 0d., and £101. 11s. 6d., making £384. 17s. 0d. in all from which £189. 0s. 0d. had to be deducted.

[4] See R. F. Metzdorf, 'Johnson at Drury Lane' in *New Light on Johnson*, ed. F. W. Hilles (1959), pp. 57–64.

The success of *Irene* fell far below Johnson's hopes, but he took his disappointment, in his well-known words, 'like the Monument'. He continued to think well of what cost him more labour and anxiety than any other composition, and eighteen quotations in the *Dictionary* (s.v. disjoint,[1] ennoble, follow, from, idler, important, imposture, intimidate, obscurely, penitence, polish, prejudice, proverbial, spare, stagnant, stormy, sultaness, vacant) testify to his parental fondness. (Though only disjoint, intimidate, stagnant, and sultaness remain in the revised edition of 1773.) Nor did he come to agree with the verdict of the public till late in life, when, on hearing part of it read out, he admitted that he 'thought it had been better'.[2] His final judgement is clearly indicated in *The Lives of the Poets*. When he said in the Life of Prior that 'tediousness is the most fatal of all faults' and 'that which an author is least able to discover', and when in his *Life of Addison* (§ 11) he drew a distinction between a poem in dialogue and a drama, and added that the success of *Cato* had 'introduced or confirmed among us the use of dialogue too declamatory, of unaffecting elegance, and chill philosophy' we cannot but think that he remembered his own *Irene*.

EDITIONS

Irene: A Tragedy. As it is Acted at the Theatre Royal in Drury-Lane. By Mr. Samuel Johnson. London: Printed for R. Dodsley at Tully's-head Pall-mall and sold by M. Cooper in Pater-noster-Row. M D CC XLIX.

Irene: A Tragedy . . . Dublin . . . M DCC XLIX.

Irene; A Tragedy . . . The Second Edition. London: Printed for R. Dodsley . . . MDCCLIV.

Irene, A Tragedy . . . A New Edition. London: Printed for J. Dodsley, in Pall-Mall. M.DCC LXXXI.

Poetical Works, G. Kearsley, 1785, pp. 37–151.

Poetical Works, W. Osborne and T. Griffin, 1785, pp. 71–152.

Works, 1787, xi. 217–315.

The present text is printed from the first edition, with slight corrections. The second and third editions, though published in Johnson's lifetime, have no independent value. Such changes as occur were made by the printer. Johnson never revised *Irene*.

The play was reprinted from the third edition in Kearsley's edition of the *Poetical Works*, 1785, and in Hawkins's edition of the *Works*, 1787.

The Prologue was reprinted in *The Gentleman's Magazine*, February 1749, p. 85; *The London Magazine*, February 1749, p. 91; *The Universal Magazine*, February 1749, p. 89; *The Scots Magazine*, March 1749, p. 116; in Davies's *Miscellaneous and Fugitive Pieces*, 1773, 1774, ii. 294; and in *The Theatrical Bouquet*, 1778, 1780, p. 303.

---

[1] This word does not occur in *Irene*, but see the First Draft, f. 13: 'With mouldering cement and with beams disjointed'. In the *Dictionary* Johnson quoted, 'Mould'ring arches and disjointed ruins' (p. 393 *post*).

[2] *Life*, iv. 5.

Twenty-six passages are quoted from *Irene* in *A Poetical Dictionary, or the Beauties of the English Poets*, 4 vols., 1761, and thirty-five in *The Beauties of the English Drama*, 4 vols., 1777.

The original manuscript of *Irene*—containing notes for the plot and the characters, and rough drafts of their speeches—was presented by Bennet Langton to George III, and is now in the British Museum, with a transcript by Langton (MS. Kings 306, 307). A copy of the 1781 edition, with a transcription and manuscript additions said to be by Langton, was sold as lot 286 in the Rosebery sale at Sotheby's, 26 June 1933.[1]

[1] Cf. *Life*, i. 108.

IRENE:

A

TRAGEDY.

As it is Acted at the

THEATRE ROYAL

I N

DRURY-LANE.

By Mr. *SAMUEL JOHNSON.*

LONDON:

Printed for R. Dodsley at *Tully's*-head *Pall-mall*
and fold by M. Cooper in *Pater-noster-Row.*

MDCCXLIX.

PROLOGUE

YE glitt'ring Train! whom Lace and Velvet bless,
    Suspend the soft Sollicitudes of Dress;
From grov'ling Business and superfluous Care,
Ye Sons of Avarice! a Moment spare:
Vot'ries of Fame and Worshippers of Pow'r!   5
Dismiss the pleasing Phantoms for an Hour.
Our daring Bard with Spirit unconfin'd,
Spreads wide the mighty Moral for Mankind.
Learn here how Heav'n supports the virtuous Mind,
Daring, tho' calm; and vigorous, tho' resign'd.   10
Learn here what Anguish racks the guilty Breast,
In Pow'r dependent, in Success deprest.
Learn here that Peace from Innocence must flow;
All else is empty Sound, and idle Show.

    If Truths like these with pleasing Language join;   15
Ennobled, yet unchang'd, if Nature shine:
If no wild Draught depart from Reason's Rules,
Nor Gods his Heroes, nor his Lovers Fools:
Intriguing Wits! his artless Plot forgive;
And spare him, Beauties! tho' his Lovers live.   20

    Be this at least his Praise; be this his Pride;
To force Applause no modern Arts are try'd.
Shou'd partial Cat-calls all his Hopes confound,
He bids no Trumpet quell the fatal Sound.
Shou'd welcome Sleep relieve the weary Wit,   25
He rolls no Thunders o'er the drowsy Pit.
No Snares to captivate the Judgment spreads;
Nor bribes your Eyes to prejudice your Heads.
Unmov'd tho' Witlings sneer and Rivals rail;
Studious to please, yet not asham'd to fail.   30

8 for] of *1785*   23 confound; *1749, 1754, Davies*

16. Quoted in the *Dictionary*, s.v. 'ennoble' as by '*Anon.*' Removed from ed. 4.
27–8. Quoted in the *Dictionary*, s.v. 'prejudice', as by '*Anonym.*', with 'mind he' for 'Judgment'. Removed from ed. 4.

He scorns the meek Address, the suppliant Strain,
With Merit needless, and without it vain.
In Reason, Nature, Truth he dares to trust:
Ye Fops be silent! and ye Wits be just!

EPILOGUE

*M*ARRY a Turk! a haughty, Tyrant King,
 Who thinks us Women born to dress and sing
To please his Fancy,—see no other Man—
Let him persuade me to it—if he can:
Besides, he has fifty Wives; and who can bear 5
To have the fiftieth Part her paultry Share?

'Tis true, the Fellow's handsome, strait and tall;
But how the Devil should he please us all!
My Swain is little—true—but be it known,
My Pride's to have that little all my own. 10
Men will be ever to their Errors blind,
Where Woman's not allow'd to speak her Mind;
I swear this Eastern Pageantry is Nonsense,
And for one Man—one Wife's enough in Conscience.

In vain proud Man usurps what's Woman's Due; 15
For us alone, they Honour's Paths pursue:
Inspir'd by us, they Glory's Heights ascend;
Woman the Source, the Object, and the End.
Tho' Wealth, and Pow'r, and Glory they receive,
These all are Trifles, to what we can give. 20
For us the Statesman labours, Hero fights,
Bears toilsome Days, and wakes long tedious Nights:
And when blest Peace has silenc'd War's Alarms,
Receives his full Reward in Beauty's Arms.

Epilogue. 'The Epilogue, as Johnson informed me, was written by Sir William Yonge. I know not how his play came to be thus graced by the pen of a person then so eminent in the political world' (Boswell, *Life*, i. 197). Murphy rejected the attribution, and described the Epilogue as 'the worst *Jeu d'Esprit* that ever fell from Johnson's pen' (*Essay on the Life*, 1792, p. 154). 'The first fourteen lines certainly deserve Murphy's censure, and could hardly have been written by the pen of Johnson; but the last ten lines are much better, and it may be suspected that these Johnson added to or altered from the original copy' (Croker, *Life*, 1831, i. 172 n. 2).

The Epilogue is printed after the Prologue in *The Gentleman's Magazine*, 1749, p. 85, and is said to be 'By another hand'.

The PERSONS

MEN

MAHOMET, Emperor of the *Turks*,	Mr. *Barry*.[1]
CALI BASSA, First Visier,	Mr. *Berry*.
MUSTAPHA, A *Turkish* Aga,	Mr. *Sowden*.
ABDALLA, An Officer,	Mr. *Havard*.
HASAN, } *Turkish* Captains,	Mr. *Usher*.
CARAZA,	Mr. *Burton*.
DEMETRIUS, } *Greek* Noblemen,	Mr. *Garrick*.
LEONTIUS,	Mr. *Blakes*.
MURZA, An Eunuch,	

WOMEN

ASPASIA, } *Greek* Ladies,	Mrs. *Cibber*.
IRENE,	Mrs. *Pritchard*.[2]

Attendants on IRENE.

---

[1] The names of the Actors are repeated in the edition of 1754, and omitted in that of 1781.

[2] 'Dr Johnson hated Mrs Pritchard: She play'd Aspasia in his Tragedy, & wonder'd He did not *flatter* her I would hardly said he flatter a *pretty* woman much less Mrs Pritchard.' (*Thraliana*, i. 133 n.)

ACT I.

SCENE I

DEMETRIUS *and* LEONTIUS *in* Turkish *Habits*.

LEONTIUS.

And is it thus DEMETRIUS meets his Friend,
Hid in the mean Disguise of *Turkish* Robes,
With servile Secrecy to lurk in Shades,
And vent our Suff'rings in clandestine Groans?

DEMETRIUS.

Till breathless Fury rested from Destruction   5
These Groans were fatal, these Disguises vain:
But now our *Turkish* Conquerors have quench'd
Their Rage, and pall'd their Appetite of Murder;
No more the glutted Sabre thirsts for Blood,
And weary Cruelty remits her Tortures.   10

LEONTIUS.

Yet *Greece* enjoys no Gleam of transient Hope,
No soothing Interval of peaceful Sorrow;
The Lust of Gold succeeds the Rage of Conquest,
The Lust of Gold, unfeeling and remorseless!
The last Corruption of degenerate Man!   15
Urg'd by th' imperious Soldier's fierce Command,
The groaning *Greeks* break up their golden Caverns
Pregnant with Stores, that *India*'s Mines might envy,
Th' accumulated Wealth of toiling Ages.

DEMETRIUS.

That Wealth, too sacred for their Country's Use!   20
That Wealth, too pleasing to be lost for Freedom!

I. i. 17–23. Gibbon quoted four of these seven lines in chap. lxviii of *The Decline and Fall*, 1788, vi. 478, as a footnote to his statement that 'the avarice of the rich denied the emperor, and reserved for the Turks, the secret treasures which might have raised in their defence whole armies of mercenaries'. Johnson, he says, 'has happily seized this characteristic circumstance'. But compare his note on II. vi. 61–4 (p. 308).

That Wealth, which granted to their weeping Prince,
Had rang'd embattled Nations at our Gates:
But thus reserv'd to lure the Wolves of *Turkey*,
Adds Shame to Grief, and Infamy to Ruin.   25
Lamenting Av'rice now too late discovers
Her own neglected, in the publick Safety.

LEONTIUS.

Reproach not Misery.—The Sons of *Greece*,
Ill-fated Race! So oft besieg'd in vain,
With false Security beheld Invasion.   30
Why should they fear?—That Power that kindly spreads
The Clouds, a Signal of impending Show'rs,
To warn the wand'ring Linnet to the Shade,
Beheld without Concern, expiring *Greece*,
And not one Prodigy foretold our Fate.   35

DEMETRIUS.

A thousand horrid Prodigies foretold it.
A feeble Government, eluded Laws,
A factious Populace, luxurious Nobles,
And all the Maladies of sinking States.
When publick Villainy, too strong for Justice,   40
Shows his bold Front, the Harbinger of Ruin,
Can brave LEONTIUS call for airy Wonders,
Which Cheats interpret, and which Fools regard?
When some neglected Fabrick nods beneath
The Weight of Years, and totters to the Tempest,   45
Must Heaven dispatch the Messengers of Light,
Or wake the Dead to warn us of its Fall?

LEONTIUS.

Well might the Weakness of our Empire sink
Before such Foes of more than human Force;
Some Pow'r invisible, from Heav'n or Hell,   50
Conducts their Armies and asserts their Cause.

36–47. Quoted in *Life*, i. 109.

DEMETRIUS.

And yet, my Friend, what Miracles were wrought
Beyond the Power of Constancy and Courage;
Did unresisted Lightning aid their Cannon,
Did roaring Whirlwinds sweep us from the Ramparts: 55
'Twas Vice that shook our Nerves, 'twas Vice, LEONTIUS,
That froze our Veins, and wither'd all our Powers.

LEONTIUS.

What e'er our Crimes, our Woes demand Compassion.
Each Night protected by the friendly Darkness,
Quitting my close Retreat, I range the City,   60
And weeping, kiss the venerable Ruins:
With silent Pangs I view the tow'ring Domes,
Sacred to Prayer, and wander thro' the Streets;
Where Commerce lavish'd unexhausted Plenty,
And Jollity maintain'd eternal Revels.—   65

DEMETRIUS.

—How chang'd alas!—Now ghastly Desolation
In Triumph sits upon our shatter'd Spires,
Now Superstition, Ignorance and Error,
Usurp our Temples, and profane our Altars.

LEONTIUS.

From ev'ry Palace burst a mingled Clamour,   70
The dreadful Dissonance of barb'rous Triumph,
Shrieks of Affright, and Wailings of Distress.
Oft when the Cries of violated Beauty
Arose to Heav'n, and pierc'd my bleeding Breast,
I felt thy Pains, and trembled for ASPASIA.   75

DEMETRIUS.

ASPASIA! spare that lov'd, that mournful Name:
Dear hapless Maid—tempestuous Grief o'erbears
My reasoning Pow'rs—Dear, hapless, lost ASPASIA!

52 Friends 1754   77 hapless] helpless 1754

LEONTIUS.

Suspend the Thought.

DEMETRIUS.

          All Thought on her is Madness:
Yet let me think—I see the helpless Maid,   80
Behold the Monsters gaze with savage Rapture,
Behold how Lust and Rapine struggle round her.

LEONTIUS.

Awake, DEMETRIUS, from this dismal Dream,
Sink not beneath imaginary Sorrows:
Call to your Aid your Courage, and your Wisdom;   85
Think on the sudden Change of human Scenes;
Think on the various Accidents of War;
Think on the mighty Pow'r of awful Virtue;
Think on that Providence that guards the Good.

DEMETRIUS.

O Providence! extend thy Care to me,   90
For Courage droops unequal to the Combat,
And weak Philosophy denies her Succours.
Sure some kind Sabre in the Heat of Battle,
Ere yet the Foe found Leisure to be cruel,
Dismiss'd her to the Sky.

LEONTIUS.

          Some virgin Martyr,   95
Perhaps, enamour'd of resembling Virtue,
With gentle Hand restrain'd the Streams of Life,
And snatch'd her timely from her Country's Fate.

DEMETRIUS.

From those bright Regions of eternal Day,
Where now thou shin'st among thy Fellow-Saints,   100
Array'd in purer Light, look down on me:
In pleasing Visions, and assuasive Dreams;
O! sooth my Soul, and teach me how to lose thee.

102 assuasive] delusive *Boswell, Life, edd. 2, 3* (ed. 1934, i. 237)

LEONTIUS.

Enough of unavailing Tears, DEMETRIUS,
I came obedient to thy friendly Summons,   105
And hop'd to share thy Counsels, not thy Sorrows:
While thus we mourn the Fortune of ASPASIA,
To what are we reserv'd?

DEMETRIUS.

                        To what I know not:
But hope, yet hope, to Happiness and Honour;
If Happiness can be without ASPASIA.   110

LEONTIUS.

But whence this new sprung Hope?

DEMETRIUS.

                        From CALI BASSA:
The Chief, whose Wisdom guides the *Turkish* Counsels.
He, tir'd of Slav'ry, tho' the highest Slave,
Projects at once our Freedom and his own;
And bids us thus disguis'd await him here.   115

LEONTIUS.

Can he restore the State he could not save?
In vain, when *Turkey*'s troops assail'd our Walls,
His kind Intelligence betray'd their Measures;
Their Arms prevail'd, though CALI was our Friend.

DEMETRIUS.

When the tenth Sun had set upon our Sorrows,   120
At Midnight's private Hour a Voice unknown
Sounds in my sleeping Ear, "Awake DEMETRIUS,
"Awake, and follow me to better Fortunes;"
Surpriz'd I start, and bless the happy Dream;
Then rouzing know the fiery Chief ABDALLA,   125

111 newsprung *1754, 1781*   125 firy *1749* (cf. III. vi. 7 and IV. i. 35: 'fiery' in
Dictionary)   ABDALLAH *1749, 1781*

Whose quick Impatience seiz'd my doubtful Hand,
And led me to the Shore where CALI stood,
Pensive and listning to the beating Surge.
There in soft Hints and in ambiguous Phrase,
With all the Diffidence of long Experience,   130
That oft' had practis'd Fraud, and oft' detected,
The Vet'ran Courtier half reveal'd his Project.
By his Command, equipp'd for speedy Flight,
Deep in a winding Creek a Galley lies,
Mann'd with the bravest of our fellow Captives,   135
Selected by my Care, a hardy Band,
That long to hail thee Chief.

LEONTIUS.

                       But what avails
So small a Force? or why should CALI fly?
Or how can CALI's Flight restore our Country?

DEMETRIUS.

Reserve these Questions for a safer Hour,   140
Or hear himself, for see the Bassa comes.

SCENE II

DEMETRIUS, LEONTIUS, CALI BASSA.

CALI.

Now summon all thy Soul, illustrious Christian!
Awake each Faculty that sleeps within thee,
The Courtier's Policy, the Sage's Firmness,
The Warrior's Ardour, and the Patriot's Zeal;
If chasing past Events with vain Pursuit,   5
Or wand'ring in the Wilds of future Being,
A single Thought now rove, recall it home.
But can thy Friend sustain the glorious Cause,
The Cause of Liberty, the Cause of Nations?

DEMETRIUS.

Observe him closely with a Statesman's Eye,   10
Thou that hast long perus'd the Draughts of Nature,
And know'st the Characters of Vice and Virtue,
Left by the Hand of Heav'n on human Clay.

CALI.

His Mien is lofty, his Demeanour great,
Nor sprightly Folly wantons in his Air,   15
Nor dull Serenity becalms his Eyes.
Such had I trusted once as soon as seen,
But cautious Age suspects the flatt'ring Form,
And only credits what Experience tells.
Has Silence press'd her Seal upon his Lips?   20
Does adamantine Faith invest his Heart?
Will he not bend beneath a Tyrant's Frown?
Will he not melt before Ambition's Fire?
Will he not soften in a Friend's Embrace?
Or flow dissolving in a Woman's Tears?   25

DEMETRIUS.

Sooner these trembling Leaves shall find a Voice,
And tell the Secrets of their conscious Walks;
Sooner the Breeze shall catch the flying Sounds,
And shock the Tyrant with a Tale of Treason.
Your slaughter'd Multitudes that swell the Shore,   30
With Monuments of Death proclaim his Courage;
Virtue and Liberty engross his Soul,
And leave no Place for Perfidy or Fear.

LEONTIUS.

I scorn a Trust unwillingly repos'd;
DEMETRIUS will not lead me to Dishonour;   35
Consult in private, call me when your Scheme
Is ripe for Action, and demands the Sword.   [*Going.*

26 these] the *1754*

DEMETRIUS.

LEONTIUS stay.

CALI.

    Forgive an old Man's Weakness,
And share the deepest Secrets of my Soul,
My Wrongs, my Fears, my Motives, my Designs:— 40
When unsuccessful Wars, and civil Factions,
Embroil'd the *Turkish* State—our Sultan's Father
Great *Amurath*, at my Request, forsook
The Cloister's Ease, resum'd the tott'ring Throne,
And snatch'd the Reins of abdicated Pow'r 45
From giddy MAHOMET's unskilful Hand.
This fir'd the youthful King's ambitious Breast,
He murmurs Vengeance at the Name of CALI,
And dooms my rash Fidelity to Ruin.

DEMETRIUS.

Unhappy Lot of all that shine in Courts; 50
For forc'd Compliance, or for zealous Virtue,
Still odious to the Monarch, or the People.

CALI.

Such are the Woes when arbitrary Pow'r,
And lawless Passion, hold the Sword of Justice.
If there be any Land, as Fame reports, 55
Where common Laws restrain the Prince and Subject,
A happy Land, where circulating Pow'r
Flows through each Member of th' embodied State,
Sure, not unconscious of the mighty Blessing,
Her grateful Sons shine bright with ev'ry Virtue; 60
Untainted with the Lust of Innovation,
Sure all unite to hold her League of Rule

---

58. Cf. *The Rambler*, No. 140, 'a late Writer has put Harvey's Doctrine of the Circulation of the Blood into the Mouth of a Turkish Statesman, who lived near two Centuries before it was known to Philosophers or Anatomists'. Harvey announced his discovery in 1616.

61. Cf. Preface to *Dictionary*, § 31: 'The words which our authors have introduced . . . by compliance with fashion or lust of innovation.'

Unbroken as the sacred Chain of Nature,
That links the jarring Elements in Peace.

LEONTIUS.

But say, great Bassa, why the Sultan's Anger,   65
Burning in vain, delays the Stroke of Death?

CALI.

Young, and unsettled in his Father's Kingdoms,
Fierce as he was, he dreaded to destroy
The Empire's Darling, and the Soldier's Boast;
But now confirm'd, and swelling with his Conquests, 70
Secure he tramples my declining Fame,
Frowns unrestrain'd, and dooms me with his Eyes.

DEMETRIUS.

What can reverse thy Doom?

CALI.

The Tyrant's Death.

DEMETRIUS.

But *Greece* is still forgot.

CALI.

On *Asia*'s Coast,
Which lately bless'd my gentle Government,   75
Soon as the Sultan's unexpected Fate
Fills all th' astonish'd Empire with Confusion,
My Policy shall raise an easy Throne;
The *Turkish* Pow'rs from *Europe* shall retreat,
And harrass *Greece* no more with wasteful War.   80
A Galley mann'd with *Greeks*, thy charge, LEONTIUS,
Attends to waft us to Repose and Safety.

DEMETRIUS.

That Vessel, if observ'd, alarms the Court,
And gives a thousand fatal Questions Birth;
Why stor'd for Flight? and why prepar'd by CALI?   85

71 Fame] Frame *1754*

CALI.

This Hour I'll beg, with unsuspecting Face,
Leave to perform my Pilgrimage to *Mecca*;
Which granted, hides my Purpose from the World,
And, though refus'd, conceals it from the Sultan.

LEONTIUS.

How can a single Hand attempt a Life   90
Which Armies guard, and Citadels inclose?

CALI.

Forgetful of Command, with captive Beauties,
Far from his Troops, he toys his Hours away.
A roving Soldier seiz'd in *Sophia*'s Temple
A Virgin shining with distinguish'd Charms,   95
And brought his beauteous Plunder to the Sultan.

DEMETRIUS.

In *Sophia*'s Temple!—What Alarm!—Proceed.

CALI.

The Sultan gaz'd, he wonder'd and he lov'd;
In Passion lost, he bad the conqu'ring Fair
Renounce her Faith, and be the Queen of *Turkey*;   100
The pious Maid, with modest Indignation,
Threw back the glitt'ring Bribe.

DEMETRIUS.

                              Celestial Goodness!
It must, it must be She; her Name?

CALI.

                              ASPASIA.

DEMETRIUS.

What Hopes, what Terrors rush upon my Soul!
O lead me quickly to the Scene of Fate;   105
Break through the Politician's tedious Forms,
ASPASIA calls me, let me fly to save her.

LEONTIUS.

Did MAHOMET reproach or praise her Virtue?

CALI.

His Offers oft repeated, still refus'd,
At length rekindled his accustom'd Fury,   110
And chang'd th' endearing Smile and am'rous Whisper
To Threats of Torture, Death and Violation.

DEMETRIUS.

These tedious Narratives of frozen Age
Distract my Soul, dispatch thy ling'ring Tale;
Say, did a Voice from Heav'n restrain the Tyrant?   115
Did interposing Angels guard her from him?

CALI.

Just in the Moment of impending Fate,
Another Plund'rer brought the bright IRENE;
Of equal Beauty, but of softer Mien,
Fear in her Eye, Submission on her Tongue,   120
Her mournful Charms attracted his Regards,
Disarm'd his Rage, and in repeated Visits
Gain'd all his Heart; at length his eager Love
To her transferr'd the Offer of a Crown.

LEONTIUS.

Nor found again the bright Temptation fail?   125

CALI.

Trembling to grant, nor daring to refuse,
While Heav'n and MAHOMET divide her Fears,
With coy Caresses and with pleasing Wiles
She feeds his Hopes, and sooths him to Delay.
For her, Repose is banish'd from the Night   130
And Business from the Day. In her Apartments
He lives——

114 lingring *1749*   125 fail. *1749, 1754*

LEONTIUS.

And there must fall.

CALI.

But yet th' Attempt
Is hazardous.

LEONTIUS.

Forbear to speak of Hazards,
What has the Wretch that has surviv'd his Country,
His Friends, his Liberty, to hazard?

CALI.

Life.   135

DEMETRIUS.

Th' inestimable Privilege of Breathing!
Important Hazard! What's that airy Bubble
When weigh'd with *Greece*, with Virtue, with ASPASIA?
A floating Atom, Dust that falls unheeded
Into the adverse Scale, nor shakes the Balance.   140

CALI.

At least this Day be calm—If we succeed,
ASPASIA's thine, and all thy Life is Rapture—
See! MUSTAPHA, the Tyrant's Minion, comes;
Invest LEONTIUS with his new Command;
And wait ABDALLA's unsuspected Visits: 145
Remember Freedom, Glory, *Greece*, and Love.
                    [*Exeunt* Demetrius *and* Leontius.

SCENE III

CALI, MUSTAPHA.

MUSTAPHA.

By what Enchantment does this lovely *Greek*
Hold in her Chains the captivated Sultan?

He tires his Fav'rites with IRENE's Praise,
And seeks the Shades to muse upon IRENE;
IRENE steals unheeded from his Tongue,   5
And mingles unperceiv'd with ev'ry Thought.

CALI.

Why should the Sultan shun the Joys of Beauty,
Or arm his Breast against the Force of Love?
Love, that with sweet Vicissitude relieves
The Warrior's Labours, and the Monarch's Cares.   10
But will she yet receive the Faith of *Mecca*?

MUSTAPHA.

Those pow'rful Tyrants of the Female Breast
Fear and Ambition, urge her to Compliance;
Dress'd in each Charm of gay Magnificence,
Alluring Grandeur courts her to his Arms,   15
Religion calls her from the wish'd Embrace,
Paints future Joys, and points to distant Glories.

CALI.

Soon will th' unequal Contest be decided,
Prospects obscur'd by Distance faintly strike.
Each Pleasure brightens at its near Approach,   20
And every Danger shocks with double Horror.

MUSTAPHA.

How shall I scorn the beautiful Apostate!
How will the bright ASPASIA shine above her!

CALI.

Should she, for Proselytes are always zealous,
With pious Warmth receive our Prophet's Law——   25

MUSTAPHA.

Heav'n will contemn the mercenary Fervour,
Which Love of Greatness, not of Truth, inflames.

CALI.

Cease, cease thy Censures, for the Sultan comes
Alone, with am'rous Haste to seek his Love.

SCENE IV

MAHOMET, CALI BASSA, MUSTAPHA.

CALI.

Hail, Terror of the Monarchs of the World,
Unshaken be thy Throne as Earth's firm Base,
Live till the Sun forgets to dart his Beams,
And weary Planets loiter in their Courses.

MAHOMET.

But, CALI, let IRENE share thy Prayers;   5
For what is Length of Days without IRENE?
I come from empty Noise, and tasteless Pomp,
From Crouds that hide a Monarch from himself,
To prove the Sweets of Privacy and Friendship,
And dwell upon the Beauties of IRENE.   10

CALI.

O may her Beauties last unchang'd by Time,
As those that bless the Mansions of the Good.

MAHOMET.

Each Realm where Beauty turns the graceful Shape,
Swells the fair Breast or animates the Glance,
Adorns my Palace with its brightest Virgins;   15
Yet unacquainted with these soft Emotions
I walk'd superior, through the Blaze of Charms,
Prais'd without Rapture, left without Regret.
Why rove I now, when absent from my Fair,
From Solitude to Crouds, from Crouds to Solitude,   20

iv. 20. The only line of twelve syllables in the play, though the alexandrine is not
uncommon in Johnson's early verse.

Still restless, till I clasp the lovely Maid,
And ease my loaded Soul upon her Bosom?

MUSTAPHA.

Forgive, great Sultan, that intrusive Duty
Enquires the final Doom of *Menodorus*,
The *Grecian* Counsellor.

MAHOMET.

                 Go see him die;   25
His martial Rhet'rick taught the *Greeks* Resistance;
Had they prevail'd, I ne'er had known IRENE.
                       [*Exit* Mustapha.

SCENE V

MAHOMET, CALI.

MAHOMET.

Remote from Tumult, in th' adjoining Palace,
Thy Care shall guard this Treasure of my Soul;
There let ASPASIA, since my Fair entreats it,
With Converse chase the melancholy Moments.
Sure, chill'd with sixty winter Camps, thy Blood   5
At Sight of female Charms will glow no more.

CALI.

These Years, unconquer'd MAHOMET, demand
Desires more pure, and other Cares than Love.
Long have I wish'd, before our Prophet's Tomb,
To pour my Prayers for thy successful Reign,   10
To quit the Tumults of the noisy Camp,
And sink into the silent Grave in Peace.

MAHOMET.

What! think of Peace while haughty *Scanderbeg*
Elate with Conquest, in his native Mountains,
Prowls o'er the wealthy Spoils of bleeding *Turkey*?   15

While fair *Hungaria*'s unexhausted Vallies
Pour forth their Legions, and the roaring *Danube*
Rolls half his Floods unheard through shouting Camps?
Nor couldst thou more support a Life of Sloth
Than *Amurath*—

CALI.

Still full of *Amurath*!   [*Aside.* 20

MAHOMET.

Than *Amurath*, accustom'd to Command,
Could bear his Son upon the *Turkish* Throne.

CALI.

This Pilgrimage our Lawgiver ordain'd—

MAHOMET.

For those who could not please by nobler Service.—
Our warlike Prophet loves an active Faith,   25
The holy Flame of enterprizing Virtue,
Mocks the dull Vows of Solitude and Penance,
And scorns the lazy Hermit's cheap Devotion;
Shine thou distinguish'd by superior Merit,
With wonted Zeal pursue the Task of War,   30
Till every Nation reverence the *Koran*,
And ev'ry Suppliant lift his Eyes to *Mecca*.

CALI.

This Regal Confidence, this pious Ardour,
Let Prudence moderate, though not suppress.
Is not each Realm that smiles with kinder Suns,   35
Or boasts a happier Soil, already thine?
Extended Empire, like expanded Gold,
Exchanges solid Strength for feeble Splendor.

MAHOMET.

Preach thy dull Politics to vulgar Kings,
Thou know'st not yet thy Master's future Greatness,   40
His vast Designs, his Plans of boundless Pow'r.

When ev'ry Storm in my Domain shall roar,
When ev'ry Wave shall beat a *Turkish* Shore,
Then, CALI, shall the Toils of Battle cease,
Then dream of Prayer, and Pilgrimage, and Peace. 45
[*Exeunt.*

ACT II

SCENE I

ASPASIA, IRENE.

IRENE.

ASPASIA, yet pursue the sacred Theme;
Exhaust the Stores of pious Eloquence,
And teach me to repell the Sultan's Passion.
Still at ASPASIA's Voice a sudden Rapture
Exalts my Soul, and fortifies my Heart.   5
The glitt'ring Vanities of empty Greatness,
The Hopes and Fears, the Joys and Pains of Life,
Dissolve in Air, and vanish into Nothing.

ASPASIA.

Let nobler Hopes and juster Fears succeed,
And bar the Passes of IRENE's Mind   10
Agaist returning Guilt.

IRENE.

        When thou art absent
Death rises to my View, with all his Terrors;
Then Visions horrid as a Murd'rer's Dreams
Chill my Resolves, and blast my blooming Virtue:
Stern Torture shakes his bloody Scourge before me, 15
And Anguish gnashes on the fatal Wheel.

ASPASIA.

Since Fear predominates in every Thought,
And sways thy Breast with absolute Dominion,

Think on th' insulting Scorn, the conscious Pangs,
The future Miseries that wait th' Apostate;   20
So shall Timidity assist thy Reason,
And Wisdom into Virtue turn thy Frailty.

IRENE.

Will not that Pow'r that form'd the Heart of Woman,
And wove the feeble Texture of her Nerves,
Forgive those Fears that shake the tender Frame?   25

ASPASIA.

The Weakness we lament, our selves create,
Instructed from our infant Years to court
With counterfeited Fears the Aid of Man;
We learn to shudder at the rustling Breeze,
Start at the Light, and tremble in the Dark;   30
Till Affectation, rip'ning to Belief,
And Folly, frighted at her own Chimeras,
Habitual Cowardice usurps the Soul.

IRENE.

Not all like thee can brave the Shocks of Fate,
Thy Soul by Nature great, enlarg'd by Knowledge,   35
Soars unencumber'd with our idle Cares,
And all ASPASIA but her Beauty's Man.

ASPASIA.

Each generous Sentiment is thine, DEMETRIUS,
Whose Soul, perhaps, yet mindful of ASPASIA,
Now hovers o'er this melancholy Shade,   40
Well pleas'd to find thy Precepts not forgotten.
O! could the Grave restore the pious Hero,
Soon would his Art or Valour set us free,
And bear us far from Servitude and Crimes.

IRENE.

He yet may live.

26, 28 create; . . . Man, *1781*

ASPASIA.

Alas! delusive Dream!   45
Too well I know him, his immod'rate Courage,
Th' impetuous Sallies of excessive Virtue,
Too strong for Love, have hurried him on Death.

SCENE II

ASPASIA, IRENE, CALI, ABDALLA.

CALI *to* ABDALLA, *as they advance.*

Behold our future Sultaness, ABDALLA;—
Let artful Flatt'ry now, to lull Suspicion,
Glide through IRENE to the Sultan's Ear.
Wouldst thou subdue th' obdurate Cannibal
To tender Friendship, praise him to his Mistress.   5

To IRENE.

Well may those Eyes that view these heav'nly Charms,
Reject the Daughters of contending Kings;
For what are pompous Titles, proud Alliance,
Empire or Wealth, to Excellence like thine?

ABDALLA

Receive th' impatient Sultan to thy Arms;   10
And may a long Posterity of Monarchs,
The Pride and Terror of succeeding Days,
Rise from the happy Bed; and future Queens
Diffuse IRENE's Beauty through the World.

IRENE.

Can MAHOMET's imperial Hand descend   15
To clasp a Slave? or, can a Soul like mine,
Unus'd to Power, and form'd for humbler Scenes,
Support the splendid Miseries of Greatness?

12, 13. Thus quoted in the *Dictionary*, s.v. 'from': 'Succeeding kings rise *from* the happy bed'.

CALI.

No regal Pageant deck'd with casual Honours,
Scorn'd by his Subjects, trampled by his Foes;   20
No feeble Tyrant of a petty State
Courts thee to shake on a dependent Throne;
Born to command, as thou to charm Mankind,
The Sultan from himself derives his Greatness.
Observe, bright Maid, as his resistless Voice   25
Drives on the Tempest of destructive War,
How Nation after Nation falls before him.

ABDALLA.

At his dread Name the distant Mountains shake
Their cloudy Summits, and the Sons of Fierceness,
That range unciviliz'd from Rock to Rock,   30
Distrust th' eternal Fortresses of Nature,
And wish their gloomy Caverns more obscure.

ASPASIA.

Forbear this lavish Pomp of dreadful Praise;
The horrid Images of War and Slaughter
Renew our Sorrows, and awake our Fears.   35

ABDALLA.

CALI, methinks yon waving Trees afford
A doubtful Glimpse of our approaching Friends;
Just as I mark'd them, they forsook the Shore,
And turn'd their hasty Steps towards the Garden.

CALI.

Conduct these Queens, ABDALLA, to the Palace: 40
Such heav'nly Beauty form'd for Adoration,
The Pride of Monarchs, the Reward of Conquest;
Such Beauty must not shine to vulgar Eyes.

SCENE III

CALI *solus*.

How Heav'n in Scorn of human Arrogance,
Commits to trivial Chance the Fate of Nations!
While with incessant Thought laborious Man
Extends his mighty Schemes of Wealth and Pow'r,
And tow'rs and triumphs in ideal Greatness;   5
Some accidental Gust of Opposition
Blasts all the Beauties of his new Creation,
O'erturns the Fabrick of presumptuous Reason,
And whelms the swelling Architect beneath it.
Had not the Breeze untwin'd the meeting Boughs,   10
And through the parted Shade disclos'd the *Greeks*,
Th' important Hour had pass'd unheeded by,
In all the sweet Oblivion of Delight,
In all the Fopperies of meeting Lovers;
In Sighs and Tears, in Transports and Embraces,   15
In soft Complaints, and idle Protestations.

SCENE IV

CALI, DEMETRIUS, LEONTIUS.

CALI.

Could Omens fright the Resolute and Wise,
Well might we fear impending Disappointments.

LEONTIUS.

Your artful Suit, your Monarch's fierce Denial,
The cruel Doom of hapless *Menodorus*—

DEMETRIUS.

And your new Charge, that dear, that heavn'ly Maid.—

LEONTIUS.

All this we know already from ABDALLA.   6

iii. 12. Quoted in the *Dictionary*, s.v. 'important'.

DEMETRIUS.

Such slight Defeats but animate the Brave
To stronger Efforts, and maturer Counsels.

CALI.

My Doom confirm'd establishes my Purpose.
Calmly he heard, till *Amurath*'s Resumption　　10
Rose to his Thought, and set his Soul on Fire:
When from his Lips the fatal Name burst out,
A sudden Pause th' imperfect Sense suspended,
Like the dread Stillness of condensing Storms.

DEMETRIUS.

The loudest Cries of Nature urge us forward;　　15
Despotick Rage pursues the Life of CALI;
His groaning Country claims LEONTIUS' Aid;
And yet another Voice, forgive me *Greece*,
The pow'rful Voice of Love inflames DEMETRIUS,
Each lin'gring Hour alarms me for ASPASIA.　　20

CALI.

What Passions reign among thy Crew, LEONTIUS?
Does chearless Diffidence oppress their Hearts?
Or sprightly Hope exalt their kindling Spirits?
Do they with Pain repress the struggling Shout,
And listen eager to the rising Wind?　　25

LEONTIUS.

All there is Hope, and Gaiety, and Courage,
No cloudy Doubts, or languishing Delays;
Ere I could range them on the crowded Deck,
At once a hundred Voices thunder'd round me,
And every Voice was Liberty and *Greece*.　　30

DEMETRIUS.

Swift, let us rush upon the careless Tyrant,
Nor give him Leisure for another Crime.

LEONTIUS.

Then let us now resolve, nor idly waste
Another Hour in dull Deliberation.

CALI.

But see, where destin'd to protract our Counsels,   35
Comes MUSTAPHA.—Your *Turkish* Robes conceal you—
Retire with Speed, while I prepare to meet him
With artificial Smiles, and seeming Friendship.

SCENE V

CALI, MUSTAPHA.

CALI.

I see the Gloom that low'rs upon thy Brow,
These Days of Love and Pleasure charm not thee;
Too slow these gentle Constellations roll,
Thou long'st for Stars that frown on human Kind,
And scatter Discord from their baleful Beams.   5

MUSTAPHA.

How blest art thou, still jocund and serene,
Beneath the Load of Business, and of Years.

CALI.

Sure by some wond'rous Sympathy of Souls,
My Heart still beats responsive to the Sultan's;
I share, by secret Instinct, all his Joys,   10
And feel no Sorrow while my Sov'reign smiles.

MUSTAPHA.

The Sultan comes, impatient for his Love;
Conduct her hither, let no rude Intrusion
Molest these private Walks, or Care invade
These Hours assign'd to Pleasure and IRENE.   15

33 idly] idle 1754

SCENE VI

MAHOMET, MUSTAPHA.

MAHOMET.

Now, MUSTAPHA, pursue thy Tale of Horror.
Has Treason's dire Infection reach'd my Palace?
Can CALI dare the Stroke of heav'nly Justice,
In the dark Precincts of the gaping Grave,
And load with Perjuries his parting Soul?   5
Was it for this, that sick'ning in *Epirus*,
My Father call'd me to his Couch of Death,
Join'd CALI's Hand to mine, and falt'ring cry'd,
Restrain the Fervour of impetuous Youth
With venerable CALI's faithful Counsels?   10
Are these the Counsels? This the Faith of CALI?
Were all our Favours lavish'd on a Villain?
Confest?—

MUSTAPHA.

Confest by dying *Menodorus*.
In his last Agonies the gasping Coward,
Amidst the Tortures of the burning Steel,   15
Still fond of Life, groan'd out the dreadful Secret,
Held forth this fatal Scroll, then sunk to nothing.

MAHOMET, *examining the Paper*.

His correspondence with our Foes of *Greece*!
His Hand! His Seal! The Secrets of my Soul
Conceal'd from all but him! All! all conspire   20
To banish Doubt, and brand him for a Villain.
Our Schemes for ever cross'd, our Mines discover'd,
Betray'd some Traytor lurking near my Bosom.
Oft have I rag'd, when their wide-wasting Cannon
Lay pointed at our Batt'ries yet unform'd,   25
And broke the meditated Lines of War.
Detested CALI too, with artful Wonder,
Would shake his wily Head, and closely whisper,
Beware of MUSTAPHA, beware of Treason.

Mustapha.

The Faith of Mustapha disdains Suspicion; 30
But yet, great Emperor, beware of Treason;
Th' insidious Bassa fir'd by Disappointment—

Mahomet.

Shall feel the Vengeance of an injur'd King.
Go, seize him, load him with reproachful Chains;
Before th' assembled Troops proclaim his Crimes; 35
Then leave him stretch'd upon the ling'ring Rack,
Amidst the Camp to howl his Life away.

Mustapha.

Should we before the Troops proclaim his Crimes
I dread his Arts of seeming Innocence,
His bland Address, and Sorcery of Tongue; 40
And should he fall unheard, by sudden Justice,
Th' adoring Soldiers would revenge their Idol.

Mahomet.

Cali, this Day with hypocritick Zeal,
Implor'd my Leave to visit *Mecca*'s Temple;
Struck with the Wonder of a Statesman's Goodness, 45
I rais'd his Thoughts to more sublime Devotion.
Now let him go, pursu'd by silent Wrath,
Meet unexpected Daggers in his Way,
And in some distant Land obscurely die.

Mustapha.

There will his boundless Wealth, the Spoil of *Asia*, 50
Heap'd by your Father's ill-plac'd Bounties on him,
Disperse Rebellion through the Eastern World;
Bribe to his Cause and list beneath his Banners
Arabia's roving Troops, the Sons of Swiftness,
And arm the *Persian* Heretick against thee; 55
There shall he waste thy Frontiers, check thy Conquests,
And though at length subdued, elude thy Vengeance.

48, 49. Quoted in the *Dictionary*, s.v. 'obscurely', but omitted in ed. 4, 1773.

MAHOMET.

Elude my Vengeance? no—My Troops shall range
Th' eternal Snows that freeze beyond *Meotis*,
And *Afric*'s torrid Sands in search of CALI.   60
Should the fierce North upon his frozen Wings
Bear him aloft above the wond'ring Clouds,
And seat him in the *Pleiad*'s golden Chariots,
Thence should my Fury drag him down to Tortures;
Wherever Guilt can fly, Revenge can follow.   65

MUSTAPHA.

Wilt thou dismiss the Savage from the Toils
Only to hunt him round the ravag'd World?

MAHOMET.

Suspend his Sentence—Empire and IRENE
Claim my divided Soul. This Wretch unworthy
To mix with nobler Cares, I'll throw aside   70
For idle Hours, and crush him at my Leisure.

MUSTAPHA.

Let not th' unbounded Greatness of his Mind
Betray my King to Negligence of Danger.
Perhaps the Clouds of dark Conspiracy
Now roll full fraught with Thunder o'er your Head.   75
Twice since the Morning rose I saw the Bassa,
Like a fell Adder swelling in a Brake,
Beneath the Covert of this verdant Arch
In private Conference; beside him stood
Two Men unknown, the Partners of his Bosom;   80

59. Cf. *The Dunciad*, iii. 87–8.

61–4. Gibbon comments thus on these lines in a footnote to chap. lxviii of *The Decline and Fall*, 1788, vi. 498: 'In the tragedy of Irene, Mahomet's passion soars above sense and reason. Besides the extravagance of the rant I must observe, 1. That the operation of the winds must be confined to the *lower* region of the air. 2. That the name, etymology, and fable of the Pleiads are purely Greek . . . and had no affinity with the astronomy of the East . . . which Mahomet had studied. 3. The golden chariot does not exist either in science or fiction; but I much fear that Dr. Johnson has confounded the Pleiads with the great bear or waggon, the zodiac with a northern constellation.'

65. Quoted in the *Dictionary*, s.v. 'follow', removed from ed. 4.

I mark'd them well, and trac'd in either Face
The gloomy Resolution, horrid Greatness,
And stern Composure of despairing Heroes;
And, to confirm my Thought, at sight of me,
As blasted by my Presence, they withdrew   85
With all the Speed of Terror and of Guilt.

MAHOMET.

The strong Emotions of my troubled Soul
Allow no Pause for Art or for Contrivance;
And dark Perplexity distracts my Counsels.
Do thou resolve: For see, IRENE comes!   90
At her Approach each ruder Gust of Thought
Sinks like the sighing of a Tempest spent,
And Gales of softer Passion fan my Bosom.
    [CALI *enters with* IRENE, *and exit with* MUSTAPHA.

SCENE VII

MAHOMET, IRENE.

MAHOMET.

Wilt thou descend, fair Daughter of Perfection,
To hear my Vows, and give Mankind a Queen?
Ah! cease, IRENE, cease those flowing Sorrows,
That melt a Heart, impregnable till now,
And turn thy Thoughts henceforth to Love and Empire.   5
How will the matchless Beauties of IRENE,
Thus bright in Tears, thus amiable in Ruin,
With all the graceful Pride of Greatness heighten'd,
Amidst the Blaze of Jewels and of Gold,
Adorn a Throne, and dignify Dominion.   10

IRENE.

Why all this Glare of splendid Eloquence,
To paint the Pageantries of guilty State?
Must I for these renounce the Hope of Heav'n,
Immortal Crowns and Fulness of Enjoyment?

6 Beauties] beauty *Osborne 1785*

Mahomet.

Vain Raptures all—For your inferiour Natures   15
Form'd to delight, and happy by delighting,
Heav'n has reserv'd no future Paradise,
But bids you rove the Paths of Bliss, secure
Of total Death and careless of Hereafter;
While Heav'n's high Minister, whose awful Volume   20
Records each Act, each Thought of sov'reign Man,
Surveys your Plays with inattentive Glance,
And leaves the lovely Trifler unregarded.

Irene.

Why then has Nature's vain Munificence
Profusely pour'd her Bounties upon Woman?   25
Whence then those Charms thy Tongue has deign'd to flatter,
That Air resistless and enchanting Blush,
Unless the beauteous Fabrick was design'd
A Habitation for a fairer Soul?

Mahomet.

Too high, bright Maid, thou rat'st exterior Grace;   30
Not always do the fairest Flow'rs diffuse
The richest Odours, nor the speckled Shells
Conceal the Gem; let female Arrogance
Observe the feather'd Wand'rers of the Sky,
With Purple varied and bedrop'd with Gold,   35
They prune the Wing, and spread the glossy Plumes,
Ordain'd, like you, to flutter and to shine,
And chear the weary Passenger with Musick.

Irene.

Mean as we are, this Tyrant of the World
Implores our Smiles, and trembles at our Feet: 40
Whence flow the Hopes and Fears, Despair and Rapture,
Whence all the Bliss and Agonies of Love?

Mahomet.

Why, when the Balm of Sleep descends on Man,
Do gay Delusions, wand'ring o'er the Brain,

Sooth the delighted Soul with empty Bliss?   45
To Want give Affluence? and to Slav'ry Freedom?
Such are Love's Joys, the Lenitives of Life,
A fancy'd Treasure, and a waking Dream.

IRENE.

Then let me once, in honour of our Sex,
Assume the boastful Arrogance of Man.   50
Th' attractive Softness, and th' indearing Smile,
And pow'rful Glance, 'tis granted, are our own;
Nor has impartial Nature's frugal Hand
Exhausted all her nobler Gifts on you;
Do we not share the comprehensive Thought,   55
Th' enlivening Wit, the penetrating Reason?
Beats not the female Breast with gen'rous Passions,
The Thirst of Empire, and the Love of Glory?

MAHOMET.

Illustrious Maid, new Wonders fix me thine,
Thy Soul compleats the Triumphs of thy Face.   60
I thought, forgive my Fair, the noblest Aim,
The strongest Effort of a female Soul,
Was but to chuse the Graces of the Day;
To tune the Tongue, to teach the Eyes to roll,
Dispose the Colours of the flowing Robe,   65
And add new Roses to the faded Cheek.
Will it not charm a Mind like thine exalted,
To shine the Goddess of applauding Nations,
To scatter Happiness and Plenty round thee,
To bid the prostrate Captive rise and live,   70
To see new Cities tow'r at thy Command,
And blasted Kingdoms flourish at thy Smile?

IRENE.

Charm'd with the Thought of blessing human Kind,
Too calm I listen to the flatt'ring Sounds.

64 Eye *1754*   74 Sounds] sound *Osborne 1785*

59–66. Quoted in *Life*, i. 110.   62–4 Cf. *Rape of the Lock*, i. 87–8.

MAHOMET.

O seize the Power to bless—IRENE's Nod 75
Shall break the Fetters of the groaning Christian;
Greece, in her lovely Patroness secure,
Shall mourn no more her plunder'd Palaces.

IRENE.

Forbear—O do not urge me to my Ruin!

MAHOMET.

To State and Pow'r I court thee, not to Ruin: 80
Smile on my Wishes, and command the Globe.
Security shall spread her Shield before thee,
And Love infold thee with his downy Wings.
    If Greatness please thee, mount th' imperial Seat;
If Pleasure charm thee, view this soft Retreat; 85
Here ev'ry Warbler of the Sky shall sing;
Here ev'ry Fragrance breathe of ev'ry Spring:
To deck these Bow'rs each Region shall combine,
And ev'n our Prophet's Gardens envy thine:
Empire and Love shall share the blissful Day, 90
And varied Life steal unperceiv'd away.

ACT III

SCENE I

CALI, ABDALLA.

CALI *enters with a discontented Air; to him enters* ABDALLA.

CALI.

Is this the fierce Conspirator ABDALLA?
Is this the restless Diligence of Treason?

84–91. Mrs. Piozzi thought that in writing these lines Johnson must have had in his mind the concluding lines of Act III of Hughes's *Siege of Damascus* and improved upon them, 'if the last four lines can admit of improvement' (Edward Mangin, *Piozziana*, 1833, p. 169). But the theme of both passages is a commonplace, and Johnson's lines have as close a resemblance to what he had written in *London*.

Where hast thou linger'd while th' encumber'd Hours
Fly lab'ring with the Fate of future Nations,
And hungry Slaughter scents Imperial Blood?   5

ABDALLA.

Important Cares detain'd me from your Counsels.

CALI.

Some petty Passion! some domestick Trifle!
Some vain Amusement of a vacant Soul!
A weeping Wife perhaps, or dying Friend,
Hung on your Neck, and hinder'd your Departure.   10
Is this a Time for Softness or for Sorrow?
Unprofitable, peaceful, female Virtues!
When eager Vengeance shows a naked Foe,
And kind Ambition points the Way to Greatness.

ABDALLA.

Must then Ambition's Votaries infringe   15
The Laws of Kindness, break the Bonds of Nature?
And quit the Names of Brother, Friend, and Father?

CALI.

This sov'reign Passion, scornful of Restraint,
Ev'n from the Birth affects supreme Command,
Swells in the Breast, and with resistless Force,   20
O'erbears each gentler Motion of the Mind.
As when a Deluge overspreads the Plains,
The wand'ring Rivulet, and silver Lake,
Mix undistinguish'd with the gen'ral Roar.

ABDALLA.

Yet can Ambition in ABDALLA's Breast   25
Claim but the second Place: there mighty Love
Has fix'd his Hopes, Inquietudes, and Fears,
His glowing Wishes, and his jealous Pangs.

8. Quoted in the *Dictionary*, s.v. 'vacant', but removed from ed. 4.

CALI.

Love is indeed the Privilege of Youth;
Yet, on a Day like this, when Expectation   30
Pants for the dread Event—But let us reason—

ABDALLA.

Hast thou grown old amidst the Croud of Courts,
And turn'd th' instructive Page of Human Life,
To cant, at last, of Reason to a Lover?
Such ill-tim'd Gravity, such serious Folly,   35
Might well befit the solitary Student,
Th' unpractis'd Dervise, or sequester'd Faquir.
Know'st thou not yet, when Love invades the Soul,
That all her Faculties receive his Chains?
That Reason gives her Scepter to his Hand,   40
Or only struggles to be more enslav'd?
ASPASIA! who can look upon thy Beauties?
Who hear thee speak, and not abandon Reason?
Reason! the hoary Dotard's dull Directress,
That loses all because she hazards nothing: 45
Reason! the tim'rous Pilot, that to shun
The Rocks of Life, for ever flies the Port.

CALI.

But why this sudden Warmth?

ABDALLA.

                              Because I love:
Because my slighted Passion burns in vain!
Why roars the Lioness distress'd by Hunger?   50
Why foam the swelling Waves when Tempests rise?
Why shakes the Ground, when subterraneous Fires
Fierce through the bursting Caverns rend their Way?

CALI.

Not till this Day thou saw'st this fatal Fair;
Did ever Passion make so swift a Progress?   55
Once more reflect, suppress this infant Folly.

49 Passions burn *1754*   51 foams *1754*

ABDALLA.

Gross Fires, enkindled by a mortal Hand,
Spread by Degrees, and dread th' oppressing Stream;
The subtler Flames emitted from the Sky,
Flash out at once, with Strength above Resistance.   60

CALI.

How did ASPASIA welcome your Address?
Did you proclaim this unexpected Conquest?
Or pay with speaking Eyes a Lover's Homage?

ABDALLA.

Confounded, aw'd, and lost in Admiration,
I gaz'd, I trembled; but I could not speak: 65
When ev'n as Love was breaking off from Wonder,
And tender Accents quiver'd on my Lips,
She mark'd my sparkling Eyes, and heaving Breast,
And smiling, conscious of her Charms, withdrew.
                    [*Enter* Demetrius *and* Leontius.

CALI.

Now be some Moments Master of thyself,   70
Nor let DEMETRIUS know thee for a Rival.
Hence! or be calm—To disagree is Ruin.

SCENE II

CALI, DEMETRIUS, LEONTIUS, ABDALLA.

DEMETRIUS.

When will Occasion smile upon our Wishes,
And give the Tortures of Suspence a Period?
Still must we linger in uncertain Hope?
Still languish in our Chains, and dream of Freedom,
Like thirsty Sailors gazing on the Clouds,   5
Till burning Death shoots through their wither'd Limbs?

CALI.

Deliverance is at Hand; for *Turkey*'s Tyrant
Sunk in his Pleasures, confident and gay,
With all the Heroe's dull Security,
Trusts to my Care his Mistress and his Life,   10
And laughs and wantons in the Jaws of Death.

LEONTIUS.

So weak is Man, when destin'd to Destruction,
The Watchful slumber, and the Crafty trust.

CALI.

At my Command yon' Iron Gates unfold;
At my Command the Sentinels retire;   15
With all the Licence of Authority,
Through bowing Slaves, I range the private Rooms,
And of To-morrow's Action fix the Scene.

DEMETRIUS.

To-morrow's Action? Can that hoary Wisdom
Born down with Years, still doat upon To-morrow?   20
That fatal Mistress of the Young, the Lazy,
The Coward, and the Fool, condemn'd to lose
An useless Life in waiting for To-morrow,
To gaze with longing Eyes upon To-morrow,
Till interposing Death destroys the Prospect!   25
Strange! that this gen'ral Fraud from Day to Day
Should fill the World with Wretches undetected.
The Soldier lab'ring through a Winter's March,
Still sees To-morrow drest in Robes of Triumph;
Still to the Lover's long-expecting Arms,   30
To-morrow brings the visionary Bride.
But thou, too old to bear another Cheat,
Learn, that the present Hour alone is Man's.

LEONTIUS.

The present Hour with open Arms invites;
Seize the kind Fair, and press her to thy Bosom.   35

19–33. A companion piece to the more famous lines in Dryden's *Aurengzebe*, IV. i.
33–44, 'When I consider life, 'tis all a cheat'. According to Burney, it was the passage
which won most applause at the first performance (Boswell, *Life*, i. 197).

Demetrius.

Who knows, ere this important Morrow rise,
But Fear, or Mutiny may taint the *Greeks*?
Who knows if Mahomet's awaking Anger
May spare the fatal Bow-string till To-morrow?

Abdalla.

Had our first *Asian* Foes but known this Ardour,   40
We still had wander'd on *Tartarian* Hills.
Rouse, Cali, shall the Sons of conquer'd *Greece*
Lead us to Danger, and abash their Victors?
This Night with all her conscious Stars be witness,
Who merits most, Demetrius or Abdalla.   45

Demetrius.

Who merits most!—I knew not we were Rivals.

Cali.

Young Man, forbear—The Heat of Youth, no more—
Well,—'tis decreed—This Night shall fix our Fate.
Soon as the Veil of Evening clouds the Sky,
With cautious Secrecy, Leontius steer   50
Th' appointed Vessel to yon' shaded Bay,
Form'd by this Garden jutting on the Deep;
There, with your Soldiers arm'd, and Sails expanded,
Await our coming, equally prepar'd
For speedy Flight, or obstinate Defence.   55
                                          [*Exit* Leont.

Scene III
Cali, Abdalla, Demetrius.

Demetrius.

Now pause, great Bassa, from the Thoughts of Blood,
And kindly grant an Ear to gentler Sounds:

2 Sounds, *1749*: Sounds. *1781*

If e'er thy Youth has known the Pangs of Absence,
Or felt th' Impatience of obstructed Love,
Give me, before th' approaching Hour of Fate,   5
Once to behold the Charms of bright ASPASIA,
And draw new Virtue from her heav'nly Tongue.

CALI.

Let Prudence, ere the Suit be farther urg'd,
Impartial weigh the Pleasure with the Danger.
A little longer, and she's thine for ever.   10

DEMETRIUS.

Prudence and Love conspire in this Request,
Lest unacquainted with our bold Attempt,
Surprize o'erwhelm her, and retard our Flight.

CALI.

What I can grant, you cannot ask in vain—

DEMETRIUS.

I go to wait thy Call; this kind Consent   15
Completes the Gift of Freedom and of Life.

[*Exit* Dem.

SCENE IV

CALI, ABDALLA.

ABDALLA.

And this is my Reward—to burn, to languish,
To rave unheeded, while the happy *Greek*,
The Refuse of our Swords, the Dross of Conquest,
Throws his fond Arms about ASPASIA's Neck,
Dwells on her Lips, and sighs upon her Breast;   5
Is 't not enough, he lives by our Indulgence,
But he must live to make his Masters wretched?

7 Master's *1749*

CALI.

What Claim hast thou to plead?

ABDALLA.

The Claim of Pow'r,
Th' unquestion'd Claim of Conquerors, and Kings!

CALI.

Yet in the Use of Pow'r remember Justice.   10

ABDALLA.

Can then th' Assassin lift his treach'rous Hand
Against his King, and cry, Remember Justice?
Justice demands the forfeit Life of CALI;
Justice demands that I reveal your Crimes;
Justice demands—But see th' approaching Sultan.   15
Oppose my Wishes, and—Remember Justice.

CALI.

Disorder sits upon thy Face—retire.
                    [*Exit* Abdalla, *Enter* Mahomet.

SCENE V

CALI, MAHOMET.

CALI.

Long be the Sultan bless'd with happy Love!
My Zeal marks Gladness dawning on thy Cheek,
With Raptures such as fire the Pagan Crouds,
When pale, and anxious for their Years to come,
They see the Sun surmount the dark Eclipse,   5
And hail unanimous their conqu'ring God.

MAHOMET.

My Vows, 'tis true, she hears with less Aversion,
She sighs, she blushes, but she still denies.

CALI.

With warmer Courtship press the yielding Fair,
Call to your Aid with boundless Promises   10
Each rebel Wish, each traitor Inclination
That raises Tumults in the female Breast,
The Love of Pow'r, of Pleasure, and of Show.

MAHOMET.

These Arts I try'd, and to inflame her more,
By hateful Business hurried from her Sight,   15
I bad a hundred Virgins wait around her,
Sooth her with all the Pleasures of Command,
Applaud her Charms, and court her to be Great.

[*Exit* MAHOMET.

SCENE VI

CALI *solus.*

He's gone—Here rest, my Soul, thy fainting Wing,
Here recollect thy dissipated Pow'rs.—
Our distant Int'rests, and our different Passions
Now haste to mingle in one common Center,
And Fate lies crouded in a narrow Space.   5
Yet in that narrow Space what Dangers rise?—
Far more I dread ABDALLA's fiery Folly,
Than all the Wisdom of the grave Divan.
Reason with Reason fights on equal Terms,
The raging Madman's unconnected Schemes   10
We cannot obviate, for we cannot guess.
Deep in my Breast be treasur'd this Resolve,
When CALI mounts the Throne ABDALLA dies,
Too fierce, too faithless for Neglect or Trust.

[*Enter* IRENE *with Attendants.*

Scene VII

CALI, IRENE, ASPASIA, &c.

CALI.

Amidst the Splendor of encircling Beauty,
Superiour Majesty proclaims the Queen,
And Nature justifies our Monarch's Choice.

IRENE.

Reserve this Homage for some other Fair,
Urge me not on to glittering Guilt, nor pour   5
In my weak Ear th' intoxicating Sounds.

CALI.

Make haste, bright Maid, to rule the willing World;
Aw'd by the Rigour of the Sultan's Justice,
We court thy Gentleness.

ASPASIA.

                    Can CALI's Voice
Concur to press a hapless Captive's Ruin?   10

CALI.

Long would my Zeal for MAHOMET and Thee
Detain me here. But Nations call upon me,
And Duty bids me chuse a distant Walk,
Nor taint with Care the Privacies of Love.

Scene VIII

IRENE, ASPASIA, Attendants.

ASPASIA.

If yet this shining Pomp, these sudden Honours,
Swell not thy Soul beyond Advice or Friendship,

2 the] thee *Osborne 1785*   10 hapless] helpless *1785*

III. viii. 'The two best *Declamatory* Scenes where the Sentiments and Language
are most perfect, seem to be the Scene between Juba & Syphax in Addison's Cato,

Not yet inspire the Follies of a Queen,
Or tune thine Ear to soothing Adulation,
Suspend awhile the Privilege of Pow'r   5
To hear the Voice of Truth; dismiss thy Train,
Shake off th' Incumbrances of State a moment,
And lay the tow'ring Sultaness aside,
                    [IRENE *signs to her Attendants to retire.*
While I foretell thy Fate; that Office done,—
No more I boast th' ambitious Name of Friend,   10
But sink among thy Slaves without a Murmur.

                            IRENE.

Did regal Diadems invest my Brow,
Yet should my Soul, still faithful to her Choice,
Esteem ASPASIA's Breast, the noblest Kingdom.

                           ASPASIA.

The Soul once tainted with so foul a Crime,   15
No more shall glow with Friendship's hallow'd Ardour:
Those holy Beings, whose superiour Care
Guides erring Mortals to the Paths of Virtue,
Affrighted at Impiety like thine,
Resign their Charge to Baseness and to Ruin.   20

                            IRENE.

Upbraid me not with fancy'd Wickedness,
I am not yet a Queen, or an Apostate.
But should I sin beyond the Hope of Mercy,
If when Religion prompts me to refuse,
The Dread of instant Death restrains my Tongue?   25

& that between the two Ladies in Johnson's Irene. I know that both are unDramatic,
the latter more particularly so, than ever was, or ever ought to have been hazarded
—but for Language & Sentiment it is most Superb.—Superieure as the French say.'
Thraliana, i. 354.

    8. Quoted in the *Dictionary,* s.v. 'sultaness'.
    15–20. Quoted in *Life,* i. 108.

ASPASIA.

Reflect that Life and Death, affecting Sounds,
Are only varied Modes of endless Being;
Reflect that Life, like ev'ry other Blessing,
Derives its Value from its Use alone;
Not for itself but for a nobler End   30
Th' Eternal gave it, and that End is Virtue.
When inconsistent with a greater Good,
Reason commands to cast the less away;
Thus Life, with loss of Wealth, is well preserv'd,
And Virtue cheaply sav'd with loss of Life.   35

IRENE.

If built on settled Thought, this Constancy
Not idly flutters on a boastful Tongue,
Why, when Destruction rag'd around our Walls,
Why fled this haughty Heroine from the Battle?
Why then did not this warlike Amazon   40
Mix in the War, and shine among the Heroes?

ASPASIA.

Heav'n, when its Hand pour'd Softness on our Limbs
Unfit for Toil, and polish'd into Weakness,
Made passive Fortitude the Praise of Woman:
Our only Arms are Innocence and Meekness.   45
Not then with raving Cries I fill'd the City,
But while DEMETRIUS, dear lamented Name!
Pour'd Storms of Fire upon our fierce Invaders,
Implor'd th' eternal Power to shield my Country,
With silent Sorrows, and with calm Devotion.   50

IRENE.

O! did IRENE shine the Queen of *Turkey*,
No more should *Greece* lament those Prayers rejected.
Again should golden Splendour grace her Cities,
Again her prostrate Palaces should rise,
Again her Temples sound with holy Musick: 55
No more should Danger fright, or Want distress
The smiling Widows, and protected Orphans.

ASPASIA.

Be virtuous Ends pursued by virtuous Means,
Nor think th' Intention sanctifies the Deed:
That Maxim publish'd in an impious Age,   60
Would loose the wild Enthusiast to destroy,
And fix the fierce Usurper's bloody Title.
Then Bigotry might send her Slaves to War,
And bid Success become the Test of Truth;
Unpitying Massacre might waste the World,   65
And Persecution boast the Call of Heav'n.

IRENE.

Shall I not wish to chear afflicted Kings,
And plan the Happiness of mourning Millions?

ASPASIA.

Dream not of Pow'r thou never can'st attain:
When social Laws first harmonis'd the World,   70
Superiour Man possess'd the Charge of Rule,
The Scale of Justice, and the Sword of Pow'r,
Nor left us aught but Flattery and State.

IRENE.

To me my Lover's Fondness will restore,
Whate'er Man's Pride has ravish'd from our Sex.   75

ASPASIA.

When soft Security shall prompt the Sultan,
Freed from the Tumults of unsettled Conquest,
To fix his Court, and regulate his Pleasures,
Soon shall the dire Seraglio's horrid Gates
Close like th' eternal Bars of Death upon thee,   80
Immur'd, and buried in perpetual Sloth,
That gloomy Slumber of the stagnant Soul;

63 Bigottry *1749* ('Bigotry' in *Dictionary*)   64 Truth? *1749, 1754*

81, 82. Quoted in the *Dictionary*, s.v. 'stagnant'.

There shalt thou view from far the quiet Cottage,
And sigh for chearful Poverty in vain;
There wear the tedious Hours of Life away,   85
Beneath each Curse of unrelenting Heav'n,
Despair, and Slav'ry, Solitude, and Guilt.

IRENE.

There shall we find the yet untasted Bliss
Of Grandeur and Tranquillity combin'd.

ASPASIA.

Tranquillity and Guilt, disjoin'd by Heav'n,   90
Still stretch in vain their longing Arms afar;
Nor dare to pass th' insuperable Bound.
Ah! let me rather seek the Convent's Cell;
There when my Thoughts, at interval of Pray'r,
Descend to range these Mansions of Misfortune,   95
Oft' shall I dwell on our disastrous Friendship,
And shed the pitying Tear for lost IRENE.

IRENE.

Go, languish on in dull Obscurity;
Thy dazzled Soul with all its boasted Greatness,
Shrinks at th' o'erpow'ring Gleams of regal State,   100
Stoops from the Blaze like a degenerate Eagle,
And flies for Shelter to the Shades of Life.

ASPASIA.

On me, should Providence, without a Crime,
The weighty Charge of Royalty confer;
Call me to civilize the *Russian* Wilds,   105
Or bid soft Science polish *Britain*'s Heroes:

106 *Britain*'s *1781 and MS.*] *Briton*'s *1749, 1754*

---

106. Quoted in the *Dictionary*, s.v. 'polish', with the spelling 'Britain's'; removed
from ed. 4. 'Briton' and 'Britain' were not regularly distinguished in the eighteenth
century. In the paragraph which George III inserted, in his own hand, in his first

Soon shouldst thou see, how false thy weak Reproach.
My Bosom feels, enkindled from the Sky,
The lambent Flames of mild Benevolence,
Untouch'd by fierce Ambition's raging Fires.   110

IRENE.

Ambition is the Stamp impress'd by Heav'n
To mark the noblest Minds, with active Heat
Inform'd they mount the Precipice of Pow'r,
Grasp at Command, and tow'r in quest of Empire;
While vulgar Souls compassionate their Cares,   115
Gaze at their Height and tremble at their Danger:
Thus meaner Spirits with Amazement mark
The varying Seasons, and revolving Skies,
And ask, what guilty Pow'r's rebellious Hand
Rolls with eternal Toil the pond'rous Orbs;   120
While some Archangel nearer to Perfection,
In easy State presides o'er all their Motions,
Directs the Planets with a careless Nod,
Conducts the Sun, and regulates the Spheres.

ASPASIA.

Well may'st thou hide in Labyrinths of Sound   125
The Cause that shrinks from Reason's powerful Voice.
Stoop from thy Flight, trace back th' entangled Thought,
And set the glitt'ring Fallacy to view.
Not Pow'r I blame, but Pow'r obtain'd by Crime,
Angelic Greatness is Angelic Virtue.   130
Amidst the Glare of Courts, the Shouts of Armies,
Will not th' Apostate feel the Pangs of Guilt,
And wish too late for Innocence and Peace?
Curst as the Tyrant of th' infernal Realms,
With gloomy State and agonizing Pomp.   135

107 shouldst] wouldst *1754*   119 Pow'rs *1749*

---

speech from the throne, 1760, he wrote 'Born and educated in this country I glory in
the name of Britain'. The passage is reproduced in A. S. Turberville's *English Men and
Manners in the Eighteenth Century*, p. 42. In the official version in *Journals of the House
of Lords* 'Britain' is printed 'Briton'.

Scene IX

Irene, Aspasia, Maid.

Maid.

A *Turkish* Stranger of majestick Mien,
Asks at the Gate Admission to Aspasia,
Commission'd, as he says, by Cali Bassa.

Irene.

Whoe'er thou art, or whatsoe'er thy Message,   [*Aside*
Thanks for this kind Relief—with Speed admit him.   5

Aspasia.

He comes, perhaps, to separate us forever;
When I am gone remember, O! remember,
That none are great, or happy, but the Virtuous.
                              [*Exit* Irene, *Enter* Demetrius.

Scene X

Aspasia, Demetrius.

Demetrius.

'Tis she—My Hope, my Happiness, my Love!
Aspasia! do I once again behold thee?
Still, still the same—unclouded by Misfortune!
Let my blest Eyes for ever gaze—

Aspasia.

                              Demetrius!

Demetrius.

Why does the Blood forsake thy lovely Cheek?   5
Why shoots this Chilness through thy shaking Nerves?
Why does thy Soul retire into herself?
Recline upon my Breast thy sinking Beauties:
Revive—Revive to Freedom and to Love.

ASPASIA.

What well known Voice pronounc'd the grateful Sounds 10
Freedom and Love? Alas! I'm all Confusion,
A sudden Mist o'ercasts my darken'd Soul,
The Present, Past, and Future swim before me,
Lost in a wild Perplexity of Joy.

DEMETRIUS.

Such Ecstacy of Love! such pure Affection,   15
What Worth can merit? or what Faith reward?

ASPASIA.

A thousand Thoughts imperfect and distracted,
Demand a Voice, and struggle into Birth;
A thousand Questions press upon my Tongue,
But all give way to Rapture and DEMETRIUS.   20

DEMETRIUS.

O say, bright Being, in this Age of Absence,
What Fears, what Griefs, what Dangers hast thou known?
Say, how the Tyrant threaten'd, flatter'd, sigh'd,
Say, how he threaten'd, flatter'd, sigh'd in vain!
Say, how the Hand of Violence was rais'd,   25
Say, how thou call'dst in Tears upon DEMETRIUS!

ASPASIA.

Inform me rather, how thy happy Courage
Stem'd in the Breach the Deluge of Destruction,
And pass'd uninjur'd through the Walks of Death?
Did savage Anger, and licentious Conquest   30
Behold the Hero with ASPASIA's Eyes?
And thus protected in the gen'ral Ruin,
O say, what guardian Pow'r convey'd thee hither.

DEMETRIUS.

Such strange Events, such unexpected Chances,
Beyond my warmest Hope, or wildest Wishes,   35

10 well-known *1781*

Concur'd to give me to ASPASIA's Arms,
I stand amaz'd, and ask, if yet I clasp thee.

ASPASIA.

Sure Heav'n, for Wonders are not wrought in vain,
That joins us thus, will never part us more.

SCENE XI

DEMETRIUS, ASPASIA, ABDALLA.

ABDALLA.

It parts you now—The hasty Sultan sign'd
The Laws unread, and flies to his IRENE.

DEMETRIUS.

Fix'd and intent on his IRENE's Charms,
He envies none the Converse of ASPASIA.

ABDALLA.

ASPASIA's Absence will inflame Suspicion;   5
She cannot, must not, shall not, linger here,
Prudence and Friendship bid me force her from you.

DEMETRIUS.

Force her! profane her with a Touch, and die.

ABDALLA.

'Tis *Greece*, 'tis Freedom calls ASPASIA hence,
Your careless Love betrays your Country's Cause.   10

DEMETRIUS.

If we must part—

ASPASIA.

No! let us die together.

Demetrius.

If we must part—

Abdalla.

Dispatch; th' encreasing Danger
Will not admit a Lover's long Farewell,
The long-drawn Intercourse of Sighs and Kisses.

Demetrius.

Then—O my Fair, I cannot bid thee goe;   15
Receive her, and protect her, gracious Heav'n!
Yet let me watch her dear departing Steps,
If Fate pursues me, let it find me here.

Reproach not, *Greece*, a Lover's fond Delays,
Nor think thy Cause neglected while I gaze,   20
New Force, new Courage, from each Glance I gain,
And find our Passions not infus'd in vain.

ACT IV

Scene I

Demetrius, Aspasia, *enter as talking.*

Aspasia.

Enough—resistless Reason calms my Soul—
Approving Justice smiles upon your Cause,
And Nature's Rights entreat th' asserting Sword.
Yet when your Hand is lifted to destroy,
Think—but excuse a Woman's needless Caution,   5
Purge well thy Mind from ev'ry private Passion,
Drive Int'rest, Love, and Vengeance from thy Thoughts,
Fill all thy ardent Breast with *Greece* and Virtue,
Then strike secure, and Heav'n assist the Blow.

15 go *1754, 1781*   18 persues *1749* (see note on *London*, l. 160, and cf. v. iii. 2
and v. ix. 36)

DEMETRIUS.

Thou kind Assistant of my better Angel,　　　　10
Propitious Guide of my bewilder'd Soul,
Calm of my Cares, and Guardian of my Virtue.

ASPASIA.

My Soul first kindled by thy bright Example,
To noble Thought and gen'rous Emulation,
Now but reflects those Beams that flow'd from thee.　15

DEMETRIUS.

With native Lustre and unborrow'd Greatness,
Thou shin'st, bright Maid, superior to Distress;
Unlike the trifling Race of vulgar Beauties,
Those glitt'ring Dew-drops of a vernal Morn,
That spread their Colours to the genial Beam,　　20
And sparkling quiver to the Breath of *May*;
But when the Tempest with sonorous Wing
Sweeps o'er the Grove, forsake the lab'ring Bough,
Dispers'd in Air or mingled with the Dust.

ASPASIA.

Forbear this Triumph—still new Conflicts wait us,　25
Foes unforeseen, and Dangers unsuspected.
Oft when the fierce Besiegers eager Host
Beholds the fainting Garrison retire,
And rushes joyful to the naked Wall,
Destruction flashes from th' insidious Mine,　　30
And sweeps th' exulting Conqueror away:
Perhaps in vain the Sultan's Anger spar'd me,
To find a meaner Fate from treach'rous Friendship—
ABDALLA—

DEMETRIUS.

　　Can ABDALLA then dissemble?
That fiery Chief, renown'd for gen'rous Freedom,　35
For Zeal unguarded, undissembled Hate,
For daring Truth, and Turbulence of Honour?

35 firy *1749* (cf. I. i. 125 and III. vi. 7)

ASPASIA.

This open Friend, this undesigning Hero,
With noisy Falshoods forc'd me from your Arms,
To shock my Virtue with a Tale of Love.   40

DEMETRIUS.

Did not the Cause of *Greece* restrain my Sword,
ASPASIA should not fear a second Insult.

ASPASIA.

His Pride and Love by Turns inspir'd his Tongue,
And intermix'd my Praises with his own;
His Wealth, his Rank, his Honours he recounted,   45
Till in the midst of Arrogance and Fondness,
Th' approaching Sultan forc'd me from the Palace;
Then while he gaz'd upon his yielding Mistress,
I stole unheeded from their ravish'd Eyes,
And sought this happy Grove in quest of Thee.   50

DEMETRIUS.

Soon may the final Stroke decide our Fate,
Lest baneful Discord crush our infant Scheme,
And strangled Freedom perish in the Birth.

ASPASIA.

My Bosom harrass'd with alternate Passions,
Now hopes, now fears—

DEMETRIUS.

                    Th' Anxieties of Love.   55

ASPASIA.

Think how the sov'reign Arbiter of Kingdoms
Detests thy false Associates black Designs,
And frowns on Perjury, Revenge and Murder.
Embark'd with Treason on the Seas of Fate,
When Heav'n shall bid the swelling Billows rage,   60

And point vindictive Lightnings at Rebellion,
Will not the Patriot share the Traytor's Danger?
Oh could thy Hand unaided free thy Country,
Nor mingled Guilt pollute the sacred Cause!

DEMETRIUS.

Permitted oft, though not inspir'd by Heav'n,   65
Successful Treasons punish impious Kings.

ASPASIA.

Nor end my Terrors with the Sultan's Death;
Far as Futurity's untravell'd Waste
Lies open to Conjecture's dubious Ken,
On ev'ry Side Confusion, Rage and Death,   70
Perhaps the Phantoms of a Woman's Fear,
Beset the treacherous Way with fatal Ambush;
Each *Turkish* Bosom burns for thy Destruction,
Ambitious CALI dreads the Statesman's Arts,
And hot ABDALLA hates the happy Lover.   75

DEMETRIUS.

Capricious Man! to Good and Ill inconstant,
Too much to fear or trust, is equal Weakness.
Sometimes the Wretch unaw'd by Heav'n or Hell,
With mad Devotion idolizes Honour.
The Bassa, reeking with his Master's Murder,   80
Perhaps may start at violated Friendship.

ASPASIA.

How soon, alas! will Int'rest, Fear, or Envy,
O'erthrow such weak, such accidental Virtue,
Nor built on Faith, nor fortify'd by Conscience?

DEMETRIUS.

When desp'rate Ills demand a speedy Cure,   85
Distrust is Cowardice, and Prudence Folly.

ASPASIA.

Yet think a Moment, ere you court Destruction,
What Hand, when Death has snatch'd away DEMETRIUS,
Shall guard ASPASIA from triumphant Lust.

DEMETRIUS.

Dismiss these needless Fears—a Troop of *Greeks*   90
Well known, long try'd, expect us on the Shore.
Borne on the Surface of the smiling Deep,
Soon shalt thou scorn, in Safety's Arms repos'd,
ABDALLA's Rage and CALI's Stratagems.

ASPASIA.

Still, still Distrust sits heavy on my Heart.   95
Will e'er an happier Hour revisit *Greece?*

DEMETRIUS.

Should Heav'n yet unappeas'd refuse its Aid,
Disperse our Hopes, and frustrate our Designs,
Yet shall the Conscience of the great Attempt
Diffuse a Brightness on our future Days;   100
Nor will his Country's Groans reproach DEMETRIUS.
But how can'st thou support the Woes of Exile?
Can'st thou forget hereditary Splendours,
To live obscure upon a foreign Coast,
Content with Science, Innocence and Love?   105

ASPASIA.

Nor Wealth, nor Titles, make ASPASIA's Bliss.
O'erwhelm'd and lost amidst the publick Ruins
Unmov'd I saw the glitt'ring Trifles perish,
And thought the petty Dross beneath a Sigh.
Chearful I follow to the rural Cell,   110
Love be my Wealth, and my Distinction Virtue.

DEMETRIUS.

Submissive and prepar'd for each Event,
Now let us wait the last Award of Heav'n,
Secure of Happiness from Flight or Conquest,

Nor fear the Fair and Learn'd can want Protection.   115
The mighty *Tuscan* courts the banish'd Arts
To kind *Italia*'s hospitable Shades;
There shall soft Leisure wing th' excursive Soul,
And Peace propitious smile on fond Desire;
There shall despotick Eloquence resume   120
Her ancient Empire o'er the yielding Heart;
There Poetry shall tune her sacred Voice,
And wake from Ignorance the Western World.

SCENE II

DEMETRIUS, ASPASIA, CALI.

CALI.

At length th' unwilling Sun resigns the World
To Silence and to Rest. The Hours of Darkness,
Propitious Hours to Stratagem and Death,
Pursue the last Remains of ling'ring Light.

DEMETRIUS.

Count not these Hours as Parts of vulgar Time,   5
Think them a sacred Treasure lent by Heav'n,
Which squander'd by Neglect, or Fear, or Folly,
No Pray'r recals, no Diligence redeems;
To-morrow's Dawn shall see the *Turkish* King
Stretch'd in the Dust, or tow'ring on his Throne;   10
To-morrow's Dawn shall see the mighty CALI
The sport of Tyranny, or Lord of Nations.

CALI.

Then waste no longer these important Moments
In soft Endearments, and in gentle Murmurs,
Nor lose in Love the Patriot and the Hero.   15

DEMETRIUS.

'Tis Love combin'd with Guilt alone, that melts
The soften'd Soul to Cowardice and Sloth;

116. Dante.

But virtuous Passion prompts the great Resolve,
And fans the slumb'ring Spark of heav'nly Fire.
Retire, my Fair, that Pow'r that smiles on Goodness   20
Guide all thy Steps, calm ev'ry stormy Thought,
And still thy Bosom with the Voice of Peace.

ASPASIA.

Soon may we meet again, secure and free,
To feel no more the Pangs of Separation.   [*Exit.*

DEMETRIUS, CALI.
DEMETRIUS.

This Night alone is ours—Our mighty Foe,   25
No longer lost in am'rous Solitude,
Will now remount the slighted Seat of Empire,
And show IRENE to the shouting People:
ASPASIA left her sighing in his Arms,
And list'ning to the pleasing Tale of Pow'r,   30
With soften'd Voice she dropp'd the faint Refusal,
Smiling Consent she sat, and blushing Love.

CALI.

Now, Tyrant, with Satiety of Beauty,
Now feast thine Eyes, thine Eyes that ne'er hereafter
Shall dart their am'rous Glances at the Fair,   35
Or glare on CALI with malignant Beams.

SCENE III
DEMETRIUS, CALI, LEONTIUS, ABDALLA.

LEONTIUS.

Our Bark unseen has reach'd th' appointed Bay,
And where yon Trees wave o'er the foaming Surge
Reclines against the Shore: Our *Grecian* Troop
Extends its Lines along the sandy Beach,
Elate with Hope, and panting for a Foe.   5

ABDALLA.

The fav'ring Winds assist the great Design,
Sport in our Sails, and murmur o'er the Deep.

CALI.

'Tis well—A single Blow compleats our Wishes:
Return with speed, LEONTIUS, to your Charge;
The *Greeks* disorder'd by their Leader's Absence,   10
May droop dismay'd, or kindle into Madness.

LEONTIUS.

Suspected still?—What Villain's pois'nous Tongue
Dares join LEONTIUS' Name with Fear or Falshood?
Have I for this preserv'd my guiltless Bosom,
Pure as the Thoughts of infant Innocence?   15
Have I for this defy'd the Chiefs of *Turkey*,
Intrepid in the flaming Front of War?

CALI.

Hast thou not search'd my Soul's profoundest Thoughts?
Is not the Fate of *Greece* and CALI thine?

LEONTIUS.

Why has thy Choice then pointed out LEONTIUS,   20
Unfit to share this Night's illustrious Toils?
To wait remote from Action, and from Honour,
An idle List'ner to the distant Cries
Of slaughter'd Infidels, and Clash of Swords!
Tell me the Cause, that while thy Name, DEMETRIUS,   25
Shall soar triumphant on the Wings of Glory,
Despis'd and curs'd, LEONTIUS must descend
Through hissing Ages, a proverbial Coward,
The Tale of Women, and the Scorn of Fools?

DEMETRIUS.

Can brave LEONTIUS be the Slave of Glory?   30
Glory, the casual Gift of thoughtless Crouds!

27–8. Quoted in the *Dictionary*, s.v. 'proverbial', but removed from ed. 4.

Glory, the Bribe of avaricious Virtue!
Be but my Country free, be thine the Praise;
I ask no Witness, but attesting Conscience,
No Records, but the Records of the Sky.   35

LEONTIUS.

Wilt thou then head the Troop upon the Shore,
While I destroy th' Oppressor of Mankind?

DEMETRIUS.

What can'st thou boast superiour to DEMETRIUS?
Ask to whose Sword the *Greeks* will trust their Cause,
My Name shall echo through the shouting Field;   40
Demand whose Force yon *Turkish* Heroes dread,
The shudd'ring Camp shall murmur out DEMETRIUS.

CALI.

Must *Greece*, still wretched by her Children's Folly,
For ever mourn their Avarice or Factions?
DEMETRIUS justly pleads a double Title,   45
The Lover's Int'rest aids the Patriot's Claim.

LEONTIUS.

My Pride shall ne'er protract my Country's Woes;
Succeed, my Friend, unenvied by LEONTIUS.

DEMETRIUS.

I feel new Spirit shoot along my Nerves,
My Soul expands to meet approaching Freedom.   50
Now hover o'er us with propitious Wings,
Ye sacred Shades of Patriots and of Martyrs;
All ye, whose Blood tyrannick Rage effus'd,
Or Persecution drank, attend our Call;
And from the Mansions of perpetual Peace   55
Descend, to sweeten Labours once your own.

CALI.

Go then, and with united Eloquence
Confirm your Troops; and when the Moon's fair Beam
Plays on the quiv'ring Waves, to guide our Flight,
Return, DEMETRIUS, and be free for ever.   60
                              [*Exeunt* Dem. *and* Leon.

SCENE IV

CALI, ABDALLA.

ABDALLA.

How the new Monarch, swell'd with airy Rule,
Looks down, contemptuous, from his fancy'd Height,
And utters Fate, unmindful of ABDALLA.

CALI.

Far be such black Ingratitude from CALI,
When *Asia*'s Nations own me for their Lord,   5
Wealth, and Command, and Grandeur shall be thine.

ABDALLA.

Is this the Recompence reserv'd for me?
Dar'st thou thus dally with ABDALLA's Passion?
Henceforward hope no more my slighted Friendship,
Wake from thy Dream of Pow'r to Death and Tortures,   10
And bid thy visionary Throne farewell.

CALI.

Name and enjoy thy Wish—

ABDALLA.

                    I need not name it;
ASPASIA's Lovers know but one Desire,
Nor hope, nor wish, nor live but for ASPASIA.

CALI.

That fatal Beauty plighted to DEMETRIUS   15
Heav'n makes not mine to give.

ABDALLA.

Nor to deny.

CALI.

Obtain her and possess, thou know'st thy Rival.

ABDALLA.

Too well I know him, since on *Thracia*'s Plains
I felt the Force of his tempestuous Arm,
And saw my scatter'd Squadrons fly before him.   20
Nor will I trust th' uncertain Chance of Combat;
The Rights of Princes let the Sword decide,
The petty Claims of Empire and of Honour:
Revenge and subtle Jealousy shall teach
A surer Passage to his hated Heart.   25

CALI.

O spare the gallant *Greek*, in him we lose
The Politician's Arts, and Heroe's Flame.

ABDALLA.

When next we meet before we storm the Palace,
The Bowl shall circle to confirm our League,
Then shall these Juices taint DEMETRIUS' Draught,   30
                                        [*Shewing a Phial.*
And stream destructive through his freezing Veins:
Thus shall he live to strike th' important Blow,
And perish ere he tastes the Joys of Conquest.

SCENE V

MAHOMET, MUSTAPHA, CALI, ABDALLA.

MAHOMET.

Henceforth for ever happy be this Day,
Sacred to Love, to Pleasure, and IRENE:

27 Art *1754*

The matchless Fair has bless'd me with Compliance;
Let every Tongue resound IRENE's Praise,
And spread the general Transport through Mankind.   5

CALI.

Blest Prince, for whom indulgent Heav'n ordains
At once the Joys of Paradise and Empire,
Now join thy People's, and thy CALI's Prayers,
Suspend thy Passage to the Seats of Bliss,
Nor wish for Houries in IRENE's Arms.   10

MAHOMET.

Forbear—I know the long try'd Faith of CALI.

CALI.

O! could the Eyes of Kings, like those of Heav'n,
Search to the dark Recesses of the Soul,
Oft would they find Ingratitude and Treason,
By Smiles, and Oaths, and Praises ill disguis'd.   15
How rarely would they meet in crouded Courts,
Fidelity so firm, so pure, as mine!

MUSTAPHA.

Yet ere we give our loosen'd Thoughts to Rapture,
Let Prudence obviate an impending Danger.
Tainted by Sloth, the Parent of Sedition,   20
The hungry Janizary burns for Plunder,
And growls in private o'er his idle Sabre.

MAHOMET.

To still their Murmurs, ere the twentieth Sun
Shall shed his Beams upon the bridal Bed,
I rouse to War, and conquer for IRENE.   25
Then shall the *Rhodian* mourn his sinking Tow'rs,
And *Buda* fall, and proud *Vienna* tremble,
Then shall *Venetia* feel the *Turkish* Pow'r,
And subject Seas roar round their Queen in vain.

ABDALLA.

Then seize fair *Italy*'s delightful Coast,   30
To fix your Standard in Imperial *Rome*.

MAHOMET.

Her Sons malicious Clemency shall spare,
To form new Legends, sanctify new Crimes,
To canonize the Slaves of Superstition,
And fill the World with Follies and Impostures,   35
Till angry Heav'n shall mark them out for Ruin,
And War o'erwhelm them in their Dream of Vice.
O could her fabled Saints and boasted Prayers
Call forth her ancient Heroes to the Field,
How should I joy, 'midst the fierce Shock of Nations,   40
To cross the Tow'rings of an equal Soul,
And bid the master Genius rule the World.
ABDALLA, CALI, go—proclaim my Purpose.
                              [*Exeunt* Cali *and* Abdalla.

SCENE VI

MAHOMET, MUSTAPHA.

MAHOMET.

Still CALI lives, and must he live To-morrow?
That fawning Villain's forc'd Congratulations
Will cloud my Triumphs, and pollute the Day.

MUSTAPHA.

With cautious Vigilance, at my Command,
Two faithful Captains, HASAN and CARAZA,   5
Pursue him through his Labyrinths of Treason,
And wait your Summons to report his Conduct.

MAHOMET.

Call them—but let them not prolong their Tale,
Nor press too much upon a Lover's Patience.
                              [*Exit* Must.

35. Quoted in the *Dictionary*, s.v. 'imposture', conflating lines 33–5.

Scene VII

Mahomet *solus.*

Whome'er the Hope, still blasted, still renew'd,
Of Happiness, lures on from Toil to Toil,
Remember Mahomet, and cease thy Labour.
Behold him here, in Love, in War successful,
Behold him wretched in his double Triumph; 5
His Fav'rite faithless, and his Mistress base.
Ambition only gave her to my Arms,
By Reason not convinc'd, nor won by Love.
Ambition was her Crime, but meaner Folly
Dooms me to loath at once, and doat on Falshood, 10
And idolize th' Apostate I contemn.
If thou art more than the gay Dream of Fancy,
More than a pleasing Sound without a Meaning,
O Happiness! sure thou art all Aspasia's.

Scene VIII

Mahomet, Mustapha, Hasan *and* Caraza.

Mahomet.

Caraza speak—have ye remark'd the Bassa?

Caraza.

Close, as we might unseen, we watch'd his Steps;
His Air disorder'd, and his Gait unequal,
Betray'd the wild Emotions of his Mind.
Sudden he stops, and inward turns his Eyes, 5
Absorb'd in Thought; then starting from his Trance,
Constrains a sullen Smile, and shoots away.
With him, Abdalla we beheld—

Mustapha.

Abdalla!

3–7. Cf. *The Rambler*, No. 60: 'Thus Sallust, the great master, has not forgot, in his account of Catiline, to remark that *his walk was now quick, and again slow*, as indications of a mind revolving something with violent commotion.'

MAHOMET.

He wears of late Resentment on his Brow,
Deny'd the Government of *Servia*'s Province. 10

CARAZA.

We mark'd him storming in Excess of Fury,
And heard within the Thicket that conceal'd us,
An undistinguish'd Sound of threat'ning Rage.

MUSTAPHA.

How Guilt once harbour'd in the conscious Breast,
Intimidates the Brave, degrades the Great. 15
See CALI, Dread of Kings, and Pride of Armies,
By Treason levell'd with the Dregs of Men.
Ere guilty Fear depress'd the hoary Chief,
An angry Murmur, a rebellious Frown,
Had stretch'd the fiery Boaster in the Grave. 20

MAHOMET.

Shall Monarchs fear to draw the Sword of Justice,
Aw'd by the Croud, and by their Slaves restrain'd?
Seize him this Night, and through the private Passage
Convey him to the Prison's inmost Depths,
Reserv'd to all the Pangs of tedious Death. 25
[*Exeunt* Mahomet *and* Mustapha.

SCENE IX

HASAN, CARAZA.

HASAN.

Shall then the *Greeks*, unpunish'd and conceal'd,
Contrive perhaps, the Ruin of our Empire,
League with our Chiefs, and propagate Sedition?

CARAZA.

Whate'er their Scheme the BASSA's Death defeats it,
And Gratitude's strong Ties restrain my Tongue. 5

14-15. Quoted in the *Dictionary*, s.v. 'intimidate'.

HASAN.

What Ties to Slaves? what Gratitude to Foes?

CARAZA.

In that black Day when slaughter'd Thousands fell
Around these fatal Walls, the Tide of War
Bore me victorious onward, where DEMETRIUS
Tore unresisted from the Giant Hand   10
Of stern *Sebalias* the triumphant Crescent,
And dash'd the Might of *Asem* from the Ramparts.
There I became, nor blush to make it known,
The Captive of his Sword. The coward *Greeks*,
Enrag'd by Wrongs, exulting with Success,   15
Doom'd me to die with all the *Turkish* Captains.
But brave DEMETRIUS scorn'd the mean Revenge,
And gave me Life—

HASAN.

                    Do thou repay the Gift,
Lest unrewarded Mercy lose its Charms.

Profuse of Wealth, or bounteous of Success,   20
When Heav'n bestows the Privilege to bless,
Let no weak Doubt the gen'rous Hand restrain,
For when was Pow'r beneficent in vain?

ACT V

SCENE I

ASPASIA *sola.*

In these dark Moments of suspended Fate,
While yet the future Fortune of my Country
Lies in the Womb of Providence conceal'd,
And anxious Angels wait the mighty Birth;
O grant thy sacred Influence, pow'rful Virtue!   5
Attention rise, survey the fair Creation,

v. i. *sola*] *solus 1749, 1781*

Till conscious of th' incircling Deity,
Beyond the Mists of Care thy Pinion tow'rs.
This Calm, these Joys, dear Innocence! are thine,
Joys ill exchang'd for Gold, and Pride, and Empire.   10
                                    [*Enter* Irene *and Attendants.*

Scene II

ASPASIA, IRENE, *and Attendants.*

IRENE.

See how the Moon through all th' unclouded Sky
Spreads her mild Radiance, and descending Dews
Revive the languid Flow'rs; thus Nature shone
New from the Maker's Hand, and fair array'd
In the bright Colours of primæval Spring;   5
When Purity, while Fraud was yet unknown,
Play'd fearless in th' inviolated Shades.
This elemental Joy, this gen'ral Calm,
Is sure the Smile of unoffended Heav'n.
Yet! why—

MAID.

              Behold, within th' embow'ring Grove   10
ASPASIA stands—

IRENE.

              With melancholy Mien,
Pensive, and envious of IRENE's Greatness.
Steal unperceiv'd upon her Meditations—
But see, the lofty Maid at our Approach,
Resumes th' imperious Air of haughty Virtue.   15
Are these th' unceasing Joys, th' unmingled Pleasures
For which ASPASIA scorn'd the *Turkish* Crown?   [*To* Asp.
Is this th' unshaken Confidence in Heav'n?
Is this the boasted Bliss of conscious Virtue?
When did Content sigh out her Cares in secret?   20
When did Felicity repine in Desarts?

4 fair] far *1754*

ASPASIA.

Ill suits with Guilt the Gaieties of Triumph;
When daring Vice insults eternal Justice,
The Ministers of Wrath forget Compassion,
And snatch the flaming Bolt with hasty Hand.   25

IRENE.

Forbear thy Threats, proud Prophetess of Ill,
Vers'd in the secret Counsels of the Sky.

ASPASIA.

Forbear—But thou art sunk beneath Reproach;
In vain affected Raptures flush the Cheek,
And Songs of Pleasure warble from the Tongue,   30
When Fear and Anguish labour in the Breast,
And all within is Darkness and Confusion;
Thus on deceitful *Etna*'s flow'ry Side,
Unfading Verdure glads the roving Eye,
While secret Flames, with unextinguish'd Rage,   35
Insatiate on her wasted Entrails prey,
And melt her treach'rous Beauties into Ruin.   [*Enter* Dem.

SCENE III

ASPASIA, IRENE, DEMETRIUS.

DEMETRIUS.

Fly, fly, my Love, Destruction rushes on us,
The Rack expects us, and the Sword pursues.

ASPASIA.

Is *Greece* deliver'd? is the Tyrant fall'n?

DEMETRIUS.

Greece is no more, the prosp'rous Tyrant lives,
Reserv'd, for other Lands, the Scourge of Heav'n.   5

37 her] the *1754*

ASPASIA.

Say, by what Fraud, what Force were you defeated?
Betray'd by Falshood, or by Crouds o'erborn?

DEMETRIUS.

The pressing Exigence forbids Relation.
ABDALLA—

ASPASIA.

    Hated Name! his jealous Rage
Broke out in Perfidy—Oh curs'd ASPASIA,   10
Born to compleat the Ruin of her Country;
Hide me, oh hide me from upbraiding *Greece*,
Oh, hide me from myself!

DEMETRIUS.

     Be fruitless Grief
The Doom of Guilt alone, nor dare to seize
The Breast where Virtue guards the Throne of Peace.   15
Devolve, dear Maid, thy Sorrows on the Wretch,
Whose Fear, or Rage, or Treachery betray'd us.

IRENE *aside.*

A private Station may discóver more;
Then let me rid them of IRENE's Presence:
Proceed, and give a loose to Love and Treason.   20
               [*Withdraws.*

ASPASIA.

Yet tell.

DEMETRIUS.

To tell, or hear, were Waste of Life.

ASPASIA.

The Life, which only this Design supported,
Were now well lost, in hearing how you fail'd.

15. Cf. *The Vanity of Human Wishes*, l. 142.

DEMETRIUS.

Or meanly fraudulent, or madly gay,
ABDALLA, while we waited near the Palace,   25
With ill-tim'd Mirth propos'd the Bowl of Love.
Just as it reach'd my Lips, a sudden Cry
Urg'd me to dash it to the Ground untouch'd,
And seize my Sword with disencumber'd Hand.

ASPASIA.

What Cry? The Stratagem? Did then ABDALLA?—   30

DEMETRIUS.

At once a Thousand Passions fir'd his Cheek:
Then all is past he cried—and darted from us;
Nor at the Call of CALI deign'd to turn.

ASPASIA.

Why did you stay? deserted and betray'd?
What more could Force attempt, or Art contrive?   35

DEMETRIUS.

Amazement seiz'd us, and the hoary Bassa
Stood torpid in Suspence; but soon ABDALLA
Return'd with Force that made Resistance vain,
And bade his new Confederates seize the Traitors.
CALI disarm'd was born away to Death;   40
Myself escap'd, or favour'd or neglected.

ASPASIA.

O *Greece*! renown'd for Science and for Wealth,
Behold thy boasted Honours snatch'd away.

DEMETRIUS.

Though Disappointment blast our general Scheme,
Yet much remains to hope. I shall not call   45
The Day disast'rous that secures our Flight;
Nor think that Effort lost which rescues thee.   [*Enter* Abd.

Scene IV

IRENE, ASPASIA, DEMETRIUS, ABDALLA.

ABDALLA.

At length the Prize is mine—The haughty Maid
That bears the Fate of Empires in her Air,
Henceforth shall live for me; for me alone
Shall plume her Charms, and, with attentive Watch,
Steal from ABDALLA's Eye the Sign to smile.   5

DEMETRIUS.

Cease this wild Roar of savage Exultation;
Advance, and perish in the frantic Boast.

ASPASIA.

Forbear, DEMETRIUS, 'tis ASPASIA calls thee;
Thy Love, ASPASIA, calls; restrain thy Sword;
Nor rush on useless Wounds with idle Courage.   10

DEMETRIUS.

What now remains?

ASPASIA.

It now remains to fly?

DEMETRIUS.

Shall then the Savage live, to boast his Insult;
Tell how DEMETRIUS shun'd his single Hand,
And stole his Life and Mistress from his Sabre?

ABDALLA.

Infatuate Loiterer, has Fate, in vain,   15
Unclasp'd his Iron Gripe to set thee free?
Still dost thou flutter in the Jaws of Death?
Snar'd with thy Fears, and maz'd in Stupefaction.

11 fly! *Works*   16 free; *1749*

DEMETRIUS.

Forgive, my Fair, 'tis Life, 'tis Nature calls.
Now, Traytor, feel the Fear that chills my Hand.   20

ASPASIA.

'Tis Madness to provoke superfluous Danger,
And Cowardice to dread the Boast of Folly.

ABDALLA.

Fly, Wretch, while yet my Pity grants thee Flight;
The Pow'r of *Turkey* waits upon my Call.
Leave but this Maid, resign a hopeless Claim,   25
And drag away thy Life in Scorn and Safety,
Thy Life, too mean a Prey to lure ABDALLA.

DEMETRIUS.

Once more I dare thy Sword, behold the Prize,
Behold I quit her to the Chance of Battle.

[*Quitting* Aspasia.

ABDALLA.

Well mayst thou call thy Master to the Combat,   30
And try the Hazard that hast Nought to stake;
Alike my Death or thine is gain to thee,
But soon thou shalt repent: another Moment
Shall throw th' attending Janizaries round thee.

[*Exit hastily* ABDALLA.

SCENE V

ASPASIA, DEMETRIUS, IRENE.

IRENE.

ABDALLA fails, now Fortune all is mine.   [*Aside.*
Haste, MURZA, to the Palace, let the Sultan
                              [*To one of her Attendants.*
Dispatch his Guards to stop the flying Traytors,
While I protract their Stay. Be swift and faithful.

[*Exit* MURZA.

24 Power *1749, 1781*   Sc. V. S.D. ASPASIA, DEMETRIUS, *all edd.*   Irene, Aspasia, Demetrius *Osborne 1785*

This lucky Stratagem shall charm the Sultan,   [*Aside.*
Secure his Confidence, and fix his Love.   6

DEMETRIUS.

Behold a Boaster's Worth. Now snatch, my Fair,
The happy Moment, hasten to the Shore,
Ere he return with Thousands at his Side.

ASPASIA.

In vain I listen to th' inviting Call   10
Of Freedom and of Love: My trembling Joints
Relax'd with Fear, refuse to bear me forward.
Depart, DEMETRIUS, lest my Fate involve thee,
Forsake a Wretch abandon'd to Despair,
To share the Miseries herself has caus'd.   15

DEMETRIUS.

Let us not struggle with th' eternal Will,
Nor languish o'er irreparable Ruins;
Come haste, and live—Thy Innocence and Truth
Shall bless our Wand'rings, and propitiate Heav'n.

IRENE.

Press not her Flight, while yet her feeble Nerves   20
Refuse their Office, and uncertain Life
Still labours with imaginary Woe;
Here let me tend her with officious Care,
Watch each unquiet Flutter of the Breast,
And joy to feel the vital Warmth return,   25
To see the Cloud forsake her kindling Cheek,
And hail the rosy Dawn of rising Health.

ASPASIA.

Oh! rather scornful of flagitious Greatness,
Resolve to share our Dangers and our Toils,
Companion of our Flight, illustrious Exile,   30
Leave Slav'ry, Guilt, and Infamy behind.

IRENE.

My Soul attends thy Voice, and banish'd Virtue
Strives to regain her Empire of the Mind:
Assist her Efforts with thy strong Persuasion;
Sure 'tis the happy Hour ordain'd above,　　　　　35
When vanquish'd Vice shall tyrannize no more.

DEMETRIUS.

Remember, Peace and Anguish are before thee,
And Honour and Reproach, and Heav'n and Hell.

ASPASIA.

Content with Freedom, and precarious Greatness.

DEMETRIUS.

Now make thy Choice, while yet the Pow'r of Choice　　40
Kind Heav'n affords thee, and inviting Mercy
Holds out her Hand to lead thee back to Truth.

IRENE.

Stay—in this dubious Twilight of Conviction,
The Gleams of Reason, and the Clouds of Passion,
Irradiate and obscure my Breast by Turns:　　　　45
Stay but a Moment, and prevailing Truth
Will spread resistless Light upon my Soul.

DEMETRIUS.

But since none knows the Danger of a Moment,
And Heav'n forbids to lavish Life away,
Let kind Compulsion terminate the Contest.　　　　50
　　　　　　　　　　　　　　[*Seizing her Hand.*
Ye Christian Captives, follow me to Freedom:
A Galley waits us, and the Winds invite.

IRENE.

Whence is this Violence?

41 Heaven *1749, 1781*

DEMETRIUS.

                    Your calmer Thought
Will teach a gentler Term.

IRENE.

                    Forbear this Rudeness,
And learn the Rev'rence due to *Turkey*'s Queen.   55
Fly, Slaves, and call the Sultan to my Rescue.

DEMETRIUS.

Farewell, unhappy Maid, may ev'ry Joy
Be thine, that Wealth can give, or Guilt receive.

ASPASIA.

And when, contemptuous of imperial Pow'r,
Disease shall chase the Phantoms of Ambition,   60
May Penitence attend thy mournful Bed,
And wing thy latest Pray'r to pitying Heav'n.
    [*Exeunt* Demetrius, Aspasia, *with Part of the Attendants.*

SCENE VI

IRENE *walks at a Distance from her Attendants.*

After a Pause.

Against the Head which Innocence secures,
Insidious Malice aims her Darts in vain;
Turn'd backwards by the powerful Breath of Heav'n.
Perhaps ev'n now the Lovers unpursu'd
Bound o'er the sparkling Waves. Go, happy Bark,   5
Thy sacred Freight shall still the raging Main.
To guide thy Passage shall th' aerial Spirits
Fill all the starry Lamps with double Blaze;
Th' applauding Sky shall pour forth all its Beams
To grace the Triumph of victorious Virtue;   10

6 Thy] The *1754*   10 triumphs *Osborne 1785*   Virtue. *1749, 1754, 1781*

61-2. Quoted in the *Dictionary*, s.v. 'penitence', but removed from ed. 4.

While I, not yet familiar to my Crimes,
Recoil from Thought, and shudder at myself.
How am I chang'd! How lately did IRENE
Fly from the busy Pleasures of her Sex,
Well pleas'd to search the Treasures of Remembrance,   15
And live her guiltless Moments o'er anew!
Come let us seek new Pleasures in the Palace,
Till soft Fatigue invite us to repose.   [*To her Attendants,*
                                                          going off.

Scene VII

Enter MUSTAPHA, *meeting and stopping her.*

MUSTAPHA.

Fair Falshood stay.

IRENE.

                    What Dream of sudden Power
Has taught my Slave the Language of Command!
Henceforth be wise, nor hope a second Pardon.

MUSTAPHA.

Who calls for Pardon from a Wretch condemn'd?

IRENE.

Thy Look, thy Speech, thy Action, all is Wildness—   5
Who charges Guilt on me?

MUSTAPHA.

                    Who charges Guilt?
Ask of thy Heart; attend the Voice of Conscience—
Who charges Guilt! lay by this proud Resentment
That fires thy Cheek, and elevates thy Mien,
Nor thus usurp the Dignity of Virtue.   10
Review this Day.

18 invites *1754*
7 Heart? *1749*

IRENE.

Whate'er thy Accusation,
The Sultan is my Judge.

MUSTAPHA.

That Hope is past;
Hard was the Strife of Justice and of Love;
But now 'tis o'er, and Justice has prevail'd.
Know'st thou not CALI? know'st thou not DEMETRIUS?   15

IRENE.

Bold Slave, I know them both—I know them Traytors.

MUSTAPHA.

Perfidious!—yes—too well thou know'st them Traytors

IRENE.

Their Treason throws no Stain upon IRENE.
This Day has prov'd my Fondness for the Sultan;
He knew IRENE's Truth.

MUSTAPHA.

The Sultan knows it,   20
He knows how near Apostacy to Treason—
But 'tis not mine to judge—I scorn and leave thee.
I go, lest Vengeance urge my Hand to Blood,
To Blood, too mean to stain a Soldier's Sabre.
[*Exit* Mustapha.

IRENE *to her Attendants.*

Go, blustring Slave.—He has not heard of MURZA.   25
That dext'rous Message frees me from Suspicion.

Scene VIII

Enter Hasan, Caraza, *with Mutes, who throw the black Robe
upon* Irene, *and sign to her Attendants to withdraw.*

Hasan.

Forgive, fair Excellence, th' unwilling Tongue,
The Tongue, that, forc'd by strong Necessity,
Bids Beauty, such as thine, prepare to die.

Irene.

What wild Mistake is this? Take hence with speed
Your Robe of Mourning, and your Dogs of Death.   5
Quick from my Sight you inauspicious Monsters,
Nor dare henceforth to shock Irene's Walks.

Hasan.

Alas! they come, commanded by the Sultan,
Th' unpitying Ministers of *Turkish* Justice,
Nor dare to spare the Life his Frown condemns.   10

Irene.

Are these the rapid Thunderbolts of War,
That pour with sudden Violence on Kingdoms,
And spread their Flames resistless o'er the World?
What sleepy Charms benumb these active Heroes,
Depress their Spirits, and retard their Speed?   15
Beyond the Fear of ling'ring Punishment,
Aspasia now within her Lover's Arms
Securely sleeps, and, in delightful Dreams,
Smiles at the Threat'nings of defeated Rage.

Caraza.

We come, bright Virgin, tho' relenting Nature   20
Shrinks at the hated Task, for thy Destruction;
When, summon'd by the Sultan's clam'rous Fury,

5 Robes *1754*

We ask'd, with tim'rous Tongue, th' Offender's Name,
He struck his tortur'd Breast, and roar'd, IRENE:
We started at the Sound, again enquir'd,   25
Again his thund'ring Voice return'd, IRENE.

IRENE.

Whence is this Rage? what barb'rous Tongue has wrong'd
    me?
What Fraud misleads him? or what Crimes incense?

HASAN.

Expiring CALI nam'd IRENE's Chamber,
The Place appointed for his Master's Death.   30

IRENE.

IRENE's Chamber! From my faithful Bosom
Far be the Thought—But hear my Protestation.

CARAZA.

'Tis ours, alas! to punish, not to judge,
Not call'd to try the Cause, we hear the Sentence,
Ordain'd the mournful Messengers of Death.   35

IRENE.

Some ill designing Statesman's base Intrigue!
Some cruel Stratagem of jealous Beauty!
Perhaps yourselves the Villains that defame me,
Now haste to murder, ere returning Thought
Recall th' extorted Doom.—It must be so,   40
Confess your Crime, or lead me to the Sultan,
There dauntless Truth shall blast the vile Accuser,
Then shall you feel what Language cannot utter,
Each piercing Torture, every Change of Pain,
That Vengeance can invent, or Pow'r inflict.   45
            [*Enter* ABDALLA, *he stops short and listens.*

Scene IX

Irene, Hasan, Caraza, Abdalla.

Abdalla *Aside*.

All is not lost, Abdalla, see the Queen,
See the last Witness of thy Guilt and Fear
Enrob'd in *Death*—Dispatch her and be great.

Caraza.

Unhappy Fair! Compassion calls upon me
To check this Torrent of imperious Rage,   5
While unavailing Anger crouds thy Tongue
With idle Threats and fruitless Exclamation,
The fraudful Moments ply their silent Wings,
And steal thy Life away. Death's horrid Angel
Already shakes his bloody Sabre o'er thee.   10
The raging Sultan burns till our Return,
Curses the dull Delays of ling'ring Mercy,
And thinks his fatal Mandates ill obey'd.

Abdalla.

Is then your Sov'reign's Life so cheaply rated,
That thus you parly with detected Treason?   15
Should she prevail to gain the Sultan's Presence,
Soon might her Tears engage a Lover's Credit;
Perhaps her Malice might transfer the Charge,
Perhaps her pois'nous Tongue might blast Abdalla.

Irene.

O let me be but heard, nor fear from me   20
Or Flights of Pow'r, or Projects of Ambition,
My Hopes, my Wishes, terminate in Life,
A little Life for Grief, and for Repentance.

Abdalla.

I mark'd her wily Messenger afar,
And saw him skulking in the closest Walks: 25

I guess'd her dark Designs, and warn'd the Sultan,
And bring her former Sentence new confirm'd.

HASAN.

Then call it not our Cruelty, nor Crime,
Deem us not deaf to Woe, nor blind to Beauty,
That thus constrain'd we speed the Stroke of Death.   30
                              [*Beckons the Mutes.*

IRENE.

O name not Death! Distraction and Amazement,
Horror and Agony are in that Sound!
Let me but live, heap Woes on Woes upon me,
Hide me with Murd'rers in the Dungeon's Gloom,
Send me to wander on some pathless Shore,   35
Let Shame and hooting Infamy pursue me,
Let Slav'ry harrass, and let Hunger gripe.

CARAZA.

Could we reverse the Sentence of the Sultan,
Our bleeding Bosoms plead IRENE's Cause.
But Cries and Tears are vain, prepare with Patience   40
To meet that Fate we can delay no longer.
                    [*The Mutes at the Sign lay hold of her.*

ABDALLA.

Dispatch, ye ling'ring Slaves, or nimbler Hands
Quick at my Call shall execute your Charge;
Dispatch, and learn a fitter Time for Pity.

IRENE.

Grant me one Hour, O grant me but a Moment,   45
And bounteous Heaven repay the mighty Mercy
With peaceful Death, and Happiness eternal.

45. Quoted in the *Dictionary*, s.v. 'spare', reading 'spare' for 'grant' in each case; removed from ed. 4.

CARAZA.

The Prayer I cannot grant—I dare not hear.
Short be thy Pains.

> [*Signs again to the Mutes.*

IRENE.

Unutterable Anguish!
Guilt and Despair! pale Spectres, grin around me,   50
And stun me with the Yellings of Damnation!
O, hear my Pray'rs! accept, all-pitying Heaven,
These Tears, these Pangs, these last Remains of Life,
Nor let the Crimes of this detested Day
Be charg'd upon my Soul. O, Mercy! Mercy!   55

> [*Mutes force her out.*

SCENE X

ABDALLA, HASAN, CARAZA.

ABDALLA *Aside.*

Safe in her Death, and in DEMETRIUS' Flight,
ABDALLA, bid thy troubled Breast be calm;
Now shalt thou shine the Darling of the Sultan,
The Plot all CALI's, the Detection thine.

HASAN *to* CARAZA.

Does not thy Bosom, for I know thee tender,   5
A Stranger to th' Oppressor's savage Joy,
Melt at IRENE's Fate, and share her Woes?

CARAZA.

Her piercing Cries yet fill the loaded Air,
Dwell on my Ear, and sadden all my Soul;
But let us try to clear our clouded Brows,   10
And tell the horrid Tale with chearful Face;
The stormy Sultan rages at our stay.

12. Quoted in the *Dictionary*, s.v. 'stormy', but removed from ed. 4.

ABDALLA.

Frame your Report with circumspective Art,
Inflame her Crimes, exalt your own Obedience,
But let no thoughtless Hint involve ABDALLA.   15

CARAZA.

What need of Caution to report the Fate
Of her the Sultan's Voice condemn'd to die?
Or why should he, whose Violence of Duty
Has serv'd his Prince so well, demand our Silence?

ABDALLA.

Perhaps my Zeal too fierce betray'd my Prudence;   20
Perhaps my Warmth exceeded my Commission;
Perhaps I will not stoop to plead my Cause;
Or argue with the Slave that sav'd DEMETRIUS.

CARAZA.

From his Escape learn thou the Pow'r of Virtue,
Nor hope his Fortune while thou want'st his Worth.   25

HASAN.

The Sultan comes, still gloomy, still enrag'd.

SCENE XI

HASAN, CARAZA, MAHOMET, MUSTAPHA, ABDALLA.

MAHOMET.

Where's this fair Trait'ress? Where's this smiling Mischief?
Whom neither Vows could fix, nor Favours bind?

HASAN.

Thine Orders, mighty Sultan! are perform'd,
And all IRENE now is breathless Clay.

MAHOMET.

Your hasty Zeal defrauds the Claim of Justice,   5
And disappointed Vengeance burns in vain;
I came to heighten Tortures by Reproach,
And add new Terrors to the Face of Death.
Was this the Maid whose Love I bought with Empire!
True, she was fair; the Smile of Innocence   10
Play'd on her Cheek—So shone the first Apostate—
IRENE's Chamber! Did not roaring CALI,
Just as the Rack forc'd out his struggling Soul,
Name for the Scene of Death IRENE's Chamber?

MUSTAPHA.

His Breath prolong'd but to detect her Treason,   15
Then in short Sighs forsook his broken Frame.

MAHOMET.

Decreed to perish in IRENE's Chamber!
There had she lull'd me with endearing Falshoods,
Clasp'd in her Arms, or slumb'ring on her Breast,
And bar'd my Bosom to the Ruffian's Dagger.   20

SCENE XII

HASAN, CARAZA, MAHOMET, MUSTAPHA, MURZA, ABDALLA.

MURZA.

Forgive, great Sultan! that by Fate prevented,
I bring a tardy Message from IRENE.

MAHOMET.

Some artful Wile of counterfeited Love!
Some soft Decoy to lure me to Destruction!
And thou, the curs'd Accomplice of her Treason,   5
Declare thy Message, and expect thy Doom.

MURZA.

The Queen requested that a chosen Troop
Might intercept the Traitor *Greek*, DEMETRIUS,
Then ling'ring with his captive Mistress here.

MUSTAPHA.

The *Greek*, DEMETRIUS! whom th' expiring Bassa   10
Declar'd the chief Associate of his Guilt.

MAHOMET.

A chosen Troop—to intercept—DEMETRIUS—
The Queen requested—Wretch, repeat the Message;
And if one varied Accent prove thy Falshood,
Or but one Moment's Pause betray Confusion,   15
Those trembling Limbs—Speak out, thou shiv'ring Traitor.

MURZA.

The Queen requested—

MAHOMET.

        Who? the dead IRENE?
Was she then guiltless! Has my thoughtless Rage
Destroy'd the fairest Workmanship of Heav'n!
Doom'd to her Death unpity'd and unheard,   20
Amidst her kind Solicitudes for me!
Ye Slaves of Cruelty, ye Tools of Rage,

                [*To* Has. *and* Car.

Ye blind officious Ministers of Folly,
Could not her Charms repress your Zeal for Murder?
Could not her Prayers, her Innocence, her Tears,   25
Suspend the dreadful Sentence for an Hour?
One Hour had freed me from the fatal Error,
One Hour had sav'd me from Despair and Madness.

CARAZA.

Your fierce Impatience forc'd us from your Presence,
Urg'd us to Speed, and bad us banish Pity,   30
Nor trust our Passions with her fatal Charms.

13 thy Message *1754*

MAHOMET.

What hadst thou lost by slighting those Commands?
Thy Life perhaps—Were but IRENE spar'd,
Well if a Thousand Lives like thine had perish'd;
Such Beauty, Sweetness, Love, were cheaply bought,   35
With half the grov'ling Slaves that load the Globe.

MUSTAPHA.

Great is thy Woe! but think, illustrious Sultan,
Such Ills are sent for Souls like thine to conquer.
Shake off this Weight of unavailing Grief,
Rush to the War, display thy dreadful Banners,   40
And lead thy Troops victorious round the World.

MAHOMET.

Robb'd of the Maid, with whom I wish'd to triumph,
No more I burn for Fame or for Dominion;
Success and Conquest now are empty Sounds,
Remorse and Anguish seize on all my Breast;   45
Those Groves, whose Shades embower'd the dear IRENE,
Heard her last Cries, and fann'd her dying Beauties,
Shall hide me from the tasteless World for ever.
                    [Mahomet *goes back and returns.*
Yet ere I quit the Scepter of Dominion,
Let one just Act conclude the hateful Day.   50
Hew down, ye Guards, those Vassals of Distraction,
                    [*Pointing to* Hasan *and* Caraza.
Those Hounds of Blood, that catch the Hint to kill,
Bear off with eager Haste th' unfinish'd Sentence,
And speed the Stroke lest Mercy should o'ertake them.

CARAZA.

Then hear, great MAHOMET, the Voice of Truth.   55

MAHOMET.

Hear! shall I hear thee! did'st thou hear IRENE?

CARAZA.

Hear but a Moment.

MAHOMET.

Had'st thou heard a Moment,
Thou might'st have liv'd, for thou hadst spar'd IRENE.

CARAZA.

I heard her, pitied her, and wish'd to save her.

MAHOMET.

And wish'd—Be still thy Fate to wish in vain.　　　60

CARAZA.

I heard, and soften'd, till ABDALLA brought
Her final Doom, and hurried her Destruction.

MAHOMET.

ABDALLA brought her Doom! ABDALLA brought it!
The Wretch, whose Guilt declar'd by tortur'd CALI,
My Rage and Grief had hid from my Remembrance.　　　65
ABDALLA brought her Doom!

HASAN.

ABDALLA brought it,
While she yet beg'd to plead her Cause before thee.

MAHOMET.

O seize me, Madness—Did she call on me!
I feel, I see the Ruffian's barb'rous Rage.
He seiz'd her melting in the fond Appeal,　　　70
And stopp'd the heav'nly Voice that call'd on me.
My Spirits fail, awhile support me, Vengeance—
Be just ye Slaves, and, to be just, be cruel,
Contrive new Racks, imbitter every Pang,
Inflict whatever Treason can deserve,　　　75
Which murder'd Innocence that call'd on me.

[*Exit* Mahomet.
[Abdalla *is dragg'd off.*

Scene XIII

Mahomet, Hasan, Caraza, Mustapha, Murza.

Mustapha *to* Murza.

What Plagues, what Tortures, are in Store for thee,
Thou sluggish Idler, dilatory Slave?
Behold the Model of consummate Beauty,
Torn from the mourning Earth by thy Neglect.

Murza.

Such was the Will of Heav'n—A Band of *Greeks*   5
That mark'd my Course, suspicious of my Purpose,
Rush'd out and seiz'd me, thoughtless and unarm'd,
Breathless, amaz'd, and on the guarded Beach
Detain'd me till Demetrius set me free.

Mustapha.

So sure the Fall of Greatness rais'd on Crimes,   10
So fix'd the Justice of all-conscious Heav'n.
    When haughty Guilt exults with impious Joy,
    Mistake shall blast, or Accident destroy;
    Weak Man with erring Rage may throw the Dart,
    But Heav'n shall guide it to the guilty Heart.   15

FINIS.

2. Quoted in the *Dictionary*, s.v. 'idler'.

DRAFTS OF 'IRENE'

THE FIRST DRAFT

Holograph in the British Museum (MS. Kings 306, 307).

Johnson's unpublished first draft of *Irene* is here reproduced with literal exactness, but the outline of the plot has been separated from the drafts of individual speeches,—a division clearly indicated in the manuscript. Folio numbers are given in square brackets in the margin, and letters covered by the binder or missing from damage to the manuscript have been added in square brackets also. Curved brackets are Johnson's, and generally show alternative readings. Words which he has underlined are printed in italics; in general these indicate that he is considering an alternative reading. Words which he has struck out are given in italics and enclosed in pointed brackets. Interlinear matter is wherever possible reduced to the normal line and enclosed in pointed brackets. Marginal numbers and letters not enclosed in square brackets usually are keys to other places in the manuscript where the speech is continued or changed. Footnotes give the place in the final form of the play where the speech, even though greatly altered, may be found.

Outline of Plot and Characters: First Draft of IRENE

[1] Mahomet
[3v] Knolles
p. 433

avaritious and
⟨avarit⟩ 338

The Turkish Emperour 3 Fol parte aversa Mahomet was learn'd especially in Astronomy could speak Greek Latin Arabick Chaldee and Persian he loved the Arts, and encourag'd a Venetian Painter. He was irreligious, perfidious, ambitious bloody cruel revengefull crafty and dissembling. He delighted in reading Histories particularly of Alexander and Julius Cæsar.

Constantinople situated on the Bosporus Thracius within half a mile of Asia.

Mahom: made a mine which was discovered 343*

A Bridge of half a mile was made over the Haven 344

Pantogles the Turkish Admiral 344

---

* The numbers on 3v refer to pages in *The Generall Historie of the Turkes*, by Richard Knolles. The references apply to any one of the first five editions from 1603 to 1638.

The Constantinopolitans would hardly leave their trades to go to the Walls the Soldiers would not fight without present pay. The people hid their Corn and their money which they were upbraided for.

The Emperour stood in the Breach to stop them and was trodden to Death

Cali Bassa was has hated by Mahomet because he had counsel'd Amurath to resume the Empire but feard his power till himself was establish'd. The Bassa knowing his ill will undertook a pilgrimage to Mecca—His correspondence with [1 con't]
Constantine was discovered by Leontares   Zoganus [t]he
                                                           second Bassa
Cali Bassa   First Vizier who had held Correspondence with [e]nvious of
              the Christians of Constantinople which he has Cali.
              reason to think by Mahomets carriage to him is
1*   not conceald from him, to try him he feigns a
2 = 11   pilgrimage to Mecca and being refused is con-
3 =   firmed in his Suspicion and enters into measures
4 =   to obviate the blow by the Death of Mahomet.
5 =   Subtle, Seditious, Impious

Mustapha   Aga of the Janizaries envious of Cali
Lascaris   A Greek Nobleman versed in Philosophy and
Demetrius   Literature, in Love with Aspasia—
Leontius
⟨Arsanes⟩   A Greek Nobleman his Friend   Muly Moluc
Sebalias A- ⎫   Hasan Aladin
    bemaza   ⎪ Turks Ferizes Solyman Mefites   Omar
             ⎬   Seremet
Turachan   ⎭ Hozza ——— Airadin   Caraza Asam
Abdalla   joint Conspiratour with Cali ⟨disappointed of a
              Government⟩
Irene   A Grecian Lady ⟨bello⟩ belov'd by Mahomet
              who for a Crown &c
Aspasia   Another Grecian Lady now Captive with Irene
              bred up in all the Learning of Greece both spar'd
              in the Sack and reserv'd for Mahomet
Euphemia   A Greek
Hazathya   A Turkish Lady

* These five numbers comprise Johnson's unfinished key to the place in the manuscript where the outline of each act begins: Act II begins on folio 11.

[10] Act 1st Scene 1st ⟨Scene a Garden near the Walls of Constant.⟩
Time ten days after the taking of it.

Demetrius and Arsanes ⟨Leontius⟩ Lament their Country,
mention Aspasia Demetrius's Mistress of whose fate he is

Demetrius dis-guised like a Turk.— ignorant, and Cali Bassa who is to come by appointment to
Demetrius, by whō Arsanes is detaind

Scene 2d Enter Cali Bassa to whom Demetrius who had been
protected by Cali recommends Arsanes. Cali thereupon

He will leave the unsettled Conquests of Greece, and establish an Empire in Asia where he has already gain'd the People by popular arts, for which reason he embarks his riches. recapitulating his kindnesses to them relates Mahomat's ill
will to him, which made favour the Christians and his Sus-
picion that he intends (either upon the knowledge of his late
treason, or out of ⟨old⟩ former anger) to cut him off, which he is
determin'd to prevent by striking first, unless he can escape
under pretence of a pilgrimage to Mecca, in which case he
shall employ them to assist him in the secret transportation
of his Treasures which he dares not trust to Turkish hands.
Then tells them that if that measure does not succeed being
assured by Mahomets refusal, of his design, he shall make
Use of their Assistance in executing his intention which they

And promises to restore the Grecian Empire may afford by their interest in Irene and Aspasia whom he gives
an account of and proposes to them to stab him in her Chamber
⟨he being there unguarded⟩ and escape in a Galley he has
prepared man'd with Christian Slaves, while he endeavours
to raise himself to empire. (perhaps he shows them how

*He resolves to precipitate the Attempt, lest the Tyrant should renew his Love lawfull it is, the Sultan having not given them quarter but
supposing them Dead.) Demetrius over-joy'd to hear of
Aspas.* engages in any thing to get her out the Tyrants hands.
Arsanes a hot Young Soldier thinks Glory and revenge

promises them and of the Hope he now has that she will quit her own Religion. which is dwelt on some time sufficient Cali seing Mustapha at a distance furnishes them
with Daggers and parts in haste from them when Scene 3d
Mustapha enters who informs Caly of Mahomets approach
makes some mention of his Passion for Irene. 13M.
Scene 4th Mahomet enters Talks of his Love, and commits
her Appartments to the care of Cali Bassa till his Seraglio
can be settled he Despatches Mustapha to see the *Death of
Leontares* and then Caly begs leave to go the Pilgrimage to

[11] Scene 5th Mecca but is refused.

Act 2d Scene 1st Scene continues in the Garden

Aspasia⎫ Aspasia encourages Irene to persist in the Faith ani- *Providence*
Irene ⎭ mates her with the Love of Virtue, with Resentment *still reigns over all to be*
showing her the ruins of her Country, with hope of Assistance *observ'd if not*
from Providence, which generally comes to our assistance in *exhausted afterwards*
extremities
45 Irene answers faintly when Cal and Abd. enter

2
Asp. Iren. ⎫ Cali and Abdalla praise Mahomet. Cali hearing
Cali Abdalla⎭ Demetrius and Arsanes at the Gate commands
Abd. to conduct the Ladies to the Palace.

3
Cali ⎫ Observes the necessity of sending away Aspasia
solus⎭

4
Cali ⎫ ⟨They reject to morrow, and determine to strike *⟨His Wealth is*
Demetrius ⎬ to day⟩ Cali takes notice that Abdalla has in- *embark'd⟩ He has won*
Arsanes ⎭ form'd them of his Conference ⟨*of*⟩ ⟨with⟩ Maho- *the Sailors*
met, ⟨mentions Amurath⟩ remands Arsanes to his Galley and
orders to win the sailors to him by kindness. Demetrius being
⟨in⟩ Turkish Dress stays with him till Mustapha approaches.
Dem. raves on Aspasia. ⟨He acquaints them with Abdallas
character who was recommended by him and refused⟩

5
Cali ⎫ Cali observing that Mustapha has uneasiness in his
Mustapha⎭ Countenance enquires the reason, affirms of himself that he neither joys nor grieves but as he observes those
passions in the Sultan Mustapha excuses it and As Mahomet
comes towards them sends him for Irene.

6
Mustapha⎫ Mustapha informs Mahomet of Cali's Treason *Mahomet then*
Mahomet.⎭ discover'd by Leontares, and his suspicion of *tells Calis request of*
Demetrius whom he has seen twice to Day consulting with *Pilgrimage*
Cali and fled ⟨15B⟩ as he approach'd in haste. and at first
heard mention of Greece Daggers &c by which he convinces
Mahomet who before slighted Cali that his danger is im-
minent, they agree that his Execution shall be private because

of his Popularity and the affair is committed to Mustapha.
[11ᵛ] ⟨*Mustapha*⟩ Cali then introduces Irene

7

17X 16.8 14L Mahomet ⎱
          15Q Irene   ⎰ Mahomet courts Irene she refuses but faintly

3

1

Cali   ⎱ ⟨Cali chides Abdalla for not returning to their
Abdalla ⎰ Counselles proper activity⟩ Abdalla declares his
passion for Aspasia, Cali reproves him for letting such softness
steal upon him at such a time Abdalla still perseveres in his
passion when Demetrius and Arsanes enter

2

Cali Abd.   ⎱ ⟨They determine on to day⟩ Cali boasts of the
Demetri Ars: ⎰ Security of Mahomet who trusts him with Irene
and himself, Arsanes describes the Chearfulness of his Sailors
Demetrius is still in pain for a sight of Aspasia which he is
promised.

3

Upbraids him Cali ⎱ Abdalla enraged at Cali's promise to Demetrius that
with mention- Abd. ⎰ he shall see Aspasia charges Cali with neglect of him,
ing justice
considering and when Cali endeavours to shew him, the unreasonableness
his present and injustice of his passion threatens to discover the whole
engagements. affair unless he is gratified

4

Cali Abd. ⎱ Mahomet boasts of his art in courting Irene
Must. Mah ⎰ and the success of it, has orderd her a train of
Christian Slaves as the first mark of Royalty to make her in
love with sovereign power, He attributes something to Calis
persuasions who thereupon boasts of his fidelity, and proposes
to remove Aspasia.

15p
5

or it may be Cali   ⎱ Laments the Slavery of Guilt, observes that a Con-
observ'd by solus ⎰ spiracy levels all when Irene enters with Aspasia and
Must. 4 Sc.
pen. her train

6
Cali   ⎫ Cali compliments Irene on her slendid attendance
Asp. Irene ⎭   16

7   [16]   II
Asp: ⎫ Aspasia endeavours to dissuade Irene from complying
Iren. ⎭ with Mah. but in vain they argue long

8
Asp. ⎫ Maid asks admission for a Stranger which Irene grants
Iren. ⎬ Demetrius enters
Maid ⎭

9
Demetrius ⎫ Demetrius and Aspasia talk over their past un-
Irene   ⎬ easinesses and future Dangers without mention
Aspasia   ⎭ of the plot and Demetrius concludes with recom-
mends to her ⟨an⟩ unshaken ⟨tr⟩ trust in Heaven. A tender
Interview. Simile at parting of *a Merchant* leaving his native an Exile
country.

4
I
Demetr: ⎫ Talk of the design while Irene is with Mahomet She
Aspasia ⎭ is distrustfull of Cali—she informs him that Irene
will yield

2
Demetrius   ⎫ Observe that the Night is coming and en- Leontius
Cali Leontius ⎬ courage each other, and determine to strike to Arsanes comes
Abd   ⎭ night because when Irene is Queen he will no to inform
more retire to so private a place. ⟨Arsa⟩ Leont. and Demetr. them that the
dispute who shall kill Mahomet.   Galley is
                                                            brought to the
                                                            Garden

3
Cali.   ⎫ Determine to poyson Demetrius just before the act, Abdalla goes
Abdal. ⎭ that he may live to strike the Blow not to enjoy to prepare
Aspasia. Mentions the remorse with which wisdom afflicts poyson
the guilty   Cali solus

4
Cali Abd   ⎫ Mahomet calls upon them all to ⟨congratu⟩ Mustapha says
Mahomet Must   ⎭ ⟨unite in⟩ joy for his Success with Irene the Soldiers
                                                            will murmur.

whom he h. n. g.* that to morrow he will espouse her as Queen. He shall hereafter conquer for Irene—sends Caly to inform Soldiers

5

Mahomets Soliloquy

Mahomet.⎫ Yet Cali lives—says Mah: and recommends to
Must.⎭ Musta—to cut him off before to Morrow. Mustapha
tells him that he has planted Hasan and Caraza about Cali

bring Cali alive [an]d ⟨kill⟩ his Companions

6 Mahom⎫ Must. examines them what they have observ'd
Must. Must.⎬ of Cali. they inform him of his hurry, his per-
Hasan Caraza⎭ turbation, incessus modo citus modo lentus¹ he
charges them to kill him and his Christian Companions.

7

Hasan⎫ Caraza relates to Hasan who enquires why in his re-
Caraza⎭ lation he said so little of Demetrius. That Demetrius
when he took him prisoner dismiss'd him, after he had been
condemn'd by way of reprisal to dye for which notwithstanding
the danger he will deliver him.

[from 16v] F 5 Scene *Irene's Appartments* // continues in the Garden.
**Scene 1 Aspasia⎫ sola She enters in and is confused at last
⎭ prays, as Her prayer ends enter Iren and att.

Scene 2
Asp ⎫ Irene praises*** the Serenity of the Night, and thinks
Iren ⎬ Heav'n shows no mark of displeasure, while Nature
Att ⎭ smiles thus around. And insults Aspasia's Melancholly.

⟨1⟩ 3
Demetrius⎫ Demetrius come in with confusion calling upon
Aspasia ⎬ Aspasia to fly, who enquiring the reason, and the
Irene ⎬ Danger, is told by D. in a few words, that as they
Attendants⎭ stood expecting Mah as Abdalla was reaching
him a cup of Wine Hasan and Caraza rush'd unawares upon
them stab'd Abdalla, seiz'd Cali and returning him his Sword
bad him fly, but whence the kindness proceeded the Night
and the Surprise suffer'd him not to know, he presses her

---

* has now gain'd *Langton.*   ** *Scenes* 1 *and* 2 *are given in the margin.*
*** praises *rewritten from* praised.

---

¹ Sallust, *Bellum Catilinarium,* xv. 5; cf. p. 343 *ante.*

departure. She desires a Moments stay for a reason which
Providence will defend them for complying with. which while
she seems telling him on the side of the Stage. Irene[9] despatches
Murza to inform Mah. that the traytors are in her appart-
ment,[8] they return and endeavour to persuade Irene to go
with them while they talk Murza goes out: She endeavours
artfully to protract their Stay.[p] but they go withou[t] her ⟨to
prevail upon them to stay she embraces Asp. and lavishes her
fondness on her⟩

[9] then first
discovering
treason.

8 saying she
will prolong
their Stay.

p by desiring
them to stay
for some
presents

⟨2⟩ 4

Irene   ⟩ She mentions her last action with remorse as being
Attendants⟩ criminal in vain. wonders she could think she
would leave Turkeys Empire to share her necessities and bear
her lofty Mien she then goes and seing the Bark going acknowledges providence, and wishes herself with them. V.6.

⟨Mahomet enters with Mustapha &c (perhaps to⟩ Asam and
Caraza) Scene ⟨Irene's appartment⟩ A Garden ⟨5⟩ Enter Irene
(in her Turkish habit) with Attendants (perhaps Christian
Slaves) speaking of what has past of Cali Bassa, Aspasia &c
and applauding herself that Mahomet shall approve her
fidelity, yet expressing her self anxious and fearfull, when
Hasan and Caraza* enter with Mutes throw over her a black
robe ⟨6⟩ and ⟨bid and⟩ ⟨Hasan bids her⟩ her prepare ⟨fo⟩ to
die, She first argues with Spirit, charges them with a conspiracy against her, calls herself their Queen, and threatning
them with Death and tortures demands to see Mahomet, and
asks her crime, they tell her that they could not presume to
question the Sultan, but must obey him, and sign to the Mutes
to lay hands on her saying they cannot afford her a Moment,
Death awaits them that linger in their task. Upon this she
turns to a submissive mien and still begs a few Moments to
recollect and pray

[6] Act 5th
V. 16F
Irene looks
after the
Galley of
Demetrius and
Aspasia.—
from the
Nature of
Guilt, and
warning that
when she is
gone they quit
not the truth.

10 9 8

10 f

allows no
pause of idle
questions

He speaks (or
nods) we listen
and obey
or but a few
Moments

Grant me one hour—oh—grant me but a Moment
    And ⟨may bounteous⟩ Heav'n repay the ⟨mighty⟩
        mercy on Your Heads
    With peacefull Death, and Happiness eternal![1]

* Hasan and Caraza *rewritten from* Asam and Cazaza.

[1] v. ix. 45–7.

They sign to the Mutes to delay—She turn herself wholly to Heav'n own's her Crime—the Justice of her punishment professes her Repentance Prays—In the⟨y⟩ midst of her Prayer Caraza or Asam excusing with humanity their act by necessity Signs again to the Mutes they drag off the Stage [6v] crying to Heav'n for Mercy. Asam and Caraza debate who shall follow them to see the Sultans orders executed each owns he cannot bear it, they hear her struggle and then she ceases. At that instant enters Mahomet (with Mustapha) raging and enquiring for the Traytress whom no degree of Power honour or favour could keep from conspiring against his Life, being told She is dead, he tell them that he was brought thither to feast upon her dying pangs, and heighten her Agonies by his presence. He then dilates upon her Beauty (wondring she could be so guilty) and her crimes, and is applauded by his Courtiers for his justice and himself expatiates upon his happiness, 9 when a Messenger arrives, who being sent from Irene ⟨to the Palace, finding him⟩ ⟨but was seiz'd by Leontius and dismiss'd when the gally set sail, then came hither being inform'd that he was not at the Palace⟩ not there is returned hither in Search of him, with an Account of the Conspiracy from Irene, upon which Mahomet finding her innocent, rages and runs in Distraction off the Stage, and Mustapha observ's the Justice of Heav'n that Man ⟨And Mortals trace th' Almighty's path in v[ain]⟩[2]

> By vice or passion driv'n
> Is but the executioner of Heavn—or Instrument
> When erring Fury throws the random dart
> Heav'n turns its point upon the guilty Heart
> Behold Irene—oe'rthrown
> 10 By crimes abhord, and treasons not her own
> Eternal justice‡ thus her doom decreed
> And in the traytress bad th' Apostate bleed[3]

Act 5th [20]

Scene 1

Aspasia sola

Marginalia:

[6v]
9 7
1 Asp. sola
2 Aspasia Irene
3 Dem. Asp. Iren.
4 Iren. Att. 8
5 Iren. Has. Car.
6 Mah. Must. Has. Car.
7 Mah &c Messeng.
8 Must. Mess.
afterwards Mustapha reflects
Some Rival's Treason
The treacher[1] Mahomet upon hearing that the Messenger name Irene takes him up supposes it some Love-story and does not hear it till many breaks
Mustapha examines the Messenger who tells him that he was stopd by Leontius
10
12y And that Heav'ns Jus-tice proceeds thr[ough] dark paths. Laborious maze— imputed guilt ‡well th'Eter-nal Mind [20]

[1] v. viii. 37.   [2] Cf. p. 385 and n. 1 *post.*   [3] v. x. 10-15.

2
Aspasia Irene &c

3
Aspasia Irene Demetrius

4
Irene etc ⟨*Unhappy Fair*⟩ ⟨*Happy Bark*⟩[2]

5
Irene. Hasan. Caraza ⟨*Unhappy Fair*⟩[3] ⟨*Grant me one*⟩[4]
Resign. Repentance

iealous Beauty[1]
Force of Woe
Relenting
Nature
shr[inks]
⟨*back*⟩ from
the hated
t[ask][5]

6
Hasan Caraza

7
Hasan Caraza Mah. Must. ⟨Yet she—fair—so shone first
Apostate⟩[6]

8
Hasan. Caraza. Mah. Must. Murza

9
Hasan. Caraza. Must. Murza.
H & C. counsel her not to dismiss her Soul discolour'd with
earthly Passions.

First Draft of IRENE

Nor think to say here will I stop
Here will I fix the Limits of transgression
Nor farther tempt the avenging Rage of Heaven
⟨*When Guilt like this once harbours in the Breast*[7]⟩
Those holy Beings whose unseen Direction
Guides through the Maze of Life the Steps of Man
Fly the Detested mansions of Impiety
And quit their Charge to Horror and to Ruin.[8]
Treat Her

[1ᵛ]

3² 2
When once
we deviate
from the path
prescribed we
wander and
rarely return.

---

[1] v. viii. 38.　　[2] v. vi. 5.　　[3] v. ix. 4.
[4] v. ix. 45.　　[5] v. viii. 20-1.　　[6] v. xi. 11.
[7] IV. viii. 14.　　[8] III. viii. 17-20. [Quoted in *Life*, i. 108.]

With all the Confidence of artless Love

T And lodge the Fate of Kingdoms in her bosom.

2 i Did Did Lightnings flash? Did Earthquakes shake our walls?[1]

(the Ramparts?)

Did aught but Luxury relax our Nerves or chill

    our blood[2] but Fear

T Sophias turrets // They call on Alla

             Altars ill-defended   Sandys

I saw thee fall

Fall in the Front of War oppress'd by Thousands

And grievd that Worth like thine should find a foe

In Mahomet, but Alla's high decrees

Dark and unchang'd, elude ⟨our⟩ weak Man's Enquiries

And Mock his idle ⟨fruitless⟩ tears. Farewell Brave Prince

           —tell to future Ages

3 b That Scythia's Barbarous Sons rever'd the Virtue

And when the wrath of Heav'n severely just

Shall Lay the Turkish Glories in the Dust

about his   And publick Spirit deemd a wild Chimæra[3]

private The airy Flights of unexperienc'd Virtue.

neglects the

publick Destruction is at Hand.[4] When every Man busied

[2] T 1 Ουδε λιθος, ουδε Σιδηρον[5]—nostro sequitur de Vulnere sanguis[6]

[H]oc fonte

deriva[t]a When Avarice corrupts th' emasculated Nation[3]—or

clades— Vain Expence the Parent of Necessity the parent of corruption

In patriam

populumque   Swear by both thy Prophets

fluxit.[7] Him thou hast chosen, ⟨*him*⟩ ⟨HIM⟩ thou hast forsaken

By Every Power that recompenses Virtue

By every Power that punishes the Wicked

And wearied   Live till the tott'ring Earth forsakes its Base

Angels rest The weary Sun forgets his Revolutions[8]

upon their

stars spheres And Time hangs his flagging Wings[9]

V. D'Herb.[10]

I wish'd

---

[1] I. i. 54–5.   [2] I. i. 56–7.   [3] I. i. 26–7.

[4] V. iii. 1.

[5] Cf. ἐπεὶ οὔ σφι λίθος χρὼς οὐδὲ σίδηρος. *Iliad*, iv. 510.

[6] Virgil, *Aeneid*, xii. 51.   [7] Horace, *Odes*, vi. 19–20.

[8] I. iv. 2–3.

[9] Cf. *Drury-Lane Prologue*, 6 (p. 107 *ante*), and Cowley's *Davideis*, iii. 329–30:

        'Bless me! how swift and growing was his wit

        The wings of *Time* flag'd dully after it.'

[10] Barthélemy d'Herbelot (1625–95), *Bibliothèque Orientale*, 1697.

To offer up my vows in the temple built by the Father of Long have
Mankind[1] ⟨see Adam⟩ ⟨long⟩ as
oblig'd by vow
9–7 Zemzem The Holy Stream which at Heavens express and drink the
command,—Flowd for the Father of our Prophets Nation holy Waters
which tasted cures diseases and drank largely procures pardon the fountain
of remission
of sins, and ⟨that⟩ purifies the ⟨spotted⟩ Soul ⟨from Sin⟩ for
Paradise
And fit her for the joys of Paradise:—And at the holy place
pour out my prayers for the long life and prosperity of my
Sovereign[2]
Build Caravanseral
Enjoy the ⟨bl⟩ Prayers and Blessings of the needy,
And give the weary Passenger refreshment.
And give the ⟨short⟩ remnant of my life to prayer, fasting,
pennan[ce] and works of goodness[3]
    Or set
The Persian Heretic in arms against Me[4]
Haly's detested hated Sect—The Mamalukes of Egypt
        Perhaps 'tis Envy To
And share the Pleasures of the World between Us[5]
To spread Civility through Russia's Forests[6] (Russian snows 3
Or bid fair ⟨soft⟩ Science polish Britains Heroes[7]
        To assist the Grecians
Virtue is fixd ⟨uncha⟩ unvarying as its Authour[8]
    nor bend to nor complies with external Circumstance⟨s es⟩
Seek out some peacefull Convents holy Shade[9]   [2ᵛ]
Thank Heav'n in daily Hymns for my ⟨our⟩ d deliverance   3V. inf. b
From splendid Wretchedness and guilty Scepters ⟨Grandeur⟩ V. inf. c.
⟨An⟩ and drop ⟨Let fall⟩ sometimes a tear for lost Irene[10]
The Common Father and the Common King
⟨Ex Exempt from the Frailties of Humanity⟩   T
Looks pitying down on ignorance and Error
Beholds the Birth of infant Indias yet unexpanded into 3
    thought
Unknown to Hope and Fear and Fraud and falshood   b
And in those Bowers of Innocence and Quiet[11]

---

[1] I. v. 9.   [2] And fit . . . Sovereign *interlined.*
[3] III. viii. 93.   [4] II. vi. 55.   [5] II. vii. 90.
[6] III. viii. 105.   [7] III. viii. 106.   [8] III. viii. 58.
[9] III. viii. 93.   [10] III. viii. 97.   [11] III. viii. 93.

Sing duly Hymns to Heaven

3 c   And as my thoughts at intervals of Prayer

Descend from future joys to   Descend from Heavn, to range the distant World

past Mis-   Oft shall I dwell on our disastrous Friendship[1]

fortunes   What will Greatness give thee? What will Greatness give a

vide inf.
d   Woman, not empire or power of Good as to men

but idle Luxury—the train of Equipage &c.[2]

Those Forms of Men that play before a Beauty

As glittring Dewdrops quiver to the Sun

And taint the Sweets of Paradise with envy

The Houries of our Prophet blush before her

d The Sparkling Ornaments, the glittring Dress (the change of
Dress

And Gold and Flattery—Thoughtless Mirth—Hurry

Crouds—For this is by Ir: given up Peace of Mind, hope of
Eter⟨nal happiness. Friendship and Fellowship of Angels⟩

Tortures shorter as Stronger

3 2 The Breast where Guilt like this has found admission

No more shall feel Religion's hallow'd ardours:[3]

—I feel the soft Infection

Flush in my cheek, and wander in my Veins

Teach me the Grecian arts of soft persuasion

[3] Sure this is Love which heretofore I conceiv'd

inf. d The Dream of idle Maids and wanton Poets[4]

The Sultan's Majesty the Warriours ⟨*fierceness*⟩ ⟨rage⟩

Sinks into mildness and softens to Submission.

And Forget (or lose) the Conquerour in the Lover

b That Scythias bands, the Sons of War and Rapine

Wild and undisciplin'd by Grecian Arts

Yet knew the Reverence due to hapless Virtue.

our savage   *the Conquerour* has spent his rage

Lords T   At length,—The Glutted sabre thirsts no more for blood

And weary Murther slumbers o'er the Carnage.[5]

                                  with dire eruption

T   Like Subterraneous Tempests ‸ burst their Caverns

And Shook the *affrighted* World Lab'ring Earth

Licentious Conquest

---

[1] III. viii. 94–6.   [2] III. viii. 71–3.   [3] IV. viii. 14–15.
[4] I. iv. 16–17. [Quoted in *Life*, i. 109.]   [5] I. i. 6–10.

In its wild Ravages distinguish'd thee
  Empire and Conquest hover or
Dominion hovers o'er their conquering Banners   T
And Terror and Confusion stalk before them
  Did we not see the Bars of Nature broken?   T
Did not our Sails receive the wondring winds
To waft our Gallies o'er the trembling Earth?
  For thee, my Fair, shall India's spices ripen
The Voice of war no more shall fright Irene
And   shade thee with   4 k
Pleasure shall ⟨*spread*⟩ her downy Pinions ⟨*o'er thee*⟩
⟨*Unboun*⟩ For thee shall Forests rise and Rivers flow   9 w
Unbounded Wealth shall flow beneath thy feet   And every
Each Day and shall be made happy with new entertain- Season croud
    ments   its blessings
And new forms of pleasure shall be invented by artists for on thee
    thee.[1]
  Adore the Beauty but despise th' Apostate.[2]
Demetrius dwells upon the insolence Oppression and cruelty [last quarter
  of the Turks then enquires why their cause prevail'd   of 3v.]
,as   A idle Tale, a Sound without a Meaning   d
And wander⟨*our*⟩ ⟨o'er⟩ the Ruins of our Country[3]   T
Wher   Where Florence gives the banish'd arts protection[4]
  Scanderbeg[5] Th' Albanian thunderbolt of War
When Genoa's faithless Sons forsook the Ramparts
  Ghastly Desolation   T
In triumph sits upon the ruin'd Spires[6]
Thy Wealth O City ill-gotten ill-preserv'd[7] shall descend ⟨in⟩ [4]   T
  a proverb among thy Enemies   a proverb and
  Why did not I dye with Palæologus and ⟨Great⟩ Shavus *a jest to* future ages
  not unreveng'd—who would not survive their Country the hiss of
Mentioning the Miseries and Slavery of the ⟨Greek⟩   12 B   T
    Oer whom the Seasons varied unperceiv'd   fenced from
Ladies introduces the mention of Aspasia.[8]   the Sun, and
  or might   Nations   shelter'd from
  There ‸ shall his boundless Wealth the Spoil of ⟨*Kindoms*⟩ the Breeze.
Ransom of Kings, the purchase of your blood

---

[1] II. vii. 81–9.   [2] IV. vii. 11.   [3] I. i. 61.
[4] IV. i. 115–16.   [5] I. v. 13.   [6] I. i. 66–7.
[7] I. i. 20.   [8] I. i. 73.

Heap'd by my Fathers illplac'd Bounties on Him
Disperse Rebellion through the Eastern World
Bribe to his Cause, and list beneath his banners
Arabia's roving troops, the Sons of swiftness
And arm the Persian Heretick against me—[1]
    Avarice Revenge Ambition and Irene
Boil in his Breast, distract his harrass'd thoughts
    Dismiss your hoary Soldier
    Hail illustrious Sultan[2]
Hail ⟨Rise⟩ Cali Bassa counsellor of Kings
k Security shall spread her shield before thee
To make thee blest each Region shall combine
And Gennah's happy ⟨to⟩ Gardens envy thine.[3] ⟨thine⟩
And India join her Aromatic Shade
            if once reduc'd to practice

9 1 3   Maxims like these, ⟨if generally persued⟩
Fierce Perse- Would break the sacred laws of peace and order
cution wears
the ⟨bleedin⟩ Guide⟨d the the⟩ the Sons dagger to the Fathers heart
bleeding world And fill the bleed[in]g world with desolation[4]
with fraud
and murder. Cali Bassa relates the Original Cause of Mahomets hatred of
[4ᵛ] him his persuasion of Amurath to resume the crown which
2 hatred he makes the reason of his Correspondence with Greek
Emperour that he might have a retreat in his Necessity here
he launches into the misery of absolute Governments, where
if a Man serves his Country counterfeit Plots and false Sus-
amidst the picions, then breaks out into the Praises of that Country (after
roarings of the having blam'd the Eastern Tyranny) which he has heard of in
Northern
Main the North[5]

    Where King and People own one common Law[6] one
      common Interest, mutual duties
    And feel one happiness and one Misfortune.

5 x Where Swain smiles over his little fields, his rising harvest
his feeding flocks, and says these are mine, and gathers his
children about him and portions out to them the acquisitions
of his Industry.

the War- Mahomet to shew Cali that a Mind usd to action and Com-
horse mand cannot be Long pleas'd with a Life of inactivity men-

[1] II. vi. 50-5.   [2] I. iv. I.   [3] II. vii. 82-3.
[4] III. viii. 60-6.   [5] I. ii. 41-55.   [6] I. ii. 56.

tions Amurath's resumtion of the abdicated imperial dignity
—which alarms Cali.[1]

think of Quiet (rest)   haughty Scanderbeg

Nor dream of peace, while (yet) *the Fierce Epirot Swoln* with Albanian
Success, ⟨secure⟩ amidst his native Rocks Prowls (like a lyon Lyon
wealthy   bleeding   Fierce
oer) the ₐ Spoils of ₐ Turkey.[2]   inf. f
The hardy Children of the Mountains
But whom I could not love, I still had trusted
Science and Arms find every where a Country.[3]
While ⟨fair⟩ yet Hungaria's inexhausted Vallies
Pour forth the Legions and the Wondring Danube
Through half his Course reflects the blaze of War[4]   5g
All the Western Kingdoms
Where unaffrighted by the din of War
They cultivate ⟨at ease⟩ the gentler Arts in quiet
Spread *wide* their ⟨kind⟩ Arms to Science and to Beauty.[5] [5]

He comforts her with the Assistance of Providence, she ⟨she⟩
She answers that she is in little care about the means of Sub-
sistence. Providence will provide for her—at least sufficient—
Let the Luxurious feel innumerable Wants—She knows that
the demands of Nature are few—Nor is Providence obliged
to provide for desires it has not created—Ingratitude charges
Providence as penurious though it satisfies their needs, because
not their desires.—Petronius—candidus esse Deus[6]—Claudian
—Verona—Martial Vitam quae faciunt[7]—she can exchange the
Pomp and Luxury she was born to, for the Magnificence of
Nature and chearful Poverty, and having drank of the River
sleep with Innocence upon its banks.[8] This Philosophy which
she was blamd for by fops and Girls, as unfit for her Sex has
taught her

But ⟨still⟩ yet my Soul detests the Bassas treason
freezes at Assassination
And my blood ⟨*freezes at Assassination*⟩[9]

Enquiring why no Comets or prodigies preceded the Ruin T
of Const:[10] is answered that the Eternal Laws are not broken inf. y

---

[1] I. vii. 19–20.   [2] I. v. 13–15.   [3] IV. i. 115.
[4] I. v. 16–18.   [5] IV. i. 115.   [6] Petronius, *Fragmenta*, xlv. 2.
[7] Martial, *Epigrammata*, X. xlvii.   [8] IV. i. 106–11.
[9] IV. i. 57–8.   [10] I. i. 35.

for temporal occasions, much less for bad Men—And marks
5 5 ⟨out⟩ the dreadfull Comets flaming path
　　　　You who tell
Irene's Crimes, forget not her Repentance.
　　　　And the ⟨wh⟩ roaring Danube
　g Pours half his Floods unheard through shouting camps[1]
[5ᵛ] y Though no Comets or prodigies fortold the ruin of Greece
　T signs which Heavn must by another Miracle enable us to
Vice the understand, yet might it be foreknown by tokens no less
Harbinger of certain by the vices which allways bring it on[2]
Ruin. 　　—Purity of prayer—Irene's Smile
Shall break the fetters of the groaning Christian[3]
　　　　　　　　(shall influence whole Nations
9y 　　　4 x 　—O Demetrius
　　　O for a Cottage in those happy regions
　　　—The gen'rous Mind contemns
　3 All fading toys, and transitory Glories
　　The poor distinctions of a ⟨ fle⟩ flying Moment[4]
　　x 　May its Kings by Heav'ns peculiar care be form'd for war
Or wouldst and its Queens for Science
thou rise the Daughter of perfection—or Beauty
Fav'rite of the
Prophet and With equal zeal Persue the task of War
share Till every Nation reverence our Prophet (his precepts)
superiour
honors in And every Suppliant lift his Eyes to Mecca.[5]
paradise see Then old in honours, and approv'd in Faith,
Religion of
Mah ⟨In⟩ Triumphant at the Head of thy new Votaries
　　Approach the 　　　　　　　and croud
　　The holy city with converted Millions—or Nations.
　　　　Exhaust the Well of Zemzem.
When the re- —Till every Constellation shines for me
volving Sea- Till ev'ry Storm in my Domain shall roar,
sons shall only
visit my 　7–7. Till evry Wave shall beat a Turkish Shore.
Dominions Then *Caly* shall the toils of Battle cease
or *Vows* Then Dream of *Prayer*, and Pilgrimage and Peace.[6]
　9 —Of prostrate Princes and adoring Nations
　　And Indias Rajas ask their Doom from thee

[1] I. v. 17–18.　　[2] I. i. 36–41. [Quoted in *Life*, i. 109.]
[3] II. vii. 75–6.　[4] IV. i. 108.　　[5] I. v. 30–2.
[6] I. v. 42–5.

Angels gaze Tickel.[1]   [7]
—For your inferiour Natures
Form'd ⟨fo⟩ to delight, and happy by delighting   Secure of
Heavn has reserv'd no future Paradise[2]   total Death,
                                                        and careless of
⟨But bids⟩ Permits the Blooming Maid secure and *thoughtless* hereafter
Cast off all idle terrours of hereafter   or gay
Quaff the full draught of each terrestrial joy   ⟨*inf.* g⟩
                    —And rove   inf. g
                  flowery
Through Shades of peace and ⟨ labyrinths of Pleasure[3] 9 x
                  unerring   the Angel of
While Heaven's high Minister whose ⟨ awfull volume   see Prid
Records each ⟨act⟩ deed each thought of sovereign Man   D Herb.
              ⟨actions⟩ your plays with inattentive
Surveys your ⟨triflings with a careless⟩ glance   Glittering
And ⟨then⟩ leaves ⟨your actions⟩ ⟨the busy trifler⟩ unregarded.[4] Reptile
                                                         Reasoning
Why then did Natures vain Munificence   Insect.—
Profusely pour her Bounties upon Woman
Why then Those charms your tongue has deign'd to flatter superiour Man
          air   descends
That ⟨Smile⟩ resistless and ⟨attractive Grace⟩ enchanting
    blush[5]
Whence all those Hopes and Fears Despair and Rapture   which
Whence all the Pleasures, and the Pains of Love.[6]
   Observe the featherd Wand'rers of the Sky   inf. d
Ordain'd like you to flutter and to shine,
And chear the weary passenger with warblings ⟨(or Musick⟩
With purple varied and bedrop'd with Gold   d
They prune the wing and spread the glossy tail ⟨(plumes⟩[7]
Freed from the harsh Severities of Virtue   g
Reward his toils, and he shall toil for you
For you shall plough the Main, and fight the Battle
   To Man bewildered in this maze of Sorrows
Now led astray by Hopes fallacious glimm'rings
Now lost amidst the gloom of disappointment
Indulgent Nature gives some transient pleasures   [7ᵛ]

---

[1] *Langton puts this at the end of 6ᵛ (p. 376) with* Laborious maze. *Tickell
has* 'the long laborious maze Of heaven's decrees, where wondering angels gaze'
(*On the death of Addison*).
[2] II. vii. 15–19.   [3] II. vii. 18.   [4] II. vii. 20–3.
[5] II. vii. 24–7.   [6] II. vii. 41–2.   [7] II. vii. 34–8.

And scatters Roses in the thorny Way
Hence from her sable wings returning Night
On the Sons On weary Mortals sheds the balm of rest
of Men And gay delusions wandring o'er the brain
Sooth the delighted Soul with empty bliss
To want give Give Wealth to Poverty ⟨and⟩ to Slavery Freedom
affluence & Such are love's joys the lenitives of Life
A fancy'd Treasure, and a waking Dream.[1]
(in honour of Then Let me once to right our injur'd Sex
our Sex Assume the boastfull Arrogance of Man
Th' Attractive softness, and th' endearing Smile
And powerfull ⟨glance,⟩ tis granted, are our own
Nor has impartial Natures ⟨generous⟩ ⟨frugal⟩ hand
Inf b Exhausted all her nobler gifts on You
Do not we share the comprehensive thought,
emendand The ⟨Sparkling⟩ ⟨enliv'ning⟩ Wit the penetrating Reason
Beats not the Female Breast with gen'rous passions
The thirst of Empire and the Love of Virtue? Glory &c[2]
b But oft conjoins in Woman's softer Mould/Frame
9-9 Greatness of Mind with elegance of Form.
7 Thou knowst not yet thy Master's future greatness
His vast designs, and plans of boundless Empire.[3]
· 8 7 And not a harvest ripen but for me
Confest—confest by dying Leontares
Amidst the In his last agonies the gasping Coward
tortures of the Still fond *of Life reveald the* dreadfull secret, groan'd out
burning Steel
forth Held *out* this fatal roll—then sunk to Nothing.[4]
—Angels—D Herb.—Herat—Empire de Genies 765 b
[8] The Wind of Heav'ns Anger that blow'd upon them—
12 P Imam— Hours of prayer—Protectress of the World
the World The Dwellings of Misfortune—
recovering When ⟨eer⟩ the tumult of unestablish'd Conquest shall give
from its
convulsion the Tyrant leisure—to fix his court, and regulate his pleasures[5]
3 inf y Soon shall the dire Seraglio's dreadful Gates
to be guilty, Close like th' eternal Bars of Death upon You
though 　　　　　　　　　　 and for ever doom'd
penitent Immured for ever—and sentence[6]

[1] II. vii. 43-8.　　　[2] II. vii. 49-58.　　　[3] I. v. 40-1.
[4] II. vi. 13-17.　　　[5] III. viii. 76-8.　　　[6] III. viii. 79-81.

⟨To range those walks of Tyranny and Lust⟩
To wander pensive in those gloomy walks   9 5
To languish out the tedious hours of life   12 v
   In   unrelenting
With every curse of angry heav'n afflicted beneath each
Despair and Slav'ry, Solitude and Guilt.[1]
    Nor think my eyes oerflow with Female Weakness[2]   3
I saw without a sigh the fierce Barbarian
Deface the Glories of my native Country   Erase
Oerthrow the Obelisks amazing height   The pompous
The pride of Roman *power*, and Grecian Art   Theatre the
                                  tow'ring Arch
Deform the Beauties of the Breathing Statue (Marble Hero   Vain Pride &
And tread the living Picture in the Dust   Wealth
Those crouds that hide a Monarch from himself   Inf g
Detested Residence of Lust and Tyranny
    The Turks never speak to their King without adding to
his name most happy, most powerful, invincible, Disposer
of Crowns &c.—Turk the Son of Japhet
When nought but mine the circling Sun shall see[3]   7
    But the sight of ⟨Friends⟩ Soul sinking into Vice (a soul that 3 g
has the Particulam) strikes me with greater horror
Than ruind Palaces or flaming Temples
A slaughter'd Nation, or a shatter'd World.
    With Cedar vaulted and inlayd with Gold
Labourd Monuments of Art.
When The Mind disentangled from the Senses   [8ᵛ]
Expands the boundless Scenes of Future Being
The glittring Vanities of empty Greatness
The Hopes and fears, the joys and Pains of Life
Fade ⟨Glide⟩ from the sight, and Vanish into nothing.[4]
        Palaces of Pleasure
Ador'd, enjoy'd, neglected, and forgot.   3
Mahom. I have tryd thee and joy to find that thou deservest 9
to be lov'd by Mahomet, with a mind great as his own—sure Select the
thou are an error of Nature, and an exception to the rest of Graces of the
                                   Day.
thy Sex and art immortal for Sentiments like thine were never Dispose the
to sink into nothing I thought all the thoughts of the fair had colours of the
                                   flaunting Robe
                                   flowing

[1] III. viii. 85–7.   [2] III. viii. 46.   [3] I. v. 42.
[4] II. i. 6–8.

been to ⟨tune the voice, &⟩ roll the eye place the Gem, chuse
the Dress, and add new roses to the fading cheek but—[1]
—Sparkling—[2]
—We oft (notwithstanding this boasted superiour Genius

3 Deceive—And make us happy by deceiving

9 7 Innocence—serene and conscious of approving Heav'n lightens
the Chain (joys of virtue) then Death comes welcome and
gives immortal Liberty while Angels hail the happy Guest
on her deliverance, and martyr'd Virgins tune celestial Lyres.

Dogs blood-   Droop at your tears and soften at your smile
hounds of War My troops—shall range the eternal snows in search of Caly
beat or search
9w every should he ascend on the Wings of the North wind, or take shel-
Cavern unin- ter in the Pleiads—wherever Fear can fly revenge can follow[3]
habited Island
cliff unprest The Extent of this Religion can be no argument, because
by human though only one Religion can be true, ⟨Chuse w⟩ no one takes
foot, beat by
3   howling in the greatest part of Mankind. Misterious Providence suffers
Storms Man to be in Darkness.

⟨Asp⟩ Ir—Then Learn since You despise us, the greatness of
a Womans Soul thus reproachd I dare despise you
⟨Amidst the⟩ Acclamations

[9] of Prostrate Princes and adoring Nations
The full-blown pride of conquest and of empire

89 Mah. Nature gives every being means of compassing its end,

9 to some force to others wiles (serpents fascination of the
Leveret) Your end is to please Man You have therefore an

Eagles Force higher instinct, as Nature ordains Man to love himself in his
sees with Resemblance, she gives you the power of copying in some
pleasure the degree his Virtues (this is the Original of yours) and act the
faint resem-
blance of his mimickry of Man
Excellencies
Like the fond So Heav'n assorts the Assassin and the Pyrate (Robber.
Boy renown'd As to the impression it makes it is because You attend only
in Grecian to one side of ⟨the⟩ Argument. Heav'n works no more Miracles
Song.[4]
inf z for us—gives us light but ⟨not⟩ forces us ⟨not⟩ ⟨to⟩ open our
eyes
Surveys his Smiling Babes, the Sons of Freedom,

2 y Beholds a long posterity of Freemen
⟨And⟩ Plants for his prattling Babes the future Shade

---

[1] II. vii. 59–66.   [2] Quoted in *Life*, i. 109.   [3] II. vi. 58–65.
[4] Narcissus.

—And Heard in my first Approach⟨ing⟩ (approaching heard)
Imperfect sounds of Greece—And Love—and Daggers
Daggers and Love? What Love but fair Irene?
Deny'd ⟨Debard⟩ each privilege of Human Nature ⟨Being⟩   3 5
The Social Gayety the improving Converse   inf p
Angels with kind assistance hover round the humble bed, drive 7
away terror and Anxiety and calling their Sister away gently,
ease the pangs of Death. And steal her from Distress.
—My troops shall range   w
The eternal Snows that ⟨freeze⟩ shine beyond Maeotis[1]
And Africs torrid shores in search of Cali
Should the fierce North upon his frozen wings
Bear him aloft, above the wondring Clouds
And seat him in the Pleiads's golden Chariot
Thence should my fury drag him down to tortures[2]
And persue coy Happiness through all the mazes of Delight x   [9ᵛ]
(of her Wandrings) and clasp her in whatever shape You find
her. Let not the lovely fugitive escape You, thus range with
out a Crime from pleasure to pleasure, while &c
As we often turn our dazled Eyes from the Sun in its meridian z
Glories to gaze uninjur'd on its *Image in the untroubled lake* so or in the
your softer Mind receiving the beams of masculine ⟨*Virtue*⟩ gentler
⟨excellence⟩ Returns the (fierce) Effulgence or Radiance of our Grandeur into
Virtue softend in gentler (milder) Lustre (Splendor) what aw'd Sweetness
before in us allures in You. what was imperious is alluring
what was awfull is charming. (or engaging

When Arsanes wonders that Heav'n should suffer the T
impious Cause to prevail—Demetr. answers that Man suffers
not Heav'n by the Loss of his Temples and ⟨altars⟩ ill-de-
fended, that The justice of Heav'n is honourd by ruin as the
Mercy by preservation. That Worlds combine in the praises
of their Maker. That bad men with the instructions of true
Religion, are worse that Bad men with a worse Religion. Vices
will have their effect then particularises the faults that brought Melancholly p3
on the Greek fall.[3]   broods or
And all the sweet varieties of Nature   pours her
That sooth the sense, and elevate the thought   influence oer
the stagnant
soul.

The gloom of
Idleness. V.
Boileau[4]

[1] Cf. Pope, *The Dunciad*, iii. 87–8.   [2] II. vi. 58–65.
[3] I. i. 35–45.   [4] Boileau, *Satire*, x, 'Les Femmes', 393–7.

And envy the Slave that toils whose labour procures her Sleep
⟨*High*⟩ Hail mighty Mustapha, Thou Soul of Armies.
lCould ⟨*f*⟩ just intention consecrate the Guilt[1]
Haste   Go Mustapha go ⟨to⟩ celebrate the Day
With Christian blood, let Leontares dye. Exit Must.
Haste to the safe Retreat, from whence Demetrius
Has heard unhurt the cries of slaughtered thousands

ₐImperial Think on Revenge and Glory Greece and Love[2]
cares and He comes from ₐ Distracting cares and crouds &c to taste
military toils
nauseous the sweets of privacy and friendship—to talk of his passion
Fastidiosa and dwell on the Beauties of his Mistress to faithfull ears.[3]
grandeur
Sure she must be no common charmer that can move him
10v thus, that has in his Seraglio the

[From 10ᵛ] the choicest beauties of every Region, which he enjoys as a
inf y ᵛ Master not a lover, and when sated with their charms leaves
them.[4]
Thou Thou chilld by sixty winter camps canst gaze on heav'nly
charms without emotion[5]

7   These Years demand—Desires more pure, and other cares
than Love.[6] Orders him ⟨Caly⟩ to prepossess her in his favour,
for awe and respect have hitherto hindred him from talking
to her of Love.

8 We wish the ⟨dreadfull⟩ task had been anothers, that another
had told the mournfull message—forbear to waste (unhappy
fair) your last Moments (or breath) in unavailing fury.[7] To
rage where we cannot resist is Madness where we can 'tis
fortitude. True Spirit is to submit to what we cannot escape.
Recollect your scatterd thou[ghts] summon your Resolution
calm your Mind, and let not Your Soul appear before the
Eternal Judge even yet sullied with this world and disturb'd
with earthly passions. ⟨But rob'd with Resignation and Repentance.⟩

5 f   allows no pause for Scruples or Enquiry
My tongue Sudden Death oertakes the Loiterer (lingring hand. ⟨*I displaid*
with am'rous
Eloquence —*Before her*⟩ all the gay Luscious Scene of costly pleasure,
displaid And all the proud magnificence of empire
3

---

[1] III. viii. 59.   [2] I. ii. 146.   [3] I. iv. 7–10.
[4] I. iv. 13–18.   [5] I. v. 5–6.   [6] I. v. 7–8.
[7] V. ix. 5–9.

And bad imperial Splendour glare (blaze) before her
I drew to my party with *alluring* promises   artfull
Each ⟨every⟩ rebel wish, each traytor Inclination   Each traytor
That raises tumults in the female Bosom seditions (mutinies   passion
And pushes feeble (thrusts defenseless) Virtue from her
        throne
The love of pow'r, of pleasure, and of Show.
Each Region where beauty shed her influence, turns the shape, g
swells the Breast or animates the Eye sends the fairest[1]
        Lost in the Deluge of impetuous War
Behold contending Nations vie for Bondage
                        Distant Mountains
Shake at my dreaded Name and the frighted World
Toils all its Languages to flatter me.
And unaccustom'd Warblings charm the Grove (pleasing
        Disson[ance]
Behold, my Fair, as my resistless Voice (hand)   [12]
D[r]ives to (holds o'er) the South or West the Storm (scourge)
        of war
How Nation after Nation falls before me
Ambitious to prevent the fatal summons
They croud my Camp with voluntary tribute
Vye for ⟨my⟩ ⟨sub⟩mission, and sollicite Bondage.
                —When of late
The Storm of Heav'ns Displeasure thundred on you. (beat Inf L
        upon   2
Those gloomy walks where Gladness never smiles   v
Gladness, fair Child, of Innocence and Freedom.   3
        Imagination hangs her weary wings
With vain (fruitless) Labour of the daring flight
                —The Mind
Rolls back upon herself—
Mecca is not to be visited by any but Mahometans.
Unjustly Mortals triumph and complain
And trace the paths of Providence in vain.
Ir. answers that the Supreme Being will accept of Virtue
whatever outward circumstances it may be accompanied with,
and may be delighted with Varieties of Worship. but is 3

        [1] I. iv. 13–15.

Answer'd That Variety cannot affect that being who infinitely
happy in his own perfections wants no external gratifications,
nor can infinite ⟨Wis⟩ Truth be delighted with falsehood. that
though he may guide or pity those he leaves in Darkness. he
abandons those who shut their eyes against the beams of Day.[1]

Demetr. the   Tore, unresisted, from the giant Hand
Soul of Greece Of stern Sebalias the triumphant Crescent,
    4   And push'd the Might of ⟨Moluc⟩ Asem from the Ramparts.[2]
    B   Fenc'd from the Sun and shelterd from the Breeze.
polish'd into   Fenc'd from the Summer breeze, and vernal show'r.
weakness Made passive fortitude the praise of Woman.[3]
    L   [12ᵛ] At my dread name the Distant Mountains shake
         Their snowy (cloudy) summits, and the Sons of fierceness
And wish That range uncivilis'd from Rock to Rock
their gloomy Distrust the Eternal Fortresses of Nature
Caverns more
obscure And terror shudders in their gloomy Caverns
Horrour This all-subduing hand, this gen'ral terror
         Unites the ⟨diss⟩ jarring Voices of Mankind
         And every Language toils to flatter me.
         He Heav'n, when its Hand pourd softness on our Limbs
Her only arms Unfit for toil, and polishd into Weakness—made passive &c
are Innocence Yet not with idle cries I fill'd the City
and Meekness
         Nor bursting through the ranks in wild Distraction
    3 Unnerv'd with Shrieks the Soldier's vig'rous arm
         But while Demetrius, dear lamented Name
         Pourd Storms of fire upon th' approaching Foe
         With supplicating tears and pure Devotion
         Implor'd the Eternal Pow'r, at Sophia's Altars
         To shield my Lover, and preserve my Country.[4]
    P   When the Confusion of new Conquests ceases
    3 And ⟨When⟩ soft Security shall prompt the Sultan
Freed from To form his Court and regulate his pleasures soon &c[5]
the tumults of   If fix'd on settled thought this Constancy
unsettled
conquests Not idly flutters on a boastfull tongue
    3 Why when Destruction rag'd around our Walls
         Why fled this haughty Heroine from the Battle?
         Why did not then this warlike Amazon

[1] Quoted in Life, i. 110.   [2] IV. ix. 10–12.   [3] III. viii. 43–4.
[4] III. viii. 42–50.   [5] III. viii. 76–8.

This fierce Virago, fearless and unshaken
Direct the loaded Cannon, grasp the Sword
Mix in the War, and shine among the Heroes.[1]
And break the galling Vow with double Guilt   [13]
⟨To look in Knolles for Amurath's resumption of the Crown⟩
                    —Still full of Amurath?[2]
Then 'tis decreed. (then Death or Empire.
    He sigh'd, He rag'd, he threatend and he flatter'd[3]   But flatterd
Thy awful air, Thy dignity of Virtue.   threatend,
                    —And Sought   sigh'd and
                                                              rag'd in vain
An easier Conquest in my softer Beauty   easy
Go Happy Bark, thy sacred Freight secures thee
—Th' Eternal Lamps—
To *Guide* thy passage shall the' ⟨Starry⟩ Aerial Spirits   5 chear
                    (Fav'ring Sky)
Fill all the Starry Lamps with double Blaze. ⟨Radiance⟩
Th⟨e⟩' Wondring ⟨Applauding⟩ Sky shall shine with Decora-
tions
To grace the triumphs of victorious Virtue.[4]
                    I see the distant Vessel
Dance o'er the Sparkling Waves—Go happy Bark[5]
Persue thy course through boiling Eddies,   Shallows
Insidious *Sands*, rough Rocks, and *whirling* Gulphs   devouring And
Thy sacred freight of Innocence and Truth   all the terrors
Shall ⟨still⟩ the whirle, and bid the Rock subside[6]   of the Dread-
                                                              ful Main
    When some neglected Fabrick nods beneath   calm
The weight of Years, and totters to the Tempest[7]   T
With mouldring Cement and with beams disjointed
And columns leaning from their central Firmness[8]   i nf 10
—Thrown beyond the verge of Providence
o'er the tide—Providence our Guide—
And bless'd with all the joy that Guilt allows[9]
    —Th' Expanded hand of lib'ral Heav'n
To linger is to dye.

[1] III. viii. 36–40.   [2] I. v. 20.   [3] I. ii. 111–12.
[4] v. vi. 5–10.   [5] v. vi. 5.   [6] v. vi. 6.
[7] I. i. 44–5.
[8] Quoted in the *Dictionary*, s.v. 'disjoint', as 'Mould'ring Arches and disjointed Columns.'
[9] v. v. 57–8.

T   To what are we reserv'd?—To what I know not
1 But hope, yet hope, to Happiness and honour,[1]
Perhaps the flood of time now rolls towards Us
A signal Hour marked out by pitying Heav'n
[13ᵛ] [t]o stop To raise our prostrate Country from its Ruins.
this raging And add new lustre to the Grecian name.
torrent of
destruction Must watchfull Providence despatch from Heav'n
That sweep 10 A Winged Messenger, or bid the Grave
away Religion
Arts and Pour forth her Dead to warn us of its fall?[2]
Freedom.   Th Attempt
2 Is hazardous but—Talk no more of Hazards[3]
                    for Greece and for
What ⟨Hazards⟩ would I shun ⟨to clasp⟩ Aspasia?
stab   What would I not endure to *strike* the Tyrant?
Celestial Fair—Maid—
T Let fierce Resentment aid Your *feeble* Virtue. (fainting)
Their Prophet   —By taunt and Insolence
ridicul'd their
Mosques pro- You may provoke but never can convince
fan'd. You perish *for* Your Folly not your Zeal.
by
         —The Hardy Soldier—May bear or break his chains
T Tell's how he first courted Aspasia but was rejected[4]
M
And wishes ⟨And dwells on the Guilt of Apostacy⟩
Irene were Extended Empire like expanded Gold
converted by *Improves it's lustre, but impairs its Strength.*
some Doctor
and the first Exchanges solid Strength for feeble splendour[5]
Gust shake[s] You are like the Sun the governour of the World but if
it into atom[s]
Your influence be too wide—Your dissipated Rays will burn
no more
My soul could animate a larger Frame
When a River is drain'd by too many Channels the Stream is
dry.
For You Fair Each Land that smiles beneath benigner Skies
Asia spreads Or boasts a happier glebe, is Yours already,[6]
her wealthy
plains. This were enough, if Caly had been Mahomet
Half were too much had Mahomet been Cali.
Hence with tedious
Forgive the frozen Narratives of ⟨Age⟩ Dotage[7]

[1] I. i. 108–9.   [2] I. i. 46–7.   [3] I. ii. 132–3.
[4] I. ii. 98–102.   [5] I. v. 37–8.   [6] I. v. 35–6.
[7] I. ii. 113.

If ⟨Dismiss⟩ yet th⟨ese⟩ glittring ⟨is⟩ ⟨train⟩ ∧ Robes these sudden Shining
    Splendors
Swell not your Soul beyond *reproof* or Counsel (Friendships 3 advice
Not yet inspire th' omniscience of a queen
Or tune your ear to soothing Adulation.
Suspend ⟨awhile⟩ (awhile) the privilege of powr (and Beauty) [14]
To hear the voice of truth, dismiss your train
Shake off th' incumbrances of State a moment,
And lay the tow'ring Sultaness aside.[1]

    And all Aspasia but her Beauty's Man.[2]   Inf. p.
        And granted all his wishes   I *discover by*
Not granted—nor deny'd—a softend Glance   this State &
A sigh, a blush inform'd him You consented[3]   Retinue
    I want alass thy steadiness of Soul[4]
Turn'd oer the page of Plato or of Tully
Enlarg'd the thought, and fortify'd the Heart
The *Coxcombs* whisper and the Fopling's Song
        Those Forms &c
They sympathise with us in every fear
Each weakness sooth and flatter ev'ry folly.
    Irene promises Aspasia that she will preserve the Law of
friendship to her inviolably: Asp: rejects[5]   17L
    To contrive some probable account of Arsanes' coming into
the private Garden as its being the Hour of prayer
    —But see Irene comes
At her approach each ruder Gust of Thought
Sinks ⟨into sighs⟩ like the sighing of a Tempest spent   Gales of softer
And softer passion steals upon my Bosom[6]   passion fan
Irene kneels—Irene rise, thou Daughter of Perfection   my Bosom
Conduct these Queens, Abdallah, to the *Palace* Attend
Such Beauty must not shine to vulgar Eyes.[7]   17B
—Illustrious Bassa—In this private Shade
A Turkish Stranger of majestic Mien   3
Intreats admittance to the fair Aspasia
Commission'd, as he says, by Cali Bassa.[8]

---

[1] III. viii. 1–8.   [2] II. i. 37.   [3] IV. ii. 31–2.
[4] II. i. 34.   [5] III. viii. 12–16.   [6] II. vi. 90–3.
[7] II. ii. 40, 44.   [8] III. ix. 1–3.

A blooming Monarch—In all the Bloom of Honour and of
    Youth
What trivial Accidents determine Fate![1]
H[ad] not my ready thought remov'd Aspasia[2]

[14ᵛ] The important Hour had pass'd unheeded by
In all the sweet *forgetfulness of Love* oblivion of Delig[ht]

In all the
fopperies of   In sighs and tears, ⟨*and*⟩ ⟨*in*⟩ transports and embraces,
meeting lovers   In soft complaints, and idle Protestations.[3]

    —Empire and Irene (Love and Empire)
                   this wretch unworthy
Claim my Divided ⟨*my*⟩ Soul; ⟨*Him I can crush at leisure.*⟩[4]

Mustapha informs him that no delay is proper for
Our Schemes He saw Arsanes and Demetrius—[5]
defeated and Our Mines discover'd, and our Battries ruind
our Mines
discoverd Disclos'd some Traytor lurking near our Bosoms[6]

L   Irene ⟨*abjures her*⟩ begins to yield at the mention of her
power to relieve the Slaves the Christians[7]
—Then mingle with your Slaves without a Murmur
Heav'n shall forgive me for the Good I'll do my power shall
stop the Rage of war, beg cityes from rapine and fire, kingdoms
from desolation Maids from Slavery Kings from Death
Asp. The Breast &c.

5   Unhappy Fair, Compassion calls upon me
To check this torrent of imperious Rage
While unavailing passion crouds your tongue
empty With *idle* threats, and fruitless Exclamation
The treacherous Moments ply their silent wings
And steal your life away. Death's horrid Angel
                   bloody
we are in Already ⟨*shakes his*⟩ ⟨shakes⟩ brandishes his ∧ Sabre o'er You
danger by this The Raging Sultan burns till our Return
pause Curses the dull delays of lingring Mercy
And thinks his bloody Mandates ill-obeyd.[8]

And add new terrors to the face of Death[9]
The Sultan comes, impatient for his Love,
Conduct her hither, ⟨*see that*⟩ ⟨let⟩ no ⟨rude⟩ intrusion
Molest these private walks or care invade

---

[1] II. iii. 2.   [2] II. iii. 10.   [3] II. iii. 12–16.
[4] II. vi. 68–71.   [5] II. vi. 80.   [6] II. vi. 22–3.
[7] II. vii. 70–6.   [8] V. ix. 4–13.   [9] V. xi. 8.

These Hours, devote to pleasure and Irene.[1]   [15]
    To mix with nobler Cares, I'll *set* apart   throw
For idle hours, and crush him at my leisure.[2]
    Thy dazzled Soul, with all its boasted Greatness
Shrinks at th' oerpowring ⟨*blaze*⟩ ⟨gleams⟩ of regal State
Stoops ⟨*at*⟩ ⟨from⟩ the Blaze like a degenerate Eagle
And flies for shelter to the Shades of life.[3]   3
Ambition is the Stamp impress'd by Heav'n
To mark the noblest Minds. With active fire
Inform'd they mount the Precipice of Power
Grasp at Command, and tow'r in quest of Empire
Then pleas'd, and conscious of Superiour Greatness
And Strength proportiond to the task of Ruling   to be clear'd
While vulgar Souls compassionate the cares
They give the Nations Laws, and view serene
The subject World, familiar to Dominion.
Thus meaner Spirits with amazement ⟨see⟩ mark
The varying Seasons, and revolving Skies   And ask what
                nearer to perfection   Guilty Pow'rs
While some Archangel ⟨*of superiour Nature*⟩   rebellious
                                      hand—
In easy State presides oer all their motions   Rolls with
Directs the Planets with a careless Nod,   eternal toil
                                    the pond'rous
Prescribes the dreadfull Comet's flaming path   Orbs.
Rolls on the Sun, and Regulates the Spheres.[4]   Conducts
    Now Mustapha *reveal* this Tale of *Horrour* (treason   persue
That clouds thy Brow and labours in thy Bosom
        at the dreadfull name of Treason
Treason so near us? ⟨*lurking in our Palace*⟩[5]
Attention rouses from the dream of Love
They put the riches of Cali Bassa on board.   [15ᵛ]
    Demetrius is much afraid lest Mahomets affection to
Aspasia should return—this He dwells often on.   2
    Mustapha observes that though neither then nor now he had B
a perfect view of him, he thinks he has seen him often upon
the wall where the danger was greatest
⟨[Ho]w blest our State could every bosom⟩
    Fidelity so firm so pure as mine[6]   ⟨3⟩
Demetrius enlarges upon the Good they shall do by teaching

---

[1] II. v. 12–15.   [2] II. vi. 70–1.   [3] III. viii. 99–102.
[4] III. viii. 111–24.   [5] II. vi. 1–2.   [6] IV. v. 17.

the Sciences particularly Nat. Phil:

Assembling Nations croud thy port.

Inferiour Beauty—Rolld undistinguish'd down the tide of Rapine[1]

L 16-8 When Mahomet ask'd Irene if she will yet consent to be his Queen, she pleads the obligations of Religion on which he preaches the Mortality of her Soul.[2]

The reason why Abdalla engages in the Conspiracy is given because he has been refused a Government to which he was recommended by Cali.[3]

p What but ⟨the⟩ Womans ⟨The imp⟩ ⟨plea?⟩ the mighty Secret Swell'd in my breast, and *labour'd* for a *vent* panted—passage I long'd for somebody with whom I might talk over the pleasures of dominion and my Schemes of Royalty. I resolve'd to anticipa[te] the Homage, and enjoy the flatteries of a throne before I ascended it—

3 'Tis yours to grant, or to refuse him Entrance

Whoe'er thou art, or whatsoe'er thy Message

Thanks for this kind relief. Conduct him hither[4]

And ⟨Strength⟩ to vanquish miseries or bear.

4 I'll give the World peace a while to indulge the pleasures of Love, then with collected force, remembring that I conquer for Irene overbear all opposition—proud Vienna trembles, and Venice in vain defended by surrounding Seas.—Rhodes.[5]

Hypocrisy 4
which I ha[ve]
worn is a bur-
then I w[ould]
have every
smile g[enu]

That hoary Villain's forc'd congratulations

Will damp my joys, and cloud the happy day[6]

ine to [morrow no] borro[wd or a]ffected [gayety][7]

[16ᵛ] He stop unmindfull of observing Crowds

in the whirl of thought

Absorb'd by thought, then waking from his dream

4 Constrains a sullen smile—and shoots away[8]

horrid joy—gloomy Resolution—his air now fearful now resolv'd.

He drew his Scymetar and lop'd the Branches.

Demetrius towrd—Above the Female pleasures of Revenge[9]

And panted on The Brink of Violation//—To linger is to dye

---

[1] Cf. *The Vanity of Human Wishes*, 346.   [2] II. vii. 1-24.
[3] IV. viii. 9-10.   [4] III. ix. 4-5.   [5] IV. v. 25-9.   [6] IV. vi. 2-3.
[7] *The insertions are taken from Langton's transcript: the leaf is torn.*
[8] IV. viii. 5-7.   [9] IV. ix. 17.

Her lofty Mien, and Insolence of Virtue—my State faded 5
before her

They dare show no suspicion of Cali lest he raise the
Soldiers[1]
With ⟨all the⟩ allurements of persuasive Wealth—Gold
And all the giddy rage of desperation
Will she yet consent to accept the' Imperial Robe, to rule with [end of 16ᵛ] 8
softer influence as the Moon sheds her cooling dews upon
the field parch by the Sun from whom she borrows her light.
and heal the wounds of War. in her palaces
The dreadfull dissonance of barbarous triumph
New joy comes rushing on me and o'erwhelms   [17
My fainting Soul with Violence of transport.[2]   3
And all the Lover rouses at her Name.
she promises to be secret but—dreads to dip her hands in
Blood. She shall be haunted in her Dreams by Phantoms, and
Murder will be always in her thoughts.

Either in the last Scene of the 3d act or the first of the fourth
Demet: tells Asp. how he was preserv'd by Cali.
What has the Wretch that has surviv'd his Country   Leont.
His Friends, his Liberty, to hazard?—Life
                              with Virtue
Whats Life when weighed with Greece ⟨or⟩ with Aspasia?   inf. b Dem
A floating Atom! dust that falls unheeded
Into the adverse Scale, nor shakes the Ballance[3]
    Our warlike Prophet loves an active Zeal
The noble flame of enterprising Virtue
Mocks the dull vows of Solitude and Penance
And scorns the lazy Hermits cheap Devotion.[4]

Demetrius's resolution to strike to day Lest Mah. may
renew his Love of Asp. may be defer'd to the Second act
Important Hazard! whats that airy Bubble[5]   b
    Will yet Irenes haughty Soul descend   X
To hear my ⟨suit⟩ ⟨vows⟩ and give a Queen to Turkey?[6]
To ⟨b⟩ Bid wasted Regions flourish at her smile (after the blast
of war[7]
And in the *paths* of War and Desolation

[1] II. vi. 42.   [2] III. x. 14.   [3] I. ii. 134–40.
[4] I. v. 25–8.   [5] I. ii. 137.   [6] II. vii. 1–2.
[7] II. vii. 72.

Bid¹ Pleasure bloom and Cities reascend.²

I'll open my breast—clasp thee—forget Greatness—

3 L And boast no title but Aspasia's Friend³

Such Heav'nly ⟨Beauty⟩ form'd for Adoration

14 B *The Pride of Monarchs* the Reward of Conquest Boast of Nature

And though built on feeble Columns—Its lofty turrets blaze amidst the Sky

With bright effulgence　　The travell afar

Surveys the Glories of the splendid Pile

But when 3 an Earthquake comes weak and unsupported It spreads the wide Plain an unregarded Ruin.

Amidst his gloomy Guards and fiery Vassals⁴

The horrid pomp of Ostentatious Woe

En[v]ies the meanest ⟨Minister of Heav'n⟩ of celestial Beings

That wafts diseases from the sleeping Infant.

[17ᵛ] That pours the dews upon the thirsty vales And burning Daemons tremble at her torments

Some soft decoy to lure me to Destruction⁵

Thou fountain of Existence I pour the Anguish of my Soul before Thee.

inf L Are these th' unceasing joys th' unmingled Pleasures

she courted Fate & For which Aspasia scorn'd the Crown of Turkey?/scornd a crown

Is this th' unshaken Confidence in Heav'n?

Is this the boasted calm of conscious Virtue?

Sigh out her care in secret? inf p When did Content⟨ment⟩ *with struggling Sorrow throb?*

Or gay Felecity retire to Desarts?⁶

The universal Smile of joyfull Nature

L Hang ⟨Sit⟩ these black clouds upon Aspasia's brow?

Does conscious Virtue shake the fainting knee?⁷

Wet the Dim eye or swell the throbbing Bosom?

Whence rise these restless cares? these strong Emotions?

These chilling Doubts, and agonizing Horrours?

From generous Piety, or abject Fear?

The Christian's Tenderness? or Womans weakness

The thoughts of happy Love, and rescu'd Greece

Flush in my cheeks, and sally in veins

---

¹ Bid *rewritten from* let.　　² II. vii. 71.　　³ III. viii. 12–14.
⁴ III. viii. 135.　　⁵ v. xii. 4.　　⁶ v. ii. 16–21.
⁷ v. ii. 19.

Exalt my soul, and swell it into Raptures.
But my Blood freezes and Weak Nature shudders
My trembling Nerves—Sink at the dreadful Scenes of Blood
    and Death
Sooner these trembling leaves shall find a Voice
To tell the Secrets of their conscious *Shades* walks
Sooner the Breeze shall catch the flying Sounds
And shock the Tyrant with a tale of Treason
Your thin Battalions and your empty tents
Your slaughter'd Multitudes that swell the Shore
And croud the fattend fields, the Ghosts that wander
Yet Strangers in some distant World proclaim
To Heav'n and Earth the Courage of Leontius
Virtue and Liberty engross his Soul
And reign without a Rival in his Bosom.[1]
Demetrius tells his concern for Aspasia and supposing her [18]
Dead calls to her to protect him.[2]
To rough—Too false too fierce *to* trust or *to* neglect for—for[3] [E]ach Hero
Ye venerable Ghosts of noble Patriots fir'd Piety or
Freedom
⟨if Human miseries or affairs yet claim your regard⟩ Both your
Ye holy Shades of—Martyrs Religion and
your country
now hover oer us and Direct our Councils are concern'd,
    bend Tyrant Adamant—melt Harlot
Cali Bassa when he determines to poyson Abd.[4] wishes he had
rather stood the Tyrants Rage than run from Crime to Crime.— 4
    How Heav'n in Scorn of Human Arrogance
Commits to trivial chance the Work of Fate!
While with incessant thought laborious Man
Extends his mighty Schemes of wealth and pow'r,
And tow'rs and triumphs in ideal Greatness
Some ⟨*sudden*⟩ ⟨fatal⟩ gust of sudden Opposition
Blasts all the beauties of his new Creation,
Oerturns the fabrick of presumptuous Reason
And whelms the swelling Architect beneath it.[5]
    To morrow Strike—Does ⟨then⟩ that experienc'd Wisdom
That Hoary Head, that Head which hungry fate 3
Marks for His own still doat upon to Morrow

[1] I. ii. 26–33.   [2] I. i. 80–103.   [3] III. vi. 14.
[4] III. vi. 13.   [5] II. iii. 1–9.

That fatal mistress of the Young the lazy
The coward and the fool, condemn'd to lose
An useless life in waiting for to morrow
To gaze with longing eyes upon to morrow

Darkness bars Till interposing Death destroys (denys) the prospect.[1]

The wily Sorc'ress ⟨b⟩⟨w⟩ears a thousand forms,

3 And various charms displays to various eyes

The Merchant sees her with wealh, the lover with his Mistress &c

The weary Soldier—Still sees to Morrow dressed in robes of triumph[2]

Wealh in her hand, and olive on her brow.

[18ᵛ] Arsanes tells that persuing to morrow is like following the meteors of a fen where

The traveller persues the (flatt'ring) wandring splendor
Still courting his embrace and still eluding
And as he seems to seize the insidious Phantom that dances before him he sinks for ever

The present hour invites with *genuine* charms
Seize the kind Fair, and press her to thy Bosom.[3]

There may be a dispute between Leontius and Demetrius who shall be employ'd in the Action of killing Mahomet[4]

—The beuteous Fiend

The shining mischief[5]—In Irene's Chamber
Said not the Villain in Irene's Chamber[6]

rouse it   If yet one Spark of Heav'nly fire remain
Unactive (unkindled) in the breast—

It must be mention'd somewhere that the Galley is now brought up to to bottom of this Garden.[7]

Mahomet upon mentioning Caly's request of pilgrima[ge]
And Must. mentioning Greece and Revenge doubt of Caly's design but determine however to kill him.[8]

Horrid as a Murd'rers Dreams, Madman's Laughter
Slumber of the Soul

3 Wilderness of waters—The sinking turrets and receding Shores

4 My Soul not oft acquainted with Remorse

[1] III. ii. 19–25.	[2] III. ii. 28–31.	[3] III. ii. 34–5.
[4] IV. iii. 25–40.	[5] V. xi. I.	[6] V. xi. 14.
[7] IV. iii. I *and* V. v. 52.		[8] II. vi. 43–86.

Shrinks from this Heap of aggregated Crime

Aspasia answers to Irenes Insult that this World is not the place where happiness is promised to Virtue, or where her Votaries obtain their Reward Virtue will cry out in torture and be anxious in Danger that yet she would not change her sorrows for Irene's Joys

Caraza concludes with exhorting all men to benevolence and ⟨Gratitude⟩ kindness—beneficium non perit—Gratitude Which is the first [19] and last Virtue of the Human Soul will reward him for it.[1]

Some angry Stratagem of jealous beawty

Mahomet dwells on the Arts which Irene would have us'd to lull him in Security with songs kisses and endearing expressions and embraces till the Sword of a traytor had taken away his Life.[2]

—Sanguinary Joy—Slaves now watch her nod

Willing to delay You here they give you on earth the pleasures
    of Paradise

Why should Cali rebel—unexpensive Age

Tell how the Tyrant flatt &c In vain

And what protecting Angel led thee hither[3]

—And loiter'd with his troop remote from Action[4]

When future Histories record the Deed.

And yet such is the condition of Human Happiness

Suspicion checks the rising transport

Will She that's false to Heavn, to me be faithfull

I love her still, but shall esteem Aspasia:

For I know
Ambition
seduc'd her.[5]

        ⟨Beauties⟩ insulted by a Slave—

An   A rebellious murmur

An angry look had sunk him into Hell[6]

        And dare not (fear to) tread upon the verge of Murder

She relates Abdalla offers of Love. he informs her ∧ that the Greeks are all devoted to him, that if they cannot serve Greece or live secure there they will go into Italy and spread Learning over the West.[7]

When she
expresses her
fears of him

    Deny'd the Savage pleasure of Oppression

And why this Dread Solemnity of Grief

---

[1] IV. ix. 18–24.   [2] V. xii. 3–4.   [3] III. x. 33.
[4] IV. iii. 22.   [5] IV. vii. 7.   [6] IV. viii. 19–20.
[7] IV. i. 34–123.

O could her boasted Saints, and powerfull Prayers
⟨*Call*⟩ ⟨Rouse⟩ from the Grave the Rivals of Pharsalia
Call forth her ancient Scipios to the field
Or bid her great Camilli
[19ᵛ] Let no distrust the gen'rous Hand restrain
For ⟨*Non*⟩ Who was e'er beneficent in vain?[1]

[20ᵛ] Accomplice of her treasons[2]

DRAFTS OF PART OF ACT V OF 'IRENE'

Manuscript in the Hyde Collection.
Works, vi (Yale ed. 1964), 229–36.

These drafts are in a small notebook which also contains two leaves of the draft of *The Vanity of Human Wishes*, and a receipt of June 1746 relating to the beginning of work on the compilation of the *Dictionary*. It is therefore associated with the later 1740s. Twelve leaves contain notes which form the raw materials of Act V of *Irene* and a few miscellaneous notes on the play. The drafts are not written out in the order in which the passages were finally printed; the Yale editors arranged them to correspond with the sequence of the published text; in the following version the original order of the manuscript has been retained but with references to the relevant parts of the play.

[12]   2
        Hasan
    ⟨*The e*⟩ Expiring Cali nam'd Irene's chamber
    The Place appointed for his Master's ⟨*mu*⟩ death
        Irene
    Irene's Chamber from ⟨*Irene's*⟩ ⟨my ⟨*Guiltless*⟩ faithful⟩ Bosom
    Far be the ⟨*horrid*⟩ ⟨Thought⟩—but here my Protestation[3]
        ⟨But who can hear thee beg without compliance⟩
    3   Abdalla
        ⟨*Is this your Ardour for your Masters safety*⟩
        Is then Conspiracy so slight a Crime
        That thus you parly with detected treason

---

[1] IV. ix. 22–23.
[2] V. xii. 5. *This single line is accompanied by figures also in Johnson's hand: 300 divided by 9 and verified. As the play was acted nine times and Johnson received, including the copyright, about £300, this may be his estimate of the average value of each night.*
[3] V. viii. 29–32.

Should She prevail to gain the Sultan's presence
Soon might her Tears engage a Lovers Credit
Perhaps her malice might transfer the charge
Perhaps her pois'nous tongue might blast Abdala

Irene

O Let me but be heard, nor fear from me,
Or flights of Pow'r, or projects of Ambition
My Hopes, my Wishes terminate in Life   [12ᵛ]
A little Life ⟨from⟩ for Grief and for Repentance.

Abdalla

I mark'd her wily Messenger afar
And saw him sculking t in the closest walks
I guess'd her dark designs, and warn'd the Sultan
And bring her former Sentence new confirm'd[1]

Abd.

Despatch ye lingring Slaves or nimbler hands
Quick at my call shall execute your Charge
Despatch, and learn a fitter time for pity.[2]

Abd

Safe ⟨her Death and⟩ in Demetrius flight, ⟨Irene's Death⟩
Abdalla bid thy troubled breast be calm
Now shalt thou shine the darling of the Sultan
The Plot all Cali's, the detection thine.[3]

4   Abdalla   [13]

Frame your report with circumspective Art
Inflame her crimes exalt your own obedience
I But let no thoughtless hint involve Abdalla

Caraza

What need of Caution to report the fate
⟨Ir⟩ Of Her the Sultan's Voice condemn'd to dye
⟨Why should the Man⟩ ⟨Or why should he⟩ whose violence of
    Duty
Has serv'd his Prince so well demand our silenc

---

[1] v. ix. 14–27.   [2] v. ix. 42–4.   [3] v. x. 1–4.

Abd.

Perhaps my Zeal too fuerce betray'd my Prudence
Perhaps my Warmth exceeded my Commission
Perhaps I will not ⟨stoop⟩ ⟨bend⟩ to plead my cause
Or ⟨reason⟩ ⟨argue⟩ with the Slave thats sav'd Demetrius

Cazaza

From his Escape learn thou the pow'r of Virtue
⟨His⟩ Nor hope his fortune while thou wantst his worth[1]
⟨Hope not thy threats shall stay the voice of⟩ truth
The tongue that forges mandates for Destruc
Nor Justice can acquit, nor mercy Spare

[13ᵛ] *blank*

[14]   Mahomet goes back and returns
Yet ere I quit the Scepter of Dominion
Let one Just act conclude the hateful Day
Hew down, ye Guards, these Vassals of Distraction
These Hounds of Blood, that catch the hint to kill
Bear off with eager haste th' unfinish'd Sentence
And speed the Blow lest Mercy should o'er take them[2]

Caraza
                         Ma
Then hear great ⟨Emper⟩ ∧ homet, the voice of Truth

Mahomet

Hear? shall I hear thee? didst thou hear Irene

Cazaza

Hear but a moment

Mahomet

Hadst thou heard a Moment
Thou mightst have liv'd, nor had I lost Irene

Caraza

I heard her, pitied her, and wish'd to save her

Mah.

And wish⟨e⟩'d,—be still thy Fate to wish in vain[3]

[1] v. x. 13-25.   [2] v. xii. 49-54.   [3] v. xii. 55-60.

Car. [14ᵛ]

I heard, and soften'd, till Abdalla brought
Her final Doom, and hurried her Destruction

Mah.

Abdalla brought her Doom? Abdalla brought it?
⟨The Wretch whose guilt declar'd by tortur⟨e⟩'d Cali [15]
My Rage and Grief had hid from my Remembrance
Abdalla brought her doom?⟩

Hasan [14ᵛ]

Abdalla brought it
While she yet beg'd to plead her cause before thee

Mah.

O seize me Madness—Did she call on me?
I Fool, I see the Ruffian's barb'rous Rage
⟨*The Wretch whose crimes declar'd by tortur'd Cali*
My Rage and Grief had hid from my remembrance⟩
He seiz'd her melting in the fond appeal
And stop'd the heav'nly Voice that call'd on me
My Spirits fail, I cannot name his death
Be Just ye Slaves and to be just, be cruel
Contrive new Racks, imbitter ev'ry Pang
               ever   the   eason
Inflict what ⟨ever⟩ ∧ ⟨Treason⟩ ∧ Tr⟨aytor⟩ ∧ can deserve
Whate'er perfidious Villainy can suffer [15]
      ich
Wh⟨o⟩ ∧ murder'd Innocence that call'd on me.[1]

                                    [16] *blank*
1 O hide me from myself   [16ᵛ]

Dem.

        Be fruitless Grief
The Doom of Guilt alone, nor dare to seize
                    Virtue guards
The Breast where ⟨*Truth supports*⟩ the Throne of Peace.
Devolve dear Maid, thy Sorrows on the Wretch
Whose Fear, or Rage, or Treachery betrayd us.[2]

            [1] v. xii. 61-76.   [2] v. iii. 13-17.

Asp.

Yet tell.

Dem

To tell or hear were waste of Life

Asp

The Life which only this design supported
Were now well lost in hearing how You fail⟨e⟩'d

Dem

Or meanly fraudulent or madly gay
Abdalla while we waited near the Palace
With ill tim⟨e⟩'d mirth propos'd the Bowl of Love
Just as it reachd my Lips a sudden Cry
Urg'd me to dash it to the Ground untouch'd
And seize me sword with disencumbred hand[1]

[17]   a Dem

[At once a thousand passions fir'd his cheek
Then all is past he cried and ⟨f⟩ darted from us
Nor at the call of Cali deign'd to turn[2]

b Dem

[Amazement seiz'd us, and the hoary Bassa
Stood torpid in Suspense, but soon Abdalla
Return'd with force that made Resistance vain
And bad his new Confed'rates seize the traytors
Cali disarm'd was born away to death
Myself escap'd or favoured or neglected[3]

a Asp

                                    had
[What Cry? what stratagem? ⟨did⟩ ᴧ then Abdalla[4]

b Asp

[Why did you stay? Deserted and betray'd
[What more could force attempt or thought contrive[5]

---

[1] v. iii. 21–9.   [2] v. iii. 31–3.   [3] v. iii. 36–41.
[4] v. iii. 30.   [5] v. iii. 34–5.

Asp

Renown'd for
O Greece ∧ science and &c¹

Dem

Though Disappointment blast our genral scheme
Yet much remains to hope, I shall not call
The day disastrous, that secures my honor²
Nor think that effort lost which rescues thee³   [17ᵛ]

Enter Abdalla

Abdalla

At length the Prize is mine—The haughty Maid
That bears the Fate of Empires in her Air
Henceforth shall live for me, for me alone
Shall play the Glance, and with attentive watch
Steal from Abdalla's Eye the Sign to smile.

Demetr.

Cease this wild Roar of Savage Exultation
Advance, and perish in the frantic boast

Aspasia

Forbear, Demetrius, 'tis Aspasia calls thee
Thy Love Aspasia calls, restrain thy Sword
Nor rush on useless wounds with idle Courage

Demetr

What now remains

Asp.

It now remains to fly

Demetr.

Shall then the Savage live to boast his Insult
Tell how Demetrius shun'd his Single hand
And stole his Life and Mistress from his sabre⁴

---

¹ v. iii. 42.   ² v. iii. 44-6.   ³ v. iii. 47.
⁴ v. iv. 1-14.

[18] ⟨*It cannot*⟩—

Abdalla

Ilfated Loiterer
ᴧ ⟨*Luckless Slave*⟩ has Fate in vain
Unclasped his iron Greip to set thee free
Still dost thou flutter in the Jaws of Death
Snar⟨*e*⟩'d with thy fears, and senseless of deliverance
Still dost thou linger in these fatal Bowrs
Frozen with Doubt, and maz'd in Stupefaction
⟨*To tire the burthen'd Rack and gorge Destruc*⟩tion
⟨To court the sword and tempt the glutted Rack⟩

Demetr

Forgive my Fair what ⟨*L*⟩ Fame what Nature prompts
Now Traytor feel the fear that chils my hand.[1]

Asp.

⟨1 *Tis*⟩
    And   dread
2 ⟨*Tis*⟩ ᴧ Cowardise to ⟨*fear*⟩ ᴧ the Boast of Folly
1 Tis Madness to provoke superfluous danger[2]

Abdalla

                  my pity
Fly Wretch ⟨*Fly*⟩ while yet ⟨*I*⟩ ᴧ grants thee flight
             waits upon
The Pow'r of Turkey ⟨*rises at*⟩ my Call
Leave   claim
⟨*Quit*⟩ but this Maid, resign a hopeless ⟨*contest*⟩
And drag away thy Life in scorn and safety
Thy Life too mean a prey to lure Abdalla

[18ᵛ]   Demetrius

Once more I dare thy sword, behold the Prize
     Behold I
⟨*Demetrius*⟩ quit⟨*s*⟩ her to the chance of Battle

Abdalla

Well mayst thou call thy Master to the combat
Alike my death or thine is gain to thee

---

[1] V. iv. 15–20.   [2] V. iv. 21–2.

> Thou shouldst lose or

Who fearst lest ⟨*I should gain, or*⟩ I possess her
But soon thou shalt lament thy daring folly
Haste, Seize them, Guards, be quick—my thoughtless hast
Has left the Slaves behind, nay then there's danger.

Exit hastily Abdal.[1]

Irene

> all is mine

Abdalla fails now fortune ⟨*is my Slave*⟩[2]

Dem.

Behold a Boaster's Worth, now snatch my Fair
The happy Moment hasten to the Shore
Ere he return with thousands at his Side

Asp.

In vain I listen to th⟨*e*⟩' inviting ⟨*Voice*⟩ ⟨Call⟩
Of Freedom and of Love my trembling Joints
Relax'd with Fear refuse to bear me forward
    Depart, Demetrius lest my Fate involve thee
Forsake a Wretch abandon'd to Despair
To share the Miseries herself has caus'd[3]

To mention Abdalla in the first act[4]   [19]
To make Aspasia and Irene name each other.[5]
    The Death of Abdalla to be produced by Caraza's necessity
of discovering him[6]

---

[1] v. iv. 23–34.   [2] v. v. 1.   [3] v. v. 7–15.
[4] Cf. i. i. 125.   [5] Cf. ii. i. 1–11.   [6] Cf. v. xii. 52 ff.

TRANSCRIPTION OF THE INCOMPLETE DRAFT OF 'LONDON'

This manuscript was preserved by Boswell and remained in the possession of his descendants until Lt.-Col. R. H. Isham obtained it from Malahide Castle in the 1930s. It is now in the Hyde Collection.

The paper is a single large leaf (12½ × 8 in.) which has been folded into four. The lower right-hand quarter contains the earlier section of the poem and was perhaps written whilst the leaf was folded up. When it was opened out Johnson wrote down the left-hand column marked by the main fold from top to bottom, and then continued in the top right-hand quarter. Occasionally he wrote line numbers beside his lines, though they do not correspond with the published tally: perhaps he miscounted, or perhaps the whole draft originally contained more lines than were ultimately printed.

Matter which has been lost at the corners and edges of the leaf is supplied in brackets; other changes are recorded in full. The text has, however, been reordered to correspond with the final version.

[*ll.* 99–106]

Illustrious Edward! from the Realms of Day
The Land of Heroes, and of Saints Survey;   100
Nor Hope the Brit⟨ons⟩ish lineaments to trace:
                surly
The rustic Grandeur and the ⟨manly⟩ Grace
But sunk in thoughtless Ease, and empty Show
Behold the Warriour dwindled to a Beau,
Sense, Freedom, Piety refind away   105
Of France ⟨an⟩ the Mimic and of Spain the prey.

[148–50]

   exalt each
⟨*Praise evry*⟩ trifle, ev'ry Vice adore
His taste in Snuff his Judgement in a Whore.
Who dwell on Balbo's courtly mien, ——   150

[198–263]

[W]ith servile Grief dependent Nobles sigh
[A]nd swell with tears the prostituted Eye

With well feignd Grattitude the pension'd Band   200
[R]efund the Plunder of the beggard land
The price of Burroughs and of Souls restore
And raise his treasures higher than before
From every part the gaudy Vassals come
And croud with sudden Wealth the rising Dome   205
Now bless'd with all the baubles of the Great
The polishd Marble and the shining Plate
Sejano sees the golden Pile aspire
And hopes from Angry Heav'n another fire.   219
   Coulds thou resign the Park and Court content   20   210
For the fair banks of Severn or of Trent
The ⟨s⟩might you find some elegant Retreat
Some hireling Senatours deserted Seat,
And Stretch your Prospects oer the fruitfull land
      rents
For less than ⟨hires⟩ the Dungeons of the Strand.   215
There prune thy shades, support the drooping flowrs
Divide the Rivulets, and plan the Bowrs
And while thy Bed a cheap Repast afford
Despise the dainties of a venal Lord.
On⟨by⟩ ev'ry Bush there artless Music sings   220
There ev'ry Breeze bears health upon its wings
On all thy Hours Security shall smile
And bless thy Evening Walk, and morn[ing] To[il]
⟨Here Life is ventur'd if the Streets You roam⟩
Prepare for Death, if here the Streets You roam
    sign
And make will before you sup from home   225
So Some fiery Fop, with new Commission vain
Who sleeps on brambles till he kils his Man
                            a
Some Gamesome Drunkard reeling from a Fe₍ₐ₎st
Provoke [a] broil, and stabs you for a jest.
Yet ev'n th[es]e Heroes mischievously gay   230
Lords of th[e] Street and terrours of the way
Flushed as they are, with Youth confu[se]d with w[ine]
Their prudent insults to the poor co[nf]ine

208 *Sejano*: Sejanus was the ambitious favourite of Tiberius, who nevertheless was
killed when he fell into disfavour. He figures in Juvenal's tenth Satire.

Mark from Afar
⟨*Afar they*⟩ mark the Flambeaus bright approach,
And Shun the shining ⟨*Co*⟩Trains and Golden Coach.   235

    In vain these dangers past, your Doors you close,
And hope the Balmy blessings of repose
Cruel with guilt, and daring with despair,   248
The midnight Murd'rer burst the faithless bar,
Invades the sacred Hour of silent rest,   240
And plants his Dagger in your slumbring Breast

    Well may we fear, such crouds at Tyburn dye
Lest scarce the exhausted should Rope supply
      Propose Your schemes, Ye Senatorian Band
      Whose Ways and Means support a sinking Lan[d]   245
[A]nd ⟨*xxx*⟩ Ropes be wanting in the tempting Spring
[To] rig another convoy for the King.
    A single Jayl, in Alfred's golden reign
[Cou]ld half the Nations Criminals contain
Fair Justice then without constraint adord   250
Sustain'd the Ballance, but resign'd the Sword
No⟨*r*⟩ Bribes were paid, no Special Juries known
Blest Age! but, ah! how diffrent from our own.
Much could I add—But seet the Boat at hand—   260
The tide retiring calls me from the Land   255
Farewell—When Youth, and Health and Fortu[ne] spent
You fly for refuge to the Wilds of Kent
And tir'd like me with Follies and with Crimes
      angry numbers
In ⟨*useful Satire*⟩ warn succeeding times
Then shall thy Friend, nor thou refuse his aid   260
Still foe to Vice, forsake his Cambrian Shade
In Virtue's Cause once more exert his Rage
Thy Satire point and animate thy Page.

        244–5. Written on the opposite half of the leaf.
        246. The second word is obliterated.

THE MANUSCRIPT DRAFT
OF 'THE VANITY OF
HUMAN WISHES'

The manuscript is in the Hyde Collection. A facsimile of the manuscript was published privately by Mrs. Hyde and the late Donald F. Hyde in New York in 1962.

The manuscript was preserved by Boswell and it was found among his papers at Malahide Castle. It is in two parts, the first comprising fifteen leaves which have been detached from a small notebook; the second is two leaves in another small notebook which included other minor pieces, notably the preliminary draft of part of Act V of *Irene*, (p. 404 *ante*).

The writing illustrates Johnson's contention that he composed in such haste that he wrote down only half lines which he completed later:

'I have generally had them in my mind, perhaps fifty at a time, walking up and down in my room; and then I have written them down, and often, from laziness, have written only half lines. I have written a hundred lines in a day. I remember I wrote a hundred lines of The Vanity of Human Wishes in a day.' (*Life*, ii. 15.)

The whole of this draft was written in half lines: each half is distinct not only because of a difference in the intensity of the colour of the ink, perhaps due to changes in the width of his pen, but also because Johnson's handwriting varies slightly in each half: in the first halves his hand is neat, consistently legible, and occasionally decorated with flourishes; in the second halves the pen is generally thicker, the writing more cramped because the first halves have pre-empted the space, and Johnson seems to have written with more haste and vigour. It is this second hand which is generally responsible for the corrections and revisions of the first halves of the lines: such alterations are often written between the lines and their legibility suffers from the crowding of the words.

There is no way of determining what time elapsed between the writing of the two halves, nor does the manuscript offer much evidence to show the stages of composition. It does not seem that Johnson wrote the whole poem out in first half lines, and then completed the whole number of second halves: by his own account one group of a hundred lines formed a unit, and there were no doubt others. The two portions of the manuscript are divided after '. . . Mortgages of Lands' (line 288), but there is not a new paragraph division until 291. The change from one notebook to another does not provide an acceptable marker for a stage in the composition.

In the following transcript the lines are numbered in relation to those of the published text of the poem as an aid to comparison: the numbers are not a true count of the lines. Johnson's own numeration of the lines is given in square brackets in the margin.

f. 1: '1'   Let Observation with extensive view
                O'erlook Mankind from China to Peru
                          ⟨eager⟩
                Explore each ⟨restless⟩ anxious toil each eager Strife
                And all the busy Scenes of Crouded Life
                         hot
                Then say how ⟨fierce⟩ desire and raging Hate   5
                Oerspred with snares the clouded Maze of Fate
                Where wav'ring Man betray'd by vent'rous pride
                To tread the dang'rous paths without a Guide
                As treach'rous Phantoms in the mist delude
                Shuns fancied ills or chases airy Good   10
                How rarely Reason guides the hasty choice
                Rules the bold hand or prompts the Suppliant voice
                          Nations sink
                How ⟨Families⟩ by darling Schemes opprest
                When Vengeance listens to the Fools Request
                Fate wings with ev'ry wish th' afflictive dart   15
                          grace
                Each Gift of Nature and each ⟨charm⟩ of art
                With fatal Heat impetuous Courage glows
                With fatal Sweetness Elocution flows
                Impeachment Stops the Speaker's pow'rful breath
          [20] And restless Enterprize impells to death.   20
                          unobserv'd
f. 2: '2'   But ⟨unregarded⟩ the Skilful and the bad
                          Fall in
                ⟨Amidst⟩ the gen'ral Massacre of Gold
                Widewasting Pest that rages unconfin'd
                And crouds with crimes the records of mankind
                          his Sword
                For Gold ⟨the Hireling⟩ the hireling Ruffian draws   25
                For Gold the Hireling Judge distorts the Laws
                    Wealth heapd on Wealth nor truth nor safety buys
                    The danger gathers as the treasures rise.
                          T⟨he⟩ell Hist'ry
                ⟨Historians tell⟩ tell where rival Kings command
                          ⟨From dubious titles⟩
                ⟨And Statutes glean⟩ And dubious title shakes the madded 30
                Land

27–8. The indented couplet is written on the blank facing page of the manuscript (f. 1ᵛ).

When Statutes glean the refuse of the Sword,
How much more safe the Vassal than the Lord [30]
Low Sculks the Hind beneath the rage of Pow'r
And leaves the b⟨a⟩onny Traytor in the Tow'r
Untouch'd
⟨Secure⟩ his Cottage, and his Slumbers sound 35
Though Confiscations Bloodhounds yelp around
 The needy Traveller secure and gay
Walks the wild Heath, and sings his toil away
Dos Envy seize thee crush th' upbraiding joy
Encrease his Riches, and his peace destroy 40
New fear⟨e⟩s in dire vicissitude invade
The Rustling Brake alarms and quiv'ring Shade [40]
Nor light nor Darkness bring his pain relief
One shews the plunder, and one hides the thief.
    the
Yet still the Gen'ral Cry ⟨from on⟩ Skies assail 45   f. 3: '3'
 And Gain and
⟨Assails the Skies⟩ Greatness load the tainted Gales
Few know the toiling Statesmans fear or Care
Th' insidious Rival and the gaping Heir
Once more Democritus arise on Earth
With chearf Wisdom, and instructive mirth 50
See Motley Life in modern trappings drest
    new born
And Feed with ⟨Change of⟩ Fools th' eternal Jest [50]
Thou who couldst laugh where want enchain'd Caprice
Toil crushd Conceit, and man was of a piece,
Where wealth unlov'd without a mourner dy'd 55
And scarce a sycophant could feed on pride,
Where ne'er was ⟨heard⟩ the form of mock debate
Or seen ⟨the⟩ a new made Mayor's unweeldy State
Where change of Fav'rites made no change of laws
And senates heard before they judg'd a cause 60
Where blasted Patriots never shrunk to peers
Nor annual Tax was rais'd by annual fears. [60]
  How would thou shake at
⟨Evn low built towns they⟩ Britain's modish tribe

37. *secure.* The printed texts agree in reading 'serene', which is a feasible
misreading of Johnson's handwriting.

         Dart the quick taunt
⟨*And unexhausted laughter*⟩ and edge the piercing Gibe
Attentive Truth and Nature to descry
And pierce each scene with philosophic eye

f. 4: '4' To thee were solemn toys or empty Shew   65
The Robes of pleasure and the veils of woe
All aid the farce and all thy mirth maintain
Whose joys are causeless, or whose Griefs are vain
    Such was the Sorn that fill'd the Sages mind

[70] Renew'd at ev'ry Glance on Humankind   70
How just that Scorn ere yet thy voice declare
Search ev'ry State and canvass ev'ry prayer.
    Unnumber'd Suppliants croud preferment's Gate
      Athirst for wealth
⟨*All fir'd with hope*⟩ and panting to be great
Delusive Fortune hears th' incessant Call   75
They mount they shine, evaporate and fall
On evry Stage the foes of peace attend,
Hate dogs their flight, and insult mocks their End
Love ends with Hope the Sinking Statesmans door
     Pours in
[80] ⟨*Shows pour*⟩ the morning Worshiper no more   80
    For growing names the weekly Scribler lies
     To
⟨*For*⟩ growing wealth the Dedicator flies.
     Room
From every ⟨*Wall*⟩ descends the painted face
     the bright
That hung ⟨*on high*⟩ Palladium of the place
And smok'd in Kitchens or in Auctions sold   85
To better Features yields the frame of Gold

f. 5: '5' For now no more we trace in ev'ry Line
Heroick worth Benevolence divine
But find the form distorted by the fall
     why should odious
[90] And ⟨*hiss the Dauber*⟩ Ruin dawb the Wall.
But will not Britain Hear the last appeal
     Fav'rites
Sign her foes doom or g[uar]d her ⟨*Patriots*⟩ zeal   90

     92. *guard*. The manuscript remains indecipherable. The published 'guard'
is a very plausible reading, but the penultimate letter does not resemble Johnson's
'r'; it is more like an 'n'.

Through Freedoms Sons no more remonstrance rings
Degrading nobles, and controling Kings
Our Supple Tribes repress their patriot throats   95
And ask no question but the price of votes
With weekly Libels, and septennial ale
Their wish is full to riot and to rail
         ⟨State⟩ Dignity see
  In Fullblown ⟨Powr see mighty⟩ Wolsey stand
Law in his Voice, and Fortune in his Hand   100 [100]
     Realm
To him the Church the ⟨State⟩ their pow'rs resign
Through him the Rays of royal bounty shine
Turn'd by his nod the stream of Honour flows
His Smile alone Security bestows
Still to new heights his restless wishes towr   105
Claim leads to Claim, and powr advances Powr
  Till Conquest
⟨Till conquest⟩ unresisted ceasd to please
And Rights Submitted left him none to seize
At length his Sovreign frowns the train of State   [110]
Mark the Keen Glance, and watch the sign to hate   110
Where'r he turns he meets a Strangers eye   **f. 6.**
His Supplians Scorn him, and his Followers fly
What then availd the pride of awful State
The golden Canopy the glittring plate
     regal
The ⟨pompous⟩ Palace—the luxurious Board   115
The livried Army, or the menial Lord
With age, with cares, with maladies opprest
He seeks the refuge of monastic rest
Grief and Disease, remember'd folly Stings
And his last words reproach the faith of Kings   120 [120]
      thoughts at humble
  Speak thou whose ‸ peace repine,
Shall Wolseys wealth, with Wolsey's end be thine
  livst thou
Or ⟨statesmens⟩ now with safer Pride content
    wealthiest Landlord
The ⟨Wisest Justice⟩ on the Bank of Trent

113. A short word is blotted illegibly after 'availd'.
124. *Wisest Justice*: after a long series of revisions: wealthiest Landlord—richest
landlord, Johnson in Dodsley's *Collection*, 1755, returned to his original reading.

⟨w⟩
For why did Wolsey by the Steeps of Fate   125
On weak foundations raise th' enormous weight
Why but ⟨th⟩to sink beneath misfortunes blow
With louder Ruin to the Gulphs below
[What gave great Villiers to th Assassins Knife
[130] ⟨W⟩ And fix'd Disease on Harley's closing life   130
What murderd Wentworth and what exile Hyde
By Kings protected and to Kings allied
        ir   indulg'd

f. 7.
What but the wish ∧ in Courts to shine
And pow'r too great to keep or to resign?
   When first the College Rolls receive his name   135
The Young Enthusiast quits his ease for fame
  Quick fires his breast
⟨Each act betrays⟩ the fever of renown
Caught from the strong Contagion of the Gown
⟨On Isis banks he waves, from noise withdrawn
[140] ⟨In sober state th' imaginary Lawn⟩
O'er Bodley's Dome his future Labours spread
And Bacon's Mansion trembles o'er his head.   140
Are these thy views, proceed illustrious Youth
And Virtue guard thee to the throne of Truth
Yet should th⟨e⟩y ⟨fate⟩ Soul indulge the gen'rous Heat
Till Captive Science yields her last Retreat
Should Reason guide thee with her brightest Ray   145
And pour on misty Doubt resistless day
Should no false kindness lure to loose delight
[150] Nor Praise relax, nor difficulty fright
Should tempting Novelty thy cell refrain
And Sloth's bland opiates shed their fumes in vain   150

f. 8: '3'
Should Beauty blunt on fops her fatal dart
Nor claim the triumph of a letter'd heart
⟨SNor⟩ Should no Disease thy torpid veins invade
Nor Melancholys Spectres haunt thy Shade
      hope
Yet ⟨dream⟩ not Life from Grief or Danger free,   155
Nor think the doom of Man revers'd for thee
  Deign   passing   to
⟨Turn⟩ on the ∧ world ⟨awhil⟩ turn thine eyes
[160] And pause awhile from Learning to be wise

There mark what ill the Scholar's life assail
                    the
Toil envy Want ⟨an⟩ Garret and the Jayl   160
    See Nations slowly wise, and meanly just,
    To buried merit raise the tardy Bust.
    Dreams
If ⟨Hope⟩ yet flatter once again attend
Hear Lydiats life and Galileo's End.
            deem when
    Nor ⟨think though⟩ Learning her last prize bestow   165
    e
Th⟨at⟩ glittering Eminence exempt from Foes
See when the Vulgar scape despis'd or aw'd
Rebellions vengeful Talons seize on Laud   [170]
From meaner minds though smaller fines content
The plundred palace or sequestred Rent   170
Mark'd out by dang'rous parts he meets the schock
And fatal Learning leads him to the Block
Around his Tomb let art and Genius weep   f. 9: '5'
But hear his death ye ⟨Block⟩heads, hear and sleep
    The festal Blazes, the triumphal Show   175
The ravish'd Standard, and the Captive Foe
The Senate's thanks, the Gazette's pompous tale
With force resistless o'er the Brave prevail   [180]
    Such
⟨These⟩ Bribes the rapid Greek o'er Asia whirl'd
    Such   a
For ⟨these⟩ the stedy Romans shook the world,   180
    such
For ⟨these⟩ in distant lands the Britons shine
And stain with blood the Danube or the Rhine
Such pow'er has praise that virtues scarce can ⟨ch⟩warm
Till Fame supplies the universal charm
Yet Reason ⟨blush⟩ Frowns on War's unequal Game   185
Where wasted Nations raise a single name
                    their Grandsires
And mortgaged States ⟨their former⟩ wreaths regret
    From age to age in everlasting
⟨Their Grandsires Glories⟩ debt   [190]

161–2. The indented couplet is written on the blank facing page of the manuscript (f. 7ᵛ).

174. The crossing out of 'Blockheads' was perhaps the effect of the proximity of 'Block' (172). Johnson let it stand, however, in the published version.

      Wreaths which at last
⟨*Great souls whose natu*⟩ the dear bought Right convey
To Rust on Medals or on Stones decay.   190

                           pride
     On what Foundation stands the Warrior's ⟨*fame*⟩
How just his Hopes let Swedish Charles decide
A frame of Adamant a soul of Fire
No dangers fright him, and no labours tire.
O'er Love o'er Fear extends his wide domain   195
Unconquer'd Lord of pleasure and of pain

f. 10.   No joys to him pacific Scepters yield
[200] War sounds the trump he rushes to the field
In vain Surrounding Kings their pow'rs combine
See One capitulate and one resign.   200
Peace courts his Hand, her Fondness he disdains
                  till
Think nothing gain'd, he cries ⟨*th*⟩ nought remains
On Moscows walls till Gothic Standards fly
And all is mine beneath the polar Sky
The march begins in military State   205
And Nations ⟨*wait*⟩ on his eye suspended wait
Stern Famine guards the solitary Coast
[210] And Winter barricades the realms of frost
He comes nor want nor cold his course delay
Hide blushing Glory, hide Pultowa's day   210
The vanquish'd Hero leaves his broken bands
      shews
And ⟨*hides*⟩ his miseries in distant lands.
Condemn'd a needy Supplicant to wait
While Ladies interpose, and slaves debate
But did not Chance at length her errour mend   215
Did no Subverted Empire mark his end
Did rival Monarchs give the fatal wound
[220] Or Hostile Millions press him to the Ground
His Fall was destin'd to a barren Strand
     petty
A ⟨*nameless*⟩ Fortress, and a nameless hand   220

f. 11.   He left the name at which the world grew pale
To paint a moral, or adorn a tale.

    222. *paint*. This contentious reading is in the first half-line and therefore to
be compared with Johnson's handwriting characteristics in similar first half-lines.

All Times their Scenes of pompous Woes afford
From Persia's Tyrant to Bavaria's Lord,
In gay Hostility, and barb'rous pride   225
With half Mankind embattled on his Side
Great Xerxes comes to seize the certain prey
And starves exhausted regions in his way   [230]
Attendant Flatt'ry counts his myriads o'er
Till counted Myriads sooth his pride no more   230
      Fresh
⟨New⟩ praise is tried till Madness fires his mind
The waves he lashes and enchains the wind
New Pow'rs are claimed new pow'rs are still bestow'd
Till rude resistance lops the spreading God
The daring Greeks deride the martial Shew   235
And heap their vallies with the gaudy foe
Th' insulted Sea with humbler thought he gains
A single Skiff to Speed his flight remains   [240]
Th' incumberd Oar scarce leaves the dreaded Coast
Through purple Billows and a floating Host.   240
    The bold Bavarian in a luckless hour
Tries the dread summits of Cesarean pow'r
[W]ith unexpected Legions pow'rs away
[An]d sees defenceless realms receive his sway
Short sway for Austria spreads her mournful Charms   245   f. 12.
The Queen the Beauty sets the world in arms
From hill to hill the Beacons rousing blaze
Spreads wide the hope of plunder and of praise   [250]
      fierce Croatian
The ⟨sons of Ravage⟩ and the wild Hussar
And all the son of ravage croud the war   250
The baffled Prince in honours flattring bloom

Though it is true that his 'oi' is rarely looped, his 'ai' is most clearly seen in
'enchain'd' (53). In this combination, which is common throughout this manuscript, he regularly makes the first letter 'a' with a small loop followed by an
upright, rather like the modern 'ei'. His 'pain' in lines 43, 196, 268, and 286
is not really comparable, for in each case the word occurs in the second half of
the line.

    The compositor of the first edition read 'point' and Johnson acquiesced in that
reading thereafter.

    243-4, 265-6. These lines are at the foot of a page on a leaf of which the
lower outer corner is torn away.

Of hasty greatness finds the hasty doom
His foes derision and his Subjects blame
And steals to Death from anguish and from Shame

Enlarge my Life with multitude of Days   255
In health, in Sickness thus the Suppliant
Hides from himself his State and shuns to know
That Life protracted is protracted woe
Time hovers o'er impatient to destroy
And s⟨to⟩huts up all the passages of Joy   260
In vain their gifts the bounteous seasons pour
The Fruit autumnal and the vernal flowr
With listless eyes the Dotard views the store
He views and wonders why they please no more
      ⟨Th⟩ Now
⟨tasted tast⟩ pall the tastless meats and joyless wines   265
[An]d Luxury with Sighs her Slave resigns

f. 13.
Approach ye minstrels try the soothing Strain
            tuneful
[270] And yield the ⟨soothing⟩ lenitives of pain.
The Notes unfelt would strike th' impervious ear
Though dancing Mountains witness'd Orpheus near   270
Nor lute nor Lyre his feeble pow'rs attend
Nor sweeter musick of a virtuous friend

                          r
But everlasting dictates c⟨ᴀ⟩oud his tongue
            or
Perversely grave ⟨and⟩ positively wrong
The still returning tale and ling'ring Jest
⟨Still rise the long tran⟩
Perplex the fawning Neice and pamper'd Guest
⟨The dull Conjecture⟩   275
While growing hopes ⟨re⟩ scarce awe the gath'ring Sneer
            scarce a Legacy
[290] And ⟨Guests are brib'd⟩ can bribe to hear
            watchful
The ⟨treachrous G⟩ Guests still hint⟨s⟩ the last offence
The ⟨ruinous⟩ Daughter's insolence the Son's expence   280
Improve his heady rage with treach'rous skill
And mould his passions till they make his will.
      Unnumberd Maladies ⟨his⟩ each joint invade
Lay siege to life and press the dire blockade

But unextinguish'd Av'rice still remains   285
And dreaded losses aggravate his pains
He turns with anxious heart and cripled hands
His bonds of Debt, and Mortgages of Lands
Or views his Coffers with suspicious eyes   f. 14.
Unlocks his Gold and counts it till he dies.   290
　But grant, the virtues of a temp'rate prime
Bless with an age exempt from scorn or crime
An Age that melts in unperceived decay
And glides in modest innocence away
Whose peaceful day benevolence endears   295
Whose night congratulating Conscience cheers
　　　　　gen'ral
The ⟨common⟩ fav'rite as the gen'ral Friend
Such Age the is, and who could wish its end   [300]

　Yet evn on this her ⟨loa⟩ loads Misfortune flings
　　　press　　　　weary　　　　　　hanging
To ⟨loade⟩ the ⟨lingring⟩ Minutes ⟨weary⟩ wings   300
　　　　New Sorrow rises as the day returns
⟨Each passing day some cause of sorrow sends⟩
　　　　　　　Daughter mourns
A Sister Sickens or a ⟨Child offends⟩
Now kindred merit fills the mournful Bier
Now lacerated Friendship claims a tear
Year chases Year Decay persues decay   305
Still drops some Joy from withring life away
New forms She sees whom different views engage
　　　And lags superfluous on th' incumbred
⟨And chearless treads the desolated⟩ stage   [310]
Till pitying Nature signs the last release
And bids afflicted worth retire to peace   310
But few there are whom hours like these await   f. 15.
Who set unclouded in the Gulphs of Fate
　From Lydia's Monarch should the search descend
By Solon caution'd to regard his end
In Lifes last Scene what prodigies surprise   315
　　　Fears of the brave
⟨The Wise man's Follies⟩ and follies of the wise
From Marlbrough's eyes the Streams of dotage flow
And Swift expires a Driv'ler and a Show.

The teeming Mother anxious for her race
Begs for each Birth the fortune of a face   320
Yet Vane could tell what ills from Beauty spring
And Sedley curs'd the form that pleasd a King
Ye Nymphs of rosy lips and radiant eye
Whom pleasure keeps too busy to be wise
Whom joys in soft vicissitudes invite   325
By day the frolick and the dance by night
Who frown with vanity who smile ⟨by⟩ with art
[330] And ask the latest fashion of the Heart
    what rules your heedless charms shall save
What care ⟨*your charms from wretchedness*⟩
Each Nymph your rival and each youth your Slave   330
 n envious
A ⟨*Rivals*⟩ Breasts with certain Mischief glow
And slaves, the Maxim tells, are always foes.

f. 16. Against your Fame with Fondness Hate combines
The Rival batters, and the Lover mines
With distant voice neglected Virtue calls
Less heard and less the faint Remonstrance falls
Tir'd with contempt ⟨*She at*⟩ She quits the Slippry reign 335
[340] And Pride and Prudence take her seat in vain
     pass
In croud at once where none the ⟨*fort*⟩ defend
The harmless freedom and the private Friend
     by
The Guardians yield ⟨*with*⟩ force resistless plied
By Intrest Prudence and by Flatt'ry Pride   340
   falls betray'd despis'd distress'd
Her Beauty'⟨*s drops her pomp betray*⟩
346] And shout Infamy proclaims the rest

Where then shall Hope and fear their Objects find
    becalm
Must dull Suspense ⟨*still e*⟩ the stagnant Mind
Must helpless Man in ignorance sedate   345
[350] Swim darkling down the current of his fate
 Must no dislike
⟨*Enquirer cease*⟩ alarm no wishes rise
No cries attempt the mercies of the skies
⟨*Which Heavn may hear*⟩

Enquirer cease, petitions yet remain
Which Heavn may hear, nor deem Religion vain   350
For Blessing, raise the supplicating voice   f. 17.
But leave to Heavn the measure and the choice
Safe in his Pow'r whose eyes discern afar
The secret ambush of a Specious pray'r
Implore his aid, in his decisions rest,   355
And hope with humble confidence the best   [360]
Yet with the sense of sacred presence prest
    When strong
⟨If Aspirations⟩ Devotion fills thy glowing breast
    Pour
⟨Breat⟩ forth thy fervours for a ⟨Soul re⟩ mind
                healthful
Obedient Passions and a will resignd   360
    which scarce
For Love ⟨whose grasp Creation⟩ collective Man can fill,
For Patience Sov'reign o'er transmuted ill,
For Hope that panting for a happier seat
Thinks Death kind Nature's signal of Retreat
These goods for Man the laws of Heav'n ordain   365
These Goods he grants who grants the pow'r to gain   [370]
With these celestial Wisdom calms the mind
And makes the Happiness she do's not find   [372]

CONTRIBUTIONS TO
POEMS BY OTHERS

Johnson was liberal in his assistance, and his advice was often sought. His earliest substantial revision was of Samuel Madden's *Boulter's Monument*, published at Dublin and at London in 1745. He told Dr. Thomas Campbell, as Boswell records, that the poem was submitted to him for castigation and that he 'blotted a great many lines'. Madden acknowledged in his Postscript that 'some hundred lines have been pruned from it, that were not quite unpardonable'. He does not mention Johnson's help, which appears to have been confined to 'pruning'; but Johnson thought him 'very thankful', and 'very generous' in his gift of ten guineas (*Life*, ed. 1934, i. 318, 545). Mrs. Mary Masters is described by Boswell as 'the poetess, whose volumes he revised, and, it is said, illuminated here and there with a ray of his own genius'. She published two volumes, *Poems on Several Occasions*, 1733, and *Familiar Letters and Poems on Several Occasions*, 1755. In the former she acknowledges the assistance of a friend who saved her from grammatical mistakes, but its date is too early for this friend to have been Johnson, unless they had met in his Birmingham days, four years before he came to London; in the later volume search has been made in vain for Johnson's illumination, though, as 'Mr. Samuel Johnson, A.M., Author of the Rambler' appears among the subscribers, he may have had the opportunity of making a few corrections. (Cf. A. Sherbo, 'Two Notes on Johnson's Revisions', *Modern Language Review*, 1 (1955), 311–15.) Grainger submitted to him the second canto of *The Sugar Cane*, but he is known only to have condemned one line when the poem was read out in a hilarious company (Boswell, *Life*, 1934, ii. 453, 533). Mrs. Thrale translated at his desire the 'metres' in the *Consolations* of Boethius, and his revision was thorough (*ante*, pp. 169–77). He revised the poems of Miss Reynolds, and 'mended some bad rhymes' by rewriting whole couplets (*Miscellanies*, ii. 279, *post*, pp. 443–4). Others of whom he knew little, such as the Revd. William Tasker, took their chance of asking his opinion (*Life*, iii. 373).

His part in the poems or passages which follow was acknowledged by himself, or is otherwise established.

REVISION OF GEOFFREY WALMESLEY'S
LATIN TRANSLATION OF JOHN BYROM'S
'COLIN AND PHEBE'

The Gentleman's Magazine, February 1745, p. 102.

Attributed to Johnson by Dr. J. M. Osborn in *The Times Literary Supplement*, 9 October 1953, p. 652, on the evidence of a notebook belonging to

Stephen Barrett who collaborated with Johnson in improving Geoffrey Walmesley's Latin translation of John Byrom's poem. The distichs for which each was responsible are here marked as 'J' and 'B'.

Barrett's notebook reports that this poem was translated into Latin one day in February 1745:

'After yᵉ Cloth was remov'd, & we had drank a Glass or two of Wine; Cave opened his budget, "Here it is, Gentlemen, a very indifferent performance, but it is just of an exact length for my purpose; and yet if yᵉ will not brush it up for me, it can not appear." "Give it to Mr Barrett (says Johnson) he'll correct it for you in a minute." "Why no (say I) that I shall not undertake alone, but if Mr Johnson will take distic for distic with me (as I have half an hour to stay before I set out for home . . .) we will endeavʳ to make it just passable." This was in return for yᵉ Main-oeuvre of throwing it all on me; & as writing Latin verse was my forte, I thought I had thereby got my Master upon yᵉ hip. But how was I mistaken wⁿ . . . I found yᵗ he was as expeditious at it, as myself! "Very well!—then (says he) do you begin." "By no means! (added I) seniores priores" and threw him yᵉ paper cross yᵉ Table. He return'd it, in a moment; and so it passed from yᵉ one to yᵉ other, like a shuttlecock; Cave chuckling all yᵉ while to see it pass & repass, so rapidly.'

J: Traduxi, Aonides! placidas quam leniter horas,
  Dum mihi *Phœbe* aderat, blandula, grata comes.

B: Pectore (vix dicam) quot, quantaque gaudia sensi!
  Quis mage quam *Corydon* sorte beatus erat?

J: Eheu! hinc abiit numquam reditura puella,   5
  Atratis facies jam nova rebus adest.

B: Cur veris perit omnis honos? Cur gloria ruris?
  En! teneo! —Has veneres, hoc decus illa dedit.

J: Pascere oves, lusuque simul cum virgine tempus
  Fallere, vel somnos cespite inire leves,   10

B: Quam mihi jucundum! præsens dum nympha juvabat,
  Lætitia insanus quo rapiebar amans!

J: Nunc tamen, infelix! —quantum, heu! mutatus ab illo!
  Fervida quam tacita viscera bile tument!

B: Nympha abiit, fugitque simul mea sola voluptas;   15
  Cor! grave cor! luctus pondera ferre nequit.

J: Qui liquido lapsu tremulus fluitare solebat
  Rivulus, et placidis saxa lavare sonis,

B: Scis puer Idalie! arrisit modo nympha, placebat
  Curriculo hisce oculis, auribus hisce sono.   20

J: Hoc absente tamen, ripæ dum margine oberro,
  Increpo sic surdis jam truculentus aquis;

B: 'Quid salis unda jocosa? quid hæc mihi murmura volvis!
    Desine; neu lacrymis obstrepe, lympha, meis!'

J: Dum teneræ circum saltarent matribus agnæ,   25
    Dum mecum indoctos risit & illa choros,

B: 'Ludite vos, alacres!—Saturnia tempora!' dixi;
    Alma viget veris jam Cytherea comes.

J: Nunc dum prætereunt—'fugite hinc! pecus ite molestum!
    'Ite'—& gramineo vellera fasce peto.   30

B: Sistite! lascivæ, facit hæc lascivia tristem;
    Cura haud tristitiæ vos tenet ulla meæ.

J: Quam mihi fidus *Hylax* placuit, dum sæpe moveret
    Caudam, & blandiloquis solveret ora sonis!

B: Huc ades, O chare, inquit, amicule, læta, manuque   35
    Permulsit nivea, molliter, illa caput.

J: Nunc, dum blanditur, petulantia verba rependo,
    Et properat duri verbera ferre pedi.

B: Verbera plura manent,—nec *Hylax*, absente puella,
    Gaudeat, at mecum triste gemente, gemat.   40

J: Qualia, Dii! vidi, dum me mea nympha secuta est!
    Floribus et campis gratia quanta fuit!

B: Hinc virgulta juvant, et opacæ frondibus umbræ;
    Hinc rident segetes—et nemus inde viret.

J: Jam formosa abiit, jamque haec decus omne reliquit,   45
    Nec mihi jam, quondam quæ nituere, nitent.

B: Fallax nympha diu magicis me lusit ocellis:
    Vana mihi mentem cepit imago diu.

J: Indocili nobis resonabant carmine sylvæ,
    Dat philomela, simul turdus, alauda, modos.   50

B: Aura susurrabat zephyri, balantibus agnis,
    Dum strepit ad nostros læta cicada pedes.

J: Abscessit—volucrum, mira dulcedine, sensus,
    Quæ tetigere prius carmina, mœsta gravant.

B: Vox erat (experto jam credite) mellea nymphæ,   55
    Quæ liquidum, ante alias, carmen ad astra tulit.

J: Quid, rosa, mutatis soliis nunc arida palles;
   Purpureum violæ quid posuere decus?

B: Quid nec habent solitos languentia germina odores?
   Nec pratis idem est, qui fuit ante, color? 60

J: Æmula! fulsistis varios induta nitores,
   Pulchrum ut ferret onus pulchrior illa, sinu?

B: Dulce fuit vobis nostræ placuisse puellæ,
   Nec non marmoreo pectore dulce mori.

J: Quam lente incedit tempus! jam nympha redito; 65
   Uror qua Zephyri frigora blanda meant.

B: Quo quæram, ut gravidis liquefiam pondera pennis,
   Ignibus emissis, quos mihi nutrit amor?

J: Ducite, Dii! *Phœben*, rapidis volet ocius alis
   Tempus, &, adducta, segnius ire licet. 70

B: Horas, ah *Corydon*! nunquam prece flectis inani,
   Æquali semper labitur hora gradu.

J: O superi, superi, moveat si nostra querela,
   Dicite, quid misero nunc medicamen erit?

B: Excute, sanus eris, *Corydon*, fera vincula amoris. 75
   Exulet at talis pectore nympha meo?

J: Haud ita; Dii! charam (semel hoc rogo) ducite *Phœben*,
   Spes prope cum vita destituere meæ.

B: Quid faciam? aut miserere, mori aut me denique coges.
   Pulchra, mei memores, ora cavete, viri! 80

ON THE DEATH OF STEPHEN GREY

Anna Williams, *Miscellanies*, 1766, p. 42.

Johnson told Boswell that of Miss Williams's original poem only two lines
remained after his revision (*Life*, ii. 26). Malone in his annotated copy, now in
the Dyce Collection in the South Kensington Museum, suggested that they were
either the first couplet or the second.

Stephen Gray—so he spelled his name—contributed twenty-one papers
to *Philosophical Translations*, nine of them on electricity. From 1719 till his
death in 1736 he was a poor brother of the Charterhouse. See a memoir by
W. P. Courtney in *Notes and Queries*, x. vi. 161, 354 (1906).

Malone detected the hand of Johnson in two other poems in Miss Williams's *Miscellanies*—'The Excursion' and 'Reflections on a grave digging in Westminster Abbey'. Johnson's alterations in her 'Verses to Mr. Richardson, on his History of Sir Charles Grandison' (*Gentleman's Magazine*, 1754, p. 40) were not adopted in the reprint in the *Miscellanies*: see *Life*, 1934, ii. 479.

On the DEATH of
STEPHEN GREY, F.R.S.

The AUTHOR of
The Present DOCTRINE of ELECTRICITY*.

LONG hast thou born the burthen of the day,
 Thy task is ended, venerable GREY!
No more shall Art thy dext'rous hand require
To break the sleep of elemental fire;
To rouse the pow'rs that actuate Nature's frame,   5
The momentaneous shock, th' electrick flame,
The flame which first, weak pupil of thy lore,
I saw, condemn'd, alas! to see no more.

 Now, hoary Sage, pursue thy happy flight,
With swifter motion haste to purer light,   10
Where BACON waits with NEWTON and with BOYLE
To hail thy genius, and applaud thy toil;
Where intuition breaks through time and space,
And mocks experiment's successive race;
Sees tardy Science toil at Nature's laws,   15
And wonders how th' effect obscures the cause.

 Yet not to deep research or happy guess
Is ow'd the life of hope, the death of peace.
Unblest the man whom philosophick rage
Shall tempt to lose the Christian in the Sage;   20
Not Art but Goodness pour'd the sacred ray
That cheer'd the parting hour of humble GREY.

---

* The Publisher of this Miscellany, as she was assisting Mr. Grey in his experiments, was the first that observed and notified the emission of the electrical spark from a human body.

THE EXCURSION

Anna Williams, *Miscellanies*, 1766, p. 49.

Though Malone detected Johnson's hand in this long (176 lines) poem in praise of rural retirement its tenor is alien to his thinking. The alleged contribution (*Life*, ii. 26) was probably confined to a few stylistic changes and possibly the following closing lines (171–6); most of the rest of the poem would have qualified for his own description: 'a despicable effusion of pastoral; a composition in which all is unnatural, and yet nothing is new.'

The EXCURSION

> With serious joy th' enlighten'd soul
> Surveys a part, admires the whole;
> Nor always silently surveys,
> But, fir'd by gratitude to praise,
> In holy confidence is blest,
> And calmly waits eternal rest.

REFLECTIONS ON A GRAVE DIGGING IN WESTMINSTER ABBEY

Anna Williams, *Miscellanies*, 1766, p. 68.

Boswell detected Johnson's hand in this poem. It is unlikely that he would write so fully of the details of exhumed corpses. His horror and revulsion at the sight of bones was often displayed: in Raasay he refused to look at a heel-bone; at Inchkenneth he told Boswell that he could not have handled human bones, and he even expressed horror at the sight of whalebones set up as gateposts. He may have helped with the first twenty and the last ten lines. Mrs. Thrale wrote in her copy (now in the Lichfield Birthplace Museum) beside the last stanza: 'These Lines are Johnson's own.'

REFLECTIONS *On a Grave digging in Westminster Abbey*

> FATIGU'D with noisy crouds and pompous show,
> To gloomy isles, and scenes of death I go,
> Where mouldering trophies hang, while falling dust
> Confutes the warrior's hope, the proud man's trust.

Where marble statues bending seem to mourn,   5
And point to flattery on the sculptur'd urn;
Detain with useless praise the wand'ring eye,
To tell where learning, greatness, beauty lye.
These all the hapless state of mortals show,
The sad vicissitude of things below.   10

Reflection dwells on images like these,
And sober thought creeps on by slow degrees;
A solemn stilness purifies my breast,
Calms all my thought, and bids my passions rest;
In contemplation deep, I seem to see   15
What now I am, what shortly I shall be;
Till by the noise of the descending spade
From studious thought recall'd, I turn my head.
Behold the gaping earth, and view beneath
Thy boasted victories, resistless death.   20
The sable chest that holds the mouldering dust,
No longer able to retain its trust,
To pieces fall'n, displays the dismal scene,
And shews the loathsome sceleton within.
Behold that eyeless scull, with ghastly stare,   25
And learn to estimate your charms, ye Fair.
Here once the curious palate; here a tongue,
On which perhaps persuasive language hung;
Here once was plac'd the sound-discerning ear;
The seat of mem'ry and of judgment here;   30
Here low'r'd the scornful look, the haughty brow,
Alas! how alter'd, how neglected now?

10. *The sad vicissitude of things*: from Richard Gifford's poem 'Contemplation', 1753,
quoted by Johnson at Nairn on hearing a girl spinning and singing a Gaelic song in
the room above:

> Verse sweetens toil, however rude the sound.
> All at her work the village maiden sings;
> Nor, while she turns the giddy wheel around,
> Revolves the sad vicissitude of things.

(27 August 1773.) Johnson's memory was not exact (*Life*, v. 117–18).
The stanza was perhaps a favourite: it is quoted, with minor variations, in the
Dictionary under 'vicissitude' and 'wheel'.

13. *solemn stilness*: cf. Gray's 'Elegy', 6, 'And all the air a solemn stillness holds'.
15. *contemplation*: see note on l. 10 *ante*.

Now on the naked bones is left no trace,
Where every feature shew'd its proper grace;
Fragments of limbs disjointed strew the floor, 35
Scarce can the eye discern the form they wore;
These once with ligaments were firmly strung,
Their veins and arteries in order hung,
Each part adapted well, complete the whole,
A dwelling suited to th' ethereal soul. 40

This monitory vault awhile survey,
Ye great, ye rich, ye giddy, proud, or gay;
Not flatter'd beauty, nor commanding state,
Can shun the general lot, or baffle fate:
The shatter'd body's ruin to survive 45
Is sacred virtue's great prerogative,
A life well spent dispels the dreadful gloom,
And cheers the terrors of the dreary tomb;
The marble dome, the sculptur'd bust shall fail,
And virtue only over time prevail. 50

VERSES ADDRESSED TO
SAMUEL RICHARDSON

The Gentleman's Magazine, xxiv (January 1754), p. 40.
Anna Williams, *Miscellanies*, 1766, p. 31.

Boswell singled this poem out as one of the pieces in Anna Williams's collection 'which have evidently received additions from his superiour pen'. The existence of a separate quarto edition of the poem, doubtless printed by Richardson himself, in the Victoria and Albert Museum seemed to support Boswell's attribution as long as the annotations on it were believed to be in Johnson's hand. It is clear they are not his and the fact that the emendations they record do not recur in *Miscellanies*, 1766, in which Johnson undoubtedly had a significant share, nullifies their importance. Malone agreed with Boswell in detecting Johnson's hand in these verses in his copy of *Miscellanies*, now in the Dyce Collection (10617) in the Victoria and Albert Museum.

VERSES addressed to Mr. RICHARDSON
ON HIS
HISTORY of Sir CHARLES GRANDISON

LONG the loose wits of a degenerate age,
  Had fill'd with ribaldry the venal page,
Scorn'd all restraints of virtue and of shame,
And rais'd the titled prostitute to fame;
Their idle novels thus the public pest,   5
Effus'd their bane, and poison'd every breast.

  THOU, zealous friend of long insulted truth,
Didst first appear the guardian of our youth,
'Twas thine a juster lesson to impart,
And move the passions, but to mend the heart.   10
Bright PAMELA, in native beauty drest,
Then burst upon the world a welcome guest;
Each fair-one read, with emulation fir'd,
All joy'd to imitate what all admir'd.

  NOR here, great mind, thy moral labours end,   15
Through life's wide round successive works extend,
From tale to tale the mighty plan pursue,
And raise new scenes before the unwearied view.

  HERE, blest with mind, with fortune, and with face,
The virgin falls, but falls without disgrace;   20
Touch'd with the woes her suffering virtue felt,
The generous kindle, and the tender melt.
In distant times, when JONES and BOOTH are lost,
BRITANNIA her CLARISSA's name shall boast.

  YET take from grateful worlds the present wreath,   25
Nor owe thy garland to the hand of death;
Even now, not rocks nor waves thy fame can bound,
The Rhine's rude banks CLARISSA's worth resound;

3 and] or *GM*   10 And . . . but to . . .] To . . . and to . . . *GM*   16 Thro'
GM

---

  23. *Jones and Booth*: the heroes of Fielding's *Tom Jones* and *Amelia*. Johnson consistently praised Richardson at the expense of Fielding.

And Tuscan bards her mournful tale relate,
In groves where VIRGIL sung of DIDO's fate. 30

As where the Alps in awful grandeur rise,
And mix their hoary summits with the skies,
All NATURE's pow'r exhausted in the past
We think, but still the greatest is the last.

THUS every mind CLARISSA's tomes rever'd; 35
Great work of art, till GRANDISON appear'd.
The firm and kind, the daring and polite,
To form one character, in one unite;
So highly finish'd, and so well design'd,
It charms with ev'ry grace of ev'ry mind. 40

IN BYRON all the softer beauties shine,
But heavenly CLEMENTINA's worth be mine;
At her distress each maid shall drop a tear,
Each pious maid her firm resolve revere,
Deplore her woes, and emulate her soul, 45
And learn from her their passions to controul.

THUS, in each character, new beauties shine,
And fresh instruction flows in ev'ry line.

THOU sweet preceptor of the rising age,
Let still another work thy thoughts engage; 50
Proceed to teach, thy labours ne'er can tire,
Thou still must write, and we must still admire.

O long may bounteous nature bid thee live,
Good to bestow, and honour to receive;
And when at fate's mild call, replete with praise, 55
Thou goest to join the great of ancient days,
Thy dust shall emblematick shades embow'r,
The hero's laurel, and the maiden's flow'r.

28. The first German translation of *Clarissa* was published between 1748 and 1751.
29. The first Italian translation was not published until 1783–6, and so the reference must be to appreciative verses in praise of Richardson.
41. Harriet Byron is the beloved and eventually the wife of Sir Charles Grandison.
42. Clementina Porretti, an Italian lady, is at first engaged to Grandison.

THE TRAVELLER
OR A PROSPECT OF SOCIETY

When Goldsmith received the proofs of this poem,—which, as the headlines show, he intended to call *A Prospect of Society*,—he asked for Johnson's help. Johnson told Reynolds that to the best of his recollection he contributed not more than eighteen lines (Leslie and Taylor's *Reynolds*, ii. 458). In 1783 he was able to identify only nine of these for Boswell. On the title-page of his copy of the 'fifth' edition of the poem, now in the Hyde Collection, Boswell wrote this note:

'In Spring 1783 Dr. Johnson at my desire marked with a pencil the lines in this admirable Poem which he furnished viz. l. 18 on p. 23 [l. 420] and from the 3 line on the last page to the end except the last couplet but one. "These (he said) are all of which I can be sure."'

The title-page and the last page are reproduced in *The R. B. Adam Library*, vol. ii, before p. 19; cf. *Life*, ii. 6.

The single line is

> To stop too fearful, and too faint to go.

It took the place of Goldsmith's

> And faintly fainter, fainter seems to go.

Other changes are pointed out, but not said to be by Johnson, in Bertram Dobell's edition of the proofs of *A Prospect of Society*, 1902.

In 'Maloniana' (J. Prior, *Life of Malone*, 1860, pp. 413–14) Akenside is reported to have attributed lines 3–4 of *The Traveller* to Johnson; no reasons are offered.

> How small, of all that human hearts endure,
> That part which laws or kings can cause or cure.   430
> Still to ourselves in every place consign'd,
> Our own felicity we make or find:
> With secret course, which no loud storms annoy,
> Glides the smooth current of domestic joy.
> *The lifted ax, the agonizing wheel,*   435
> *Luke's iron crown, and Damien's bed of steel,*
> To men remote from power but rarely known,
> Leave reason, faith and conscience all our own.

THE DESERTED VILLAGE

'The four last lines were marked at my desire by Dr. Johnson spring 1783 as all that he wrote of this admirable Poem.' This note was written by Boswell on the last page of his copy of the 1777 reprint of the poem bound with the preceding copy of *The Traveller*, in the Hyde Collection. The reproduction of the page in *The R. B. Adam Library*, vol. ii, opposite p. 19, shows Johnson's mark. Cf. *Life*, ii. 7.

> That trade's proud empire hastes to swift decay,
> As ocean sweeps the labour'd mole away;
> While self dependent power can time defy,
> As rocks resist the billows and the sky.

SIR ELDRED OF THE BOWER

Early in January 1776 Johnson invited himself to drink tea with Hannah More in order that they might read together *Sir Eldred*, a legendary tale which she had just published along with *The Bleeding Rock*. She describes the evening in a letter written on the following day (? 6 January): 'Our tea was not over till nine, we then fell upon Sir Eldred: he read both poems through, suggested some little alterations in the first, and did me the honour to write one whole stanza; but in the Rock, he has not altered a word. Though only a tea visit, he stayed with us till twelve' (W. Roberts, *Memoirs of Hannah More*, 1834, i. 64).

In 1959 Mr. H. W. Liebert elaborated Johnson's contribution to this poem in his 'We Fell upon Sir Eldred' in *New Light on Johnson*, ed. F. W. Hilles, pp. 233–45, and argued that the following revisions of the first edition of 1776 which were published in the second in 1778 were attributable to him.

Part I

ii. Where gliding *Tay* her stream sends forth,
    To feed the neighbouring wood . . .

vi. And every deed of lofty worth
    Is but a claim for more.

viii. When *merit* raised the sufferer's name,
    He show'r'd his bounty *then*;
    And those who cou'd not prove that claim,
    He succour'd still as *men*.

Hannah More's original versions were as follows:

Part I.

ii. 2 feed] crown
vi. 2 claim] tax
viii. 2] He *doubly* served him *then*;
    4] He thought they still were *men*.

xi.   Yet if the passions storm'd his soul,
            By jealousy led on;
        The whirlwind rage disdain'd controul
            And bore his virtues down.

xviii. The birds their vernal notes repeat,
            And glad the thick'ning grove,
        And feather'd partners fondly greet
            With many a song of love;

xxxiii. For wisdom, by a father's care,
            Was found in every field.

xxxvii. While the sweet-scented rose shall last,
            And boast its fragrant power,
        When life's imperfect day is past,
            And beauty's shorter hour.

xl.   When sailing thro' the cloudless air,
            She sheds her silver light;

xli.   So BIRTHA shone!—But when she spoke
            The Muse herself was heard, . . .

xlv.   The virgin blush which spreads her cheek
            With Nature's purest dye,
        And all those dazzling beams which break
            Like Morning, from her eye.

xi.] Yet if distrust his thoughts engage,
            Or jealousy inspires,
        His bosom wild and boundless rage
            Inflames with all its fires:
xviii. 1 vernal] amorous
       2 thick'ning] vernal
       3 And] Their
xxxiii. 1 by] with
xxxvii.] While the sweet pink, and scented rose,
            In precious odours last;
        And when no more the colour glows,
            The sweetness is not past.
xl. 1 cloudless] liquid
    2] It pours its lambent light:
xli. 1 So] Such
xlv. 1 The virgin blush which spreads] The mountain breeze which paints
     3 those] the   beams] fires
     4 Like morning] Illustrious

xlvi.   And still his raptur'd eye pursued,
     And feasted on the sight.

xlix.   My scorn has oft the dart repell'd
     Which guileful beauty threw,
    But goodness heard, and grace beheld,
     Must every heart subdue.

l.   Quick on the ground her eyes were cast,
     And now as quickly rais'd:—
    Her father haply that way past,
     On whom she trembling gaz'd.

Part II

iii.   Together did we learn to bear
     The casque and ample shield; . . .

lxiv.   And dying BIRTHA close he found
     In brother's blood imbru'd.

THE VILLAGE

Crabbe asked Reynolds to submit *The Village* to Johnson, and on 4 March 1783 Johnson returned the manuscript to Reynolds with a letter expressing his 'great delight'. 'The alterations which I have made', he wrote, 'I do not require him to adopt, for my lines are, perhaps, not often better than his own; but he may take mine and his own together, and perhaps between them produce something better than either.' Boswell says in his Journal under 3 April 1783: 'I got the Poem home with me and copied all the Doctor's fragments.' His *Life* preserves

xlvi. 1 raptur'd] ravish'd
xlix.] *Beauty* with coldness I've beheld,
    And 'scap'd the shaft divine;
   But what my guardless heart can shield
    From *piety* like thine?
l.   She cast her mild eyes on the ground,
    And rais'd their beams as fast;
   And close her Father dear she found,
    Who haply that way past.

Part II.
iii. 2 casque] targe
lxiv. 2 imbru'd] inbued. Cf. p. 24 n. *ante.*

what is now known of Johnson's revision (ed. 1934, iv. 175, 509). Crabbe had
written:

> In fairer scenes, where peaceful pleasures spring,
> Tityrus, the pride of Mantuan swains, might sing:
> But charmed by him, or smitten with his views,
> Shall modern poets court the Mantuan muse?
> From Truth and Nature shall we widely stray,
> Where Fancy leads, or Virgil led the way?

He adopted Johnson's recast of the passage:

> On Mincio's banks, in Cæsar's bounteous reign,
> If Tityrus found the golden age again,
> Must sleepy bards the flattering dream prolong,
> Mechanick echoes of the Mantuan song?
> *From Truth and Nature shall we widely stray,*   5
> Where Virgil, not where Fancy, leads the way?

A MOTTO IN 'THE RAMBLER'

A notable instance of unacknowledged revision is provided by the motto to
No. 130 of *The Rambler*. Johnson ascribed the translation to the Edinburgh
Edition (see p. 128), but what he printed is not so much Elphinston's as his own.
The Edinburgh Edition gives this:

> No mist so blights the vernal meads,
> When summer's sultry heat succeeds,
> As one fell moment blasts the blow
> That gave the tender cheek to glow.
> Some beauty's snatch'd each day, each hour;
> For beauty is a fleeting flow'r:
> Then who that's wise, will e'er confide
> In such a frail, so poor a pride?

Enough of Elphinston's version was retained to account for the attribution. The
motto is from Seneca's *Hippolytus*, ll. 764–71.

> Not faster in the summer's ray
> The spring's frail beauty fades away,
> Than anguish and decay consume
> The smiling virgin's rosy bloom.
> Some beauty's snatch'd each day, each hour;
> For beauty is a fleeting flow'r:
> Then how can wisdom e'er confide
> In beauty's momentary pride?

LINES IN HAWKESWORTH'S TRAGEDY

Manuscript of a letter from R. Ryland to William Hayley, 7 April 1809, in the Hyde Collection.

The letter from Hawkesworth's nephew describes various of his uncle's literary papers, some of which were missing. Johnson had contemplated an edition of them in 1777, but no such edition ever appeared and the papers remain untraced. Ryland wrote:

'The greatest Loss is the Tragedy, which I really think was a very fine One—that Johnson thought so & Mrs Thrale, I have Evidence in his own hand writing—it was a perfectly fair Copy . . . the Scene was laid in Spain & among peruvian[1] Connections. The Story is much in my memory but no lines of it wholly except 2 which Johnson substituted at the Close of one of the Acts for a Couplet which did not please his Ear, without altering the sentiment . . .'

Mrs. Thrale thought it 'capital; if want of Probability in the story be excusable', and added that it was 'call'd the *Rival*'. (*Thraliana*, i. 328.)

> Thy mind which Voluntary doubts molest
> Asks but its own permission to be blest.

VERSES BY FRANCES REYNOLDS

Manuscript of Frances Reynolds's *Recollections* in the Hyde Collection. *Johnsonian Miscellanies*, ed. G. B. Hill, 1897, ii. 279–80.

The entry containing these verses is undated in the manuscript, but on 16 June 1780 Johnson wrote to Frances Reynolds, 'Do not, my Love, burn your papers. I have mended little but some bad rhymes. I thought them very pretty, and was moved in reading them.' (*Letters*, ed. Chapman, ii. 374, no. 682.) Birkbeck Hill noted that Johnson had soon wearied of the task of correction, for his changes were confined to the early lines. Of her poem Croker wrote that 'Johnson read it attentively, and made numerous corrections; but after all it is not worth much' (*Life*, 1848, p. 649 n.).

Frances Reynolds recorded Johnson's aid, and added that he had also 'honoured two more poems by the same Author with his corrections and inserted them in Mrs. Williams's collection of poems, without knowing who was the Author till many years after' (MS. Hyde, f. 40; *Johns. Misc.* ii. 279 n.). On the assumption of the identity of the signature 'Stella', A. T. Hazen attributed *Rasselas to Imlac* (pp. 97–101), and *An Ode* ('The man devoid of care and strife . . .', pp. 102–3) in Anna Williams's *Miscellanies*, to Frances Reynolds, but Malone in his copy (now in the Dyce Collection) attributed the former to 'Mrs.

---

[1] Miss R. Roberts acknowledged Hawkesworth's aid in correcting the proofs in the preface to her *The Peruvian Letters. Translated from the French. With an additional original volume*. London, 1774, p. v.

Greville'—Frances, the wife of Richard Fulke Greville (*Life*, iv. 535). The extent of Johnson's revision is not readily discoverable.

The verses recorded with his amendments are in two parts: the first of ten lines, the second a couplet. Frances Reynolds's original versions were:

> As late disconsolate in pensive mood,
> I sat revolving Life's vicissitude
> Oft sigh'd to think how Youth had pass'd away,
> And saw with sorrow Hopes diminish'd ray,
> In prospect view the dismal scene to come,
> Of gloomy age should Fate my Days prolong,
> Yet whilst I linger on the doubtful steep
> Where youth declining seems with age to meet
> Nature to her own Laws appears averse
> Still prompts resistance where there's no redress;
>
> Chears every sense the common air I breathe
> Each common bounty prompts to prayer and praise.

Johnson's alterations begin with the fifth line:

> View'd the dark scene with melancholy gaze
> Should Fate to helpless Age prolong my Days
> Yet whilst I linger in the middle way
> Where Life's high vigour verges to decay
> Sure Nature acts, I cry'd, by wondrous Laws
> She prompts resistance yet all hope withdraws.
>
> The springing grass, the circulating air
> Each common bounty prompts to praise and prayer.

POEMS OF DOUBTFUL AUTHORSHIP

ON 'THE GENTLEMAN'S MAGAZINE'

The Gentleman's Magazine, 1736, following title.

Nichols, in the Preface to the *General Index* to *The Gentleman's Magazine*, 1821, p. xiii, said that he believed these verses to be by Johnson. The verses are signed 'Rusticus'. In the 'Autobiography of Sylvanus Urban' in *The Gentleman's Magazine* for September 1856, p. 271 n., it was pointed out that the same signature is attached in 1735 and 1736 to several pieces, some of which are certainly not by Johnson. So far as is known, no verses by Johnson appeared in the *Magazine* before April 1738, but he had been in communication with Cave as early as 25 November 1734.

In Locupletissimum ornatissimumque SYL. URB. *Thesaurum.*

M ENSTRUA concinnat SYLVANUS, & ANNUA *Dona*,
Quantus ubique Lepos! quantus ubique Decor!
Apte antiqua novis miscentur, et utile dulci:
  PALLAS ubique docet; ridet ubique VENUS.
*Talis in æterno felix Vertumnus Olympo,   5
  Mille habet Ornatus, mille decenter habet.

  * Tibull., Lib. IV.

ON THE GIN-ACT

The Gentleman's Magazine, July 1736, p. 420.

In *The Genuine Works of William Hogarth*, 1808, i. 291 n., John Nichols gives these lines, with this introduction: 'The following verses on the Gin Act, in 1736, I have reason to think were the production of Dr. Johnson.' In the absence of Nichols's reasons they must be placed among the doubtful poems. They are signed 'Ardelio'.

P ENSILIBUS fusis, cyatho comitata supremo,
Terribili fremitu stridula mœret anus.
O longum, formosa, vale, mihi vita decusque,
  Fida comes mensæ, fida comesque tori!

Eheu! quam longo tecum consumerer ævo!   5
  *Heu! quam tristitiæ dulce lenimen eras!
Æternum direpta mihi! sed quid moror istis?
  Stat: fixum est: nequeunt jam revocare preces.
I, quoniam sic fata vocant: liceat mihi tantum
  Vivere, te viva, te moriente, mori.   10
                    * Ovid.

VENUS IN ARMOUR

The Gentleman's Magazine, April 1738, p. 214.

   This unsigned Latin epigram was attributed to Johnson in the 'Autobiography
of Sylvanus Urban' in *The Gentleman's Magazine* for September 1856, p. 272,
but no reasons were given. Whether the translation was also attributed to Johnson
is not clear.

Epigramma

ARMATAM *Pallas Venerem* conspexit, et eia
  Nunc age, certamen nunc ineamus, ait;
Dulce *Venus* ridens, lorica nil opus, inquit,
  Vincere te potui nuda, quid arma geram?

Englished

VENUS in armour *Pallas* chanc'd to view,
  And dar'd her much th' old quarrel to renew;
Love's queen reply'd, and smil'd a world of charms,
Naked I conquer'd you, what need of arms?

FROM 'THE SONG OF SOLOMON'

The Gentleman's Magazine, April 1738, p. 215.

   This unsigned poem was attributed to Johnson in the 'Autobiography of
Sylvanus Urban' in *The Gentleman's Magazine* for September 1856, p. 272, but
no reasons were given.

Ex Cantico Solomonis

SURGE, soror dilecta, mihi lux, gaudia, vita;
    Haud mora, surge, soror!
Aspice, diffugiunt ignavæ frigora brumæ;
    Ver geniale venit.
Turbidus imber abest; mittit rosa roscida gemmas,   5
    Sole fovente, suas.
Veris, io! venit alma dies! *Philomela* canorum
    Fundit ab ore melos,
Aeriæque columbæ, dantes oscula, jungunt
    Oribus ora suis.   10
Jam teneros fructus detrudit lactea ficus
    Arboreasque comas;
Munera luxurians dat pampinus, et generoso
    Subrubet uva mero.
Suaviter exhalant violaria grata, *Sabæo*   15
    Spirat odore botrus.
Huc, soror alma, veni! pernicibus ocyor *Euris*
    Huc, soror alma, veni!

THE LOGICAL WAREHOUSE

The Gentleman's Magazine, May 1738, p. 271.

This epigram was said to be by Johnson in the 'Autobiography of Sylvanus Urban' in *The Gentleman's Magazine*, September 1856, p. 272, but no reasons were given. It is signed 'Philologus'.

THE

LOGICAL WAREHOUSE:

Occasioned by an Auctioneer's *having the Groundfloor of the Oratory in* Lincoln's-Inn-Fields.

DISSIMILI domus una duos tenet arte tumentes;
    Præcones ambo, Nummus utrique Deus.
Quæris, Quis prior est fama meritisve; superna
    Cui pars verbosæ, vel datur ima, domus?
Supra *Præco Dei*—strepit infra *Præco Bonorum*:   5
    HIC Bona queis opus est venditat, ILLE Sonum.

ON THOMAS BIRCH

The Gentleman's Magazine, January 1739, p. 4.

This Latin paraphrase of Johnson's Greek epigram on Dr. Birch (*ante*, p. 84) was hesitatingly ascribed to Johnson by Croker, *Life*, 1831, i. 110, on the ground that Johnson had made a similar paraphrase of his Greek epigram on Eliza. Croker was followed in the 'Autobiography of Sylvanus Urban' in *The Gentleman's Magazine*, September 1856, p. 275, where no doubt is suggested.

In BIRCHIUM

ARTE nova, raraque fide perscripserat ausus
   Birchius egregius, claraque gesta virum.
Hunc oculis Veri Fautrix lustravit acutis,
   Et placido tandem hæc edidit ore, Dea:
'Perge modo, atque tuas olim post funera laudes   5
   'Qui scribat meritas, Birchius alter erit.'

TRANSLATION OF A WELCH EPITAPH ON PRINCE MADOC

The Gentleman's Magazine, October 1740, p. 519.
The St. James's Chronicle, 26 May 1787.
The European Magazine, June 1787, p. 451.
Works, 1788, xiv. 546.
Works, 1823, i. 415.

The original epitaph—found in Sir Thomas Herbert's *Travels*, 1638, p. 360 —was printed in *The Gentleman's Magazine* for March 1740, p. 105, and an English translation sent in by 'Riverius' was printed in August, p. 409. The Latin was given this editorial introduction: 'As we have never been favour'd with the *Latin* translation of the remarkable *Welch* epitaph [mentioned by 'Riverius'] . . . we insert the following, which has lain by us some time.'

The Latin translation, signed 'I', was said to be 'clearly Johnson's' by John Nichols in an editorial note in the *Magazine* for May 1787, p. 441.

In the *European Magazine* edited by Isaac Reed it was appended to the Latin and English versions of the Epilogue to the *Carmen Seculare* (pp. 218–19 *ante*) 'Written by Doctor Johnson', and described as 'By the Same'. Evidently Reed had no doubts and since he was almost certainly the editor of *Works*, 1788, xiv, he made the same attribution on two distinct occasions.

INCLYTUS hic hæres magni requiescit *Oeni*,
   Confessus tantum mente manuque patrem;
Servilem tuti cultum contempsit agelli,
   Et petiit terras per freta longa novas.

ON LORD LOVAT'S EXECUTION

The Gentleman's Magazine, April 1747, p. 194.
Boswell, *Life*, 1791, i. 97 (1934, i. 180).

Johnson repeated these verses 'with great energy' at Ullinish on 21 September 1773 (*Boswell's Journal*, ed. Pottle and Bennett, p. 197; *Life*, i. 180). Boswell, who quotes them in the *Life*, seems to have been inclined to think that they were by Johnson, but admits that he had no authority to say that they were his. He adds that 'one of the best critics of our age' had suggested to him 'that "the word *indifferently* being used in the sense of *without concern*", and being also very unpoetical, renders it improbable that they should have been his composition'. But one of the meanings of the word given in the *Dictionary* is 'in a neutral state; without wish or aversion'; and Shakespeare's *Julius Cæsar*, I. ii. 87 is quoted as an example. (This casts doubt on the identification of the critic with Malone.) That Johnson was able to repeat these verses some twenty-six years after their appearance in *The Gentleman's Magazine* may suggest that he wrote them; but, in view of his remarkable memory, additional evidence is required before they can be definitely assigned to him. The question still remains as Boswell left it. The attribution was again made in *The Gentleman's Magazine*, lxiv (July 1794), pp. 623–5, by 'Protoplastides'. See also lxv (January 1795), pp. 6–8.

Simon Fraser, twelfth Baron Lovat, was beheaded on Tower Hill on 9 April 1747, at the age of eighty. The number of *The Gentleman's Magazine* containing the verses begins with an 'Account of the Behaviour and Execution of the late Ld Lovat, and some further particulars of his Life' in which Croker found 'strong internal evidence, both in matter and manner, of having been written by Johnson'. He added, 'The interest which he took in this transaction may have fixed in his memory the lines on Lord Lovat, which certainly do not resemble his own style' (*Life*, 1848, p. 55).

The Earl of Kilmarnock and Lord Balmerino were executed on Tower Hill on 18 August 1746, and Charles Radcliffe, titular Earl of Derwentwater, on 8 December, all for participating in the Jacobite Rebellion. See *The Gentleman's Magazine*, 1746, pp. 391, 666, 676. Balmerino is pronounced Balmĕr′ino (locally Bamir′nie).

On Lord LOVAT's Execution

PITY'D by *gentle minds* KILMARNOCK dy'd;
The *brave*, BALMERINO, were on thy side;
RADCLIFFE, unhappy in his crimes of youth,
Steady in what he still mistook for truth,
Beheld his death so decently unmov'd,   5
The *soft* lamented, and the *brave* approv'd.

But LOVAT's end indiff'rently we view,
True to no *king*, to no *religion* true:
No *fair* forgets the *ruin* he has done;
No *child* laments the *tyrant* of his *son*;   10
No *tory* pities, thinking what he *was*;
No *whig* compassions, for he *left the cause*;
The *brave* regret not, for he was not brave;
The *honest* mourn not, knowing him a *knave*.

A SONG

The Gentleman's Magazine, June 1747, p. 290.
Pearch, *Collection of Poems*, 1770, iii. 245; 1775, iii. 243; 1783, iii. 245.
The Charmer, Edinburgh, 1782, ii. 207.
Poetical Works, 1785, p. 163.
Works, 1787, xi. 362.

This poem was first attributed to Johnson in Pearch's *Collection*, the authority
of which is not beyond question. There is some reason, however, for believing
that this collection was edited by Isaac Reed, a reliable and indefatigable literary
antiquary who was also a friend of Johnson. (See *ante*, p. xv n. 3.)

A Song

NOT the soft sighs of vernal gales,
   The fragrance of the flow'ry vales,
The murmurs of the crystal rill,
The vocal grove, the verdant hill;
Not all their charms, tho' all unite,   5
Can touch my bosom with delight.

Not all the gems on *India*'s shore,
Not all *Peru*'s unbounded store,
Not all the pow'r, nor all the fame
That heroes, kings, or poets claim,   10
Nor knowledge, which the learn'd approve,
To form one wish my soul can move.

Yet nature's charms allure my eyes,
And knowledge, wealth and fame I prize;

7 end] fate *Boswell*

Fame, wealth and knowledge I obtain,   15
Nor seek I nature's charms in vain:
In lovely *Stella* all combine,
And, lovely *Stella!* thou art mine.

THE NATURAL BEAUTY

The Gentleman's Magazine, February 1748, p. 89.
The Scots Magazine, February 1748, p. 83.
Pearch, *Collection of Poems*, 1770, iii. 247.
Poetical Works, 1785, p. 165.
Works, 1787, xi. 359.

This poem was attributed to Johnson in Pearch's *Collection*, but not reprinted in it in 1775. The octosyllabic couplets recall Johnson's translation
from Anacreon.

THE
NATURAL BEAUTY

To STELLA

WHETHER *Stella*'s eyes are found
      Fix'd on earth, or glancing round,
If her face with pleasure glow,
If she sigh at others woe,
If her easy air express   5
Conscious worth, or soft distress,
Stella's eyes, and air, and face
Charm with undiminish'd grace.

If on her we see display'd
Pendant gems and rich brocade;   10
If her chintz, with less expence,
Flows in easy negligence,
Still she lights the constant flame,
Still her charms appear the same.
If she strikes the vocal strings,   15
If she's silent, speaks, or sings,
If she sit, or if she move,
Still we love, and still approve.

13 constant] conscious *Pearch, 1785, 1787.*

Vain the casual transient glance,
Which alone can please by chance,   20
Beauty, which depends on art,
Changing with the changing heart,
Which demands the toilet's aid,
Pendant gems, and rich brocade!
I those charms alone can prize,   25
Which from constant nature rise,
Which nor circumstance, nor dress
E'er can make or more or less.

AN EVENING ODE

The Gentleman's Magazine, January 1750, p. 38, and
The Gentleman's Magazine, September 1754, p. 428.
The Scots Magazine, September 1754, p. 425.
Fawkes and Woty, *The Poetical Calendar*, 1763 [2nd ed. 1764], ix. 11.
Pearch, *Collection of Poems*, 1770, iii. 246; 1775, iii. 244; 1783, iii. 246.
The Charmer, Edinburgh, 1782, ii. 206.
Poetical Works, 1785, p. 164.
Works, 1787, xi. 358.

Pearch's *Collection* is again the earliest authority for Johnson's authorship.
An engraved song sheet entitled 'EVENING. A favorite BALLAD by Haydn,
The WORDS by Dr. Johnson. DUBLIN. Published by E. RHAMES, at her MUSICAL
CIRCULATING LIBRARY, N? 16, Exchange Street' is undated [*Works*, vi (Yale ed.
1964), 369 suggests *c.* 1790; but there are perhaps different versions]. It exhibits
minor textual variants and omits lines 5–6 and 21–22.

AN
EVENING ODE

To STELLA

EV'NING now, from purple wings,
Sheds the grateful gifts she brings;
Brilliant drops bedeck the mead,
Cooling breezes shake the reed;

Title] An Evening Ode to Delia. *GM '54, Scots Mag., 1763*   1 from] with *Song*
sheet   3 Pearly *Song sheet*

Shake the reed, and curl the stream,   5
Silver'd o'er with *Cynthia*'s beam.
Near, the chequer'd, lonely grove
Hears, and keeps thy secrets, Love.—
Stella! thither let us stray,
Lightly o'er the dewy way;   10
Phœbus drives his burning car
Hence, my lovely *Stella*, far;
In his stead, the Queen of Night
Round us pours a lambent light;
Light that serves but just to show   15
Breasts that beat, and cheeks that glow.
Let us now, in whisper'd joy,
Ev'ning's silent hours employ;
Silence, best, and conscious shades
Please the hearts that Love invades;   20
Other pleasures give them pain,
Lovers all but Love disdain.

THE VANITY OF WEALTH

The Gentleman's Magazine, February 1750, p. 85.
The Scots Magazine, February 1750, p. 86.
Pearch, *Collection of Poems*, 1770, iii. 249; 1775, iii. 245; 1783, iii. 247.
Poetical Works, 1785, p. 166.
Works, 1787, xi. 360.

The subject is more Johnsonian than that of the previous piece (it owes something to Horace, *Odes* II. xviii), but the attribution again rests only on the authority of Pearch's *Collection*.

8 Cupid Oh approve our Love *Song sheet*   9, 12 *Stella*] Delia *GM '54, Scots Mag., 1763*   9 Thither, Delia, *GM '54, SM, 1763*   14 Round us pours] Sheds around *GM '54, SM, 1763*   15 serves] seems *1785, 1787*   17 now] there *GM '54, SM, 1763*   18 Ev'ning's] All the *GM '54, SM, 1763* 19 conscious] dusky *GM '54, SM, 1763*   20 heart *GM '54, SM, 1763* 21–2 Other passions then at rest, Love possesses all the breast *GM '54, SM, 1763*.

THE
VANITY of WEALTH

An ODE

To a Friend

No more thus brooding o'er yon heap,
  With Av'rice painful vigils keep.
Still unenjoy'd the present store,
Still endless sighs are breath'd for more.
O! quit the shadow, catch the prize,   5
Which not all *India*'s treasure buys!
  To purchase heav'n, has gold the pow'r?
Can gold remove the mortal hour?
In life, can *Love* be bought with gold?
Are *Friendship*'s pleasures to be sold?   10
No—all that's worth a wish, a thought,
Fair *Virtue* gives, unbrib'd, unbought.
Cease, then, on trash thy hopes to bind,
Let nobler views engage thy mind.
  With *Science* tread the wond'rous way,   15
Or learn the *Muse*'s moral lay;
In social hours indulge thy soul,
Where *Mirth* and *Temp'rance* mix the bowl.
To virtuous *Love* resign thy breast,
And be, by blessing *Beauty*, blest.   20
  Thus taste the feast by Nature spread,
Ere Youth and all its joys are fled;
Come, taste with me the balm of life,
Secure from pomp, and wealth, and strife.
I boast whate'er for man was meant,   25
In health, and *Stella*, and content:
And scorn, oh! let the scorn be thine!
Mere things of clay, that dig the mine.

VERSES IN 'THE IDLER'

The Universal Chronicle, 27 January 1759, p. [25].
The Idler, 1761, 1767, 1783, i. 229; (Dublin) 1762, p. 124.
Works, 1787, viii. 163 (Yale ed. 1963, ii. 128; vi (1964), 387).

These lines introduced the original No. 42 of *The Idler* (renumbered 41 in the collected editions). The verses are unattributed except by the editor, F. P. Walesby, of the 'Oxford' edition of Johnson's *Works*, 1825, iv. 270, who named Ovid as the author; but the lines are not in Ovid, and the Yale editors attributed them to Johnson himself. The essay was published on 27 January 1759, and was given (in 1761) the title 'On the Death of a Friend'.

Sarah Johnson died in her ninetieth year on 20/1 January 1759; it would have been entirely characteristic of Johnson to express his feelings in Latin verse. The Dublin edition of *The Idler* (1762) supplied a verse translation.

> Whoe'er bewails the wretched poets doom,
> And sheds a tear of pity on his tomb;
> May he no more of sorrow taste, or weep;
> Calm be his life, his death a pleasing sleep.

> AT tu quisquis eris, miseri qui cruda poetæ
> Credideris fletu funera digna tuo,
> Hæc postrema tibi sit flendi causa, fluatque
> Lenis inoffenso vitaque morsque gradu.

THE HAPPY LIFE

Anna Williams, *Miscellanies*, 1766, p. 18.

Boswell attributed this poem to Johnson on the basis of internal evidence (*Life*, ii. 25), and Malone marked it as Johnson's in his copy of Miss Williams's book.

The theme was one of Johnson's favourites; but some lines are at variance with his usual style. It may be that they remain from a poem which was written by Miss Williams and, like her poem *On the Death of Stephen Grey* in the same volume, underwent his thorough revision. The French motto supports the view that, at most, he only revised the poem.

2 tuo] tua *U.Chron.*

THE
HAPPY LIFE

Las d'esperer, et de me plaindre
De l'amour des Grands et de sort,
C'est ici que j'attends la mort,
Sans la desirer ou la craindre.   St. Amand.[1]

THRICE happy they, who in an humble state
    Contented live, and aim not to be great;
Whose life not sunk in sloth is free from care,
Nor tost by change, nor stagnant in despair;
Who chearfully receive each mercy given,   5
And bless the lib'ral hand of bounteous Heaven;
Who with wise authors pass the instructive day,
And wonder how the moments stole away;
Who gently taught by calm experience find
No riches equal to a well form'd mind;   10
Who not retir'd beyond the sight of life,
Behold its weary cares, its noisy strife;
And safe in virtue's philosophick cell,
Content with thinking right, and acting well,
Mark rashness sporting on perdition's brink,   15
And see the turrets of ambition sink;
Of life without a pang dissolve the tie,
In peace decay, with resignation die;
Breathe out the vital flame in humble trust,
And mingle blameless with their native dust.   20

TRANSLATION OF VERSES BY CRASHAW

Transcript, *c.* 1775, by or for Thomas Percy (Bodleian Library: Percy 87).

In the first three editions of the *Dictionary* Johnson quoted under 'Curtain',
'Peace', and 'Sleep' the last ten lines of Crashaw's 'Epitaph upon Husband and
Wife, which died, and were buried together'. This translation of the last eight
lines, with the heading 'Part of a Latin translation of Crashaw's Verses under
the word peace in the English Dict.', is written on a fly-leaf of a collection of
some of Johnson's pieces formed about 1765 by Thomas Percy (*Irene*, 1754;

----

[1] The quatrain is not in the collected works of St. Amant.

London and *The Vanity of Human Wishes*, extracted from Dodsley's *Collection*, 1765; 'The Vision of Theodore' from *The Grand Magazine of Magazines*, 1750, &c.). On the preceding fly-leaf Percy drew up, between 1772 and 1775, a list of other publications by Johnson;[1] and immediately below the translation from Crashaw is written the translation of Pope's verses on his Grotto (pp. 92–3). The inclusion of the translation from Crashaw in these surroundings indicates that Percy believed it to be by Johnson.

INNOCUA hic membris permistas membra columbas
  Supremis junxit nexibus arctus amor.
Hic jaceant; donec Nox transeat horrida nimbis,
  Et cortina novum det revoluta diem!
Tunc alacres demum surgent, et crastinus ortus
  Æternum Æternâ Luce juvabit opus!

EPIGRAM ON SIR THOMAS MORE
ERASMUS, AND MICYLLUS

Manuscript, British Museum, Add. MS. 12070.
Diary of a Journey into North Wales, in the year 1774, ed. R. Duppa, 1816, p. 17.

This Greek distich occurs in Johnson's Diary of his Welsh tour in a right-hand column, opposite the entry in the left-hand column for 15 March 1774, and appears to be unrelated to the context. Johnson wrote ἦρεν [i.e. ᾗρεν] in front of εἶλεν, as if doubtful which word to use, and this may be cited as evidence that the couplet was composed by him; but it is equally good evidence of imperfect memory. No other reference to Micyllus has been found in the whole body of Johnson's work. But the editors have also failed to find this couplet among the considerable quantity of verse written in praise of the learning of Micyllus (Jacob Moltzer, 1503–88).

Τὸ πρῶτον Μῶρος, τὸ δὲ δεύτερον εἶλεν Ἐρασμός,
  Τὸ τρίτον ἐκ Μουσῶν στέμμα Μίκυλλος ἔχει.

VERSES WRITTEN AT CALAIS

Transcript deriving from Frederick Hendriks, in Cornell University Library.
Notes and Queries, 25 April 1891, VII. xi. 329.

The poem was published in *Notes and Queries* by Frederick Hendriks, who wrote that the manuscript 'although unsigned, seems in the autograph of

---

[1] The Bodleian list is shorter than that sent to Boswell in May 1772 (Waingrow, *Correspondence*, pp. 5–8) but varies in some details so that it is not obviously a preparatory draft.

Johnson. At the end are the words, "From Mr. Langton", in the handwriting of Boswell.' The manuscript is not mentioned in Sotheby's catalogue of the Hendriks Sale on 11 and 12 November 1909, and Mr. Hendriks's son has been unable to trace it. An album of autographs collected by Hendriks was lot 208 at Messrs. Puttick and Simpson's, 29 January 1914. It remains untraced. If the poem is Johnson's, the explanation why Langton did not print it with the others that he edited in 1787 may be that the manuscript came into his possession after that date. The Cornell transcript was sometime owned by Thomas Caldecott.

Johnson reached Calais with the Thrales on 10 November 1775, on his return from his only visit to France, and crossed with them to Dover next morning. 'Verses left at the White-Lion, Calais, supposed to be written by Mrs. Piozzi', are printed in *The European Magazine* for May 1787, p. 370. They are on much the same subject. But Mrs. Thrale's Journal shows that, though the sea was rough, the crossing was not delayed. The title is suspicious; the verses were certainly not written by Johnson on a window. Mrs. Thrale's silence is also suspicious; had she known of the verses, she would have claimed a copy of them, and could hardly have failed, if not to print them, at least to allude to them somewhere.

Verses wrote on a Window of an Inn at Calais

EURE veni.   Sua jamdudum exoptata morantur
Flamina; Te poscit Votis Precibusque Viator
Impatiens, qui longa moræ fastidia sensit.
Interea, ad curvas descendens Littoris oras,
Prospicit in Patriam, atque avidis exhaurit Ocellis,   5
Nec dulci faciem de Littore dimovet unquam:
Illic Dubrenses in Cœlum assurgere Colles
Aspicit, excelsamque Arcem, grandesque Ruinas,
Et latè ingentes Scopulorum albescere tractus:
Nequicquam; videt hæc, nec fas attingere visa;   10
Obstat Hyems inimica, et Vis contraria Venti.

TRANSLATION FROM CALLIMACHUS

A Letter to Samuel Johnson, L.L.D. on the Subject of A Future State, by John Taylor, L.L.D., 1787, pp. 11–12.

The substance and the larger part of the composition of this *Letter* were first attributed to Johnson by R. W. Chapman (*Review of English Studies*, ii (1926), 338–9); J. H. Hagstrum (*Modern Philology*, xl (1943), 255–6) and J. Gray (*Johnson's Sermons*, Oxford 1972, pp. 29 ff.) concur. It is unlikely that Taylor was completely incapable of quoting and translating Callimachus, but the possibility remains that Johnson was responsible. This version in the *Letter* is original to that publication.

There is no copy of Callimachus reported in the sale catalogue of Johnson's library. Langton recorded only one comment and that a disparagement, but it was a reference to the Causes rather than to the Hymns or the Epigrams (*Life*, iv. 2).

The 25th Epigram of Callimachus was included in the *Greek Anthology* (vii. 471) whence Johnson translated it into Latin (p. 244 *ante*). The reading of the last word of line 2 of the Greek implies that this version was not taken from the *Anthology* but rather from some edition of Callimachus' works.

Taylor's prefatory note to the *Letter* refers to Johnson's *Prayers and Meditations* for 14 October 1781 for the period of this work, which was therefore mainly composed at Ashbourne. (*Life*, iii. 296 n. 2; *Works*, i (1958), 310–11).

Translation of Epigram XXV of Callimachus

Εἴπας, "Ηλιε χαῖρε, Κλεόμβροτος Ὠμβρακιώτης
"Ηλατ᾽ ἀφ᾽ ὑψηλοῦ τείχεος εἰς Ἀΐδην,
Ἄξιον οὐδὲν ἰδὼν θανάτου κακόν, ἀλλὰ Πλάτωνος
Ἕν τὸ περὶ ψυχῆς γράμμ᾽ ἀναλεξάμενος.

2 Ἀΐδαν *Greek Anthology*.

Cleombrotus exclaim'd, 'Farewell, O light!'
From the high tow'r then plung'd to Stygian night,
No ills he felt that urg'd the desp'rate thought,
But wish'd to realize what Plato taught.

POEMS WRONGLY ATTRIBUTED TO JOHNSON

EPITAPH ON A DUCK

Mrs. Piozzi included in her *Anecdotes* (p. 11) the 'epitaph upon the duck he killed by treading on it at five years old', and described it as 'a striking example of early expansion of mind, and knowledge of language':

> Here lies poor duck
> That Samuel Johnson trod on;
> If it had liv'd it had been good luck,
> For it would have been an odd one.

The story was first told by Anna Seward in *The Gentleman's Magazine*, lv (February 1785), p. 100.

Hawkins in his *Life* (p. 6) printed a different version, with a more circumstantial account: 'When he was about three years old, his mother had a brood of eleven ducklings, which she permitted him to call his own. It happened that in playing about he trod on and killed one of them, upon which, running to his mother, he, in great emotion, bid her write. Write, child? said she, what must I write? Why write, answered he, so:

> Here lies good Master Duck,
> That Samuel Johnson trod on,
> If 't had liv'd 'twould have been good luck,
> For then there'd been an odd one.

and she wrote accordingly.'

Boswell inquired into the truth of the story, and made these jottings in his *Note Book* (1925, pp. 3, 4): 'Miss Porter told me in his presence at Litchfield Monday 25 March 1776 . . . that his mother told her that when he was in petticoats he was walking by his father's side and carelessly trode upon a duck one of thirteen and killed it. So then this duck it was said to him must be buried, and he must make an epitaph for it. Upon which he made these lines

> Under this stone lyes Mr Duck
> Whom Samuel Johnson trode on
> He might have liv'd if he had luck;
> But then he'd been an odd one.

Dr. Johnson said that his Father made one half of this epitaph. That he was a foolish old man, that is to say was foolish in talking of his children. But I trust to his mother's relation of what happened in his childhood rather than to his own recollection; and Miss Porter assured him in my presence upon his mother's authority that he had made this epitaph himself. But he assures me 21 Septr. 1777 that he remembers his Father's making it. So I am convinced.'

These notes are the basis of what Boswell says in the *Life* (i. 40), where he rejects the epitaph, but gives a slightly different version of it—a composite version founded partly on those of Hawkins and Mrs. Piozzi.

TRANSLATION OF LORD HERVEY'S EPITAPH ON QUEEN CAROLINE

In his *Young Samuel Johnson* (1955), p. 183, Professor J. L. Clifford suggested that Johnson helped Henry Hervey Aston to translate the Latin epitaph on Queen Caroline by his brother John, Lord Hervey. The Queen died on 20 November 1737, and the translation is mentioned by his father Lord Bristol in a letter to Lord Hervey on 12 June 1738:

'may you not modestly urge the zealous affection he [i.e. Henry Hervey] so early discovered to the memory of that truly great woman and your particular friend and patroness, (and for which I loved her also) the late Queen, by attempting, and not without success, an imitation of your Latin epitaph in English Verse.' (*Suffolk Green Books*: Letter Book of John Hervey, first Earl of Bristol, 1894, ii. 1081.)

The Yale editors (*Works*, vi (Yale ed. 1964), 362–5) doubted Johnson's part in the translation but published a modernized text from a manuscript which they allege to be in the British Museum. There is a manuscript copy docketed 'J. M. W. Scrip. 1769' in the Bodleian (MS. Add. A. 190) from which a limited edition was printed in the Bibliography Room at the Bodleian Library in 1968.

On stylistic grounds there is nothing to associate the piece with Johnson, who was composing his *London* about this time, and it is hard to see him contributing to some bad verses in memory of a Queen who had long favoured Walpole, at that time regarded with deep hostility by Johnson. Although the topic was occasional, Hervey was a friend, anonymity was assured, and the result never published, this was a period of Johnson's life when his political attitudes were strong and uncompromising. (See *Life*, i. 164 and D. J. Greene, *The Politics of Samuel Johnson* (1960), pp. 81–111.)

TO A YOUNG LADY EMBROIDERING

These verses (beginning 'Arachne once, ill-fated Maid') were printed in *The St. James's Chronicle* for 26 May 1787 as 'by Dr. Johnson', and followed the version in *The Gentleman's Magazine* for September 1740, p. 464, where the signature is 'G'. They were written by David Garrick. They were included as by 'D. G.' in Dodsley's *Collection*, 1748, iii. 238, and in Garrick's *Poetical Works*, 1785, ii. 502, but with the title 'Upon a Lady's Embroidery', and with new readings in the first of the two stanzas.

EPITAPH ON SAVAGE

In the undated letter in which Johnson told Cave that he was ready to begin the Life of Savage (who died 1 August 1743) there is a reference to an inscription: 'I have no notion of having any thing for the Inscription. I hope you don't think I kept it to extort a price. I could think of nothing, till to-day.' Hill hazarded the suggestion that it might perhaps be the 'Epitaph on the late R—d S—e, Esq.' (beginning 'Whom *Phœbus* favour'd') published in *The Gentleman's Magazine* for September 1743, p. 490; but the suggestion is untenable in view of the quality of the verse. The inscription may have had nothing to do with Savage, nor need it have been in verse; and it may not have been intended for *The Gentleman's Magazine*.

AD ORNATISSIMAM PUELLAM

This poem (beginning 'Vanæ sit arti, sit studio modus, Formosa virgo') was printed in *The Gentleman's Magazine* for October 1743, p. 548, and reprinted in Popham's *Selecta Poemata Anglorum*, Bath, 1774, i. 81, unsigned, and in the second edition 1779, i. 67, where it is signed 'R. L.' It was correctly assigned to 'Dr. Lowth' in *The New Foundling Hospital for Wit*, 1773, vi. 46, in the heading of an English translation by William Duncombe. On the authority of James Bindley, Malone mistakenly ascribed it to Johnson in the third edition of Boswell's *Life*, and printed it in a footnote (1799, i. 130). Cf. Croker, *Life*, 1831, i. 134 n., and *Notes and Queries* 15 June 1872, IV. ix. 482.

EPILOGUE SPOKEN AT DRURY LANE, 1747

The Epilogue spoken on the first night of Garrick's management of Drury Lane theatre, 15 September 1747 (beginning 'Sweet doings truly! we are finely fobb'd'), was published along with Johnson's Prologue. It was attributed to Johnson in *The New Foundling Hospital for Wit*, 1771, iv. 99, and later editions. It was written by Garrick.

WINTER. AN ODE

(No more the *Morn*, with tepid rays,)

THE MIDSUMMER WISH

(O *Phoebus!* down the western sky,)

AUTUMN. AN ODE

(Alas! with swift and silent pace,)

These three poems were printed in *The Gentleman's Magazine* for December 1747, p. 588, May 1748, p. 232, and September 1748, p. 422. The first and third were included in Fawkes's and Woty's *The Poetical Calendar*, 1763: 'Winter' in No. 1, January, pp. 3–4, and 'Autumn' in No. 9, September, pp. 5–6. They were first ascribed to Johnson in Pearch's *Collection*, 1770, iii. 238–43, and since 1785 have appeared in all collections of Johnson's poetry. They were written by Hawkesworth.

His poems have never been collected, though Johnson in 1777 contemplated an edition of his works for the benefit of his widow (see Johnson's letter of 12 April 1777 to John Ryland, Hawkesworth's brother-in-law and cf. p. 443 *ante*). They were the subject of a letter in *The Gentleman's Magazine* for January 1779, p. 72:

'A writer in your Supplement, p. 664, having desired a list of Dr. Hawkesworth's detached pieces in your Magazine, he may depend on the following being correct, viz. in Vols. XLVI [XVI, 1746] and XLVII [XVII, 1747] all the Poems said in the Indexes to be *by Mr. Greville*. XLVIII [XVIII, 1748]. Midsummer Wish, p. 232; Solitude, 278; The Two Doves, 326; Autumn, 422 XLIX [XIX, 1749]. Insulted Poverty, p. 424; and all the Poems by *H. Greville.*'

The letter is signed 'Crito', the usual signature of the Rev. John Duncombe, who was a regular contributor to the Magazine for twenty years till his death in 1786 (Nichols, *Literary Anecdotes*, viii. 277) and as a friend could speak with authority. In his list of twenty-six poems, 'Winter', 'The Midsummer Wish', and 'Autumn' are all included. Another poem in the list, 'Life, an Ode'—ascribed to Hawkesworth in Pearch's *Collection*, 1770, iii. 143—is said to have been read aloud by Hawkesworth to Johnson, who memorized it before it was printed (W. Cooke, *Life of Johnson*, 1785, p. 107). This is independent support for the accuracy of the list. But that all the twenty-six poems were by the same author is not likely to be challenged when they are examined.

Poems are rarely indexed in *The Gentleman's Magazine* under the name or pseudonym of their author, and to no other author are so many poems assigned. Clearly someone connected with the *Magazine* had a special interest in these poems. They were indexed at the time when the man who edited the poetical section of the *Magazine*, or, in the words of John Ryland, 'generally compiled Cave's poetical Miscellany' (*ante*, p. 94), was Hawkesworth.

TO MR. URBAN, ON HIS COMPLEATING THE XVIIITH VOLUME OF 'THE GENTLEMAN'S MAGAZINE'

This piece (beginning 'Arts, to compleat what *Nature* but began') was printed after the preface to *The Gentleman's Magazine* for 1748. It was contributed to *The Bee* for 9 March 1791 by 'A. B.' (the Earl of Buchan, as is shown by a later communication), and was thus introduced: 'The inclosed I many years ago tore out of a magazine, and have always intended sending it to some public paper. I am certain that it has been written by Dr. Johnson. I need not tell a judge like you that it is excellent. It has escaped all his collectors, and well deserves to be reprinted.' See also *Notes and Queries*, 1914, 11. x. 304 and 1915, 11. xi. 7. There is no reason for this attribution. There were many such annual tributes in the *Magazine*.

A HINTED WISH

This epigram (beginning 'You told me, Maro, whilst you live') is ascribed to Johnson in Mark Van Doren's *Anthology of World Poetry*, New York, 1928, p. 439 (London, 1929, p. 387). It is F. Lewis's translation of Martial's epigram, xi. 47, the motto of *The Rambler*, No. 198.

TRANSLATION OF LATIN VERSES BY BUBB DODDINGTON

In *The Scots Magazine* for May 1806, p. 367, appeared this unsigned contribution:

'The following Ode [Ad Amicum] was composed by the celebrated Bubb Doddington, afterwards Lord Melcombe, and given by him to a young friend then sent into Scotland under the tuition of the late ingenious and learned Dr. Chapman, who, at that young gentleman's request, corrected it. It was afterwards, by his Lordship, put into the hands of Dr. Johnson, who corrected it also, and translated it into English.'

Both Doddington's and Chapman's versions are given in full before the English translation (beginning 'The traveller, when a storm draws nigh'), of which the last stanza is a sample:

> By art, he forms a snug retreat,
> Whither he can with ease retire,
> Whene'er intolerably wet,
> And cuddle round the kindly fire.

There seems to be no authority for this attribution. Hawkins quotes part of a letter from Doddington to Johnson expressing a desire to receive a visit from him (*Life*, 1787, p. 329); and Cave refers to it in his letter to Samuel Richardson of 29 August 1750: 'Mr. Doddington sent a letter directed to the Rambler, inviting him to his house, when he should be disposed to enlarge his acquaintance. In a subsequent number [14] a kind of excuse was made, with a hint that a good Writer might not appear to advantage in conversation' (*Literary Anecdotes*, v. 40). They are not known to have had any further dealings.

EPITAPH ON RICHARD CHILDREN

Northcote (*Reynolds*, 1813, p. 43) says that Roubiliac asked Reynolds to introduce him to Johnson in the hope of obtaining an epitaph for a monument on which he was engaged for Westminster Abbey, and that Johnson was prepared to write it in the presence of both at Gough Square, where he lived from 1749 till January 1759. Only the epitaph on Goldsmith in Westminster Abbey is by Johnson, but Mrs. Katherine Esdaile in her *Life of Roubiliac*, 1928, p. 118, proposed the epitaph on Richard Children (d. 1753) in the parish church of All Saints, Tonbridge ('O thou, whose Manners unadorned by Art'). This epitaph is largely derived from lines 289–96 of *The Vanity of Human Wishes* and *Pope's Epistle to Robert Earl of Oxford and Mortimer*; and it violates Johnson's precept that an epitaph should name the person concerned.

Οὐκ ἔστι Διὸς κλέψαι νόον

This is the title of a Latin poem of twelve lines (beginning 'Nequicquam Danaen includit ahenea turris') printed in *The Universal Visiter* for March 1756, p. 142, with the signature '* *'. Hawkins says that Johnson's contributions 'have this mark' (*Life*, 1787, p. 352 n.). Boswell, who apparently read into this statement more than it contains, says that 'all the essays marked with two *asterisks* have been ascribed to him' (*Life*, i. 306), and proceeds to point out exceptions. He does not name this Latin poem, but it must be included among the pieces not by Johnson.

SONG

(The silver rain, the pearly dew)

This sentimental song was printed in *The Universal Visiter* for April 1756, p. 192, with the signature 'T'. It was reprinted as 'By Mr. S. Johnson' in *The St. James's Magazine* for February 1764, p. 365, and was attributed to Dr. Johnson by Messrs. Elkin Mathews in their catalogue No. 5, 1925, p. 74. In theme and tone it bears no resemblance to any known poem by Johnson. It is more like the work of Samuel Johnson of Shrewsbury, whose *Poems on Several Occasions* appeared in 1768; but it is not included in that volume.

TO MYRTILIS. THE NEW YEAR'S OFFRING

(Madam, Long have I look'd my tablets o'er)

Printed in Anna Williams's *Miscellanies*, 1766, p. 13; assigned to Johnson in Bell's *Classical Arrangement of Fugitive Pieces*, 1789, vi. 53; included in Thomas Park's edition of Johnson's *Poetical Works*, 1811, p. 89. There seems to be no reason for this attribution.

THE THREE WARNINGS

(The Tree of deepest root)

Malone at one time thought that Johnson had a hand in this poem by Mrs. Thrale, which was published in Anna Williams's *Miscellanies*, 1766, pp. 74-80. In his 'Maloniana' Sir James Prior printed the following note:

> Mr. Lysons, though a great friend of hers, showed Dr. Laurence who dined with us this day, a little account of her pretty poem, *The Three Warnings*. Of this piece, Lysons said, from some information he had got, that 'the first hint was given to her by Johnson; that she brought it to him very incorrect; and that he not only revised it throughout, but supplied several new lines.' Under this account, which was written by Lysons and shown to Mrs. Piozzi, she has added with respect to the statement of its being suggested by Johnson, '*That is not true*', acknowledging by the exception that the rest was true. But she was careless about truth, and therefore not to be trusted. (Prior, *Life of Edmond Malone*, 1860, p. 413.)

Despite this, Malone did not deny authorship to Mrs. Piozzi in his own copy of the *Miscellanies*, nor did he communicate any objections to Boswell, who credited the poem to her (*Life*, ii. 26). She herself said that the story was told to her by Capt. Conway (*Thraliana*, i. 225).

If Johnson really wrote part of the poem, there is no clear evidence by which it can be identified. Malone's belief seems not to have lasted and he probably found that his first inference was unwarranted.

VERSES ON A COTTAGE IN WALES

'Johnson's cottage', on the Gwaynynog estate, Denbighshire, bears a slab with six verses (beginning 'Around this peaceful cot, this humble shed') attributed to Johnson by local tradition and guide-books. The attribution is repeated by E. W[alford] in *Notes and Queries*, 1895, VIII. viii. 488. They are dated 1768. Johnson's only visit to Wales was with the Thrales in the summer of 1774. See *Notes and Queries*, 1873, IV. xi. 438. The urn commemorating Johnson's association with Gwaynynog was erected in or after 1777.

INSCRIPTION ON DR. TAYLOR'S HOUSE AT ASHBOURNE

This inscription was printed as Johnson's in Nichols's *Literary Anecdotes*, x. 62, in a footnote signed by the Rev. Samuel Pegge:

> Stet domus hæc donec Testudo perambulet orbem,
> Et donec fluctus ebibat Formica marinos.

Pegge remarked on the false metre of the second line, which he corrected to read 'Ebibat et donec fluctus', &c. Johnson was supposed to have supplied the inscription on one of his many visits to his friend Dr. Taylor at Ashbourne; but there is no evidence that the house bore any inscription till about 1930, when Pegge's corrected version was inscribed by Dr. Ernest Sadler, the then owner. Nor is it known how Johnson should ever have been associated with an inscription which was in use in France before his lifetime. It is found on the Lycée at Tarbes, Hautes Pyrénées (where Marshall Foch was educated), with the date 1699, the year in which the Lycée was founded:

> Stet domus hæc fluctus donec formica marinos
> Ebibat et totum testudo perambulet orbem.

A similar and earlier example, dated 1669, is on the Église des Cordeliers at Toulouse:

> Durabit donec fluctus formica marinos
> Ebibat et totum testudo perambulet orbem.

(Information supplied by Le Proviseur of the Lycée at Tarbes.) Dr. L. F. Powell has pointed out to the editors that an earlier form of the couplet is printed at the end of *La Bibliothèque d'Antoine du Verdier*, 1585, p. 1227:

> Stet liber hic donec fluctus formica marinos
> Ebibat, aut totum testudo perambulet orbem.

VERSES ON THE APPROACH OF WINTER

These verses (beginning 'Autumnal leaves apace do fade') were printed in *The New Foundling Hospital for Wit*, 1771, iv. 155, without attribution, and in the edition of 1784, vi. 60, were said to be 'by the same', i.e. Johnson. They were included in *The County Magazine* for September 1788, p. 133, with the signature 'G. W.' They were obviously not written by Johnson.

VERSES TO GOLDSMITH

'Verses from Doctor Johnson to Doctor Goldsmith, occasioned by the new Comedy, intitled, *The Mistakes of a Night*' (beginning 'No wonder the *Vis Comica* is scarce') were printed in *The London Chronicle* for 1 April 1773, over the initials 'S. J.' Internal evidence is decisive against Johnson's authorship.

In the errata to Cooke's *Life of Johnson*, 1785, two pieces are deleted from the list of Johnson's poems given on the last page of the volume—'To a Bush Fighter' (beginning 'In rancour's dark, obscene, sequester'd seat') and 'To Dr. Goldsmith, on the Success of his Comedy, called "She Stoops to Conquer"' (beginning 'Long have our comic writers try'd to move'). Both had been printed without attribution in Davies's *Miscellaneous and Fugitive Pieces*, 1774, iii. 290, 291—the latter with the title 'To Doctor Goldsmith, on the Success of his Comedy, called the Mistakes of a Night'. It is not the same poem as that printed in *The London Chronicle*.

ODE TO MRS. THRALE, '1784'

These verses beginning 'Cervisial coctor's viduate dame', are contained in a quarto pamphlet entitled *Ode by Dr Samuel Johnson to Mrs Thrale, upon their supposed approaching Nuptials*, dated 1784. They were composed by Boswell, apparently on 12 April 1781, the day after Henry Thrale's funeral (Pottle, *Literary Career*, No. 72, pp. 131 ff.), and printed in 1788. Boswell quoted the first stanza in the *Life*, iv. 387, and described them as 'not without characteristical merit'. Wyndham Lewis suggested, and the possibility may be conceded, that John Wilkes may have had a hand in them (*The Hooded Hawk* (1946), p. 158).

THE PATRIOT

The Patriot, a Tragedy. From a Manuscript of the Late Dr. Samuel Johnson, Corrected by Himself. 1785. This blank-verse tragedy by Joseph Simpson bears little evidence of Johnson's correction. Boswell denied his authorship (*Life*, iii. 28). Boswell's copy was lot 2594 in 'Bibliotheca Boswelliana' at Sotheby's, 24 March 1824. It contained a 'note by Mr. Boswell relative to the Author', but its present whereabouts is unknown. A manuscript fair copy at Harvard is entitled 'Leonidas' and bears the date '1750'.

THRENODIA

This Latin threnody, purporting to have been written after Culloden, was printed in *The European Magazine* for October 1785, p. 312. It was contributed by 'G. T.' with the following note: 'When Jacobitism received its death's-wound, the following THRENODIA was composed, it is said, by the late celebrated Dr. J—n. The elegance of the composition may, perhaps, make amends for the virulence of the matter; as at any rate it shews the spirit of the party for whom it is composed.' Six lines at the conclusion are in verse, beginning 'Cum temerata fides, pietasque inculta jaceret'. There is no reason for including them among Johnson's poems.

ODE TO MRS. THRALE

This Ode, beginning 'Arbores nudos generare posse Scotiae montes' is printed in *The Morning Chronicle* for 24 April 1786 under this heading, 'The following Ode addressed to Mrs. Thrale, and given us as a genuine production of Dr. Johnson's, is published, that it may have a place in the next Edition of Mr. Boswell's Book'. It is a *jeu d'esprit*, suggested by a perusal of the *Tour to the Hebrides*.

VERSES ON LOVE

A piece of fourteen lines on love (beginning 'How fleet is the hour, when love's folding arms') was contributed by 'T. B.' to *The Morning Chronicle* of 25 April 1786 as a 'small Fragment of the late Dr. Johnson's . . . that the world might not lose any thing of so valuable a man'. Neither sentiment nor style merits the attribution, which may not have been made seriously.

EPITAPH ON MRS. JANE WRIGHT

An epitaph which begins 'If virtuous acts, a great tho' humble mind' and consists of ten rhyming couplets which end:

> Learn here thy fate, and this great precept know,
> There's no Repentance in the grave below.

is printed in the section 'Letters' of *The Hampshire Repository*, ii [1801], pp. 111–12, under the title 'Epitaph on Mrs Jane Wright, a descendant of the ancient Scotch family of Auchinleck, upon her Monument in Bishop's Waltham Church'. A footnote adds, 'The above composition is attributed to Dr Johnson and not without some internal evidence from the stile and the sentiments, as well as from his connection with the family.' Mrs. Wright's ancestry is obscure, and Johnson's authorship improbable.

TRANSLATION OF AN INSCRIPTION ON SELDEN'S BIRTHPLACE

Above the lintel in the house called 'Lacies' at Salvington, Sussex, John Selden (1584–1654) at the age of ten, is reputed to have carved the following lines

> Gratus, honeste, mihi; non claudar; invito sedeque.
> Fur, abeas; non sum facta soluta tibi.

According to Augustus Hare, *Sussex* (1894), p. 170, the couplet was rendered by Johnson

> Walk in and welcome; honest friend, repose.
> Thief, get thee hence; to thee I'll not unclose.

There is nothing to connect Johnson with the translation.

VERSES WRITTEN IN A COPY OF MURPHY'S 'LIFE OF GARRICK'

An incredibly bad quatrain (beginning 'Dear is memory whene'er we wish to trace') was contributed as Johnson's to *Notes and Queries*, 1902, 9. ix. 330. The contributor [James Hayes] said that he found these 'unpublished (?) lines of Dr. S. Johnson (in the calligraphy of a lady) in an old copy of Arthur Murphy's *Life of David Garrick*, as a kind of note or introduction to Murphy's remarks on *Irene* . . . The lady's remarks below the lines are: "Johnson wrote those lines for you M. W. D., with the very nice pen you made me—Adieu".'

THE EAGLE AND ROBIN RED-BREAST

This poem (beginning 'The Prince of all the feather'd kind') is printed in Warton's *The Union*, 1753, p. 28, and in a bookseller's catalogue (May 1935) is said to be by Johnson. It is an anglicized version of 'The Eagle and Robin Red-breist', printed in *The Ever Green*, 1724, ii. 232, and signed 'AR. SCOT', i.e. Allan Ramsay, not 'Mr. Archibald Scott', as expanded in *The Union*.

LINES ON AN HOUR-GLASS

A manuscript of verses beginning 'See! from the glass the sandy minutes pour . . .' was lot 422 in Messrs. Sotheby's sale, 18 July 1949, It was said to be in Johnson's hand but was returned by Messrs. Maggs Bros., the purchasers.

CITY OF GOD

The misattribution of the well-known Hymn 'City of God, how broad and far, &c.' to Johnson is a recurrent vulgar error. It seems not to have appeared in print save in Bartlett's *Familiar Quotations*, 11th ed., Boston, 1938 (*Works*, vi (Yale ed. 1964), 393). The author was Samuel Johnson (1822–82).

ON MRS. THRALE'S SECOND MARRIAGE

Manuscript verses, beginning 'Whether from Love of Fame or Love of Ale', are preserved in the National Library of Wales (MS. 4734B). They are confusingly docketed: 'Mrs Piozzi's Brynbella Marr with Mr Thrayle by Dr Johnson'. The verses are indecent and were not composed by Johnson.

LOST OR UNIDENTIFIED POEMS

UNTRACED MANUSCRIPTS

In the Ridgeway sale at Sotheby's, 30 June 1879, lot 237 was described as Johnson's 'MS Piece of Poetry. s. 1 pp. 4to.' That it was signed implies a school or college exercise. In the same rooms on 21 June 1881, lot 118 was described as 'Latin Verse, 2 pp. 8vo. in his Autograph . . .'.

VERSES TO OLIVIA LLOYD

'When at Stourbridge school', says Boswell, 'he was much enamoured of Olivia Lloyd, a young quaker, to whom he wrote a copy of verses, which I have not been able to recover.' There is no reason to think that the verses were ever printed. See *Life*, ed. 1934, i. 92, 529.

THE GLOW-WORM

'He told us', says Boswell, 'one of his first essays was a Latin poem upon the glow-worm. I am sorry I did not ask where it was to be found' (*Life*, ii. 55). Malone in 1799 added in a footnote that 'whether it be any where extant, has not been ascertained' (ii. 232). It may not have been printed, but Boswell seems to have got the impression that it had been; and 'Latin Verses on a Glow-worm' is one of the titles in the manuscript list of Johnson's writings drawn up by Percy, and now in the Bodleian Library (see pp. 456–7).

SOMNIUM

Boswell talked with Dr. William Adams of Johnson's time as an undergraduate. His notes include: 'It was near the 5 of Novr. which was then kept as a great day at Pembroke. Johnson failed. I [Boswell] am sorry for it—a Poem by him on the Gunpowder plot would have been sublime. He gave in an excuse titled *Somnium* a common thought that the muse came to him and said it did not become him to write on such high subjects as politicks but should confine himself to humbler themes. But it was in Virgilian Verse.' (*The Correspondence and other Papers of James Boswell relating to the making of the 'Life of Johnson'*, ed. M. Waingrow, 1969, p. 23; cf. also *Life*, i. 60.)

VERSES IN DODSLEY'S 'COLLECTION'

Mrs. Thrale included in *Thraliana* 'a Catalogue of such Writings as I *know* to be his, there are many that *I do not* know—scattered about the World'. It ends with 'a Copy of Verses in Dodsley which he never would tell me, though he trusted me with Secrets of far greater Importance' (ii. 81; ed. 1941, p. 205). In all its other items the Catalogue is correct. This 'Copy of Verses' may have been ascribed in the *Collection* to another author.

LATIN VERSES ON TORRÉ'S FIREWORKS

Tyers records that 'on the fireworks of Torré he wrote a Latin poem' (*The Gentleman's Magazine*, liv (December 1784), p. 910; *Johnsonian Miscellanies*, ii. 377). The poem is undiscovered.

TO DELIA

The manuscript of a poem 'To Delia', in four quatrains, unsigned, and inscribed 'To Mr. Humphrey, from the Author', was sold as by Johnson in the Hagen sale at the Anderson Galleries, New York, on 14 May 1918. It begins:

> Thou whose love-inspiring air
> Delights, yet gives a thousand woes—
> My Day declines in dark despair,
> And Night hath lost her sweet repose.

It was afterwards sold by the Brick Row Book Shop, New York. The editors have not succeeded in tracing it.

CORRECTIONS IN A BIRTHDAY ODE BY CIBBER

On 25 June 1763 Boswell recorded Johnson on Cibber:

Colley Cibber, Sir, was by no means a blockhead; but by arrogating to himself too much, he was in danger of losing that degree of estimation to which he was entitled. His friends gave out that he *intended* his birth-day Odes should be bad: but that was not the case, Sir; for he kept them many months by him, and a few years before he died he showed me one of them, with great solicitude to render it as perfect as might be, and I made some corrections, to which he was not very willing to submit. I remember the following couplet in allusion to the King and himself:

> 'Perch'd on the eagle's soaring wing,
> The lowly linnet loves to sing.'

Sir, he had heard something of the fabulous tale of the wren sitting upon the eagle's wing, and he had applied it to the linnet. Cibber's familiar style, however, was better than that which Whitehead has assumed. *Grand* nonsense is insupportable. (*Life*, i. 402.)

On another occasion Johnson said, 'I remember when he brought me one of his Odes to have my opinion of it, I could not bear such nonsense, and would not let him read it to the end' (*Life*, ii. 92–3). Evidently Johnson remembered the occasion well, for he later added the circumstance that Cibber had 'abused Pindar to me, and then shewed me an Ode of his own, with an absurd couplet, making a linnet soar on an eagle's wing' (*Life*, iii. 72–3), but he also added that it was Cibber who terminated the reading: 'I objected very freely to several passages. Cibber lost patience, and would not read his Ode to an end' (*Life*, iii. 184).

Cibber was appointed Poet Laureate in 1730; he died in December 1757. George II's birthday was 30 October [1683]. The ridiculous couplet mentioned by Johnson seems not to have been published, and the ode which Johnson revised is unidentified.

INDEX OF FIRST LINES

INDEX OF TITLES

GENERAL INDEX